Facts On File
NATIONAL PROFILES

Scandinavia

FACTS ON FILE
NATIONAL PROFILES

Scandinavia

GEORGE THOMAS KURIAN

Facts On File
New York • Oxford • Sydney

Facts On File National Profiles: Scandinavia

Facts On File, Inc.	Facts On File Limited	Facts On File Pty Ltd
460 Park Avenue South	Collins Street	Talavera & Khartoum Rds
New York, NY 10016	Oxford OX4 1XJ	North Ryde NSW 2113
USA	United Kingdom	Australia

Library of Congress Cataloging-in-Publication Data

Kurian, George Thomas.

   Facts on file national profiles. Scandinavia / George Thomas Kurian.
     p. cm.
   Bibliography: p.
   Includes index.
   ISBN 0-8160-1998-3
   1. Scandinavia—Handbooks, manuals, etc. I. Title. II. Title:
Scandinavia.
DL5.5.K87   1990   89-33090
948—dc20

British and Australian CIP data available on request from Facts On File.

Facts On File books are available at special discounts when purchased in bulk quantities for businesses, associations, institutions, or sales promotions. Please contact the Special Sales Department of our New York office at 212/683-2244 (dial 800/322-8755 except in NY, AK or HI).

Composition by Logidec
Manufactured by R.R. Donnelley & Sons
Printed in the United States of America

10 9 8 7 6 5 4 3 2 1

This book is printed on acid-free paper.

CONTENTS

CONTENTS

INTRODUCTION

Part of an ongoing series of national profiles derived from the larger Encyclopedias of the First, Second and Third Worlds, *Facts On File National Profiles: Scandinavia* is a survey of five of the northernmost countries of Europe—Denmark, Sweden, Norway, Finland and Iceland. Properly, three of these countries—Denmark, Sweden and Norway—are known as Scandinavia. When Iceland is added, the name Nordic countries is commonly used. Finns, being ethnically different, are not considered as Nordics or Scandinavians, but Finland is bound to this region by shared traditions of history and culture. For the sake of convenience, all five countries are grouped together as Scandinavia in this study.

There are few regions more homogeneous than Scandinavia. Like Siamese quintuplets, the five countries are linked organically and have functioned together throughout history as one group. Physically the Danes, Swedes, Norwegians and Icelanders belong to what is loosely called the Nordic type, typically tall, blond and dolicephalic, although there are some regional variations. Further, because of their geographical isolation, Scandinavians have been able to preserve their ethnic uniqueness and insular characteristics to a greater degree than southern or middle Europeans and have been less exposed to immigration and intermixture.

Geographically, the five countries exhibit considerable similarities. The cold, near-Arctic climate; the rugged and deeply indented coastlines; and the absence of long rivers are common geographical features. The mountainous and inhospitable interiors have influenced the development of all major urban settlements on the coast. The influence of the sea has been even more critical. All the five countries have rich maritime traditions, and Scandinavian sailors and sailing ships are part of the legends of the early centuries of the Christian era. Some of them are reputed to have discovered the New World before Columbus, but if they did, they missed one of the great prizes of history by not recording their discovery and founding a settlement.

Historically, all five countries have been part of one another at some point in their history. Sweden and Norway were part of Denmark under the Union of Kalmar of 1397, and Norway and Denmark were united until the end of the Napoleonic wars. Norway and Sweden were part of one Kingdom from 1814 to 1904. Iceland was a part of Norway from 1263 to 1814 and of Denmark from 1814 to 1944. Finland was a province of Sweden until 1809. Except for Gustavus Adolphus's campaigns in Germany and Eastern Europe in the 17th century, Scandinavia has played only a small role in modern European history. In turn, it has been spared much of the vicissitudes of foreign conquest and domination by their southern neighbors, except for two interludes: the Nazi occupation of Norway, Denmark and Finland during World War II, and the Russian occupation of Finland from 1809 to 1919.

The religious unity of Scandinavia is even more striking. The five countries are bastions of Lutheranism, which is the official confession in all of them. As a result, Scandinavia has been spared the agony of religious conflict that rent larger countries such as Germany and France well into the 20th century. However, the Scandinavians as a group have lacked the religious intensity that characterized other European nations, such as Poland, Ireland, Italy and Spain. Scandinavian countries were among the last to be Christianized in Europe, and paganism survived in this region as late as the 12th century. The lateness of the conversion perhaps explains the looseness of religious affiliations and weakness of religious traditions.

Politically, all five countries subscribe to a form of liberal-socialist democracy, even though Norway, Sweden and Denmark are constitutional monarchies. (Finland almost became a monarchy at the end of World War I, when a German prince was placed briefly on the throne.) They also are among the most advanced welfare states in the world, with an exemplary record in such areas as women's rights, environmental protection, freedom of speech and social welfare. Scandinavia is the home of the institution of ombudsman, which is one of the most important innovations in modern public administration. Unlike larger countries, Scandinavia has faced few challenges to its open society. With small, homogeneous populations, the Scandinavian countries could adopt radical social and political experiments with greater success than other countries with more diverse or larger populations. In fact, the so-called Scandinavian Way or Middle Way has been much admired but little emulated by the rest of the world.

The only clearly demarcated cultural boundaries among the five countries are those of language. Finnish belongs to the Uralic family of languages, while Norwegian, Swedish, Danish and Icelandic belong to the Indo-Aryan group. Language loyalties are strong—a carryover from the 19th century, when language controversies provided the grist for warring intellectual camps in struggles as fierce as political struggles in other countries. In Scandinavia language is not merely a medium of communication, it also is a standard around which to rally, a symbol of national heritage.

It is surprising that in a region bound by such strong common ties, economic linkages developed only very late. Economically, Scandinavia is overshadowed by its southern neighbors, particularly since the founding of the European Community, of which only Denmark among the Scandinavian countries is a member. With a combined population of 22.7 million (about the same as Canada) and a combined GNP of $302.3 billion in 1986, Scandinavia is not in the big leagues. The idea of a Nordic Union was first mooted by Denmark in 1938, but is was not until 1962 that the Treaty of Cooperation was signed in Helsinki providing the legal basis for the organization. This treaty was revised in 1971 and 1974, creating a separate Nordic Council of Ministers with jurisdiction over the whole field of interstate cooperation. The Nordic Council serves as the legislative arm of the union.

The Nordic Council of Ministers holds formal and informal meetings and is attended by ministers with responsibility for the subject under discussion. Each member state also appoints a minister in its own cabinet as minister for Nordic cooperation. Decisions of the Council of Ministers are unanimous, except for procedural questions, and are binding on the individual countries provided no parliamentary approval is necessary under the constitution of any of the countries. The Council of Ministers reports each year to the Nordic Council.

The principal avenues of economic cooperation are:
- the Nordic Investment Bank, founded in 1975
- the Nordic Industrial Fund, founded in 1973
- the Nordic Economic Research Council, founded in 1980
- NORDTEST, founded in 1973 for technical testing and standardization
- the Nordic Project Fund

Communications. A Nordic agreement for transport and communications went into force in 1973.

Labor. Since 1954 a free labor market has been in force among Denmark, Finland, Norway and Sweden.

Environment. The Nordic Convention on the Protection of the Environment was signed in 1974. The coastal states also have signed the Convention on the Marine Environment of the Baltic, which went into force in 1980. Special agreements have been concluded between Denmark and Sweden on pollution in the Øresund and between Finland and Sweden on pollution in the Gulf of Bothnia. The Nordic Institute for Advanced Studies on Occupational Environment was established in 1982.

Energy. A common authority for electricity supply (NORDEL) was set up in 1963.

Citizenship. Citizens of one Nordic country working in another are in many respects given the status of nationals and have the right to vote in local elections in the country of residence.

Social welfare and health. Under the 1955 Convention on Social Security (renewed in 1981), Nordic citizens have the same rights, benefits and obligations in each Nordic country. In 1981 an agreement was concluded for doctors, dentists, nurses and pharmacists on the standards of competence required for obtaining work in other Nordic countries.

Educational and scientific cooperation. This covers secondary education, adult education and vocational training. Joint projects include those on journalism, languages and medical education. National research programs are coordinated, and research findings and information are shared. There are 24 joint Nordic research institutions.

Cultural activities. These are sponsored by 16 joint projects dealing with arts, literature, theater, music, film and Sami language. The Nordic Cultural Fund was founded in 1966 to promote cultural cooperation by making grants for Nordic cultural projects within the region.

The Nordic Council was founded in 1952 as a forum for cooperation among Nordic parliaments. It consists of 87 members elected annually by and from the parliaments of the respective countries as follows: Denmark, 16; Faeroe Islands, 2; Greenland, 2; Finland, 18; Åland Islands, 2; Iceland, 7; Norway, 20; and Sweden, 20. The various parties are proportionately represented in accordance with their representation in the national parliaments. The council initiates and follows up cooperative efforts among Nordic countries by issuing recommendations and statements of positions to the Nordic Council of Ministers. Nordic Council members are assigned to six standing committees. The Presidium of the Nordic Council, in which all five countries have two parliamentary representatives, is the supreme executive body.

The author wishes to acknowledge the support and encouragement of Edward W. Knappman, publisher of Facts On File. Thanks also are due to Kate Kelly, editor, for overseeing the project and to William Drennan for his superb copyediting.

George Thomas Kurian
Yorktown Heights

DENMARK

DENMARK

BASIC FACT SHEET

OFFICIAL NAME: Kingdom of Denmark (Kongeriget Danmark)

ABBREVIATION: DE

CAPITAL: Copenhagen

HEAD OF STATE: Queen Margrethe II (from 1972)

HEAD OF GOVERNMENT: Prime Minister Poul Schluter (from 1982)

NATURE OF GOVERNMENT: Parliamentary democracy

POPULATION: 5,125,676 (1988)

AREA: 43,076 sq. km. (16,627 sq. mi.) (excluding Greenland and the Faeroe Islands)

ETHNIC MAJORITY: Scandinavian

LANGUAGE: Danish

RELIGION: Protestant; Evangelical Lutheran

UNIT OF CURRENCY: Krone

NATIONAL FLAG: The Dannebrog or "Danish cloth," the oldest national symbol in continuous use in the Western world; a white cross, off-center toward the hoist, on a field of red

NATIONAL EMBLEM: Denmark has a simple state emblem—three lions on a gold shield with nine red hearts—and a much older royal arms. In the royal arms three shields are imposed upon one another. The "Heart Shield" contains the ancestral arms of the ruling family, two red bars on gold (Oldenburg) and a gold cross on blue (Delmenhorst). On the medium shield are devices against red backgrounds representing duchies absorbed by the realm: a silver nettle shield (Holstein), a silver swan (Stormarn), a mounted knight in gold armor (Ditmarsh) and a gold horsehead (Lauenburg).

The chief escutcheon is quartered by a large Dannebrog cross. One quadrant bears the 12th-century royal state emblem. In another, two blue lions on gold signify Schleswig. Below the arm of the silver cross, four devices in blue appear on one side, displaying three golden crowns commemorating the union of Denmark, Norway and Sweden in 1397, and three silver figures representing Danish dependencies: a falcon for Iceland, a ram for the Faeroe Islands and a polar bear for Greenland. A blue lion on a gold background surrounded by red hearts mark the royal title as the ruler of the ancient tribe of the Wends; underneath is a gold wivern, a fabled winged creature with a dragon's head, representing dominion over the Goths. Two Norse giants stand beside the arms. Gold chains of Danish orders circle the shield with pendants dangling. A red ermine-lined gold-fringed cape topped with a bejeweled royal crown frame the ornate emblem.

NATIONAL ANTHEMS: "Kong Kristian Stod Ved Hojen Mast" (King Christian Stood by the Lofty Mast) and "Der er et Yndigt Land" (There Is a Lovely Land)

```
┌─────────────────────────────────────────────────────────────────────┐
│                    BASIC FACT SHEET (continued)                       │
└─────────────────────────────────────────────────────────────────────┘
```

BASIC FACT SHEET *(continued)*

NATIONAL HOLIDAYS: Constitution Day, June 5; birthday of the queen, April 16; all major Christian festivals

NATIONAL CALENDAR: Gregorian

PHYSICAL QUALITY OF LIFE INDEX: 98 (on an ascending scale with 100 as the maximum)

DATE OF INDEPENDENCE: 800

DATE OF CONSTITUTION: June 5, 1953

WEIGHTS & MEASURES: Metric

GEOGRAPHICAL FEATURES

Located in southern Scandinavia, the Kingdom of Denmark consists of Denmark proper, the Faeroe Islands and Greenland. Denmark itself comprises the peninsula of Jutland (Jylland) and some 406 islands with a total land area of 43,076 sq. km. (16,627 sq. mi.) extending 402 km. (250 mi.) north to south and 354 km. (220 mi.) east to west. The only land boundary, with West Germany, is 68 km. (42 mi.) long. The country is surrounded by water on the other three sides: the Skaggerak on the north; the Kattegat, the Øresund and the Baltic Sea on the east; and the North Sea on the west. The total length of the coastline is 7,403 km. (4,600 mi.). There are no border or other territorial disputes.

The precise size of Denmark proper is subject to constant variation owing to marine erosion and deposit and reclamation work. Moreover, when the tides are active, the coastline shifts twice daily, up to 16 km. (10 mi.) on the western coast of South Jutland. Not included in the land area are inlets or fjords directly connected with the sea, among them the lagoon of Ringkøbing, which is linked with the North Sea by the sluices of Hvide Sande. The 406 islands (of which only 97 are inhabited) account for over one-third of the land area. The largest are Zealand (Sjaelland, 7,015 sq. km.; 2,709 sq. mi.), Fünen (Fyn, 2,984 sq. km.; 1,152 sq. mi.), Lolland (1,234 sq. km.; 480 sq. mi.), Bornholm (588 sq. km.; 227 sq. mi.) and Falster (514 sq. km.; 198 sq. mi.). Geographically, Denmark may be described as a virtual archipelago, the only one in northern Europe.

The capital is Copenhagen (København), on the island of Zealand (Sjaelland) and the adjoining island of Amager on the western shore of the Øresund. A small village in the early Middle Ages called Havn, it received town privileges in 1254 and a royal residence in 1445. It is the site of the great castles of Rosenborg, Charlottenborg, Christiansborg (now the seat of the Parliament, the Folketing), Amalienborg and Fredericksborg; all were built in the 17th and

```
PRINCIPAL CITIES (estimated population,
1983)

København (Copenhagen, the capital)     1,372,019*
Århus (Aarhus)                             182,645
Odense                                     137,606
Ålborg (Aalborg)                           114,437
Esbjerg                                     70,825
Randers                                     56,288
Horsens                                     46,949
Helsingør (Elsinore)                        43,867
Vejle                                       43,592
Kolding                                     41,468
Roskilde                                    39,747
Næstved                                     38,290
* Including Frederiksberg and Gentofte.
```

18th centuries. There are only three other cities with a population of over 100,000 inhabitants, and 16 with a population of over 20,000 inhabitants.

Denmark is a low-lying country, with its highest point, Yding Skovhoj in East Jutland, only 173 m. (568 ft.) above sea level. The surface relief is characterized by glacial moraine deposits, which form undulating plains with gently rolling hills interspersed with lakes. The largest lake is Arreso (40.6 sq. km.; 15.7 sq. mi.). The moraines consist of a mixture of clay, sand, gravel and boulders, carried by glaciers from the mountains of Scandinavia and raised from the bed of the Baltic, with an admixture of limestone and other rocks. During the last glaciation, only the northern and eastern parts of the country lay under the icecap. The ice limit followed a line running from Viborg to Bovbjerg on the western coast and southward to the national boundary near Tinglev. The country west and south of this line formed a polar landscape during the final glaciation. Between the hills are extensive level outwash plains of the meltwater formed from stratified sand and gravel outside the ice limit. These heathland plains are the site of the country's densest settlements.

The boundary line between the sandy West Jutland and the loam plains of East and North Denmark is the most important geographical dividing line in the country. West of the line is a region of scattered farms; to the east, villages with high population density.

Valleys, both tunnel and regular, furrow the moraine landscape. The East Jutland inlets were created by the intruding sea in the lowest part of the tunnel valleys, to which glacial erosion also contributed. The inlets form natural harbors, making maritime activities easy means of livelihood. The Gudenå River, the longest river in Denmark (158 km.; 98 mi.), follows the intersecting valley systems.

Flat sand and gravel tracts make up one-tenth of the total land area. They are particularly numerous in the northern part of the country, such as in the Limfjorden area. Where draining is rendered difficult in these flat and low-lying regions, the land often is swampy. Along the coast of South Jutland, where there is a strong tidal range, there are salt marshes formed by clay deposited by tidal waters. Dune landscapes form an almost unbroken belt along the entire coast of Jutland.

The substratum on which Danish soils have developed are chiefly moraine and meltwater sand. There are two basic types: loam and podsol. Loam is dark-colored, porous and highly organic and thus is rich in plant food. It is common in eastern Denmark. Podsol occurs chiefly in open, sandy tracts, where the earth is subject to drying out, as in West Jutland. Tillage and regulation of the water table have considerably improved the Danish soil, which is not intrinsically well suited to agriculture. With deep plowing and the use of fertilizers, more than three-fourths of the land surface can be efficiently cultivated.

Denmark is in the North Temperate Zone, where the natural type of vegetation is the deciduous forest, but as it borders on the coniferous belt, spruce and fir thrive in plantations. About 11% of the land area is forest. Beech, oak, elm and lime thrive in a few locations.

Natural plant communities include dune vegetation and heathland plants, which occur chiefly on the sandy heaths of West Jutland. Heather vegetation also is found on steep hill slopes, on the granite terrain of Bornholm and on gravelly beach ridges. Dunes, heath and bogs together cover 7% of the land surface.

As in other densely populated countries, the original stock of large mammals have been wiped out. The largest wild species is the red deer. The freshwater fauna are heavily affected by pollution, but the marine fauna form the basis of a large fishing industry.

Greenland, the largest island in the world, has a total land area of 2,173,600 sq. km. (840,000 sq. mi.). Of this area, 1,833,900 sq. km. (708,100 sq. mi.) lie under its icecap. Of the ice-free area, some 150,000 sq. km. (38,000 sq. mi.) are inhabited. The greatest north-to-south distance is 2,670 km. (1,660 mi.), and the greatest east-to-west distance is 1,290 km. (800 mi.). Greenland is bounded on the north by the Arctic Ocean, on the east by the Greenland Sea, on the southeast by Denmark Strait, on the south by the Atlantic Ocean and on the west by Baffin Bay and Davis Strait. The coastline runs 39,090 km. (24,289 mi.).

Greenland is a mountainous country with lofty fringes, the highest point of which is Gunnbjorns Fjaeld, 7,700 m. (12,140 ft.). The average thickness of the ice field is 1,515 m. (4,971 ft.).

The Faeroe Islands are in the Atlantic, six degrees to the northwest of Denmark. The Faeroes' 19 islands, of which 18 are inhabited, cover an area of 1,399 sq. km. (540 sq. mi.). Among the larger islands are Strømø (374 sq. km.; 174 sq. mi.), Østerø (266 sq. km.; 110 sq. mi.), Vågø (178 sq. km.; 69 sq. mi.), Syderø (153 sq. km., 59 sq. mi.) and Sandø (114 sq. km.; 44 sq. mi.). The maximum length of the islands is 120 km. (70 mi.) north to south and 79 km. (49 mi.) northeast to southwest. The total coastline is 1,117 km. (694 mi.).

The Faeroe landscape is characterized by a stratified series of basalt sheets, with intervening thinner layers of solidified volcanic ash (tufa). Glacial action has carved the valleys into trough-shaped hollows and formed steep peaks, the highest being Slaettaretindur (882 m.; 2,894 ft.) on Østerø. Millions of seabirds nest on the rocky coastal ledges.

CLIMATE & WEATHER

Denmark lies on the western fringe of the Eurasian continental block, where the Gulf Stream or the North Atlantic Westerly Drift brings warmth to the northern regions. The westerly winds temper the winter climate. The mean temperature in the coldest month is 12°C (54°F) higher than the average for Denmark's latitude. At the same time, the waters of the Baltic separate Denmark from the continental climate of Eastern Europe. However, in exceptional winters, when ice closes the Baltic, cold air streams from the east can spread over the country, causing hard winters. During one such winter in 1940, the air temperature was the lowest ever recorded in Denmark, at –31°C (–23.8°F).

Conversely, easterly air streams during periods of high pressure in summer may hold off the westerly sea winds. The sun then shines for a longer period in a cloudless sky, the temperature rises and there is a heat wave. The highest temperature recorded under such conditions was 35.8°C (96.4°F).

Generally, however, the climate is in the intermediate range. The mean temperature of the coldest month, February, is –0.4°C (about 31°F); that of the warmest, July, 16.6°C (61.5°F): but there are great variations from the normal, especially in winter. The number of annual frost days ranges from 70 on the coasts to 120 in the interior.

The weather is very changeable, as the country is in a temperate zone at the meeting point of extremely diverse air masses. When, for example, humid, relatively warm and hence light Atlantic air encounters Arctic air that is dry, cold and heavy, they do not mix, but remain separate on a front that is generally oblique to the ground. As the fronts swing over the Danish region throughout the year, the weather is constantly changing. Westerly winds predominate, especially in gales. Gale damage is most common in West Jutland, particularly in spring.

The mean annual precipitation is 60 cm. (23.6 in.), ranging from about 80 cm. (31.3 in.) in Southwest Jutland to about 40 cm. (15.8 in.) in the area of the Great Belt, which is a rain shadow. The number of days with precipitation fluctuates between 120 and 200. Snow falls from January through March, six to nine days a month. Although rain falls throughout the year, the heaviest is during August and October and the lowest during the spring and winter months, which are relatively dry. This has negative implications for agriculture, which needs more rain in the spring and less in the fall.

The length of the day ranges over the year between seven and 17½ hours. Denmark's latitude determines that the sun stands at noon at midsummer at 57½° above the horizon and at midwinter at only 10½°. At summer midnights, the sun is low under the northern horizon, giving the light nights that are characteristic of northern Scandinavia and Alaska. There is a difference of 7°7′ between the eastern and the western extremities, corresponding to about half an hour in time. Danish Standard Time follows Central European Time.

POPULATION

The population of Denmark was estimated in 1988 at 5,125,676, based on the last census, held in 1983, when the population was 5,116,454. Denmark ranks 91st in the world in size of population. The population is expected to increase to 5,137,000 by 1990 and to 5,165,000 by 2000.

The population of Greenland is 54,000, with a growth rate of 1.1% annually; that of the Faeroe Islands is 46,000, with a growth rate of 0.7% annually.

Denmark has reached a zero population rate. The rate was 0.7% during 1965–73, but it declined to 0.2% during 1973–84 and will remain at the zero level for the rest of this century. The population is expected to reach a stationary level of 5 million by 2010.

The decline in population growth rate is a 20th-century phenomenon. In the 19th century Denmark experienced a big increase in population, from 900,000 in 1800 to 1,400,000 in 1850 and to 2,500,000 in 1920, all despite considerable emigration, especially to the United States. In the 1880s alone, one Dane in every 11 left the country.

Denmark was one of the first countries to liberalize abortion law, although the Maternity Aid Act was designed to encourage women to go through with their pregnancies to avoid a further fall in birth rates. In 1956 the Family Planning Association was formed to monitor health legislation and to provide practical guidance to couples. A 1966 law makes it a doctor's duty to discuss family planning with his patients. In 1969 sex education, adapted to the children's age, was made a compulsory subject in schools.

Population, 1925–70 (000)			
Year	Total	Male	Female
1925	3,435	1,676	1,758
1930	3,551	1,736	1,814
1935	3,706	1,824	1,882
1940	3,844	1,900	1,944
1945	4,045	2,002	2,043
1950	4,281	2,123	2,158
1960	4,585	2,273	2,312
1970	4,938	2,451	2,486

Since 1968 there has been a massive influx of asylum-seekers to Denmark. In that period over 18,000 persons have sought asylum in Denmark, including Sri Lankan Tamils, Iranians and Lebanese. The influx of non-Danish people has placed strains on the already overburdened welfare system. The rights of these groups are protected by the Refugee Board, with authority to reverse decisions of the Aliens Directorate. Denmark has only a moderate number of guestworkers relative to many other European countries.

The Equal Rights Council has worked successfully to eliminate sex discrimination. Women hold positions of authority at all levels. In 1986, they held about 26% of the seats in the Folketing and headed three cabinet ministries.

DEMOGRAPHIC INDICATORS, 1986

Population: 5,125,676 (1988)
Year of last census: 1983
Sex ratio: male, 49.29; female, 50.71
Population trends (000)
1930: 3,542   1960: 4,581   1990: 5,137
1940: 3,832   1970: 4,938   2000: 5,165
1950: 4,281   1980: 5,123
Population doubling time in years at current rate: Over
   100 years
Hypothetical size of stationary population (million): 4
Assumed year of reaching net reproduction rate of 1:
   2030
Age profile (%)
0–14: 17.9   30–44: 22.7   60–74: 13.8
15–29: 22.8   45–59: 16.2   Over 75: 6.6
Median age (years): 37.1
Density per sq. km. (per sq. mi.): 119 (308.1)
Annual growth rate (%)
1950–55: 0.77   1975–80: 0.25   1995–2000: –0.08
1960–65: 0.76   1980–85: 0.08   2000–5: –0.18
1965–70: 0.71   1985–90: 0.03   2010–15: –0.29
1970–75: 0.52   1990–95: –0.02   2020–25: –0.45

DEMOGRAPHIC INDICATORS, 1986 (continued)

Crude birth rate, 1/1000: 10.8
Crude death rate, 1/1000: 11.4
Change in birth rate, 1965–84: –43.9
Change in death rate, 1965–84: 10.9
Dependency, total: 48.5
Infant mortality rate, 1/1000: 11.4
Child (0–4 years) mortality rate, 1/1000: insignificant
Maternal mortality rate, 1/100,000: 7.7
Natural increase, 1/1000: –0.6
Total fertility rate: 1.4
General fertility rate: 43
Gross reproduction rate: 0.72
Marriage rate, 1/1000: 5.7
Divorce rate, 1/1000: 2.8
Life expectancy, males (years): 71.6
Life expectancy, females (years): 77.5
Average household size: 2.0
% illegitimate births: 43
Youth
  Youth population 15–24 (000): 760
  Youth population in 2000 (000): 616
Women
  Of childbearing age 15–49 (000): 1,314
  Child/woman ratio: 223
Urban
  Urban population (000): 4,499
  % urban 1965: 77   1985: 86
  Annual urban growth rate (%)
  1965–80: 1.1   1980–85: 0.3
  % urban population in largest city: 32
  % urban population in cities over 500,000: 32
  Number of cities over 500,000: 1
  Annual rural growth rate –2.1 (1985–90)
Vital statistics

ETHNIC COMPOSITION

Denmark is one the most ethnically homogeneous nations in the world. Racially, there is no special Danish type. The present population is based on a racial mixture of the New Stone Age and various groups that have immigrated since. The Nordic group is, nevertheless, more prominent, being characterized by blond, curling hair and blue eyes.

The only non-Danish minority is a German community in South Jutland numbering about 40,000, or less than 0.8% of the population. Industrial expansion in the 1970s caused a large immigration of foreign workers, numbering about 54,000.

The population of Greenland is partly Eskimo but consists chiefly of Green-landers, a Mongoloid-Caucasian mixture of Eskimos and Danes.

LANGUAGE

The official language is Danish, a branch of the East Scandinavian group of the Gothonic (Germanic-Teutonic) family of languages derived from Primitive Norse. The territorial core of Primitive Norse extended from Trondelagen to the north to the Ejder River and the Danish islands to the south. This language community had broken up by the ninth century into the West Scandinavian and East Scandinavian groups. In about the 12th century, Danish began to evolve separately from Swedish, becoming the language of the Danish kingdom, which emerged as a political unit at that time. Simultaneously with this geographical delimitation, Danish evolved from a lending language to a borrowing language. Also, linguistically, Danish became a bridge for those cultural influences that from the Middle Ages to modern times flowed from south to north. The main cultural influence was Christianity, which was introduced by Harald Bluetooth (c. 985), who is reported on the stone at Jelling "to have made the Danes Christians." With Christianity came the Latin script, which came to be widely employed by the scribes, although the traditional orthography survived until the Reformation. Another cultural influence was German, which filtered through the Hanseatic merchants and brought in its wake hundreds of new words for products and merchandise and also ethnic and abstract words. The central stock of native words was, however, largely preserved, and most foreign words were largely assimilated and adapted to Danish patterns.

Another wave of German influence began with the Reformation and the invention of printing, although on a more modest scale. The Danish translation of the Bible—Christian III's Bible of 1550— is astonishingly free of Germanisms and thoroughly Danish in style, thanks to the translators, especially a noted canon at Lund, Christiern Pedersen. The High German words were used primarily in literary or scientific works and did not penetrate popular speech.

The period of early Modern Danish (1500–1700) saw the written language become fixed in more or less the form it has today. An orthographic reform adopted by the typesetters resulted in drastic simplification and the introduction of greater consistency. From the end of the 17th century, Romance loan words began to be adopted, such as musical and banking terms from Italian, cooking and fashion words from French and scientific terminology from classical languages. Maritime words also were adopted from Dutch. More recently, Danish has borrowed heavily from English.

Until 1700, the written and spoken languages varied considerably, and dialects dominated spoken Danish. However, with the growing centralization of the kingdom, a standard spoken language began to take shape, called Rigsma-let.

Modern written Danish (Rigssproget) is governed by a ministerial spelling reform of 1889 and its subsequent minor amendments. This language is taught in schools and used in public administration. A consultative body appointed by the Ministry of Education, Dansk Sprognaevn, provides advice and guidance on language issues. Although it employs the Latin alphabet, it has many peculiarities, such as special vowels (æ, ø and ä). Phonetically, the most characteristic feature of Danish is the glottal stop that normally occurs in single-syllable words when the word has a long vowel or ends in a voiced sound. Standard spoken Danish in not fixed or sanctioned in every detail of pronunciation, and many small differences are acceptable.

RELIGION

The national church *(folkekirken)* of Denmark, under paragraph 4 of the Constitution, is Evangelical Lutheran. It subscribes to the three creeds of the early church—the Apostles' Nicene, and Athansasian and the Augustine Confession—as well as the Shorter Catechism of Luther.

Christianity was introduced in 826 by the Benedictine monk Ansgar, from northern France. But it was not nationally adopted until about 960, when, according to the Saxon chronicler Widukind, the monk Poppo converted King Harald Bluetooth after miraculously carrying red-hot iron in his hands. The story of the Danish church in the Middle Ages reflects the continental struggle between the crown and the church. From about 1520 a reform movement gathered strength and resulted in the smooth adoption of Lutheranism in 1536 under the leadership of Johan Bugenhagen, Peder Palladius and Hans Tausen. From 1660 the Lutheran State Church was headed by the absolutist king.

Religious life in the 19th century was influenced by three outstanding personalities: Bishop J.P. Mynster, Søren Kierkegaard and N.F.S. Grundtvig. The Danish service was established from the Reformation in pure Lutheran form with few fixed liturgical features but with a rich hymnology. The hymn tradition was renewed by Grundtvig. The Grundtvigian revival was followed in the latter half of the 19th century by a pietistic revival, which had a strong sacramental character.

As absolutism gave way to constitutionalism in 1849, religious freedom was introduced and the state church became the national, or people's church. The state supports the church as a national institution and as part of the Danish heritage and upholds Sunday legislation and noncompulsory religious teaching in schools in accordance with Evangelical Lutheran doctrines. Financially, the church is maintained by a state tax, which is levied on church members along with an ordinary income tax. In addition, the state extends grants for the maintenance of old churches as national monuments. At the same time all other religious groups enjoy full freedom of association and worship.

Paragraph 73 of the Constitution states that "The Constitution of the national church shall be ordered by law." This has been interpreted to mean that the affairs of the church should be determined by parliamentary legislation. This authority is exercised by the politically appointed minister for ecclesiastical affairs, who need not be a member of the national church. Spiritually, the Danish church has no single authority. The juridical character of the regular Assembly of Bishops, under the presidency of the bishop of Copenhagen, remains ambiguous. Bishops are appointed by the queen on presentation of a candidate elected by the pastors and delegates of the parish councils, which are themselves elected by universal suffrage. Clergy are trained in the theological faculties of the Universities of Copenhagen and Århus. Numbers of new ordinations have been steadily declining in recent years. To make up for the lag, laymen and laywomen are being ordained in more numbers.

Theoretically, the national church is limited to the frontiers of the kingdom. The Danish Church Abroad was founded in 1919 to care for Danish communities outside the kingdom, the largest of which is in South Schleswig. Although weekly church attendance is estimated at less than 5% of the population, the national church exercises a strong influence on many aspects of social and cultural life. Until recently, the parish minister also was president of the local commune's school commission. Free church movements in Denmark have generally been less successful in winning adherents than their counterparts in other Scandinavian countries.

The Roman Catholic Church has maintained a presence in Denmark since 1849. Most of the 32,000 Catholics live in or around Copenhagen. Some 25% of the Catholics are descendants of immigrant Slavs. The majority of the guest workers of the 1970s are Muslims.

No religious statistics have been collected since 1921, when about 97% of the population belonged to the national church. Civil data, especially baptismal records, show that more than 90% still are nominally affiliated with the national church. In Denmark, a newborn child is declared simply as a boy or a girl, and the child's name becomes official only after baptism or a similar ceremony, within a year. Civil data also show that there are 2,336 churches and 110 deaneries in the nation's 10 dioceses. Data on other religious communities are not particularly reliable.

HISTORICAL BACKGROUND

Little is known of Denmark's early history. Harald Bluetooth (d. 985), the first Christian king of Denmark, conquered Norway, and his son Sweyn conquered England. Under Canute (1018–35) Norway, England and Denmark were united, but shortly after his death the union with England came to an end and Norway seceded. Danish hegemony was reestablished over Norway and Sweden by the Union of Kalmar in 1397. In 1523 Sweden broke free, but the union with Norway remained until 1814. The Reformation was established in Denmark during the reign of Christian III (1534–59). A series of wars with Sweden resulted in the loss of southern Sweden as well as Danish control of the Øresund. Meanwhile, under Frederick III (1648–70) and Christian V (1670–99), absolute monarchy was reestablished and remained in force until 1849. Denmark was on the losing side in the Napoleonic wars and as a result lost Norway by the Peace of Kiel (1814). Within the next half century Denmark had lost to Prussia her southern provinces of Scheswig, Holstein and Lauenburg. North Slesvig was returned to Denmark through a plebiscite after World War I. The Virgin Islands were ceded to the United States in 1917. A democratic constitution was introduced in 1849 and a revised one adopted in 1915. Denmark was invaded by the Germans in 1940 and served as a springboard for the invasion of Norway. Iceland became an independent republic in 1944.

CONSTITUTION & GOVERNMENT

Denmark is one of the oldest monarchies in Europe, completing its first millennium in 1985. On the adoption of the nation's first written Constitution, in 1849, absolute monarchy gave way to representative democracy. The so-called June Constitution (Junigrundloven) established three seminal principles: Judicial authority should reside in independent courts; legislative authority should rest jointly with king and parliament; and executive authority should be vested in the king, but he would not perform any act of state except on the authority of a minister. The lower chamber could impeach the ministers in the National Court (Rigsret). The king could not levy any taxes without the consent of the Folketing.

The June Constitution was for its time one of the most liberal in Europe. The two chambers of the Folketing were elected under universal suffrage by all independent men over 30. But the conservatives did not give up without a struggle, and it was not until 1901 that their power was broken, when King Christian IX signed "the change of system" *(systemskifte)* and appointed a ministry based on the majority only in the lower chamber. This principle was written into the Constitution in 1953.

A constitutional amendment in 1915 gave women and servants the vote and reduced the voting age to 25. The electoral privileges of the upper chamber were abolished. Proportional voting was introduced. Dissolution of the chamber was made more difficult. Another constitutional amendment, in 1920, authorized the incorporation of North Schleswig into the kingdom.

After World War II, a radical amendment was spearheaded by the Social Democrats and Radical Liberals and became law on June 5, 1955. The new Constitution abolished the upper chamber. The voting age was reduced from 25 to 23. Later amendments, confirmed by referendums, further reduced it, to 21 in 1961 and to 20 in 1971. To safeguard minorities, a provision was included for referendums on parliamentary bills when demanded by one-third of the members. Parliamentary rule was constitutionally guaranteed by the provision that no minister may remain in office after a vote of no confidence and that a government must resign if a vote of censure is passed against the prime minister. Together with the new Constitution, the new Act of Succession was passed, permitting female succession to the throne. It was under this act that Queen Margrethe II succeeded her father, King Frederik IX, as head of state in 1972.

The executive is the cabinet, headed by the prime minister, who is the head of government. Ministers are the administrative heads of their respective ministries. Most ministries consist of a single department, but two comprise several departments, the largest being the Ministry of Economic and Budget Affairs, with six departments. Departments are divided into offices.

Since 1901 it has been the unfailing constitutional practice that a government must step down if it finds itself without a plurality in the Folketing. In the course of the 20th century this principle has been developed into a grand and elaborate set of constitutional norms. When the Constitution was revised in 1953, the principle was confirmed and incorporated in Section 15. This is the only written rule governing the formation of a cabinet.

Since the turn of the century, no Danish government has commanded a majority in the Folketing. Governments as a rule are minority governments made up of a number of parties. The only time in the past decade when a government has approximated to the ideal of a majority government was for a brief period in 1978–79 when a coalition government composed of Social Democrats and Liberals commanded 86 of 176 members in the Folketing. Nevertheless, governments function because they receive the support of one or several other parties on major issues. These are called supporting parties. A supporting party adopts a position of considerable flexibility to keep the government in office, often without a formal agreement. Often the government is unsure of the extent of support it can receive from these parties but carries on its work in the expectation of such support. Interparty negotiations, including compromises, take up much a cabinet's time and tax its skills. Determinations of how much a party can give and how much it can get without abandoning its traditional platforms affect every issue and parliamentary vote. Thus cabinet crises are frequent in Danish political life.

A cabinet may be brought down in several ways. The most clear-cut is a direct censure or a vote of no confidence. Such a censure has not occurred since 1909. The second is when the cabinet chooses to resign when faced with a large-scale erosion of support. A third is when the government chooses to resign after defeat in the Folketing on a major issue, as happened in 1950. The fourth and probably the most common is when the government triggers a cabinet crisis by using the right of dissolution. This may be done to precipitate an election at a most auspicious time for the ruling parties.

Following an election a new government is formed through a process called *regeringsdannelsessituation.* In most Western countries it is fairly easy to form a government after a general election. Not so in Denmark, where the parties themselves determine the composition of the cabinet and form new alignments, permutations and combinations that may not reflect the will of the voters, or reflect it less than perfectly. Over the years, a complicated procedure has been evolved for installing a new government. Its three main purposes are to ensure that the new government has a "reasonable" chance of survival, that all parties had a chance of participating in the negotiations and that the constitutional role of the monarch is not violated through personal royal predilections.

Formation of a cabinet begins with the departing prime minister advising the queen on the probable courses of action. He will also ask her to invite the politician most likely to succeed to form the cabinet. If this person agrees to do so and obtains the necessary support, the queen recedes from the picture. More commonly, however, the queen may be advised to summon more than one party leader, and with their counsel she appoints a royal investigator *(kongelig undersoger),* who is asked to preside over the negotiations among the parties. Often the royal investigator emerges as the prime minister in the next coalition. In other cases, he recommends to the queen a realistic proposal for forming a new government and clarifying the political situation. In making his recommendation, the royal investigator must conform to his mandate from the queen and also achieve the broadest possible government.

The cabinets thus formed are true party creations, not necessarily popular governments. Their success is dependent on the fragile unity achieved through political horse-trading. Yet, the democratic character of the institution has been preserved through numerous crises and changes in government.

The number of ministers is not laid down in the Constitution and has varied over the years. Apart from ministers without portfolio, each minister heads a department. Legally, the ministers are responsible for their own actions individually. Cabinet decisions are based on consensus, not vote.

All government bills and administrative measures come before the Council of State (Statsradet), which consists of the cabinet under the presidency of the monarch. The heir to the throne participates when he or she is of age. In addition to Folketing bills, the Council of State also ratifies international treaties and agreements and reprieves certain long-term prison sentences. Other matters requiring the monarch's signature are submitted by the royal private secretary.

The Constitution of 1955, following a Swedish precedent, provided that the Folketing appoint one or two persons as ombudsman, and this office was established in 1955. The powers of the ombudsman are defined in Order 342 of 1961, Act 258 of 1971 and Order 48 of 1982. The ombudsman is directed to see that no one in public service pursues unlawful activities, makes arbitrary or unjust decisions or is guilty of error or neglect. His terms of reference do not extend to judges, the Fokleting or the national church. Anyone, not necessarily an interested party, may complain to the ombudsman. He is not, however, obliged to deal with every complaint, but uses his own discretion as to whether a complaint warrants investigation. The complaint must be in writing and within certain time limits. In investigating complaints, the ombudsman is invested with semijudicial powers, including the right to subpoena witnesses. If he believes there is reason to institute criminal charges, he may direct the public prosecutor to do so. Where a minister or former minister is involved, the ombudsman may direct the Folketing to proceed against him. In addition, the ombudsman may make recommendations to the Folketing on measures to improve the administration and correct deficiencies in current laws and administrative regulations.

CABINET LIST

Prime Minister	Poul Schluter
Minister of Agriculture	Laurits Toernaes
Minister of Ecclesiastical Affairs	Torben Rechendorff
Minister of Culture	Ole Vig Jensen
Minister of Defense	Knud Enggaard
Minister of Economic Affairs	Niels Helveg Petersen
Minister of Education and Research	Bertel Haarder
Minister of Energy	Jens Bilgrav-Nielsen
Minister of Environment	Lone Dybkjaer
Minister of Finance	Palle Simonsen
Minister of Fisheries	Lars P. Gammelgaard
Minister of Foreign Affairs	Uffe Ellemann-Jensen

CABINET LIST *(continued)*	
Minister of Health	Elsebeth Kock-Petersen
Minister of Housing	Agnete Lausten
Minister of Industry	Niels Wilhjelm
Minister of the Interior and Nordic Cooperation	Thor Pedersen
Minister of Justice	Erik Ninn-Hansen
Minister of Labor	Henning Dyremose
Minister of Social Affairs	Aase Olesen
Minister of Taxation	Anders Fogh Rasmussen
Minister of Traffic and Communications	Hans Peter Clausen
Governor, Central Bank of Denmark	Eric Hoffmeyer

Up to 1953 Greenland was governed as a colony. The 1953 Constitution accorded it the status of a fully integrated part of the Kingdom of Denmark. Greenland sends two members to the Folketing. Greenland affairs are the responsibility of the minister for Greenland, while local affairs are handled in part by a democratically elected Provincial Council (Landsradet) and in part by a Danish governor *(landshovding)*. The two correspond to the Danish County Council and county prefect, respectively. Special legislation applies to Greenland in certain areas.

The Faeroe Islands were a Danish county until 1948, when self-government was introduced. The democratically elected assembly (Lagting) has legislative powers in all local affairs. The local government (Landsstyre) handles all local affairs. The Danish government is represented on the islands by a commissioner *(rigsombudsmand)*.

ORGANIZATION OF DANISH GOVERNMENT

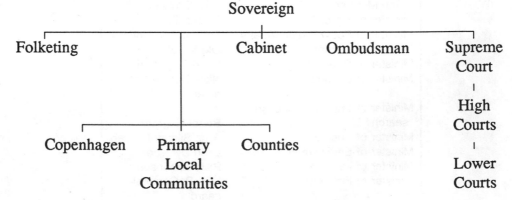

RULERS OF DENMARK

King/Queen (from 1947)

April 1947–February 1972:	Frederik IX
February 1972– :	Margrethe II

Prime Ministers (from 1945)

May–November 1945:	Vilhelm Buhl (Social Democratic Party)
November 1945 –November 1947:	Knud Kristensen (Agrarian Party)
November 1947 –October 1950:	Hans Hedtoft (Social Democratic Party)
October 1950 –September 1953:	Erik Eriksen (Agrarian Party)
September 1953 –February 1955:	Hans Hedtoft (Social Democratic Party)
February 1955 –February 1960:	Hans Hansen (Social Democratic Party)
February 1960 –September 1962:	Viggo Kampmann (Social Democratic Party)
September 1962 –February 1968:	Jens-Otto Krag (Social Democratic Party)
February 1968 –October 1971:	Hilmar Baunsgaard (Radical Party)
October 1971 –October 1972:	Jens-Otto Krag (Social Democratic Party)
October 1972 –December 1973:	Anker Jørgensen (Social Democratic Party)
December 1973 –February 1975:	Poul Hartling (Liberal Party)
February 1975 –September 1982:	Anker Jørgensen (Social Democratic Party)
September 1982– :	Poul Schluter (Conservative People's Party)

HUMAN RIGHTS

Human rights are well protected in Denmark and enforced by the office of the ombudsman. Arrested persons must be brought before a judge within 24 hours of detention. In serious crimes, the accused is placed in solitary confinement. All trials are public except in divorce and paternity trials, or rape and child molestation cases. The rights of aliens are protected by the 1983 Alien Act. Natives of Greenland and the Faeroe Islands enjoy all the rights and privileges of Danish citizens.

In 1987 the Human Rights Center, mandated by the Folketing, was establishes with state funding to conduct research and provide information on a broad range of human rights issues. The Equal Rights Council deals with sex discrimination. Women hold strong representation in both the cabinet and the Folketing.

CIVIL SERVICE

Civil servants number over 800,000 and account for about 28% of the labor force. There is no unified civil service under a central agency, but each department has considerable autonomy in matters of public employment. However, in the central government, the Ministry of Finance is responsible for the biannual wage negotiations with unions, and these wage agreements are binding on all departments. Local governments conduct their own wage negotiations with unions representing their personnel, but these are coordinated with those of the central government. The civil service is heavily unionized. Most civil servants belong to unions affiliated with one of three labor federations: the Joint Council of Danish Public Servants and Salaried Employees' Organizations, the Central Organization of Civil Servants or the Joint Council of Danish Supervisors' and Technical Officers' Societies. Permanent civil servants enjoy security of tenure and may not be dismissed other than as laid down in civil service regulations. These regulations also provide for 40 grades, each with its corresponding wage scale. Promotions are based on seniority as well as informal assessments. Recruitment is based on informal interviews, and there are no elaborate tests or procedures except for admission to the police or defense forces. The age of retirement is 70 for the higher civil servants and 67 for others.

LOCAL GOVERNMENT

Danish local government was thoroughly reorganized in 1970. Local government boundaries, which in many cases had been untouched for over 800 years, were abolished, and the number of local government units was reduced from 1,387 to 277. Previously, the country was divided into 89 boroughs (kobstaeder) and 23 county authorities *(amstkommuner)*, the latter being subdivided into over 1,500 urban and rural districts *(sogne kommuner)*. The reform did not affect the national capital, which continues to be governed by the elected City Council (Borgerrepraesentation) of 55 members and an executive consisting of a chief burgomaster *(overborgmester)*, five burgomasters *(borgmester)* and five aldermen *(radmaend)*. At the same time, the distinction between urban and rural boroughs was abolished, the number of primary local governments *(primaerkommuner)* was reduced to 277 and the number of county authorities was reduced to 14. The primary local governments are chosen by the Elected Council (Kommunalbestyrelse) chaired by a mayor or *borgmester*.

Counties are governed by the elected County Council (Amtsrad) chaired by the county mayor *(amtsborgmester)*. The jurisdiction of the county councils includes roads, hospitals, schools and other public buildings. Central county government responsibilities are discharged by a prefect as chairman of a special council consisting of four members appointed by the County Council.

Greenland is divided administratively into the subprovinces *(landsdele)* of West Greenland, East Greenland and North Greenland. There are 16 provincial districts *(landsradaskredse)*, each of which elect one member of the Greenland Provincial Council by direct vote every four years. The 159 habitations are grouped in to 19 local districts *(kommuner)*, each with a local council *(kommunalbestyrelse)* of from three to 13 members; 19 judicial districts *(retskredse)*, each having a district court *(kredsret)*; 13 police divisions; 17 medical districts; 19 parochial districts; and 19 school districts.

The Faeroe Islands are divided into seven regions *(sysler)*, each under a sheriff *(sysselmand)*, who constitutes the local authority with some judicial functions. There are 50 local districts with 120 settlements *(bygder)*, some with as few as 30 inhabitants.

FOREIGN POLICY

Danish foreign policy is thoroughly pro-Western and is based on close links with four organizations: the United Nations, NATO, the Nordic Council and the EC. There is a remarkable consensus among all major political parties on foreign policy issues.

Although committed to collective security, Denmark has consistently resisted pressures by NATO to increase defense spending. In 1984, the Social Democrats and their allies secured legislation making Denmark the first NATO nation to withdraw completely from missile employment. Denmark was admitted to the EC in 1973 and remains the only Nordic member of that organization. It places great emphasis on relations with developing countries and is one of the few nations to meet the U.N. goal of contributing 0.7% of the GNP as de-

POLITICAL SUBDIVISIONS				
		Area		Population
Counties	Capitals	sq. km.	sq. mi.	(1984 est.)
Århus	Århus	4,561	1,761	579,800
Bornholm	Rønne	588	227	47,200
Frederiksborg	Hillerød	1,347	520	332,900
Fyn	Odense	3,486	1,346	453,900
København	—	522	202	616,200
Nordjylland	Ålborg	6,173	2,383	482,100
Ribe	Ribe	3,132	1,209	215,200
Ringkøbing	Ringkøbing	4,853	1,874	264,100
Roskilde	Roskilde	891	334	207,100
Sønderjylland	Åbenrå	3,930	1,517	249,800
Storstrøm	Nykøbing	3,398	1,312	257,600
Vejle	Vejle	2,997	1,157	326,700
Vestjælland	Sorø	2,984	1,152	277,800
Viborg	Viborg	4,122	1,592	230,600
Cities				
Copenhagen (København)	—	88	34	482,900
Frederiksberg	—	9	3	88,100
TOTAL		43,081	16,633	5,112,100
Source: Official government figures.				

velopmental assistance. As a member of the Nordic Council, Denmark maintains close relations with the other members of the Council—Norway, Iceland, Sweden and Finland. In 1982 Denmark joined Norway and Sweden in resuming diplomatic relations with the Vatican, ending a four-century rupture.

PARLIAMENT

The national legislature is the unicameral Folketing, whose members are elected every four years by universal suffrage under a modified proportional representation system. Of its current membership of 179, a total of 135 are elected in 17 districts, with 40 additional seats divided among those parties that have secured at least 2% of the vote but whose district representation does not accord with their overall strength. There also are two representatives each from Greenland and the Faeroe Islands.

Parliamentary sessions begin on the first Tuesday in October and average about 300 plenary sitting hours a year until May, spread over 117 days. The Folketing recesses at Christmas, Easter and for sessions of the Nordic Council in February and March. Much of the work is done in 23 standing committees, whose competence corresponds to those of the ministries. There also are committees on standing orders, proof of elections, scientific research, energy policy and the EC.

Parties are the legislative catalysts. They choose members of committees, party floor leaders and spokesmen. Danish parliamentary behavior is characterized by high cohesion and discipline. Nevertheless, shifting majorities have made government formation difficult. Because of volatile electoral opinion, continuity of parliamentary membership is low, and elections have been held every second year since 1971.

With the abolition of the upper chamber, the Landsting, in 1953, provision was made in the Constitution for holding referendums. Within three working days of the passage of a bill, one-third of the Folketing members may apply to the speaker for a referendum to be held on the proposed measure. The prime minister is responsible for initiating the referendum, which must take place not earlier than 12 and not later than 18 working days after he has announced it. The bill is annulled if it is opposed by a majority of the Folketing electors and at least 30% of those entitled to vote. Certain types of bills, such as money bills, are excluded from this provision. The first referendum took place in 1963.

Under the Constitution, no taxes may be levied until the finance bill or interim measures have been approved by the Folketing. Similarly, no expenditures may be incurred without such authority. However, because the finance bill is drafted some months before the fiscal year, it is impossible to foresee income or expenditures. Consequently, the practice has developed whereby the government requests the Folketing's Finance Committee (Finansudvalget) to approve unforeseen items. This practice makes this committee one of the most powerful parliamentary organs. At the end of the year all the allocations are incorporated into a supplementary estimates bill, thereby meeting constitutional requirements.

The Danish electoral system is one of the most complex in the world. It has been described as an "ingenious mathematical system" understood by less than 40 people in the whole of Denmark. At the core of the system is proportional representation (forholdstalsvalg), which replaced single-member constituencies in 1920. The electoral system is characterized by two kinds of seats, four different geographical levels for holding elections, three or four different ways to nominate candidates, and a number of ways to designate the persons chosen. Also, the votes are tabulated at various stages based on several different distribution principles.

Suffrage is equal and universal for all adults over 18. The 175 seats (excluding those of Greenland and the Faeroe Islands) in the Folketing are distributed in advance among the three election areas (amrader) into which the country is divided—metropolitan Copenhagen, the islands and Jutland—and of these, 135 constituency seats are subdivided into 14 county constituencies and three metropolitan constituencies in Copenhagen, making up the basic elements of the electoral system. The distribution is mostly determined by population totals and density, subject to constant adjustment.

Danish elections are dominated by political parties. Only a few people run as independents, and no independent candidate has been elected in recent years. The parties normally put forward one candidate in each of the 103 nomination districts. However, several parties put up candidates in the larger county/metropolitan constituencies in a process called parallel nomination, which is important in tabulating election returns.

In recent years 12 to 13 parties have put up candidates in the elections. Parties already represented in the Folketing are automatically entitled to nominate candidates and participate in the election campaign, which is partly financed by public funds. Parties that are new or not represented are accorded these privileges only if they collect signatures totaling 1/175th of the votes cast in the previous election.

Voting practices are standard. Polling is organized and supervised by the local authorities. Balloting is secret, and tabulation is done in the presence of participating party representatives. A voter may cast his ballot in different ways: either for a party by putting a mark next to the party's name, or for one of the party candidates by putting a mark next to his name. It is possible to vote either for the candidate nominated in one's own district or for any candidate in the county/metropolitan constituency.

In recording the returns, the most important geographical unit is the county/metropolitan constituency, where the first distribution of seats takes place. This is determined by the so-called Modified Lague method, in which the party votes are successively divided by 1.4-3-5-7-9, etc. The 15 biggest quotients indicate the party allotment by the first method. This method is common to all countries with proportional representation. To increase the proportionality, Denmark uses a system of equalizing that involves a subsequent distribution of 40 supplementary seats among some of the parties that have received at least 2% of the valid votes in the entire country. This is known as the threshold rule. The supplementary votes are then distributed among the different county/metropolitan constituencies following very complicated mathematical procedures.

It now remains to be determined which candidates have been elected in each party, and this is done through even more complicated procedures. Within each constituency, each party has a choice of three different methods of nomination; sometimes the three methods may be mixed at the party's discretion. The most common method is putting forward a single candidate in each nomination district within each constituency. The second method is listing candidates in a specific order of preference, called the party list, determined before an election. Voters in this case may vote either for the party or for one of the party candidates. If a party candidate fails to reach the so-called distribution figure, a redistribution takes place involving the transfer of votes from candidates who have received fewer votes to those at the head of the list. The party list may be broken if a great many personal votes are cast for a low-priority candidate. The third method is called the parallel nomination, and this is the one most widely adopted. In this method party candidates all receive parallel nominations in a constituency, i.e., no candidate is put up in a particular district, and his election is determined by the personal votes he obtains in the entire constituency. Party votes in a constituency thus get distributed among individual candidates in exact proportion to the number of personal votes received in each nomination district within the constituency. Under this method party candidates are a shoo-in in safe districts where a party had historically dominated.

The Danish electoral system has undergone few changes in the past 60 years. The older parties have sought to raise the threshold limit to reduce the proliferation of new parties, while the smaller ones have called for the elimination of the threshold rule altogether. While the proportional system has added to the instability of Danish governments, Danes cherish this principle as making their democracy more democratic.

Normal voter turnout ranges from 80% to 90%, with invalid or blank votes less than 0.6%. An electoral register is kept by each municipal authority and is renewed every January. There are no by-elections, as vacancies are filled by candidates of the same party who have received the next largest number of votes. Party strength in the Folketing thus remains fixed from one election to the next unless a member breaks away from a party.

POLITICAL PARTIES

The four "old" parties in Danish politics are the Social Democrat, the Liberal, the Radical and the Conservative People's covering the ideological spectrum from left to right. They also have dominated government coalitions during most of the 20th century. During the 1946–86 period the Social Democrats were represented in the government 67% of the time, the Radicals 27%, the Liberals 36% and the Conservatives 25%. The Justice Party, Center Democrats and the Christian People's Party have been co-opted into coalitions mainly as supporting parties. The 1973 elections marked an end to this quadrumvirate. The Communist Party, the Left Socialists and the Justice Party (unrepresented in the Folketing since 1960) were returned to the Folketing, and in addition, three new parties gained representation for the first time: the Center Democrats, the

FOLKETING ELECTION RESULTS, 1987
(metropolitan Denmark only)*

Party	Votes	%	Seats
Social Democratic Party .	985,906	29.32	54
Conservative People's Party	700,886	20.84	38
Socialist People's Party .	490,176	14.58	27
Liberals	354,291	10.54	19
Radical Liberals	209,086	6.22	11
Center Democrats	161,070	4.79	9
Progress Party	160,461	4.77	9
Christian People's Party .	79,664	2.37	4
Common Course Party ..	72,631	2.16	4
Others	148,386	4.41	—
Total	3,362,557	100.00	175

* The Folketing also has two members from Greenland and two from the Faeroe Islands.

Christian People's Party and the Progress Party, all at the expense of the traditional parties. This fragmentation has meant more power-sharing and greater instability, a process that has continued into the 1980s.

The Social Democrats were the first mass organization in Danish history and one of the first to establish youth groups. Over the years party activity has tended to shift from the local to the national level. Nevertheless, grass-roots local units remain the sources of party influence and power. Local party branches also are important sources of funds, especially at election time. The advent of television has reduced the power of the party bosses and enabled smaller and newer organizations to appeal directly to the national electorate. This explains the success of the Radical Liberals, the Center Democrats and the Progress Party, which do not have the organizational strength of the older parties. In fact, they may be characterized as cadre, rather than mass, parties. Party discipline also is stronger among the older parties, which uphold norms of party solidarity more stringently.

The Liberal Party (Venstre, Danmarks Liberale Parti, V) is the oldest Danish political party, founded in 1870 in opposition to the ruling conservative elite. It spearheaded the struggle against the monarchy to secure the principle of parliamentary government. This they achieved in 1901 after a bitter struggle against the Conservatives. Since 1945 the Liberal Party has shared power in minority or coalition governments six times. The party is organized at four levels: local commune associations; constituency organizations; county associations; and the national-level Executive Committee. It hews to classic liberal positions in its platform, upholding individual freedoms in a pluralistic society. In its economic policy the Venstre stands for a free-market economy with a strong private sector, an incomes policy to secure competitiveness, and restraints on trade union power. Its monetary policy supports expanded production, improved supply of capital and reduced interest rates. It supports existing social welfare provisions. In foreign policy it is pro-NATO and pro-EC and advocates closer Nordic cooperation.

The bastion of Liberal strength is made up of farmers, and the decline in the number of farmers is reflected in the party's membership decline from 129,000 in 1971 to 89,500 in 1984. Yet the ratio of members to voters is 22%, which is the second-highest among all political parties. Because of its close ties to the agricultural sector—often serving as its voice and spokesman—the party sometimes is known as Agrarian Liberal Party.

The Social Democrats (Socialdemocratiet, SD) were founded in 1871 a year after the Liberals, as a Marxist party. In its early years it concentrated on trade union organization and won its first parliamentary seat in 1884. From 1920 it began to attract voters from outside the ranks of labor and became the largest political party in the Folketing in 1924—a position it has maintained since, although it has never won an outright majority. The Social Democrats laid the foundations of the modern Danish welfare state while in office with the Radical Liberals from 1929 to 1943. Since 1945 the Social Democrats have given the country six of its 11 prime ministers and have led 14 of its 19 governments.

The Social Democrats have a highly developed party organization with 700 local units at the local level; 103 constituency organizations; 15 county organizations; and a national congress, which elects an executive committee. The main catchment area of the party is the trade union movement, whose interests the party has historically espoused. Party ideology has long shed its Marxist tenets and may best be described as democratic socialism, in the tradition of the British Labor Party. The socialist bias of the SD is strongest in the economic field, where it advocates public ownership of means of production, higher wages and benefits for workers, nationalization of health services, and state housing. In foreign policy it is slightly left of center, supporting both NATO and the EC while opposing an increase in power of the European Parliament and U.S. plans to employ cruise and Pershing missiles on Danish soil.

SD support is heavily concentrated among blue-collar workers and lower classes, but the party has been losing support among the younger age groups and among the Copenhagen electorate. Its membership has been declining since 1948, when it peaked at 38% of SD voters. Actual membership in 1984 was 107,000.

The Conservative People's Party (Det Konservative Folkeparti, KF) was formed in 1876 as the United Right, a group of landowners and upper-class supporters of monarchical rule. It led a losing fight against the Liberals to retain the Landsting (upper house), on the abolition of which in 1901 it regrouped to form the KF in 1915. Apart from the united-front wartime coalitions of 1940–43 and 1945, the KF was not a member of a coalition government until 1950. When in alliance with the Liberals, they carried out a major reform of the Constitution. The KF was again out of office until 1968, when it joined a Radical-led coalition that included Liberals. This coalition was responsible for the abolition of censorship on pornography, which earned conservatism a bad name. In 1982, Poul Schluter became the first Conservative prime minister at the head of a coalition that included Liberals, Center Democrats and the Christian People's Party.

The KF is heavily centralized and is led by two national-level bodies: the national council and the directorate. All parliamentary and local council candidates are nominated by the directorate.

The KF is a pro-free enterprise group that advocates low taxes, low wages and low inflation. Predictably, it supports both NATO and the EC more than other parties do. Always in coalition with the Liberals, the KF has adopted some of the classic Liberal stances in domestic policy as well. Membership in 1983–84 was reported at 52,000.

The Center Democrats (Centrum-Demokarterne, CD) are a splinter party that broke away from the Social Democrats in 1973 in protest against the latter's drift to the left. The party's main organizational units are the National Assembly, the National Council and the National Executive. The CD draws on the middle-class support of "suburban socialists" who subscribe to social-democratic values but wish to retain many of the economic advantages of petty capitalism. It opposes the excessive influence of trade unions and favors a balance between capitalism and socialism. In foreign policy the CD is both pro-NATO and pro-EC.

The Progress Party (Fremskridtspartiet, FP) was founded in 1972 as a populist movement protesting excessive taxation and "paper-shuffling bureaucracy." In the 1973 elections the FP gained 16% of the vote to become the second-largest party in the Folketing, but its support has sharply declined since then. The FP has never participated in the government, and its role has been limited to that of a gadfly. The party's main plank is opposition to the income tax, which is perceived as regressive. The party program is equally iconoclastic in other areas: abolition of the county governments, reduction of the number of parliamentary members from 179 to 40, with elections in a single national constituency in which voting would be for individuals and not for parties; weighting of parliamentary votes on the basis of votes received by each member in the elections; the use of the referendum for any law that did not receive a 60% vote in the Folketing; and the abolition of the diplomatic service in favor of electronic diplomacy by telephone. The party draws mainly on protest votes from traditional party members.

The Socialist People's Party (Socialistisk Folkeparti, SF) was founded in 1959 by Aksel Larsen, former leader of the Danish Communist Party for 26 years before being expelled for espousing a Danish version of socialism in preference to a hard Moscow line. It has never joined the government because of its opposition to NATO and the EC, but it has been a supporting party for successive SD governments. A mass party, it has achieved periodic success at the polls but has been riven by factions. The SF's ideology is unabashedly Marxist, although it pursues less militant programs. It participates in most popular movements as a means of broadening its appeal. With only 7,100 members, SF membership represents only about 2% of its electoral strength. The bulk of its strength is concentrated in the Copenhagen area, where it attracts both intellectuals and blue-collar workers.

The Christian People's Party (Kristeligt Folkeparti, KrF) was founded in 1970 and gained its first representation in the Folketing in 1973. Its orientation is similar to that of Christian political parties in Nordic countries, with a heavy bias in favor of traditional moral integrity and values that are being eroded by legislated permissiveness. Pornography, which is legal in Denmark, is one of the major targets of its programs. On other issues the KrF tends to side with the Conservatives. The KrF supports not only the EC and NATO but also increased aid to developing countries.

The Danish Communist Party (Danmarks Kommunistike Parti, DKP) was founded in 1919 and gained its first parliamentary seat in 1932. After a brief period of resurgence from 1945 to 1947, it was gradually isolated from mainstream politics because of its hard-line Stalinist stance. It regained parliamentary representation from 1973 to 1979, but the breakaway of the Socialist People's Party led the DKP into the political wilderness once again.

The Justice Party (Danmarks Retsforbund, DRF) was founded in 1919 and gained its first parliamentary seat in 1926. The party is based on the economic and social ideas of Henry George, author of *Progress and Poverty*, who advocated a single tax on increases in land values—hence the party's alternative name of Single-Tax Party. In other respects the Justice Party resembles laissez-faire liberals and libertarians. Its electoral fortunes have waxed and waned, and for a brief period from 1957 to 1960 it was a member of the Radical Liberal-led coalition government.

The Left Socialists (Venstresocialisterne, VS) were founded in 1967 as a splinter group of the left wing of the SF. Partly libertarian and party Marxist, it appeals to students and professionals rather than workers. The party does not cooperate with others in the Folketing but uses the forum to propagate its ideas, occasionally proposing imaginative policies.

The Radical Liberals (Det Radicale Venstre, RV) are one of the four "old" parties. They split from the Liberals in 1905 but participated in the government from 1909 to 1910 and from 1913 to 1920. Wedged between socialists and non-socialists, the RV has had a humanizing influence on both. In intermittent alliance with both the SD and the Conservatives, it has been in and out of governments between 1920 and 1964, and it led a majority coalition government from 1968 to 1971. Since 1982 it has actively supported the Conservative-led coalition. In foreign policy the RV's policies are more in line with those of the socialists, opposing excessive military expenditures.

There are no illegal political parties or known terrorist groups in Denmark.

ECONOMY

Denmark is a free-enterprise economy with a dominant private sector.

The Danish economy shares some of its characteristics with its northern Nordic neighbors and some with southern EC neighbors. Its basic strengths are in industry and agriculture, and its major problem is its overdependence on exports. Both are rooted in the history of the economy.

Denmark emerged from World War II with most of its economy intact, although considerably depleted. The devaluation of the kroner in 1949 (following that of the British pound) helped to boost exports, while the Marshall Plan helped to stimulate the weaker sectors. Nevertheless, the country's terms of trade deteriorated by almost 20% annually from 1949 to 1951, and Denmark had no means of servicing its foreign debt. The balance of payments was the top priority among government planners, even at the expense of consumer goods. At the beginning of the 1950s Danish exports were primarily farm products. As a result, the farmers favored liberalization of trade and removal of import restrictions. Industry, however, was more protectionist. Relatively late in getting started, its range of products was designed mostly for the home market. Even by the 1920s, industrial exports accounted for only 20% of total export earnings. In the 1930s it survived mostly because of heavy import restrictions. However, faced with growing competition from abroad, Danish industry surged in the 1950s, increasing production, employment and share of exports. By the end of the 1950s Denmark had established itself as a significant industrial exporter, helping to swing the balance of payments into Denmark's favor. During the period from 1958 to 1962, the GNP at fixed prices increased by a total of 26%, a rate unequaled since. As a result of strong growth, Denmark achieved full employment in 1962. For the rest of the decade and well into the early 1970s, the

Danish economy was in fine fettle. The public sector alone more or less doubled during this period, exhibiting the fastest growth of all sectors. The state also laid the foundations of a welfare society, initiating large-scale income transfers to households in the form of pensions, unemployment benefits, etc. The economic consequences of the welfare society were to become evident only much later.

To pay for welfare services, the state needed more tax revenues. Consequently taxes soared, making Danes some of the most taxed people in the world. The balance of payments also deteriorated, forcing the government to borrow heavily. Inflation, declining agricultural exports and stagnation in industrial exports all contributed to the onset of a severe economic crisis. In conjunction with a devaluation of the krone in 1967, the Social Democrat government tried to put a brake on rising wages by applying an incomes policy.

The year 1973 was a watershed in Danish economic history. In that year, Denmark joined the Common Market, along with Great Britain, and the first oil crisis hit Denmark—a traditional oil importer—with the severity of an earthquake. The 1973 elections reflected the fact that "something was rotten in the state of Denmark." Dissatisfied voters elected numbers of candidates of protest parties, beginning an era of political instability that lasted well into the mid-1980s. During 1973–75 inflation climbed by 20% annually; unemployment was at an all-time high; and the balance of payments deficit increased from Kr3 billion in 1975 to Kr12 billion in 1976, equal to 5% of the GNP. The problem was exacerbated by the second oil crisis, of 1978–80, which brought about a worsening of Denmark's terms of trade by 10%. Interest payments on the country's net foreign debt of Kr150 billion limited the room for fiscal maneuvers. Government efforts to keep the lid on inflation and improve the balance of payments produced other equally unpleasant side effects: lower wages, higher interest rates, high unemployment, deteriorating public finances and higher taxes.

Danish economic policy has changed course in the 1980s to tackle these chronic problems, which have defied conventional solutions. Long-term wage and price restraints, low interest rates and increased industrial competitiveness are among the main thrusts of the new policy. Danish oil and gas production in the North Sea also has contributed toward reducing the balance of payments deficits. Social benefits have been curtailed as austerity became the official watchword.

Nevertheless, Danish leaders have not abandoned the earlier philosophy that social values should pervade the economy rather than the other way around. Significantly, Denmark still tops the list of countries measured by "social progress." As a result, there are no depressed regions, no slums, no ghettoes in the country.

PRINCIPAL ECONOMIC INDICATORS

Gross National Product: $64.610 billion (1986)
GNP per capita: $12,640
GNP average annual growth rate: 1.5% (1973–86)
GNP per capita average annual growth rate: 1.4% (1973–86)
Average annual rate of inflation: 7.3% (1980–86)
Consumer Price Index: (1980 = 100)
    All items: 162.6 (February 1988)
    Food: 156.0 (February 1988)
Wholesale Price Index
Average annual growth rate, (1980–86) (%)
    Public consumption: 0.9
    Private consumption: 2.5
    Gross domestic investment: 7.1

BALANCE OF PAYMENTS, 1987 ($ million)

Current account balance: –2.975
Merchandise exports: 25.618
Merchandise imports: –24.806
Trade balance: 812
Other goods, services & income +: 10.586
Other goods, services & income –: –14.152
Other goods, services & income net: —
Private unrequited transfers: –56
Official unrequited transfers: –164
Direct investment: —
Portfolio investment: —
Other long-term capital: 8,333
Other short-term capital: –835
Net errors & omissions: –80
Counterpart items: 1,370
Exceptional financing: —
Liabilities constituting foreign authorities' reserves: –712
Total change in reserves: –5,102

GROSS DOMESTIC PRODUCT, 1985

GDP nominal (national currency): 605.3 billion
GDP real (national currency): 414.3 billion (1980 prices)
GDP per capita ($): 11,174

Average annual growth rate of GDP, 1980–86: 2.8%

GDP by type of expenditure (%)
    Consumption
        Private: 54
        Government: 26
    Gross domestic investment: 18

GROSS DOMESTIC PRODUCT, 1985 *(continued)*
Gross domestic saving: 22

Foreign trade
Exports: 37
Imports: −36

Cost components of GDP (%)
Net indirect taxes: 15
Consumption of fixed capital: 9
Compensation of employees: 55
Net operating surplus: 22

Sectoral origin of GDP (%)
Primary
Agriculture: 6
Mining: 1

Secondary
Manufacturing: 20
Construction: 6
Public utilities: 1

Tertiary
Transportation & communications: 8
Trade: 15
Finance: 2
Other services: 19
Government: 23

Average annual sectoral growth rates, 1980–86 (%)
Agriculture: 4.6
Industry: 2.6
Manufacturing: 2.9
Services: 2.4

OFFICIAL DEVELOPMENT ASSISTANCE

In $ Million

13	59	205	481	415	395	449	440	695	855
1965	1970	1975	1980	1982	1983	1984	1985	1986	1987

As Percentage of GNP

0.13	0.38	0.58	0.74	0.77	0.73	0.85	0.80	0.89	0.87
1965	1970	1975	1980	1982	1983	1984	1985	1986	1987

PUBLIC FINANCE

The Danish fiscal year is the calendar year.

The public sector in Denmark includes the central government and local administrations as well as quasi-public organizations that discharge functions laid down by legislation. The combined expenditures of these public bodies average annually 45% of the GNP at factor cost. This is about five times the percentage obtained before World War I. By the end of the 1930s the share had risen to 15%, and by the late 1950s to 25%.

The basic factors in this quintuple explosion in the national budget have been a steady improvement in the traditional public services—education, health and transportation—and a great expansion in social welfare and an improvement in the standards of social benefits. Since the end of World War II there have also been greatly increased defense spending as well as expenditures for the development of Greenland. Demographic changes led to slow growth of the tax base but entailed rapidly increasing costs for educating the young and taking care of the old. Because of an agricultural slump beginning in the 1960s, the government had to extend substantial subsidies to this sector until Denmark joined the EEC in 1973. Finally, aid to developing countries and budgetary allocations to the EEC began to grow in size and importance.

Until the late 1930s, expenditures of state and local governments were about equal, but those of the former have grown three times in size since then. This disparity is the result of deliberate policy. The central government has borne an increasing share of local government expenditures to level the differences among local government services and revenues. Along with the administrative reorganization of local government units in 1970 came a reordering of financial relations between the state and local governments. The state assumed the cost of Social Security pensions. Also, a number of state allocations are measured according to the revenue levels and expenditure needs of individual local governments. These allocations are aimed at harmonizing the tax levels in various parts of the country and are supplemented by direct equalization programs for transferring funds from local governments with high income levels to those with low ones.

Until the beginning of this century, central government revenues were derived principally from taxes on real property, customs duties and a few consumer taxes. The present system of income and capital taxes was introduced in 1903, when the property tax also was modernized and reduced. As a result, property taxes now account for a little under 5% of all direct taxation; consumer taxes and customs duties account for about 35%. The past 40 years have witnessed a gradual broadening of the scope of consumer taxes, which now include those for tobacco, beverages, motor vehicles and gasoline. Typically they amount to 50% to 80% of the retail value of these goods. Customs duties, on the other hand, have scarcely any fiscal significance. The scale of public expenditures rose to supplement these consumer taxes with even more broadly based ones. A wholesale tax was introduced in 1962, replaced five years later by the value-added tax, the first such levy in the world. In 1975 new-house building was included in this tax. The value-added tax is paid by all businesses. Typically they add about 15% to the prices of goods and services in the home market. Exporters are compensated by the state for their payment of what is meant to be a tax on consumption only. Revenue from the value-added tax accounts for over 45% of total indirect taxation.

The personal income tax averages about 35% of the taxable income. The share of local government income tax averages about 40% of the total. The highest rate of combined state and local income tax normally is about 60% to 65%, and it cannot exceed two-thirds of taxable income over Kr100,000. The income tax is supplemented by a tax on wealth, introduced in 1903, levied at the rate of 9% on all taxable wealth over Kr500,000. This tax has greatly diminished in fiscal importance, accounting for only 2% of the revenue from the income tax. The income tax is deducted at the source through withholdings on wages and pensions. On nonwage incomes, demands are issued to the taxpayers directly. Tax on dividends is withheld at a flat 30% rate.

Capital gains are not normally included in assessments of personal income tax but are taxed separately. There also is a company tax at the rate of 35% of annual earnings, whether paid out as dividends or placed in reserve. In calculating the assessment, an allowance of 2.5% of the share capital is made, up to a maximum of half the taxable earnings. Real-estate taxes are now important only in local government taxation and account for about 15% of revenues at that level. The average rate is about 3½%.

As a background to its economic policy, the government publishes an economic survey, which is submitted to the Folketing each year in March just before final adoption of the budget, and in September before the level of the state income tax is finally fixed.

With revenues and expenditures amounting to 45% of the GNP, public finances exert considerable influence on the national economy. There was a surplus in public budgets throughout most of the 1960s and early 1970s. For a decade following the first oil crisis, of 1973, both budget deficits and public debt worsened. In 1983 spending on social services accounted for 42% of all expenditures, compared to 48% a decade earlier. Gross interest payments on public debt had risen to 12½% of total expenditures, compared to 2½% in 1974. Revenues grew less strongly than expenditures, although direct taxes are higher in Denmark than in most OECD countries. The new Conservative-led government initiated a tight fiscal policy in 1982, emphasizing public sector spending restraint. As a result, the growth in public sector expenditures has stabilized at about 5½% a year. The general government deficit has been reduced significantly since its peak in 1982 and as rapidly as it was built up. The improvement of the general government balance has been impressive by international standards.

The main contribution to the improvement in the public sector financial balance has come from the revenue side, from a strong growth in the tax bases and an increase in tax rates. After a decline in 1982 to 52.2%, the ratio of public sector revenue to the GDP rose to 57.3% in 1985. This has been accompanied by a shift in tax burdens away from households and toward business, through higher Social Security contributions and a higher corporate tax rate of 50% introduced in 1985. The 1986 the central government budget brought the deficit down to 4½% of the GDP, compared to 6% in 1985.

In 1985 the Folketing approved a tax reform bill that abolished or reduced a number of deductions, introduced a flat tax rate of 50% on capital income, and divided taxable profits into return on capital and personal income. A new expenditure control system also was introduced in 1986 to achieve zero growth in the net real public expenditure level. The incomes policy also was intensified by suspending the indexation system until 1987, limiting public and private sector wage increases, and limiting profit margins and price increases in the private sector.

CENTRAL GOVERNMENT EXPENDITURES, 1986
% of total expenditures

Defense: 5.2
Education: 9.2
Health: 1.0
Housing, Social Security, welfare: 40.0
Economic services: 6.8
Other: 37.8
Total expenditures as % of GNP: 39.5
Overall surplus or deficit as % of GNP: –3.8

CENTRAL GOVERNMENT REVENUES, 1986
% of total current revenues

Taxes on income, profit & capital gain: 37.2
Social Security contributions: 3.7
Domestic taxes on goods & services: 41.7
Taxes on international trade & transactions: 0.1
Other taxes: 3.8
Current nontax revenue: 13.5
Total current revenue as % of GNP: 43.8
Government consumption as % of GNP: 24
Annual growth rate of government consumption, 1980–86: 0.9%

CURRENCY & BANKING

Denmark has a highly developed financial system, dating back to 1846, when the first commercial bank was founded. At the apex of the system is the National Bank of Denmark, which is the central bank. Below it are three levels of banks, as follows:

Banks of Deposit	Specialized Credit Institutions	Insurance Companies and Pension Funds
Commercial banks	Mortgage societies	Life assurance companies
Savings banks	Ship credit fund	Pension programs and funds
Cooperative banks	Industrial and credit finance companies	Unit trusts
Post office giro	Local government mortgage societies	

The National Bank of Denmark was established by statute in 1936. Its management consists of a board of directors, a committee of directors and a board of governors. The minister for economic affairs, as Royal Bank commissioner, presides over the board of directors, of whose 25 members eight are members of the Folketing. The committee of directors comprises seven members and the board of governors of three members. The National Bank is authorized to issue currency notes, short-term securities, deposit certificates and debentures. Commercial and savings banks may borrow from the National Bank at varying interest rates. The National Bank is the state's banker; the Ministry of Finance holds a current account with it, which reflects the effect of government finance on the volume of money.

Commercial and savings banks are governed by the Bank Act of 1906. There is heavy concentration in this sector, with the five largest commercial banks accounting for two-thirds of total advances and deposits. These five are the Copenhagen Commercial Bank, the Danish Farmers Bank, the Private Bank, the Danish Provincial Bank and the Cooperative Bank. Nearly 65% of commercial bank advances are for trade, industry and construction.

Savings banks are required to be self-governing institutions in which neither founders, guarantors nor other participants may own resources or surplus. A savings bank must have at least 25 guarantors, who may not draw interest except on their paid-up guarantee capital. The largest savings banks are members of the Amalgamated Danish Savings Banks, whose combined deposits account for nearly 60% of all savings bank deposits.

The mortgage societies date back to the middle of the 19th century. The formerly large number of mortgage societies was reduced by law in 1970 to seven. The law distinguishes between first and second mortgages. In the case of the former, the maximum loan is 40% of the value of the property, and the maximum repayment period is 40 years. The Industry and Crafts Finance Institute provides medium-term loans for industry to finance machinery, buildings, vehicles, etc.

A license is not required to carry on an insurance business, but a number of statutory requirements laid down in the Insurance Act of 1959 must be complied with. A company may not begin business until it has been enrolled in the *Insurance Register* and its statutes have been ratified by the minister of commerce. A company may not conduct both life insurance and general insurance business. Only limited liability and mutual companies may engage in the insurance business. Insurance company funds must be invested in accordance with the guidelines laid down in the Insurance Act. Since the 1970s, pension funds have acquired great importance and command substantial resources.

The Copenhagen Stock Exchange is the only stock exchange in Denmark. It is governed by the law of 1972 and by a committee of 11 members. The Exchange has 35 members.

The Danish national currency is the krone (Kr), divided into 100 ore. Coins are issued in denominations of 5, 10 and 25 ore and 1, 5 and 10 krone; notes are issued in denominations of 20, 50, 100, 500 and 1,000 krone.

Denmark went over from the silver to the gold standard in 1873 but several times had to abandon the fixed rate of exchange identified with the gold standard. Denmark is a member of IMF, the EMS (European Monetary System) and other bodies. The krone was devalued in 1949 and again in 1982. At present the krone is tied to the Common Market's exchange system, which restricts fluctuations in mutual exchange rates to 2% of the parities determined by the rates notified to the European Fund.

EXCHANGE RATES OF THE KRONE AGAINST THE DOLLAR									
1979	1980	1981	1982	1983	1984	1985	1986	1987	1988
5.365	6.015	7.425	8.384	9.875	11.280	8.969	7.342	6.096	6.448

The years 1983 to 1985 witnessed fundamental changes in fiscal policy in response to crises. These changes included a tighter incomes policy, the adoption of a hard currency option and the progressive dismantling of controls on capital flows. In 1985 a more market-oriented system of controlling bank credit expansion, relying on marginal reserve requirements, was introduced. In 1982, despite an interest rate differential of 8% over international capital market rates, there was a sizable flight of private capital from the country. Moreover, very high long-term interest rates had adverse effects on private investment and government debt servicing. Since 1982, interest rates have declined, from 22% in 1982 to 10% in 1986. The interest rate differential has narrowed to some 4% vis-à-vis West Germany and to zero vis-à-vis the United States. Increasing confidence in the Danish currency is reflected in sizable capital inflows, mainly in the form of purchases of government bonds by foreign investors. Given the financial environment of 1982, the government committed itself to a stable exchange rate and rejected devaluation of the krone as an option. At the same time, steps were taken to dismantle existing controls on capital movements, particularly those governing company borrowing abroad and nonresident access to the Danish bond market.

One of the features of the 1982 economic crisis was monetary expansion beyond the National Bank guidelines. The growth of the broadly defined money supply (M^2) reached 26% in 1983, and although it declined to 16% to 18% in 1984, it still was in excess of the National Bank target. Therefore, brakes were put on the expansion of bank lending to bring the expansion of money supply to 10% annually. However, this control system was worn down by company borrowing abroad and large purchases of bonds by banks. The counterpart was a large increase in contract deposits (individually negotiated short-term deposits), resulting in an upward pressure on deposit rates. In 1985, therefore, the National Bank introduced a new policy framework that (1) replaced the ceiling on bank lending by a system of marginal reserve requirements on deposits and (2) introduced a new system of bank liquidity control based on sales to banks of three-month certificates of deposit, which may serve as collateral for borrowing at the National Bank. In the second half of 1985 M^2 continued to grow at an annual rate of 13% to 14%, while there was a strong acceleration in the growth of the narrow money supply (M^1). However, the new liquidity controls had not yet been reflected in the bank balance sheets.

FINANCIAL INDICATORS 1987

International reserves minus gold: $ 10.066 billion
  SDRs: 304
   Reserve position in IMF: 175
   Foreign exchange: 19.587 billion
Gold (million fine troy oz): 2
Ratio of external debt to total reserves: —

Central bank
  Assets

FINANCIAL INDICATORS 1987 *(continued)*

Foreign assets: 37.8 (%)
Claims on government: 0.6 (%)
Claims on bank: 38.1 (%)
Claims on private sector: 23.5 (%)

Liabilities
Reserve money: 28.2 (%)
Government deposits: 44.9 (%)
Foreign liabilities: 5.3 (%)
Capital accounts: 31.6 (%)

Money supply
Stock in billion national currency: 215
M^1 per capita: 42060DKr
U.S. liabilities to: $4.061 billion
U.S. claims on: $986 million

Private banks
Assets
Loans to government: 7.2 (%)
Loans to private sector: 66.5 (%)
Reserves: 2.5 (%)
Foreign assets: 24.8 (%)

Liabilities: deposits: 554.2 billion DKr
Of which
Demand deposits: 36.6 (%)
Savings deposits: 33.6 (%)
Government deposits: 5.4 (%)
Foreign liabilities: 24.4 (%)

GROWTH PROFILE (Annual Growth Rates, %)

Population, 1985–2000: –0.1
Crude birth rate, 1985–90: 10.9
Crude death rate, 1985–90: 11.2
Urban population, 1980–85: 0.3
Labor force, 1985–2000: 0.2
GNP, 1975–86: 1.5
GNP per capita, 1965–86: 1.4
GDP, 1980–86: 2.8
Inflation, 1980–86: 7.3
Agriculture, 1980–86: 4.6
Industry, 1980–86: 2.6
Manufacturing, 1980–86: 2.9
Services, 1980–86: 2.4
Money holdings, 1980–86: 16.9
Manufacturing earnings per employee, 1980–85: –0.4
Energy production, 1980–86: 55.8
Energy consumption, 1980–86: 1.1
Exports, 1980–86: 4.5

GROWTH PROFILE (Annual Growth Rates, %) *(continued)*

Imports, 1980–86: 3.9
General government consumption, 1980–86: 0.9
Private consumption, 1980–86: 2.5
Gross domestic investment, 1980–86: 7.1

AGRICULTURE

Despite a small population and an even smaller size, Denmark claims a number of superlatives in agriculture: It is the world's number one exporter of pig meat, number three in cheese and number four in butter. Two-thirds of the farm production is exported to about 150 countries. Danish agriculture was the first in the world to eradicate such cattle diseases as bovine tuberculosis (1952) and undulant fever (1959). In its ownership structure also, Denmark stands out in having 96.7% of its holdings farmed by owners.

It took three stages of modernization to bring Denmark to this prominence. Down to the mid-18th century, all agricultural land was owned by the crown and by large landholders, the majority of the peasants being copyhold tenants. The cultivated land was usually divided according to the open-field system, one field for winter grain, one for summer grain and the third fallow. Each field was divided into strips of different quality, and each strip was further subdivided. Family holdings were scattered over a large number of narrow strips, often 50 to 100 each. Land reforms initiated in about 1760 brought radical changes both in the social position of the peasants and in the agricultural structure. Among other things, they promoted a transition from copyhold to freehold farming, together with consolidation of individual holdings. Common cultivation ceased, and as a general rule farmers moved out of the village to their new consolidated holdings. These reforms placed Denmark ahead of most other European countries in regard to agrarian structure. The abolition of villeinage in 1788 by King Frederik VI is a benchmark in Danish social as well as agrarian history.

The second phase of modernization came toward the end of the 19th century. The great expansion of railways in North America and Eastern Europe enabled vast quantities of cheap grain to be shipped from these regions to Western Europe. Most countries in Europe tried to protect their farmers from the effects of falling grain prices by high tariffs. Denmark, on the other hand, turned the low prices into an advantage by switching to livestock production and importing cheap grain to feed cattle. As much as 90% of the crop was processed for livestock, which now became the main activity in the farm sector. A network of slaughterhouses and dairies was established, and large export markets were found, especially in Great Britain.

The third phase of modernization began with the introduction of agrotechnology, which reduced the number of farmers on the one hand and increased their per capita income and productivity on the other. In 1946 there were 208,000 farms compared to 110,800 today. In 1950 one in every five Danes was a farmer; today there are fewer than one in 20. In 1960 there were 110,000 farm laborers; today, only 24,000. In 1950 one Danish farmer produced enough to feed 35 people; today he produces enough for 128 people.

It is difficult to understand the Danish agriculture or economy without reference to the famed Danish cooperative movement. This movement has developed under three heads: agricultural cooperatives, retail cooperatives and urban cooperatives. The cooperative movement was first developed by the weavers of Rochdale, England, in 1844. The idea spread quickly to Denmark, where the first cooperative store was set up in 1866 at Thisted by a clergyman, H. C. Sonne. The movement gained strength in 1870 with the large-scale production and export of animal-based foodstuffs. By the establishment of agricultural cooperatives, the small and medium-size farmers were able to meet the requirements of standardization and quality, especially for the British market. The cooperative enabled the family holding to compete with the large-scale farmer. The first cooperative dairy was founded in 1882 at Hjedding in West Jutland, and by 1890 there were more than 700. The first cooperative bacon factory was built in 1887 at Horsens in East Jutland. From 1890 to 1914 farmers established a network of purchasing, processing and marketing associations: the Danish Egg Export Committee was the first such, in 1895. The growing number of cooperatives entailed greater coordination among them. In 1896 the retail cooperatives became associated with the Cooperative Wholesale Society. The Central Cooperative Committee, formed in 1899, coordinated the agricultural cooperative movement, including the retail cooperatives, under the direction of Anders Nielsen. In 1919 a second body, the Federation of Danish Cooperative Societies, was founded.

After World War II, the cooperative movement was enabled by technology to become leaner and more concentrated. While there were 1,400 coop dairies in the days of the horse-drawn cart, now there are only 139, with motorized milk tankers. Similarly, the number of cooperative abattoirs has declined from 72 in 1962 to 16. The extent of concentration in cooperatives is brought out in the table on page 43.

Urban cooperation was started by the cooperative bakeries, the first of which was started in 1884. They were followed by the building trades and milk supply. In 1917 Copenhagen societies formed the Greater Copenhagen Cooperative So-

Sector	Number of Cooperatives	Share of Business (%)
Milk	149	87
Butter	1	92
Cheese	1	79
Abattoirs	16	90
		(pigs, 50; cattle, 40)
Poultry	2	45
Eggs	1	60
Seeds	1	45–50
Fruits, Vegetables and Flowers	1	50
Grain and Chemicals	3	50
		(grain, feedstuffs);
		43
		(fertilizers);
		40
		(field seed)
Agricultural Machinery	1	15

ciety, which has since developed into one of the biggest retail businesses in Denmark. In 1922 the urban cooperatives were federated into the Union of Urban Cooperative Societies, and there was considerable growth between the wars, especially in provincial cities. Since 1945, the urban movement has been characterized by structural rationalization, with concentration of resources. Although urban cooperation has never had the same social and economic importance as its agricultural counterpart, it is particularly strong in the housing field. While the agricultural cooperative movement has traditionally been neutral in social matters, the urban movement has had a close historical association with the labor movement, the Social Democrats and the trade unions.

In the modern period, the most important piece of land legislation stemmed from the Agricultural Commission of 1960. Government policy is to keep farm ownership in family ownership. Therefore there is a statutory ban on the acquisition of agricultural properties by companies and institutions, and the purchase of holdings by individuals. Provisions governing joint operations have been substantially liberalized, and the amalgamation of holdings with a combined acreage of less than 200 ha. (494 ac.) is permitted. Agricultural loans are provided for acquiring supplementary holdings when the area after amalgamation does not exceed 35 ha. (86 ac.), or 50 ha. (124 ac.) in the case of poor-quality land. Farmers under 40 years of age who purchase a holding can obtain a depreciation loan, an establishment grant and a five-year operating grant under a 1967 law. In 1973 certain amendments were made in the Agricultural Act to bring it into conformity with EEC agricultural policy. Purchasers of farmland now must live permanently on the holding and pursue farming as a principal occupation.

The number of farm properties remained for many years at about 200,000. However, since 1960 the number has fallen sharply, to 134,000, as a result of amalgamations and sale of land for other purposes. Since Denmark's entry into the EEC, however, the number has stabilized somewhat. In the early 1970s there were 41,000 small holdings of less than 10 ha. (24.7 ac.), 84,000 medium-size farms of 10 to 50 ha. (24.7 to 123.5 ac.) and 9,000 large holdings of over 50 ha. As a result of amalgamation, the average farm size has risen from 15 ha. (37.1 ac.) to 22 ha. (54.3 ac.). The predominant ownership form since the beginning of the 19th century has been freehold, with over 95% of farms in this category. The owner and farmer are almost always one and the same person, the family doing most of the work. The great majority of the farms are fairly comprehensive, producing grain and coarse fodder and raising cattle, pigs and poultry. Specialization in any area is restricted to the larger holdings.

The agricultural area of Denmark is estimated at 2.9 million ha. (7.2 million ac.), or about 64% of the total land area. Nearly 11% is forest, with 8% meadow and pasture. Of the farmland, nearly 90% is in normal crop rotation; the balance is in permanent grass.

Farm production supplies 80% to 90% of the fodder needs of the large livestock population, as well as total domestic consumption of seed grain, bread grain, industrial grain, sugar and potatoes. Exports of these items constitute about 10% of total agricultural exports. About 60% of the agricultural area is devoted to cereals, 26% to grass and green fodder, 7% to root fodder and 7% to commercial crops. The yield per hectare is high by international standards: The grain yield is about 35 to 40 crop units per ha. (86.5 to 98.8 per ac.), grass 40 to 50 per ha. (98.8 to 123.5 per ac.) and root fodder 80 to 90 per ha. (197.6 to 222.3 per ac.).

About 90% of the value added in agriculture is in livestock production. Of this, dairy cattle account for 30%, fat stock 15%, pigs 45% and poultry 10%.

Cattle are kept on 70% and dairy cows on 65% of the holdings. The average size per herd is about 19 cows, but the trend is toward larger herds. The chief breeds are Red Danish Dairy (40%), Black and White Danish Dairy (35%), Jersey (18%) and pure beef breeds such as Charolais and Hereford (2% to 3%). The average yield is about 4,700 kg. (10,362 lb.) of milk of 4.4% fat and nearly 200 kg. (441 lb.) of butter fat. About 53% of all milk is used for making butter; about 16% for cheese; about 7% for preserved milk; about 4% for feed; and about 20% for liquid milk and cream, ice cream and various specialties. About half of all skimmed milk and buttermilk obtained during the buttermaking process is returned to the farmer as feed. The dairy industry produces 30 to 40 different cheeses, some 11 of which are marketed under Danish names such as Samso, Danbo and Havarti.

Meat production consists partly of discarded cows and partly of fattened calves. Approximately 1 million head of cattle are slaughtered annually, producing 250,000 tons of beef and veal, of which two-thirds are exported. Carcasses also provide skins and intestines for pharmaceutical production as well as raw materials for the paint and varnish industries.

Pigkeeping is the mainstay of Danish farm production. The country is noted for one of the finest specimens in the world: the Danish Landrace, a long pig with a fine bone structure, thin layer of fat and meaty hams. There are 9.8 million of these at any given time, the average piggery having a stock of 158. A total of 10 million pigs are slaughtered annually. Roughly 40% of the pig meat is sold to Great Britain; 22% is marketed as pork in Denmark; and the remaining 38% is converted to canned meat, sausages and meat cuts. Other parts also are commercially valuable: skin for leather, blood for plywood, bristles for toothbrushes, pancreases for insulin and pituitary glands for hormones. Nothing is wasted.

There are 5 million egg-layers in the poultry sector. Denmark has banned battery-cage hens. Egg production has declined, especially since Great Britain became self-sufficient in eggs. The production of table chickens is relatively new and, unlike egg production, is restricted to large farms.

An impressive feature of Danish agriculture is the scrupulous monitoring and inspection of livestock and products and constant efforts to improve breeding strains and product quality. Much of this work is done by the farmers' associations, but the government also enforces stringent quality and health regulations and grading standards. Danish farm products are among the most uniform and quality-guaranteed in the world.

A Danish farmer is required to obtain a "green license." To do so, he must attend a school of agriculture for three months and spend three years as a trainee on at least two farms. The training concludes with a nine- to 12-month course in farm management. The green license is required to obtain the many government benefits and subsidies available to the farmer.

The Danish farming industry is represented at the national level by a number of organizations, of which the largest is the Agricultural Council (Landbrugsradet), which is a federation of the Farmers' Union, representing large farmers, and the Smallholders' Union. The Agricultural Council has a permanent committee, the Agricultural Marketing Committee, to promote agricultural farm products abroad. The Federation of Danish Agricultural Associations represents medium-size farmers. Each agricultural sector has its own national federation. Agricultural research takes place principally at the Royal Veterinary and Agricultural University.

Horticulture and fruit growing take place all over Denmark, although they have developed most intensively near the major cities, especially Odense and Copenhagen. Of the businesses in this field, 36% are in the islands east of the Store Baelt, 36% in Fünen and 28% in Jutland. Horticulture and fruit growing account for 8% to 9% of the value added in agriculture. Of the productive area, fruits account for 48%, vegetables for 34%, nurseries and outdoor flowers for 15% and hothouses for 3%. The total area devoted to this sector is 26,500 ha. (65,455 ac.), or 14.8 ha. (36.6 ac.) per 1,000 inhabitants. The industry is noted for the dominance of family units and hothouse culture. The average size of the business is 2.65 ha. (6.55 ac.). About 25% of the production is exported. Domestic sales take place through cooperative marketing associations.

Forests cover 472,000 ha. (1,165,840 ac.), or about 11% of the land area. The annual timber yield is made up equally of hardwood and softwood. Two-thirds of the forest area is under private ownership, 30% is state-owned and 3% belongs to local governments. Of the 33,000 forest properties, only 3% exceeds 50 ha. (123.5 ac.) and less than 0.4% exceeds 500 ha. (1,235 ac.). In about 1800 the area under forest had fallen to 4% of the land area, leading to passage of legislation to prevent further depletion. The Forest Act of 1805, which made forests a protected national reserve, is still in force today.

The native stands are all deciduous, with beech, oak, ash and sycamore predominating. In the 18th century, conifers were planted on a large scale: Scotch pine, Norway spruce, silver fir and larch. Later came mountain pine as well as Douglas fir and Sitka spruce, the latter two from the United States. In the latter half of the 19th century the Japanese larch was introduced. More than two-thirds of the forest area has been planted within the past 150 years.

State forests are administered by the Directorate of State Forestry. The Danish Heath Society, founded in 1866, administers its own lands, totaling 12,500 ha. (30,875 ac.) of forests as well as 35,000 ha. (86,450 ac.) of private forests. A forest district of 1,000 ha. (2,470 ac.) is directed by a forest superintendent, who usually is a graduate in forestry.

As a nation surrounded on three sides by water, Denmark has a well-developed fishing industry. A characteristic feature of Danish fishing is that it is carried on exclusively from cutters of less than 50 gross tons. These cutters, generally made of wood, are owned by their skippers, and the crew is paid with part of the catch while sharing in some of the costs. Fishing is carried on year-round. About a third of the catch is sold at public auctions, which take place in all major fishing ports. Since domestic consumption is low—about 25 kg. (55 lb.) per head per annum—much of the catch is exported. The chief fishing ports are on the western and northern coasts of Jutland: Esbjerg, Hirtshals, Skagen, Thyborøn, Hanstholm, Hvide Sande, Strandby and Grenå. The Ministry of Fisheries operates the Bureau of Fishery Control, Danish Fisheries and Marine Research and a research laboratory. Fishing also is a major commercial activity in the Faeroe Islands and Greenland. Of the Faeroe Islands' catch, cod constitutes 30%, herring 32% and fish for fodder 22%. Greenland fisheries are chiefly centered in Davis Strait, between Greenland and Canada.

AGRICULTURAL INDICATORS, 1986

Agriculture's share of GDP: 6%
Average annual growth rate: 4.6% (1980–86)
Value added in agriculture: $3.980 billion
Cereal imports (000 tons): 349
Index of Agricultural Production (1979–81=100): 119.2 (1985)
Index of Food Production (1979–81=100): 119.2 (1985)
Index of Food Production per capita (1979–81=100): 123 (1984–86)
Number of tractors: 169,700
Number of harvester-threshers: 35,400
Total fertilizer consumption: 669,600 tons
Fertilizer consumption per ha. (per ac.) (100 g.): 2,418 (979)
Number of farms: 90,000
Average size of holding, ha. (ac.) 31.4 (77.5)
Size class (%)
   Below 1 ha. (below 2.47 ac.): 19.4
   1–5 ha. (2.47–12.35 ac.): 19.4
   5–10 ha. (12.35–24.7 ac.): 19.4
   10–20 ha. (24.7–49.4 ac.): 64.4
   20–50 ha. (49.4–123.5 ac.): 64.4
   50–200 ha. (123.5–494 ac.): 16.2
   Over 200 ha. (over 494 ac.): 16.2
Activity (%)
   Mainly crops: 49.2
   Mainly livestock: 24.0
   Mixed: 26.8
% of farms using irrigation: 15.2
Total area under cultivation: 2,819,000 ha. (6,965,749 ac.)
Farms as % of total land area: 65.4
Land use (%), total cropland: 92.4
   Permanent crops: 1.2
   Temporary crops: 98.7
   Fallow: 0.1
Meadows & pastures: 7.1
Woodland: —
Other: —

```
┌─────────────────────────────────────────────────────────┐
│          AGRICULTURAL INDICATORS, 1986 (continued)      │
│   Yields, kg./ha. (lb./ac.)                             │
│      Grains: 5,015 (4,476)                              │
│      Roots & tubers: 36,419 (32,506)                    │
│      Pulses: 4,302 (3,840)                              │
│      Milk, kg. (lb.) animal: 5,808 (12,804)             │
│                                                         │
│   Livestock (000)                                       │
│      Cattle: 2,495                                      │
│      Horses: 33                                         │
│      Sheep: 89                                          │
│      Pigs: 9,321                                        │
│                                                         │
│   Forestry                                              │
│      Production of roundwood: 2,693 million cu. m.      │
│         (94.75 million cu. ft.)                         │
│         of which industrial roundwood (%): 87           │
│      Value of exports ($ 000): 186,020                  │
│                                                         │
│   Fishing                                               │
│      Total catch (000 tons): 1,696                      │
│         of which marine (%): 98.6                       │
│      Value of exports ($ 000): 952,712                  │
└─────────────────────────────────────────────────────────┘
```

MANUFACTURING

Manufacturing contributes 17% to the GNP. Manufacturing's growth rate during 1973–84 was 2.4%. Compared with other Western countries, Danish manufacturing had a late start. It was not until the mid-19th century that the industrial revolution reached Denmark, and the early plants were built under the umbrella of a protectionist law of 1863. This principle was maintained in a new law of 1908, when a substantial tariff was imposed on imported goods competing with Danish products. Under its aegis, the biggest industrial establishments were founded in Denmark. The most rapid development has taken place since the 1960s, when the range and quality of Danish manufactures established a niche for the country in international export markets.

The great majority of manufacturing plants employ fewer than 500 people. Production is labor-intensive. With a few exceptions, there are no capital-intensive enterprises in the country. As a result, Danish firms can adapt their production lines quickly. Manufacturing is innovation-oriented. Companies are constantly looking for special lines in which they can secure a strong competitive position through product development.

Danish manufactures range over a wide field, but two groups stand out in terms of volume of production and employment: food and drink, which leads in value added, and engineering in employment. The prominent position of food and drink is not surprising considering the input from agriculture. Its share in manufacturing production has risen to 23%, from 21% in 1973. The share of engineering has grown to 24%, and it provides the keen edge of Danish productivity and export drive. The chemicals industry occupies third place with 9%, much of its growth coming from the three oil refineries built with foreign initiative. The other major industrial sectors are textiles and clothing, woodworking, paper, stone, clay and glass, and transportation.

To a greater extent than elsewhere Denmark has maintained these traditional industries rather than move toward technology-based industries. Denmark is meagerly represented in the so-called knowledge-intensive industries, though this may reflect the absence of massive military and aerospace programs. The efficiency of the agricultural sector has been a disincentive for venturing into areas where skills and inputs of a different order are required. On the other hand, Denmark has never been heavily engaged in the "sunset industries" (shipbuilding, petrochemicals, steel and automobiles), which have caused severe problems in other advanced countries. There are no manufacturing centers of any significant size.

Denmark markedly lags behind its EC partners in technological competitiveness. It devotes just over 1% of its GDP to research and development. In 1983 the manufacturing sector employed some 2½ man-years per 1,000 man-years of its total work force for R&D. This may be due to the fact that Denmark has none of the internationally large corporations that lead in R&D expenditures, and particularly no firms engaged in military, aeronautic or space research. Industries with a low R&D intensity dominate the Danish industrial structure. Almost two-thirds of the value added is produced, and more than half of the manufacturing employment is accounted for by industries that spend only 17% of national R&D costs. On the other hand, R&D-intensive enterprises that spend more than 50% of R&D costs produce only 14% of the value added and employ 10% of the work force in manufacturing. There also is a strong concentration of R&D expenditures among large firms. In small enterprises, technological progress often is made through adaptation of existing techniques because the lack of economies of scale makes it unprofitable to maintain independent research units.

Government industrial policy is geared toward greater dynamism in the private sector. The state has traditionally maintained a hands-off policy toward the private sector. State subsidies to business constituted only 1% of the GDP in 1984, whereas the average was about 3% in other Scandinavian countries in that year. A key principle in the formulation of industrial policies has been to rely on correct market mechanisms as much as possible. The "forward-looking" industrial strategies of the sort implemented in Japan and France, for example, have not been on the Danish agenda. Direct state intervention is applied only to market failures. Support has been given in specific cases, where the small size of the Danish firms discouraged them from undertaking attractive investments that required a long lead time for payoff. Unlike in many other countries, in Denmark public procurement has not been used as an instrument of industrial policy. The much-disputed "picking the winners" approach has been rejected in Denmark, and the "saving the losers" policy has been applied to a limited extent only (notably in shipbuilding). The main thrust of industrial policy is defensive: to preserve jobs and promote exports.

Since its peak in 1982, industrial support has been cut back by 43%, from Kr3.5 billion to Kr2 billion. However, an increasing share of available funds has been allocated to technology development, especially to ensure the transfer of knowledge in various scientific fields.

The state-owned industrial and trading sector is small. The state has limited equity participation in a few major companies, such as Det Danske Staatvalsevaerk (DDS), a steel company. There is only one state trading company, the Royal Greenland Trade Department, which is responsible for the supply of consumer and capital goods to Greenland. In addition, the state owns and operates most airports, the rail system, the post office (including part of the telephone service) and broadcasting.

The major constraints on Danish industry are low growth of productivity and limited manpower resources to meet the demand for highly skilled workers. The central industrial organization is the Federation of Danish Industries, which looks after the economic, political and commercial interests of the industry but does not concern itself with industrial relations.

Denmark has long had a liberal foreign investment policy (both direct and portfolio) because of its heavy dependence on foreign trade. Foreign direct investment generally is limited to manufacturing, trade, handicrafts, transportation and hotels. There are certain restrictions on foreign participation in the shipping industry and arms manufacture. There are no restrictions on ownership, and foreign investors may have full control. Also, there are no restrictions on the repatriation of profits to foreign countries. Investments in development areas, primarily West and North Jutland and the smaller islands, are encouraged through incentives available equally to foreign and domestic investors. U.S. direct investment is estimated at close to $1.5 billion.

MINING

Denmark has no significant mineral resources. Greenland has lead and zinc concentrates and cryolite.

MANUFACTURING INDICATORS, 1986

Average annual growth rate, 1980–86: 2.9%
Share of GDP: 20%
Labor force in manufacturing: 27%
Value added in manufacturing, 1986: $9.729 billion
   Food & agriculture: 22%
   Textiles: 6%
   Machinery: 24%
   Chemicals: 10%
Earnings per employee in manufacturing, 1980–85
   Growth Rate: –0.4%
   Index (1980=100): 97 (1985)
Total Earnings as % of value added: 52
Gross output per employee (1980=100): 109 (1985)
Index of Manufacturing Production: (1980=100): 123 (1987)

ENERGY

Until 1973 Denmark was one of the most vulnerable countries in the world in the energy sector, with 93% of its energy needs being met by oil imported from the Middle East. By the mid-1980s the energy picture has brightened. Dependence on imported oil has been substantially reduced, and both oil and natural gas from Denmark's North Sea fields have made Denmark 40% to 50% self-sufficient in energy by the late 1980s. The demand for primary energy will be reduced by a more widespread utilization of surplus heat from coal-fired combined heat and power plants. More than one-third of Danish homes will be supplied by combined heat and power (CHP) before the end of the century.

Danish energy policy, already smarting under the sting of the 1973 crisis, took a further buffeting with the second oil crisis, in 1978–79. In fact, 1979 was the most momentous year in the history of Danish energy. The Folketing adopted legislation initiating a state-backed natural-gas project—one of the most expensive construction projects the nation has ever undertaken. In the same year, the Ministry of Energy was set up and the Heat Supply Act was passed. Development of a national oil and gas company also was pushed ahead in earnest in 1979. Passage of the Natural Gas Act of 1979 gave DONG, as this company was called, the capital to undertake capital exploration and transmission projects. Meanwhile, energy conservation programs were beginning to pay off handsomely. New buildings required less energy. Industry had cut back its consumption levels considerably, partly as a result of state subsidies for oil substitution. Danish consumption of gasoline has dwindled in recent years as a result of speed limits and improved mileage performance, and there has been a corresponding increase in use of mass transportation. Electricity consumption, on the other hand, has increased since the oil crises, although the government has countered with a penal levy of almost 30%.

Exploration for oil and gas has been conducted in Danish fields for almost 50 years. In 1966 the first offshore deposits were found in Anne Field in the North Sea. The sole rights for drilling had been granted in 1962 to Danish ship-builder, A. P. Moller, who operated the Danish Underground Consortium (DUC) with Mobil, Shell, Chevron and Texaco as partners. Gorm, a second oil field, went into production in 1981, followed by Skjold in 1982. The three fields, of which Gorm is the largest, produce 2.5 million tons of oil annually, almost one-fourth of Denmark's oil needs. The DUC also is tapping the gas reserves in these fields as well as two new gas fields, Tyra and Roar. To intensify explora-tion, the state has bought back from the DUC all unexplored areas, which have been reassigned to seven groups of new companies.

Oil and gas are brought onshore on the western coast via two state-owned pipelines. There are three oil refineries: a Shell plant near Fredericia, an Esso plant at Kalundborg and a former Gulf refinery at Stigsnaes.

Because of the efficiency of Denmark's power-generating systems—which use 90% coal—Denmark did not follow other countries into nuclear power. The decision to go nuclear was postponed a number of times in the Folketing and is expected to be defeated if submitted to a national referendum. Mean-while, Denmark appears to have sufficient power capacity until the 1990s.

Under the Heat Supply Act of 1979 a total of 50% of Danish households will be supplied with district heating from heating plants, power plants and refuse incinerators, 15% of the households will be heated by natural gas and the re-mainder by oil-burning plants.

Denmark is acknowledged as one of the international leaders in harnessing windmill energy. There are approximately 1,000 windmills. Because of the na-ture of the Danish climate, the country has had only moderate success with so-lar power. The use of livestock manure to generate biogas is at the experimental stage. On the other hand, agricultural straw is being converted into fuel in spe-cially designed burners. Denmark now has close to 20,000 straw-burning heat-ing plants on farms. Thosands of heat pumps have been installed to draw heat from the soil and from the air.

ENERGY INDICATORS, 1986

Total energy production, quadrillion BTU: 0.21
  Crude oil: 0.16
  Natural gas, liquid: 0.0
  Natural gas, dry: 0.5
  Coal: 0.0

ENERGY INDICATORS, 1986 *(continued)*

Hydroelectric power: 0.0
Nuclear power: 0.0
Average annual energy growth rate, 1980–86: 55.8%
Public utilities' share of GDP: 1.0%
Energy consumption per capita, kg. (lb.) oil equivalent: 3,821 (8,430)
Energy imports as % of merchandise imports: 10
Average annual growth rate of energy consumption, 1980–86: 1.1%

Electricity
  Installed capacity: 8,651,000 kw.
  Production: 29.064 billion kw.-hr.
    % fossil fuel: 99.7
    % hydro: 0.1
    % nuclear: 0.3
  Consumption per capita: 5,764 kw.-hr.

Natural gas
  Proved reserves: 76 billion cu. m. (2.684 trillion cu. ft.)
  Production: 1.756 billion cu. m. (62 billion cu. ft.)
  Consumption: 671 million cu. m. (23.696 billion cu. ft.)

Petroleum
  Proved reserves: 516 million bbl.
  Years to exhaust proved reserves: 19
  Production: 27 million bbl.
  Consumption: 76 million bbl.
  Refining capacity: 166,000 bbl. per day

Coal
  Reserves: 63 million metric tons
  Production: —
  Consumption: 12,146 million metric tons.

LABOR

In 1987 the Danish labor force was estimated at 2,860,000, up from 2,713,000 in 1984. Women constitute about 45.1% of the labor force. Although discrimination on the basis of sex is actively opposed, women are generally paid less. During periods of recession, the unemployment rates for women are double those for men. Nearly half of the married women are employed part time. Distribution of women in the various sectors differs widely from that of men. Women account for half of the work force in trade and distribution, two-thirds in administration and services, 25% in manufactures and handicrafts and 20% in transportation.

```
┌─────────────────────────────────────────────────┐
│             LABOR INDICATORS, 1986                │
│                                                   │
│ Total economically active population: 2.86 million (1987) │
│                                                   │
│ As % of working-age population: 66                │
│                                                   │
│ % female: 45.1                                    │
│ Activity rate (%)                                 │
│    Total: 53.9                                    │
│    Male: 59.4                                     │
│    Female: 48.6                                   │
│                                                   │
│ Employment status (%)                             │
│    Employers & self-employed: 9.3                 │
│    Employees: 87.9                                │
│    Unpaid family workers: 2.3                     │
│    Other: 0.5                                     │
│    Organized labor: 65                            │
│                                                   │
│ Sectoral employment (%)                           │
│    Agriculture, forestry, fishing: 6.4            │
│    Mining: 0.2                                    │
│    Manufacturing, construction: 27.0              │
│    Electricity, gas, water: 0.7                   │
│    Trade: 15.3                                    │
│    Transportation, communications: 6.9            │
│    Finance, real estate: 7.3                      │
│    Services: 36.2                                 │
│                                                   │
│ Average annual growth rate of labor force, 1980-2000: │
│ 0.2%                                              │
│                                                   │
│ Unemployment (%): 9.3                             │
│ Labor under 20 years: 9.6%                        │
│                                                   │
│ Hours of work                                     │
│    Manufacturing: 34.5                            │
└─────────────────────────────────────────────────┘
```

The minimum age for employment of children is 15. The Working Environment Act of 1975 applies to the types of work that may be performed by those between 15 and 18. The act also established the Labor Inspections Service to enforce current regulations regarding work, rest and safety. The minimum wage is about $6.40 per hour. The workweek was reduced in the mid-1980s to 39 hours. The "11-hour rule" stipulates that a worker has the right to 11 hours of rest between work periods.

Immigration never has been an important factor in Denmark's labor history. It added 0.8% to the population between 1969 and 1979 but since has become insignificant. Reduced labor demand and tighter immigration rules have stopped the modest inflow of foreign workers.

Although Denmark has a very low population growth rate, the active labor force (16 to 66 years) grew twice as fast as usual during the 1970s, at an annual rate of 1.2%. The labor participation rate rose from 67% in 1970 to 79% in

1983 but declined to 66% in 1986. This development was entirely due to the increasing participation of women in the labor market.

In 1970 the labor force was almost fully employed. The unemployment rate was a minimal 1%. But as cutbacks in state budgets began to take effect, unemployment rose sharply—to 7% in 1980, 9% in 1981, 10% in 1982 and 10.8% in 1983. It fell to 10.5% in 1984; to 9% in 1985; and rose slightly, to 9.3%, in 1986. Workers under 25, especially women, have been particularly vulnerable to unemployment. In 1984 their unemployment rate was 17%, although it fell to 10.4% in 1985. Whereas recruitment in the public sector has been virtually frozen as a result of the government's budgetary restraint program, the manufacturing and construction sectors have been able to create more jobs. The new jobs were primarily wage-earner jobs, whereas the number of self-employed continues its downward trend. Unfortunately, most students grew up during the past quarter century with their skills oriented to public sector service, and many of them need retraining to enter other sectors. The problem is compounded by the relative immobility of Danish labor. Despite comparatively favorable developments since 1984, unemployment looms as a troubling domestic political issue over the remainder of this century. It is a destabilizing factor in both Danish politics and public finance.

During the 1960s and 1970s Danish wages rose more rapidly than those abroad—in the mid-1970s at annual rates of close to 20%. The inflation rate was correspondingly high, about 15%. With 1970 as the basis, Danish unit costs were 10% to 15% above the international average. The situation was partly mitigated when the then Social Democratic government devalued the krone successively while, by a series of incomes policy measures, holding Danish wage increases on a par with those abroad. The center-right coalition government that took office in 1982 has managed to bring Danish wage increases below those abroad. During 1986 and 1987 wages rose by 4% to 5%. A price moderation in 1985 resulted in moderate real wage gains, although real wages have declined since the 1970s.

Denmark has extensive labor legislation, but no code defines the rights and obligations of management and labor or prescribes procedures for collective bargaining or the election and certification of a bargaining unit. Factory legislation and welfare legislation are comprehensive, the former in regulations governing working conditions and the latter in benefits. A 1975 law on work environment authorized the creation of joint industrial committees and the election of shop safety stewards. Workers' representation on company boards was introduced in 1974.

Industrial relations are governed by the so-called September Agreement of 1899 between the central organizations of labor and management. Under this agreement, such issues as hours of work, wage changes, holidays and cost of living adjustments are subject to agreement between the two organizations, who may bargain freely on local issues only. Special boards deal with dismissals. Government conciliators are available if labor-management negotiations break down. If conciliation fails, labor disputes on contract interpretation go to a joint industrial arbitration committee, whose decision is binding. If the collective agreement has been violated, the case goes to the Labor Court.

The principal labor organization is the Danish Federation of Trade Unions (Landsorganisationen i Danmark, LO) with over 1.3 million members organized in to 40 affiliates, mostly craft unions. There has been a steady reduction in the number of affiliates through mergers encouraged by the LO. The General and Special Workers' Union and the Women's General Workers' Union are peculiar to Denmark.

The highest body in the LO is the Congress, which consists of the executive councils of individual national unions; it meets every four years. Between congresses the highest policy-making body is the 24-member Executive Committee. The Social Democrats appoint two members of the Executive Committee, and the LO appoints two members of the SD Executive Committee. The 31 national unions are comprised of about 1,800 local unions. At the local level, workers of each craft as well as unskilled workers form clubs, each headed by a shop steward, and elect club committees, which in larger firms combine into a joint club headed by a chief steward. Shop stewards are protected from being fired.

Efforts to restructure the LO into a federation of industrial unions have met strong opposition from the largest union, General Workers, as well as the union of unskilled women workers, who fear dilution of their influence, and also because of conflicting interests between skilled and unskilled workers.

There are two national trade union federations outside the LO: The Federation of Civil Servants and Salaried Employees (FTF) is a group of predominantly white-collar worker organizations, mostly in the public sector. In contrast to the LO, the FTF has no political affiliations, although it tends to take sides with the LO on most union issues. The Central Organization of Academicians (AC) is another union of white-collar workers employed in the private and public sectors.

There has traditionally been close cooperation between workers and employers in educational matters. In 1974 a joint training fund was established, to which employers contribute a sum based on the number of man-hours. The Workers' Educational Association was founded in 1924, and today it is the largest adult education organization in Denmark. It prepares its own educational materials. The first Labor College was opened in 1910 at Esbjerg, followed by another at Roskilde and the Trade Union Center College at Elsinore. The three largest trade unions maintain their own schools.

The Danish Employers' Confederation is the principal spokesman for management in trade, commerce and industry. It has over 150 affiliated associations. Its highest authority is the General Assembly, which elects the General Council of 55 members and the Executive Committee of 15 members. Although the number of employers' associations far exceeds the number of national unions, the percentage of organized employers is rather small (less than 25%). Nevertheless, as a statutory body it has enormous powers, and it polices its members quite effectively.

FOREIGN COMMERCE

Foreign trade is critical for the Danish economy, and the balance of payments figures are among the closely watched indicators of the nation's economic health. As a corollary, Denmark has traditionally been one of the champions of free trade, and its memberships in the EEC and the OECD have reinforced its free-trade philosophy.

From 1968 through 1975 manufactured goods overtook agricultural products as the primary merchandise export revenue earners. Since then, their relative shares have remained fairly stable. Nevertheless, by OECD standards Denmark's export base remains highly agricultural; only Greece and Ireland show higher ratios of agricultural export values to total merchandise export values. The end of the shrinkage of the agricultural export sector may be traced, in part, to the EEC's Common Agricultural Policy (CAP). After a period of weak export performance from 1965 to 1980, Denmark has outperformed the rest of the OECD since 1980. Denmark's foreign trade is vulnerable on two fronts: Its exports are mainly of "niche" or traditional products characterized by small-scale production, high input of fixed capital, and unskilled labor. Its imports, on the other hand, are characterized by a relatively high input of R&D.

FOREIGN TRADE INDICATORS, 1986

Exports: $21.3 billion
Imports: $22.9 billion
Balance of trade: –$1.6 billion
Annual growth rate 1980–86 exports: 4.5%
Annual growth rate 1980–86 imports: 3.9%
Ratio of international reserves to imports
   (in months): 2.0: 1
Value of manufactured exports: $12.334 billion
Terms of trade (1980=100): 106 (1986)
Import Price Index (1980=100): 86.9
Export Price Index (1980=100): 91.9

FOREIGN TRADE INDICATORS, 1986 *(continued)*		
Import of goods as % of GDP: 33.2		
Export of goods as % of GDP: 30.9		
Direction of Trade (%)		
	Imports	Exports
EEC	51.7	45.3
U.S.A.	4.8	8.4
East European economies	2.8	1.9
Japan	5.7	3.4
Composition of Trade (%)		
	Imports	Exports
Food		
Agricultural raw materials	15.3	35.6
Fuels	8.9	3.2
Ores and minerals	0.6	0.6
Manufactured goods	75.3	60.6
of which chemicals	10.5	8.9
of which machinery	31.7	24.3

TRANSPORTATION & COMMUNICATIONS

The Danish transportation system has developed in the form of a large H, crossing east to west from Copenhagen via Odense to Esbjerg, and north to south from Elsinore and Copenhagen to Lolland and Falster and from northern Jutland via Ålborg and Århus to the frontier with West Germany. Of the 66,482 km. (41,319 mi.) of highways, 64,551 km. (40,119 mi.) are concrete, bitumen, stone or black-surfaced. The principal components of the system are the European motorways E3, E4 and E66; primary roads; and subsidiary roads and streets. Four-lane roads exist only on a modest scale, mostly on the E roads. Due to the expansion of motor traffic, there is heavy congestion in and around Copenhagen, the major provincial cities and at ferry crossings, creating the need for new construction. A law of 1972 divides the country's roads into three categories: state highways, county roads and local government subsidiary roads. At a number of points bridges have been built across sounds and fjords, the two largest being Storstrum, connecting Zealand and Falster, and Lille Baelt Bridge between Fünen and Jutland. In the 1960s a bridge was constructed between Fünen and Langeland and a tunnel under Limfjorden at Ålborg. A second bridge across the Store Baelt was opened in 1970.

There are ferry services across the Øresund, the Store Baelt, the Kattegat, the Baltic and many other waterways. Most of the major ferry services are operated by Danish State Railways.

As in other advanced countries, mass transit is declining, but a dense network of coach services for commuters covering the entire country is provided by the State Railways and private operators. Large towns have private or public bus services. Copenhagen had tram services until 1972.

Rail transportation is concentrated in Danish State Railways, which operates 2,120 km. (1,318 mi.) of track. Of these, 1,999 km. (1,242 mi.) are rail lines, including 736 km. (457 mi.) double track and 97 km. (60 mi.) electrified. There also are 121 km. (75 mi.) of rail ferry services. In addition to the state railways there is network of private branch lines with 650 km. (404 mi.) of track, controlled mostly by local governments. About two-thirds the passengers are carried by the Copenhagen suburban rapid transit system, and about 7% are car drivers crossing by ferry. During most years, the State Railways shows an annual deficit, which is made up by the Treasury.

The administrative status of Danish ports varies. Esbjerg, Frederickshavn, Elsinore, Skagen and Thyborn are state-owned and directly under the Ministry of Public Works. Copenhagen Port and Copenhagen Free Port have special status. Most provincial ports are owned by the municipalities. Three large oil-refinery ports were built in the late 1960s.

After declining to 3.314 million GRT in 1970, the Danish merchant marine rebounded to 5.211 million GRT in 1984. More than 80% of the ships are less than 10 years old. Three large companies control three-fourths of the combined tonnage, while the smaller ships are owned by partnerships.

The national flag airline is the Scandinavian Airlines System (SAS), owned by Denmark, Norway and Sweden. It is a consortium in which Denmark holds two-sevenths interest, Norway two-sevenths and Sweden three-sevenths. Danair, a subsidiary of SAS, operates domestic flights in Denmark. Since 1965 there has been regular air service between Copenhagen and the Faeroe Islands, where there is an airport at Vagar. The major international airport in Denmark is at Kastrup, 10 km. (6 mi.) from the center of Copenhagen. Other important airports are at Tirstrup in Århus; Ålborg, Billund, Esbjerg, Karup, Skrydstrup, Stauning, Sønderborg and Thisted in Jutland; Rønne in Bornholm; and Odense in Fünen. On the whole, there are 131 airfields, of which 116 are usable, 25 with permanent-surface runways, and nine with runways over 2,440 m. (8,006 ft.).

TRANSPORTATION INDICATORS, 1986

Roads
Length, km. (mi.): 70,147 (43,587)
Paved (%): 100

Motor vehicles
Automobiles: 1,500,946
Trucks: 346,431

TRANSPORTATION INDICATORS, 1986 *(continued)*

Persons per vehicle: 2.8
Road freight, ton-km. (ton-mi.): 9.400 billion (6.4 billion)

Railroads
Track, km. (mi.): 2,471 (1,535)
  Passenger-km. (passenger-mi.): 4.508 billion (2.801 billion)
  Freight, ton-km. (ton-mi.): 1.749 billion (1.198 billion)

Merchant marine
  Vessels: 1,063 (over 100 GWT)
  Total deadweight tonnage: 6,805,200
  Oil tankers: 2,311,000 GRT

Ports
  4 major
  15 secondary
  41 minor
Cargo loaded: 11,244,000 tons
Cargo unloaded: 32,952,000 tons

Air
Km. (mi.) flown: 41.3 million (25.6 million)
Passengers: 4,126,000
Passenger-km. (passenger-mi.): 3.204 billion (1.991 billion)
Freight, ton-km. (ton-mi.):129.3 million (88.6 million)
Mail, ton-km: 14.6 million (9 million)
Airports with scheduled flights: 12
Civil aircraft: 58

Pipelines
Refined, km. (mi.): 578 (359)
Natural gas, km. (mi.): 700 (434.7)
Crude, km. (mi.): 110 (68.3)

Inland waterways
Length, km. (mi.): 417 (259)
Cargo, ton-km. (ton-mi.): 1.7 billion (1.2 billion)

COMMUNICATION INDICATORS, 1986

Telephones
Total: 4,005,000
Persons per: 1.3

Phone traffic
Local: 2.445 billion
Long distance: 1.510 billion
International: 55 million

Post office
  Number of post offices: 1,293
  Domestic mail: 1.570 billion

COMMUNICATION INDICATORS, 1986 *(continued)*

Foreign mail received: ⎫
Foreign mail sent: ⎭   1.570 billion

Telegraph
Total traffic: 329,000
National: 211,000
International: 118,000

Telex
Subscriber lines: 13,307
Traffic (000 minutes): 55,673,000

Telecommunications
  9 Submarine coaxial cables
  2 earth satellite stations

TOURISM & TRAVEL INDICATORS, 1986

Total tourist receipts: $1.326 billion
Expenditures by nationals abroad: $1.410 billion
Number of hotel beds: 20,370
Average length of stay: 2.5 days
Tourist nights: 8,577,000
Number of tourists: 5 million
  of whom from : (%)
  West Germany: 40.4
  Sweden: 14.2
  Norway: 11.6
  U.S.A.: 6.1

DEFENSE

The sovereign is the constitutional head of the armed services. The operational command is vested in the Ministry of Defense. Denmark has a unified defense ministry and a single defense command. The chief of defense, the head of the Defense Command, is a serving officer whose deputy is the chief of the defense staff. Both are members of the Defense Council, along with the chiefs of the army, navy and air force and the commander of the Danish operational forces. The Chief of Defense is the operational head of the army but, in time of conflict, he may transfer command to the commander of the Danish operational forces, who also is the NATO Baltic approaches commander (COMBALTAP). The head of the army is not an operational commander but is commander of the army training school. The home guard is directly subordinate to the Ministry of Defense through its own commander.

Conscription is authorized by the Constitution. The period of service is nine months in peacetime. The right of conscientious objection is recognized, and about 15% of eligible Danes invoke the right annually. Defense legislation is extensive and includes the Acts of 1950, 1960, 1969 and 1973 and the Royal Decree of 1952, amended in 1961.

Defense personnel are trained at specialized schools: artillery personnel at the Army Fire Support School at Varde, West Jutland, and infantry personnel at the Army Combat School at Oxboel, West Jutland. Regular officers are trained at the Defense College, Copenhagen, a triservice institution that also is the staff college.

Reserves are formed, for the most part, of complete units of ex-conscripts who have completed their nine months' training. They are incorporated either into the Augmentation Force, where they remain for 18 months or directly into the Field Army Reserve or the Local Defense Force, where they remain for five years. At the end of this period their reserve liability effectively ceases.

The army is organized into supply troops, signal corps, engineers, artillery, army aviation, infantry and armored troops. The latter include old regiments of infantry and cavalry. The first battalion of these regiments belongs to the standing force and is manned by regulars, while the second to the fourth battalions are training units or belong to the local defense forces. The field army consists of three elements: the standing force and the augmentation force (together known as the covering force) and the field army reserve. The covering force comprises five small armored infantry brigades, three on Jutland and two on Zealand, each of which consists of an armored infantry battalion, a tank battalion, an artillery battalion and an armored reconnaissance squadron. In addition, there is one infantry battalion on Bornholm and a royal lifeguard battalion in Copenhagen. The major army training schools are the Army Fire Support School in Varde, the Army Combat School in Oxboel and the Defense College in Copenhagen.

DEFENSE PERSONNEL, EQUIPMENT & BUDGET, 1986

Defense budget: $1.406 billion
% of GNP: 2.4
% of national budget: 5.2
Defense expenditures per capita: $275
Defense expenditures per soldier: $45,355
Defense expenditures per sq. km. of national territory: $32,698 ($84,710 per sq. mi.)
Total military manpower: 31,000
Reserves: 162,200
Army: 17,000; 2 division headquarters; 5 mechanized infantry brigades; 6 regiments; 8 independent infantry battalions; 1 army aviation unit

```
┌─────────────────────────────────────────────────┐
│      DEFENSE PERSONNEL, EQUIPMENT & BUDGET,       │
│              1986 (continued)                     │
│  Navy: 5,700; submarines; frigates; fast attack craft; patrol │
│         craft; minelayers; coast defense unit; naval bases │
│         at Copenhagen; Korsor and Frederikshavn   │
│  Air Force: 6,900; Tactical Air Command; Air Defense │
│              Group; Air Matériel Command          │
│  Arms imports: $70 million                        │
│  Arms exports: —                                  │
└─────────────────────────────────────────────────┘
```

Operationally, the kingdom is divided into the Western Land Command, the Eastern Land Command and the Bornholm Region. The Eastern Land Command has two standing force brigades; the Western Land Command, three. For territorial defense Denmark is divided into seven regions: three in Jutland, one in Fünen, two in Zealand and one in Bornholm.

Although a member of NATO, Denmark does not permit the stationing of foreign troops on its soil (except in Greenland) or NATO troop exercises in Bornholm. Denmark does not allow the stationing of nuclear weapons on its territory.

The principal naval bases are at Copenhagen, Kørsør and Frederickshavn. The navy is charged with guard duties off the Faeroe Islands and Greenland. The air force consists of a tactical air command.

Denmark receives no military aid and has no arms industry.

EDUCATION

The earliest Danish schools were established from the 10th to the 12th centuries. The University of Copenhagen was established in 1479 through a papal bull of Sixtus IV. In 1536 the state took over the grammar schools from the Catholic Church, and the history of national education may be said to begin from that date. From the 15th to the 19th centuries the most decisive influence on education was the national Lutheran Church. The Lutheran belief in individual salvation and the concomitant Christian duty to read the Bible led to the promotion of compulsory schooling under church auspices. The state, for its part, acknowledged its obligation to provide the physical facilities for such schooling. King Frederik IV (1699–1730) established schoolhouses throughout the country. In 1689 a high commission reorganized the entire school system, requiring townships to pay for primary schools, maintain evening classes for adults and make school attendance compulsory for children between ages seven and 14. It also created the first normal schools.

The Enlightenment and the rise of the merchant class, who needed a more practical type of school, led to dissatisfaction with the church's role in education. The impact of the new philosophies of education was felt in two directions: first, the expansion of the curriculum to include modern languages and science, and second, an emphasis on freedom of choice in education. The latter development is associated with the Free School Movement, which owes its origins to N.F.S. Grundtvig, poet, clergyman and philosopher. In 1852 Kristen Kold founded the country's first free school to put Grundtvig's ideas into practice. These schools had no entrance or leaving examinations, instruction was confined to the lectures, and the curriculum was unstructured.

At the turn of the century, the modern system of education had already taken shape, comprising the *folkeskole* at the elementary level, the *mellomskole* at the middle level, universities at the upper level and folk high schools at the nonformal level. The old Latin grammar schools had been converted into *realskoler* (lower secondary schools), and a three-year gymnasium, or upper secondary school, prepared students for the university. The system represented in some cases a fusion and in other cases a coexistence of differing national traditions.

The constitutional basis of education is established through extensive legislation, such as the Grammar Schools Act of 1809; the Act of 1857, abolishing the control of crafts training by the guilds; and the Apprenticeship Act of 1889 and the Act of 1814, introducing seven years of compulsory education. Section 76 of the Danish Constitution specifies that education shall be compulsory. The Act of 1958 established the 10-year *folkeskole*, the elementary *hovedskole* and the lower secondary *realafdeling*. In 1976 a new education act came into effect. It introduced nine years of comprehensive primary and lower secondary education for all, a noncompulsory 10th year and an optional preschool year.

Danish education is characterized by a rich variety of options for the schoolgoer. There are about 80 residential folk high schools. For the 14 to 18 age groups there are continuation schools *(efterskoler)* and youth schools *(ungdomskoler)*. The former have the flavor of folk high schools and teach young people practical subjects for a year beyond their compulsory schooling. Youth schools are designed for school-leavers who lack particular aptitudes. commercial schools and higher commercial schools offer courses leading to proficiency in commercial subjects. The agricultural *landbrugsskoler* accept students for agricultural training.

Nearly 13% of all Danish schools are private, and they enroll about 6% of all students. All private schools are entitled to receive state subsidies covering 85% of their operational expenditures, provided they meet a minimum enrollment standard and their instructional standards are comparable to those of the state schools.

The school year starts in August and ends in June. Lessons last 50 minutes each, and the number of lessons per year varies from 720 in the first year to 1,200 after the fourth year.

A notable development in Danish education is the abandonment of annual examinations. Pupils are encouraged to proceed at their own pace and are promoted automatically from grade to grade. The former division of pupils in grades eight to 10 into academic achievers and nonachievers has been abolished. Under law, marks based on numerals are not allowed from the first to the seventh year of classes, but schools are required to inform pupils and their parents regularly of the student's progress.

Although compulsory education begins at age seven, more than 85% of children from five to seven attend one of four types of preschools: *bornehaver* (kindergartens) for five- to seven-year-olds; *vuggestuer* (day nurseries) for children up to three; *integrerede institutioner* (integrated schools); and *bornehaveklasser* (preschool classes) for five- to seven-year-olds. Preschool classes are run by the Ministry of Education; the others come under the Ministry of Social Affairs and are run by local authorities or private groups.

The term *folkeskole* covers both primary and lower secondary education, both of which are governed by the Folkeskole Act of 1975. Although primary education is compulsory and free, parents have the right to teach children at home, and 6% of the children are so taught. Although the *folkeskole* is comprehensive, there are two courses of different content but with the same number of lessons per week in certain subject groups. The spectrum of school subjects is very broad, and there is wide range of optional subjects, especially in the last three years. Contemporary studies have been introduced more recently, including sex education, road safety, non-Christian religions and philosophies of life, and health and drug education. Camping, field trips and work experiences occupy 10 days each year from the first to the seventh year, 20 days in the eighth year and 30 days in the ninth and 10th years. Religious education normally is compulsory, but pupils may be excused under certain circumstances. The school year normally comprises 200 school days, and the number of lessons per week must not exceed 20 for the youngest and 34 for the oldest pupils. The average size of a classroom is 19 pupils and the legal limit is 26.

The Folkeskole Act of 1975 introduced a new examination system with four principal features: (1) There is no overall examination; (2) in most subjects there is only one examination level; (3) the decision to present oneself for an examination is voluntary by a student; and (4) there is no passing mark. The *folkeskole* leaving examination may be taken in 11 subjects and the advanced leaving examination in five subjects. The period of compulsory education is deemed to be over when a pupil has completed nine years of schooling, or on July 31 of the year of the student's 17th birthday.

Education at the secondary level is divided into two main types: general upper secondary education, which prepares students for higher education; and EFG (Erhvervsfagige Grunduddanneiser), a vocational training course that prepares students for work in trade and industry. The two types have developed independently of each other. It is far easier to be admitted to the general level or the gymnasium than to the EFG because admission to the latter depends on the number of seats available.

The two most common types of general upper secondary education are the three-year courses at the gymnasium, which lead to the *studentereksamen* (upper secondary school leaving examination), and the two-year courses leading to the HE (higher preparatory examination). In addition, there is the possibility of taking the *Hojere handelseksamen* (higher commercial examination) or attending two-year day or evening courses leading to the *studentkurser* (upper secondary school leaving examination).

The HF, introduced in 1967, can be taken by anyone over 18. A pass gives the student access to most types of higher education. This examination can be taken on a single-subject basis, so it is possible to pass the examination in parts over three or four years. The examination is written and oral.

Vocational education was thoroughly overhauled in the 1950s. Before 1950 the only vocational training available was apprenticeship training, which took three to four years and was based on a contract between the employer and the apprentice. The Apprenticeship Act of 1956 gave apprentices the right to attend day classes and gave national trade committees oversight over apprenticeship programs in their respective trades. In the early 1970s the EFG was introduced, and it gained parliamentary sanction in 1977. However, apprenticeship training continues to function as a parallel system.

For centuries the country's only university was the University of Copenhagen, which celebrated its 500th anniversary in 1979. The second was established at Århus in 1928. Odense followed in 1964, Roskilde in 1972 and Ålborg in 1974. The Universities of Copenhagen and Århus have five faculties each (theology, social sciences, medicine, natural sciences and humanities), Roskilde and Odense have three each and Ålborg is a congeries of schools and colleges. Roskilde is an experimental university based on student participation and innovative instruction. On the whole, universities are fairly autonomous, with the general control of the Ministry of Education limited to examinations, degrees, enrollment and staffing.

In principle, admission to institutions of higher education is open to all who have passed the upper secondary school leaving examination, the higher preparatory examination or the higher commercial examination. However, admission to professional schools is regulated through a numerus clausus.

University courses generally last from five to eight years. Theology, medicine and law award candidate degrees while arts and sciences award magister degrees. Generally the student is left free to decide what, how and how long to study. Lectures are open to all, and there are no structured courses, regular assessments or advice on progress. Accordingly, dropout rates are high. Postgraduate doctorates often taken up to 15 years.

Traditionally, power in the universities lay with the professors who held established chairs and from among whom the rector and deans were elected. Protests by junior staff and students during the 1960s resulted in breaking this power structure. Between one-third and one-half of all university committees are now made up of student delegates, and the remainder represent the teaching staff, regardless of rank. The national student–professor ratio is 12:1, which is high even by European standards.

Education is a state responsibility, shared by the central government, counties and municipalities. Primary and lower secondary schools are under local government control, while gymnasia and HF courses are run by the counties. The majority of preschools, engineering colleges, schools of social work and teacher training colleges are privately owned. The state subsidizes both municipal and private educational institutions, including folk high schools, agricultural schools and continuation schools.

While the constitutional authority over education is vested with the Folketing, the Ministry of Education has oversight over all educational activities, programs and policies. The ministry comprises three main sections and five directorates. Section I deals with legislation and administration, Section II with pay and staffing and Section III with planning budget statistics and international relations. The five directorates deal with (1) primary, lower secondary and adult education and teacher training; (2) upper secondary; (3) vocational; (4) higher education; and (5) building. The ministry directs and controls the system through regulations, ministerial orders, departmental circulars, guidelines, directives and recommendations. It also determines the allocation of funds, approves curricula and appoints permanent educational personnel. The powers of the central government are historically strong, especially in the areas of policy-making and planning.

Each of the country's 14 county councils oversee the HF courses, gymnasia and single-subject examination courses for adults. The county councils also exercise certain supervisory functions over municipal schools and the day and evening courses under the Leisure-Time Act.

Each municipal council, or Byrad, has an education committee in charge of educational administration. One of its principal functions is the preparation of the school plan, mapping the distribution of schools, their catchment areas, staff, health and welfare facilities, as well as the teaching plan. Municipal councils report directly to the ministry.

Rural district councils (Sognerad) also have school commissions which work in conjunction with the county school council and the county school directorate. Copenhagen has an independent status that dates back to 1658. Its city council is responsible for all schools within the city limits and reports directly to the minister of education.

At the school level, the principal supervisory bodies are the school board, the teachers' council and the pupils' council.

Different regulations apply to the administration of vocational schools. The overall responsibility is placed with different ministries, such as those for labor, agriculture, interior and social affairs. Technical and commercial schools are self-governing institutions administered by boards comprising representatives of both trade unions and employers.

University administration is governed by the Act of 1970 as amended in 1973 and 1976. Under this act each institution of higher education is administered by a rector assisted by collegial boards and committees. Each university has a supreme governing body (Konsistorium) as well as a council for research and studies, and councils for each discrete discipline. Both teaching staff and students are represented on these committees.

Public education, including higher education, is free and largely financed by public funds, the two exceptions being vocational training financed by industry and private schools that charge fees. Higher education is financed entirely by the central government, and primary and secondary education are financed partly by the central government and partly by local authorities. A complicated system of reimbursement is designed to redress regional inequalities. In general, central government aid is given for teachers' salaries and for capital projects. In 1970 local governments were given a greater financial stake, under which they receive a per capita sum per pupil and in return must defray 40% of teachers' salaries. Teachers' salaries absorb over two-thirds of the recurrent costs.

During the 1960s and 1970s, education was one of the highest budgetary priorities, with the result that the amount of the GNP spent on education rose from 3% in 1966 to 8.2% in 1975. Since then, there has been a rollback in expenditures until the amount reached 6.9% in 1984. Administrative costs accounted for 14.9%, teaching materials for 5.5%, scholarships for 4.4% and welfare services for 3.8%. The share of the first level was 56.5%, that of the second level 17.3% and that of the third level 16.9%.

Nonformal education programs fall into four categories: (1) general youth education programs, including continuation schools, home economics schools and agricultural schools; (2) education programs of voluntary youth and sport organizations; (3) general adult education programs, comprising folk high schools, evening schools, extramural departments of universities, mass education associations and the media and (4) recurrent or lifelong education.

Teachers are trained in institutions specializing at various levels: 26 colleges of education for preschool teachers, 31 training colleges for primary and lower secondary teachers, and universities for gymnasium and HF course teachers. Teachers for vocational schools are trained at the State Institute for the Educational Training of Vocational Teachers. Most adult education teachers are part-time workers with varying educational backgrounds or are trained at the Royal Danish School of Educational Studies.

EDUCATION INDICATORS, 1986

Literacy
   Total (%): 100
   Males (%): 100
   Females (%): 100

First level
   Schools: 2,557
   Students: 415,148
   Teachers: 34,541
   Student–teacher ratio: 12:1
   Net enrollment rate: 101%
   Females (%): 49

Second level
   Schools: 3,247
   Students: 339,835
   Teachers: 36,105
   Student–teacher ratio: 9:1
   Net Enrollment rate: 75%
   Females (%): 51

Vocational
   Schools: 282
   Students: 144,024
   Teachers: —
   Student–teacher ratio: —
   Vocational enrollment rate: —

Third level
   Institutions: 96
   Students: 124,144
   Teachers: 10,411
   Student–teacher ratio: 12:1
   Gross enrollment ratio: 29.2%
   Graduates per 100,000 ages 20–24: 2,209

EDUCATION INDICATORS, 1986 *(continued)*

% of population over 25 with post-secondary education:
—

Females (%): 49

Foreign study
  Foreign students in national universities: 3,084
  Students abroad: 882
  of whom in
  U.S.A.: 382
  West Germany: 267
  U.K.: 29

Public expenditures
  Total: 35.589 billion Kr
  % of GNP: 6.5
  % of national budget: 9.2
  % current: 88.7

GRADUATES, 1982

Total: 19,112

Education: 5,710
Humanities & religion: 1,326
Fine & applied arts: 319

Law: 423
Social & behavioral sciences: 683
Commerce & business: 957

Mass communication: 422
Service trades: 89

Natural sciences: 182
Mathematics & computer science: 147
Medicine: 4,107

Engineering: 1,662
Architecture: 304
Industrial programs: 538

Transportation & communications: 261
Agriculture, forestry, fisheries: 531
Other: 1,451

LEGAL SYSTEM

Denmark has a civil law system that goes back to about 1200. After the introduction of absolute rule in 1660, the king decreed in 1683 a general code applicable to the whole country, the Danish Code of Christian V. Danish law is based primarily on the Jutland Code, which does not break from the former law.

The text of the Danish Code has never been altered, nor did new laws appear as amendments in the initial period after 1683. All legislation since then has been in the form of separate statutes. Few of the provisions of the Danish Code are still in force. But no attempt has been made to codify the mass of legislation in a comprehensive code, so it may be said that Denmark does not possess a general civil code.

The Constitution of 1953, like its predecessors, is based on the doctrine of the separation of powers and lays down rules governing the organization and powers of the courts. The current rules are contained in the Administration of Justice Act of 1916, printed with numerous subsequent additions in 1969. Judges are constitutionally independent, although appointed by the crown on the recommendation of the minister of justice. Judges can be dismissed only by the Special Court of Indictment.

The highest court is the Supreme Court (Hojesteret), with 19 judges, which also functions as a court of appeals. The court usually sits in two divisions of at least five judges each. All matters not specifically assigned to a lower court fall within the purview of one of the two high courts (Landsretter) under the Supreme Court, the eastern wing sitting in Copenhagen with jurisdiction over the islands and the western sitting in Viborg with jurisdiction over Jutland. The eastern wing has 36 judges; the western, 20. On the next lower level are the lower courts (Underret), of which there are 84. Each lower court has only one judge, except in Copenhagen and Århus, which have 29 and eight, respectively. The lower court judge also functions as a bailiff, estate administrator and notary and is responsible for records and registrations.

Cases may be reopened by the Special Court of Indictment in the event of fresh evidence after a final judgment. There is a special high court for Greenland. There are also special courts, such as the Tax Tribunal, the Maritime and Commercial Court and the Labor Court. Only professional judges sit on ordinary civil benches, but lay judges may participate in criminal proceedings both as jurors and as assessors, except on the Supreme Court. On the other hand, the Supreme Court cannot, in penal cases referred to it, set aside the assessment of the evidence for the accused person's guilt by a high court. Free legal aid, including counsel, is provided for the indigent, whether defendants or plaintiffs.

The final decision on whether to prosecute is made by the chief public prosecutor and public prosecutors. The chief public prosecutor appears only before the Supreme Court. Public prosecutors appear before the high courts, and the police act as prosecutors in lower courts.

To practice as a lawyer *(advokat)* requires a special letter of appointment from the minister of justice, a degree in law from a Danish university and three years of practical training. There is no distinction between lawyers and solicitors. All lawyers are members of the Society of Counsels, which is governed by the Board of Counsels.

No data are available concerning Danish prisons.

LAW ENFORCEMENT

The first full-time police force in Denmark was created in Copenhagen in 1590. Other towns followed suit during the 17th and 18th centuries. Law enforcement was a municipal function until the State Police (Rigspolitiet) were created in 1919. All existing municipal police forces were absorbed into the State Police in 1933.

The State Police are headed by a chief of police *(rigspolitichefen)* who reports to the Ministry of the Interior. Denmark is divided into 72 police districts, each under a director of police. Below the districts are the divisions (each commanded by a police master) and stations.

The State Police comprise four main branches: the Civil Police or the municipal police; the Land Police or the rural police; the Criminal Police; and the Order Police, in charge of public order, crowd control and ceremonial functions. There also is a flying squad.

The uniform is a dark blue jacket and trousers worn with a blue forage cap or a peaked cap with a white cover. Police training is conducted at the Police College in Copenhagen.

No statistics are available concerning crime in Denmark.

HEALTH

Primary health service in Denmark is defined as all noninstitutional health service facilities. General medical and dental practice developed as liberal professions. In the late 19th century a cooperative health service developed, which subsequently through state grants and regulations came to influence the extent and quality of health care delivery. In 1973 the National Health Security Act transferred to the county councils and the city of Copenhagen the responsibility for initiating and running a primary health service financed by local taxes.

In primary health service, the citizen has a choice of two programs. One provides health services completely free of charge by the doctor chosen by the individual for one year. Specialist care is available to this group of patients only on referral from their own general practitioner, whose remuneration is governed by agreement between the Health Security Service and the medical associations.

The second option (used by less than 10% of the population) gives the citizen a freedom of choosing his own doctor or specialist, but he must pay all medical bills directly, though two-thirds of the amount eventually will be refunded by the Health Security Service. All patients pay a proportion of their dental bills. Patients under both programs are granted a 50% subsidy on drugs dispensed by pharmacies and a 75% subsidy on vital drugs.

Traditionally, the Danish general practitioner worked alone. Now more than half the GP's work in group practice. Outside of Copenhagen a group practice may be purchased, but the purchaser has to be approved by a county council committee.

The hospital service has been a public responsibility since 1806. The state is directly involved in the operation of only one hospital, Rigshospitalet, in Copenhagen. The few private hospitals are financed by public funds. Under the Hospital Services Act, the county councils and the city of Copenhagen are responsible for maintaining an adequate hospital service. Since the 1950s, central hospitals, serving a county or part of a county, have been set up throughout the country. The smaller hospital units have been phased out. There are only 20 hospitals with fewer than 100 beds, and 30 hospitals with from 100 to 200 beds. Examination and treatment are free of charge to all patients, except foreigners, unless they are involved in an accident or are suffering from an acute illness. Admission normally is on the referral of a medical practitioner. Some of the other free services include examination of pregnant women, school medical examination and treatment, industrial medical facilities, preventive health screening of children through health visitors, and family planning counsel.

The Ministry of the Interior is responsible for legislation governing medical personnel, hospital service and preventive measures; the Ministry of Social Affairs for the primary health service; the Ministry of the Environment for environmental protection and food safety; and the Medico-Legal Council of the Ministry of Justice for forensic affairs. The National Health Service is a separate body under the Ministry of the Interior and is headed by a physician. The health profession is well organized, and their principal association wields great influence in the formulation of medical policies.

HEALTH INDICATORS, 1986

Health personnel
  Physicians: 12,975
  Population per: 394
  Dentists: 4,519
  Nurses: 29,892
  Pharmacists: 1,470
  Midwives: 915

Hospitals
  Number: 127
  Number of beds: 35,976

HEALTH INDICATORS, 1986 *(continued)*
  Per: 10,000:70
  Admissions/discharges per 10,000: 1,992
  Bed occupancy rate: 82%
  Average length of stay: 11 days

Type of hospitals (%)
  Government: 91.3
  Private Nonprofit: 8.7
  Private profit: —

Public health expenditures
  As % of national budget: 1.2
  Per capita: $48.20

Vital statistics
  Crude death rate per 1,000: 11.4
  Decline in death rate, 1965–84: 10.9%
  Life expectancy at birth
    Males: 71.6
    Females: 77.5
  Infant mortality rate per 1,000 live births: 11
  Child mortality rate ages 1–4 year per 1,000:
    insignificant
  Maternal mortality rate per 100,000 live births: 7.7

Causes of death per 100,000
  Infectious & parasitic diseases: 4.9
  Cancer: 283.9
  Endocrine & metabolic disorders: 19.5
  Diseases of the nervous system: 11.6
  Diseases of the circulatory system: 523.8
  Diseases of the respiratory system: 89.3
  Diseases of the digestive system: 37.1
  Accidents, poisoning & violence: 78.3

FOOD & NUTRITION

The average Dane consumes 3734 calories and 122.7 g. (4.3 oz.) of protein per day. This food supply is 128% of FAO food requirements. Food expenditures account for 21.3% of total household expenditures. The total available calorie supply is derived as follows: 18.5% from cereals; 4.3% from potatoes; 19.5% from meat and poultry; 2.9% from fish; 11.3% from eggs and milk; 3.4% from fruits and vegetables and 18.9% from fats and oils.

**PER CAPITA CONSUMPTION OF FOODS,
kg. (lb.), 1986**

Potatoes: 68.1 (150.1)
Wheat: 46.0 (101.43)

```
┌─────────────────────────────────────────────────────────┐
│ PER CAPITA CONSUMPTION OF FOODS (continued)             │
│ Rice: 2.0 (4.4)                                         │
│ Fresh vegetables: 58.5 (129)                            │
│ Fruits (total): 41.1 (90.6)                             │
│    Citrus: 9.0 (19.8)                                   │
│    Noncitrus: 32.1 (70.7)                               │
│ Eggs: 14 (30.8)                                         │
│ Honey: 0.7 (1.5)                                        │
│ Fish: 20.6 (45.4)                                       │
│ Milk: 150.1 (330.9)                                     │
│ Butter: 7.9 (17.4)                                      │
│ Cream: 8.1 (17.8)                                       │
│ Cheese: 12.3 (27.1)                                     │
│ Yogurt: 9.0 (19.8)                                      │
│ Meat (total): 76.7 (169.1)                              │
│    Beef & veal: 13.3 (29.3)                             │
│    Pig meat: 53.0 (116.8)                               │
│    Poultry: 9.8 (21.6)                                  │
│    Mutton, lamb & goat: 0.6 (1.3)                       │
│ Sugar: 39.3 (86.6)                                      │
│ Chocolate: 4.5 (9.9)                                    │
│ Ice cream: 7.5 l. (15.8 pt.)                            │
│ Margarine: 20.0 (44.1)                                  │
│ Biscuits: 5.9 (13.0)                                    │
│ Breakfast cereals: 2.4 (5.2)                            │
│ Canned focds: 6.3 (13.9)                                │
│ Beer: 136.9 l. (301.8 pt.)                              │
│ Wine: 18.1 l. (38.2 pt.)                                │
│ Alcoholic liquors: 1.6 l. (3.3 pt.)                     │
│ Soft drinks: 40 l. (84.5 pt.)                           │
│ Mineral waters: 7.6 l. (16 pt.)                         │
│ Fruit juices: 15.1 l. (31.9 pt.)                        │
│ Tea: 0.5 (1.1)                                          │
│ Coffee: 10.4 (22.9)                                     │
│ Cocoa: 0.5 (1.1)                                        │
└─────────────────────────────────────────────────────────┘
```

MEDIA & CULTURE

The Danish press dates back to 1666, when the first Danish paper, *Den Danske Mercurius,* was published by the crown as an official bulletin. Press censorship existed until 1849, but since then the Danish press has been one of the freest. Four papers founded in the 18th century still publish today: *Berlingske Tidende* (1749, Copenhagen), *Stiftstidende* (1767, Ålborg), *Stiftstidende* (1772, Fyens) and *Stiftstidende* (1794, Århus).

Article 77 of the Constitutional Act states: "Any person shall be at liberty to publish his ideas in print, in writing and in speech, subject to his being held responsible in a court of law." The legal limits of fair comment and speech are

wide, constrained only by laws protecting individual honor and good reputation. Neither journalists nor newspapers are required to register or be licensed.
In fact, the principle of press freedom has been extended even to pornographic
publications. Article 77 of the Constitutional Act also bans any kind of censorship. Even military information can be published unless the government prohibits it.

There is no truly national press. Most of the dailies are concentrated in
Copenhagen, which claims roughly 16% of all dailies and about half of the total
daily newspaper circulation. Although the number of newspapers has been falling, circulation has remained stable enough to make per capita circulation one
of the world's highest. The Danish media audience also is well educated, sophisticated, affluent and well interested in a wide range of political and social affairs.
With a few exceptions, urban dailies and provincial papers appeal to all educational and interest levels with a good balance of local news, foreign news and
commentary. The typical newspaper avoids extremes of sensationalism and
staid facticity. The nearest approaches to sensationalism are found in the midday tabloids *B.T.* and *Ekstra Bladet*, while both *Information* and *Aktuelt* may
be considered heavy. In general, Danish papers are informal but warm and dig-
nified. Their makeup is pleasing, typography attractive and the use of pictures
generous and interesting. The language is conversational, not stuffy.

Ownership of the Danish press has traditionally been in the hands of local
private families or limited-liability companies. But that phenomenon has been
changing in recent years. Since 1945 there has been increasing concentration of
ownership in the hands of a few publishing houses or chains. Some 25% of total
circulation of all dailies plus two large weeklies, numerous district papers, a
book publishing business and a printshop are controlled by the Berlingske
Group. Another large newspaper chain is owned by the Berg Group, which
publishes six dailies. A fair portion of the Danish press operates on a nonprofit
basis. In some cases, such as that of *Information*, the staff has taken over the paper. The Social Democratic press is owned and run by the trade unions, which
actually subsidize it. At least 16 small Liberal and Radical provincial papers are
published by nonprofit companies. In fact, only 10 small papers are privately
owned by a single person or family today.

Special interest and political party affiliations are other old traditions in the
Danish press. Beginning in 1849, newspapers began to be tied to, or strongly espouse, first the Conservatives, then the Liberals, the Social Democrats and the
Radicals. The rivalry among political party papers has continued to the present
day. In Copenhagen, for example, *Berlingske Tidende* is the Conservative voice
while *Politiken* supports the Radicals and *Aktuelt* supports the Social Democrats. Since World War II, economic pressures have taken a heavy toll on the

political press, and a number of newspapers have gone out of business. Today the Social Democrats own only *Aktuelt* and two provincial papers. The national Lutheran Church is represented by *Kristeligt Dagblad*. The church also runs a news bureau called Kristeligt Pressebureau. With the weakening of the political press, the independents have grown stronger. This has led to greater objectivity in reporting and less editorializing, even at the expense of less political clout. As a result of these forces of change, Denmark's present 46 dailies might be classified according to their political views as follows: Social Democratic, three; Independent Social-Liberal, two; Conservative, two; Independent Conservative, two; Liberal, 15; Independent Liberal, seven; Communist, two; and apolitical, 13.

Most Danish dailies have a similar size and format, a 22 x 5.5-inch, seven- or eight-column page, with up to 40 pages for the larger dailies, 20 pages for the provincials and 12 to 14 pages for the smaller dailies. (The exceptions are the Copenhagen tabloids.) Advertisements take up between one-third and two-thirds of the space, with ads even on the front pages. Color is employed well. In general, makeup is lively but neither lurid, light nor frivolous. In Copenhagen all dailies are either morning or midday papers. The 10 largest newspapers with their circulations are:

Ekstra Bladet	250,000
Politiken	230,000
B.T.	220,000
Berlingske Tidende	198,000
Jyllands Posten	109,040
Stiftstidende (Århus)	73,000
Stiftstidende (Odense)	70,000
Vestkysten	56,000
Aktuelt	55,000
Stiftstidende (Århus)	20,000

The country's most influential newspapers are *Berlingske Tidende*, *Aktuelt* and *Politiken*, and the first is well regarded abroad. Among serious newpapers *Information* has a place of its own. Among provincial papers, *Jyllands Posten* is the best known.

Denmark's besk known weekly magazine is *Billed Bladet*, with a circulation of 280,000. It is followed by the family magazine *Familie Journalen* (366,600), *Ide-nyt Hus Og Have* (1,300,000), *Se Og Har* (315,000) *TV Bladet* (280,000), *Samvirke* (685,000), *Hjemmet* (244,000), *Helse-Familiens Laegeblad* (355,000), and the children's magazine *Anders & Co.* (142,000).

The major publishers' association is the Danish Newspaper Publishers' Union. The Association of Danish Newspaper Employers reprensents the publishers in collective bargaining with unions. The Joint Council of Danish Newspapers is the general spokesman of the industry and also runs the Danish Press Council. Working journalists are organized in the Danish Union of Journalists. Industrial disputes were frequent in the business in the 1970s, but relative peace has prevailed since the economic crisis of the early 1980s.

As more and more newspapers have failed or have merged into chains or groups, the government has expanded its program of indirect subsidies to the press in several ways: through low-interest loans, relief from value-added taxes, postal and telephone concessions and public sector advertisements. The government also has set up the Financial Institution of the Daily Press, to which it contributes annually.

MEDIA INDICATORS, 1986

Newspapers
  Number of dailies: 47
  Circulation (000): 1,837
    Per 1,000: 359

  Number of nondailies: 11
  Circulation (000): 1,249
    Per 1,000: 244

  Number of periodicals: —
  Circulation: —

  Newsprint consumption
    Total: 165,100 tons
    Per capita: 32.23 kg. (71 lb.)

Book publishing
  Number of titles: 7,296

Broadcasting
  Annual expenditures: Kr 686 million
  Number of employees: 3,179

Radio
  Number of transmitters: 49
  Number of radio receivers: 2,052,000
  Persons per receiver: 2.5
  Annual total program hours: 14,909

Television
  Television transmitters: 32
  Number of TV receivers: 1,953,000
    Persons per receiver: 2.6
  Annual total program hours: 2,486 (public only)

Cinema
  Number of fixed cinemas: 453
  Seating capacity: 92,000
    Seats per 1,000: 18
  Annual attendance (million): 13.8
    Per 1,000: 2,700

```
┌─────────────────────────────────────────────────────┐
│          MEDIA INDICATORS, 1986 (continued)           │
│  Gross box office receipts: Kr 286.8 million          │
│ Films                                                 │
│   Production of long films: 11                        │
│   Import of long films: 233                           │
│       % from U.S.A.: 51.1                             │
│       % from France: 6.9                              │
│       % from Italy: 7.7                               │
│       % from Soviet Union: 7.3                        │
└─────────────────────────────────────────────────────┘
```

The national news agency is the Ritzaus Bureau, cooperatively owned by the Danish press. It has a working relationship with multinational agencies much as Reuters, AFP and dPA, which have bureaus in Denmark.

Broadcasting is a monopoly of Danmarks Radio, which began operating in 1925. Although technically under the Ministry of Cultural Affairs, it is an independent institution governed by the Radio Council of 27 members elected by the Folketing. Danmarks Radio broadcasts over 16,000 hours of radio programs annually from one long-wave, three medium-wave and 40 VHF transmitters, and 2,400 hours of television programs from 30 color transmitters. About half of the telecasts are imports. Revenues are derived solely from licenses, as there is no advertising. Faeroese Radio and Greenland Radio are independent. Greenland Televion is cable only.

Denmark's largest libraries are the University Library at Copenhagen, founded in 1482, and the Royal Library. There are public libraries in each of the local government areas governed by the Public Library Law of 1920.

```
┌─────────────────────────────────────────────────────┐
│   CULTURAL & ENVIRONMENTAL INDICATORS, 1986           │
│ Public Libraries                                      │
│   Number: 249                                         │
│   Volumes: 33,408,000                                 │
│   Registered borrowers: —                             │
│   Loans per 1,000: 17,087                             │
│                                                       │
│ Museums: 277                                          │
│   Annual attendance: 7,828,000                        │
│   Attendance per 1,000: 1,530                         │
│ Performing arts facilities: 77                        │
│   Number of performances: 9,727                       │
│   Annual attendance: 2,522,000                        │
│   Attendance per 1,000: 490                           │
│ Ecological sites                                      │
│   Number of facilities: 23                            │
│   Botanical gardens & zoos: 19                        │
└─────────────────────────────────────────────────────┘
```

SOCIAL WELFARE

Danish social security legislation differs in several respects from the social security legislation of other countries. This is particularly true as regards eligibility for social benefits. In the majority of cases there is no stipulation of membership in an insurance program, or payment of premiums or fees. It is sufficient merely to be a resident of Denmark, which means that to a large extent foreigners can obtain these benefits on the same terms as Danish citizens.

The Danish system of social welfare is financed largely by government revenues. The share of employers is limited to coverage for industrial injuries, five weeks' sickness benefits in the event of illness, and a small proportion of the cost of the disablement pension program. Another feature is that legislation dealing with social welfare is simple and few, despite its broad scope.

The Constitution of 1849 contained a provision committing the public to assist anyone unable to support himself or his family. This provision is reaffirmed in the current Constitution, but with broader implications. The reform of the system in 1964 was based on two principles: that of local assistance and that of single authority. To satisfy these two principles, the social security administration is now delegated to local authorities, and all decisions on aid for the individual and his family are handled by a single office.

Social benefits fall into two main categories: universal benefits available to everyone and contingency benefits granted in response to individual needs. Government spending in this field can be subdivided into (1) income transfers, such as children's allowances, pensions, unemployment and sickness benefits, etc., and (2) general forms of cash assistance plus service facilities, such as institutional care, foster care, home help, etc. About 40% of state assistance is in the form of income transfers, with the balance in the form of service facilities. The breakdown of the expenditures is as follows:

EXPENDITURES	%
Old-age and disablement—retirement pensions, disablement pensions, nursing homes, home help, special care services	42
Illness—hospitals, health service, dental care, mental illness	30
Families with children—family allowance, rent subsidies, advanced child maintenance, day-care institutions, special measures for children	15
Unemployment benefits—job training, upgrading	9
Public assistance	1
Industrial accident insurance	1
Administrative charges	2

The family allowance is granted to families with income below a certain level and is paid to the mother. A special youth allowance may be added for children aged 16 to 18. Rent subsidies are available on the basis of a means test. Virtually all expenses arising from serious illnesses are covered by the state. Below a certain maximum sum, unemployment benefits can be up to 90% of a person's previous income and can be paid for a maximum of 3½ years, after which assistance is granted under the 1976 Social Assistance Act. When the loss of earnings is due to illness or accident, sickness benefits are paid for the first five weeks by the employer and after that by the state. If an individual is unable to resume work after an illness or accident, the state provides retraining and rehabilitation. If he is unable to resume work permanently, he can be awarded a disablement pension according to the degree of incapacity. Maternity benefits are paid to wage-earning wives for 14 weeks and to others for four weeks. Disablement compensation and death benefits are paid to industrial accident victims and their dependents.

The 1976 Social Assistance Act combines various pieces of social legislation under one heading. The act also provides for an advisory service for individuals faced with economic hardship. It includes provision for defraying expenses not covered by other social legislation, such as the extra cost of caring for handicapped children under 18 years of age. A home-help service is extended during illness, maternity and convalescence. Assistance is made available to juveniles under 18 to enable them to remain at home if they run into difficulty at school or are faced with a crisis. In some cases juveniles may be placed in foster homes without parental permission. Other facilities are offered for expectant mothers, single mothers, the mentally ill, the homeless, the physically handicapped and others unable to fit into ordinary society.

A retirement pension is financed by the state at the rate of 60% of the average income to everyone over 67, irrespective of means. Certain supplementary benefits are extended according to the recipient's means.

There is no private welfare system in Denmark.

CHRONOLOGY

1945—V. Buhl's second coalition government takes office; on the coalition's fall, Knud Kristensen heads a Liberal government.
1947—Hans Hedtoft forms his first Social Democrat government.
1948—Faeroe Islands granted home rule.

1949—Denmark joins NATO. . . . Krone is devalued.

1950—Erik Eriksen leads Liberal/Conservative coalition into office.

1953—Hans Hedtoft forms his second Social Democrat goverment. . . . A new Constitution is promulgated along with a new Act of Succession permitting female succession to the throne. . . . Electoral Act is passed. . . . Greenland is integrated into the Kingdom of Denmark.

1955—H. C. Hansen forms his first Social Democrat government. . . . Parliament approves appointment of a national ombudsman on the Swedish model.

1957—H. C. Hansen leads a coalition government consisting of Social Democrats, Radical Liberals and the Single-Tax Party.

1958—Education Act is passed incorporating far-reaching reforms.

1959—Socialist People's Party is founded.

1960—Viggo Kampmann forms his first coalition government consisting of Social Democrats, Radical Liberals and the Single-Tax Party. . . . Agricultural Commission initiates reform of land tenure. . . . Single-Tax Party leaves the coalition.

1962—Helsinki Agreement on Nordic Cooperation is signed, with Denmark as a founding member. . . . J. O. Krag forms his first Social Democrat/Radical Liberal coalition.

1964—J. O. Krag leads Social Democrat government.

1966—Odense University is founded.

1968—H. Baunsgaard heads a Radical Liberal/Conservative/Liberal coalition.

1969—Pornography is legalized in Denmark.

1970—Local government reform reduces the number of local administrative units and rationalizes their finances. . . . Christian People's Party is founded.

1971—Helsinki Agreement is revised. . . . Baunsgaard coalition steps down and J. O. Krag returns to office as Social Democrat prime minister.

1972—King Frederik IX dies; his daughter succeeds to the throne as Queen Margrethe II. . . . Roskilde University is founded. . . . Progress Party is founded. . . . New Primary Education Act is passed. . . . J. O. Krag resigns and is succeeded in office by Anker Jørgensen.

1973—Denmark joins the EEC. . . . Abortion is legalized. . . . Center Democrats form a separate party as a protest against the Social Democrats' move to the left. . . . Jørgensen is ousted and Poul Hartling forms a Liberal government.

1975—Jørgensen returns to office, to remain in power until 1982 as head of four cabinets.

1976—Social Assistance Act is passed. . . . Government decides to raze the "Free City," the hangout of drug addicts and counterculturists.

1982—Jørgensen quits; Poul Schluter heads a Conservative/Liberal coalition. . . . Krone is devalued. . . . Greenland leaves the EEC.

BIBLIOGRAPHY

BOOKS

Anderson, Robert T. and Edward Hohfeld. *Denmark: Success of a Developing Nation.* Cambridge, Mass., 1973.

Danstrup, John. *A History of Denmark.* Copenhagen, 1944.

Einhovn, Eric, and John Logue. *Welfare States in Hard Times: Policies and Politics in Denmark and Sweden.* Kent, Ohio, 1982.

Fitzmaurice, John. *Politics in Denmark.* New York, 1983.

Harder, Eric. *Local Government in Denmark.* Copenhagen, 1973.

Jones, W. Glyn. *Denmark.* New York, 1970.

Lauring, P. *Denmark: A History.* Copenhagen, 1981.

MacHaffie, Ingeborgs, and Margaret A. Nielsen. *Of Danish Ways.* New York, 1984.

Manniche, Peter. *Living Democracy in Denmark.* Westport, Conn., 1952.

Marcussen, Ernst. *Social Welfare in Denmark.* Copenhagen, 1980.

Miller, Kenneth E. *Government and Politics in Denmark.* Boston, 1968.

Oakley, Stewart. *A Short History of Denmark.* New York, 1972.

Rovnholt, Henning. *The Danish Cooperative Movement.* Copenhagen, 1950.

Rutland, Jonathan. *Looking at Denmark.* Philadelphia, 1968.

Stareke, Viggo. *Denmark in World History.* Philadelphia, 1963.

UNESCO. *Dominant Ways of Life in Denmark; Alternative Ways of Life in Denmark.* Paris, 1980.

OFFICIAL PUBLICATIONS

Statistik Årbog (Statistical Yearbook).

Danmarks Variendforsel og-udforsel (External Trade of Denmark).

Folke og Holigtaellingen (Population and Housing Census).

Ministry of Finance

Statsregnskabet (Central Government Accounts).

Other Units of the Central Government

Accounts of extrabudgetary units.

Regnskaber for Kirkelige Fonde (Church Funds Accounts).

Regnskaber for de Sociale Kasser og Fonde (Social Security Funds Accounts).

Skatter og Afzifter (Taxes and Duties), *Danmarks Statistik* (Danish and English).

Statistisk Årbog (Statistical Yearbook), *Danmarks Statistik* (Danish and English).

Statistisk Tiaarsoversigt (Statistical Ten-Year Review), *Danmarks Statistik.*

Statistiske Efterretninger (Statistical Bulletin), *Danmarks Statistik.*

Local Government

Amtskommunernes regnskaber (county government accounts).

Primaer kommuneregnskaber (municipal accounts).

Institutions regnskaberne (local government extrabudgetary units accounts).

De Kommunale Finanser for Regnskabsaaret 19– (Municipal Finances for Fiscal Year 19–), *Danmarks Statistik.*

Note: All sources are annual and in Danish only except as indicated.

FINLAND

FINLAND

GEOGRAPHICAL FEATURES

A far northern country on the European continent, Finland has an area of 337,032 sq. km. (130,128 sq. mi.). Its length, one-third of which lies above the Arctic Circle, is 1,165 km. (724 mi.) north to south, and its width is 542 km. (337 mi.) east to west. It shares its borders on the west with Sweden (586 km.; 364 mi.), on the north with Norway (716 km.; 445 mi.) and on the east with the Soviet Union (1,269 km.; 789 mi.). Finland's total coastline of 1,100 km. (684 mi.), on the Gulf of Finland, the Baltic Sea and the Gulf of Bothnia, is deeply fragmented and studded with islands. The total boundary length is 3,671 km. (2,282 mi.).

The capital is Helsinki, on a peninsula on the Gulf of Finland west of the estuary of the Vantaanjoki (the Wanda River). It also is the capital·of the department of Uusimaa. Helsinki was founded in 1550 by Gustavus Vasa about four miles north of its present site, to which it was transferred when the old site was destroyed by fire in 1640. It became the capital in 1812. During the Russo-Finnish War of 1939–40 it was bombarded several times but escaped serious damage. The population of the principal cities was as follows in 1985:

Helsinki (Helsingfors) (capital)	484,480
Tampere (Tammerfors)	167,732
Turku (Åbo)	163,449
Espoo (Esbo)	148,689
Vantaa (Vanda)	139,144
Oulu (Uleåborg)	96,887
Lahti	94,778
Pori (Björneborg)	78,970
Kuopio	76,882
Jyväskylä	64,658
Kotka	60,045
Vaasa (Vasa)	54,545
Lappeenranta (Villmanstrand)	54,005
Joensuu	45,950
Hämeenlinna (Tavastehus)	42,489

The Finnish landscape is characterized by a rather asymmetric distribution of hills and plains, with the highest elevation (1,324 m.; 4,344 ft.) in the extreme Northwest. Most of the higher landforms, referred to as mountains, have rounded ridgetops averaging between 457 and 762 m. (1,500 and 2,500 ft.) above sea level, but there is a major interruption around Lake Inari, which occupies a plain at elevations of 91 to 183 m. (300 to 600 ft.). More than half of eastern Finland is hilly, with the land gently sloping toward the southwest. Paralleling the coast of the Gulf of Bothnia is a belt of plains about 97 km. (60 mi.) wide with elevations from 5 to 18 m. (15 to 60 ft.). The separation between these plains and the hills is rather sharp in the North compared to the Southwest.

The surface of the land has been scoured and gouged in recent geological times by glaciers that have left thin deposits of gravel, sand and clay. The relief of Finland has been considerably affected by the continental glacier, which on retreating left the bedrock littered almost everywhere with morainic deposits. The resulting formations can be seen most clearly in the shape of complex features such as the Salpausselka ridges and of numerous eskers running north to west to south to east. Another reminder of the Ice Age is the fact that Finland still is emerging from the sea, so that its area grows by 7 sq. km. (2.7 sq. mi.) annually. In Ostrobothnia the land rises by 90 cm. (3 ft.) and in the Helsinki area by 30 cm. (1 ft.) every 100 years.

The entire Finnish coast is paralleled by an island zone. The zone reaches its greatest breadth and complexity in the Southwest. Finland's offshore islands are numbered by the tens of thousands—the Åland Archipelago alone has nearly seven thousand. The Åland and Turku archipelagoes are rich in flora and fauna and abound in fish. They also were the first inhabited parts of the country. However, in more modern times some of the less accessible islands have become deserted while others have become haunts of sportsmen and tourists. In the inner skerries, summer cottages have proliferated, used by those commuting between the coastal cities and their tributary islands. A network of ferries also brings a summer surge of visitors. In the outer skerries, deserted farmsteads have been restored by vacationers.

Finland's coastal zone is known appropriately as the "golden horseshoe." It is dominated by the two cities of Helsinki and Turku (Åbo), the former capital of the country, situated on the mouth of the Aurajoki. Turku was the site of the first university and Finland's first place of religious pilgrimage. The developed coastal zone extends northward from Turku through the so-called *vakka suomi* and on to the Kokemäki River, which drains the lakes of Häme to the port of Pori. Eastward the coastal plain extends to the Russian border. Here successive little rivers open up fertile valleys behind old, established settlements.

Ostrobothnia (Pohjanmaa to the Finns) also has its coastal zone. It is a land of little relief but of many rivers. Its southern coastal plains, the broadest in Finland, are traversed by a series of parallel flowing rivers that originate in Suomenselka, the highest point. Between the Oulu Valley and the Swedish border, the character of the rivers changes. Oulujoki, its formerly impressive falls now harnessed for power, is Finland's most impressive river. Beyond its broad and rapid-strewn estuary are those of the Ijoki, Simojoki, Kemijoki and Tornionjoki. Ostrobothnia's coastline is actively changing as the waves of a tideless sea break upon its coast.

Lakes cover the greater part of southern Finland. In relation to its size, Finland has more lakes than any other country. There are 55,000 lakes that are at least 200 m. (656 ft.) in breadth and 19 large lakes, including the artificial reservoirs of Lokka and Portipahtta, that are more than 200 sq. km. (77 sq. mi.) in area. The largest, Lake Saimaa (4,400 sq. km., 1,698 sq. mi.), is the fifth-largest lake in Europe. Most of these lakes are quite shallow, the average depth being only 7 m. (23 ft.) and the greatest depth just over 100 m. (328 ft.). The lakes are dominated by long, sinuous esker ridges, rising scores of feet above the lake surface and generally clad with lofty pines and flanked by sandy beaches. Such ridges as Punkaharju, Pyynikki and Pulkkila are nationally renowned. The lake districts have more forests than the coasts do.

The easternmost part of Finland is Karelia, part of which was ceded to the Soviet Union by the Armistice of 1944 and the Peace Treaty of 1947. It is dominated by the Saimaa Canal, one of the most impressive structures in Finland.

Nearly half of Finland's land area is described as North Country or Nordkalotten (Pohjoiskalotti in Finnish), including the most elevated parts of the country. It is the land of the Lapps. It also is one of the coldest zones in Europe, with the timberline passing through it. Below and above the tree line, North Country has extensive swamps, and about a third of the area is covered with bogland. The vast expanses of swamp are the least attractive elements in the northern landscape.

The North Country also is intersected with some of the country's longest and most impressive rivers, such as the Kemi and the Tornionjoki, the latter shared with Sweden. Many of these rivers empty into the freshwater Bothnian Gulf, but some, such as the Paatsjoki and the Tenojoki, drain into the Arctic, and others have carved dramatic gorges through to Russian Karelia. These torrents are among the most unspoiled in the country.

Drainage patterns are directly related to the surface features. The North is drained by long rivers, such as the Muonio, the Tornio and, the Kemi. In the central part of the country the streams become shorter, except for the Oulu. They also are more sluggish and flow across land that must be ditched before it can be used for cultivation. In the lake district in the Southeast, rivers are long and narrow and dammed by the great east-to-west double ridge called the Salpausselka, which runs parallel to the Gulf of Finland coast eastward from Helsinki. The area south of the lake district and westward along the coast is drained mostly by a series of short streams.

CLIMATE & WEATHER

The Finnish climate is considerably warmer than the country's location might seem to warrant. Temperatures are ameliorated by the Baltic Sea, the inland waters and, in particular, by west winds that bring air currents from the Atlantic warmed by the Gulf Stream. In contrast, winds from the Eurasian continent bring cold spells in winter and heat waves in summer.

Winter is the longest season. Its short, dark days are made up for by the long, light night of summer. The darkless summer of most of Lapland, when the sun does not go below the horizon, lasts more than 70 days. The snow cover lasts for over 90 days in the Ahvenanmaa Islands off the southwestern coast and up to 250 days in the North. There is precipitation in all seasons. In the South the annual rainfall is 600 to 700 mm. (24 to 28 in.) and in the North 500 to 600 mm.

(20 to 24 in.), much of it snow. Winter temperatures range from -3°C to -13°C (27°F to 9°F), while summer temperatures range from 13°C to 20°C (55°F to 68°F).

POPULATION

The population of Finland was estimated in 1988 at 4,949,716, based on the last census, held in 1980, when the population was 4,784,710. Finland ranks 93rd in the world in size of population. The population is expected to cross the 5 million mark by 1990 and to reach 5,073,000 by 2000.

The 1950 census was the country's first true census, previous counts commonly being based on total enrollments in church and civil registers.

POPULATION GROWTH, 1749–1980			
Year	Total (000)	Year	Total (000)
1749	420	1920	3,147
1808	900	1930	3,463
1843	1,500	1940	3,695
1879	2,000	1950	4,030
1890	2,380	1960	4,446
1900	2,656	1970	4,707
1910	2,943	1980	4,784

In the decade from 1950 to 1960 the growth rate was only 0.9%. Since then the growth rate has declined further. During the early 1970s the country's total population declined under peace conditions for the first time since the 1866–68 famine. The overall growth percent of 0.4% was the lowest, with Sweden, for northern Europe. This reflected emigrational strains as well as other factors common to the rest of Europe.

The settlement of Finland has progressed generally northward. By 1550 the southern fifth of the country, including the southern coast, the Bothnian shores and inland around Lake Oulu were settled. Settlements spread rapidly to the north, reaching the northern border the by mid-19th century. Despite this historical pattern, nearly half of the population is concentrated in the southernmost portion of the country, and most of the remainder are distributed south of the 66th parallel. Moreover, all the major cities are to be found in the South. Since 1910 the population center has remained at a point roughly 170 miles north of Helsinki. Most Finns also live near the water, along the southern and Bothnian coasts, in the lake districts and along the rivers. Also contributing to the concentration of population in the South are certain elements of the lanscape, such as lower elevation and good soil. Climatically as well, the South has advantages over the North. The summers are longer and the winters not as cold.

Snow covers the ground for about three months in the extreme Southwest, whereas at Rovaniemi in Lapland it covers the ground for seven months. Annual precipitation is higher and mean temperatures are lower in the South. One result of these physical characteristics is a more valuable forest cover in the South than in the North.

On a regional scale, population distribution has a cultural basis as well. Much of the linearity of settlement is a reflection of transportation routes. In the patterns of both railroads and roads there is a general north-to-south orientation, followed by connections inland toward the coast. Occupations also are broadly regional. Agriculture is spread most continuously in the most southern strip, fishing extends along the southern and southwestern coasts, industry is scattered along the southern half and most productive forestry is in the southwestern fifth. The concentration of agriculture is related to the southern soils, while the concentration of industry is related to the proximity to the Baltic ports. Mining is concentrated in the Southwest, near Lake Oulu, and the Ivalo part of northern Lapland.

Finland has suffered demographic losses for several decades as a result of emigration, particularly to Sweden. Since Finland joined the Nordic Council in 1956, Finns could travel to and take jobs in any of the member countries without passports or work permits. There also are internal factors in this emigration, such as the field reservation program, which discouraged certain forms of agriculture. Altogether, over 300,000 Finns have emigrated since 1956. There is no significant immigration to Finland.

The internal rural-to-urban migration also has accelerated since the end of World War II. At the turn of the century, the country was predominantly rural, and even as late as 1940 only 23% was urban. By 1980 the majority of the inhabitants were urban, but the rate of urbanization has slowed since. The migration is an economic phenomenon, reflecting the combined attractions of more job opportunities and a higher quality of life in urban areas. While most of the southern communes lost population since the 1960s, the large cities have experienced unbroken growth.

The prevailing form of settlement in the inland regions is found in scattered dwellings. In these areas the density of population is the lowest in Europe, outside Norway and Iceland. Along the coastal strips there are pockets of heavy population density. Variety characterizes the city layouts. Nearly every urban area is on water, and some have two shorelines if they are situated between two lakes or on a peninsula or combine stream-mouth and coastal locations. Patterns of settlement in rural areas range from unplanned settlements to contemporary planned groups in colonies. The majority of the colonies are made up of resettled Finns who were displaced during or after World War II. Each colony was a group settlement primarily on state-owned land. The result was to fill in many blank spots on the population map in the North.

The feminist movement is historically strong in Finland. Women are well represented in the professions and in the Edushunta (Parliament). The Council for Equality coordinates and sponsors legislation to reduce gender-based discrimination. A comprehensive Equal Rights Bill to ensure equal treatment of women in the workplace went into effect in 1987. Under the bill, an equal-rights ombudsman monitors official programs in this field. A new surname law permitting women to retain their maiden name after marriage as their only surname (and a husband to take his wife's surname) took effect in January 1986.

Information is not available on birth control policies or activities in Finland.

DEMOGRAPHIC INDICATORS, 1986

Population: 4,949,716 (1988)
Year of last census: 1980
 Sex ratio: male, 48.3; female, 51.7
Population trends (million)
 1930: 3.463   1960: 4.446   1990: 5.000
 1940: 3.695   1970: 4.707   2000: 5.073
 1950: 4.030   1980: 4.784
Population doubling time in years at current rate: over
    100 years
Hypothetical size of stationary population (million): 4
Assumed year of reaching net reproduction rate of 1:
    2030
Age profile (%)
 0–14: 19.5   30–44: 23.6   60–74: 12.4
 15–29: 22.9   45–59: 16.7   Over 75: 4.9
Median age (years): 36.6
Density per sq. km. (per sq. mi.): 16.2 (42.0)
Annual growth rate (%)
 1950–55: 1.10   1975–80: 0.32   1995–2000: 0.05
 1960–65: 0.60   1980–85: 0.37   2000– 5: –0.02
 1965–70: 0.18   1985–90: 0.21   2010–15: –0.13
 1970–75: 0.45   1990–95: 0.12   2020–25: –0.32
Vital statistics
Crude birth rate, 1/1,000: 12.4
Crude death rate, 1/1,000: 9.6
Change in birth rate, 1965–84: –21.6%
Change in death rate, 1965–86: –5.2%
Dependency, total: 46.4
Infant mortality rate, 1/1,000: 6.3
Child (0–4 years) mortality rate, 1/1,000: insignificant
Maternal mortality rate, 1/100,000: 3.0
Natural increase, 1/1,000: 2.8
Total fertility rate: 1.6
General fertility rate: 47
Gross reproduction rate: 0.78

```
┌─────────────────────────────────────────────────┐
│         DEMOGRAPHIC INDICATORS, 1986 (continued)  │
│  Marriage rate, 1/1,000: 5.3                      │
│  Divorce rate, 1/1,000: 2.0                       │
│  Life expectancy, males (years): 70.3             │
│  Life expectancy, females (years): 78.6           │
│  Average household size: 2.8                      │
│  % illegitimate births: 16.4                      │
│  Youth                                            │
│   Youth population 15–24 (000): 648               │
│   Youth population in 2000 (000): 630             │
│  Women                                            │
│   Of childbearing age 15–49 (000): 1,271          │
│   Child/woman ratio: 242                          │
│   % women using contraception: –                  │
│   % women married 15–49: –                         │
│  Urban                                            │
│   Urban population (000): 3,482                    │
│   % urban 1965: 44    1985: 60                    │
│   Annual urban growth rate (%)                    │
│   1965–80: 2.5    1980–85: 2.9                    │
│   % urban population in largest city: 27          │
│   % urban population in cities over 500,000: 27   │
│   Number of cities over 500,000: 1                │
│   Annual rural growth rate: –2.2%                 │
└─────────────────────────────────────────────────┘
```

ETHNIC COMPOSITION

The overwhelming majority of the population is Finnish. The only significant national minorities are the Swedish-Finns and the Lapps. There are scattered groups of Russians and Germans. Some 5,000 Gypsies live chiefly in Vaasa Province and adjoining localities.

The origins of the Finns are obscure, but their ancestors probably were central Asians mixed somewhat with Germanic and Slavic peoples. Moving northward, they occupied the Finnish peninsula, displacing the aboriginal Lapps.

The Swedish-speaking minority trace their origins to the Swedish colonists between the 12th and the 19th centuries, when Finland was under varying degrees of Swedish rule. Until this century, they were a dominant group, with political and economic power disproportionate to their numbers. The Swedish culture is strongest in the Ahvenanmaa Islands and around Turku, but it blends with Finnish culture around Helsinki. Until recently most Swedish-Finns belonged to their own political party, the Swedish People's Party, which, although still active, wields much-diminished influence, reflecting a growing weakening of the political cohesiveness of the Swedish-Finns. Nonetheless, Swedish-Finns continue to identify with Swedish rather than Finnish heritage.

The number of Lapps is estimated at less than 1,500. Generally, Lapps are divided into two groups: mountain Lapps, who are reindeer herders, and forest Lapps, who are farmers and fishermen. Younger Lapps are giving up their traditional lifestyles and adopting Finnish customs and lifestyles. Many leave their homes to acquire higher education in the southern cities, marry non-Lapps and rarely return home. Other than reindeer, there are few status symbols, no wide variations in wealth and no formal political organizations. Kinship is the strongest social bond. Great emphasis is placed on neighborliness, hospitality, pleasant demeanor and practical cooperation in such activities as hunting, fishing and reindeer herding. Cooperative efforts are directed by a council consisting of one man from each family, with an elected council chief.

There are no significant numbers of ethnic aliens in Finland.

LANGUAGES

Until 1863 Swedish was the sole official language of Finland. However, growing nationalist sentiment from the 1840s onward resulted in a strong push for the adoption of Finnish as an official language. The national debate led to the Language Decree of 1863, placing Finnish on an equal footing with Swedish as an official language. The advocates of Finnish continued to press for the adoption of Finnish as the sole official language and the displacement of Swedish as an official language. Their efforts were rewarded when in 1883 all courts were ordered to use Finnish in their transactions in districts where it was the predominant language. Some Swedes helped to make the transition easier by voluntarily giving up their language and surnames.

The larger social changes taking place after 1945 pushed the language controversy into the background. In any case the supremacy of Finnish over Swedish was more or less assured by that time. Although Swedish enjoys equal official status with Finnish, and although Swedish is used as a medium of instruction in the national education system, the dream of the 19th-century Finnish nationalists has more or less been realized. However, Swedish-Finns have separate schools where Swedish is the primary medium of instruction.

Lappish is not widely used, even by the Lapps.

RELIGION

The central fact of Finnish religious life is the dominance of Lutheranism. The Evangelical Lutheran Church of Finland is the state church. Its bishops are appointed by the president of the republic and the church law is enacted by the Eduskunta, cementing the ties that bind state and church. Significantly, parliamentary services open and close with a Lutheran service in Helsinki Cathedral.

Both the Eastern and Western branches of Christianity reached Finland by the 12th century. Finland was largely pagan before the crusade by Eric IX of Sweden in 1155. A Catholic bishop of English birth, Henry of Uppsala, came to the country with Eric and stayed behind to consolidate the new religion. He was murdered by an irate Finnish peasant on the ice of Lake Koylio and later became the patron saint of the church and its apostle. Orthodoxy was introduced into eastern Finland from Russia in the middle of the 12th century. Dominicans entered in 1249, and in 1219 Magnus, a Finn, was appointed bishop of Åbo (Turku). Finland was attached to Sweden at the time of the Reformation and followed King Gustavus Adolphus in accepting Lutheranism, particularly through the efforts of Michael Agricola. Catholicism did not return until the middle of the 19th century, when the free churches also were introduced.

A fundamental feature of the Reformation was the translation of the Bible into indigenous languages. Agricola himself translated all of the Old Testament and part of the New Testament into Finnish and thus helped to develop literary Finnish. Lutheranism thus stimulated the growth of literacy in Finland. Second, it strengthened the civil authority and developed the concept of both the separation and the interconnection of church and state that has governed church-state relations since.

The church is divided into eight dioceses, each diocese into deaneries (of which there are 68), and deaneries into parishes. Despite the apparent episcopal nature of church organization, congregational life is emphasized and local parishes are quite independent.

A diocese is the territorial jurisdiction of a bishop, who is appointed by the president of the republic from a list of three candidates elected by the clergy and a committee of laymen. The country's eight dioceses include seven Finnish-speaking and one Swedish-speaking. Each is headed by a chapter composed of the bishop as chairman, the dean and three assessors. The dean is the rector of the cathedral parish. Every five years the bishop calls all the clergy of his diocese to a conference in preparation for the church assembly. Each deanery is headed by a rural dean, who is the liaison between the chapters and the parish clergy. The parishes are both administrative areas and religious communities. Each parish is governed by a parish council and the parish potentiaries, both selected at parochial meetings.

The only source of income for the parish is the church tax, which ordinarily is 1% of taxable income. Joint stock companies and firms also must pay church taxes. Since 1960 this tax has been deducted at the source and passed through the treasury to the parishes. The parishes themselves pay about 7% of their earnings to the central church fund.

The parish leadership comprises the rector assisted by the chaplain, who supervises youth work; association activities; curates; and deaconesses, who perform nursing and social work for the poor.

The three main administrative organs of the state church are the Church Assembly, the Enlarged Bishops' Conference and the Ecclesiastical Board. The Church Assembly is the highest of these bodies, responsible for approving new liturgical books, hymnals, catechisms and revised versions of the Bible. It also proposes amendments to existing church laws as well as new laws, which must be approved by the Eduskunta to be legally binding. The Church Assembly meets once in every five years. The Enlarged Bishops' Conference consists of one bishop, one assessor, two laymen from each diocese and the members of the Ecclesiastical Board. The Enlarged Bishops' Conference, traditionally presided over by the archbishop of Turku, selects members of the Ecclesiastical Board, controls central funds, makes recommendations to the government on ecclesiastical matters and arranges ecumenical contacts. The Ecclesiastical Board is the permanent organ or cabinet of the Conference. It consists of six members: one theologian; one jurist; one administrator; two laymen; and the archbishop, who presides. One of these members must come from the Swedish-speaking areas.

There are two Lutheran mission societies: the Finnish Missionary Society and the Lutheran Evangelical Association of Finland. Mission work is funded by donations, not taxes. Finnish missionaries are particularly active in Tanzania, Namibia, Kenya, Ethiopia, Israel, Taiwan and Japan. Diaspora work among Finns abroad and ecumenical and foreign relations are conducted by the Committee for Foreign Affairs. The main forum for ecumenical relations at home is the Ecumenical Council of Finland.

The status of the church is defined in both the Constitution and common law and may best be described as a "special relationship." Questions affecting mutual interests are called "mixed matters." These include laws relating to marriage, divorce, oaths, the care of the poor and religious instruction. The government is required to consult the Church Assembly on issues touching on these matters. The state, in turn, has an important voice in church administration. It decides whether new dioceses and parishes should be founded and whether new churches should be built. The president and the minister of education invariably attend notable church occasions, such as the consecration of bishops and church jubilees.

The church and the state also cooperate on other programs. The church keeps records of births, marriages and deaths of all members and cares for most of the country's cemeteries. For those who have withdrawn from the national church there is a civil register, which applies to about 5% of the population.

Non-Lutherans can register with their own church. On its side, the state pays the salaries of the theological faculty of the National University and provides chaplains and religious instructors for the army, navy, prisons and hospitals.

With growing secularization, church-state relations have been subjected to serious debate. A gradual process of detachment began after World War II and is continuing. Nevertheless, surveys show that a great majority of the people support continuing official connection between the two institutions.

Although there is a state religion, complete freedom of religion is granted under the Freedom of Religion Act of 1923. Everyone over age 18 may freely join or leave any religious association. Children under 15 have the same religious affiliations as their parents, or if these belong to separate religions, as their mother. Religious freedom also guarantees the right to organize religious groups, as long as this does not break the law of the land or offend good manners. Most of the religious associations are on a state-maintained register. However, some groups, such as the newer Pentecostals, who do not wish to be included in the register, are incorporated under the general law governing nonprofit organizations.

The second-largest church is the Finnish Orthodox Church, an autonomous body governed by its bishops and a central board. It is divided into two dioceses, Karelia and Helsinki. At the end of World War II the church lost most of its constituency when the greater part of Karelia was ceded to the Soviet Union, but it received considerable compensation from the state. Since then it has slowly rebuilt its membership and in the early 1980s constituted 1.2% of the churchgoing population. The head of the church, the archbishop of Karelia, has his see in the middle of the new Orthodox settlement in Kuopio, where its theological seminary also is located.

The growth of the Roman Catholic Church is reflected in the fact that in 1977 Finland was transferred from the jurisdiction of Propaganda at the Vatican to that of the Congregation for Bishops. Nonetheless, the diocese of Helsinki has the smallest membership of any Catholic diocese in Europe, with only five parishes.

The free churches include Baptist, Methodist, Adventist, Congregationalist and other groups. The Pentecostal movement expanded rapidly until 1965, when it began to decline.

As elsewhere in Europe, the church in Finland is undergoing a crisis of indifference. Changing times and social mores have raised fundamental questions regarding its relevance and role. Although conventional adherence is still largely unchallenged, outward manifestations of piety and devotion are largely absent, and public criticism of the church is being increasingly and more stridently voiced. Regular Sunday attendance is low, averaging about 4% of the population over 15, with some parishes recording only 1%. However, Sunday services never were traditionally paramount in Finnish religious life. Distance is another decisive factor. In inland regions churches are many miles away from farms, and in some places the journey is impossible in winter. The parish of Inari in Lapland covers 25,907 sq. km. (10,000 sq. mi.), while the parish of Velkua in the Turku Archipelago covers 265 islands. Under these conditions, services may sometimes be held in homes, schools, in the main room of a farmstead, the rocky bank of an island or the temple of a birch grove. Despite declining church attendance there are few apostates. Even a great majority of Communist voters are church members, and some are professing Christians. They pay church taxes, get married in church, have their children baptized and send them to Sunday school. The proportion of civil marriages has, in fact, declined.

HISTORICAL BACKGROUND

Finland was a province of Sweden from the 1150s to 1809. By 1293 Swedish rule had extended as far east as Karelia and along the Gulf of Bothnia. After Sweden's military defeats by Russia in 1808–9, Finland was transferred to Russia. Alexander I granted Finland a privileged autonomous status as a grand duchy. During the 19th century an independence movement gathered strength in the country, propelled by Russian moves to extinguish all vestiges of internal autonomy. After the Bolsheviks seized power in Russia in 1917, Finland declared its independence. A short civil war followed in which both Germany and the Soviet Union intervened. In July 1919 Finland declared itself a democratic republic with a parliamentary system of government. In the following two decades disputes were settled with both Sweden over the Aland Islands and the Soviet Union over East Karelia. However, relations with the latter continued to deteriorate, and two wars followed the breakdown of negotiations: the Winter War of November 30, 1939, to March 13, 1940, and the Continuation War of June 26, 1941, to September 19, 1944. The armistice terms of 1944, later confirmed by the Paris Peace Treaty of February 10, 1947, provided for the cession of territory, payment of reparations to the Soviet Union and expulsion of German troops on its soil. The last provision led to the German-Finnish War of October 1944 to April 1945.

CONSTITUTION & GOVERNMENT

Finland is one of the youngest republics in Europe; Finland's Constitution dates back only to 1918. Much of its earlier constitutional history is linked to that of Sweden or Russia. Few constitutional structures of the Russian and Swedish periods survive.

The two fundamental bases of government are the Constitution and 1919 and the Parliament Act of 1928. These laws derive from the Parliament Act of 1907, which is considered to be the first truly constitutional law of modern time in Finland. The act called for a bicameral legislature elected on the basis of universal suffrage and proportionate representation. Thus Finland was one of the first Western countries to extend suffrage to women. The act remains substantially intact, with only minor changes in the 1928 version. A strange footnote to Finnish history is that under the 1918 Constitution, the Eduskunta elected a German prince as king of Finland. But after Germany's defeat in World War I, the election was annulled and the Eduskunta finally passed a republican Constitution in 1919.

Other fundamental laws enacted since 1919 include that of 1922 creating the High Court of Impeachment, that of 1918 creating the Supreme Court and the Supreme Administrative Court, that of 1951 granting internal autonomy to the Ahvenanmaa Islands, that of 1922 prescribing the personnel strength of ministries, that of 1924 on presidential election and that of 1955 creating the presidential electoral college.

The Constitution vests executive power in the president and his council of ministers. Although in practice his powers are circumscribed, he wields substantial powers as commander in chief and head of state, including the right to appoint cabinet ministers, department heads, provincial governors and judges.

The individual rights of citizens are guaranteed in Part II of the Constitution. They encompass freedom of movement, speech, religion and association, and freedom from arbitrary arrest. The Constitution, however, omits what are called "social rights," and no mention is made of the quality of life. Social rights legislation began to enter the statute books extensively after World War II.

Interpretation of the Constitution is not delegated to the judiciary. The Constitution states only that "if a provision in a decree is contrary to a constitutional or other law, the Eduskunta, it shall not be applied by a judge or other official." Within the Eduskunta the Constitutional Committee reviews all major legislative proposals.

To amend any provision of a fundamental law requires a simple majority in the first reading. A second approval is necessary, and if the proposed amendment is carried forward from one legislature to another, approval by two-thirds of the votes is required.

A more delicate and uniquely Finnish form of constitutional alteration is the so-called exception to fundamental law. Exceptional laws are temporary suspensions of particular constitutional clauses. The procedure for making an exceptional amendment is the same as that for fundamental amendments. If the action is urgent, the Parliament Act of 1928 provides a quicker procedure in which the proposed legislation becomes an emergency bill. An emergency may be declared by five-sixths of the Eduskunta and the declaration then may be approved by a two-thirds majority.

The executive branch is charged with the administration and execution of all laws passed by the Eduskunta. A system of checks and balances exists within the executive. The State Council's decisions must be approved by the president, but his signature is valid only when countersigned by a minister. The State Council's powers are limited by the Eduskunta. Over the years it has also lost powers to the president, who is not bound by parliamentary control.

The president is elected by universal suffrage indirectly for six years. His term cannot be cut short by the Eduskunta, but he may be impeached by a three-fourths vote there. Traditionally he has no party ties while in office. His powers are extensive including suspensive veto and the right to issue decrees, dissolve the Eduskunta, conduct foreign affairs, command the armed forces and grant citizenship, immunity and pardons. Generally the suspensive veto is exercised with the concurrence of the State Council but may be overridden by a two-thirds vote in the Eduskunta. The right to issue decrees is based on Article 28 of the Constitution, but a presidential decree may not change an act of the Eduskunta. The power to dissolve the Eduskunta is used only rarely and also is done with the concurrence of the State Council. In general the conduct of foreign affairs is delegated to the foreign ministry, although top-level negotiations usually are carried out by the president himself. In appointing members of the State Council the president is traditionally guided by party strengths in the Eduskunta, but occasionally he may appoint caretaker governments without reference to party politics. Although he is the supreme commander, the president may transfer command during wartime to a military officer. This was the case when President Kyosti Kallio named Marshal Carl Gustav von Mannerheim as commander in chief in 1939 at the outset of the Winter War.

The prestige of the presidency is the single most effective factor in governmental stability and continuity. It is a result of not only the fragmentation of the political parties but also of the influence and ability of the men who have held it in recent times, Urho Kekkonen in particular.

The State Council has no more than 16 members, including the prime minister. The permanent ministers are for defense, finance, education, justice, interior, foreign affairs, social affairs, commerce and industry, and communications and public works. A minister may head more than one ministry, and a ministry may have coministers. The president may appoint ministers without portfolio, but this practice has not been followed since the 1940s. The chief government prosecutor, or chancellor of justice, sits on the State Council but bas no vote. He also differs from ministerial appointees in that his post is guaranteed for an entire interelection period. Although the principle of joint cabinet responsibility requires all ministers to support cabinet decisions, ministers may dissent publicly. However, if dissent reaches critical proportions, the prime minister may resign, forcing the dismissal of the entire State Council.

The duties and powers of the State Council are both administrative and legislative. Virtually all legislation is initiated by the State Council. Moreover, the State Council may independently legislate on the basis of broad parliamentary decisions.

Within the State Council, three forums have evolved for formal and informal discussion: the "evening school," the ministerial committee and the plenary session.

The "evening school" dates from the late 1930s and is an informal session to discuss and negotiate proposals that if openly discussed would generate conflict. This forum is particularly important in coalition governments. There are two permanent ministerial committees, one dealing with foreign policy and the other with finance, both chaired by the prime minister. The committees' decisions are binding. The effective importance of the plenary sessions has diminished with the growth in importance of the other forums. Nevertheless, final decisions, by vote or acclamation, lie in the plenary sessions.

The State Council's responsibility to the Eduskunta is expressed primarily through interpellations from the floor of the Eduskunta. There also is a question hour, introduced in 1966, when members may cross-examine ministers once a week.

ORGANIZATION OF THE FINNISH GOVERNMENT

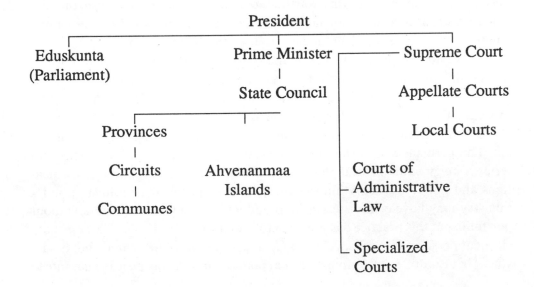

RULERS OF FINLAND (from 1944)

Presidents

August 1944–March 1946:	Gustav von Mannerheim
March 1946 –February 1956:	Julio Paasikivi
February 1956 –October 1981:	Urho Kekkonen
October 1981– :	Mauno Koivisto

Prime Ministers

November 1944 –March 1946:	Julio Paasikivi (no party)
March 1946–July 1948:	Mauno Pekkala (Finnish People's Democratic League)
July 1948–March 1950:	Karl Fagerholm (Finnish Social Democratic Party)
March 1950 –November 1953:	Urho Kekkonen (Agrarian League)
November 1953–May 1954:	Sakari Tuomioja (no party)
May–October 1954:	Ralf Torngren (Swedish People's Party)
October 1954–March 1956:	Urho Kekkonen (Agrarian League)
March 1956–May 1957:	Karl Fagerholm (Finnish Social Democratic Party)
May–November 1957:	Vaino Sukselainen (Agrarian League)
November 1957–April 1958:	Rainer von Fieandt (no party)
April–August 1958:	Reino Kuuskoski (no party)
August 1958–January 1959:	Karl Fagerholm (Finnish Social Democratic Party)
January 1959–July 1961:	Vaino Sukselainen (Agrarian League)
July 1961–April 1962:	Martti Miettunen (Agrarian League)
April 1962–December 1963:	Ahti Karjalainen (Agrarian League)
December 1963 –September 1964:	Reino Lehto (no party)
September 1964 –May 1966:	Johannes Virolainen (Center Party)
May 1966–March 1968:	Rafael Paasio (Finnish Social Democratic Party)

```
┌──────────────────────────────────────────────────────┐
│        RULERS OF FINLAND (from 1944) (continued)       │
│ March 1968–May 1970:       Mauno Koivisto (Finnish     │
│                            Social Democratic Party)    │
│                                                        │
│ May–July 1970:             Teuvo Aura (no party)       │
│ July 1970–October 1971:    Ahti Karjalainen (Center    │
│                            Party)                      │
│                                                        │
│ October 1971                                           │
│ –February 1972:            Teuvo Aura (no party)       │
│ February–September 1972: Rafael Paasio (Finnish So-    │
│                            cial Democratic Party)      │
│                                                        │
│ September 1972                                         │
│ –June 1975:                Kalevi Sorsa (Finnish Social│
│                            Democratic Party)           │
│                                                        │
│ June–November 1975:        Keijo Liinamaa (Finnish So- │
│                            cial Democratic Party)      │
│ November 1975–May 1977: Martti Miettunen (Center       │
│                            Party)                      │
│ May 1977–May 1979:         Kalevi Sorsa (Finnish Social│
│                            Democratic Party)           │
│ May 1979–January 1982:     Mauno Koivisto (Finnish     │
│                            Social Democratic Party)    │
│ January 1982–May 1987:     Kalevi Sorsa (Finnish Social│
│                            Democratic Party)           │
│ May 1987– :                Harri Holkeri               │
└──────────────────────────────────────────────────────┘
```

Finnish cabinets have a relatively short life span. In the 71 years since independence there have been 57 cabinets yielding an average tenure of 14 months. Many have lasted just few months, and one, the third cabinet of Julio Vennola in 1931, lasted less than a month. In light of this record the third administration of Kalevi Sorsa, which took office in 1982, set a record for longevity.

```
┌──────────────────────────────────────────────────────┐
│                   CABINET LIST (1989)                  │
│ President:                     Mauno Koivisto          │
│ Prime Minister:                Harri Holkeri           │
│ Minister of Agriculture and For-                       │
│   estry:                       Toivo T. Pohjala        │
│ Minister of Communications:    Pekka Vennamo           │
│ Minister of Defense:           Ole Norrback            │
│ First Minister of Education:   Christoffer Taxell      │
│ Second Minister of Education:  Anna-Liisa Piipari      │
│ Minister of Environment:       Kaj Barlund             │
│ First Minister of Finance:     Erkki Liikanen          │
│ Second Minister of Finance:    Ulla Puolanne           │
│ Minister of Foreign Affairs:   Kalevi Sorsa           │
│ Minister of Foreign Trade:     Pertti Salolainen       │
│ Minister of Government:        Ilkka Kanerva           │
│ Minister of the Interior:      Jarmo Rantanen          │
│ Minister of Justice:           Matti Louekoski         │
└──────────────────────────────────────────────────────┘
```

```
┌─────────────────────────────────────────────────┐
│           CABINET LIST (1989) (continued)         │
│  Minister of Labor:              Matti Puhakka     │
│  First Minister of Social Affairs                  │
│    and Health:                   Helena Pesola     │
│  Second Minister of Social Affairs                 │
│    and Health:                   Tarja Halonen     │
│  Minister of Trade and Industry  Ilkka Suominen    │
│  Chancellor of Justice :         Jorma S. Aalto    │
│  Governor, Bank of Finland:      Rolf Kullberg     │
└─────────────────────────────────────────────────┘
```

FREEDOM & HUMAN RIGHTS

As a constitutional republic based on the rule of law, Finland has experienced no major violations of human rights in recent years. Since January 1989 pretrial procedures have been reformed, shortening the detention period to seven days and giving the accused access to a lawyer during that time. The institutions of habeas corpus and bail do not exist as such in Finland. Those accused of serious crimes must by law remain in custody. Preventive detention is authorized only during a declared state of war for narrowly defined offenses such as treason, mutiny and trafficking in arms. New legislation on the status of conscientious objectors to obligatory military service was passed in 1985 and took effect in 1987. It abolished the investigative board that formerly conferred the status of conscientious objector. The new law lengthened the alternative civilian service for conscientious objectors to 16 months, and those who refuse both civilian and military service are sentenced to jail. Jehovah's Witnesses are exempted from this obligation altogether. While freedom of public association is guaranteed, only Finnish citizens may belong to political groups. Public demonstrations require notification to the police.

Repatriation of Soviet citizens seeking asylum in Finland has become a sensitive issue raised by Amnesty International.

Finland passed a comprehensive Equal Rights Bill, which took effect in 1987. The Council for Equality and the equal-rights ombudsman monitor the progress of equal rights. A new surname law permits women to retain their maiden names after marriage as their only surname and also for the husband to take the wife's surname.

CIVIL SERVICE

In general, the president makes all high-level appointments, the Supreme Court makes the lower judicial appointments, and the State Council and the central and regional offices fill the remaining jobs. The majority of the posts are filled on the basis of application, examination and recommendation. Patronage appointments are common, especially to higher administrative posts, but the practice is less prevalent than in other countries. Salary and retirement benefits are determined by the Eduskunta but are not competitive with those in private industry. No tenure is assured by law, except in judicial posts. All civil servants retire at age 67.

LOCAL GOVERNMENT

The main units of local administration are the provinces *(laani)* and communes or municipalities *(kunta)*. Circuits or counties are strictly census units rather than centers of regional administration.

Finland is divided into 12 provinces. In each province the general administrative authority is the Provincial Board, headed by a governor appointed by the president. The boards combine general and financial duties and also are the highest police authorities. Under the boards there are local sheriffs *(nimismies)* in each of the 225 districts and magistrates in the "old" cities—cities founded in medieval times.

Local self-government is based on the Communal Law of 1948 and the Local Government Act of 1976. Under the broad control of the central government the local authorities have limited powers of taxation and are responsible for education, health, social welfare and other local matters. The legislative authority of the *kunta* is the Municipal Council, elected by direct and proportional representation, with from 17 to 85 members, depending on the size of the municipality. The whole municipality is constituted as a single electoral district. The executive organ is the Municipal Board, elected by the Municipal Council for a two-year term. In addition, the Municipal Council elects a large number of statutory and non-statutory bodies. The executive officer of the board is the municipal manager, called the town manager in cities. There are about 400 intermunicipal corporations for coordinating multimunicipality programs. In 1987 there were 461 municipalities, of which 84 were cities.

The Swedish-speaking Ahvenanmaa Islands have a semi-autonomous status under law. The power of the governor in this province is nominal and subordinate to that of an elected Assembly. The Assembly elects the seven-member Regional Board for a three-year term. The Assembly also has legislative powers applicable to the province. In addition, it has special taxing powers beyond those pertaining other regions, including the right to levy an increment on state income revenues.

AREA AND POPULATION				
		Land Area		Popu-lation
Prov-inces	Capitals	Sq. Km.	Sq. Mi.	(1984 est.)
Ahvenanmaa	Mariehamn	1,527	590	23,400
Häme	Hämeenlinna	17,010	6,568	672,700
Keski-Suomi	Jyväskylä	16,230	6,266	246,400
Kuopio	Kuopio	16,511	6,375	255,100
Kymi	Kouvola	10,783	4,163	342,300
Lappi	Rovaniemi	93,057	35,929	200,200
Mikkeli	Mikkeli	16,342	6,310	209,100
Oulu	Oulu	56,866	21,956	430,200
Pohjois-Karjala	Joensuu	17,782	6,866	177,700
Turku ja Pori	Turku	22,170	8,559	710,700
Uusimaa	Helsinki	9,898	3,822	1,165,400
Vaasa	Vaasa	26,447	10,211	442,600
TOTAL		304,623	117,615	4,875,800

Source: Official government figures.

FOREIGN POLICY

Finnish foreign policy has three main determinants: neutrality, friendship with the Soviet Union and Nordic cooperation.

Finnish neutrality is not derived, as in the case of Switzerland, from a long historical tradition, nor is it the result of an international treaty. It was adopted as the official policy as a result of geographical reality (proximity to the Soviet Union) and bitter experiences during World War II, in which it ended on the losing side. After the war, the country's international position was very fragile. It was isolated and bound by the terms of an unfavorable peace treaty signed February 10, 1947. The immediate task in the postwar period was to devise a modus vivendi with the Soviet Union, and the efforts in this direction came to be known as the Paasikivi Line (later the Paasikivi-Kekkonen Line) after the Finnish presidents of that era. The Agreement of Friendship, Cooperation and Mutual Assistance signed in 1948 between the two countries was a first step. The agreement, subsequently reaffirmed in 1955, 1970 and 1983, is not a mutual defense alliance. Finland is only obliged to defend its territory against an attack by West Germany or allies of West Germany and to forestall an attack on the Soviet Union mounted through Finland, and even in such a case, only after consultation between both parties had determined that such a threat existed. On the other hand, the preamble states that the Soviet Union respects "Finland's desire to remain outside the conflicting interests of the Great Powers." Although the Finns did not characterize their official foreign policy as neutral until the 1950s, this agreement was the first international recognition of Finland's nonalignment.

The easing of world tensions in the 1950s, the withdrawal of Soviet troops from their military bases in Porkkala on the southern coast and Finland's entry into the Nordic Council strengthened Finland's neutral role and posture. President Kekkonen, who succeeded Paasikivi in 1956, was an extremely forceful exponent of Finland's brand of active (as contrasted with Switzerland's passive) neutrality. Finland has avoided taking sides on issues involving the superpowers. Its positions on other issues, such as Vietnam, Korea, German reunification and South Africa, have been cautious and restrained. An example of Finland's active neutrality was the Kekkonen Plan for establishing a denuclearized zone in the Nordic region. Another was its support for SALT talks, which took place in Helsinki. Finland also was the host to the Conference on Security and Cooperation with Europe involving both the East and the West. Finland has held back from joining the EEC from a desire not to compromise its nonalignment.

Economic relations between Finland and the Soviet Union are coordinated by the Permanent Intergovernment Finnish-Soviet Commission on Economic Cooperation. In this context, the Soviet Union agreed to lease its half of the Saimaa Canal to Finland. Finland enjoys a most favored nation treatment by the Soviet Union and ranks fourth among trade partners of the Soviets outside the Warsaw Pact.

Nordic cooperation is the second most important plank of Finnish foreign policy. Although Finns are not Scandinavians by race, they have been accepted into the Nordic community because of the historical ties between Finland and Sweden. Finland joined the Nordic Council in 1955 after the Soviet Union modified its earlier opposition. The Council is concerned primarily with economic and social cooperation. It has no political or military policy. In contrast to the EEC, there are no supranational organizations associated with the Council, which functions only as an advisory body; its decisions are not binding on its members. The charter of the Council is not an international agreement but is approved by the member parliaments. The organs of the Council are the Presidium, the Council Assembly of 78 members and various committees. Each member nation sends 18 members to the Council Assembly except Iceland, which sends six. Outside of the Council there are periodic consultations among the member countries on political and military matters.

As a member of the Nordic Council, Finland enjoys a number of advantages. The Passport Union allows Finns to travel to other Nordic countries without passports, to work in them without work permits and to obtain Social Security benefits on the same scale as nationals. However, Finland is not a partner in the Scandinavian Airlines System (SAS).

Historical ties to Germany, muted during the 1950s as a result of Soviet suspicions, flourished again with the establishment of diplomatic relations with East Germany and West Germany in 1973. West Germany is a major trade partner, accounting for more than half of Finland's trade with the EEC.

Relations with the United States, the United Kingdom and other Western countries are primarily cultural and economic. As a member of the United Nations since 1955, Finland has participated in a number of U.N. peacekeeping operations, particularly in Cyprus, where a Finn was named the U.N. commander, as well as in Lebanon and India.

Finland is one of the leading European contributors to development aid to the Third World. In addition to participation in joint development projects, Finland has its own programs in Tanzania, Zambia, Vietnam, Kenya, Egypt and Sri Lanka. Official appropriations for this work totaled 0.4% of the GNP in 1984 and are expected to reach 0.7% by 1990.

The conduct of foreign policy is vested solely in the president by the Constitution. Because he is elected for a six-year renewable term, he is the guarantor of a stable foreign policy, with the leeway to make bold initiatives without being fettered by party squabbles. The State Council has the Foreign Affairs Committee, whose role has diminished since World War II and now is purely advisory. The Ministry of Foreign Affairs, however, is one of the most powerful in the cabinet. Finland maintains 44 embassies abroad; a legation in South Africa; and two permanent missions, one at the United Nations in New York and the other at the United Nations in Geneva.

PARLIAMENT

The national legislature is the unicameral Eduskunta (Riksdag in Swedish) of 200 members, elected by universal suffrage in a proportional representation system. Elections are held every four years, and the average turnover of seats in each election is about one-fourth of the total.

The Eduskunta is in session almost year-round, except in the summer and on state holidays. The average age is 50, and about 20% of the representatives are women. According the Article 11 of the Parliamentary Act of 1928, members are not bound to follow party dictates, nor is there any mention of party activity within the act. Nevertheless, parliamentary activity takes place strictly along party lines. The degree of party solidarity varies. Communists particularly tend to stick together, while the Swedish People's Party is loosely knit. In votes of confidence, the cohesion of the party groups is total. Based on the number of seats held in the Eduskunta, each party receives subsidies.

At the outset of each session the Eduskunta chooses a speaker and a committee of 45 electors to decide on membership on the various legislative committees. Committee work undergirds all legislative activity. All important bills must pass through one or more appropriate committees. The speaker determines which committee will receive a particular bill for study. Often statements and further study are required from another related committee, resulting in reports that present together all government and individual proposals and opinions on a particular issue.

Committees are of two kinds: permanent and extraordinary. The Parliament Act of 1928 specifies the following permanent committees: constitutional, legislative, foreign affairs, finance and banking. Extraordinary committees, which are reestablished every year, deal with education, agriculture and forestry, social affairs, defense, transportation and other matters. Subcommittees are permissible by law but are rare. Committees usually divide into sections for particular matters, then reconvene to approve or reject the committee report. Subcommittees report directly to the Eduskunta in the name of the entire committee.

The supervisory Grand Committee of 45 members is appointed by the committee of electors to oversee the Eduskunta's legislative process. In effect it represents an upper house and makes up for Finland's lack of one.

The ultimate forum is the plenary session, in which party groups are seated from left to right in ideological order. Usually sessions are held twice a week. The agenda is prepared by the speaker. Government proposals always take precedence on the calendar and must be acted on before discussion of private bills. Discussion precedes vote and no time limit is placed on speeches, interjections or replies. Members vote by standing, but when the majority is not clear, the speaker may request a machine-recorded vote or a secret ballot.

Individual bills must be introduced within two weeks of a new session, but government bills may be introduced at any time. Bills are presented in one of three forms: legislative bills, financial resolutions and petitions. Legislative bills concern the passage of a new law or the rescinding or amendment of an existing one; financial resolutions concern requests for budgetary operations; and petitions concern individual requests on which legislation is called for. Less than 10% of private bills are voted on in any session, and about 50% never come to the floor.

Outside of its legislative function, the Eduskunta supervises certain sectors of the administration. Its Banking Committee oversees the work of the Bank of Finland. The Eduskunta also elects the directors of the National Pensions Institute and the Finnish Broadcasting Corporation.

The electoral system was first devised in 1906 and, although challenged at regular intervals, has survived with few changes.

All Finnish citizens over 18, with the exception of persons convicted of a crime and others mentioned in Article 6 of the Parliament Act of 1928, have the right to vote. All eligible voters are registered on the basis of census lists that are open to public inspection and correction.

The country is divided into 15 electoral districts, with seats varying in number based on the census figures. Election boards are appointed at the communal and regional levels, and all parties are represented. Candidates are nominated mainly by the political parties on the basis of primaries. Parliamentary elections are held every four years. Polls are open for two days beginning on the third Sunday in March. The candidates are listed by number on the list of each electoral alliance. Therefore the voter can vote for both the alliance and the candidate by writing his number on the ballot. If only the nominee's name is filled in, the alliance does not benefit from the vote but the candidate does. The number of votes for each list and/or bloc is recorded, and each candidate is then assigned a "comparison number" based on the following formula: The leading individual vote-getter in each bloc is assigned the total vote of that bloc, the runner-up one-half, the third one-third and so on. Once these computations are made, all candidates are ranked and available seats assigned on the basis of rank. In effect, the vote for the individual candidate helps to determine his ranking within the bloc, while the simultaneous vote for the party list helps to determine the party's share of the available seats. This system is weighted in favor of the larger parties; nevertheless, small parties have been able to hold their own in recent years.

Presidential elections are held every six years on the basis of indirect universal suffrage. Eligible voters go to the polls to vote for electors on January 15 and January 16 of an election year, and electors convene one month later in Helsinki for the electoral convention. A candidate must win a majority of the votes. If this is impossible on the first and second ballots, the two candidates receiving the most votes on the second ballot are pitted against each other for a final round. A new president is inaugurated on March 1 following the election. In times of crisis, presidents may be elected directly by the Eduskunta, as was the case with Marshal Mannerheim in 1944.

Generally, voter turnouts are lower for presidential elections than for parliamentary ones. The latter is generally in the high 80% range while the former is in the low 70% range.

POLITICAL PARTIES

Political parties are the principal channels of political participation in Finland. They are not mentioned in the fundamental laws and generally are considered civil organizations with the same legal status as other associations. All major

PARTIES IN THE EDUSKUNTA After 1987 Elections			
Party	Votes	%	Seats
Social Democratic Party .	694,666	24.14	56
National Coalition Party .	665,477	23.13	53
Center Party	507,384	17.63	40
Finnish People's Demo-			
cratic League	269,678	9.37	16
Swedish People's Party .	153,141	5.32	12
Finnish Rural Party	181,557	6.31	9
Finnish Christian Union .	74,011	2.57	5
Democratic Alternative . .	122,115	4.24	4
Green Party	115,830	4.03	4
Others	93,661	3.25	1*
Total	2,877,520	100.00	200
* Åland delegate.			

parties are considered mass parties with large, dues-paying memberships. However, they are narrowly based, appealing to particular sections or classes or geographical areas. Thus they tend to be fragmented as well as numerous, inhibiting the formation of stable governments.

Eight parties are represented in the Eduskunta.

The Center Party (Keskustapuolu), founded as the Agrarian Union in 1906, adopted the present name in 1965. It is the leading nonsocialist party, and it the was third-ranking in number of seats in the Eduskunta in 1983. Its pivotal ideological position has enabled it to serve in 90% of coalition governments and to supply more presidents and prime ministers than any other party. The party leadership favors cooperation with the left and moderate socialist parties, while a minority, estimated at one-fourth (and known as the "Black Dozen"), opposes such cooperation. Historically pro-agrarian and pro-private enterprise, it nevertheless opposes concentration of wealth and supports state ownership and regulation in certain areas on pragmatic grounds. Party membership is estimated at over 300,000, of whom some 60% are farmers, 20% upper white-collar and 20% lower blue-collar. Although it receives fairly even support in all electoral districts, it is strongest in the northern provinces of Oulu and Lapland and the Southeast and weakest in the urbanized districts of Häme, Uusimaa and Helsinki, where it receives less than 5% support. It picked up its first deputy from Helsinki proper only in 1983. The Center Party merged with the Liberal People's Party in 1982 and since then has begun to stress ecological issues in an effort to attract younger voters.

The Finnish Christian League (Suomen Kristillinen Liitto, SKL), founded in 1958, won its first parliamentary seat in 1966 and by 1979 had expanded its representation to nine seats, but it lost six seats in 1983. The SKL derives its support exclusively from the more devout Lutherans. As a defender of traditional family values it has moved to the right in recent years. Party membership is listed as 20,000, mainly in the Pietist strongholds of Vaasa and Mikkeli.

The Finnish People's Democratic League (Suomen Kansan Demokraattinen Liitto, SKDL) was formed in 1944 by dissident Social Democrats, independent Socialists and Communists and is a grand coalition of the left. Its principal segment is the Finnish Communist Party (Suomen Kommunistien Puolue, SKP) while the Democratic League of Finnish Women and the Socialist League of Students are minor partners.

Founded in 1918, the SKP became a legal party in 1922 but was eliminated as an effective political group by the fascists until 1944. Since the end of World War II the SKDL coalition has enjoyed considerable success, winning an average of 20% of the votes in general elections. However, its popularity has steadily declined since 1966, and its parliamentary representation fell from a peak of 50 in 1958 to 16 in 1987. It lost further ground in the municipal elections of 1984. From 1966 to 1983 it participated in all but two of the non-caretaker governments but was forced to leave in 1983 when it voted against a modest increase in the defense budget.

The SKDL and the SKP maintain separate organizational networks and membership lists. Since 1969 the SKP was divided into Eurocommunist and Stalinist factions, with the latter in the majority. The alliance pursues long-range goals through the SKP and short-term and more pragmatic goals through the SKDL. The alliance espouses a broad range of radical and not-so-radical programs, such as expansion of state enterprises, worker participation in management, enlargement of rural holdings, increasing unemployment benefits, a 35-hour workweek, lowering the retirement age and payment of wages to housewives. SKDL is second only to the Center Party in membership, with an estimated strength of 176,000 members, of whom 60,000 are members of the SKP. The twin pillars of SKDL strength are urban and industrial labor, and landless laborers and small farmers of the North and East. Although the former are becoming less radical, the backwoods remain the bastion of Marxist influence. However, the SKDL suffered one of its worst electoral defeats in 1983, losing the cities to Social Democrats and losing much of the backwoods vote to the Finnish Rural Party.

The Finnish Rural Party (Suomen Maaseudun Puolue, SMP) was founded in 1956 by a group of dissidents from the Agrarian Union (Center Party). The SMP gained its first seat in 1966 and broke into the big league in 1970 by winning 10.5% of the vote and 18 seats in the Eduskunta. In the mid-1970s internal dissensions led to a split into two factions, resulting in the loss of 16 seats. By 1983 it had recovered and staged a comeback, winning 17 seats and 9.7% of the votes. SMP ideology is a curious mixture of socialism and antisocialism, but its basic appeal is to backwoodsmen, who constitute the backbone of the party. In 1983 it was successful in wooing backwoods voters from the SKDL. The SMP espouses a number of populist planks, and it mobilizes public outrage against the abuses of power by conventional parties. It has over 15,00 organizational units, including 150 communal and 14 district organizations. Party policies are decided by the leadership, especially by the party chairman, Pekka Vennamo. Membership, estimated at 35,000, is concentrated in the eastern provinces, where Kuopio and Pohjois-Karjala are party strongholds. It joined the government in 1983.

The Finnish Social Democratic Party (Suomen Socialidemokraattinen Puolue, SDP), founded in 1899 as an outgrowth of the labor movement, the SDP changed radically after World War I. Under the leadership of Vaino Tanner, the party transformed itself from an orthodox Marxist group into a mainline socialist party, espousing the same goals as the other Scandinavian Social Democratic parties. The trend continued after World War II under Vaino Leskinen. Centralized economic planning was the party's key objective, with socialization limited to key sectors of the economy. This pragmatic approach met with firm resistance within the left wing of the party, which, led by Aarre Simonen, broke away to form the Social Democratic League of Workers and Small Farmers (Tyovaen ja Pienviljelijain Sosialidemokraattinen Litto, TPSL), also known as the Simonists. In 1969 the TPSL disbanded and was reabsorbed into the SDP. The SDP is the first preference of the industrial blue-collar workers. It also has an important support base in the urban middle class and in addition attracts the new left and the professionals. A major source of strength is the Confederation of Finnish Trade Unions, which although formally nonpolitical counts 63% of its membership as pro-SDP. With about 100,000 members, the SDP ranks third in numerical strength. Party support is weakest in the northern provinces and in Vaasa Province to the west. Membership is organized in 1,350 basic units, of which 176 are communal organizations and 16 are district organizations. Between triennial congresses the party is run by the 50-member Party Council and the 15-member Executive Committee. With much of its earlier factionalism behind it, the SDP has headed most governments since 1966. The SDP is moderate reformist and anti-Communist in outlook but pursues much the same economic goals as the SKDL. In foreign policy the SDP has given up its earlier hostility to the Soviet Union and become more amenable to the Kekkonen Line. SDP fortunes and prospects were bolstered by Mauno Koivisto's easy victory in the 1982 presidential elections, its electoral success in 1983 in capturing 57 seats, and Prime Minister Kalevi Sorsa's track record as party leader. It is emerging as Finland's "natural" ruling party.

The Liberal People's Party (Liberaalinen Kansanpuollue, LK) was founded in 1956 as a coalition of the Finnish People's Party and the Liberal Union, also known as the League of Independents. It is essentially a middle-class party, favoring government economic planning but upholding the need for private enterprise. The LK concentrates on social goals, particularly democratization of education and extension of Social Security benefits.

The LK's constituency is spread thinly throughout the country, but the bulk of its votes comes from the more populous southern Uusimaa and Turku provinces, where it attracts mainly urban white-collar workers. Although relatively homogeneous, the LK suffers from organizational weakness, low membership and fewer basic organizations (about 300) and district organizations (14) and the absence of communal organizations. Policy is set at the biennial party congresses while the Party Board manages day-to-day affairs. The party merged with the Center Party in 1982 although retaining its separate identity.

The National Coalition Party (Kansallinen Kokoomus, KK) is the most important conservative party. Founded in 1918 as a continuation of the pre-independence "Old Finns," a nationalist group, its first taste of power came when its leader P.E. Svinhufoud was president from 1931 to 1937. It participated in most governments until 1946, supplying 10 prime ministers. Since then it has participated in only three governments (1958–59, 1962–63 and 1964–66) and was in the political wilderness during the Kekkonen years. Even though out of power, the KK has steadily held on to its share of the national vote, its Eduskunta strength reaching 47 seats in 1979, but dipping slightly to 44 in 1983 as a result of inroads by the Finnish Rural Party with its greater appeal to populist right-wingers.

The KK pursues a policy of Reaganomics, which it describes as "people's capitalism." As a defender of private enterprise, it seeks to dismantle the machinery of government regulations, cut business taxes, Social Security and unemployment benefits, and shift from income taxes to consumption taxes to encourage saving. The KK also is anti-Soviet and pro-Western, making it an unacceptable coalition partner for the generally left-of-center governments.

Historically, KK support comes primarily from big business, large landowners and a broad spectrum of antisocialists. Another important support base comprises interest groups such as the Federation of Finnish Industries, the Confederation of Finnish Employers, the Central Chamber of Commerce, the Confederation of Agricultural Producers and veterans' organizations. More recently the KK has made significant inroads into the urban middle class.

The Swedish People's Party (Svenska Folkparteit) was founded in 1906 as the institutional continuation of the Swedish interest group in the Eduskunta for promoting the interest of the Swedish-speaking minority. With the decline in the percentage of Swedes in the population, the fortunes of the party have waned, but still it obtained 12 seats in the 1987 Eduskunta. The party has joined all of the coalition governments since 1968. Although racially homogeneous, the party embraces a broad range of political opinions. It has 97 basic units and four district organizations in Swedish-speaking areas. Generally the party tends toward conservatism (reflecting earlier dominance of large landowners) tempered by the growing influence of social liberalism. Party membership is about 50,000 and is concentrated in Uusimaa and Vaasa provinces and the Åland Islands. Support also comes from the 25,000 member Central Association of Swedish Agricultural Producers and Swedish Cooperative Association.

Minor parties include the Constitutional Right-Wing Party (POP), formed in 1973 to oppose the reelection of President Kekkonen; the People's Unity Party, a breakaway group of the Finnish Rural Party; and the Greens, and ecology-oriented party that doubled its representation in the Eduskunta between 1983 and 1987, from two to four seats.

There are no illegal political parties or known terrorist groups in Finland.

ECONOMY

Finnish economic performance in recent years has displayed many positive features, particularly high and stable growth of output and employment by European standards. Both the budget and the current external account deficits have been contained at sustainable levels, thus avoiding a large buildup of public and external debt. Moreover, inflation is down to the OECD average. At the same time, through 1987, external competitiveness and export performance have continued to worsen, resulting in a further edging up of unemployment, which has become a focus of policy debates. While the marked fall in energy prices in the mid-1980s buoyed up Finnish exports to Western markets, exports to Eastern markets have declined.

Macroeconomic policies have played a role both directly and indirectly in stabilizing growth since the second oil crisis of the late 1970s. Fiscal planning, monetary exchange rates and income policies have been directed toward breaking the "devaluation cycle." Finnish economic stability is reflected in the fact that since 1981 the annual rate of real GDP growth has hardly deviated from 3%. Although this is 1% below the average growth rate over the past 25 years, the manufacturing productivity growth rate has accelerated during the same period, from 4% to 5% annually.

Part of the explanation for the comparatively rapid and balanced output growth in the first half of the 1980s lies in the active pursuit of countercyclical demand management policies. Other stabilizing elements have included:

- the declining share of the timber, paper and pulp industry (the "flex price" sector) in total export earnings, from 55% in 1970 to 38% in 1985, and the growing share of the metal and engineering industry (the "fix price" sector) from 19% to 31% during the same period
- the growing share of trade with the Soviet Union during 1979–82, when the Western export markets were shrinking
- the strength of the U.S. and Canadian dollars, which protected until 1985 raw-material–producing sectors, notably timber, paper and pulp, from North American competition
- the rapid pickup in consumption, both public and private

The smooth growth of output since the second oil shock has been associated with a relatively strong expansion of employment despite better productivity growth. Indeed, Finland is among the few countries where the employment/population ratio was higher in 1984 than in 1970. As in other OECD countries, it is mainly the service sector that has absorbed the growth in the labor force, with about three-quarters of the increase in the public sector. The share of industrial employment declined through the 1980s, but less than in other OECD countries, and employment levels still exceed the average of the preceding decade. Nevertheless, the rate of unemployment has been on balance broadly unchanged at about 6% for the past five years. This "stickiness" reflects a strong growth of the labor force, owing to a continuing rise in the participation rates as well as to a boost to population growth by a return of migrants, especially from Sweden.

Although public deficits have emerged recently, they are modest by international standards. The deterioration in the public sector was more than offset by an overall improvment of the aggregate financial position of the private sector. As a result, Finland has maintained faster economic growth than the OECD average, with less deterioration in the real foreign balance.

At the same time there are some less encouraging features, which could act as brakes on future growth. These include an erosion in the competitiveness of industrial products, a decline in the share of gross fixed investment in the GDP, and a lack of structural readjustments in the productive sectors to meet new technological advances. Performance against inflation also has been less satisfactory. Although the inflation growth rate was slower in the first half of the 1980s than in the preceding decade, Finland has lost the favorable inflation differential vis-à-vis the OECD average that it had in the 1970s. By 1985 inflation was being brought again under control as a result of lower wage inflation and more moderate increases in officially set prices. As in other Scandinavian countries, inflationary pressures are built into the wage-setting mechanisms. Also, the system of agricultural price setting and the general administration of price controls provide little incentive to resist inflation.

Although total fixed investment has grown in line with real output in recent years, the level is low by historical standards. The share of real private fixed investment in the GDP fell to 22% in the 1980s from 25% in the 1960s and 27% in the 1970s. A decline has been recorded in virtually all sectors, though it is particularly pronounced in the residential construction and nonmanufacturing production sectors. Industrial investment in plant and equipment has been replaced in part by increased R&D expenditures and direct investment abroad.

Because Finland was less severely hit by increases in oil prices in the past than other countries, it is not expected to benefit from oil price decreases to the same extent either. Such decreases are likely to result in a fall in Finnish exports to the Soviet Union. Even so, the net terms-of-trade gains associated with lower oil prices are large (on the order of 1.5% of the GDP), and the impact on consumer prices (at some 2% in 1986) also is significant.

After a rather good performance in 1984, with a good trade surplus equivalent to 11.1% of export revenues, the export balance deteriorated in 1985 to just over half as vigorous growth of domestic demand increased imports. The balance on services also deteriorated as Finnish tourists spent more abroad. Interest payment on foreign debt also remained high despite favorable exchange rate changes. In 1986 and 1987 the trade balance improved, mainly due to the terms-of-trade gain in 1986. The current account deficit, however, is projected to remain at about 1% of the GDP. The services account continues to deteriorate and may remain in deficit for some time to come.

Finland is predominantly a free-market economy, with the private sector accounting for close to 70% of the GNP. Ownership remains largely in private hands in commerce, agriculture, forestry, housing, manufacturing, and banking and insurance. Government investment is concentrated in mining, nonresidential construction, public utilities and transportation and communications. There are joint ventures by the private and the public sectors, some with foreign collaboration, in high-technology sectors such as automobiles and chemicals. In all, government-controlled firms account for only about 16% of industrial production. In the private sector, no single group or company dominates any sector of the economy, although several large cooperatives dominate wholesale trade.

To combat growing disparities in regional economic development, the government has established the Regional Development Board. Two development zones are designated, covering the entire country outside the South. The largest amount of assistance is reserved for the northern region. Three broad tactical approaches are adopted: investment incentives, such as loans and tax deductions; promotion of labor mobility; and government investments in infrastructure in selected communities that offer potential for future expansion.

Under the Supervision of the Ministry of Economics, the Economic Council and its subcommittees help to formulate general economic policies. Participation is limited to government administrators and representatives of major economic groups, such as the Central Union of Agricultural Producers (MTK), the Central Federation of Finnish Employers (STK), the Finnish Central League of Trade Unions (SAK) and the Central Federation of Officials and Civil Servants (TVK). Appointments are made by the Eduskunta. All these groups exercise varying degrees of pressure tactics to impose their views on government and to shape economic decisions. The SAK uses its ties with the Social Democrats, the MTK its ties with the Center Party, and the STK its control of the commercial press and private research. The rise of the Economic Council reflects the declining importance of the Eduskunta as a forum where the more esoteric aspects of economic policy can be discussed.

Decisive changes have occurred in the past 50 years in the national distribution of income. In general, income from wages, other labor income, corporate profits and surpluses of government enterprises has risen, while income from unincorporated enterprises and interest and rent has declined. Much of the decline in income from unincorporated enterprises has resulted from the diminishing role of agriculture, where most workers are self-employed.

PRINCIPAL ECONOMIC INDICATORS

Gross National Product: $60.040 billion (1986)
GNP per capita: $12,180 (1986)
GNP average annual growth rate: 2.8% (1973–86)
GNP per capita average annual
    growth rate: 2.4% (1973–86)
Average annual rate of inflation: 8.1% (1980–86)
Consumer Price Index (1980=100)
    All items: 165.9 (February 1988)
    Food: 169.9 (February 1988)
Wholesale Price Index (1980=100) 136 (1988)
Average annual growth rate (1980–86) (%)
    Public consumption: 3.7
    Private consumption: 3.1
    Gross domestic investment: 1.0

```
┌─────────────────────────────────────────────────────────┐
│          BALANCE OF PAYMENTS, 1987 ($ million)          │
│                                                          │
│  Current account balance: −1,949                         │
│  Merchandise exports: 19,026                             │
│  Merchandise imports: −17,703                            │
│  Trade balance: 1,323                                    │
│  Other goods, services & income +: 4,717                 │
│  Other goods, services & income −: 7,524                 │
│  Private unrequited transfers: −162                      │
│  Official unrequited transfers: −304                     │
│  Direct investment: −813                                 │
│  Portfolio investment: 1,366                             │
│  Other long-term capital: −216                           │
│  Other short-term capital: 6,219                         │
│  Net errors & omissions: −585                            │
│  Counterpart items: 609                                  │
│  Exceptional financing: —                                │
│  Liabilities constituting foreign authorities reserves: 11 │
│  Total change in reserves: −4,642                        │
└─────────────────────────────────────────────────────────┘
```

PUBLIC FINANCE

In 1985 central government revenues represented 29% of the GNP, placing Finland in the middle among developed countries in this respect. The gross tax burden is less than in countries such as Sweden, Norway, the Netherlands and the United Kingdom but higher than in Japan, Switzerland, Australia and the United States. Central government revenues are heavily dependent on indirect taxes, although the share of these taxes in total revenue has gradually declined. Sales tax makes up half of indirect taxes, and the other half comes from excise duties on alcohol and fuel oil. Income and inheritance taxes yield only one-third of all tax revenues but have been steadily gaining in importance. The corporation tax is a flat rate, whereas the personal income tax is progressive, up to a maximum of 80% of taxable income. The sales tax is, with some exceptions, about 16% of the sale price. The state share of taxation is about 60%; that of local authorities, 25%; and that of other taxes, chiefly Social Security payments, 14%. The gross tax level is 36% to 38%, and the net tax level is about 20%. Income transfers and subsidies play a considerable part in the public economy, but less so than in other welfare societies. The local tax is a flat percentage of personal income, varying with the commune, and there is a 1% church tax payable by both individuals and corporations. Many types of exemptions are available.

The fiscal year is the calendar year. Each fall the Ministry of Finance submits the budget to the Eduskunta accompanied by a survey of the economy and the outlook for the coming year. Early in the following year, while the budget is be-

GROSS DOMESTIC PRODUCT, 1985

GDP nominal (national currency): 334.9 billion
GDP real (national currency): 219.4 billion (1980 prices)
GDP per capita ($): 10,998
Average annual growth rate of GDP, 1980–85: 2.6%

GDP by type of expenditure (%)
Consumption
Private: 53
Government: 19
Gross domestic investment: 24
Gross domestic saving: 24

Foreign trade
Exports: 31
Imports: –29

Cost components of GDP (%)
Net indirect taxes: 11
Consumption of fixed capital: 14
Compensation of employees: 54
Net operating surplus: 21

Sectoral origin of GDP (%)
Primary
Agriculture: 8.6
Mining: 0.5

Secondary
Manufacturing: 25.3
Construction: 7.4
Public utilities: 3.0
Tertiary
Transportation and communications: 7.8
Trade: 11.4
Finance: 15.6
Other services: 5.3
Government: 15.1

Average annual sectoral growth rate, 1980–86 (%)

Agriculture: 0.2
Industry: 2.8
Manufacturing: 3.0
Services: 2.4

ing debated, the ministry publishes a revised version of the survey, estimating the overall fiscal impact on aggregate demand, incomes and money supply. After the approval of the final budget, the government may return several times during the year with requests for supplementary appropriations.

Not only has government spending become much more significant since World War II in terms of GDP, but also there have been major changes in re-

---

OFFICIAL DEVELOPMENT ASSISTANCE

In $ Million

2	7	48	110	144	153	178	211	313
1965	1970	1975	1980	1982	1983	1984	1985	1986

As Percentage of GNP

0.02	0.06	0.18	0.22	0.29	0.32	0.35	0.40	0.45
1965	1970	1975	1980	1982	1983	1984	1985	1986

CENTRAL GOVERNMENT EXPENDITURES, 1986
% of total expenditures

Defense: 5.2
Education: 13.7
Health: 10.6
Housing, Social Security, welfare: 35.7
Economic services: 21.0
Other: 13.7
Total expenditures as % of GNP: 31.1
Overall surplus or deficit as % of GNP: –0.5

CENTRAL GOVERNMENT REVENUES, 1986
% of total current revenues

Taxes on income, profit and capital gain: 31.5
Social Security contributions: 9.6
Domestic taxes on goods and services: 45.7
Taxes on international trade and transactions: 0.8
Other taxes: 4.4
Current nontax revenue: 7.9
Total current revenue as % of GNP: 29.8
Government consumption as % of GNP: 21
Annual growth rate of government consumption: 3.7%
(1980–86)

---

source allocation. Until 1953 temporary expenditures associated with the war—such as reparations and compensation for evacuees from lands ceded to the Soviet Union—dominated the budget. Since then, the fastest-growing items are education, social welfare and capital allocations.

Fiscal policy—the management of aggregate demand by changes in government tax receipts and expenditures—has not played a significant part in stimulation of the economy. Indeed, failure to use it probably has contributed to the cyclical instability of the economy. This weakness is common to many democratic societies because of political considerations. Increase or decrease in taxes requires parliamentary approval and may be subjected to long interparty squabbles. It was only with the adoption of the 1977–82 medium-term stabilization program that fiscal policy began to be used as a tool to achieve economic stability. The strict requirement for balancing the state budget each year was extended to cover a five-year cycle. The Ministry of Finance had great room for maneuver because of the relatively small size of the public sector in relation to the GDP and the low level of domestic indebtedness by international standards. During 1982–83 a moderate fiscal stimulus was given to the economy to absorb the slack induced by the international recession. During 1984–85 a somewhat restrictive stance was adopted as international and domestic recovery got under way. During 1985–86 and expansionary policy was adopted as both the domestic economy and exports weakened.

An interesting feature of fiscal policy is the use of tax instruments, including adjustment of tax brackets, sales tax, Social Security contributions and energy tax. Even more striking is the rapid growth of government spending, at about 4% of the GNP since 1980, fueled by implementation of new welfare programs. The result has been an equally rapid buildup of government indebtedness, though at 14% of the GDP, its level still is low by international standards.

CURRENCY & BANKING

The national monetary unit is the Finnmark or markka, divided into 100 pennia (singular: penni). Coins are issued in denominations of 5, 10, 20 and 50 pennia and notes in denominations of 5, 10, 50, 100 and 500 markkas.

EXCHANGE RATE Markkas per U.S. Dollar						
1982	1983	1984	1985	1986	1987	1988
5.291	5.810	6.530	5.417	4.794	3.946	4.079

The central bank is the Suomen Pankki (Finlands Bank, the Bank of Finland), which is the bank of issue under the guarantee and supervision of the Eduskunta. The Bank's Board of Management is appointed by the president of the republic, and its nine supervisors are elected by the Eduskunta.

The commercial banking system comprises two large and five small banks with 928 branches, and 270 savings banks with 1,050 branches. In addition, there are 371 cooperative banks and five mortgage banks. The Postipankki collects small savings through 3,250 local post offices and 12 offices of the Bank of Finland as well as through its own head office and 36 branches. There are several nonbank institutions in the financial sector, including the National Pensions Fund, two institutions that finance corporate R&D, and a large number of insurance companies.

As a rule, banks do not offer specialized services. Few institutions operate in capital markets. Commercial banks have limited portfolio holdings, and the market in short-term government notes and bonds is small.

FINANCIAL INDICATORS, 1986

International reserves minus gold: $1.787 billion
   SDRs: 204.6
     Reserve position in IMF: 165.2
     Foreign exchange: $1.417 billion
Gold (million fine troy oz): 1,912
Ratio of external debt to total reserves: —

Central bank
   Assets (%):
   Foreign assets: 75.8
   Claims on government: 2.4
   Claims on bank: 9.0
   Claims on private sector: 12.8
   Liabilities (%):
   Reserve money: 65.9
   Government deposits: 2.2
   Foreign liabilities: 0.3
   Capital accounts: 16.6

Money supply
Stock in billion national currency: 30.342
M^1 per capita: 6,140
U.S. liabilities to: $835 million
U.S. claims on: $1.009 billion

Private banks
   Assets (%):
   Loans to government: 0.8
   Loans to private sector: 73.6
   Reserves: 3.7
   Foreign assets: 21.9
   Liabilities of which (%): deposits (billion national currency): 313,653
   Demand deposits: 6.8
   Savings deposits: 46.6
   Government deposits: 3.2
   Foreign liabilities: 31.4

GROWTH PROFILE (Annual Growth Rates, %)

Population, 1986–2000: 0.2
Crude birth rate, 1985–90: 12.1
Crude death rate, 1985–90: 10.6
Urban population, 1980–85: 2.9
Labor force, 1985–2000: 0.3
GNP, 1973–86: 2.8

```
+------------------------------------------------+
| GROWTH PROFILE (Annual Growth Rates, %) (con-  |
|                    tinued)                     |
| GNP per capita, 1973–86: 2.4                   |
| GDP, 1980–86: 2.7                              |
| Inflation, 1980–86: 8.1                        |
| Agriculture, 1980–86: 0.2                      |
| Industry, 1980–86: 2.8                         |
| Manufacturing, 1980–86: 3.0                    |
| Services, 1980–86: 2.4                         |
| Money holdings, 1980–86: 14.3                  |
| Manufacturing earnings per employee, 1980–85: 1.9 |
| Energy production, 1980–86: 9.5                |
| Energy consumption, 1980–86: 3.6               |
| Exports, 1980–86: 2.8                          |
| Imports, 1980–86: 1.9                          |
| General government consumption, 1980–86: 3.7   |
| Private consumption, 1980–86: 3.1              |
| Gross domestic investment, 1980–86: 1.0        |
+------------------------------------------------+
```

AGRICULTURE

Finnish farming is characterized by the relatively small proportion of arable land (9%) under cultivation, adverse climatic and soil conditions and the small size of the holdings. Farming is concentrated in southwest, where wheat, oats, barley and rye are grown. The small, independent farmer is the bulwark of agriculture. Small-scale farms were created by a series of land reforms beginning with the Lex Kallio of 1922. The Land Use Act of 1928 sought to improve the conditions of existing farms by increasing the farm size, consolidating smaller farms and introducing new land-use patterns. The average farm is about 9 ha. (22 ac). A total of 99% of all farms are privately owned and operated.

The cooperative movement is strong in the agricultural sector. There are over 3,000 cooperative associations, which handle both crops and livestock produce. Cooperative banks are major sources of rural credit.

One goal of agricultural policy that has met with considerable success is self-sufficiency in basic foodstuffs. The country is self-sufficient in grains, and it exports livestock surpluses. There are quota restrictions on the import of agricultural commodities. There also is a system of government-subsidized price supports and income supplements paid directly to the producer. In view of the growing difficulties in exporting agricultural surpluses, agricultural production has been cut since 1960. The volume of farm production has therefore increased very little since that date. In particular, the field reservation program led to the demise of many farming communities and to a large-scale exodus of unemployed farmers to the cities.

Livestock provides 75% of the gross value of agricultural output. Horses and sheep have become rarities, but dairy and beef cattle, pigs and chickens are raised in large numbers. The most common breed of cattle is the Ayrshire. In Lapland some 200,00 reindeer are herded. Dairy products account for some 45% of the gross value of agricultural production, and beef and pork another 25%.

AGRICULTURAL INDICATORS, 1986

Agriculture's share of GDP: 6%
Average annual growth rate: (1980–86) 0.2%
Value added in agriculture: $5.030 billion
Cereal imports (000 tons): 98
Index of agricultural production (1979–81=100): 113.8
Index of food production (1979–81=100): 113.8
Index food production per capita: (1979–81=100): 110 (1984–86)
Number of tractors: 238,000
Number of harvester-threshers: 46,000
Total fertilizer consumption: 507,900 tons
Fertilizer consumption per ha. (per ac.) (100 g.) 2,104 (852)
Number of farms: 200,000
Average size of holding (ha.): 60 (148.2 ac.)
Size class (%)
  Below 1 ha. (below 2.47 ac.): —
  1–5 ha. (2.47–12.35 ac.): 15.2
  5–10 ha. (12.35–24.7 ac.): 25.6
  10–20 ha. (24.7–49.4 ac.): 30.2
  20–50 ha. (49.4–123.5 ac.): 23.2
  50–200 ha. (123.5–494 ac.): ⎫
  Over 200 ha. (over 494 ac.): ⎬ 5.8

Tenure (%)
  Owner-operated: 79.9
  Rented: 19.3
  Other: 0.8
% of farms using irrigation: 3

Farms as % of total land area: 39.5

Cultivated area: 12,025,000 ha. (29,713,000 ac.)

Land use (%)

  Total cropland: 20.1
  Permanent crops: 0.3
  Temporary crops: 97.6
  Fallow: 2.1
  Meadows and pastures: 1.1
  Woodland: 58.1
  Other: 20.7

AGRICULTURAL INDICATORS, 1986 *(continued)*

Yields kg./ha. (lb./ac.)
  Grains: 2,911 (2,598)
  Roots and tubers: 19,624 (17,515)
  Pulses: 2,120 (1,892)
  Milk kg. (lb.)/Animal: 5,048 (11,129)

Livestock (000)
  Cattle: 1,576
  Horses: 35
  Sheep: 116
  Pigs: 1,211

Forestry
Production of roundwood: 41,782 million cu. m. (1.476 billion cu. ft.)
  of which industrial roundwood (%): 92.8
Value of exports ($ 000): 4,603,703
Fishing
Total catch (000 tons): 160.6
  of which marine %: 78.8
Value of exports ($ 000): 16,559

Livestock products have faced the same problems of surpluses as crops. Beginning in the latter half of the 1960s, the government began cutting production incentives. Slaughtering bonuses were offered to reduce the size of herds and a soil bank was established to take pastureland out of production. Producer prices were lowered by imposing a supplementary tax on the sale of certain dairy products. Quotas were placed on the import of feed and fodder for cattle. These policies have succeeded in cutting down the size of the national herd.

About 75% of the total land area is covered by 54.5 milion acres of forestland, making Finland one of the world's largest wood-producing nations. One-third of the forest lands are publicly owned. The main tree species are pine (44%) spruce (36%), birch (18%) and aspen and elder (2%). Pine, spruce and birch provide the raw materials for the sawmilling, cellulose, and paper industries, while aspen is used in the manufacture of matches.

Most of the wooded area is taken up by farm forests with an average size of roughly 36 ha. (90 ac.). In the North the average size is slightly larger, at 53 ha. (132 ac.), but it is somewhat smaller in the South, at 27 ha. (67 ac.). As agriculture became less labor-intensive, large number of farmers turned to forest farming. The so-called forest money constitutes more than one-third of total farm income and in some areas more than half. Nevertheless, mechanization has made inroads, causing a rapid decline in the work force. However, in the wintertime, when there is little work to be done on the farms, farmhands work as lumberjacks.

Horses continue to be used to haul logs to the roadside or onto ice-covered lakes. When the ice melts, the logs are floated downstream, from where the bundled timber is towed across the larger lakes by small tugs. Some of the raw wood also is hauled by truck.

The volume of the growing stock is estimated at 1.5 billion m. (4.9 billion ft.), but the volume of felling in recent years has been slightly under capacity. Since the middle 1960s, overcutting of the natural stock has resulted in a small decline in the country's forest reserves. In response to clear signs of a timber shortage, Finland was converted from a net exporter to a net importer of raw timber, particularly from Sweden and the Soviet Union. In 1965 the Finnish government launched its first five-year silviculture improvement plan for expanding the cultivated forest area to 295,547 ha. (730,000 ac.), the enlargement of the drainage area to 325,911 ha. (805,000 ac.), the replacement of slow-growing trees with high-yield varieties, the introduction of high-intensive cultivation techniques and the construction of new roads between lumber regions and factories.

Fishing is an insignificant sector in terms of value of output. There are only a few thousand professional fishermen, and most of the catch is caught by amateur anglers. The most important species is the Baltic herring, white fish and salmon in the sea and vendace in the inland waters.

MANUFACTURING

Finland entered the industrial age only in the 1950s. Until then, manufacturing was limited to the production of paper and paper products. Contributing to rapid industrial expension were a medley of factors: forced reparations to the Soviet Union, which stretched the productive capacity of the heavy engineering sector; growing world demand for Finnish quality products; better transportation and communication into the productive interior of the country; and enormous hydroelectric capacity.

The wood and paper industry is historically the bellwether of Finnish manufacturing, although since 1958 it has yielded first place in value added and employment to metals and engineering. The mechanical wood branch of the industry differs from the pulp and paper branch. In the 1960s the former showed signs of slowdown as the domestic supply of timber leveled off and the climbing price of wood began to menace the industry's heretofore competitive cost structure, which helped it to penetrate foreign markets that absorbed two-thirds of the output. Producers then turned to higher degrees of processing to increase the value added but faced formidable capital investment requirements, in the raising of which Finland does not have much of a competitive edge.

> **MANUFACTURING INDICATORS, 1986**
>
> Average annual growth rate, 1980–86: 3.0%
> Share of GDP: 25%
> Labor force in manufacturing: 32.3%
> Value added in manufacturing: $12,199 billion
>   Food & agriculture: 13%
>   Textiles: 7%
>   Machinery: 24%
>   Chemicals: 7%
> Earnings per employee in manufacturing
>   Growth rate: 1.9% (1980–85)
>   Index (1980=100): 110 (1985)
> Total earnings as % of value added: 44
> Gross output per employee (1980=100): 119
> Index of Manufacturing Production: (1980=100) 116.5

On the other hand, the paper branch is already capital-intensive and very efficient. Its international competitive position is not threatened, nor is its share in total exports. The pulp and paper industry includes mechanical pulp mills, semichemical pulp mills, sulfite and sufate pulp mills, paperboard and cardboard mills, fiberboard mills, wallpaper factories, cardboard box factories, bag and envelope factories and so on. Production has evolved more sluggishly in the mechanical wood branch, which includes sawmills and planing mills, plywood mills, bobbin and spool factories and a number of other woodworking factories.

The metal industry owes its origin to the forest industry, for which it made machinery and equipment. The greatest successes in recent years have been in the basic metal industries. Steel plate and sheet steel are produced in Rauarukki in northwestern Finland, and nickel, chromium, cobalt and zinc by the firm Outokumpu. The automobile industry was founded in 1969 in Uusikaupunki (Nystad) in southwestern Finland by a combine of the Swedish Saab Company and the Finnish Valmet. Also toward the end of the 1960s, the production of elevators was started by the firm of Kone. Finland also subcontracts fabrication of parts for large projects, such as atomic power stations in Sweden. Since it is essential that shipping routes be open throughout the year, Finland took the lead in manufacturing icebreakers, in the production of which Finland is now the unchallenged leader. Dominated by the three companies of Wartsila, Rauma-Repola and Valmet, the Finnish shipbuilding industry specializes in container ships, refrigerator ships, passenger ferries and luxury liners. Another sector of growing importance is electronics, which covers domestic appliances and electrical machinery. The basic metals and engineering industries use much of the domestically mined metals, but these metals meet only about half of the raw materials requirements of the basic metals industry, which in turn meets only half the requirements of the engineering industry.

The chemical industry is the fastest-growing and one in which public companies have a strong position. Neste, the biggest oil refinery in Scandinavia, and Rikkihappo, producer of sulphuric acid, superphosphates and nitrogen fertilizers, are both state-owned companies. The forest industries also make chemical products, such as ethyl alcohol, pine oil and turpentine. The cellulose industry is predominantly in private hands. The petrochemical company Pekima, which manufactures raw materials for plastics, is owned partly by the state and partly by private interests.

Finnish design, characterized by classic simplicity, has helped to enhance the appeal of Finnish industrial and consumer products throughout the world. Although Finland is relatively less developed in hi-tech industries, there is considerable export of technological know-how in the more conventional areas, such as the flash melting method for the production of copper devised by Petri Bryk, and the meteorological radio balloon for wind direction plotting devised by Vilho Vaisala.

The food industry is the third largest in terms of value added, but much of its production is consumed domestically. The textile industry, one of the country's oldest, has fallen on lean days but still commands strong foreign markets because of superior design and fabrics.

The government industrial sector contributes about 15% of the GDP and 20% to exports. Government ownership takes the form of shareholdings in companies that are set up and run just as private companies are. State corporations are administered by the Companies Division of the Ministry of Trade and Industry. Finnair Oy (the national airline) and Oy Alko Ab (the state alcoholic beverage monopoly) are subordinate to the Ministry of Communication and the Ministry Social Affairs and Health, respectively. Besides Neste Oy, which is partially owned by the state, other state corporations include Enso Gutzeit Oy (pulp, paper and paper products), Finnlines (ocean freight lines), Outokumpu Oy (copper and primary metals), Valmet Oy (machinery and ships), Rautaruukki Oy (steel) and Kemira Oy (chemicals). State plants also account for more than half the electricity production.

Industrial development is financed by a variety of sources but primarily by the Industrialization Fund, which is a source of loan capital for small and medium-size industries. Other credit institutions include the Regional Development Fund, the Investment Fund of Finland and the Nordic Investment Bank. SITRA (the Finnish National Fund for Research and Development) provides financial assistance for research and development projects undertaken by Finnish corporations.

About 900 Finnish companies have at least 20% foreign equity. These include subsidiaries of U.S. manufacturing companies in chemicals, textiles and cosmetics. In general, foreign investment is welcome and receives the same treatment as domestic businesses. There are a few regulations that limit the extent of foreign membership on boards of directors and foreign ownership of shares. Certain economic activities are reserved to the state. No foreign investments are allowed in industries using natural resources as raw materials. Foreign ownership of shipping and aviation also is restricted. Other economic activities from which foreigners are excluded include real estate, insurance, pharmacies and trading in foreign currency.

Finland is a member of the "Paris Union," or the International Convention for the Protection of Industrial Property. Under the Patents Act of 1968, patents are granted for 17 years but are not renewable. Trademarks are protected under the Trademarks Act of 1964 for renewable 10-year periods. Finland follows the Nice International Classification System for registration purposes. Industrial designs are protected under the Registered Designs Act of 1971 for five years, renewable for two further periods of five years.

MINING

Finland's mineral resource endowment is not abundant. The most important metal by volume is iron. The richest deposits are at Outokumpu, near the Soviet border. Previously unknown deposits of cobalt, uranium and chromium have been discovered since the 1950s. There also are commercially valuable quantities of zinc, nickel, gold and silver.

The short-term outlook for the minerals industry is good, but unless new mineral deposits are found, only two mines are expected to remain in operation by the end of the century and all others will be depleted. In 1983 alone two mines, Outokumpu's Virtasalmi and Myllikoski Oy's Luikonkahti copper mines, were closed. Mining production accounts for less than 0.5% of the GDP.

Chromium is produced at Tornio at the top of the Gulf of Bothnia by Outokumpu. Production in 1986 had risen to 170,000 tons per year. Cobalt is produced at Outokumpu's plant at Kokkola on the Bothnian coast, with a capacity of 1,800 tons per year. Outokumpu also is the sole producer of copper from seven of its nine mines. In 1985 it signed an agreement with A/S Sydvaranger of Norway for the purchase of the Bidjovaggi copper mine in northern Norway near the Finnish border. Rautaruukki, the state steel company, operates three iron-vanadium mines that deliver iron concentrates to the Rahe steelworks on the Gulf of Bothnia. Of these, two are expected to be closed because of depletion of deposits. A molybdenum discovery was made in the 1970s in Inari, east of Ivalo at Kivijarvi. Outokumpu's nickel mine at Kotalahti was depleted in 1987, but its new Enonkoski nickel mine went on stream in 1985. The mine's ore reserves are estimated at 500,000 tons, sufficient for 10 years. Production of titanium and vanadium has been decreasing since 1980. Until its closure in 1984, Rautaruukki's Mustavaara vanadium mine was the largest in Europe.

There is no foreign participation in the minerals industry in Finland.

ENERGY

Finland has no known deposits of coal, petroleum or natural gas and is not likely to discover any significant domestic sources of these fuels in the future. As a result, imported fuels provide between 70% and 80% of energy requirements. Waste fuel, derived principally from waste wood and the residual caustic sodas originating in the pulp industry, is being increasingly utilized but has not kept pace with expanding consumption. Most of the petroleum supplies comes from the Soviet Union at competitive prices.

The maximum hydroelectric power potential from all lakes and streams is rated at 19 billion kw-hr. per year. Over half of the capacity comes from three major dams: the Kemi River complex in the Far North, the Oulu Dam in the East and the Vironkoski Project in the Southeast. There is considerable undeveloped potential in the North. Since the 1970s, fuel- and coal-operated thermal plants have become more important than hydroelectric plants.

Peat is a largely underexploited source of fuel. Finland has one of the largest known reserves in the entire world, estimated at 600 million tons. The cost of exploitation is cheap, but transportation costs are high because it is a bulky commodity. Therefore it is competitive only within a short radius of the site deposits.

The first atomic power plant began operations in 1972, and another three have been built since then, using domestic uranium discovered in 1959. These plants produce some 40% of electrical energy. Two of the plants, Loviisa I and Loviisa II, built by the Soviet Union, are pressurized water reactors; the other two, Olkiluoto I and Olkiluoto II are heavy-water–type reactors.

Natural gas is delivered through a new pipeline from the USSR. The line extends from Imatra on the Soviet border for 125 m. (78 mi.) to Kouvola.

LABOR

The Finnish labor force is estimated 2.437 million, of whom almost half are women. The proportion of women in the labor force has increased steadily since World War II and is particularly strong in areas such as the textile industry and the services sector. However, women continue to receive lower pay than men for most jobs. The unemployment rate has varied from 4% to 7.5% in recent

---

ENERGY INDICATORS, 1986

Total energy production
quadrillion BTU:
  Crude oil: 0.31
  Natural gas, liquid: 0.0
  Natural gas, dry: 0.0
  Coal: 0.0
  Hydroelectric power: 0.13
  Nuclear power: 0.18
Average annual growth rate of energy production,
1980–86: 9.5%
Public utilities' share of GDP: 3%
Energy consumption per capita, kg. (lb.) oil equivalent:
5,475 (12,070)
Energy imports as % of merchandise imports: 14
Average annual growth rate of energy consumption
(1980–86): 3.6%

Electricity
  Installed capacity: 11,313,000 kw.
  Production: 47.098 billion kw.-hr.
    % fossil fuel: 36.0
    % hydro: 25.8
    % nuclear: 38.2
  Consumption per capita: 10,588 kw.-hr.

Natural gas
  Proved reserves: —
  Production: —
  Consumption: 971 million cu. m. (34.291 billion cm. ft.)

Petroleum
  Proved reserves: —
  Years to exhaust proved reserves: —
  Production: —
  Consumption: 84 million bbl.
  Refining capacity: 241,000 bbl. per day

Coal
  Reserves: —
  Production: —
  Consumption: 5,207,000 tons

---

years and was estimated at 6.7% in 1985 (7.5% for men and 6.0% for women).
Paradoxically, there is an equally high shortage of skilled personnel in times of
economic upturns. There also is a strong regional imbalance in employment because 70% of production is concentrated in the South around Helsinki, Turku,
Lappeenranta, Lahti, Jyväskylä and the valleys of the Kymi and the Kokemaki
rivers. Through employment exchanges and other mechanisms, the government seeks to make it easier for the northern unemployed to go south.

The Nordic free labor market provides a safety valve for the unemployed. More than 250,000 Finns are reported to have emigrated to Sweden since the 1950s. On the other hand, there is little immigration into Finland.

Finnish labor is highly organized, with over 80% of workers unionized. Employers' associations also represent an equally high percentage of employers. The four central labor confederations are:

- The Central Organization of Finnish Trade Unions, SAK
- The Confederation of Salaried Employees of Finland, TVK
- The Finnish Confederation of Academic Professional Associations, AKAVA
- The Confederation of Technical Employee Organizations of Finland, STTK

The main employers' organizations in the private sector are:
- The Finnish Employers' Confederation, STK
- The Confederation of Commercial Employers, LTK
- The Federation of Agricultural Employers, MTL

The main labor negotiating entities in the public sector are:
- The Department of Public Personnel Management, VTML
- The Local Authorities Negotiating Commission, KSV
- The Church of Finland Negotiating Commission, KiSV
- The Collective Bargaining Commission for Institutions, YSV

The SAK is by far Finland's largest labor union and represents primarily blue-collar workers. It was founded in 1907 but assumed its present form only in 1969, when a split in the Social Democratic Party was healed. It has 28 affiliated unions with a total membership of 1,041,619, of which the largest is the Finnish Municipal Workers and Salaried Employees' Union. The overwhelming majority of SAK unions are controlled by the Social Democrats, and only five are dominated by Communists. However, some unions, notably the Metalworkers' Union and the Rubber and Leather Workers' Union, have significant Communist minorities. The largest Communist union is the Construction Workers' Union, with 65,638 members.

The TVK was organized in 1922 and represents white-collar and clerical workers in 15 member unions with a total of 371,614 members, about 60% of whom are public employees. The federation is politically independent but often swings toward Social Democratic positions.

The AKAVA, founded in 1950, is the central organization of professional employees, with a total of 206,713 members in 44 affiliated member unions. Many of its member organizations would be classified in other countries as professional associations rather than trade unions. In some ways the federation is the most militant, as it refused to sign the 1984 central incomes policy agreement and struck for higher salaries for its teachers and doctors. The AKAVA also is the most apolitical of the four labor federations.

The STTK was founded in 1946 and represents 120,420 members in 15 unions. Most of its members are foremen and technicians. Although formally apolitical, the Social Democrats are prominent.

The STK has 30 affiliated associations representing 5,300 firms, most of them small or medium-sized. It was founded in the same year as the SAK. The LTK, dating from 1945, has seven member associations; the MTL, founded in 1946, has 1,400 member companies. The VTML covers 202,000 civil servants, the KSV 365,000 municipal employees and the KiSV 15,000 clergymen of the Evangelical Lutheran Church.

Since 1968, centralized incomes policy agreements have governed labor-management relations. Only in 1973, 1977–78 and 1980 has there not been such a nationwide umbrella agreement. The incomes policy process is essentially trilateral, involving the government as well as workers and management. The central agreement covers the general level of wage and salary increases; other terms of employment; and a "social policy package," which provides for vacation, holidays, sick pay, maternity leave, taxes, travel costs, rent, etc. The agreement also obliges the parties to refrain from any labor strife while its terms are in force. However, the central agreement provides only the basic guidelines, which are fleshed out in lower-level negotiations, first between the labor federations and the employer associations and then between management and the workers at the individual plants.

An example of how the process works is provided by the 1984 Pekkanen (after Matti Pekkanen) Agreement, covering 1984 and 1985. It granted a 2.2% wage and salary increase in 1984 and a 3.6% increase in 1985. In addition, workers at the lower end of the pay scales received an extra 0.2% to 0.25% increase. The agreement also contained an uncapped index clause that would become effective when the CPI, deflated for terms of trade, rose to more than 5.8%. In January 1985 the SAK and the TVK worked out an implementing agreement whereby the working year was reduced by 32 hours for those working 40 hours a week. These workers will receive four extra days of vacation. The agreement also raised unemployment compensation to a base of 70 markka a day, indexed to inflation. In turn the government pledged to increase the fines for illegal and wildcat strikes by nine times per strike, to a maximum of 90,000 markka for organizations and 900 markka for each individual worker. In agriculture, the agreement proposed the expenditure of 310 million markka for price supports in 1984 and 345 million markka in 1985.

In general, the central incomes policy agreements have helped to guarantee labor peace. However, there have been exceptions in most years. For example, of the total of 1,940 strikes in 1983, 82.8% occurred despite a valid collective bargaining agreement, 99.7% occurred without the consent of the trade union involved, and 99.7% occurred without the required legal notice being given. Most of these strikes involved either Communist-dominated unions or small firms with a history of such confrontations.

The future of central incomes policy agreements is not clear. Generally employers are not enthusiastic about them because the divergences of interests of the groups involved usually work against management. Further, unions may refuse to abide by the agreements and still go on strike, as AKAVA did in 1984. The agreements also have been criticized for inflating the influence of labor and management at the expense of the Eduskunta, whose influence on economic policy decisions has, as a consequence, been whittled away.

In addition to the collective agreements, there are "general agreements" dealing with broader issues of industrial democracy, usually negotiated between the central organizations. These include the agreement defining fundamental rights and duties of employers and employees; the agreement of protection against dismissal; the agreement on shop stewards; the agreement on labor protection; and other agreements covering training, information and work organization.

When disputes arise, the services of the National Conciliation Office and the Labor Court are available to both parties. The nine-member Labor Court is the last resort, and its decisions are binding.

A new law on industrial democracy became effective in 1979 and applies to all enterprises employing 30 or more workers. It obliges employers to consult employee representatives on important questions regarding job classification and working conditions within the existing collective bargaining framework. The law has no provision for corporate board representation for employees.

The average earnings of Finnish workers is low relative to other Western or Scandinavian countries. In 1984 the average hourly wage in the manufacturing sector was $3.62, which represents an increase of 54% in total current terms and 1.4% in average annual real terms since 1980. The highest-paid group overall are construction workers, who receive an average of $5.40 per hour, and the lowest are female farm workers, whose hourly earning is only $2.85.

The earnings of blue-collar workers have risen by 49.3% in current terms (1.4% in average annual real terms) since 1980, while those of white-collar workers in general have risen by 50.3% in current terms (1.4% in average annual real terms) during the same period. During this time workers in the private sector fared better (49.8% in current terms and 1.4% in average annual real terms) than their counterparts in the central government (47.1% in current terms and 1.2% in average annual real terms). Within the public service sector, municipal employees fared better.

Although women's earnings are only 77.7% of men's earnings, the gap is closing fast, as the former is increasing 3.0% faster than that of men.

As in other countries, a significant proportion of the wage bill is for indirect labor costs, such as Social Security fees, holiday and illness pay and unemployment insurance. According to data published in 1985, indirect labor costs average 56.1% of wages and salaries, higher at 59.5% for blue-collar workers and lower at 50% for white-collar workers. Half of the indirect costs cover employers' payments mandated by law, such as pensions and medical, accident and unemployment insurance premiums. Another 40% is due to wages and to payments for time off from work. The remaining 10% represent voluntary payments for occupational safety, measures to increase job satisfaction and housing subsidies.

Retirement age normally is 63 for women and 65 for men. Persons engaged in difficult or heavy work may retire at age 55. The workweek is 40 hours, although 37 hours is the norm. Work for more than eight hours per day or 40 hours per week is paid at the rate of time and a half for the first two hours of overtime per day and double time for all additional hours. Double time also is paid for work on Sundays and state holidays.

The annual paid vacation is two days per calendar month or four weeks per year the first six years, and thereafter 2.5 days per month.

Despite the persistently high unemployment rate, it is only recently that nominal wage increases have come down from close to double-digit levels. This may seem to indicate that wages are rather slow to adjust in Finland, although wage flexibility in Finland is relatively high by international standards. One concept that is widely used in the analysis of wage behavior is the so-called Nonaccelerating Inflation Rate of Unemployment (NAIRU). From 1950 to 1970 NAIRU was about 2½%, in the next decade from 3½% to 4%, and 5% in the 1980s. On this basis, the rise in wages has contributed only marginally to the rise in inflation. The level of Social Security contributions also has been used as a tool of incomes policy. Payroll taxes have been steadily reduced to increase wage flexibility.

FOREIGN COMMERCE

Foreign trade is an extension not merely of Finnish industry but also of the nation's foreign policy. Accordingly, the Soviet Union is the principal trading partner and the most favored country. Finland did not join the EEC out of concern not to jeopardize relations with the Soviet Union, but, with tacit Soviet ap-

```
┌────────────────────────────────────────────────────┐
│              LABOR INDICATORS, 1986                  │
│                                                      │
│  Total economically active population: 2.57 million  │
│  As % of working-age population: 67                  │
│  % female: 46.7                                      │
│  Activity rate (%)                                   │
│     Total: 53.6                                      │
│     Male: 58.2                                       │
│     Female: 49.3                                     │
│                                                      │
│  Employment status (%)                               │
│     Employers & self-employed: 12.6                  │
│     Employees: 84.0                                  │
│     Unpaid family workers: 1.4                       │
│     Other: 2.0                                       │
│     Organized labor: 80                              │
│                                                      │
│  Sectoral employment (%)                             │
│     Agriculture, forestry, fishing: 11.3             │
│     Mining: —                                        │
│     Manufacturing, construction: 32.3                │
│     Electricity, gas, water: —                       │
│     Trade: 14.4                                      │
│     Transportation, communications: 7.4              │
│     Finance, real estate: 6.1                        │
│     Services: 28.5                                   │
│                                                      │
│  Average annual growth rate of labor force, 1980–2000: │
│  0.3                                                 │
│                                                      │
│  Unemployment (%): 5.4                               │
│  Labor under 20 years: 5.3%                          │
│                                                      │
│  Hours of work                                       │
│     Manufacturing: 32.4 hours                        │
└────────────────────────────────────────────────────┘
```

proval, joined the EFTA in 1961. There are no trade barriers with COMECON countries. Sweden and Norway also have become important trading partners.

During the same period there have been structural changes in the composition of foreign trade. In the first half of this century exports were almost exclusively limited to forest products. In the 1950s the share of metals and engineering began to grow and since that time have become the leading exports. The share of forest products has correspondingly dropped in export value, to 40% from 45%. Imports consist mainly of raw materials, fuels and crude oil. Again, this has strengthened the role of the Soviet Union, as most of the crude oil is imported from that country in the framework of a bilateral agreement.

```
┌─────────────────────────────────────────────────┐
│            FOREIGN TRADE INDICATORS, 1986          │
```

FOREIGN TRADE INDICATORS, 1986

Exports: $16.36 billion
Imports: $15.33 billion
Balance of trade: $1.03 billion
Annual growth rate exports 1980–86: 2.8%
Annual growth rate imports 1980–86: 1.9%
Ratio of international reserves to imports (in months): 1.5
Value of manufactured exports: $13.188 billion
Terms of trade (1980=100): 114 (1986)
Import Price Index (1980=100): 93.2
Export Price Index (1980=100): 77.7
Import of goods as % of GDP: 24.5
Export of goods as % of GDP: 26

Direction of trade (%)

	Imports	Exports
EEC	42.9	37.8
U.S.A.	4.8	5.4
East European economies	18.0	21.7
Japan	6.5	1.5

Composition of trade (%)

	Imports	Exports
Food } Agricultural raw materials	9.5	14.1
Fuels	15.3	2.4
Ores and minerals	2.3	0.4
Manufactured goods	72.8	83.2
of which chemicals	10.2	5.5
of which machinery	35.5	27.6

TRANSPORTATION & COMMUNICATIONS

Valtionrautatiet, the Finnish state railways, operates 6,071 km. (3,773 mi.) of track of 1.524-m. (5-ft.) gauge, of which 480 km. (298 mi.) are multiple-track and 1,257 km. (781 mi.) are electrified. Trains do mostly long-distance hauling. Rail services are not normally self-sustaining financially and are subsidized by a special allocation from the central budget. A subway opened in Helsinki in 1982.

Railroad shipping westbound to Europe always has presented problems because the 1,524-m. gauge does not match the gauge prevailing elsewhere in Europe. Containerization and improved ferry services to Sweden and West Germany are changing the situation. Tornio and Naantali have railroad ferry transshipment points. Rail transportation eastward is not a problem because the track gauge in Finland is the same as that in the Soviet Union.

There are 105,663 km. (65,670 mi.) of roadways, of which 37,663 km. (23,388 mi.) are public and paved and 38,000 km. (23,617 mi.) are public and unpaved. In addition, there are 30,000 km. (18,645 mi.) of state-subsidized private roads. Of the 75,663 km. (47,025 mi.) of public roads, 11,173 km. (6,944 mi.) are main roads (I and II Class), 29,465 km. (18,313 mi.) are other highways and 35,025 km. (21,768 mi.) are local roads. These roads support an extensive trucking industry as well as bus routes. The country is divided into 13 roads and waterways districts under the supervision of the Roads and Waterways Administration.

Inland waterways are the historic medium of summer transportation. Unfortunately, they freeze in winter, requiring considerable communication adjustments. Most rivers are not only short—the Kemi being the notable exception—but also intercepted by waterfalls, rapids and shallows. In their natural condition they are mostly nonnavigable and present hazards that militate against large-scale use. Nevertheless, they may be used even in winter, and buses often drive over ice several feet thick.

The most vital elements in the inland waterways are the canals, such as the Vesijarvi and the Kalkkinen on Lake Päjänne and the Konnus and the Taipale on Lake Saimaa. There are 40 open canals and 25 lock canals with a total length of 76 km. (47 mi.). In 1963 the Soviet Union leased to Finland the right to use the southern part of the Saimaa Canal. In 1968 the rebuilt Saimaa Canal was opened for vessels.

There are 30 ports open for maritime traffic, of which 20 have a minimum depth of 27 feet (8.2 m.). Nine icebreakers patrol the shipping lanes during the winter months. The ice is worst in February. Usually only three ports—Turku, Helsinki and Kotka—can be kept open year-round, and during severe winters only one or two are open for large ships. The chief export port is Kotka; the main import port is Helsinki, which has five specialized harbors. The West Harbor handles most of the transatlantic traffic, the East Harbor most of the coastal and North Sea freight and most passenger traffic and the North Harbor local launch traffic. Sornainen is the timber and coal harbor, while Herttoniemi specializes in oil. Other ports include Honkalahti, Pori, Rauma and Oulu.

The Finnish merchant marine is a major foreign currency earner. Slightly less than half of Finland's sea cargoes are transported in domestic bottoms. Regular car and ferry services connect the southern ports with Scandinavia and West Germany.

Finland's network of domestic air services is the second densest per capita in Europe. The national flag line, the state-owned Finnair, operates 21 domestic services as well as 34 international flights. Finnaviation, a subsidiary of Finnair, operates scheduled domestic services. A new international airport has been built at Malmi, 19 km. (11.8 mi.) from Helsinki.

The postal and telegraph services are entirely state-owned, while telephone lines are partly state-owned and partly private. There are approximately 4,000 post offices, 3,300 telegraph dispatch offices and 800 joint offices. Telecommunications facilities include three submarine cables.

TRANSPORTATION INDICATORS, 1986

Roads
   Length, km. (mi.): 76,061 (47,262)
   Paved (%): 55

Motor vehicles
   Automobiles: 1,546,094
   Trucks: 230,375
   Persons per vehicle: 2.8
   Road freight, ton-km. (ton-mi.): 22 billion (15 billion)

Railroads
   Track, km. (mi.): 5,906 (3,670)
   Passenger-km. (passenger-mi.): 3,224 billion
   (2.003 billion)
   Freight, ton-km. (ton-mi.): 8.072 billion (5.529 billion)

Merchant marine
   Vessels: 276 (over 100 gross tons)
   Total dead weight tonnage: 1,907,800
   Oil tankers: 948,000 GRT

Ports: 4 major, 7 secondary 34 minor
   Cargo loaded: 20,244,000 tons
   Cargo unloaded: 29,952,000 tons

Air
   Km. (mi.) flown: 37 million (22.9 million)
   Passengers: 2,991,000
   Passenger-km. (passenger-mi.): 2.916 billion (1.812 billion)
   Freight, ton-km. (ton-mi.): 92.9 million (63.6 million)
   Mail, ton-km. (ton-mi.): 7.1 million (4.4 million)
   Airports with scheduled flights: 21
   Civil aircraft: 39

Pipelines
   Refined: 0
   Natural gas: 580 km. (360 mi.)
   Total: 580 km.

Inland waterways
   Length, km. (mi.): 6,057 (3,764)
   Cargo, ton-km. (ton-mi.): 4.2 billion (2.9 billion)

```
COMMUNICATION INDICATORS, 1986

Telephones
   Total: 3,028,000
   Persons per: 1.6
   Phone traffic
      Local: 1,914,390,000
      Long distance: 407,470,000
      International: 18,110,000

Post office
   Number of post offices: 3,632
   Domestic mail:          ⎫
   Foreign mail received:  ⎬  1,098,005,000
   Foreign mail sent:      ⎭

Telegraph
   Total traffic: 662,000
   National: 586,000
   International: 76,000

Telex
   Subscriber lines: 8,400
   Traffic (000 minutes): 26,202

Telecommunications
   2 submarine cables

      TOURISM AND TRAVEL INDICATORS, 1986

Total tourist receipts: $501 million
Expenditures by nationals abroad: $776 million
Number of hotel beds: 10,886
Average length of stay: 5.5 days
Tourist nights: 2,097,000
Number of tourists: 460,000
   of whom from (%)
   Sweden: 25.6
   West Germany: 13.2
   Soviet Union: 11.6
   Norway: 7.9
```

DEFENSE

Although Finland did not achieve independence until 1917, its military traditions go back 300 years when, as part of Sweden, Finland supplied the Swedish armies with some of their most effective units of foot soldiers and officers. On various battlefields they achieved a reputation for bravery, which increased the national self-confidence. Their most valiant performance was against their traditional enemy, Russia, under whose domination they fell in 1809. Even as a grand duchy under Russia, the Finnish military traditions persisted. Between 1809 and 1903 the Finnish Military Academy in Hanuna trained over 1,000 officers, many of whom served with great distinction in the Imperial Russian Army. Among them was Carl Gustav von Mannerheim, the hero of the Finnish Resistance and the struggle for independence.

Defense was not a major preoccupation of the leaders of independent Finland, so they were not quite prepared when the Soviet Union invaded the country in November 1939. Nevertheless, the Finnish Army destroyed thousands of invading troops in few weeks, and for a while it looked as if Finland could turn back the aggressor. However, massive Soviet reinforcements soon ended the conflict, and on March 12, 1940, an armistice confirmed most of the initial Soviet demands, including the loss of some national territory. But unlike the Baltic states, Finland was not occupied, nor did it suffer further infringements. In the Continuation War from 1941 to 1944, Finland fought first the Russians as a German ally, and then the Germans.

Considering the magnitude of the defeat, Finland did not fare too badly when the terms of a peace treaty were drawn on February 10, 1947. The terms of this treaty as well as the 1948 Agreement of Friendship, Cooperation and Mutual Assistance signed with the Soviet Union imposed certain restrictions on the Finnish Army. The former limited the size of the armed forces to 41,900 while the latter obliged Finland to use all her forces against aggression directed at the Soviet Union through Finnish territory. An earlier agreement with Sweden (1929 and 1940) demilitarized the Åland Islands and exempted their inhabitants from military service.

Supreme command of the armed forces is vested in the president of the republic assisted by the Defense Council comprising the prime minister; the ministers of defense, external affairs, finance, and trade and industry; the chief of the defense forces; and the chief of staff. On the operational side there is the Defense Staff heading all the three services, with a total of 16 subdivisions. On the same level as the Defense Staff is the Ministry of Defense. The army has its own chief of general headquarters and chief of staff, while the navy and the air force have their own chiefs and staffs subordinate to the commander in chief.

Finland is divided into seven military areas, each with a brigade and some with additional units: the Armored Brigade, with headquarters at Parola; the Swedish-speaking Nylands Brigade, with headquarters at Dragsvik; the Pohjan Brigade, with headquarters at Oulu; the Kainuun Brigade, with headquarters at Kajaani; the Porin Brigade, with headquarters at Sakyla; the Karjalan Brigade, with headquarters at Kouvola; and the Savon Brigade, with headquarters at Mikkeli. There also is a guard battalion at Helsinki and light infantry battalions at Häme, Pohjois-Karjala, Kymi, Nyland and Lappi.

The obligatory period of military service for all males is eight months, which may be extended up to 11 months. After 240 days the conscripts pass to the reserves, in which they remain to age 50, with periodic refresher training. Those selected for technical training, as reserve NCOs, or as reserve officers, serve for 330 days and remain in the reserves until age 60. Regular officers and NCOs (there are virtually no private soldiers) enter as conscripts and then transfer either to the officer corps or to the NCO corps.

Regular army officers are trained at the Cadet School in Santahamina, Helsinki. The final stage in military education is the War College, which conducts two-year courses for the general staff and three-year courses for the technical staff. Each of the other arms of service has at least one school, such as the Infantry Combat School, the Parachute School, the Artillery School, the Engineer School, the Signal School, the Logistics Training Center and the Ordnance School. The percentage of conscientious objectors has remained at less than 0.5%, one of the lowest in the Western world.

DEFENSE PERSONNEL, EQUIPMENT & BUDGET, 1985

Defense budget: $848 million

% of GNP: 1.5

Military expenditures per capita: $174

Military expenditures per soldier: $15,143

Military expenditures per sq. km. of national territory: $2,516 ($6,518 per sq. mi.)

Total military manpower: 36,500

Reserves: 700,000

Army: 30,900; 7 military areas; 23 military districts; 1 armed brigade; 7 infantry brigades; Field artillery: 2 regiments; 2 independent battalions. Coastal artillery: 2 regiments; 3 independent battalions; 1 anti-aircraft artillery regiment; 4 independent antiaircraft artillery battalions; 2 engineer battalions

Navy: 2,700; fast attack craft; corvettes; patrol craft; minelayers; naval bases at Upinniemi (Helsinki) and Turku

Air Force: 2,900; 64 combat aircraft; 3 air defense wings; 3 fighter wings

Arms exports: $0

Arms imports: $90 million

The Frontier Guards are a paramilitary constabulary trained in guerrilla war and act in peacetime as a border security force and coast guard. There are seven Frontier Guards units, of which the four land units are in the northern, western and eastern military areas and the three coast guard units in the three coastal military areas. They are trained in special schools. Within each area the Frontier Guards exercise police powers as well.

Finland does not manufacture military equipment other than small arms and a few vehicles. Finland receives no military aid, and there are no foreign military bases in the country.

EDUCATION

As in other Western countries, the history of Finnish education is bound up with that of the church. The first schools, begun in the 13th and 14th centuries, were attached to cathedrals. The country's first university was founded in Turku in 1640, followed nine years later by the first secondary school, based on the model of Jan Comenius. The primary-school system was first delineated in an 1866 ordinance that required every commune to establish a sufficient number of primary schools for all children between ages eight and 14. In 1683 the Luthern bishop Gezelius made the first proposal for the reorganization of general education. A law passed in that year declared that it was the duty of all citizens to learn to read, and those who could not were barred from communion and marriage. Until the mid-19th century all postprimary education was in Swedish hands; the first Finnish-language secondary school did not open until 1858. Since then, Finnish-language schools have virtually displaced Swedish-language ones except in Swedish-speaking areas.

An act of 1872 removed secondary schools from ecclesiastical control and placed them under civil authority. It also grouped them under three types: *lyceer* (lycea), *realskoler* and higher schools for girls. The *lyceer* offered both a four-year course leading to the technical high school and an eight-year course leading to the university.

The first efforts to introduce compulsory education were resisted by the Russian rulers until 1893, when the Compulsory School Founding Act was passed, requiring each district to set up a primary school. After independence came the 1921 law on compulsory school attendance that mandated an eight-year compulsory schooling consisting of six years of primary school and two years of lower secondary school. This basic pattern survived until 1962, when an extra year was added at the primary level.

Basic regulations regarding education are incorporated into the Finnish Constitution and parliamentary legislation. The Constitution stipulates that all children between seven and 16 should receive free and compulsory education in Finnish except in Swedish-speaking areas, where they may receive instruction in their mother tongue. The Educational System Act of 1978 affirms the principle of comprehensiveness, which means that all children will attend the same basic school and follow the same curriculum. Educational legislation is part of social legislation. Two amendments to the Comprehensive School Decree of 1978 came into force in 1980. One amendment stipulates that the maximum size of the basic study group in the first and second grades be reduced from 32 to 25 pupils; the second requires the maintenance of a minimum teacher–pupil ratio of 1:10. A third amendment, in 1981, extends to the fifth and sixth grades the right enjoyed by teachers in the third and fourth grades to divide their classes into two groups—regular and advanced—for certain subjects, such as language and mathematics.

The 1978 Act for the Development of Secondary Education created a basis for the reform of the second level beginning in 1982 and extending until 1988. In 1983 legislation was passed creating a board of seven members for comprehensive schools. For upper-level schools there are nine members, including two pupils who have the right to speak but not to vote. Experiments in vocational education are governed by a March 1981 decree and are conducted by the National Board of Vocational Education.

An amended decree of 1980 governs curricula in upper secondary schools. The decree provides for courses of 38 hours each. Subjects are divided into compulsory and optional, and the latter are further divided into elective and advanced elective.

The school year runs from mid-August to May 31 and consists of 190 days of attendance, five days a week, five to seven hours per day. The year is divided into two terms, with a one-week holiday at Christmas and 10 weeks in the summer in addition to breaks at Easter and during February/March for skiing. The university year runs from September 1 to March 31 and is divided into two terms.

Only about 10% of preprimary enrollment is in private schools, but the proportion rises in elementary and secondary schools. About two-thirds of the secondary schools are privately run.

The senior secondary school culminates in *ylioppilastutkinto*, the matriculation examination taken at about age 19. It not only ensures admission to the university but also entitles those who pass it to wear the student cap. The importance of this examination is such that it overshadows even sports events in newspapers. Finnish pupils are very grade-conscious, remembering them clearly later in life. Generally examinations are written rather than oral, as a result of which students characteristically are reticent to offer personal judgments in public and shy away from group discussions. The authoritarian attitude of many teachers does not improve matters.

During the period since World War II, education has expanded rapidly. Although hundreds of rural primary schools were being closed, urban schools were experiencing an explosion in enrollments. As a result, the Ministry of Education embarked on a still-continuing comprehensive reform of the education system. The thrust of these reforms has been felt at every level of education. Since 1968 preschool classes and kindergarten have been included in the municipal school system. Major priorities at the basic school level have been (1) integration of subject-divided curricula, (2) development of education content to reflect technological and social changes, (3) development of teaching materials (4) reform of pupil grading and (5) development of special education.

At the secondary and vocational levels, the major goal has been to balance the academic and the vocational wings. To reduce regional and urban-rural imbalances, vocational educational facilities were expanded in remote rural areas, and free accommodation and transportation were provided for students.

The 1966 Act for the Development of Higher Education stipulated the annual number of places in each institution and the percentage to be enrolled in each discipline, in a move to encourage more students to study medicine, science and technology. A centralized and standardized admission system also was introduced, with several faculties joining together to conduct joint entrance examinations. The reform of the degree programs involved the phasing out of the lower first degrees, the rationalization of the basic first degrees and the restructuring of postgraduate courses. The 1976 Committee on the Regional Extension of Higher Education divided the country into six planning areas (with the Swedish-speaking area as a separate unit) and made recommendations for equalizing educational opportunities and for making higher education relevant to economic needs.

Preprimary education. There is no compulsory education for preschool children, but preschool education is provided by day-care centers for children under three and by kindergartens for three- to six-year-olds. These facilities are mostly concentrated in the cities and are financed by municipalities, industrial enterprises or voluntary associations, some of which receive state subsidies.

Primary education. This consists of nine years of compulsory and free education available to every child between ages seven and 16 and guaranteed by the Constitution. The new basic school for this age group came into being in 1977–78. Primary schools comprise 5,687 comprehensive schools, of which 3,950 are lower-level, 590 are upper-level, 795 are remedial and special schools, 12 are practice schools for teacher trainees, 20 are private schools, 10 are schools run by foreign embassies and 310 are Swedish-language schools. The curriculum as well as the distribution of hours are regulated by law. Pupils receive marks during the school year for every subject taught, together with marks for conduct and application, and these marks are recorded from grade 4 on. Marks are awarded on a scale of 0 to 10. Those with marks of 5 or more in all subjects proceed to the next grade; those with marks of only 4 in two subjects need to pass a supplementary examination to be promoted; those who receive marks of 4 or less in three or more subjects must repeat the year.

Secondary education. The upper secondary school *(lukio)* is a three-year general educational establishment, the primary function of which is to prepare students for higher education. In practice, however, less than half of those who complete the *lukio* enter an institution of higher education. Only 46% of those leaving the basic school continue their education in the *lukio*.

The new curriculum for the *lukio* is based on 38 hours of teaching per week. The maximum size of a *lukio* class is 36. The *lukio* culminates in the *ylioppilas-tutkinto*, or matriculation examination, consisting of four compulsory and two optional written tests. The four compulsory papers are composition in the native tongue, first foreign language and second national language, and either mathematics or a general paper *(reaalikoe)*. Papers are graded in descending order, such as magna *cum laude approbatur (laudatur), cum laude approbatur, lubentur approbatur* and *approbatur.* The fail rate is relatively low. Successful candidates receive two certificates: the Matriculation Board Certificate and the Secondary School Leaving Certificate. Outside the general school system, there are four foreign-language schools in Helsinki.

Vocational and technical education is the cutting edge of the state educational reform and is being developed as an alternative route to higher education. There are some 600 vocational education institutions, of which 30% are state-owned, 48% are municipal and 22% are private. There are two types of vocational institutions: municipal vocational schools and vocational institutes. The former take students straight from basic schools and offer them training in at least six areas: metalwork, machine repairs, electrical work, building and construction, carpentry, and catering. Vocational instiues primarily prepare students for technical management in a course that lasts three or four years. There is no apprenticeship tradition in Finland, and apprenticeship programs run by vocational schools draw a small number of students.

As part of the reform of vocational education, "basic lines" have been introduced as units of study. A basic line is divided into two segments: a general period and a specialization period. The latter is further divided into detailed branches of specialization. The general period and one specialization line constitute a unit of educational content called "trained vocation." The government has listed 24 basic lines with a total of 222 lines of specialization or trained vocations. Separate study lines, not part of any basic line, number 23. Another key educational strategy in this field is called "dimensioning." It is designed to ensure that the number of upper secondary graduates moving on to vocational education will correspond roughly to the number of openings available to them for further study.

Similarly, technical institutions are divided into technical schools *(teknillinenkoulu)* and technical institutes *(teknillinenopisto)*, and commercial institutions into commercial schools *(kauppakoulu)* and commercial institutes *(kauppaopisto)*. The technical schools offer the lower diploma and the technical institutes the higher diploma. Commercial schools offer the *mercantti* certificate, while the commercial institutes offer the *merkonomi* certificate after two and three years, respectively. Agricultural education is offered by general and specialized schools.

HIGHER EDUCATION

There are 18 universities in Finland, as follows:

University	Year Founded
University of Helsinki (founded as the Academy of Turku and transferred to Helsinki in 1809)	1640
Helsinki University of Technology	1908
The Swedish University of Turku	1908
University of Turku	1920
University of Oulu	1959
University of Joensuu	1966
University of Kuopio	1966
University of Jyväskylä	1966
University of Tampere	1966
Lappeenranta University of Technology	1966
Tampere University of Technology	1972
University of Lapland	1979
Helsinki School of Economics	1911
Helsinki Swedish School of Economics	1927
Swedish University of Turku School of Economics	1927
College of Veterinary Medicine	1945
Turku School of Economics	1950
Vaasa School of Economics	1968

Other institutions include the College of Industrial Design; Sibelius Academy; the Swedish School of Social Science and Local Administration; and the Ateneum, or School of Fine Arts.

At present fewer than half the matriculants find places at universities, and hence a numerus clausus restriction is in effect. The annual university entrance examinations are held in June or July.

University courses include two levels of first degree and two levels of a higher degree—all obtained by passing examinations and presenting dissertations. In a degree course, each subject may be studied at one of three levels—*approbatur, cum laude approbatur* and *laudatur*—and a certain number of passes is required at each level to gain the appropriate certificate. The basic or first degree is the *kandidatti*, the lower postgraduate degree is the *licensiaatti* and the third level is the *maisteri*.

The degree courses were reorganized under the reform of higher education beginning in 1975. The length of a program leading to a basic degree averages 160 to 220 credit units, corresponding to four to six years of study, one credit unit being equivalent to 40 hours of full-time study. Each degree program is divided into general or introductory studies (25%), subject-oriented or core studies (50%) and specialized or research studies (25%).

University teachers are ranked in five categories: full professors, associate professors, docents, lectors and assistants. Full professors and associate professors are appointed by the president of the republic. Docents are part-time, honorary teachers paid per lecture. Lectors and assistants are often postgraduate students.

Each university has a student organization composed of all students, which acts as a lobbying organization and also runs housing, health care and food service facilities. Invariably they are active in politics and environmental issues. The national umbrella organization for all student associations is the National Union of Finnish Students.

The preferences of Finnish students run heavily to humanities, social sciences, law, business and education, which together account for 56% of the enrollment. Only 20% of the students turn to natural sciences or agriculture, 17% to technology or applied sciences and 7% to medicine. However, natural sciences dominate doctoral degree recipients, who constitute 12.5% of all degree awardees.

Independent research institutes are few in Finland, and much of the research is carried out in universities. Some 70% of research funds are directly allocated from the state budget; the rest come from external sources, such as the Academy of Finland. Basic research accounts for 60%, applied research for 30% and product development for 10%.

Administration. Except for preschool education, which is partly under the Ministry of Social Affairs and Health, all other levels of education comes under the jurisdiction of the Ministry of Education. The ministry is divided into six departments—General, International Relations, School, Higher Education & Research, Arts, and Youth & Sports—and is assisted by four advisory bodies: the Council for School Affairs, the Advisory Board for Secondary Education Reform, the National Council for Higher Education and the National Council for Teacher Education. Subordinate to this ministry are two powerful agencies: the National Board of General Education and the National Board of Vocational Education. Each of the 12 provinces has a school department responsible for all types of education except vocational education. Each school department has its own inspection staff, and in bilingual provinces there also is a Swedish department. At the municipal level there are school boards consisting of eight to 12 members elected for four-year terms, of whom at least two are teachers. All basic and senior secondary schools have school councils with representatives of parents, pupils and teachers in varying proportions.

In 1966 the Bureau of Educational Planning was set up within the National Board of General Education to help draw up five-year medium-term plans. Educational planning also occurs at the provincial level through regional development plans. A third planning mechanism is the Development Program for Secondary Education, which is revised biennially.

EDUCATION INDICATORS, 1986

Literacy
  Total (%): 100.0
  Males (%): 100.0
  Females (%): 100.0

First level
  Schools: 5,687
  Students: 369,047
  Teachers: 25,139
  Student-teacher ratio: 15:1
  Net enrollment rate: 103%
  Females (%): 49

Second level
  Schools: 1,082
  Students: 316,740
  Teachers: 22,356
  Student-teacher ratio: 14:1
  Net enrollment rate: 101%
  Females (%): 53

Vocational
  Schools: 550
  Students: 116,906

EDUCATION INDICATORS, 1986 *(continued)*

Teachers: 15,000
Student-teacher ratio: 8:1
Vocational enrollment rate: N.A.

Third level
Institutions: 21
Students: 119,902
Teachers: 5,191
Student-teacher ratio: 23:1
Gross enrollment rate: 30.6%
Graduates per 100,000 ages 20–24: 2,459
% of population over 25 with postsecondary
education: 11.9
Females (%): 48

Foreign study
Foreign students in national universities: 766
Students abroad: 1611
    of whom in
        U.S.A.: 470
        West Germany: 719
        U.K.: 26

Public expenditures
Total: 15.355 billion markka
% of GNP: 5.7
% of national budget: 13.1
% current: 92.6

Graduates, 1982

Total: 24,736
Education: 1,615
Humanities & religion: 1,923
Fine & applied arts: 174

Law: 497
Social & behavioral sciences: 857
Commerce & business: 5,422

Mass communication: 51
Home economics: 24
Service trades: 197

Natural sciences: 1,179
Mathematics & computer science: 507
Medicine: 4,725

Engineering: 6,089
Architecture: 113

Transportation & communications: 67
Agriculture, forestry, fisheries: 557
Other: 739

Institutions of higher education are under the direct supervision of the Department of Higher Education and Research at the Ministry of Education, with the exception of arts education, which is controlled by the Arts Department of the same ministry. The Department of Higher Education and Research is divided into six bureaus and is assisted by three advisory bodies: the Council for Higher Education, the Council for Teacher Education and the Science Policy Council. All universities are public but enjoy considerable internal autonomy, although some, such as the University of Helsinki, are more autonomous than others. The new educational reforms have whittled down some of this autonomy by having degrees for each field of study regulated at the national level. University administration consists of six units: the University Council, the Administrative Council, the rector, the administrative office, the faculty or departmental councils and the institute councils. The University Council consists of 18 to 60 members elected for two-year terms. It drafts regulations, makes budget proposals and elects the rector, vice rector and members of the Administrative Council. The latter council, with six to 12 members and chaired by the rector, is responsible for general administration and is assisted by the administrative office. At the University of Helsinki and some other universities the chancellor *(kansilieri)* is the highest university official and is appointed by the president of the republic. Departmental councils consist of six to 16 members, of whom half are faculty members and half are students. In larger universities there also are faculty and institute councils consisting of the head of departments and two representatives from each departmental council. The faculty councils draw up syllabi, supervise the selection of students, approve admission, organize entrance examinations and recommend candidates for the faculty.

The financial costs of education are borne by both the state and the municipalities. As it is the right and duty of every citizen to be educated, all municipalities are required by law to provide education of equal standard irrespective of financial capacity. The municipalities are classified into 10 categories according to capacity and reimbursed according to schedule. Such reimbursement amounts to 75% of recurrent costs in the vocational and adult sectors, 85% of the recurrent costs for senior secondary schools and 80% for basic schools. At the university level all recurrent and capital costs are met by the state budget. Municipalities receive 60% to 95% of the construction costs of each school building. The state also refunds two-thirds of the amount spent on libraries and equipment and guarantees 90% of the teachers' salaries. In technical institutions over 80% of the teachers' salaries and 50% of other expenses are covered by state subsidies.

At the basic level everything is free. In senior secondary schools students pay a small fee, which is reduced or waived in the case of financial difficulties. Textbooks, however, have to be purchased by the students. At the university level there is no tuition and housing and health services are subsidized, but students must meet the cost of course materials and living expenses. Through the State Center for Aid to Education, grants and low-interest loans are made available to students in universities as well as in senior secondary schools.

The adult education system is guided by the 1971 Adult Education Committee Report. The programs are supervised by a number of official bodies, such as the Ministry of Education, the Ministry of Labor, the National Board of General Education and the National Board of Vocational Education. Provincial and municipal governments are also involved, particularly the latter. A number of nonofficial organizations also are active, such as the Institute of Adult Education of the University of Tampere, the Finnish Folk High School Association, the Union of Civic and Workers' Institutes and the Finnish Association of Adult Education Institutions.

General adult education is provided in adult education centers (formerly civic and workers' institutes), folk high schools, folk academies, study centers, correspondence schools and secondary evening schools. They receive state subsidies covering 70% to 90% of their operating expenses.

There are 276 adult education centers, usually owned by municipalities and run by boards elected by municipal councils, with a full-time headmaster. More than simply learning centers, they have developed over the years into social and cultural centers as well. There are over 41 evening schools, the majority run by municipalities, designed for grown-up and employed young people to help prepare them to take examinations leading to the lower or upper secondary school certificate. Folk high schools are boarding schools that train students between ages 16 and 30 living in rural areas, as a preliminary to more advanced studies. A full course for basic school graduates lasts one to three years, but the schools also offer condensed courses lasting six to nine months or one month. Both the schools and the folk academies have the right to grant certificates. There are 89 folk schools in Finland, the majority of them private. Of these, 34 are Grundtvigian (after Nikolai Grundtvig, a Danish pedagogue), 40 are Christian, 12 are run by labor unions or political organizations and three are special schools for the disabled. Most of them charge modest school fees. Study centers consist of a number of study circles run by voluntary educational organizations. There are nine study centers, five of them Finnish, two Swedish and two bilingual. The circle does not have a teacher in the proper sense of the term, but a leader elected by the participants. Correspondence schools are run by nonprofit groups. A student is entitled to receive from the state a refund of 80% of his course fees after a successful final examination. Distance education is provided by the adult education section of the Finnish Broadcasting Company, which produces nearly 300 transmissions annually. The Joint Examination Board for Adult Education conducts examinations based on these courses and issues certificates to those who pass. Open university programs are conducted by university consortia, primarily on a regional basis, permitting students to complete parts of academic degrees. The minimum age limit is 25 years, and work experience may be required.

Vocational adult education, which is 100% subsidized by the state, is provided mainly in vocational course centers and in vocational institutes and evening classes of vocational schools. There are 42 vocational course centers, offering programs lasting three to 18 months. Trainees are provided free tuition, meals, accommodation and travel in addition to a training allowance. Vocational institutes arrange complementary courses and in-service training for the employed.

Teacher education is the responsibility of the Council for Teacher Education of the Ministry of Education and is based on the 1971 Act on Teacher Education. All private kindergarten teacher education schools were taken over by the state in 1977 and renamed kindergarten institutes. Kindergarten teachers also are trained by certain university faculties of education. Training takes three years (40% devoted to practical work) and leads to a preprimary teachers' certificate. Training at the basic and upper secondary levels is conducted by education departments at 10 universities. That of basic school class teachers (grades 1 through 6) lasts five years and leads to a master's degree. Because teachers in vocational education comprise a very heterogeneous group, they are required in most cases to have only a degree in higher education and a vocational education certificate from a vocational institution. Generally, participation in in-service training is incorporated into collective bargaining agreements. The educational reforms of the 1970s necessitated considerable retraining of teachers in new pedagogic methods and technology, for which the Center for In-Service Training and Retraining was established. Basic and upper secondary school teachers are required to attend for three training days a year. Many teachers also attend summer universities and participate in weekend schools and study days.

The principal teachers' union is the Suomen Opettajaln Liitto, founded in Helsinki in 1893.

LEGAL SYSTEM

The legal system operates on four levels: the supervisory officers, the general courts, the specialized courts and the courts of administrative law.

The supervisory offices, comprising the offices of the chancellor of justice and the judicial delegate or ombudsman, guarantee the legal rights of citizens and the legality of state actions. The chancellor of justice is a nonvoting member of the State Council and also is the top prosecutor before the highest courts. The office of the ombudsman, officially known as the judicial delegate, was created in 1957 on the Swedish model through an amendment to Article 49 of the Constitution. The ombudsman is elected to a four-year term by the Eduskunta soon after every general election.

The administration of justice is vested with the three-tier general courts, comprising local courts, appellate courts and the Supreme Court. The judges of the local courts are appointed by the Supreme Court, whereas the judges of the appellate courts and the Supreme Court are appointed by the president of the republic. Local judges are assisted by municipally elected lay boards that serve as juries and whose unanimous opinion cannot be overruled by a judge. The appellate courts are in Helsinki, Turku, Vaasa and Kuopio. All courts of appeal are divided into sections, which pronounce decisions in the name of the entire court. Each section consists of four judges, three of whom constitute a quorum. Important issues are referred to the plenary session. The Supreme Court is the highest court, although the right to appeal beyond the appellate courts is limited to important matters. The Supreme Court also supervises the administration of justice and gives advisory opinions on petitions for pardon and on legislative matters. It consists of a president and 21 justices divided into three sections, each of which speaks for the entire court, with five justices constituting a quorum.

There is a parallel system of administrative courts headed by the Supreme Administrative Court, established by Article 56 of the Constitution Act of 1919. The court is in Helsinki; consists of a president and 21 justices and is divided into three sections, which render decisions on behalf of the entire court. Tax questions fill the major part of the court's docket. A special court of administrative law is the highest level of appeal for civil servants concerning loss of jobs. Under a 1955 law a network of regional administrative courts deal with complaints of maladministration at the local or regional level.

A number of specialized courts have been set up over the years. These include:

- Military courts *(sotaoikeus)* consisting of a professional judge as chairman and four military members.
- Land partition courts *(maanjako-oikeus)*, three in number and set up in 1766, with a judge as chairman and four experts.
- Water courts *(vesioikeus)*, founded in 1961. Appeals from these courts lie with the Supreme Water Court.
- The Insurance Court (Vakuutusoikeus), in Helsinki, with jurisdiction in cases concerning social insurance and Social Security. It is headed by a chief insurance judge and is composed of six members.

- The Labor Court (Tyotuomioistuin), founded in 1946 and consisting of a chairman and six members.
- The High Court of Impeachment (Vaitakunnanoikeus), founded under Article 59 of the Constitution Act of 1919 to try members of the Council of State, the president of the republic, justices of the Supreme Court and the Supreme Administrative Court as well as the chancellor of justice arraigned for illegal acts in the exercise of their official functions. Charges are brought by the president of the Eduskunta, speaking for a three-fourths majority.

Finland is a Scandinavian civil law country. The Swedish General Code of 1734 still is in force in Finland. No general codification of laws has been carried out. New legislation consists mostly of separate acts. The Union of Finnish Lawyers has privately published a systematic collection of laws titled *Suomen Laki* (The Law of Finland), in two volumes. These volumes are published in both Finnish and Swedish. *Bibliographic Juridica Fennica*, a two-volume legal bibliography, has been published by Suomalainen Lakimiesyhdistys.

Customary law is important, especially in matters of real estate and commerce, but is binding only where the legal issue is not covered by statute, which always takes precedence. Legal precedents have less force, and prior decisions by law courts are not binding on the subsequent administration of justice. However, Supreme Court and Supreme Administrative Court decisions have considerable influence, and lower court judges generally tend to follow trends rather than depart from them radically.

Information is not available on the criminal justice system and the prisons in Finland.

LAW ENFORCEMENT

The Finnish police system dates back to the Middle Ages as part of a structure that developed in the Scandinavian countries. Its basic form has been maintained during the centuries of Swedish and Russian domination and is manifested in a highly centralized administration under the Ministry of the Interior. The Police Division within the ministry is headed by a commander in chief and an inspector general. In each of the 12 provinces there is a provincial command under a superintendent. These commands are, in turn, divided into districts, of which there are roughly 240. Senior officers of urban districts are called police chiefs; those of rural districts, sheriffs. Local authorities provide one-third of the cost of maintaining police forces in their area but have no authority over them.

The general police are responsible for maintaining law and order, while other branches have specialized functions. The Mobile Police are charged with anti-smuggling operations and traffic duties; the Central Criminal Police, located in Helsinki, investigate serious crimes; the Security Police, another specialized group, conduct counterespionage. All equipment and supplies are centrally controlled.

Police personnel are ranked in a three-step hierarchy: officers, noncommissioned officers and enlisted men or constables. Most officers are trained in the Police School, but those with university degrees may be admitted directly. Training in law is important because police officers may be required to act as prosecutors in some instances.

Helsinki has the largest and most organized police unit in the country. Its police chief holds the rank of police commander and heads an establishment of over 2,000 employees. The city is divided into nine precincts.

Personnel of all ranks wear a dark blue uniform consisting of trousers and either a tunic or hip-length blouse. Headgear consists of either a blue peaked cap or a blue Scandinavian-type forage cap. In summer the uniforms may be discarded in favor of a blue, long-sleeved shirt worn with a black tie.

Data are not available on incidence and types of crime in Finland.

HEALTH

Generally the Finns are healthy people. The leading indicators conform to the Scandinavian norm. The infant mortality rate is among the lowest in the world. The incidence of communicable diseases has steadily declined since the 1930s, while polio and diphtheria have virtually disappeared. (The only exception is gonorrhea, reported cases of which grew from 8,805 in 1938 to 10,848 in 1978). Tuberculosis, a serious problem in the 1930s and 1940s, affecting some 80% of 20-year-old men and accounting for nearly 30% of deaths, has been brought under effective control.

One serious problem is disability. Of the population aged 45 to 64, a total of 19.5% are on disability pensions, as compared with 10% in Sweden, 10.8% in Norway and 10.6% in Denmark. The most common causes of disability are disorders of the locomotive musculoskeletal system (28.7%), cardiovascular diseases (28.6%) and mental disorders (18%).

In terms of smoking and alcohol consumption Finland ranks more or less on a par with other Scandinavian countries.

Finns drink more spirits than their neighbors in Scandinavia—less often, perhaps, but in larger quantities at a time. This accounts for a mortality rate from alcohol poisoning that is double that of other Nordic countries. Tobacco consumption has been drastically cut since 1974, when deaths from lung cancer

Country	Tobacco, kg. (lb.)/inh.	Alcohol, 100% l. (qt.)/inh.
Finland	1.51 (3.33)	6.31 (6.67)
Denmark	1.65 (3.64)	9.23 (9.75)
Iceland	2.93 (6.46)	2.86 (3.02)
Norway	1.44 (3.17)	4.28 (4.52)
Sweden	1.67 (3.68)	6.11 (6.46)

were 89.4 per 10,000 inhabitants, the highest in Scandinavia. In the first half of this century cigarette smoking in Finland was the highest in the world. The antismoking campaign is slowly taking effect, particularly among the young. In five years, the incidence of smoking among 14-year-olds came down to 9%, from 19% in 1973.

Nutrition is generally satisfactory, except that the Finns eat too much fat and too few vegetables.

Although there are no specific provisions on health in the Constitution, health care is regarded as a citizen's natural right and its provision a state obligation. The first health care regulations date from 1879. Until 1945 the emphasis was on elimination of communicable diseases. Immediately after World War II the emphasis changed to maternal and child care. In the 1950s the priority was creation of a network of district hospitals. As a result of this program Finland now has 21 district hospitals. The next phase began with the passage of the Primary Health Care Act in 1972.

Health care is organized regionally, with primary responsibility resting with local authorities. Each commune receives a subsidy for provision of health services ranging from 39% of costs for the richest to 70% for the poorest. Communal hospitals are generally free, except for a small fee charged for certain services. Health care costs in the private sector are covered by social insurance, which pays daily allowances and subsidiary allowances up to a maximum of 50 weeks. Maternity allowance is equal to the daily allowance and is paid for 35 weeks. State compensation is 60% for doctors' fees and 50% for medicine. Travel costs also are compensated. All these payments are tax-free.

Health administration is hierarchic. At the apex is the Ministry of Social Affairs and Health, assisted by three national boards: the Board of Health, the Board of Social Welfare and the Board of Labor Protection. The degree to which the administration is decentralized is evident from the fact that the ministry has a personnel strength of less than 20 and that the entire staff of the national Board of Health is only 200. There are departments of social affairs and health in each of the 12 provincial administrations, and boards of health in each of the communes. Small communes form federations for health care delivery. A health board is in charge of a primary health care unit or center, which conducts primary medical, nursing and ambulance services, dental care, health education, health care for the elderly, school health services, and maternal and child health services. There are 213 primary health care units in the country, half of them run by federations of communes.

The goals of the Primary Health Care Act of 1972 were coverage of the entire population, comprehensive and integrated scope of medical services, equality in the distribution of resources, free services for the individual and community participation. Under the act primary health centers (PHC) have been established for every 10,000 inhabitants, although in some sparsely inhabited areas they serve fewer people. Most PHC's have at least four doctors and 40 other personnel. The centers have an average of 2.5 beds per 1,000 inhabitants and account for 75% of primary health contacts.

With the growth of PHC's, the number of doctors solely in private practice has fallen to about 5%, although 30% of hospital physicians run a small private practice outside working hours. A PHC doctor receives a salary for 36 hours a week and overtime on a fee-for-service basis.

Free dental care is given to all under 17. For adults, dental work is not subsidized or covered by social insurance. Finland has a large number of dentists (one per 1,300 inhabitants), of whom 68% are women.

The modern network of hospitals dates only from 1950, when the Eduskunta passed an act making hospital construction a state responsibility. At the same time all hospitals (with a few exceptions) were transferred to communal ownership. For specialized treatment the country is divided into 21 hospital districts Each central hospital handles at least four of the most common clinical specialties. Five of the central hospitals are university teaching hospitals (Helsinki, Turku, Kuopio, Oulu and Tampere). The 21 hospital districts are grouped into these five university hospital regions. A large-scale building program for mental hospitals was put through in the 1950s. Finland has a high ratio of hospital beds to inhabitants, and therefore no expansion of hospital services is envisioned.

FOOD & NUTRITION

The average Finn consumes 3,080 calories and 93.4 g. (3.29 oz.) of protein per day. This food supply is 111% of FAO food requirements. Food expenditures account for 25.5% of total household expenditures. Of total daily calories, 23.9% is derived from cereals, 5.3% from potatoes, 15.7 from meat and poultry, 1.8% from fish, 17.0% from milk and eggs, 3.9% from fruits and vegetables and 14.1 from fats and oils.

HEALTH INDICATORS, 1986

Health personnel
  Physicians: 10,193
    Population per: 481
  Dentists: 3,916
  Nurses: 43,989
  Pharmacists: 7,057
  Midwives: 1,179

Hospitals
  Number: 367
  Number of beds: 61,082
    Per 10,000: 125
  Admissions/discharges per 10,000: 2,080
  Bed occupancy rate: 81.7%
  Average length of stay: 19 days

Type of hospitals (%)
  Government: 94.9
  Private nonprofit: ⎫
  Private profit: ⎬ 5.1

Public health expenditures
  As % of national budget: 9
  Per capita: $37.80

Vital statistics
  Crude death rate per 1,000: 9.6
  Decline in death rate, 1965–84: –5.2%
  Life expectancy at birth (years)
    Males: 70.3
    Females: 78.6
  Infant mortality rate per 1,000 live births: 6.3
  Child mortality rate ages 1–4 years per 1,000:
    insignificant
  Maternal mortality rate per 100,000 live births: 3.0

Causes of death per 100,00

  Infectious & parasitic diseases: 8.1
  Cancer: 198.6
  Endocrine & metabolic disorders: 12.0
  Diseases of the nervous system: 11.9
  Diseases of the circulatory system: 531.5
  Diseases of the respiratory system: 79.7
  Diseases of the digestive system: 26.7
  Accidents, poisoning & violence: 79.7

MEDIA & CULTURE

The Finnish press has its origins in the Swedish era. The first publication, in 1771, *Tidningar Utgifne Af Et Sallskap i Åbo* (News Published by a Society in Åbo), was itself in Swedish. The first Finnish-language publication, called *Suomenkieliset*, appeared in Turku four years later and was edited by a rural clergyman. By 1840, when Finland lad already passed from under Sweden to Russia, Helsinki emerged as the main center of Finnish journalism. In 1847 the first Finnish-language newspaper was founded in this essentially Swedish-speaking city. Called *Suometar*, it was the first to emphasize current news. By the end of the 1840s the Finnish-language press had not only struck roots but also displayed vigorous growth. Of the 16 newspapers in 1860, half were in Finnish. Despite this development, Finland ranked among the bottom five countries in Europe in both the number of newspapers and their circulation per capita. Of the 16 newspapers published in 1860, only five had circulations exceeding 1,000.

The 1860s were a time of vigorous press activity following a brief thaw in the repressive rule of the tsars. The Young Pro-Finns were responsible for the creation of Finland's first modern newspaper, *Helsingfors Dagblad*, edited by Robert Lagerborg, the first full-time professional journalist in Finnish press history. After Lagerborg's early death in 1882, the daily began to decline, and seven years later it ceased publication. One reason for its demise was its adoption of a neutral attitude in the Swedish-Finnish controversy, which had become the central concern of the 1880s. The Pro-Finns pressed their claims in a new newspaper, *Uusi Suometar*, which soon assumed leadership of the Finnish-language press. Because this paper espoused conservative causes (conservatives came to be known as "Suometarians"), radicals broke with it and in 1890 founded their own organ, *Paivalehti*, the country's first liberal newspaper. By the 1890s the press had clearly split along party lines, with the three main groups—the Swedish nationalists, the conservatives or Old Finns and the radicals or Young Finns—having their own newspapers. A fourth group was added in the 1890s, when the Social Democrats began establishing newspapers within the labor movement. *Tyomies* (The Workman), founded as a weekly in 1895 and converted into a daily in 1899, developed into the leading spokesman for Finnish socialism. By the turn of the century it was the country's largest newspaper in circulation if not in influence.

The number of newspapers grew continuously in the latter decades of the 19th century, but the turnover also was great. Between 1890 and 1900 alone, 153 publications were founded, whereas only 81 survived the turn of the century. By the same period, the Finnish-language press had overtaken the Swedish-language press in both the number of newspapers and issues per week. Own-

```
┌─────────────────────────────────────────┐
│     PER CAPITA CONSUMPTION OF FOODS Kg. (Lb.),│
│                    1986                   │
│ Potatoes: 65.0 (143.3)                    │
│ Wheat: 46.6 (102.7)                       │
│ Rice: 3.9 (8.6)                           │
│ Fresh vegetables: 32.8 (72.3)             │
│ Fruits (total): 35.9 (79.1)               │
│     Citrus: 14.6 (32.2)                   │
│     Noncitrus: 21.3 (46.9)                │
│ Eggs: 11 (24.2)                           │
│ Honey: 0.5 (1.1)                          │
│ Fish: 4.3 (9.4)                           │
│ Milk: 194.4 (428.6)                       │
│ Butter: 12.1 (26.6)                       │
│ Cream: 8.2 (18.9)                         │
│ Cheese: 8.2 (18.9)                        │
│ Yogurt: 8.9 (19.6)                        │
│ Meat (total): 55.0 (121.2)                │
│     Beef & veal: 21.7 (47.8)              │
│     Pig meat: 31.0 (68.3)                 │
│     Poultry: 2.0 (4.4)                    │
│     Mutton, lamb & goat: 0.3 (0.66)       │
│ Sugar: 41.0 (90.4)                        │
│ Chocolate: 3.7 (8.1)                      │
│ Ice cream: 9.4 l. (19.8 pt.)              │
│ Margarine: 8.0 (17.6)                     │
│ Biscuits: 4.9 (10.8)                      │
│ Breakfast cereals: 3.9 (8.5)              │
│ Pasta: —                                  │
│ Canned foods: 2.5 (5.5)                   │
│ Beer: 56.8 l. (125.2 pt.)                 │
│ Wine 8.0 l. (16.9 pt.)                    │
│ Alcoholic liquors: 2.5 l. (5.2 pt.)       │
│ Soft drinks: 38.0 l. (80.3 pt.)           │
│ Mineral waters: 5.2 l. (10.9 pt.)         │
│ Fruit Juices: 28.1 l. (59.4 pt.)          │
│ Tea: 0.2 (0.44)                           │
│ Coffee: 13.9 (30.6)                       │
│ Cocoa: 0.1 (0.22)                         │
└─────────────────────────────────────────┘
```

ership and editorial patterns also were changing, as the printer-publisher was replaced by the joint stock company and as the academics who moonlighted as journalists were replaced by permanent and professional full-time newspeople. Newsgathering also improved with the establishment of the first national news agency in 1887, followed by a second one in 1898. The first rotary press was acquired by *Hafvudstadsbladet* in 1896 followed by *Uusi Suometar* in 1899, but the old hand presses remained in use until the early decades of the 20th century.

In appearance the papers had a medieval look, with black gothic letters and heavy borders. It was not until 1912 that *Uusi Suometar* set all its text in roman. Violent protests were raised, but gradually the example was followed by the others.

During the "years of oppression" from 1899 to 1905, the Russian administration of Nicholas Ivanovitch Bobrikov clamped down on the free press, closing 24 publications and suspending another 47 for varying lengths of time. When the repression came to an end in 1905 following Bobrikov's assassination and the November Manifesto, the press began to experience another period of vigorous growth. In 1917—the last year of Russian sovereignty—382 newspapers were published, and the aggregate circulation of newspapers had grown six times since 1900. Another stage in press history was marked in the same year when the Newspaper Publishers' Association was founded, with a membership of 60.

The history of the press in Finland since 1917 has been marked by the rise and fall of party newspapers. By 1970 the party press had declined by over two-thirds, from 105 in 1918 to 38 in 1970. In addition to newspapers, political parties run their own news agencies. The political press still accounts for nearly half of the total circulation.

As a nation with total literacy, Finland ranks high in both newspaper circulation and newsprint consumption per capita. In 1984 a total of 67 dailies were published in the country, with an aggregate circulation of 2,599,000 or 535 copies per 1,000 inhabitants. In the same year 311 nondailies were published, along with 4,432 periodicals. Twelve of the dailies were published in Swedish. Finland is the second-largest exporter of newsprint in the world, and domestic consumption generally accounts for only 7% of production. Because of the export priorities, newsprint prices are relatively high.

Dailies are published in 57 towns, of which 18 have competing dailies. The nation's media capital is Helsinki, but its dominance is being challenged by the provincial press, which exhibits a greater growth rate. Evening papers play only a minor role. Only one evening paper appears in Helsinki. There are no special Sunday papers.

From a journalistic point of view, Finnish dailies tend to be staid and sober rather than sensationalist. Crime and sex usually are downplayed, and scandals are shunned. Even political criticism is gentle and moderate. Typographically, the papers have a slightly old-fashioned appearance, with only small concessions to modernity in makeup and layout. Too many stories are crammed into the first page and continued inside after only a few sentences. More often than not, letters to the editor are banal. Two unusual features are the birthday list and a daily summary of the editorial comments of competitors. Foreign news is covered in depth, as a result of which the Finnish reader is better informed about world affairs than his counterparts in the rest of Europe.

Only one newspaper can claim a national character and circulation: *Helsingin Sanomat*, which appears among *The World's Great Dailies*. Owned by the Erkko family, it is an independent paper that usually comes out on the side of liberal and democratic ideas. With a circulation of 418,000, it is read by every fourth adult in the country.

As in other countries, the Finnish press represents only a small fraction of the industrial sector, its aggregate assets making up 1.4% of all industrial assets. As newspaper publishing by itself is not financially profitable, many press enterprises have other diversified interests, which provide up to 70% of their total annual revenues. Even so, only 65% of the companies report a profit. Furthermore, the larger newspapers claim a lion's share of the profits, leaving the small- and medium-sized papers in dire financial straits. Of total revenues, nearly 73% comes from advertising and 27% from subscription and single-copy sales. Of sale revenues, 90% comes from subscriptions and 10% from newsstand sales. More than 60% of all advertising is channeled through newspapers, while television receives only 10%. (There is no commercial radio.) As a result, newspapers are overdependent on advertising.

Finland has no chains except in one or two cases, where a daily issues a part edition under another name in a neighboring locality. There also is very little concentration in ownership, with the largest company, Sanoma Oy, the publisher of *Helsingin Sanomat*, accounting for only 10% of total circulation. Likewise, the 10 largest dailies have only 46% of national circulation. However, there is strong geographic concentration in the South, with the northern press comparatively underdeveloped.

One of the first laws of independent Finland was the Press Freedom Act of 1919, which has remained the foundation of the country's free press. Its basic principle, contained in Section I, guarantees every Finnish citizen the right to publish printed material "without public authorities being allowed to set any obstacles to this in advance." All citizens also are granted the right to carry on a printing business after notifying the authorities, to edit publications and to sell or circulate them without hindrance. The law also provides for the right of rectification for individuals and institutions who wish to correct false statements about themselves. Chapters 6 and 7 of the act deal with forfeiture of criminally offensive printed works—particularly obscene ones—and suspension of periodicals and newspapers of the same nature.

Subsequent legislation has advanced press freedom. The Act on Publicity of Official Documents of 1951 confirms the right of Finnish citizens to obtain access to any public official document. Most public documents come automatically into the public domain 25 years following their original date. An amendment to the Code of Procedure in 1966 accorded journalists the right, except in serious criminal cases, to refuse to divulge to the court their sources of information. In 1971 this right of anonymity was extended to radio and television. Another amendment, in 1974, stipulated punishment for publications that discriminated against or incited hatred against any population group of defined race, color, nationality or religious affiliation. Chapter 24 prohibits illicit eavesdropping and illicit surveillance by both public officials and private citizens. Chapter 27 deals with libel in print, for which a prison term is prescribed. Violation of privacy also is classified as a crime, except when it relates to the public life of a public official. A new act, in 1970, revised the old regulations against blasphemy, which still is punishable. The Criminal Code contains provisions against defamation. Other restrictions on the press include the duty to maintain secrecy in matters relating to national defense; to report only facts without comments on matters that are sub judice; and to avoid harsh criticism of the Soviet Union, which is extremely sensitive on this score.

Press self-regulation started in 1957, when the Finnish Association of Journalists established a code of conduct known as Rules for Journalists. Accuracy and fairness in media also are enforced by an ombudsman body known as the Board of Opinion for Mass Media.

Finland has no information ministry or department, and the government plays a low-key role in news management. The principal element of state-press relations is the subsidy system. The media receive four types of subsidies: the so-called general subsidy for transportation of newspapers, the direct transportation and delivery subsidy, the subsidy for news agencies and the subsidy for the political press.

The national news agency is the Suomen Tietotoimisto Finska Notisbyran (STT), founded in 1915 and owned cooperatively by Finnish newspapers and the Finnish Radio Company. The four major political parties—National Coalition, Center, Finnish Social Democratic and Finnish People's Democratic League—maintain their own news agencies, subsidized by the state.

The sole licensed broadcasting company is the Finnish Broadcasting Corporation (Oy Yleisradio, YLE) owned 99.9% by the state, with the remaining 0.1% divided among 88 shareholders. The highest executive authority of the YLE is the Administrative Council, elected by the Eduskunta for a four-year term. While the YLE has a monopoly over radio broadcasting, it is assisted by OY Mainos TV—Reklam (MTV), a joint stock company that broadcasts over 900 hours of commercials on the YLE networks annually. The YLE operates two television channels, the first for about 45 hours a week and the second for about 40 hours a week. Some 100,000 homes are linked by cable television.

There are three programming councils: one for radio, one for television and the third for Swedish-language broadcasting. Although Swedes make up only 7% of the population, Swedish programs account for 20% of the total.

Broadcasting revenues are derived from license fees and advertising. The former provide 80% of the revenues because advertising is limited to 15% of airtime.

Regular film production started in 1906, and the first sound film was produced in 1931. Film production was heavily cut down in the 1950s, reflecting the inroads of television and the changes in people's leisure habits. At present some four feature films are produced annually, subsidized by the Finnish Film Foundation.

Finland ranks high in the number of theaters and theatergoers. There are over 40 professional theaters in addition to a great many semiprofessional and amateur theaters, summer theaters and student and youth theaters.

The volume of book publishing is enormous, with an annual output in 1986 of 6,268 titles. Relative to the population, this is one of the highest rates in the world. Three publishing giants dominate the book industry: Werner Soderstrom, Otava and Tammi.

MEDIA INDICATORS, 1986

Newspapers
   Number of dailies: 67 (1984)
   Circulation (000): 2,599 (1984)
     Per capita: 0.54 (1984)

   Number of nondailies: 311 (1984)
   Circulation (000): —
     Per capita: —

   Number of periodicals: 4,432 (1984)
   Circulation: —

   Newsprint consumption
   Total: 146,000 tons
   Per capita: 30.2 kg. (66.6 lb.)

Book publishing
   Number of titles: 6,268

Broadcasting
   Annual expenditures: 1,353.9 million markka
   Number of employees: 4,355

Radio
   Number of transmitters: 101
   Number of radio receivers: 2,500,000
     Persons per: 2.0
   Annual total program hours: 17,535

MEDIA INDICATORS, 1986 *(continued)*

Television
  Television transmitters: 172
  Number of TV receivers: 1,792,000
    Persons per: 2.7
  Annual total program hours: 4,507

Cinema
  Number of fixed cinemas: 378
  Seating capacity: 86,000
    Seats per 1,000: 17.5
  Annual attendance (million) per 1,000: 1,400
  Gross box office receipts: 172.5 million markka

Films
  Production of long films: 15
  Import of long films: 212
  % from U.S.A.: 48.6
  % from France: 3.8
  % from Italy: 4.7
  % from Soviet Union: 2.1

MASS MEDIA CIRCULATION, 1983

	Total Circulation	Household Coverage
TV licenses	1,723,000	96%
Major newspapers		
Helsingin Sanomat (national)	418,000	23%
Turun Sanomat (regional)	132,000	7%
Aamulehti (regional)	137,000	8%
Maaseudun Tulevaisuus (national)	128,000	7%
Uusi Suomi (national)	87,000	5%
Ilta-Sanomate (evening)	147,000	8%
Major magazines		
Valitut Palat (Reader's Digest)	309,000	
Seura	314,000	
Apu	304,000	
Nykyposti	226,000	
Suomen Kuvalehti	121,000	
Women's Magazines		
Kotiliesi	215,000	
Kodin Kuvalehti	169,000	
Anna	144,000	

```
┌─────────────────────────────────────────────┐
│ CULTURAL & ENVIRONMENTAL INDICATORS, 1986    │
│ Public Libraries                             │
│   Number: 461                                │
│   Volumes: 29,900,000                        │
│   Registered borrowers: 2,100,000            │
│   Loans per 1,000: 15,567                    │
│                                              │
│ Museums: 572                                 │
│   Annual attendance: 2,897,000               │
│   Attendance per 1,000: 590                  │
│                                              │
│ Performing arts facilities: 47               │
│   Number of performances: 11,242             │
│   Annual attendance: 2,588,000               │
│   Attendance per 1,000: 527                  │
│                                              │
│ Ecological sites                             │
│   Number of facilities: 33                   │
│   Botanical gardens & zoos: 7                │
└─────────────────────────────────────────────┘
```

SOCIAL WELFARE

The first social insurance (employees' accident insurance) was introduced in 1895. General, statutory old age and disability insurance appeared with the National Pensions Act of 1937. The cost of social insurance is divided among employers, employees, the state and local authorities. In terms of the size of expenditures, Finland is one of the world leaders in Social Security.

Pension benefits include old age, disability, unemployment and survivors' pensions. They are covered by several acts, such as the Employees' Pension Act, the Temporary Employees' Pension Act, the Farmers' Pension Act, and the Self-Employed Persons' Pension Act. Old-age benefits begin at age 65, and if the insured has no other income he or she also may receive an additional support pension, support allowance and a housing supplement.

Unemployment insurance is voluntary and organized on a vocational basis. Unemployment funds charge membership fees. The maximum daily allowances, which are paid for up to 150 days, do not exceed two-thirds of the last received daily wages.

Universal statutory sickness insurance was introduced in 1963. Compensation is given in two ways: 60% of the cost of medical treatment, and a daily allowance for each day of sickness. Social insurance covers much of the cost of maintaining health. Accident insurance, introduced in 1948, is compulsory. It may be a lump-sum compensation or a series of allowances covering medical care, rehabilitation, etc.

Social allowances are subsidies paid from public funds irrespective of the beneficiaries' past or present employment record. Unlike social welfare, social allowances are not paid on a case-by-case basis, but automatically. Family assistance includes maternity benefits, child allowances, family allowances, housing subsidies and tax relief. Persons wishing to receive vocational training through apprenticeships or vocational schools receive state aid.

Social welfare is designed to supplement social insurance and social allowances. Social welfare programs come under local administration and thus are financed mainly through local taxes. Child welfare and care of the mentally ill are the two most important areas of social welfare. Child welfare includes day-care centers, crèches, day nurseries for preschoolers and day homes for school-going children, playgrounds and kindergartens. Communes also are responsible for the care of the aged. Every commune maintains either by itself or jointly with other communes at least one old people's home. Under Finnish law, the care of vagrants and alcoholics is a matter for welfare and not for the courts.

There is no private welfare system in Finland.

CHRONOLOGY

1946—Marshal Carl Gustav von Mannerheim retires as president; Prime Minister Julio Paasikivi is named president, and Mauno Pekkala becomes prime minister.

1948—Agreement of Friendship, Cooperation and Mutual Assistance is signed with the Soviet Union; Finland cedes parts of eastern Karelia to the Soviet Union and agrees to pay war reparations. Karl Fagerholm forms first Social Democratic ministry.

1950—Urho Kekkonen heads Agrarian League government.

1953—Sakari Tuomioja heads no-party government.

1954—Ralf Torngren of Swedish People's Party heads brief government.

1955—Finland joins the United Nations and the Nordic Council.

1956—Karl Fagerholm heads his second government; Urho Kekkonen is president.

1957—Vaino Sukselainen heads the government, followed by Rainer von Fieandt.

1958—Raino Kuuskoski forms a no-party government but yields to Karl Fagerholm's third government.

1959—Vaino Sukselainen forms his second government.

1961—Martti Miettunen forms his first government. Finland joins the European Free Trade Association.

1962—Ahti Karjalainen forms his first government.

1963—Reino Lehto forms a no-party government.

1964—Johannes Virolainen forms a Center Party government.

1966—Rafael Paasio heads a Finnish Social Democratic government.

1968—Mauno Koivisto heads a Finnish Social Democratic government.

1970—Teuvo Aura heads a brief no-party government but is replaced by Ahti Karjalainen's second government.

1971—Teuvo Aura heads his second no-party government.

1972—Rafael Paasio heads a brief Finnish Social Democratic government but yields to Kalevi Sorsa of the same party.

1975—Keijo Liinamaa heads a brief government but is replaced by Martti Miettunen's second government. Finland hosts the Conference on Security and Cooperation in Europe.

1977—Kalevi Sorsa heads his second government.

1979—Mauno Koivisto heads his second government.

1981—Urho Kekkonen dies. Mauno Koivisto is elected president.

1982—Kalevi Sorsa heads his third government.

1987—Finland's first conservative-led government takes office under Harri Holkeri as prime minister.

BIBLIOGRAPHY

BOOKS

Allison, Roy. *Finland's Relations with the Soviet Union, 1944–1984*. New York, 1985.

———— *Cultural Policy in Finland*. Paris, 1972.

Darby, H. C. *The Changing Finland*. New York, 1983.

De Biasi, M. and G. Stenius. *Finlandia: Profile of a Country*. London, 1967.

Edwards, G. R., and G. W. Abbott. *The Agricultural Economy of Finland*. Washington, D.C., 1966.

European Research Association and Sakari Jutila. *Finlandization for Finland and the World*. London, 1983.

———— *Finnish Foreign Policy: Studies in Foreign Politics*. Vammala, Finland, 1963.

Hall, W. *The Finns and Their Country*. London, 1967.

Harmaja, Leo. *Effects of the War on Economic and Social Life of Finland*. London, 1933.

Hodgson, John H. *Communism in Finland: A History and an Interpretation*. Princeton, 1966.

Jakobson, Max. *Finnish Neutrality*. New York, 1969.

Jutikkala, Eino, and Kauko Pirinen. *History of Finland*. New York, 1973.

Kekkonen, Urho. *A President's View*. London, 1982.

Kirby, D. G. *Finland in the Twentieth Century: A History and an Interpretation*. Minneapolis, 1980.

Knoellinger, C. E. *Labor in Finland*. Cambridge, Mass., 1961.

Mannerheim, Carl Gustav Emil. *The Memoirs of Marshal Mannerheim.* New York, 1954.

Maude, George. *The Finnish Dilemma.* London, 1976.

Mazour, Anatole G. *Finland Between East and West.* Westport, Conn., 1976.

Mead, William R. *Finland.* New York, 1968.

Nickels, Sylvie. *Finland: An Introduction.* London, 1973.

Nousiainen, Jaakko. *The Finnish Political System.* Cambridge, Mass., 1971.

Pantila, L. A. *The Political History of Finland, 1809–1966.* New York, 1976.

Platt, R. R. *Finland and Its Geography.* New York, 1955.

Rajanen, Aini. *Of Finnish Ways.* New York, 1984.

Screen, J.E.O. *Finland* (World Bibliographical Series). Santa Barbara, Calif., 1981.

Sentzke, G. *Finland: Its Church and Its People.* Helsinki, 1963.

Stover, William J. *Military Policies in Finland.* Washington, D.C., 1982.

Upton, A. F. *Finland in Crisis, 1940–41.* Ithaca, N.Y., 1964.

———— *The Finnish Revolution.* Minneapolis, 1981.

Vloyantes, John P. *Silk Glove Hegemony: Finnish-Soviet Relations, 1944-74.* Kent, Ohio, 1975.

Wuorinen, John H. *Finland and World War II, 1939–44.* Westport, Conn., 1983.

———— *A History of Finland.* New York, 1965.

OFFICIAL PUBLICATIONS

Ministry of Finance

Cash Receipts and Expenditures of Central Government (monthly)
Report on Management and State of Public Finance

Other Units of Central Government

Annual Report of the Social Insurance Institution
Closed Accounts of Central Government and of the Funds, State Treasury Office
Local Government Financial Statistics, Central Statistical Office
Monthly Accounts of Central Government and of the Funds, State Treasury Office

Bank of Finland

Monthly Bulletin (English)

Note: All sources are annual and in Finnish and Swedish only except as indicated.

ICELAND

ICELAND

BASIC FACT SHEET

OFFICIAL NAME: Republic of Iceland (Lýthveldith Island)

ABBREVIATION: IC

CAPITAL: Reykjavik

HEAD OF STATE: President Vigdis Finnbogadottir (from 1980)

HEAD OF GOVERNMENT: Prime Minister Steingrimur Hermannsson (from 1988)

NATURE OF GOVERNMENT: Parliamentary democracy

POPULATION: 246,526 (1988)

AREA: 103,000 sq.km. (39,768 sq. mi.)

ETHNIC COMPOSITION: Primarily Nordic-Celtic

LANGUAGES: Icelandic

RELIGION: Evangelical Lutheran

UNIT OF CURRENCY: Krona

NATIONAL FLAG: A red cross (with an extended right horizontal) bordered in white on a blue field

NATIONAL EMBLEM: A red-tongued silver vulture with gold claws and beak and a black dragon, also red of tongue and with gold crest and claws and white teeth, sit back to back on top of the shield; a black bull with golden hooves and glowing eye paws the rocky land beside it. A white-bearded giant with black and gold belt, black staff, golden sandals and gold-lined cape stands in front with his right hand resting on the shield.

NATIONAL ANTHEM: "O Goth Vors Lands" (O God of Our Land)

NATIONAL HOLIDAYS: National Day, June 17; New Year's Day; First Day of Summer; Labor Day; major Christian festivals

NATIONAL CALENDAR: Gregorian

PHYSICAL QUALITY OF LIFE INDEX: 100 (on an ascending scale with 100 as the maximum)

DATE OF INDEPENDENCE: June 17, 1944

DATE OF CONSTITUTION: 1944

WEIGHTS & MEASURES: Metric

GEOGRAPHICAL FEATURES

The westernmost country of Europe, Iceland is an island in the North Atlantic Ocean just below the Arctic Circle, 322 km. (200 mi.) east of Greenland, 1,038 km. (645 mi.) west of Norway and 837 km. (520 mi.) northwest of Scotland. Its area is 103,100 sq. km. (39,797 sq. mi.), extending 490 km. (304 mi.) east to west and 312 km. (194 mi.) north to south. The total length of the coastline is 4,970 km. (3,088 mi.). The mainland comprises 102,950 sq. km. (39,739 sq. mi.), (including 408 sq. km. [157 sq. mi.] of lakes). The islands and

skerries comprise 150 sq. km. (58 sq. km.). Of the many islands, the most notable are the Westman Islands, off the southern coast.

The capital is Reykjavik, on a bay on the southwestern coast. With a 1983
population of 87,106, Reykjavik contains 35% of the national population. The
other major towns are:

Town	Population
Kópavaogur	14,433
Akureyri	13,742
Hafnarfjördhur	12,700
Keflavik	6,874
Garoabaer	5,753
Akranes	5,351

Iceland consists mainly of a central volcanic plateau with elevations ranging
from 700 to 800 m. (2,297 to 2,625 ft.) ringed by mountains, the highest of
which is Hvannadalshnukur (2,119 m.; 6,952 ft.) in the Oraefajokull glacier.
Lava fields cover about one-ninth of the country; glaciers, about one-eighth.
Geologically the country is still very young and bears signs of still being in the
making. It appears on the whole roughly hewn, abrupt and jagged, without the
softness of outline that characterizes more mature landscapes. The average
height is 500 m. (1,641 ft.) above sea level, and one-quarter of the country lies
below the 200-m. (656-ft.) contour line. The largest lowland areas include Ar-
nessysla, Rangarvallasysla and Vestur-Skaftafellssysla in the South and Mýrar
in the West. In the plateaus, land is broken into more or less tilted blocks, with
most leaning toward the interior of the country. Glacial erosion has played an
important role in giving the valleys their present shape. In some areas, such as
between Eyjafjorour and Skagafjorour, the landscape possesses alpine characteristics. There are numerous and striking gaping fissures within the postgla-
cially active volcanic belts.

Icelandic coasts can be divided into two main types. In regions not drained
by the debris-laden glacial rivers, the coasts jut irregularly, incised with numerous fjords and smaller inlets. They offer many good natural harbors where the
fjords have been deepened by glacial erosion. The other type of coast is sandy,
with smooth outlines featuring extensive offshore bars with lagoons behind
them. The beaches from Djupivogur in the Southeast to Olfusa in the Southwest
belong in this category.

Glaciers cover an area of 11,200 sq. km. (4,323 sq. mi.), or 11% of the total
land area. Nearly all types of glaciers, from small cirque glaciers to extensive
plateau icecaps, are represented. The biggest of these icecaps, Vatnajökull, with
an area of 8,300 sq. km. (3,204 sq. mi.) and a maximum thickness of 1,000 m.

(3,281 ft.), is larger than all the glaciers in continental Europe put together. One of its southern outlets, Breidamerkurjökull, reaches more than 120 m. (394 ft.) below sea level. Other large icecaps are Langjökull (1,025 sq. km.; 396 sq. mi.) and Hofsjökull (953 sq. km.; 368 sq. mi.). in the Central Highlands, Mýrdalsjökull (700 sq. km.; 270 sq. mi.) in the South and Drangajökull (160 sq. km.; 62 sq. mi.) in the Northwest. The altitude of the glaciation limit is lowest, about 600 m. (1,969 ft.) in the Northwest and highest, over 1,500 m. (4,922 ft.) in the highlands north of Vatnajökull. Since about 1890, the glaciers have greatly thinned and retreated, and some of the smaller ones have almost disappeared. During the 1960s the retreat began to slow down, but some of the glaciers are now advancing again.

Because of the heavy rainfall, Icelandic rivers are numerous and relatively large. Pjorsá, the longest river, has a length of 237 km. (147 mi.) and Jökulsá á Fjöllum, the second longest, a length of 206 km. (128 mi.). Other major rivers include Skjálfandafljót, Jökulsá á Brú, Lagarfljót, Skeidara and Kuoafljót. These rivers belong to three types. The debris-laden glacial rivers usually divide into a great number of interlinked tributaries that constantly change course and flow through the outwash plains that lie below the glaciers. Skeidara is a typical example. The maximum discharge in the glacial rivers usually occurs in July or early August. Direct-runoff rivers drain the old basalt areas in summer and autumn, while spring-fed rivers drain the regions covered by postglacial lava fields. Swift currents make Icelandic rivers unnavigable for the most part.

The wealth of waterfalls is typical of the young landscape. The largest, Dettifoss (44 m.; 144 ft.), is in Jökulsá á Fjöllum. The others are Gullfoss (32 m.; 105 ft.) in Hivita, Godafoss in Skjálfandafljót, Skogafoss and Fjallfoss.

Iceland possesses numerous lakes, mostly of tectonic origin. Others resulted from the deepening of valleys by glacial erosion or damming by lava flows, glacial deposits and rock slides. Small crater lakes are common in explosion craters, especially in the Landmannalaugar-Veidivotn area, where the Lake Oskjuvatn caldera has an area of 11 sq. km. (4.2 sq. mi.) and a depth of 217 m. (712 ft.). On the sandy shores lagoon lakes are common, the biggest being Hop (30 sq. km.; 12 sq. mi.).

The soils may be roughly grouped into mineral soils and organic soils, with a number of intermediate types. The mineral soils are loessial, formed by materials supplied by explosive volcanic eruptions and glacier erosion. Because of the cool climate, the chemical and biological processes in the soil are slow, and their properties strongly reflect those of volcanic rocks. Most soils are suitable for agriculture but require heavy fertilizer applications.

Earthquakes are frequent in the country. The largest ones occur within a fracture zone that runs through the Southern Lowlands, where disastrous earthquakes were recorded in 1784 and 1896. Earthquakes also are frequent on the Reykjanes Peninsula and in the districts around Skjálfandia, Eyjafjordur and Skagafjordur in the North.

Iceland is very rich in natural heat, as the regional heat flow within the neo-volcanic areas averages two or three times the global average. Two main types of thermal areas can be distinguished on the basis of the maximum subsurface temperature of thermal water. The low-temperature areas where the maximum temperature is less than 150°C (302°F) have few springs. The hot springs are common all over the country except in the East and Southeast and number over 300. The largest is Deildartunguhver in Borgarfjordur.

The English word "geyser" comes from the most famous Icelandic hot spring, at Geysir in Haukadalur in South Iceland. At times Geysir is quiescent, while at others it spouts water to a height of about 60 m. (197 ft.). A nearby famous spouter is called Strokkur. Beautiful silica sinter terraces are displayed around the hot springs at Hveravellir in the Central Highlands. The total natural heat discharge of the high-temperature areas reaches several thousand megawatts.

Nearly every type of volcano is found in Iceland. Lava-producing fissures forming so-called center rows are the most common. It was one of these, the Ladagigar, that in 1783 poured out the most extensive lava flow in the world in historical times. It covers 565 sq. km. (218 sq. mi.) and has a volume of about 12 sq. km. (4,6 sq. mi.). The crater rows follow the same direction as the Pleistocene ridges. Shield volcanoes such as Skjádbreidur also have produced a great amount of lava but have not been active for the past 1,000 years. Iceland also has active volcanoes of the central type fed by magma chambers higher up in the earth's crust. Many of them are blanketed by perpetual ice, including two that have erupted most frequently in historical times, Grimsvotn and Katla. The latter, which has Iceland's largest caldera (80 sq. km.; 31 sq. mi.), has erupted about 20 times in the past 1,000 years. Each eruption of these volcanoes is accompanied by a water flood *(jokulhlaup)*. These floods occur every five to 10 years, sometimes without volcanic eruptions. The eruption of Oraefajökull in 1362 devastated the settlement at the foot of the volcano. Another large caldera, at Askja in the Dyngjufjoll massif, erupted in 1875, causing great damage in East Iceland. The most famous of Icelandic volcanoes is Hekla, which was renowned during the Middle Ages as the abode of the damned. Since its first recorded eruption in 1104, Hekla has erupted 14 times, the last in 1970.

Explosion pits are found throughout the country. Submarine eruptions often occur off the coasts, especially in the Reykjanes ridge. The last one, which began in 1963 and lasted until 1967, built up the island of Surtsey, which now covers an area of 2.8 sq. km. (1.1 sq. mi.). On January 23, 1973, the Vestmannaey-jar crater erupted, burying one-third of the town of the same name.

CLIMATE & WEATHER

The climate of Iceland is influenced by the situation of the country as a boundary zone between two very different air masses, one polar and the other tropical. It also is affected by the confluence of two ocean currents. Because of the submarine ridge between Iceland and Scotland, a branch of the North Atlantic Drift—a continuation of the Gulf Stream—is deflected westward and flows clockwise around the southern and western coasts. Consequently the harbors on these coasts are free from ice year-around. Some Atlantic water reaches the northern coast, where it is submerged in a branch of the East Greenland Polar Current, which curves southeastward around the eastern coast and meets the Atlantic waters off the southeastern coast.

A third factor affecting Icelandic climate is the Arctic driftice carried by the East Greenland Polar Current, but the influence of this ice varies greatly from season to season and from year to year. In most years, the northern coast of Iceland is completely ice-free. In other years, the ice approaches the northern coast, especially in the winter and early spring. The advance of the drift ice means a considerable fall in temperature and usually some decrease in precipitation.

The seasonal fluctuations in temperature and precipitation chiefly depend, however, on the tracks of atmospheric depressions crossing the North Atlantic. The passage of a depression south of Iceland brings relatively cold weather, especially in northern districts, while a depression moving northeast between Iceland and Greenland brings mild and rainy weather.

Considering the northern situation of the country, Iceland's climate is much warmer than might be expected.

The lowest temperature noted in Iceland at sea level was -36.2°C (-33.2°F), in Siglufjorour in March 1881; the highest, 30.5°C (86.9°F) at Teigarhorn in June 1939. High temperatures in North and East Iceland usually are due to the foehn effect.

Because of the frequent passage of depressions, Iceland is very windy. The average annual numbers of days with wind force of 9 on the Beaufort scale are 13.5 in Reykjavik and 3.5 in Húsavík but 70.7 in Vestmannaeyjar. Thunderstorms are rare, with an average of one every three years in West Iceland and an average of two every year in the East. Fogs also are not very frequent. The annual average of foggy days is 10 on the western coast and 60 on the eastern coast. The northern lights are often visible, especially in autumn and early winter.

On the southern slopes of Vatnajökull and Mýrdalsjökull, the annual rainfall exceeds 4,000 mm. (157 in.), but in the highlands just north of Vatnajökull it is less than 400 mm. (16 in.). Snow cover as a percentage of total cover for every day in winter is 17 in Fagurholsmyri on the southern coast and 53 in Húsavík on the northern coast.

There was a marked climatic amelioration from about 1919 to 1964, resulting in improved fishing conditions, birdlife and vegetation. During this time sea ice was practically absent, but the climate began to deteriorate after 1965, and sea ice began to reappear in considerable masses.

POPULATION

The population of Iceland was estimated at 246,526 in 1988. It ranks 157th in the world in size of population. The last census was held in 1983, when the population was 235,537. The population is expected to reach 252,000 by 1990 and 270,000 by 2000.

Immigration to Iceland began in about A.D. 870 and the next 60 years are known in Icelandic history as the Age of Settlements. Nothing is known for certain about the size of the population during the first eight centuries after the Age of Settlements, and estimates range from 60,000 to 100,000. It appears that there was a steady increase in population during the first two or three centuries, but famine and epidemics became more frequent in and after the 13th century. Years are sometimes named after epidemics in Iceland; smallpox usually raged once in a generation and the Plague or Black Death visited Iceland twice—in 1402 and 1495. During the "Little Ice Age" climatic conditions deteriorated, and during the 17th and 18th centuries several famines occurred when the hay crop or the fish crop failed. By 1703, when the nation's first census was taken, the population had declined to 50,358. Soon after the census, the worst smallpox epidemic in the country's history took the lives of 8,000 people, bringing the population down to about 43,000. It did not exceed 50,000 again until the 19th century. Despite adverse living conditions throughout most of the 19th century, the population began to grow at last. The last years with more deaths than births were 1882–83 when measles raged. The last epidemic to curtail the population was the Spanish influenza in 1938 and the last smallpox epidemic in 1839. The import of grains has prevented the incidence of famines in this century.

Emigration was insignificant for many centuries until the 1870s, when emigration to America began. However, during the 20th century, emigrants have exceeded immigrants by only a small number.

Iceland is the most sparsely populated country in Europe, with a density of 2.3 inhabitants per sq. km. (6 inhabitants per sq. mi.), but since more than one-third of the nation lives in the capital, the rest of the country has an even lower density. This is a consequence of the fact that nearly four-fifths of Iceland is uninhabitable. Habitation is restricted to areas below the 200-m. (656-ft.) contour line. Urbanization also has led to greater disparities in regional populations as the center of population moved closer to Reykjavik.

Urban localities did not develop until the 19th century. The early fishing villages had some urban characteristics but could not be described as true towns. Reykjavik became a town in 1786 with a mere 302 inhabitants. Simultaneously, more harbors began to develop as towns. It was not until 1930 that, with the development of mechanized agriculture, towns began to develop in the interior. Thus the change from an entirely rural population to a predominantly urban population took place within less than 100 years. This transition was accompanied by the virtual disappearance of farming communities, especially in the West Peninsula, as well as in the North and East. A reversal of this process began in the late 1970s. Reykjavik's share of the national population, estimated at 41% from 1954 through 1973, has declined since to 35%.

Iceland had a female majority through most of recorded history. The sea took a big toll of the male fishermen, and of the infants, more girls than boys managed to survive. However, during the past 100 years the males have been gaining, and sex parity was achieved during the 1950s. In more recent years there has been a slight male surplus.

The age composition underwent frequent changes until this century. The annual number of births ranged from 2,200 to 2,800 from 1901 through 1941; the rate rose steeply, to 4,000 in 1950 and to 4,900 in 1960, and it has remained in that range since. More recent age composition has been affected by the declining death rate and increased emigration of younger adults. During the 10 years from 1974 to 1984, when the population rose by 11%, the number of children under 15 actually declined by 4%. The growth of the 15 to 24 age group was 5%, that of the 40 to 64 age group 10% and that the 65 to 84 age group 18%, while the number of people age 85 or over grew by 90%.

Consensual marriage remains the traditional norm in Iceland. It represents a throwback to earlier times, when only a minority lived together in formal bonds of matrimony. Between 1974 and 1984, the proportion of marrieds among 25-year-olds fell from 61% to 30% for men and from 75% to 44% for women. As a result, Iceland has one of the highest illegitimacy rates in Europe. Most young people do not care for religious or civil sanctions for their cohabitation. Of the firstborn children, about two-fifths are born to married couples, two-fifths to single mothers and one-fifth to consensual marriage partners. Both infant and adult mortality rates have dropped significantly during this century; as a result, life expectancy rates for both men and women are as high as in other Scandinavian countries.

Emigration was not a significant demographic phenomenon except from 1870 to 1914, when over 10,000 Icelanders settled in Canada or the United States. Emigration spurted again to a record high from 1968 to 1970, when over 1% of the population left the country, this time to Australia or elsewhere in Scandinavia. Some of these emigrants returned to Iceland during the 1970s.

By 1984 the Icelandic birth rate was reduced to the replacement level. If the trend remains, the population would become stationary at 335,000 by the middle of the 21st century. This population would have birth and death rates of 13 per 1,000. Children under 15 would constitute only 19% of the total population, while those over 60 would constitute 24%. No information is available regarding birth control activities or official birth control policies in Iceland.

DEMOGRAPHIC INDICATORS, 1986

Population: 246,526 (1988)
Year of last census: 1983
 Sex ratio: male, 50.24; female, 49.76
Population trends (000)

1930: 109	1960: 177	1990: 252
1940: 121	1970: 204	2000: 270
1950: 144	1980: 229	

 Population doubling time in years at current rate: 76
 Hypothetical size of stationary population (million):
    N.A.
 Assumed year of reaching net reproduction rate of 1:
    N.A.
 Age profile (%)

| 0–14: 25.5 | 30–44: 20.8 | 60–74: 9.9 |
| 15–29: 26.1 | 45–59: 13.2 | Over 75: 4.5 |

Median age (years): 30.5
Density per sq. km. (per sq. mi.): 2.4 (6.2)
Annual growth rate (%)

1950–55: 2.0	1975–80: 1.07	1995–2000: 0.62
1960–65: 1.74	1980–85: 0.99	2000–05: 0.53
1965–70: 1.22	1985–90: 0.86	2005–15: 0.36
1970–75: 1.32	1990–95: 0.72	2020–25: 0.17

Vital statistics
 Crude birth rate, 1/1000: 16
 Crude death rate, 1/1000: 6.9
 Change in birth rate, 1973–83 (%): N.A.
 Change in death rate, 1973–83 (%): N.A.
 Dependency, total: 50.7
 Infant mortality rate, 1/1000: 5.7
 Child (0–4 years) mortality rate, 1/1000: insignificant
 Maternal mortality rate, 1/100,000: 0.0
 Natural increase, 1/1000: 9.1

DEMOGRAPHIC INDICATORS, 1986 *(continued)*

Total fertility rate: 1.9
General fertility rate: 6.2
Gross reproduction rate: 0.92
Marriage rate, 1/1000: 5.2
Divorce rate, 1/1000: 2.2
Life expectancy, males (years): 74.9
Life expectancy, females (years): 80.2
Average household size: 3.3
% ilegitimate births: 48
Youth
 Youth population 15–24 (000): 42
 Youth population in 2000 (000): 40
Women
 Of childbearing age 15–49 (000): 66
 Child-woman ratio: 328 per 100 women
 % women using contraception: N.A.
 % women married 15–49: N.A.
Urban
 Urban population (000): 229
 % urban 1986: 89.7
 Annual urban growth rate (%)
 1965–70: 1.7   1985–90: 1.1
 % urban population in largest city: 35
 % urban population in cities over 500,000: —
 Number of cities over 500,000: —
 Annual rural growth rate: –1.3%

Population, 1703–1984*

Year	Population	Year	Population
1703	50,358	1860	66,987
1734	43,400†	1870	69,763
1751	48,800†	1880	72,445
1755	48,300†	1890	70,927
1759	42,800†	1901	78,470
1762	44,845	1910	85,183
1769	46,201	1920	94,690
1778	49,900†	1930	108,861
1783	48,900†	1940	121,474
1785	40,623	1950	143,973
1786	38,400†	1960	177,292
1801	47,240	1965	193,758
1811	48,800†	1970	204,578
1823	50,100†	1975	219,033
1835	56,035	1980	229,187
1850	59,157	1984	240,443

* 1703–1950 according to census results and estimates.

† 1955–84 as of December 1 according to the National Registry.

ETHNIC COMPOSITION

The population is entirely Icelandic, descended from the original settlers who came chiefly from Norway in the late 9th and early 10th centuries, with a mixture of Scots and Irish. Information on the early settlers is given in the Landnamabok (Book of Settlements); believed to have been compiled in the 12th century. According to this source, the great majority of settlers came from western Norway and some from other parts of Scandinavia. A sizable number arrived from the Celtic areas of the British Isles, some of them slaves of free settlers. Blood group investigations show a close similarity between the Irish and the Icelandic peoples.

Less than 1% of the inhabitants are foreign-born, most elsewhere in Scandinavia.

LANGUAGE

The official language is Icelandic, derived from the Old Norse that was spoken by the 10th-century settlers. It has changed little through the centuries because of the country's isolation and because of the strength of the country's literary heritage.

The Nordic language group to which Icelandic belongs is characterized by a number of linguistic innovations that occurred mainly from A.D. 400 to 800. Among these are certain manifestations of the umlaut and breaking. From the ninth century onward, the Nordic language began to split in two: East Nordic, comprising Swedish and Danish; and West Nordic, comprising Norwegian, Icelandic and Faeroese. From the end of the 10th century Icelandic began to evolve separately from Norwegian but did not become markedly different until the 14th century. As Norwegian changed, Icelandic became increasingly resistant to change. The first Icelandic grammars appeared in the 12th century, although the first printed grammar was published only in 1651. The earliest dictionary, *Specimen Lexirunici*, based on a glossary of Old Icelandic by Magnus Olafsson, was published in 1650.

The basic vocabulary of Old Icelandic consisted of words inherited from Norwegian, and most of them have been preserved to this day in their pure form. The only genuine loanwords were Celtic. The introduction of Christianity marked a turning point. In its wake, the language was enriched by neologisms of all kinds. It also brought the Latin alphabet and the arts of reading and writing. The Reformation, together with the introduction of printing, marked another turning point. In the earliest Icelandic Bible and other religious literature, considerable foreign influence is evident, especially from Low German through Danish mediation. In the following centuries Danish influence became more and more prominent, both in vocabulary and style. After the establishment of a Danish trade monopoly in 1602, Danish virtually displaced Icelandic in the capital, Reykjavik. But it did not penetrate the everyday language of the common people outside of Reykjavik. During the 18th and 19th centuries, spurred by the so-called National Awakening, a nationalist movement, Icelandic reasserted itself with the help of language purists who waged successful campaigns against both Danishisms and Germanisms.

Although Icelandic is a remarkably uniform language, there are geographical dialectal differences. Thus, for instance, a tomcat is called *hogni* in the North, *steggur* in the West and *fress* in the South and East. Some words are peculiar to certain regions. Certain dialectal differences also exist in the grammar. But the most notable differences are in pronunciation. An interesting feature is that all dialects, both standard and substandard, enjoy the same social reputation and are considered equally good and correct.

Until the 20th century the government was not concerned with matters of language and generally kept away from the Purist Movement, a movement to keep Icelandic pure from Danish influence. The first direct official intervention in this area was in 1913, when the Personal Names Act and the Farm Names Act were passed. The former was amended in 1925, when the adoption of new family names was declared illegal. The earliest official orthography prescribed by government regulations dates from 1918. It was replaced by a new statutory orthography in 1929 and was revised again in 1973. The 1973 law abolished the use of the letter z except in marginal cases and laid down the first official rules of punctuation. The first official lexicographic effort was the establishment of the Dictionary Committee of the University of Iceland in 1951. This was followed for a brief period by the informal New Words Committee until the Icelandic Language Committee was formally founded in 1965 by ministerial decree.

RELIGION

The national church is the Evangelical Lutheran Church according to the Constitution. The church, however, plays only only a muted role in national life, although statistically it is the home church for 90% of the population. There are no significant religious minorities in Iceland.

Iceland was converted to Christianity in the year 1000, about 130 years after the initial settlement. The Christian religion was adopted by an act of the Althing (Parliament) as a result of missionary activity by Norwegian evangelists. Some of the early settlers were Christians, and the first known inhabitants of the country were Irish monks. Two bishoprics were established: one in the South in 1066, the other in the North in 1106. From then until the end of the Middle Ages, the church dominated the cultural and political life of the country. Monasteries played an important role in the creation of Iceland's rich medieval literature. The foundation of church power was the Tithe Law of 1096, which secured the church an extensive economic base. Through the church Icelandic culture became internationalized via wandering clerics and monks.

The Reformation represented the culmination of a political as well as a religious struggle. The last Roman Catholic bishop, Jon Arason, was beheaded in 1550, signalizing the Protestant ascendancy. Although Arason became a symbol of Icelandic nationalism, the new Protestant doctrines found ready acceptance among the intelligentsia. The new translation of the Icelandic Bible, printed in Iceland by Bishop Guobrandur Porlaksson at Holar in 1584, is still cherished as an outstanding monument of Icelandic prose. The Bible also became the wellspring of the indigenous Icelandic culture. Among the other masterpieces of Icelandic religious literature of this period are the Passion Hymns of Hallgrimur Petursson (1614–74).

During the bleak and pestilential centuries until 1900, the religious tradition achieved a unity and strength never surpassed. With the introduction of Pietism in the 1740s, the practice of regular religious exercises on the farms became universal. Apart from regular church attendance, prayers were said daily together with reading and singing, particularly during Lent. On Sundays, the sermon of the day was read to those unable to attend church from the collection of Jon Vidalin, first printed in 1718. The churches of the period were mostly small and made of turf and stone, with interiors decorated with primitive art.

In spite of the common reading of religious literature, the Bible was little known. The numerous issues of the Bible from 1584 to 1747 were far too expensive for the common man. It was not until 1813, when the British and the Foreign Bible Society printed and distributed 5,000 copies, that the Bible became affordable for every Icelander. In the absence of the Bible, the liturgy of the church and the piety of its members were shaped through Guobrandur Porlaksson's Graduale, a service book and hymnbook that was the companion of every churchgoer. Its music was of medieval ecclesiastical song in the ancient modes. When the Graduale was officially replaced in 1801, the quality of the church service declined. Today the congregation remains passive while the choir sings the responses and the hymns.

Since the 19th century, the decline of the church as a force in national life has been hastened by social and economic as well as demographic changes. There were a few positive developments, such as the establishment of a theological seminary in 1847, new translations of the Bible in 1866 and 1912, new hymnbooks in 1886 and 1972, new laws by the Althing granting congregations greater powers in church government, and the establishment of the YMCA in 1899.

The national church comprises 287 congregations grouped into 15 district assemblies, each supervised by a dean. The supreme authority is the president of the republic, who delegates power to the minister of justice and ecclesiastical affairs. In religious affairs, the church is governed by the bishop of Iceland (since 1802 Iceland has had only one bishop), the Synodical Conference, the Church Assembly and the Executive Council of the Church Assembly.

There is complete religious freedom in Iceland.

HISTORICAL BACKGROUND

Iceland's first settler was Ingolfur Arnarson, who sailed from Norway to Iceland in 874 and settled in what is now Reykjavik. Others followed in the succeeding centuries, and in 930 a republic was established under the authority of the Althing. In 1263, torn by civil strife, the Althing decided to submit to the rule of Norway by a treaty that established a purely nominal union under the Norwegian crown. In 1381 Iceland passed, together with Norway, under the rule of the king of Denmark and remained so after Norway was separated from Denmark in 1814. Gradually Iceland lost much of its former autonomy. Exclusive trading rights were given in 1602 to a private Danish trading company, and Danes had a complete monopoly of trade with Iceland until 1786. The ensuing economic ruin was compounded by epidemics and volcanic eruptions, particularly that of 1783, which reduced the population to 38,400 by 1786, half of the number before the union. In 1800 the Danish king abolished the Althing. After a long constitutional struggle, the Althing was reestablished as an advisory body in 1843, limited home rule was granted in 1874 and complete home rule was given in 1903. In 1918 Iceland was declared a free and independent state linked to the Danish king as head of state and with complete autonomy except in foreign affairs. During World War II, cut off from Denmark (which was under German occupation), Iceland assumed control over its defense and foreign affairs. In a referendum held in 1944, over 97% of those participating voted to end the union with the crown of Denmark, and Iceland was declared an independent republic in that year.

CONSTITUTION & GOVERNMENT

According to historical records, chiefly the *Islendingabok*, a state organization was set up in Iceland in about A.D. 930, at the end of the so-called Settlement Period. In the same year a legal and uniform code was promulgated, and the Althing was established. The code presumably was based on the laws in force in western and central Norway but was not committed to writing. Shortly thereafter, an ecclesiastical code was enacted. The laws of this period, known as the

Free State Period, are found in two 13th century manuscripts, commonly called *Gragas* (Dragon). *Gragas* describe at length the constitutional system of the Free State. Unlike all other states of the time, no king or other dignitary held supreme political or administrative power, which was vested in the 39 *godar* who served as local leaders or chieftains. Assemblies were held both locally and nationally. There existed 13 local *things*, each under the superintendence of three *godar*. The national assembly, or the Althing met for two weeks each summer at Thingvellir, 50 km. (31 mi.) east of Reykjavik, and performed both legislative and judicial functions.

Legislative power also was exercised by the Logretta, a council on which the 39 *godar* held seats together with nine titular *godar*; the two bishops; and an elected president, the *logsogumadur*. In addition, 96 advisers to the *godar* had a place in the Logretta. The judicial power of the Althing was vested in five courts, of which four were regional courts of middle instance and the fifth a supreme court. Judges were appointed by a *godar*. Outside the *things* there were local units called *hreppar* charged with the care of paupers, compulsory mutual insurance of houses and livestock, and supervision of communal lands.

When Iceland passed under the rule of Denmark in 1262, these political and judicial institutions were radically altered under the new legal code, known as Jarnsioa. Representatives of the Danish king took over the administration, and a hierarchy of government officials appeared. The Althing survived as an assembly comprised of the representatives of the king, the bishops and the clergy, the chief justices and 84 houseowner-farmers appointed for life. As time passed, the power of the Althing dwindled. A formal assent to the king's absolute power was given in 1662, and by 1700 the Althing had surrendered the last vestiges of its legislative power, although it remained as a judicial body until 1800. By the 16th century, a division of the country into *sýslur* (counties) had emerged, strengthening the authority of the king.

The Althing was reestablished in 1845 as a consultative assembly and granted legislative power in the "special affairs" of Iceland in 1874. The power, however, was subject to royal veto. The executive power remained in the hands of the Danish government. Limited home rule was introduced by constitutional amendment in 1903. This meant the introduction of a parliamentary government with a minister resident in Iceland responsible to the Althing. But home rule was not considered an acceptable solution by Icelanders and, after complicated negotiations, the Act of Union of 1918 was negotiated. By this act Denmark recognized Iceland as a sovereign state in personal union with Denmark. The Act of Union resulted in the new Icelandic Constitution of 1920. The Constitution granted Denmark the right to conduct Iceland's foreign affairs and to guard its territorial waters. Under its terms, the Act of Union could be revised or terminated in 1943. When Denmark was occupied by the Nazis in 1940, the althing seized the opportunity to pass two resolutions: one investing the cabinet with the power of the head of state, and the other declaring that henceforth Iceland would conduct its own foreign affairs. A special regent took over from the cabinet as temporary head of state in 1941. Three years later, on June 17, 1944, the Act of Union was terminated unilaterally, a republic was proclaimed, and a new Constitution was approved in a popular referendum.

The present Constitution dates from the establishment of the republic in 1944. It has been amended three times: in 1959, 1968 and 1984. These amendments are limited in scope, and a thorough revision is being debated. Amendments to the Constitution are introduced in the Althing in the same way as ordinary legislation; if adopted, the Althing is dissolved and a new election is called. The amendment comes into force if adopted again by the new Althing session.

The Constitution consists of 81 articles grouped in seven chapters. The first chapter is a preamble; the other six deal with the president and the cabinet, elections, functions of the Althing, the courts, the state Evangelican Lutheran Church and human rights.

The Constitution defines the powers, status and mode of election of the president who is the head of state. All laws require the signature of the president and the countersignature of a cabinet member. The president is granted veto power and the right to issue decrees when the Althing is not in session. Certain administrative acts also need presidential sanction. These include the opening and termination of sessions of the Althing, dissolution of the Althing, appointment of senior members of the civil service and judiciary and the conclusion of international treaties. Government-sponsored legislation must receive presidential sanction before being placed on the floor of the Althing.

The Constitution provides for the Council of State, presided over by the president and comprising the prime minister and cabinet members. Although placed above politics, the president has played a key role in modern times in cabinet-forming. When no political party has an absolute majority in the Althing, as is invariably the case in recent history, the president chooses the person to be in charge of the negotiations for a coalition, a choice that carries considerable political clout.

The president is elected by direct, popular vote for a term of four years. There is no vice president. When necessary, presidential functions are discharged by a committee of three consisting of the prime minister, the speaker of the Althing and the president of the Supreme Court.

The administration is headed by the prime minister as the head of government, and a cabinet consisting of 13 ministries. The ministers are formally appointed by the president by an act countersigned by the prime minister. There is no election of a new prime minister. As no single party has held a working majority in the Althing for decades, the country is almost always ruled by coalition governments, and sometimes long negotiations have proven necessary before they could be formed. Lack of progress in such negotiations has occasionally led to the appointment of minority cabinets and, in one instance, of a nonpolitical caretaker cabinet. After the ministers have been appointed, a parliamentary vote of confidence is not compulsory. A motion of no confidence may be tabled at any time with respect to the whole cabinet or its individual members. If such a motion is adopted, the cabinet or the minister in question has to resign. The size of the cabinet is not specified in the Constitution but usually there are 10 ministers, some heading more than one ministry.

Cabinet meetings are frequent and are held to discuss new legislative proposals or important political measures, or when a minister so desires. The prime minister presides over such meetings. Neither the Council of State, which meets infrequently, nor the cabinet act on a collegial basis. The minister has the authority to make relevant decisions and to assume responsibility for them. Other ministers, the prime minister and the president usually are informed about acts of political importance and are legally responsible if they do not protest, but they have no de jure power to enjoin a minister from a certain course of action. Political considerations do, of course, set limits as to what individual ministers undertake, but nevertheless they have significant autonomy.

Ministers are, according to the Constitution, *eo ipso* members of the Althing. On the rare occasions when a minister has not been elected a member, he assumes a seat on the ministerial bench with the full rights of a member except for the right to vote.

ORGANIZATION OF ICELANDIC GOVERNMENT

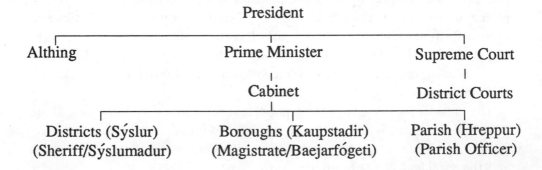

President

Althing   Prime Minister   Supreme Court

                 Cabinet   District Courts

Districts (Sýslur)   Boroughs (Kaupstadir)   Parish (Hreppur)
(Sheriff/Sýslumadur)   (Magistrate/Baejarfógeti) (Parish Officer)

RULERS OF ICELAND (from 1944)

Presidents

June 1944–January 1952:	Sveinn Björnsson
January–August 1952:	Presidential Council: Steingrimur Steinthórsson/ Jón Pálmason/Jón Asbjörnsson
August 1952–August 1968:	Ásgeir Ásgeirsson
August 1968–August 1980:	Kristján Eldjárn
August 1980– :	Vigdis Finnbogadottir

Prime Ministers

December 1944 –February 1947:	Ólafur Thors (Independence Party)
February 1947 –December 1949:	Stefan Stefansson (Social Democratic Party)
December 1949 –March 1950:	Ólafur Thors (Independence Party)
March 1950 –September 1953:	Steingrimur Steinthórsson (Progressive Party)
September 1953–July 1956:	Ólafur Thors (Independence Party)
July 1956–December 1958:	Hermann Jonasson (Progressive Party)
December 1958 –November 1959:	Emil Jónsson (Social Democratic Party)
November 1959 –November 1963:	Ólafur Thors (Independence Party)
November 1963–July 1970:	Bjarni Benediktsson (Independence Party)
July 1970–July 1971:	Johann Hafstein (Independence Party)
July 1971–August 1974:	Ólafur Jóhannesson (Progressive Party)
August 1974–August 1978:	Geir Hallgrimsson (Independence Party)
August 1978 –October 1979:	Ólafur Jóhannesson (Progressive Party)
October 1979 –February 1980:	Benedikt Groendal (Social Democratic Party)
February 1980–May 1983:	Gunnar Thoroddsen (Independence Party)

```
┌─────────────────────────────────────────────────────┐
│          RULERS OF ICELAND (from 1944) (continued)    │
│  May 1983–May 1987:      Steingrimur Hermannsson      │
│                          (Progressive Party)          │
│  May 1987–October 1988:  Thorsteinn Palsson (Inde-    │
│                          pendence Party)              │
│  October 1988– :         Steingrimur Hermannsson      │
└─────────────────────────────────────────────────────┘
```

```
┌─────────────────────────────────────────────────────┐
│                    CABINET LIST                       │
│  President:                  Vigdis Finnbogadóttir    │
│  Prime Minister:             Thorsteinn Palsson       │
│  Minister of Agriculture:    Jon Helgason             │
│  Minister of Commerce:       Jon Sigurdsson           │
│  Minister of Communications: Matthias Mathiesen       │
│  Minister of Education                                │
│  and Culture:                Birgir Isleifur Gunnar-  │
│                              sson                     │
│  Minister of Finance:        Jon Baldvin Hannibal-    │
│                              sson                     │
│  Minister of Fisheries:      Halldór Asgrimsson       │
│  Minister of Foreign Affairs: Steingrimur             │
│                              Hermannsson              │
│  Minister of Health and Social                        │
│    Security:                 Gudmundur Bjarna-        │
│                              son                      │
│  Minister of Industries                               │
│  and Energy:                 Fridrik Sophusson        │
│  Minister of Justice and                              │
│  Ecclesiastical Affairs:     Jon Sigurdsson           │
│  Minister of Social Affairs: Johanna Sigurdardot-     │
│                              tir                      │
│  Chairman, Board of Directors,                        │
│    Central Bank of Iceland:  Jonas G. Rafnar          │
└─────────────────────────────────────────────────────┘
```

FREEDOM & HUMAN RIGHTS

Iceland has an exemplary record in human rights. There is a long-standing respect for the autonomy of individuals. Persons detained are brought before a judge within 24 hours. Defendants are guaranteed the right of free and competent legal counsel if they are indigent. The independence and fairness of the court system is carefully guarded by the Supreme Court. There are no restrictions on civil and political rights. The only human rights violation referred to the European Commission on Human Rights is that raised by a single Icelander who questioned the practice of one traffic official serving as both prosecutor and judge in traffic courts.

Iceland is perhaps the only country in the world with an all-woman political party, the Women's Alliance. In 1987 it captured 10.1% of the popular vote and 10% of the seats in the Althing. The head of state is a woman. Nevertheless, women continue to be underrepresented in all areas of national life.

CIVIL SERVICE

Under the direction of the cabinet minister, each ministry is headed by a secretary-general or permanent under secretary, who always is a civil servant. Under him there is a deputy and several divisional chiefs. In two ministries the divisions are grouped into so-called offices, each headed by deputy under secretary. A divisional chief may be politically appointed to work on special assignments, but he leaves his post when the minister who appointed him resigns. The number of ministries and the subjects handled by them are regulated by Central Administration Act of 1969.

The structure of the administration below the level of the ministries has been built up over a long period and varies from one sector to another. There are a number of central agencies and institutions, of which the oldest are the Bishop's Office and the National Bureau of Public Health. Both are supervisory bodies. Other agencies and institutions, such as the Public Road Administration and the State Social Security Institute, are directly engaged in administering state programs. A few institutions, such as the Agricultural Society and the Fisheries Association are quasi official. A number of state-owned corporations fall outside the administrative structure as generally defined. These include the Central Bank, the three state-owned commercial banks and certain other business enterprises.

Most administrative authorities also operate on the local level distinct from organs of local government. The state administrative divisions do not correspond entirely to local government divisions. The authority of cabinet ministers over such local bodies is not absolute. For example, members of local administrative boards or committees are elected by the Althing and do not answer to central government officials.

LOCAL GOVERNMENT

For administrative purposes Iceland is divided into 18 districts or provinces *(sýslur)* and 23 towns or boroughs *(kaupstadir)*, headed by a sheriffs *(sýslumadur)* in a district and a magistrate *(baejarfógeti)* in a borough. In Reykjavik the duties of a magistrate are divided among several officials. In some cases the same person serves as the sheriff and magistrate in a district and a borough. Borough magistrates are assisted by a town council made up of one representative from each parish *(hreppur)*. Each parish also has its own council and administrative officers. Town councils are elected by proportional representation and rural councils by a simple majority.

The legal basis of local government is Article 76 of the Constitution, which grants local authorities the right to manage their own affairs. Other legislation relating to local government includes the Local Government Act of 1961 and the Local Finance Act of 1983.

The present system of local government was established by a royal decree in 1972 and distinguishes three levels: 23 municipalities, 200 rural districts and 18 provinces. There is wide disparity in the population of the various local units. Some rural districts have populations of under 50 inhabitants, and 160 of the least populated districts account for only 10% of the national population.

The scope of local authority is defined in the Local Government Act. Local authorities can engage in any activity or service not prohibited by law or by the central government. Many engage in private enterprises, such as fishing.

In the towns a town manager is elected and appointed by the council. If elected, his legal status is that a mayor; if appointed, it is that of town manager. Committees play a major role in deciding policies and programs.

The scope of local authority activities covers statutory functions such as social welfare, health, education, sanitation and road construction but may expand into areas such as bus transportation, land use, fire service, libraries, museums, sports, garbage collection and traffic. In coastal municipalities, the local authorities are responsible for maintenance of harbors and fishing vessels, and in rural districts for inspection of livestock and other matters relating to farming. In all units, they are responsible for fostering employment by operating small or medium-size commercial enterprises.

Under the Local Government Act, local government revenues are derived from two sources: direct local taxation, consisting of personal income tax, real estate tax and local operation tax; and general or special central government grants. Total municipal expenditures as a proportion of the GNP has risen in recent years, from 5.3% in 1950 to 7.5% in 1980. Of the expenditures, 18% goes to social welfare, 17% to education and 10% to public health.

Central government control over local authorities is exercised by the minister of social affairs. Usually he delegates much of this task to the regional supervisory councils, presided over by the county sheriff.

The great number of small rural districts has led to frequent attempts to amalgamate them, so far unsuccessfully. For a number of years the Althing has been considering without taking any action proposals for a new Local Government Act.

AREA AND POPULATION

Regions Counties*	Adminis- trative centers	Area sq. mi.	Area sq. km.	Popu- lation 1984 estimate
Austurland		8,683	22,490	13,100
Austur- Skaftafel- lssýsla	Höfn	2,347	6,080	2,300
Nordhur- Múlasýsla	Seydhisfjödhur	4,799	12,430	3,300
Sudhur- Múlasýsla	Eskifjördhur	1,537	3,980	7,500
Nordhurland eystra		8,370	21,680	26,200†
Eyjafjardhar- sýsla	Akureyri	1,602	4,150	19,000
Nordhur- Thingey- jarsýsla	Húsavik	2,077	5,380	1,700
Sudhur- Thingey- jarsýsla	Húsavik	4,691	12,150	5,400
Nordhurland vestra		4,973	12,880	10,700†
Austur- Húnavatns- sýsla	Blönduós	1,900	4,920	2,600
Skagafjard- harsýsla	Saudhárkrókur	2,077	5,380	6,500
Vestur- Húnavatns- sýsla	Blöduós	996	2,580	1,500
Rekjavíkursvaedhi og Reykjanes- svaedhi		741	1,920	142,600
Gullbrin- gusýsla	Keflavík	405	1,050	32,600
Kjósarsýsla	Hafnarfjördhur	336	870	110,000
Sudhurland		9,649	24,990	20,100
Árnessýsla	Selfoss	3,401	8,810	10,400
Rangárval- lasýsla	Hvolsvõllur	3,197	8,280	8,300
Vestur- Skafta- fellssýsla	Vik	3,050	7,900	1,300
Vestfirdhir		3,676	9,520	10,400

AREA AND POPULATION *(continued)*				
Austur-Bardhastran-darsýsla	Patreks-fjördhur	444	1,150	400
Nordhur-Isafjard-harsýsla	Isafjördhur	1,181	3,060	5,200
Strandasýsla	Hólmavik	1,015	2,630	1,100
Vestur-Bardhas-trandarsýsla	Paterks-fjördhur	598	1,550	2,000
Vestur-Ísafjard-harsýsla	Ísafjördhur	436	1,130	1,700
Vesturland		3,676	9,520	15,100
Borgarfjard-harsýsla	Borgarnes	753	1,950	6,800
Dalasýsla	Budhardalur	815	2,110	1,100
Mýrasýsla	Borgarnes	1,262	3,270	2,600
Snaefellsnes-sýsla	Stykkishólmur	846	2,190	4,600
TOTAL		39,768	103,000	238,200

FOREIGN POLICY

The Ministry of Foreign Affairs was established in 1941, three years before the full establishment of the Republic of Iceland in 1944. In 1971 the Althing passed a new law regarding foreign service that updated many of the provisions of the 1941 act on the ministry. At present Iceland maintains embassies in nine countries, although ambassadors are accredited to 60 countries.

European cooperation plays a central role in the country's foreign policy. Nordic ties also are important and are strengthened by Iceland's membership in the Nordic Council. Iceland also was one of the founding members of NATO, The Council of Europe and the Organization of European Economic Cooperation (OEEC). Iceland became a member of the United Nations in 1946.

For a country whose economy is heavily dependent on fisheries, the conservation of the overexploited fishing grounds is a key concern. In 1948 the Althing extended the national fishing limits, which now are maintained at 322 km. (200 mi.). This act triggered a series of conflicts with neighboring countries, known in diplomatic history as the "cod wars." The first cod war resulted from the proclamation of a 19-km. (12-mi.) limit in 1958 and was terminated by agreements with Great Britain, Ireland and West Germany in 1961. A second period of hostilities followed the proclamation of an 80-km. (50-mi.) limit in 1961 and was ended by a temporary agreement with Great Britain in the same year. In 1975 a third cod war erupted following Iceland's extension of the limit to 322 km. despite an adverse ruling on the 80 mi. limit by the International Court of Justice at The Hague. In 1980 an agreement was concluded with Norway on fishing in overlapping 322-km. fishery zones.

Historically opposed to the establishment of an indigenous military force, Iceland announced in 1973 its intention to close the United States-maintained NATO base at Keflavik. The decision was rescinded in 1974 by the conservative Hallgrimsson coalition. In 1985 the government announced that it planned to set up an Office of Defense.

PARLIAMENT

The national parliament is the Althing, one of the oldest legislatures in the world, dating back to A.D. 930. It is a bicameral body of 63 members elected for a four-year term by a mixed system of proportional and direct representation. The members elect one-third of their number to constitute the Upper Chamber (Efri Deild), while the remainder make up the Lower Chamber (Nedri Deild).

New rules were enacted in 1984 on elections to the Althing. According to these rules: the voting age is fixed at 18. In addition, the country is divided into eight constituencies. Of 62 of the seats, 54 are distributed according to proportional representation as follows: Reykjavik, 14; Reykjanes, eight; and five or six to each of the remaining six constituencies. From the nine seats that are left, eight are divided beforehand among the constituencies according to the number of registered voters in the previous election. Finally, one seat is given to a constituency after the election to compensate the party with the fewest seats in relation to its number of votes.

Party seats are allocated on the following basis: First, 75% of the seats are awarded in proportion to each party's share of the votes in the constituency itself, but only if it has captured at least 7% of the votes there. The remaining seats are distributed among the parties according to a formula that aims at equitable representation in the Althing. Finally, the seats allotted to each party are given to candidates according to the number of votes gained by each of them for the seat in question. The votes for each seat are counted separately. Thus the place of the candidate on the party list determines his selection, except in cases where the voters have struck his name from the ballot.

These rules reflect a compromise between the traditional rural constituencies and the two urban ones of Reykjavik and Reykjanes. They have prevented any one party from dominating the political landscape in recent years.

In each constituency the unsuccessful candidate becomes the alternate member of the Althing. They take a seat there if the regular member in unable to sit for two weeks or more.

Both chambers of the Althing sometimes sit as one chamber, the United Althing and sometimes as two chambers. The United Althing considers and approves the budget and most draft resolutions. A bill may be tabled in either chamber and has to pass three readings before it is sent to the president for signature. If the two chambers fail to agree, three more readings are required, the last of these in the United Althing. If a draft statute is rejected by a simple majority, it cannot be tabled again in the same session. Should a draft reach a ninth reading (something that has not happened for many years), two-thirds of the votes become necessary for its approval.

An important part of parliamentary work takes place in committees. A draft statute is almost always sent to a standing committee for review, which usually happens after the first reading in either chamber. Draft resolutions normally are also received by one of the standing committees of the United Althing. The committees submit written comments on the issues sent to them. In each of the two houses, there are nine standing committees, dealing with finance and trade, communications, agriculture, fishing, industry, local government and social affairs, health and welfare, education, and general affairs. The United Althing has a credentials committee, which deals with remuneration of Althing members, and four committees concerned with finance, foreign affairs, economic affairs and general affairs, respectively. The first two are considered so important that they are required to be active between sessions as well.

Regular sessions of the Althing begin on October 10 and usually end in April or May. Meetings are held between Monday and Thursday each week, and the remaining days are set aside for constituency work. In an average session the United Althing holds 87 meetings, the Nedri Deild 104 and the Efri Deild 94. The average number of bills per session is 170, of which 97 are proposed by the cabinet and 73 by individual members. The average sessional output consists of 85 statutes approved (81% tabled by the cabinet), 26 resolutions approved, and 80 questions answered by a cabinet member.

The party groups in the Althing meet regularly—as a rule at least twice a week during the sessions, but only infrequently between sessions. The parliamentary party meetings are attended by other party leaders on a relatively regular basis. The party groups enjoy legal status, which governs the allocation of time in certain debates, especially those that are broadcast. Party discipline is fairly strict, as reflected in voting patterns.

ALTHING ELECTION RESULTS, 1987		
Party	% of Votes	Seats
Independence Party	27.2	18
Progressive Party	18.9	13
Social Democratic Party	15.2	10
People's Alliance	13.3	9
Citizens' Party	10.9	7
Women's Alliance	10.1	6
Others	4.4	1*
Total	100.0	63

* Independent member elected with 1.2% of the total votes.

POLITICAL PARTIES

The foundations of the present-day political party system were established by 1930, when the major parties had already been established. The introduction of the universal franchise in 1915 had led to the formation of political groups covering the entire gamut of the ideological spectrum. The Labor Party became the first to achieve a nationwide organization, as it was founded by people outside the Althing intent on gaining seats in there. The Progressives and the Independents, on the other hand, started out as parliamentary groups. Rules of association for the Progressive Party on a national basis were not introduced until 1933 and for the Independence Party not until 1936. As in other countries, a number of small short-lived and issue-oriented parties have appeared on the stage periodically, but these generally have resulted from splits within the major parties.

The four major Icelandic parties are commonly ranked from right to left as the Independence Party, the Progressive Party, the Social Democratic Party and the People's Alliance. Two minor parties that hold seats in the current Althing are the Social Democratic Alliance and the Women's Alliance, both founded in 1983.

The Independence Party (IP, Sjalfstaedisflokkurinn) was founded in 1929 through a merger of the Conservative Party (founded in 1924) and the Liberal Party (founded in 1926). It has remained the largest party in the country, usually polling about 40% of the votes. Until 1942 the IP was in opposition, but the electoral reform of that year enabled it to capture more seats, and since that time it has contributed four prime ministers: Ólafur Thors (1942, 1944–47, 1953–56 and 1959–63), Bjarni Benediktsson (1963–1970), Johann Hafstein (1970–71) and Geir Hallgrimsson (1974–78). Compared to its socialist rivals, the IP displays considerable homogeneity despite the disparate groups that constitute its core. Nevertheless, the party suffered a serious breach in 1980 when its deputy leader, Gunnar Thoroddsen, formed a coalition government, leaving the bulk of the party in opposition. With the retirement of Thoroddsen in 1983, party unity was restored.

The IP is the best-organized party in Iceland in terms of electoral machinery and breadth of constituency. It combined strong leadership with remarkable tolerance in party discipline. Rarely have IP members been expelled for breach of discipline. It is strongest in urban areas but also has a strong following in rural districts. It is supported by and has close connections with *Morganbladid*, Iceland's largest daily.

Although conservative by historical tradition, the IP does not oppose the welfare state and economic planning. The party's ideology, labeled "social liberalism" is characterized by pragmatism. It has maintained a prolabor image and thus has succeed in not alienating the working class. The younger IP members, however, favor a more aggressive free-market approach. In foreign policy the IP is a consistent supporter of NATO and its Western allies.

The IP claims about 25,000 members, drawn from both white- and blue-collar workers. In fact, about one-fourth of the delegates to recent conventions of the Icelandic Federation of Labor have been IP supporters. The party is strongest in the capital, where it attracts 45% of its national vote, and weakest in the East, where the relative percentage is only 20%.

The People's Alliance (PA, Althydubandalagid) is descended from the Communist Party and breakaway groups from the Social Democratic Party (SDP). The Communist Party was founded in 1930 by radical SDP members and won its first seat in the Althing in 1937 with 8.5% of the vote. When the SDP refused to join it in a popular front, the left wing of the SDP broke off and joined the Communists to form the United Socialist Party (USP). In its first elections, in 1942, the USP polled 16.2% of the vote, more than the SDP. The USP participated in the IP-SDP-USP coalition from 1943 to 1947. In 1956, after another split in the SDP, the PA was created as a loose electoral alliance between the USP and the dissident SDP members. It was a member of the coalition government from 1956 to 1958. After a decade in political wilderness, the PA re-created itself as a formal political party in 1968, and the USP was dissolved. The PA took part in the governing coalitions of 1971–74, 1978–79 and 1980–83, but it has never held the key portfolios of prime minister, foreign affairs or justice. The 1968 reorganization led to a serious split in PA ranks; dissidents then formed the now-defunct Union of Liberals and Leftists.

The PA is not formally a Communist Party and steers clear of orthodox Leninism in economic matters. Nevertheless, its core is strongly socialist, with a sprinkling of environmentalists and anti-establishment intellectuals. Not surprisingly, it advocates public ownership of all major private enterprises while rejecting the Soviet style of economic centralization. In foreign policy the PA opposes NATO and the U.S. military presence at Keflavik. On the other hand, it has proved its independence by opposing the Soviet invasions of Czechoslovakia and Afghanistan and the violations of human rights in Eastern Europe.

The PA is stronger in urban than in rural areas. Although it has only 3,000 card-carrying members, it has a better national coverage than the SDP in both voting support and local organization.

The Progressive Party (PP, Framsoknarflokkurinn) was founded as a parliamentary party in 1916. In its early years it was almost exclusively a farmers' party, with close ties to the cooperative movement. Polling about 25% of the vote in national elections, the PP is Iceland's second-largest party. Before the electoral reforms of 1942, the PP was the "natural party of government," dominating all coalition governments from 1917 to 1942 (except 1924–27) and held the premiership from 1927 to 1942. Although the PP has lost its dominant role, it has headed four coalitions since the end of World War II.

The PP has about 105 local branches and a women's wing. It publishes a national daily, *Timinn*. Historically a centrist farmers' party, the PP has over the years broadened its appeal as the party of the "middle ground." It supports a mixed economy and emphasizes state-sponsored rural development. In foreign policy the PP supports NATO but falls short of approving the U.S. military base at Keflavik.

In its early years, as an exclusively agrarian party, the PP did not even run candidates in urban areas. Despite some urban penetration in recent years, the PP remains weak in the towns, polling only 14% to 18% in these areas compared to 30% to 50% in rural areas. Despite its electoral weakness, the PP has been continuously in government since 1971.

The Social Democratic Party (SDP, Althyduflokkurinn) was founded in 1916 as the political arm of the labor movement. Until 1942 it had close organizational ties with the Icelandic Federation of Labor. As Iceland's first mass party, its early years were impressive, gaining 20% of the vote in the 1934 elections. As a result of major party schisms, the party began to lose ground since then and is now the smallest of the four major parties, polling an average of 14% to 16% of the vote. The SDP first joined a coalition government in 1934 after having supported the PP government from 1927 to 1931. The SDP has been in government for almost two-thirds of the years since then, holding the prime ministership (Stefan Stefansson, 1947–49) and minority representation in two cabinets (Emil Jónsson, 1958–59 and Benedikt Groendal, 1979–80). Its ideological flexibility is demonstrated by its partnership with the conservative IP from 1959 to 1971. After a short decline in its fortunes in 1971 and 1974, the party returned with a triumphant electoral victory in 1978, when its share of the vote increased from 9.1% to 22%.

The SDP is a member of the Socialist International and has both youth and women's wings. Its very democratic organizational structure has spawned numerous splits and frequent ousters of party leaders. In 1975 the SDP added a clause in its constitution making open primaries compulsory before every Althing election.

The SDP is more centrist than other European social democratic parties and deemphasizes class struggle and nationalization in favor of a mixed economy and a welfare state. As a result, the SDP has lost its left wing three times in its history. In 1978, the year in which it won a stunning electoral victory, the SDP refurbished its waning socialist image with the slogan "A New Party on an Old Base" and supported various populist causes. In foreign policy the SDP is closer to the IP, supporting both NATO and the U.S. base at Keflavik, despite flak from its youth wing.

The SDP claims about 5,000 members, drawn mostly from urban workers. The party has never been able to win a good following in the rural districts.

Minor parties have had only fugitive success in Icelandic politics. The two that hold seats in the post-1987 Althing are the Women's Alliance and the Social Democratic Alliance, which together gained 21% of the vote. Both were founded in 1983. Their success is attributed to protest votes rather than a shifting of political loyalties. There are no illegal political parties or known terrorist groups in Iceland.

ECONOMY

Iceland has a free-enterprise economy with a dominant private sector.

For almost two decades Iceland has been faced with the serious problems of inflation and an endemic external deficit. Consumer prices rose on an average of 35% annually in the 1970s. Exogenous factors related to fluctuations in terms of trade, sluggish export demand and a depleted fish catch played a role in promoting the inflationary process. Internally, inflation was fueled by a wage indexation system and exchange rate depreciation. The coalition government that took office in 1983 made a dertermined effort to break the wage-price spiral. They embraced an incomes policy, limiting wage increases to 8% in June and 4% in October and suspending wage indexation until 1985. This was combined with a policy of exchange rate stability following an initial 15% devaluation of the krona. These measures were accompanied by Social Security and tax changes intended to mitigate their effects on living standards. In the second phase of this program, the incomes policy was phased out from 1984 and monetary policy was to be tightened. As a more general aim, the government declared its intention to establish a framework of decentralized decision-making through financial and economic deregulation.

Indexation of wages has a long history in Iceland. Over the years reforms have aimed at its modification, particularly through removal of certain price changes from the index. These reforms culminated in the Economic Management Act of 1979, which provided for proportional wage indexation at three-month intervals based on the Cost of Living Index. It excluded the effects of changes in the terms of trade resulting from higher import prices, the prices of alcohol and tobacco and the wage component of the publicly administered domestic farm prices. The legislation was not binding. It allowed unions and employers to agree on other terms of indexation through collective bargaining. By 1983 indexation threatened to generate an annual inflation rate of 130% to 140%. Mounting bankruptcies and a shortfall in fish catches in 1983 added to the economy's problems. Deindexation therefore became a priority in the government's economic policy.

The initial incomes policy phase of the counterinflation program was successful. The inflation rate had been brought down to 15% by the third quarter of 1984. The pace of nominal wage increases had decelerated to 7% by the same period.

However, following a public sector strike in October 1984, wage settlements were agreed that granted a wage rise of 25% to the end of 1985. This settlement immediately resulted in a 12% devaluation of the krona, pushing the Cost of Living Index up by 29%. As a result, the Wage Index rose at an annualized rate of 50% in the closing months of 1984.

The government's new economic strategies were implemented against the background of a supply shock caused by a fall in marine production in 1982 and 1983. The favorable growth performance of the 1970s, when the GNP rose by an annual rate of 4% in real terms, gave way to a more modest growth rate in the early 1980s as the amount of the fish catch (which contributes between 15% and 20% of the GNP) stagnated. The dramatic drop in the fish catch led to a fall in the GNP. A ban on capelin (a low-value fish used for fish meal and oil) fishing was enforced in 1983. The more valuable cod catch declined from a peak of 461,000 tons in 1981 to 294,000 tons in 1983 and 281,000 tons in 1984. In overall tonnage, the 1984 catch represented a recovery to 1981 levels.

The year 1984 marked an upturn for the hard-pressed economy. Domestic demand continued to be vigorous: Real consumption increased by 3% and investment by 7% over the 1983 levels. Accumulating fish stocks (as a result of a larger catch of capelin) contributed to the strength of the total domestic demand. The improvement in the fish catch raised the total export production by

11.25%. The output of the manufacturing and construction sectors also recovered significantly.

The recorded current account deficit narrowed from 10% of the GNP in 1982 to 2.25% of it in 1983 but deteriorated again in 1984, particularly as a result of a 12% rise in merchandise imports and stiffer export competition. In response, the government devalued the krona again, by 3%. With a further worsening of the service account, the current external deficit widened to $130 million, or 6% of the GNP.

A major contributing factor has been the growth of debt interest payments, which have doubled in dollar terms since 1979. In 1983 Iceland's long-term debt rose by 10% of the GNP to 60% by the end of the year, up from 35% in 1980. The traditional practice of financing the current account deficit by long-term credit explains only part of this development.

The aim of improving the profit position of the more hard-pressed sectors of the economy has been only partially attained. The profitability of the fisheries sector has been reduced by heavy investment in new fishing vessels, causing serious cash deficits. However, the profitability of the manufacturing sector has improved, with industries producing for the domestic market recording 6% to 7% higher profits than in 1983. Export industries have been even more profitable, showing 11% more profits than in 1984. The profit of retail and wholesale industries also improved significantly as a result of lower real wages and increased turnover.

Inflation in 1984 was brought down without any significant increase in the rate of unemployment, which only slightly exceeded 1% of the work force. Signs of labor shortage emerged in the Reykjavik area.

A substantial increase in the fish catch in 1986 brought a more buoyant outlook to the economy. Catches of other demersal fish than cod were more abundant than expected, and sales abroad increased considerably. Changes in the composition of production and shifts in sales volume from the U.S. market to Europe also brought more revenues. Increased domestic production and the higher overall level of economic activity contributed to a strong demand for labor, with unemployment falling to 0.7%. Earnings increased substantially faster in 1986, on an average by 31%. Wages rose by 21%. Inflation rose by 10% and prices by 21%. The overall terms of trade improved by 4%, mainly as a result of the sharp fall in oil prices, rising fish prices in the foreign markets, lowering interest rates and depreciation of the U.S. dollar. The merchandise trade balance showed a suplus or IKr 2.4 billion, up from IKr 1.3 billion a year earlier. The services account (excluding interest payments) showed a surplus of IKr 1.5 billion. Net interest payments abroad amounted to IKr 5 billion. The current account deficit stood at IKr 2.2 billion or 1.5% of the GNP, and the long-term foreign debt at IKr 74.5 billion or 52% of the GNP. The debt service is estimated at 19% of export earnings.

While Iceland has rich natural resources, they are narrowly based and vulnerable to supply shocks, which make export income, living standards and the balance of payments highly variable. This variability is greater in Iceland than in other OECD countries. As a result of unpredictable changes in the marine environment, national expenditures have exhibited large fluctuations. Foreign borrowing has often been used to cushion living standards from these abrupt changes. But burdened with a high foreign indebtedness, the government is attempting to reduce the economy's vulnerability through diversification, especially into energy-intensive industries. The diversification program also includes an extension of the country's manufacturing, processing and service base. Since Iceland has virtually fully employment, job creation and import substitution are not major issues. However, there are several constraints on Iceland's capacity to engage in a rapid industrialization program, given its small economy and labor force and limited financial resources.

After taking office in 1983, the new government appointed a committee to examine the possibility of expanding power-intensive industries and to discuss new joint ventures with foreign companies. The government hopes to triple the power-intensive sector by the end of the century. It has focused its attention on the aluminum industry, where Iceland has a distinct advantage in terms of duty-free access to the Common Market as well as low energy and transportation costs. The principal projects are a smelter at Staumsvik and a 25,000-ton silicon metal smelter at Reydarfjordur in East Iceland. The government also is seeking joint ventures with foreign companies that could employ geothermal energy directly in their industrial production. With steam costing an estimated $1.50 per ton, Iceland, with its hot springs, has a distinct advantage in this respect.

Iceland does not receive foreign aid.

PRINCIPAL ECONOMIC INDICATORS

Gross National Product: $3.260 billion (1986)
GNP per capita: $13,370 (1986)
GNP average annual growth rate: 2.1% (1973–86)
GNP per capita average annual
   growth rate: 1.0% (1973–86)
Average annual rate of inflation: 1%
Consumer Price Index: (1980=100)
   All items: 1,190.2 (February 1988)
   Food: 1,383.7 (February 1988)
Wholesale Price Index: N.A.

```
┌─────────────────────────────────────────────┐
│        BALANCE OF PAYMENTS, 1986 ($ million)  │
│                                               │
│  Current account balance: 16.9                │
│  Merchandise exports: 1096.8                  │
│  Merchandise imports: −1,024                  │
│  Trade balance: −72.8                         │
│  Other goods, services & income +: 472.9      │
│  Other goods, services & income −: −532.8     │
│  Other goods, services & income net: —        │
│  Private unrequited transfers: 5.7            │
│  Official unrequited transfers: −1.7          │
│  Direct investment: 6.4                       │
│  Portfolio investment: —                      │
│  Other long-term capital: 150.3               │
│  Other short-term capital: −56.5              │
│  Net errors & omissions: −5.8                 │
│  Counterpart items: 3.4                       │
│  Exceptional financing: —                     │
│  Liabilities constituting foreign             │
│     authorities reserves: —                   │
│  Total change in reserves: −114.8             │
└─────────────────────────────────────────────┘
```

PUBLIC FINANCE

The history of Icelandic public finance goes back to 1874, when under the new Constitution of that year the king of Denmark granted Iceland the right to manage its own national budget. The first budget was presented to the Althing in 1875. The intervening years have witnessed the growth of the share of public expenditures in national income from less than 4% to over one-third and a reversal of the share of central and local governments in total public expenditures.

The budget of the central government is presented to the Althing at the beginning of each regular session, usually in October as the finance bill. The bill is given three readings in the United Althing. After each reading the bill goes to the Appropriations Committee where it generally undergoes considerable amendment. Since 1922 the fiscal year has coincided with the calendar year.

The major direct taxes are income and net wealth taxes and Social Security contributions: The indirect taxes are excise and sales taxes, levies on production, profits of the liquor and tobacco monopoly and import duties; other indirect taxes are stamp duties, taxes on bank transactions and a payroll tax. The national income tax is progressive for individuals but is levied at a flat rate for companies.

The tax structure is characterized by a heavy dependence on import duties. The tariff structure is highly progressive, with luxury goods such as automo-

GROSS DOMESTIC PRODUCT, 1985

GDP nominal (national currency): 111.023 billion
GDP real (national currency): 15,293 billion (1980 prices)
GDP per capita ($): 11,123
Average annual growth rate of GDP, 1980–85: 0.3%

GDP by type of expenditure (%)
  Consumption
    Private: 59
    Government: 17
  Gross domestic investment: 23
  Gross domestic saving: —

  Foreign trade
    Exports: 42
    Imports: –42

Cost components of GDP (%)
  Net indirect taxes: 22
  Consumption of fixed capital: 13
  Compensation of employees: 65
  Net operating surplus: 65

Sectoral origin of GDP (%)
  Primary
    Agriculture: 21.8
    Mining: —

  Secondary
    Manufacturing: 13.4
    Construction: 7.6
    Public utilities: —
  Tertiary
    Transportation and communications: 9.9
    Trade: 20.6
    Finance: —
    Other services: 26.8
    Government: 26.8

biles taxed most heavily, while the rates on materials for agriculture and fishing are low or nonexistent. Another big revenue item is the net profit from the state monopoly of tobacco and alcohol. Other state enterprises generally do not return profits to the Treasury but receive state subsidies and grants to cover their losses.

Of public expenditures, the biggest category covers welfare, a large proportion of which represents the central government contribution to the National Insurance System. The other categories, in the order of their respective shares, are education; culture and church; health; communications, including roads; consumer subsidies; agriculture; fisheries; manufacturing; energy; justice; foreign service; and government pensions.

State enterprises also form part of the national budget. Besides the alcohol and tobacco monopoly, the state runs the postal service, national radio and television, fertilizer and cement plants, herring factories, a barrel factory, an engineering works, a shipping service and several farms.

The finances of the central and local governments are interrelated in many ways. Many local projects are financed in common, and local governments share some taxes with the central government that are distributed among the municipalities through the Municipal Equalization Fund. In addition to disbursements from this fund, the major sources of local government revenue are the personal income tax levied at a flat rate on gross income; the property tax; and the business tax, which is levied on gross business expenditures. The largest slice of local government expenditures goes to social services. Other budgetary claims include environmental services, fire protection and police. In cities, road-building may account for up to 25% of the total budget.

In addition to the main or the "A" budget, there is a parallel "B" budget, which includes government enterprises, and funds that finance their operations from public revenues. It also incorporates the Loan and Relending Account, which manages the lending operations of the government. The two budgets are combined in the "Credit Budget," which forms part of the Investment and Credit Program. In 1982 and 1983 the combined "A" and "B" budget borrowings amounted to 3.25% to 4% of the GNP.

To counter the growing central government deficits, the 1984 budget incorporated one of the most ambitious reductions in state spending. Total public consumption was reduced by 4%, to 5% in real terms, and current expenditures on goods and services were reduced by 2%. Government investment declined by 17%, and overall government spending volume dropped by 10%. The outcome was a cash surplus of 0.5% of the GNP. The 1985 budget proceeded to consolidate the gains by phasing out agricultural export subsidies. Central government expenditures remained at or slightly above their 1984 level of about 29% of the GDP. The 1985 budget also incorporated the first of three steps toward phasing out the state income tax on average wage earnings, a concession estimated to amount to IKr 600 million to IKr 700 million, representing a reduction in the rate of direct taxes to the GNP. To compensate for this revenue loss, indirect taxes were raised.

Foreign indebtedness in relation to the GNP has increased substantially since 1978. The 1983 the net debt rate approached 60%, exceeded only by Ireland in the OECD, the average for the smaller OECD countries being about 35%. Central government external debt, which amounted to 40% of the GNP in 1983, also exceeded that of all other OECD countries except Ireland. As a consequence, overseas debt interest payments are relatively high, at 6% of the

---

CENTRAL GOVERNMENT EXPENDITURES, 1984
% of total expenditures

Defense: —
Education: 11.99
Health: 23.02
Housing, Social Security, welfare: 16.19
Economic services: 29.24
Other: 19.56
Total expenditures as % of GNP: 25.82
Overall surplus or deficit as % of GNP: —

CENTRAL GOVERNMENT REVENUES, 1984
% of total current revenues

Taxes on income, profit & capital gain: 9.20
Social Security contributions: 4.73
Domestic taxes on goods & services: 47.12
Taxes on international trade & transactions: 15.90
Other taxes: 8.28
Current nontax revenue: 14.77
Total current revenue as % of GNP: —
Government consumption as % of GNP: 26.81
Annual growth rate of government consumption: N.A.

GNP. The origins of the problem lie not so much in rising capital imports (most of which have been used to finance capital investment) but in the increasing divergence between the real rates of interest on debt and domestic GNP growth rates, as well as a low rate of domestic savings. Of the borrowings under the 1985 budget of IKr 9.868 billion (11.5% of the GNP), foreign borrowing made up three-quarters. However, of the total, the greater part is earmarked to refinance existing overseas debt, so that net foreign borrowing amounted to only 3% of the GNP.

CURRENCY & BANKING

The Icelandic monetary unit is the krona (plural: kronur), divided into 100 aurar (singular: eyrir). Coins are issued in denominations of 5, 10 and 50 aurar and 1 and 5 kronur and notes in denominations of 10, 50, 100 and 500 kronur.

The banking system comprises a central bank, commercial banks and savings banks; public investment credit funds; insurance companies; private pension funds; and social insurance institutions.

The Central Bank of Iceland was established in 1961, when it took over the central banking functions previously performed by the National Bank of Iceland, the oldest and largest of the commercial banks. The Central Bank is an in-

EXCHANGE RATE, kronur per U.S. dollar						
1982	1983	1984	1985	1986	1987	1988
16.625	28.670	40.545	42.060	40.240	35.660	39.460

dependent government-owned institution administered by a three-man Board of Governors.

The National Bank of Iceland, founded in 1885, also is owned by the government, as are the Fisheries Bank and the Agricultural Bank. The state holds a minority interest in the Industrial Bank. There are three private commercial banks: the Bank of Commerce, the Cooperative Bank and the People's Bank. There are about 50 savings banks, many of them small, private, nonprofit institutions. In recent years many have been amalgamated with commercial banks and have become their branches.

Public investment credit funds play an important role in the supply of long-term finance. Usually they are administered by banks. Financing is obtained through special taxes, treasury grants and outside borrowing. Currently there are three major funds: the Fisheries Loan Fund, the Agricultural Loan Fund and the Industrial Loan Fund. Home mortgages are handled by the Mortgage Department of the National Bank. The Development Fund of Iceland was established in 1966 and is administered by the Economic Development Institute.

Under a new Central Bank rule of November 1986, the banks set the interest rates on deposits and loans by themselves. The Central Bank will intervene only if real lending rates exceed those in major trading countries and if interest rate margins become too large. A new law also was passed regulating the operations of private finance companies, trust funds and brokers. In the same year the Central Bank established Iceland's first stock exchange, and operations commenced on a limited scale.

Despite a deceleration of money supply (M3) in 1985 to 25%, the Central Bank had persistent difficulties in monetary control. However, money supply has risen at a slower rate than either the nominal GNP or inflation. High rates of inflation and negative interest rates tended to lower the demand for money. Domestic credit has expanded along with monetary growth. Easy recourse to central bank credit has led to a poor liquidity position for the deposit money banks. Rapid domestic credit expansion has fueled demand pressures on the economy, which have been met by imports. To accommodate these demands, banks increased their overdrafts at the central bank, and when the latter imposed a system of escalating penalty rates on overdrafts in 1982, the banks sought accommodation by short-term borrowing abroad. To correct this problem, the Central Bank required commercial banks to generally match their foreign liabilities with foreign assets.

Until 1983 real interest rates on nonindexed bank deposits were negative. By 1984 interest rates fell to 20% on loans and to 17.5% on deposits. However, these rates have fluctuated widely in response to changes in monetary policy.

With a domestic rate of inflation substantially greater than in OECD countries, the krona had to be devalued a number of times in the early 1980s: by 33% in 1982, by a further 11% in 1983 and by 14.5% in 1983. In 1984 and 1985 the authorities envisaged an effective depreciation of 5% based on trends in profit margins and balance of payments. However, as wages rose by 34.5% in 1984, the krona was again devalued, by 12%.

The government that took office in 1983 initiated a number of monetary reforms, including deregulation of interest. The Treasury was permitted to auction bills. The rediscounting system was reformed, and stricter reserve requirements were laid down to discourage overdrafts. In spite of these reforms, the monetary system has remained accommodating.

FINANCIAL INDICATORS, 1986

International reserves minus gold: $309.8 million
    SDRs: 0.2
    Reserve position in IMF: 4.9
    Foreign exchange: $304.7 million
Gold (million fine troy oz): 0.049
Ratio of external debt to total reserves: —

Central bank
Assets (%)
    Foreign assets: 55.1
    Claims on government: 28.7
    Claims on bank: 15.6
    Claims on private sector: 0.6
Liabilities (%)
    Reserve money: 58.2
    Government deposits: 12.0
    Foreign liabilities: 6.9
    Capital accounts: —

Money supply
Stock in billion national currency: 22.556
M^1 per capita: 91,970
U.S. liabilities to: $86 million
U.S. claims on: —

```
┌─────────────────────────────────────────────────┐
│         FINANCIAL INDICATORS, 1986 (continued)    │
│  Private banks                                    │
│  Assets (%)                                       │
│      Loans to government: 2.8                     │
│      Loans to private sector: 78.4                │
│      Reserves: 15.4                               │
│      Foreign assets: 3.5                          │
│  Liabilities: deposits: 71.610 billion kronur     │
│      of which (%)                                 │
│      Demand deposits: 28.9                         │
│      Savings deposits: 40.9                        │
│      Government deposits: —                        │
│      Foreign liabilities: 23.5                     │
│      Other: 6.7                                   │
└─────────────────────────────────────────────────┘
```

AGRICULTURE

Icelandic agriculture is conditioned by the country's northern latitude and the nature of its landscape. Lying just south of the Arctic Circle, it offers little scope for crop cultivation. With its Oceanic climate—short, cool summers and long but not very cold winters—there is little difference between the highest and lowest temperatures. The warmest month is July, with an average of about 11°C (52°F), and the coldest is February, with an average temperature just below the freezing point. Rapid changes in temperature can take place throughout the year, however, with consequent damage to vegetation.

Grass grows for no more than four months, from May to September, and because of the comparatively short and chilly summers it is practically the only crop that can be cultivated. Grain once was grown in the country, but that came to an end in the 16th century because of the deteriorating climate. The state recently has undertaken afforestation, and it supports tree-planting with grants, mainly to combat erosion. Agricultural land is devoted almost entirely to grass for the production of hay and silage as feed for the sheep and dairy cattle that are the mainstays of Icelandic farming.

The amount of arable land is small. According to altitude, the total area is as follows:

below 200 m. (650 ft.): 27,500 sq. km. (10,615 sq. mi.) or 26.7%

between 200 and 800 m. (650 and 2,600 ft.): 37,000 sq. km. (14,282 sq. mi.) or 35.9%

over 800 m. (2,600 ft.): 38,500 sq. km. (14,861 sq. mi.) or 37.4%

Arable land with comparatively dense vegetation covers between 15,000 and 20,000 sq. km. (5,790 and 7,720 sq. mi.) and sparse vegetation a similar area.

The soil of the agricultural land varies widely in quality. Much of the grassland is wet and marshy and interspersed with gravel and lava fields. Use of mechanized processes has proved capable of reclaiming these marshes using track-laying tractors and bulldozers. The development was encouraged by an act of the Althing in 1945, providing government grants for the purchase of heavy machinery by farm federations.

Grass is the staple crop of the farmer, providing pasture in summer and feed in winter. In winter cattle have to be fed for as long as eight months and sheep for five to six months.

Since 1860 the proportion of the population dependent on agriculture has been enormously reduced. It was 79.1% in 1860, 42.9% in 1920, 30.5% in 1940, 14.0% in 1960, 11% in 1970 and 7.1% in 1982. Despite this fall in numbers, productivity has multiplied. With 1882–90 as 100, the Index of Agricultural Production had climbed to over 1,000 by 1980. However, the number of farms remained stable until the past few decades. For the past 250 years the number of farms ranged from 6,150 to 5,350, but between 1953 and 1970 the number fell by an average of 32 a year, from 5,210 to 4,660, despite the establishment of 100 new market gardens and smallholdings during the period. Much of the phased-out farms were in the Northwest or the Northeast. Between 1936 and 1971 the government helped to establish 750 new farms and to rebuild 180 abandoned farms.

Farms vary in average size between 150 and 1,200 ha. (371 and 2,964 ac.), with the average being 300 ha. (741 ac.). The average stock per farm is 180 sheep and 13 cattle, including eight dairy cows. The area of cultivated grassland per farm varies from five to 100 ha. (12 to 247 ac.). Three of four farmholders are freeholders. About half of the leaseholds are government- or institution-owned, but their tenants have extensive legal protection and low rents. The use of fertilizers has steadily risen since 1950, when it was only 4,200 tons, to 35,300 tons in 1984. Fertilizers now account for 10% of the farming costs. Icelandic farms are heavily mechanized, and every farm has at least one tractor and one haymaking machine.

Iceland's natural hot water and steam resources allow hothouse cultivation of various fruits, vegetables, flowers and plants. In the years since 1924, when the first hothouse was built, this has become an important sector of Icelandic agriculture. Some farmers concentrate entirely on hothouse production.

The principal livestock animals are cattle (both dairy and beef), sheep and horses. Income from farm production is divided as follows: cattle, 50%; sheep, 33%; horses, 2%; hothouse and garden produce, 5%; pigs and poultry, 7%; and subsidiary income, 3%.

```
┌─────────────────────────────────────────────────┐
│         AGRICULTURAL INDICATORS, 1986             │
│                                                   │
│ Agriculture's share of GDP: 5.7%                  │
│ Index of Agricultural Production (1979–81=100): 101.0 │
│ (1985)                                            │
│ Index of Food Production (1979–81=100): 100.8 (1985) │
│ Number of tractors: 14,000                        │
│ Number of harvester-threshers: 100                │
│ Total fertilizer consumption: 26,600 tons         │
│ Number of farms: 7,000                            │
│ Size class (%)                                    │
│    Below 1 ha. (below 2.47 ac.): 15.7             │
│    1–5 ha. (2.47–12.35 ac.): 9.3                  │
│    5–10 ha. ( 12.35–24.7 ac.) 11.7                │
│    10–20 ha. (24.7–49.4 ac.): 23.7                │
│    20–50 ha. (49.4–123.5 ac.) 35.8                │
│    50–200 ha. (123.5–494 ac.):  ⎫                 │
│    Over 200 ha. (over 494 ac.):  ⎬  3.7           │
│                                  ⎭                 │
│ Yields                                            │
│    Roots & Tubers, kg./ha. (lb./ac.): 12,500 (11,157) │
│    Milk, kg.(lb.)/animal: 3,719 (8,199)           │
│                                                   │
│ Livestock (000)                                   │
│    Cattle: 64                                     │
│    Horses: 54                                     │
│    Sheep: 770                                     │
│    Pigs: 13                                       │
│ Fishing                                           │
│ Total catch (000 tons): 1,680                     │
│    of which marine (%): 100                       │
│ Value of exports ($000): 617,355                  │
└─────────────────────────────────────────────────┘
```

The bulk of agricultural production is consumed domestically. Only in favorable years is the surplus production exported. Milk and dairy products are distributed by the dairies. Meat is distributed by the Federation of Cooperative Societies and the South Iceland Meat Packing Cooperative. The Market Gardeners Sales Organization looks after the sales of greenhouse and garden vegetables. There are approximately 50 legally authorized slaughterhouses, owned mostly by farmers' cooperatives. Agricultural prices are regulated by the Agricultural Production Board.

As fishing is Iceland's single most important industry, contributing between 15% and 20% of the GNP, its fortunes govern the state of the economy. Fishing also is an important determinant in foreign policy. Few nations are as dependent on trawlers for their economic health as Iceland is.

Iceland is on a platform or continental shelf whose outlines roughly follow those of the country down to great depths. This platform rests, in turn, on a submarine ridge stretching as far as Scotland to the southeast and Greenland to the northwest. The shelf and its slopes provide ideal conditions for the spawning of many important species of fish. These favorable conditions are mainly created by the mixture of warm water carried to the coasts of Iceland by the Gulf Stream and cold, nutrient currents from the Arctic. More than 100 species of fish have been caught in Icelandic waters, but most of them are of little or no commercial value. There are in Icelandic waters between 15 and 20 species of fish currently considered commercially valuable, of which the largest are capelin, cod, herring, saithe, haddock and redfish. The majority of the exploited stocks are coastal.

The Icelandic fishing grounds are exploited by at least seven other nations. The most vigorous competition comes from the United Kingdom and West Germany. As a result of overfishing by these nations, important changes have occurred in the patterns of fish spawning and migration and consequently in the fish harvest. Iceland has tried to protect its own crucial stake in these fishing grounds by extending its economic limits to 322 km. (200 mi.), a step in conformity with U.N. recommendations for coastal states.

Although total catch and the number of fishermen have remained fairly stable over the years, the composition of the catch and its value have fluctuated widely over the same period. Until 1968 herring was the most valuable, and Icelandic fishermen introduced a number of innovations, such as side propellers to increase the maneuverability of the vessels and optimize the herring catch. After the decline of the herring fishery by the late 1960s, demersal fishing increased by about 50%, with cod and capelin emerging as the principal money-earners.

The first whaling station was established in 1948. Operations are strictly controlled. Whaling is permitted for four months only each year, and the number of catches also is limited, to four.

Cod and other demersal species are mainly processed into frozen, salted or dried unsalted products. Filleting and freezing of demersal fish account for 65% of fish processing operations. About 25% is salted; the rest is exported on ice or used fresh in the home market. Capelin is processed into oil and meal. Most of the scallops are frozen for the U.S. market. Lobster and shrimp are steadily growing in importance.

Despite efforts to diversify the economy, Iceland remains heavily dependent on fishing for income, employment and export earnings. Marine products represent approximately 75% of the country's exports, and the sector employs roughly 25% of the work force. However, the fish catch, particularly of whitefish such as cod and haddock, as well as of herring and capelin, have been characterized by large swings, resulting in "boom" or "bust" cycles in the industry. Capelin catches, for example, rose from 200,000 tons annually in the early 1970s to 1 million tons annually by the late 1970s but declined to 15,000 tons in

1982, when a total ban was imposed on capelin fishing; then it rose to 800,000 tons in 1985.

In addition the fluctuations in catch, the industry suffers from fluctuations in foreign demand and price. The export price of capelin products is generally more volatile than that of whitefish. In addition, since capelin is used largely for fish meal, which is used lagely as a substitute for soybean meal in animal feed, the dollar price of capelin is subject to developments in the international soybean market. Iceland also faces stiff competition from other fish-exporting countries, particularly Norway and Canada, both of which subsidize their national fisheries.

The robust growth of the fish harvest during the 1970s stimulated strong investment in the fishing industry, leading to serious current problems of overcapacity. In 1984 the size of the fishing fleet stood at 113,000 GRT, compared with 79,000 GRT at the end of 1971, a 43% increase. In addition to expanding gross tonnage, substantial investments have been made in navigation equipment, fishing gear and the processing industry. In the early 1980s the trawler fleet comprised 103 vessels in the size range of 250 GRT and over and accounted for 43.7% of the fishing fleet by weight. Investment in new deep-sea trawlers was stepped up after the extension of the fishing zone to 322 km. But by the early 1980s signs of excess capacity began to appear. The new trawlers had an adverse effect on fish stocks, and the resulting drop in the fish catch left many boatowners high and dry, unable to meet their debt service payments. Because the fishing industry exercises such a heavy weight in the economy, widespread bankruptcies in this sector could have serious consequences. The government has responded with several measures: by augmenting the resources of the intra-industry Catch Equalization Fund, reduced interest rates for the Fisheries Loan Fund, setting quotas for individual vessels rather than for the whole industry and banning the import of new fishing vessels.

MANUFACTURING

Manufacturing is a small sector, contributing about 15% to the GNP. The limited domestic market cannot support a large industrial base, and as a result industrial growth has been moderate and slow. Of the total number of manufacturing firms, fewer than 200 employ more than 20 workers. The major manufacturing sectors include dairy; beverages and food chemicals; textiles; carpets; leather; hides and skins; shoes; garments; fishing gear; furniture; chemicals; shipbuilding; plastics; and ceramics.

Government efforts to diversify the industrial base have resulted in a number of large power-intensive plants. Among the most important of these are the Staumsvik smelter and the Gufunes State Fertilizer Plant. The only other plant of note is Kisiliojan, which utilizes the diatomite deposits at the bottom of Lake Mývatn in the North.

There is no significant foreign investment in Iceland.

MINING

Iceland has no significant mineral resources, apart from limited amounts of diatomite and pumice.

ENERGY

Iceland has no fossil fuel resources. On the other hand, it has substantial harnessable hydro and geothermal reserves, estimated at 35,000 gw.-hr. per year. Only a fraction of this energy potential is being utilized now.

Nearly 99.7% of total population has access to electricity. Total production in 1985 was 4.332 billion kw.-hr. or 17,975 kw.-hr. per capita, placing Iceland among the top 10 in this respect. Electrification began in 1904 when a small stream in the fishing and market town of Hafnarfjördhur was harnessed and a small plant of 9 kw. was built. The first power plant, on the Sog River, began operating in 1937 with an 8,800 kw. installed capacity. The next important step was the 1946 Electricity Act, which made electrification a state responsibility. The State Electricity Authority was established on the basis of this legislation. By another act, passed in 1965, the National Power Company was set up, jointly owned by the state and the city of Reykjavik. In 1967 the Energy Act was passed, establishing the National Energy Authority to take over the functions of the State Electricity Authority.

After many years of intensive research, the utilization of geothermal resources is advancing rapidly. Natural hot water is used for domestic heating in Reykjavik. The water is obtained from wells in the city and in the thermal area of Reykir. The temperature of the water ranges from 80°C to 140°C (176°C to 284°C) at the wellhead, and it is 75°F to 80°F (167°F to 176°F) when it enters radiators in the houses. The cost of natural hot water heating is only 40% that of fuel oil heating and 70% of the cheapest electrical heating. Nine other communities in various parts of the country use natural hot water heating systems of the same design. Overall, about 57% of the population, 10 ha. (24.7 ac.) of greenhouses, most of the schools and 80 public swimming pools are heated by thermal water. The use of oil for space heating is expected to be eliminated effectively by the end of the 1980s. A geothermal electricity generating plant is in operation near Krafla in North Iceland.

Despite these considerable achievements, imported fuels continue to constitute a major drain on foreign exchange resources, accounting for 15.1% of total merchandise imports. However, there is little room for further substitution, since at present there is no alternative fuel for the fishing fleet and the transportation system.

ENERGY INDICATORS, 1986

Public utilities' share of GDP: Insignificant
Energy consumption per capita, kg. (lb.) oil equivalent: 5,105 (11,254)

Electricity
  Installed capacity: 947,000 kw.
  Production: 4.044 billion kw.-hr.
    % fossil fuel: 0.1
    % hydro: 95.2
    % nuclear: 4.7
  Consumption per capita: 16,642 kw.-hr.

Petroleum
  Consumption: 4 million bbl.

Coal
  Consumption: 69,000 tons

LABOR

Since the end of World War II Iceland has had a unique record of full employment, which has led to a national intolerance of even the slightest indication of impending unemployment. Nevertheless, seasonal unemployment or underemployment is typical of the country's major industries, fishing and fish processing.

The current labor force of about 115,000 (a participation rate of almost 47%) is expected to grow to about 167,000 by 2023. Providing the additional 52,000 jobs that will be needed by then, but no more, presents policymakers with the delicate task of balancing a necessary drawdown of fishing capacity with just enough commercial and industrial enterprises to absorb the increase. The labor force may remain stable in the decades to come, given Icelandic reluctance to emigrate on the one hand and the virtual absence of foreign labor on the other. Some shifts in employment patterns are inevitable as traditional employment sectors shrink and as newer ones are being slowly wet-nursed. One shift that is already evident is toward public employment, where one of every three new entrants finds a job.

Iceland has not experienced any general strike, and the last major strike, by public sector employees, was in 1984. Given the sensitivity of the economy to labor unrest, any strike threat by either of the two major federations receives immediate political attention. The federations wield considerable clout because they can block the ports to press their demands. A March 1985 walkout by teachers in secondary schools who employed the Nordic tactic of mass resignations rather than a declared strike achieved only mixed results. It was unsuccessful in terms of immediate wage improvements, and it provided the then minister of education, Ragnhildur Helgadottir, with a chance to demonstrate a tough government stance toward further work stoppages.

Virtually all Icelandic workers belong to unions. The national federation covering private sector workers, the Icelandic Federation of Labor, is a rather loose federation having both regional conferences through which local unions adhere to the national body and some direct member-unions whose concentration in functional fields does not fit neatly into regional groupings. This federation undertakes annual master wage negotiations with the Federation of Icelandic Employers; conducts worker education projects; manages its own and some of the government's social benefit programs; and represents Icelandic labor on the Nordic Labor Council, the ETUC and the ICFTU. The Federation of State and Municipal Employees (BSRB) represents public employee member unions. In the past, BSRB wage settlements have tended to trail behind those in private industry, but the experience of 1984 may indicate a change to a more active BSRB role in the future. A number of small unions in small sectors of the economy such as air transportation and printing, remain unaffiliated with either national federation.

Unlike in other Nordic countries, the unions do not profess an exclusive loyalty to the socialist party but espouse divergent political ideologies, including conservatism. Each political party, in turn, contains a labor council, which handles issues relating to labor.

For a high-cost country, Iceland is paradoxically a low-wage one. Indeed, the prime minister caused a considerable furor in 1984 by citing low wages as an inducement to foreign industries to choose Iceland for their operations. The basic wage rates ($300 to $500 per month being the lower end of the scale), however, understate considerably the actual compensation levels for most wage earners (except hapless civil servants receiving only one salary, fully visible to the tax collector). Aside from a black or underground economy, which does not appear in official statistics (and which is the primary explanation for the evident signs of prosperity despite "official" hard times), two-income families are the norm in Iceland. Most Icelanders pursue more than one gainful occupation, and the private sector has a bewildering system of flexible bonus payments and extra payment programs that make determination of actual individual earnings difficult, especially for the Tax Office.

Nominally, national master wage agreements are negotiated for the private sector between the Icelandic Federation of Labor and the Icelandic Federation of Employers and for the public sector between the Federation of Government and Municipal Employees and the Ministry of Finance. These master agreements are then supplemented by local agreements involving conditions of work, social benefits and extra wage payments at the enterprise or local level for subordinate labor organizations. As a result, analysis of actual wage trends usually lags behind the claims made in each contract negotiation, and only gross percentage figures and perceptions of the parties' satisfaction with one or another wage settlement enter into discussions of the wage picture in Iceland. As is normal in Nordic welfate state economies, periodic calls for upgrading lower-paid workers' wages disproportionately to those of higher-paid workers in the name of social justice usually run head-on into resistance from higher-paid union members objecting to the wage compression implicit in this tactic.

Iceland has extensive labor legislation. Collective bargaining is governed by Law 80/1938, which also specifies the circumstances under which a strike or lockout is legal and outlines the means of official intervention. The law draws a sharp distinction between legal differences and differences of interest in labor disputes. Legal differences concern matters of interpretation of labor contracts and should be resolved without resort to strikes. On the other hand, the right to strike is guaranteed where differences of interest arise over wages and conditions of work. The role of the authorities, embodied in the state arbitrator, is small. It is not his duty to mediate, and usually he does not interfere unless negotiations have either broken down or the dispute appears to be heading for a strike or a lockout. The arbitrator has no authority to order a cooling-off period, although he may offer a compromise solution to be voted on by workers or employers. The government can, however, ban any strike by passing a law.

A separate law governs the collective bargaining of civil servants. Civil servants are forbidden to strike by law, but they defied the law in 1984 and won significant concessions.

FOREIGN COMMERCE

In 1986 the merchandise trade showed a surplus of IKr 2.4 billion, compared to IKr 1.3 billion in 1985. This is attributable to a considerable increase in the export value of fish products on the export side and a fall in oil prices and a contraction in the special imports for the aluminum smelter on the import side. Lower oil prices and improved fish prices are expected to maintain favorable terms of trade for the rest of the decade.

Iceland has been a member of the GATT since 1968 and the EFTA since 1970. As an EFTA member Iceland has a free-trade agreement with the EEC that includes a special provision for tariff reductions for fish products.

LABOR INDICATORS, 1985

Total economically active population: 122,800
As % of working-age population: 56.4
% female: 43.6
Activity rate (%)
  Total: 48.7
  Male: 60.6
  Female: 44.5
  Organized labor: 60%

Sectoral employment (%)
  Agriculture, forestry, fishing: 20.3
  Manufacturing, construction: 33.9
  Trade: 14.5
  Services: 31.3

Unemployment (%): 1.7
Labor under 20 years: 10.1

Hours of work
  Manufacturing: 41.2

FOREIGN TRADE INDICATORS, 1986

Exports: $1.096 billion
Imports: $1.115 billion
Balance of trade: -$19 million
Terms of trade (1980=100): 83.8
Import Price Index (1980=100): 82.4
Export Price Index (1980=100): 69.1

Direction of Trade (%)

	Imports	Exports
EEC	52.9	54.2
U.S.A.	7.0	21.7
East European economies	6.5	5.5
Japan	6.5	4.8

Composition of Trade (%)

Food and	Imports	Exports
Agricultural raw materials	11.7	80.6
Fuels	9.6	—
Ores & minerals	2.8	0.9
Manufactured goods	75.9	18.6
of which chemicals	7.9	—
of which machinery	33.1	1.3

TRANSPORTATION & COMMUNICATIONS

Iceland has no railways, and all land transportation is by motor vehicle. Road-building did not begin until about 1900, and the early roads were narrow, intended only for horse-drawn vehicles. Gradually construction improved as traffic increased. By 1930 all districts were linked by some roads, although in winter many of them were impassable. By the mid-1980s there were 12,343 km. (7,671 mi.) of roads, of which 166 km. (103 mi.) were bitumen and concrete, 1,284 km. (798 mi.) bituminous-treated and gravel, and 10,893 km. (6,770 mi.) earth. In the quality of its highway system, Iceland still is underdeveloped. Since the population is small and the country large, roadbuilding is relatively expensive. It is made even more difficult by natural barriers, inhospitable terrain and many small rivers. There are 35 bridges of 100 m. (328 ft.) or more, and about 770 bridges between 10 and 100 m. (33 and 328 ft.). The ring road around the country is complete except for a small gap south of Vatnajökull. In this area there are glacial rivers that change their courses across wide, sandy stretches, and roads are submerged under glacial floods.

Marine transportation is important, especially in trade. The first Icelandic shipping company was founded in 1914 and now operates most of the coastal services. After World War II a new fleet was created. In 1984 it had a GRT of 179,000, up from 35,000 in 1974. In 1946 the Federation of Icelandic Cooperative Societies launched its first ship. Other Icelandic shipping companies maintain services between Iceland and other countries, mostly with ships of small size. The fishing fleet accounts for a large percentage of the total tonnage.

Iceland has many good natural harbors. The largest are at Reykjavik and Vestmannaeyjar. There are three secondary harbors, at Akureyri, Hafnarfjördhur and Seydhisfjördhur. The one at Hafnarfjördhur serves the aluminum plant there and has a spring tide depth of 12 m. (39 ft.)

Domestic aviation began in 1919. In 1938 Icelandair was formed and has since served as the national flag line. Another company, Icelandic Airlines, was formed in 1944. Both companies were merged into Icelandair in 1973. It operates a fleet of three Boeings and four Fokkers both on domestic flights and on international flights to the United States and elsewhere in Europe. The principal international airport is at Keflavik, 47 km. (29 mi.) from Reykjavik. There are 97 other airfields, of which 91 are usable, three with permanent-surface runways and 12 with runways over 1,220 m. (4,003 ft.) Three international airlines—BEA, SAS and Pan American—operate flights to Iceland.

The telecommunications system consists of two submarine cables linking Iceland with Canada and Scotland, one satellite station and two Atlantic Ocean antennas. Postal service is hampered by weather and terrain; in sparsely populated areas mail is delivered only once a week, while in Reykjavik and larger towns it is delivered twice a day.

Tourism is a major revenue earner, although tourist traffic in unevenly distributed over the year, with more than half the tourists arriving in the summer. During the peak season many boarding schools are used as hotels. Most tourists come to Reykjavik, but Akureyri and Lake Mývatn in the North also are favorite tourist centers. Safari tours into the interior are popular as well. Many tourists also visit Greenland from Iceland. About 40% of the tourists come from the United States, and most of the remainder from West Germany, Great Britain and elsewhere in Scandinavia. The Iceland Tourist Bureau coordinates tourist promotion activities.

TRANSPORTATION INDICATORS, 1986

Roads
   Length, km. (mi.): 12,343 (7,671)
   Paved (%): 12

Motor vehicles
   Automobiles: 103,100
   Trucks: 13,160
   Persons per vehicle: 2.0
   Road freight, ton-km. (ton-mi.): 464 (318)

Merchant marine
   Vessels: 389
   Total dead weight tonnage: 161,600

Ports
   1 major, 3 secondary
   Cargo loaded: 600,000 tons
   Cargo unloaded: 1,400,000 tons

Air
   Km. (mi.) flown: 16.5 million (10.4 million)
   Passengers: 710,000
   Passenger-km. (passenger-mi.): 2.268 billion
   (1.409 billion)
   Freight, ton-km. (ton-mi.): 25 million (17.1 million)
   Mail, ton-km.: 4.3 million (2.6 million)
   Airports with scheduled flights: 24
   Civil aircraft: 20

COMMUNICATION INDICATORS, 1986

Telephones
   Total: 125,000
   Persons per: 1.9
   Phone traffic
      International: 1,323,000

```
┌─────────────────────────────────────────────────┐
│      COMMUNICATION INDICATORS, 1986 (continued)  │
│ Post office                                       │
│   Number of post offices: 150                     │
│   Domestic mail:                 ⎫                │
│   Foreign mail received:         ⎬  38,823,000   │
│   Foreign mail sent:             ⎭                │
│                                                   │
│ Telegraph                                         │
│   Total traffic: 571,000                          │
│   National: 555,000                               │
│   International: 16,000                            │
│                                                   │
│ Telex                                             │
│   Subscriber lines: 442                           │
│   Traffic (000 minutes): 1,730                    │
│                                                   │
│ Telecommunications: 2 submarine cables; 1 satellite sta- │
│ tion; 2 Atlantic Ocean antennas                   │
│        TOURISM AND TRAVEL INDICATORS, 1985        │
│ Total tourist receipts: $41 million               │
│ Expenditures by nationals abroad: $76 million     │
│ Number of hotel beds: N.A.                        │
│ Average length of stay: 4 nights                  │
│ Tourist nights: N.A.                              │
│ Number of tourists: 97,000                        │
│   of whom from (%)                                │
│   U.S.A.: 32.6                                     │
│   U.K.: 10.2                                       │
│   West Germany: 9.7                               │
│   Denmark: 9.6                                    │
└─────────────────────────────────────────────────┘
```

DEFENSE

Iceland does not maintain a defense force. There is a U.S. military base at Keflavik.

EDUCATION

The history of the Icelandic school system starts with the establishment of organized Christianity during the 11th century. The Central Grammar School or Gymnasium at Reykjavik can be traced back to the foundation in 1056 of a cathedral school at Skalholt in South Iceland. The grammar school or the Latin school tradition is one of the two central pillars of the country's educational history. The other is the old custom of teaching the three R's to young children at home. This type of education was strong during the latter half of the 18th century after two eminent scholars, the Danish bishop Ludwig Harboe and Jon Thorkelsson, made a tour of inspection in 1741–45 that revealed widespread deficiencies in literacy. In their report they charged the parents to teach their children from age five under the general supervision of clergymen. The result was that by 1800 most of the population could read. The Education Act of 1880 made such instruction an officially approved obligation.

In 1907 the Althing passed the first major piece of educational legislation, which set the direction and course for schooling to the present time. The act established educational districts in rural areas and school districts in towns and villages, each with a school board. It also created the Office of Education under a commissioner. Primary education (from ages 10 to 14) was made compulsory and free. Primary schools were to be established in all towns and funded and run by local authorities, with subsidies from the central government and under the overall supervision of the Office of Education.

In addition to the Act of 1907, the constitutional foundations of education are found in the Education Acts of 1926, 1936 and 1946; the School Systems Act of 1974; the Basic Education Act of 1974; the Act on Financing of Schools of 1967; the University of Iceland Act of 1979; the Teachers University Act of 1971; the Grammar School Act of 1970; and the Act Permitting the Establishment of Comprehensive High Schools of 1973 as amended in 1977 and 1980. The Constitution itself makes only a passing reference to education.

The language of instruction is Icelandic. At the secondary level, and even more so at the university level, textbooks in both English and other Scandinavian languages frequently are used, and these languages also are employed for lectures. As a rule, the academic year is nine months long. The school year begins in September and ends in May. In rural areas, primary schools may be operated for a shorter time, or for a minimum of seven months a year. Also in rural areas, schools may be operated for six days a week, but other schools maintain a five-day schedule. In a nine-month school, the school days vary from 170 to 210. At the secondary and university levels, the academic year is divided into two semesters. At the University of Iceland, the fall semester lasts from September 15 until January 23 and the spring semester from January 24 to May 31.

According to the School Systems Act, there are three interrelated levels of schooling: the primary school; a unified comprehensive school of nine grades, for ages seven to 16; and the secondary school of four years. Compulsory education starts at age seven. Under the Basic Education Act of 1974, local authorities operate preprimary classes for children of age five or six.

Generally examinations are given at the end of each school year. At the university and secondary levels, examinations are held at the end of each semester. At the primary level, examinations are given by each school. The schools may adopt any grading system they choose but may not employ a letter grade scale, which is used only for the standardized test given at the end of the ninth grade. Most schools use a grade scale of 1–10, sometimes taken to decimal points.

There are no private schools in Iceland except one secondary boarding school run by the Seventh-Day Adventists and a few primary schools run either by that church or by the Catholic Church.

At the secondary and university levels the choice of textbooks in Icelandic is extremely limited, and foreign textbooks in English and other Scandinavian languages are extensively used. Primary and secondary textbooks are published by the National Center for Educational Materials.

In all urban areas, primary schools comprise grades one through nine as well as classes for six-year-olds. Grades one through six are commonly distinguished as the first stage and grades seven through nine as the second stage. In rural areas the trend has been toward larger schools, usually with boarding facilities. In remote rural areas a system of alternate teaching is practiced, with children spending one or two weeks alternately at school and at home.

The weekly load of classwork in grades one through nine ranges from 22 to 35 classes, each class lasting 40 minutes. All primary schools have a coordinated syllabus covering Icelandic, mathematics, social studies, religion, home economics, arts and crafts, music, physical education, science, Danish and English. English is introduced in the sixth grade. In grades seven through nine pupils may take electives from 10 to 14 hours per week. Students who work may count their work experience toward elective credits at the time of the final examination.

Primary classes are not integrated, and students are not grouped according to ability. Supplementary and special education are provided for gifted students as well as for problem learners and the handicapped.

The main types of schools at the secondary level are grammar schools, comprehensive high schools and vocational schools. Grammar schools are four-year schools leading to the *studentsprof* (matriculation examination). They offer programs in modern languages, the classics, physics, mathematics and natural sciences and, more recently, music, social sciences and business education. The older grammar schools offer the course-points system with fixed credits for each course. Courses to be taken for matriculation are grouped in three categories: mandatory subjects, course-related subjects and electives, counting 70%, 20% and 10%, respectively, toward a diploma.

Comprehensive high schools were first established in 1975. Today there are 10 such high schools. Unlike grammar schools, comprehensive high schools offer both academic and vocational courses as well as special programs in health and hygiene, home economics, social services, business education and fine arts.

Vocational schools comprise commercial schools as well as trade schools. Among the special areas served by these schools are fish processing and management, catering, navigation, aviation, radiography, assistance to the handicapped, customs work and drama.

Until recently, the University of Iceland was the only institution of higher learning. In 1971 the former Teachers Training College was raised to university status, as were later the Technical College and the School of Agriculture at Hvanneyri. There are no private institutions of higher education. All higher education is free of charge.

The University of Iceland was founded in 1911, although three of its constituents—the Theological Seminary, the School of Medicine and the Law School were founded earlier, in 1847, 1876 and 1908, respectively. Departments added since founding are Economics, Philosophy and Liberal Arts, Engineering, Social Sciences, and Dentistry.

Teacher training is offered at the Teachers University, which has three-year programs for primary and preprimary schoolteachers and special programs for in-service teachers, music teachers, crafts teachers, and physical education teachers. Secondary teachers must receive a university degree in their major field and complete a one-year course in education.

The school system is highly centralized under the Ministry of Education. Responsibility for primary education is shared among eight regional education authorities. Each authority appoints a school council for a four-year term. School directors are appointed by the minister of education. The school system is financed from the national budget.

Each of the eight regions is divided into school districts. There are 152 school districts on the whole, their numbers in each region ranging from one to 29. Although most of the secondary schools are directly run by the state, a few are run jointly by the state and local authorities. In such cases the state pays the teachers' salaries, half of administrative costs and 60% of initial costs.

There are four departments within the Ministry of Education: Primary Education, Vocational and Technical Education, Higher Education and International Education and Educational Research. The Center for Educational Materials, founded in the early 1980s, is gradually taking over many of the responsibilities formerly vested in the Department of Educational Research.

Adult education is governed by the Adult Education Act of 1979. The Reykjavik School of Adult Education, founded in 1939 by the city, offers a great variety of evening and afternoon courses. Similar schools have been established in other towns. A number of private schools also offer evening and afternoon courses for adults. The trade unions and the cooperative societies operate a correspondence school. There are no open university programs. International programs are conducted by the University of Iceland in modern Icelandic and its literature, funded by the Nordic Culture Fund.

```
┌─────────────────────────────────────────────────┐
│            EDUCATION INDICATORS, 1986             │
│                                                   │
│ Literacy                                          │
│   Total (%): 100.0                                │
│   Males (%): 100.0                                │
│   Females (%): 100.0                              │
│                                                   │
│ First level                                       │
│   Schools: 187                                    │
│   Students: 25,000                                │
│   Teachers: 2,600                                 │
│   Student–teacher ratio: 10:1                     │
│   Net enrollment rate: 101%                       │
│   Females (%): 49                                 │
│                                                   │
│ Second level                                      │
│   Schools: 157                                    │
│   Students: 21,800                                │
│   Net enrollment rate: 90%                        │
│   Female (%): 47                                  │
│                                                   │
│ Vocational                                        │
│   Schools: 44                                     │
│   Students: 4,280                                 │
│                                                   │
│ Third level                                       │
│   Institutions: 4                                 │
│   Students: 4,780                                 │
│   Teachers: 280                                   │
│   Student–teacher ratio: 17:1                     │
│   Gross enrollment rate: 22.8%                    │
│   Students per 100,000 ages 20–24: 2,136          │
│   % of population over 25 with postsecondary      │
│   education: 3.7                                  │
│   Females (%): 52                                 │
│                                                   │
│ Foreign study                                     │
│   Foreign students in national universities: N.A. │
│   Students abroad: 1,392                           │
│      of whom in                                   │
│          U.S.A.: 473                              │
│          West Germany: 170                        │
│          U.K.: 41                                 │
│                                                   │
│ Public expenditures                               │
│   Total: Icelandic krona 6.457 billion (1986)     │
│   % of GNP: 4.1                                   │
│   % of national budget: 12.2                      │
│   % current: N.A.                                 │
└─────────────────────────────────────────────────┘
```

LEGAL SYSTEM

In 1920 the present legal administration came into being when the government of Iceland decided to abolish the power of the Supreme Court in Copenhagen in Icelandic cases and set up the High Court in Reykjavik as the Supreme Court of Iceland. Since then, Iceland has had a court system of two instances only, with appeals going directly from the district courts to the Supreme Court. The Supreme Court has eight judges appointed by the president of the republic upon the advice of the minister of justice. A case usually is heard by a panel of five judges, but sometimes by a group of three. The Supreme Court can rule on questions pertaining to both fact and law. On an average it hands down 170 judgments annually.

Each district—Reykjavik, 22 boroughs, 18 counties and the Keflavik airport area—has a number of district courts. The most important contain a general civil court, a criminal court, a probate court, a court of auctions and a sheriff's court. The general civil courts are known as town courts in Reykjavik and the boroughs and special sessions in other districts. A Labor Court the entire country tries cases on trade union law, and no appeal can be made from its decisions on points of substance. There also is the High Court of State, which has never been convened since being established. The court has the power to impeach cabinet ministers, and its judgments are final. Iceland has no administrative courts, but the legality of administrative acts can be adjudged by the regular courts. However, some administrative boards exercise quasi-judicial functions, such as the Tax Board.

The justices of the Supreme Court and the district judges are appointed for life and cannot be removed from office except by court judgment. Although there are no juries, lay judges sometimes sit with regular judges. If a case demands expert knowledge on questions of fact, the judge appoints two experts, who then sit as judges and who can outvote the regular judge even on points of law.

The rules of court procedure follow Scandinavian models. Proceedings are generally oral, except in petty cases in the district court, which constitute the majority of all cases handled. There are few restrictions on evidence, and judges exercise wide discretion in their interpretations and evaluations. In civil case the parties, not the judge, decide what evidence should be produced, whereas in criminal cases the judges must make independent investigations from the bench. The burden of proof in criminal cases rests with the prosecution. No doctrine of contempt of court is applied.

Written statutes form the principal source of Icelandic law. According to customary law, the courts can declare a statute unconstitutional, which has occurred on a few occasions. Administrative rules constitute an important source of law in the form of delegated legislation. In Icelandic jurisprudence, the law is generally divided into two categories: private and public. In this context, private law includes commercial law. A comprehensive legal code has never been promulgated in the country; number of statutes of varying vintage serve in its stead. These include the Penal Code of 1940, the Civil Procedure Code of 1936 and the Criminal Procedure Code of 1974.

No information is available on prisons in Iceland.

LAW ENFORCEMENT

The Icelandic Police was a municipal force until 1972, when it was brought under central government authority. For police purposes the country is divided into 26 districts, each under a chief of police. In Reykjavik, police functions are divided between the chief judge of the Criminal Court, who also is the head of the CID, and the chief of police. Chiefs of police are almost always lawyers, and they carry out other quasi-judicial functions. Since there is no army in Iceland, the police perform certain defense functions as well.

The regular police handle the enforcement of administrative regulations in addition to traffic duties and enforcement of law and order. Criminal investigation divisions exist only in the largest towns. The Mobile Police Force is called upon to assist rural police forces in emergencies. The police are not normally armed and carry only batons or nightsticks.

In Reykjavik the Narcotics Surveillance Section is under the chief of police, who also heads the Aliens Office and the Police Training College. The National Central Bureau of Interpol is a division of the Ministry of Justice.

Police uniforms consist of black trousers and a black jacket with brass buttons along with white peaked caps and white shirts for inspectors and above and light blue shirts for the lower ranks.

No data are available on incidence and types of Prime in Iceland.

HEALTH

Under the Ministry of Health, the medical administration is headed by a director of health. Under him are chief medical officers at the headquarters and district physicians at the regional level. At present the country is divided into 57 districts. Each administrative community has a sanitary board, the members of which are elected by the local council. Larger towns have sanitary inspectors.

General health conditions in Iceland have vastly improved since the turn of the century. Throughout history, Iceland has been ravaged by epidemics of all kinds. Common infectious diseases such as diphtheria, scarlet fever, measles and influenza often caused high mortality until the first decades of the 20th century. Today, however, these diseases have been brought under control. Leprosy and hydatid diseases, widely prevalent in past centuries, have become extinct.

HEALTH INDICATORS, 1986

Health personnel
  Physicians: 574
    Population per physcian: 420
  Dentists: 191
  Nurses: 2,724
  Pharmacists: 168

Hospitals
  Number: 45
  Number of beds: 2,677
    Per 10,000 population: 111
  Admissions/discharges per 10,000: 2,087
  Bed occupancy rate: 101%
  Average length of stay: 19 days

Type of hospitals (%)
  Government: 71.6
  Private nonprofit: 28.4
  Private profit: 28.4

Public health expenditures
  As % of national budget: 23
  Per capita: $690

Vital statistics
  Crude death rate per 1,000: 6.9
  Life expectancy at birth (years)
    Males: 74.9
    Females: 80.2
  Infant mortality rate per 1,000 live births: 5.7
  Child mortality rate ages 1–4 years per 1,000: insignificant
  Maternal mortality rate per 100,000 live births: 0.0

Causes of death per 100,000
  Infectious & parasitic diseases: 4.2
  Cancer: 162.0
  Endocrine & metabolic disorders: 5.0
  Diseases of the nervous system: 10.9
  Diseases of the circulatory system: 293.9
  Diseases of the respiratory system: 79.8
  Diseases of the digestive system: 18.4
Accidents, poisoning & violence: 53.4

FOOD & NUTRITION

The average Icelander consumes 3,122 calories and 129.9 g. (4.6 oz.) of protein per day. This food supply is 113% of FAO food requirements. Food expenditures account for 23.8% of total expenditures. Of calorie consumption, 19.6% is derived from cereals, 4.0% potatoes, 16.4% from meat and poultry, 6.0% from fish, 19.5% from eggs and milk, 3.2% from fruits and vegetables and 9.7% from fats and oils.

PER CAPITA CONSUMPTION OF FOODS, Kg. (Lb.), 1986

Potatoes: 54 (118.8)
Fruits
   Citrus: 12.5 (27.5)
Eggs: 17 (37.4)
Milk: 299.6 (660.6)
Butter: 3.8 (8.3)
Cheese: 7.6 (16.7)
Meat (total): 59 (130)
   Beef and veal: 8.3 (18.3)
   Pig meat: 4.2 (9.2)
   Poultry: 3.1 (6.8)
   Mutton, lamb and goat: 43.4 (95.6)
Sugar: 45.3 (99.8)
Beer 15.5 l. (32.7 pt.)
Wine 7.7 l. (16.2 pt.)
Alcoholic liquors: 2.1 l. (4.4 pt.)
Coffee: 8.3 (18.3)
Cocoa: 1.7 (3.7)

MEDIA & CULTURE

Newspaper publishing started in 1848 in Iceland with the weekly *Thjoolfur*, which served the 1,100 residents of Reykjavik with reports of foreign and domestic affairs. Some 25 years later, the newspaper *Isafold* was founded. It has survived to this day as part of a weekly paper in Akureyri, *Islendingur-Isafold*. The first daily newspaper to appear was *Visir*, in 1910. It is now an afternoon daily with a circulation of about 21,000 and an average size of about 20 pages. There are five morning dailies, of which the largest is *Morganbladid*, a conservative paper with a circulation of 40,000. It is the oldest morning daily, founded in 1913. The second-oldest morning daily is *Timinn*, organ of the Progressive Party. The paper was founded in 1916. With an average size of 26 pages, it has a circulation of about 20,000. Founded in the same year, *Althyubladid* is the organ of the Social Democratic Party. Selling only 5,000 copies per issue, the paper has the smallest circulation of all dailies and is published only on weekdays. Slightly to its left is *Thjokviljinn*, organ of the left-wing Socialist People's Union. Founded in 1935, the paper normally runs 16 pages and has a circulation of 12,000. The youngest of the dailies is *Dagbladid*, founded in 1975. An independent paper, it managed to become within five years the nation's second-largest-selling daily, with a press run of 25,000 copies.

In addition, most political parties publish weeklies in the regional centers. The Social Democratic Party publishes *Althyudumadurinn in Akureyri* and the Progressive Party *Dagur in Akureyri* and *Einherji in Siglufjordur*. The Independence Party publishes *Siglfirdingur*. Two of the morning papers, *Morganbladid* and *Timinn*, publish special Sunday supplements of 12 to 16 pages. All Icelandic dailies are tabloids. All the dailies except *Morganbladid* share common printing facilities, established in 1972. All leading journalists are members of the the Union of Icelandic Journalists. Iceland has no national news agency.

The first Icelandic periodical was founded in 1781, and it held out for 15 years. Then came *Skirnir*, the oldest surviving periodical in Scandinavia. First published in 1827, *Skirnir* was printed in Copenhagen until 1890, when it moved to Iceland. From 1887 to 1966 more than 1,400 periodical titles appeared in Iceland.

Iceland was a country of books even before the invention of printing. Even though the largest collection of Icelandic manuscripts, the Arni Magnusson Collection in Copenhagen, was partially destroyed by fire in 1728, enough survive to attest to the vitality of Icelandic book activity in the Middle Ages. The printing press was introduced into the country in the 16th century. The first book to be published, *Brevarium Holense*, bears the date 1534. In the 17th century, total output reached 225, of which 198 were printed in the country. The annual output in the 1980s has varied from 500 to 600. Per capita, Iceland is among the top five countries of the world in book publishing, outdistancing both the United States and sister Scandinavian countries.

The state-owned *Rikisutvarpid* (Icelandic State Broadcasting Service) was founded in 1930 as a state monopoly. It runs a 100-kw. longwave station in Reykjavik and one longwave station in East Iceland, with relay stations around the country broadcasting on medium-wave and FM. There is a single radio program on the radio for about 16.5 hours. The weekly television program is some 22 hours long (there is no program on Thursdays), of which only one-third is of Icelandic origin. Both radio and television carry commercials. Annual license fees are payable for each radio and television set.

The U.S. Navy operates a radio station (24 hours a day) and a television service (80 hours a week) on the U.S. base at Keflavik.

MEDIA INDICATORS, 1986

Newspapers
  Number of dailies: 5
  Circulation (000): 114
  Per capita: 1,000 inhabitants: 507

  Newsprint consumption
  Total: 5,000 tons
  Per capita: 21 kg. (46.3 lb.)

Book publishing
  Number of titles: 1,121

Radio
  Number of transmitters: 26
  Number of radio receivers: 73,000
    Persons per: 3.3

Television
  Television transmitters: 130
  Number of TV receivers: 65,000
    Persons per: 3.7

Cinema
  Number of fixed cinemas: 39
  Seating capacity: 12,000
    Seats per 1,000: N.A.
  Annual attendance (million): 2.2
    Per 1,000: 9,400

Films
  Production of long films: 4

CULTURAL & ENVIRONMENTAL INDICATORS, 1986

Libraries
  Number: 238
  Volumes: 1,426,000

Museums: 16
  Annual attendance: 108,000
  Attendance per 1,000: 462

Performing arts
  Number of facilities: 4
  Number of performances: 528
  Annual attendance: 154,000
  Attendance per 1,000: 658

Ecological sites
  Number of facilities: 21
  Number of botanical gardens & zoos: 2

SOCIAL WELFARE

Iceland has a long history of social welfare legislation, going back to 1890, when the first law on old-age insurance was enacted, partly replacing general poor relief, which for centuries had been locally administered. As the fishing industry grew, a law providing industrial injuries compensation was passed in 1903 followed, three years later, by a law introducing sickness insurance. Comprehensive social insurance legislation was enacted in 1936, and since then these programs have been expanded and new ones introduced.

Social insurance accounts for about 80% of net Social Security expenditures and for an even higher percentage of the finance. It is divided into five branches: pensions, insurance, industrial injuries insurance, family allowances and unemployment insurance. The plans are administered by the State Social Security Institute. The Social Security Board, with five members elected by the Althing, supervises the finances and operations of the Institute. Unemployment insurance is supervised by a special board of seven members elected by the Althing and nominated by the Icelandic Federation of Labor and the Confederation of Icelandic Employers.

The central government bears 86% of the cost of pension insurance; employers cover the balance. The cost of health insurance is divided between the central government, which bears 90%, and the local governments, which bear 10%. Health benefits are paid in full by the central government. The cost of employment injuries insurance is borne by employers and employees. The unemployment insurance fund receives equal contributions from employers and local authorities, making up 50%, with another 50% from the central government. Family allowances are paid in full by the central government.

Iceland has no supplementary pensions program. On the other hand, a large number of salaried employees have long been entitled to supplementary pensions from special pension funds, most of which have been established either by law or by collective agreements. These programs are financed through contributions of employers and employees, the total contributions as a rule being 10% of the basic salary or wage. Supplementary sickness funds also have been established by collective agreements and pay daily allowances over and above the health insurance benefits.

CHRONOLOGY (from 1944)

1944–Iceland proclaims itself a sovereign republic with a new Constitution; Independence and Labor parties coalition under Ólafur Thors forms a government.

1947–Labor, Independence and Progressive parties form a coalition government under Stefan Stefansson.

1949–Iceland joins NATO . . . . Independence Party forms a minority government under Ólafur Thors.

1950–Progressive and Independence parties form a coalition government under Steingrímur Steinthórsson.

1951–U.S. base at Keflavik begins operations.

1953–Independence and progressive Parties form a coalition government under Ólafur Thors.

1956–Progressive, Labor and Labor Union parties form a coalition government under Hermann Jonasson.

1958–Iceland extends territorial limits to 19 km. (12 mi.) triggering the first cod war with the United Kingdom . . . . Labor Party a forms minority government under Emil Jonsson.

1959–Independence and Labor parties form a coalition government under Ólafur Thors.

1961–Central Bank of Iceland is founded . . . . Iceland extends territorial limits to 80 km. (50 mi.), triggering second cod war.

1963–Ólafur Thors steps down and is replaced by Bjarni Benediktsson.

1968–Iceland joins the EFTA.

1970–Benediktsson steps down as prime minister in favor of Johann Hafstein.

1971–Progressive, Lavor Union and Liberal and Left Alliance form a coalition government under Ólafur Jóhannesson.

1974–Independence and Progressive parties form a coalition government under Geir Hallgrimsson.

1975–Iceland extends territorial limits to 322 km. (200 mi.), triggering third cod war.

1978–Progressive, Labor and Labor Union parties form a coalition government under Ólafur Jóhannesson.

1979–Labor Party forms a minority government under Benedikt Groendal.

1980–A breakaway group from Independence Party, and Progressive and Labor Union parties form a coalition government under Gunnar Thoroddsen.

1983–Progressive and Independence parties form a coalition government under Steingrimur Hermannsson.

1987–Hermansson coalition loses election; Thorsteinn Palsson of the Independence Party forms coalition government.

1988–Steingrimur Hermannsson returns to office as prime minister.

BIBLIOGRAPHY

BOOKS

Ahlmann, Hans. *Land of Ice and Fire*. London, 1938.

Briem, Helgi. *Iceland and the Icelanders*. New York, 1945.

Cary, Sturges. *Volcanoes and Glaciers: The Challenge of Iceland*. New York, 1959.

Chamberlin, William Charles. *Economic Development of Iceland Through World War II*. New York, 1947.

Gjerset, Knut. *History of Iceland*. New York, 1925.

Griffiths, John C. *Modern Iceland*. New York, 1969.

Grondal, Benedikt. *Iceland: From Neutrality to NATO Membership*. Oslo, 1971.

Horton, John. *Iceland* [World Bibliographical Series]. Santa Barbara, Calif., 1983.

Iceland 1986. Reykjavik, 1986.

Jensen, Amy Elizabeth. *Iceland: Old-New Republic*. New York, 1954.

Jonsson, Hannes. *Iceland and the Law of the Sea*. Reykjavik, 1972.

Lindroth, Hjalmar. *Iceland: A Land of Contrasts*. Princeton, N.J., 1937.

Malmstrom, Vincent. *A Regional Geography of Iceland*. Reykjavik, 1958.

Nuechterlain, Donald. *Iceland: Reluctant Ally*. Ithaca, 1961.

Rothery, Agnes. *Iceland: New World Outpost*. New York, 1948.

Rutherford, Adam. *Origin and Development of the Icelandic Nation*. London, 1938.

Scherman, Katherine. *Daughter of Fire: Portrait of Iceland*. Boston, 1976.

Stefansson, Vilhjalmur. *Iceland: The First American Republic*. New York, 1939.

Thomasson, Richard. *Iceland: The First New Society*. Minneapolis, 1980.

Thorardson, Bjorn. *Iceland: Past and Present*. London, 1945.

Thorgilsson, Ari. *Book of the Icelanders*. Ithaca, N.Y., 1936.

OFFICIAL PUBLICATIONS

Accountant General

Rikisreikningur (Central Government Account) (annual).

Mánadaryfirlit Rikisbókhalds (Monthly Survey of Ministry of Finance Transactions) (unpublished).

Bókhaldsgögn ríkisbókhalds (Accounting Records of the Ministry of Finance) (unpublished).

Other Units of the Central Government

Arsreikningur Almannatryggingakerfisins (Annual Report of the Social Security Institutions).

Arsreikningur Ríkisábyrgdasjóds (Annual Report fo the State Guarantee Fund).

Arsreikningur Vidlagasjóds (Annual Report of the Contingency Insurance Program).

Communal Finance, Statistical Bureau of Iceland (special issues containing three years of local government data) (Icelandic with English headings).

Central Bank of Iceland

Arsskýrsla (Annual Report) (Icelandic and English).

Hagtölur Mánadarins (Monthly Statistical Bulletin).

Local Government

Arsreikningar Sveitarfélaga (Local Government Accounts) (annual).

Note: All sources are in Icelandic only except as indicated.

NORWAY

NORWAY

BASIC FACT SHEET

OFFICIAL NAME: Kingdom of Norway (Kongeriket Norge)

ABBREVIATION: NO

CAPITAL: Oslo

HEAD OF STATE: King Olav V (from 1957)

HEAD OF GOVERNMENT: Prime Minister Gro Harlem Brundtland (from 1986)

NATURE OF GOVERNMENT: Parliamentary democracy; constitutional monarchy

POPULATION: 4,190,758 (1988)

AREA: 324,220 sq. km. (125,149 sq. mi.)

ETHNIC MAJORITY: Nordic

LANGUAGE: Norwegian

RELIGION: Evangelical Lutheran

UNIT OF CURRENCY: Krone

NATIONAL FLAG: A blue cross with an extended right horizontal outlined in white on a red field

NATIONAL EMBLEM: A gold-crowned lion on a red shield holding the silver-headed battle ax of St. Olaf in its forepaws. The shield is crested with a gold crown bearing an orb and a plain gold cross at its peak. When shown as the royal arms, the shield is surrounded by the chain and order of St. Olaf and displayed on a red, gold-fringed ermine pavilion with a more elaborate crown, repeating the lion and ax them at its crest.

NATIONAL ANTHEM: "Ja, Vi Elsker Dette Lander" ("Yes, We Love This Country")

NATIONAL HOLIDAYS: Constitution Day (May 17); New Year's Day; Labor Day; all major Christian festivals

NATIONAL CALENDAR: Gregorian

PHYSICAL QUALITY OF LIFE INDEX: 99 (on ascending scale with 100 as the maximum)

DATE OF INDEPENDENCE: June 7, 1905

DATE OF CONSTITUTION: May 17, 1814

WEIGHTS & MEASURES: Metric

GEOGRAPHICAL FEATURES

Norway is in the western part of the Scandinavian peninsula, with almost one-third of the country north of the Arctic Circle. Norway's total land area, including Svalbard and Jan Mayen, is 386,958 sq. km. (149,009 sq. mi.). Svalbard, with 62,700 sq. km. (24,202 sq.mi.), constitutes 16.20% of the land area; Jan Mayen, with 380 sq. km. (147 sq. mi.), has 0.10% of the land area. Norway extends 1,752 km. (1,089 mi.) NNE to SSW, the greatest length of any European country outside the Soviet Union. Norway's greatest width is 430 km. (267 mi.)

ESE to WNW, but in places it is less than 8 km. (4.97 mi.). Norway is bounded on the north by the Arctic Ocean, on the northeast by Finland and the Soviet Union, on the west by the Norwegian Sea of the Atlantic Ocean, on the east by Sweden, on the south by the Skagerrak and on the southwest by the North Sea. The land boundaries are 716 km. (455 mi.) with Finland, 196 km. (122 mi.) with the Soviet Union and 1,619 km. (1,006 mi.) with Sweden. Traveling northward from the Skagerrak, the sea boundaries consist of the North Sea as far as the Stadt; the Atlantic, called the Norwegian Sea, as far as the North Cape; and then the Arctic Ocean. The total coastline is 1,995 km. (1,240 mi.) when measured as an unbroken line but more than seven times that length with the inclusion of the fjords and the greater islands. There are no border or other territorial disputes.

The capital is Oslo, formerly Christiania, in the Southeast, on the Oslo fjord. There are only two other cities over 100,000 inhabitants: Bergen in the Southwest, on the Pudde Fjord; and Trondheim, in West Norway, on the Trondheim fjord. Trondheim is the place of coronation and the place of burial of Norwegian kings.

PRINCIPAL CITIES (population, 1984)			
Oslo (capital)	447,257	Stavanger	92,883
Bergen	207,332	Kristiansand	61,704
Trondheim	134,143	Drammen	50,809

The Scandinavian peninsula slopes abruptly toward the Atlantic coast, giving a rugged appearance to the Norwegian side of the border with Sweden. This ruggedness takes on a grander scale to the south of the Trondheim depression, which forms an effective boundary zone between the northern and southern halves of the country. In general, Norway is a mountainous country, with average elevations exceeding 457 mi. (1,500 ft.). Its upland character is most clearly seen in the high fells. The fell area is commonly divided into six areas: Jostedalsbreen, the Jotunheim and the western *vidder* and Dovrefjell, Trollheimen and the eastern *vidder*. Fully 3,000 sq. km. (1,158 sq. mi.) of the fells are under icefields, the most extensive of which is the Jostedalsbreen. The ice surfaces range from 914 to 1,829 m. (3,000 to 6,000 ft.) in height. Mountains clutter the topographical map of Norway, and an array of suffixes indicate mountainous features: *egg* (crest); *hammer* (precipice); *hord* (a broad summit); *kamp* (a broad top); *knat* (a crag); *koll* (a rounded top).

Deep troughs are incised into the plateau surfaces. The troughs take the form of narrow gorges in the interior. Seaward, they broaden into fjords. The fjord heads commonly are characterized by deltaic flats; their central stretches are of great depth, but their mouths are relatively shallow. The fjord zone reaches its greatest breadth in Sogne and Hardanger. Arctic fjords such as Tana, Lakse and Varanger are broader and shorter. The fjords are complemented by deeply entrenched valleys on the landward side. Glaciated valleys such as Setesdal, Numdal, Hallingdal and Valdres, with their extended ribbon lakes, frequently give the illusion of inland fjords. The pattern of alternating valleys and plateaus suggests that Norway is a collection of fjords, as many geographers have described it.

Much of the landscape is dominated by steep gradients. Verticality also has resulted in deep scouring of the land and its continual denudation. Thus water moves in cataracts, scarring the weathered precipices. It is said that in western Norway the sound of the erosion can be heard in the form of a roar or a rumble.

Except in the Southwest and the Far North, the coast to which the plateaus fall has a girdle of islands. The island zone reaches its broadest width of over 60 km. (37 mi.) at the southern approaches to the Trondheim fjord. The outer islands, protruding from relatively shallow waters, rarely exceed 30 m. (100 ft.) in height, while the inner islands may rise to 305 m. (1,000 ft.). These islands are characterized by a series of rock terraces known as strandflats.

In the extreme Southwest, the Jaeren Peninsula has been described as a bit of Denmark clinging to Norway. Viewing the coast in its entirety, there is an interesting contrast between the longer fjords of the South and the shorter fjords of the North, and the larger islands of the North and the smaller islands of the South.

Complementary to the islands are numerous lakes, which are more diverse in form than those of Finland. Because of altitudinal variations, Norway's lakes are at many different levels. In the Southeast, Lake Mjosa is the largest, while Lake Rosvann is the highest in North Norway.

Between the southwestern massif and the southeastern fells of the Swedish borderlands is a rich valley complex focusing upon Gudbrandsdal and Østerdal. These two great dales open up routes to the Trondheim lowland and also drain into the Oslo fjord through flights of broad and fertile terraces. Here is the dividing line between Østfold and Vestfold, characterized by continuous levels of level lowland. Østland is the most Swedish part of Norway in its landscapes. Trondelag also bears resemblance to Østland in its lowlands. Extending from Stavanger fjord to Skien on the margins of Østland is Sorlandet. North Norway is described by geographers as the fifth major unit of the country, and it is as dissected as any other part of Norway. Some of the largest islands in Scandinavia—Hinnøy, Senjaa, North Kvaløy, South Kvaløy and Sorey—are in this region. The two most extensive and detached island groups are those of Lofoten and Vesterålen. Much of the land is bare of vegetation.

Norwegian mountain ranges are roughly divided into three groups. The most northerly, the Kjölen, is by far the greatest and forms a natural barrier between Norway and Sweden, receding with decreasing height northward to the Finnish border. The Dovrefjell range marks the division between North and South Norway. The Langfjell, consisting of several ranges, contains the highest peaks in the peninsula. Galdhøpiggen, in this group, is the highest peak in the country, at 2,560 m. (8,399 ft.). At an altitude of 1,830 m. (6,004 ft.) lies the Hardangervidda, a desert plateau of some 6,477 sq. km. (2,500 sq. mi.), with steep sides scarred and grooved by waterfalls and valleys.

Throughout Norway, the sound of falling water is the natural accompaniment to the landscape. The melting snow from the great fields of the Hardanger and Jostedalsbreen mountains releases vast amounts of what the Norwegians call "white coal." Among the most magnificent falls are the 253-m. (830-ft.) Vettisfos, east of Sogne; and the 162-m. (530-ft.) Vøringfos, which falls from the heights of Fossli to the Maabodal Valley.

Most of the northern end of the Norwegian Plateau is covered by icecaps. They are, on the whole, uninterrupted by peaks rising above them and are almost without crevasses. Jostedalsbreen, 1,503 sq. km. (580 sq. mi.) in area and possibly 457 m. (1,500 ft.) thick, is the largest glacier in Europe. The next two largest are the Svartisen, about 1,036 sq. km. (400 sq. mi.) in area; and Folgefonn, about 280 sq. km. (108 sq. mi.) in area, the top of which is over 1,524 m. (5,000 ft.) above sea level. Other large snowfields include Hallinskarvet in Hardanger, Snohetta in Dovrefjell, Store Borgefjell overlooking the Namsen Valley, Seiland near Hammerfest and Oksfjordjokel near Kvanangen. Most of the glaciers are clean, with little of the loose dirt that spoils the appearance of the Alpine glaciers.

The rivers of Norway are swift and turbulent, rushing through steep valleys and rocky gorges. Generally the rivers are not navigable, but they are valuable as flumes for the timber coming down from forest districts. The only navigable rivers are the Glomma and the Dramselv. The Glomma, the largest river in Scandinavia, is 563 km. (350 mi.) long and rises more than 610 m. (2,000 ft.) above sea level at Aursunden Lake, north of Røros. Many lakes widen the stream, and the river is famous for its fine waterfalls. Dramselv rises in Valdres and enters Oslofjord at Drammen. The other major rivers are the Numedalslagen, the Nidelv, the Rauma, the Driva, the Sand, the Bjoreia and the Evanger.

Lakes abound in Norway. Nearly one-twelfth of the country is under fresh water, sometimes so deep that the waterbed is far below the level of the sea. By far the greatest of these lakes is the Mjøsa, 363 sq. km. (140 sq. mi.) in area and 452 m. (1,482 ft.) deep. Hornindaisvann, although only 32 km. (20 mi.) in area, has the same depth as Mjøsa. Among the more beautiful lakes are Loen, Olden,

Bygdin, Tyin, Femundsjon, Rosvann, Randsfjord, Tyrifjord, Snaasenvatn, Tansjon and Altevatn. The levels of the lakes differ greatly, by as much as 396 m. (1,300 ft.) in altitude. Most of the larger lakes are 122 m. (400 ft.) above the sea and were perhaps heads of fjords that have since disappeared.

In 1920 the Spitsbergen archipelago was placed under Norwegian sovereignty and given the name Svalbard. Bear Island (Björnoya, 178 sq. km.; 69 sq. mi.) usually is included in the Svalbard group. Norwegian sovereignty over Jan Mayen Island (372 sq. km.; 144 sq. mi.) was recognized in 1930. Compared with the mainland, the islands have a complex geology, with a much greater range of rocks. It shares some of the basalt features common to Iceland and the Faeroes. Icefields cover extended areas and the surface is covered by permafrost. Svalbard is the most northerly human settlement in Europe.

The richest vegetation is found in the Southeast, around Oslofjord, and is dominated by conifers (spruce, fir and pine). At lower levels there are deciduous trees such as maple, oak, ash, elm and silver birch. Above the conifer timber line at 900 m. (2,952 ft.) extends a zone of birch trees; above that, a zone of dwarf willow and dwarf birch; and beyond that grow lichens, especially the variety known as reindeer moss and other arctic plants. Higher still, the rocks are bare. The world's northernmost tree grows at Hammerfest.

Arctic flowers are found wherever the climate is dry and warm. Gentian and mountain avens grow in clusters, and ice ranunculus and wild azaleas flourish beside the delicate harebell. The flora becomes scarcer toward the coast.

Animal species are sharply divided into arctic and boreal. In the North, the reindeer, polar fox, wolverine, polar hare, lemming and snow bunting are relics of the period when arctic animals roamed the country. Toward the South, elk is found, along with red deer, bear, lynx, fox, marten and stoat. Bears and beaver have almost died out. Seabirds dominate avian life. Inland birds are mostly migratory, flying South in the autumn. Most of the reptiles are immigrants from the South. The circumfluent Gulf Stream is rich in fish life and abounds in cod, herring, haddock, whiting and flounder.

CLIMATE & WEATHER

Norway covers an area of over 13 degrees of latitude, and the climatic conditions vary accordingly, but generally the coast enjoys a mild winter and a cool summer while the interior has a cold winter and a hot summer. Considering its northern situation, Norway has a remarkably equable climate mainly due to the currents of tropical air and the warm waters of the Gulf Stream. In the western coastal area, from the land's end at Lindesnes to the Lofoten Islands protruding into the Arctic Sea in the North, the climate is mild during the winter months from November to March/April, with mean temperatures of 1°-2°C (34°-36°F).

In the Lofoten Islands, the mean temperature is over 20°C (68°F) above the average for its latitude. The coastal levels also have the highest levels of precipitation, as clouds blown in from the west lose much of their humidity when they encounter the high mountains close to the sea. Inland Norway has, in general, less precipitation and larger temperature variations between summer and winter. The highest mean temperatures are registered in districts around Oslofjord at 15°-17°C (59°-63°F). The highest temperature ever recorded in Norway is 35.6°C (96.1°F); the lowest, -51°C (-59.8°F). The most exposed cold spots are in the inland valleys and mountain districts of South-Central Norway and on the plateau of Finnmarksvidda in the North.

In the summer the prevailing winds blow from the sea; in winter, from the land. Thunderstorms are not common.

During part of the summer, the midnight sun, a popular attraction of foreign tourists, shines over Norway north of the Arctic Circle. At Tromsø, the largest city in the North, it lasts from May 20 till July 23. At Longyearbyen, in Svalbard, it lasts from April 21 till August 8. Conversely, there are long winter nights from the end of November to the end of January, during which the sun does not rise above the horizon and in which the northern lights, or aurora borealis, are visible.

POPULATION

The population of Norway was estimated at 4,190,758 in 1988, based on the last census, held in 1986, when the population was 4,145,845. Norway ranks 62nd in the world in land size and 96th in size of population. The population is expected to be 4,224,000 by 1990 and 4,356,000 by 2000.

Patterns of settlement suggest that while the national density is low, it also is uneven. The Vik region, coextensive in certain respects with the coastal zone of Sweden, has the greatest population concentration of Norway. It extends southwestward, into the southern coastlands of Sorlandet. Outside the South, the population distribution is closely related to physical accessibility, with distinct concentrations near rivers and other waterways. Another characteristic of these settlements is the predominance of isolated farmsteads. Called *tatorts*, these loose clusters of dwellings constitute the most common form of settlements in other Scandinavian countries as well.

Emigration is part of Norwegian population history and began as early as 1825, when the first group of emigrants left Norway for the United States on board the 50-ton sloop *Restorationen*. Within the next 35 years over 44,000 Norwegians had found their way to the New World, mostly to midwestern states such as Minnesota. There also was limited emigration to South

America and Australia. Since the beginning of this century there also has been a sizable return emigration.

Urbanization has moved more slowly in Norway than in Sweden or Denmark but it gathered momentum as a result of the clustering of industries in the major cities of Oslo, Trondheim and Bergen. Between 1965 and 1985 the urban population share grew from 37% to 73%. During 1965-80 Norway had one of the highest rates of urban growth in Western Europe, at 5.0%.

Norway has been less exposed to non-Nordic immigration than Sweden, West Germany, France, the United Kingdom and the Netherlands. In 1984 the 101,000 foreign nationals in the country constituted less than 2.5% of the population. Of these, 32% were citizens of other Nordic countries, 31.5% nationals from the rest of Europe, 19% Asians, 11.6% North Americans, 3.0% Africans, 2.3% Latin Americans and 0.6% Australians and Pacific islanders. In 1975 severe restrictions were imposed on non-Nordic immigration. Although their rights are protected by law, many non-Nordic immigrants face discrimination in public and social life, particularly Pakistanis, Turks, Vietnamese and Africans.

Women, who constitute over 40% of the work force, are protected under the Equal Rights Law of 1978 and other regulations. The state Equal Rights Council monitors enforcement of the law, and the equal rights ombudsman processes complaints of sexual discrimination. Norway has a woman prime minister, and it is far ahead of other Nordic countries in the number of women legislators. Eight of the 18 cabinet portfolios are held by women, one of the highest percentages in the world. No information is available on birth control activities or official birth control policies in Norway.

DEMOGRAPHIC INDICATORS, 1986

Population, 1988 (000): 4,191
Year of last census: 1986
 Sex ratio: male, 49.4; female, 50.6
Population trends (million)
 1930: 2,807   1960: 3,581   1990: 4,224
 1940: 2,973   1970: 3,877   2000: 4,356
 1950: 3,265   1980: 4,086
Population doubling time in years at current rate: Over
   100 years
Hypothetical size of stationary population (million): 4
Assumed year of reaching net reproduction rate of 1:
   2030
Age profile (%)
 0–14: 19.8   30–44: 21.3   60–74: 14.7
 15–29: 23.2   45–59: 14.4   Over 75: 6.6
Median age (years): 35.7
Density per sq. km. (per sq. mi.): 12.9 (20.8)

```
┌─────────────────────────────────────────────────────┐
│        DEMOGRAPHIC INDICATORS, 1986 (continued)      │
│  Annual growth rate (%)                              │
│    1950–55: 0.97    1975–80: 0.42    1995–2000: 0.06 │
│    1960–65: 0.78    1980–85: 0.27    2000–05: 0.03   │
│    1965–70: 0.81    1985–90: 0.18    2010–15: 0.07   │
│    1970–75: 0.66    1990–95: 0.12    2020–25: 0.01   │
│  Vital statistics                                    │
│    Crude birth rate, 1/1,000: 12.6                   │
│    Crude death rate, 1/1,000: 10.5                   │
│    Change in birth rate, 1965–84: –25.5              │
│    Change in death rate, 1965–84: 7.4                │
│    Dependency, total: 52.9                           │
│    Infant mortality rate, 1/1,000: 8                 │
│    Child (0–4 years) mortality rate, 1/1,000: Insignificant │
│    Maternal mortality rate, 1/100,000: 2.0           │
│    Natural increase, 1/1,000: 2.1                    │
│    Total fertility rate: 1.7                         │
│    General fertility rate: 48                        │
│    Gross reproduction rate: 0.77                     │
│    Marriage rate, 1/1,000: 4.8                       │
│    Divorce rate, 1/1,000: 1.9                        │
│    Life expectancy, males (years): 72.8              │
│    Life expectancy, females (years): 79.5            │
│    Average household size: 2.4                       │
│    % illegitimate births: 25.8                       │
│  Youth                                               │
│    Youth population 15–24 (000): 650                 │
│    Youth population in 2000 (000): 530               │
│  Women                                               │
│    Of childbearing age 15–49 (000): 1,051            │
│    Child/woman ratio: 2.57 per woman                 │
│    % women using contraception: N.A.                 │
│    % women married 15–49: N.A.                       │
│  Urban                                               │
│    Urban population (000): 3,641                     │
│    % urban 1965: 37    1985: 73                      │
│    Annual urban growth rate (%)                      │
│    1965–80: 5.0    1980–85: 0.9                       │
│    % urban population in largest city: 18            │
│    % urban population in cities over 500,000: 62     │
│    Number of cities over 500,000: 3                  │
│    Annual rural growth rate: –8.0%                   │
└─────────────────────────────────────────────────────┘
```

ETHNIC COMPOSITION

Except for the approximately 25,000 Asian, African and Latin American immigrants as will as small numbers from other non-Nordic areas, Norway has an extremely homogeneous population, consisting almost entirely of Nordics.

The only historical ethnic minority is the Sami or Lapp group. They number not more than 30,000 to 40,000 in Norway, constituting about about two-thirds of the global Lapp population. Norwegian Lapps are classified into three groups: Mountain Lapps, River Lapps and Sea Lapps. The Mountain Lapps are seminomads living in a wide area from Varanger to Fermunden. The River Lapps live in the vicinity of the watercourses in the interior of Finnmark and combine agriculture with animal husbandry and hunting. The Sea Lapps, who make up the largest group, inhabit the northern Norwegian fjords from Varanger to Tysfjord. They are fishers and farmers whose lifestyles are not markedly different from those of their non-Lapp neighbors.

LANGUAGE

The national language is Norwegian, which belongs, along with Danish and Swedish in Scandinavia, to the Germanic language group. In addition to the letters of the English alphabet, it has three additional letters: æ, å and ø.

Historically, there are two language forms: Bokmaal and Nynorsk. The conflict between these forms has played a large part in the literary and social history of Norway. It has been a controversial issue in Norway for more than a century and has not been resolved to this day.

Both Bokmaal (literally, the language of the book) and Nynorsk (New Norwegian) are closely related, and both are mutually comprehensible. There is a large overlap between them, their main differences being in orthography, pronunciation and vocabulary, although these are being continually eroded. The aim of the official language policy is to blend these two forms into Common Norwegian (Samnorsk).

Although the language controversy dates chiefly from the 19th century, the origin of the language division is much older. In the 12th and 13th centuries, the language of Norway was the Old Norse of the sagas, the Eddaic lays and the skaldic poems. Although much of the Old Norse literature was written in Iceland, the dialects of Trondelag and western and eastern Norway dominated in Norway itself.

Changes began to appear in the language after most of the clergy perished during the Black Death of 1349–50 and Norway was united with Sweden and Denmark. The influence of Swedish was strong up to 1450 and that of Danish after that date. After 1500 the bishops of Oslo and Nidaros (Trondheim) used only Danish. Combined with the decline of the Norwegian literary tradition, this development enabled Danish to become the only written language of Norway after the Reformation. However, Norwegian continued to be the spoken form of native-born Norwegians. The country became, in effect, bilingual.

The influence of Danish was reinforced by the advent of printing in Norway 163 years after it reached Denmark in 1480. This meant that throughout the period all Bibles, catechisms and hymnals were available only in Danish. Further, since the kingdom's only university was in Copenhagen, the clergy and the literati were educated in Danish. For example, Ludvig Holberg, the most distinguished writer in Danish in the 18th century, was a Norwegian by birth.

Even during this Danish period, Norwegian was kept alive by lexicographical works such as *Den Norske Dictionarium* (1646) by Christen Jensson, *Glossarium Norvagicum* (1749) by Bishop Erik Pontoppidan and *Norsk Ordsamling* (1802) by Laurents Hallager, as well as literary works of Thomas Rosing de Stockfleth and Edvard Storm. Norwegians also used their own pronunciation when reading Danish aloud. Thus a curious reading pronunciation of Danish developed in Norway, especially in the church and among the upper classes. As a result there were not only two languages but also two types of pronunciation for each language.

When the union with Denmark was dissolved in 1814, the position of Danish as the national language still was strong. Indeed, its position was strengthened as the sole medium of instruction in schools, although its name was changed to Modersmaalet (mother tongue). Further, the schools taught a pure Danish uncorrupted by Norwegianisms. Writers such as Mauritz Hansen and H.A. Bjerregaard were criticized for the use of Norwegian words in their works.

The first blow for language reform was struck by poet Henrik Wergeland (1808–45), whose *Om Norsk Sprogreformation* (On Norwegian Language Reform), published in 1835, called for the adoption of Norwegian as the language of the country. The case of Norwegian was put forth even more strongly by Ivar Aasen and Knud Knudsen. The researches of Aasen into Norwegian rural dialects was a turning point. In 1848 he published his *Det Norske Folkesprogs Grammattik* (A Grammar of the Norwegian Folk Language) and in 1850 *Ordbog over det Norske Folkesprog* (Dictionary of the Norwegian Folk Language), revised in 1864 and 1873, respectively. Aasen was the first to christen dialectal Norwegian Landsmaal, meaning both country language and national language. It corresponded most closely to the dialects of western Norway and eschewed all loan words and forms derived from Danish and German.

Knud Knudsen, a teacher, developed a practical plan, explained in his *Det Norske Malstraev* (The Norwegian Language Struggle) of 1867 to work step by step for the Norwegianization of Dano-Norwegian. His campaign for orthographic changes bore fruit in the publication of J. Aars's *Norske Retskrivnings Regler* (Spelling Rules for Norwegian), and Knudsen's program for the substitution of the unvoiced consonants p, t and k for the voiced b, d and g of Danish was realized after his death. Allying himself with Henrik Ibsen and Bjornstjerne

Bjornson, Knudsen combated the influence of Danish on Norwegian pronunciation in *Den Landsgyldige Norske Uttale* (A Norwegian Pronunciation Valid for the Whole Country) in 1876. To encourage the substitution of Norwegian for loanwords, he compiled a massive dictionary called *Unorsk og Norsk* (Un-Norwegian and Norwegian) in 1881. In it he proposed Norwegian equivalents, some of which were neologisms of his own devising, for foreign words.

Meanwhile, Landsmaal gained new converts in writers such as Aasmund Olafsen Vinje and Arne Garborg. The movement was promoted by periodicals such as *Dolen* and *Fedraheimen*.

It was not long before the language question came into the political arena. In 1885 the Storting (Parliament) gave Landsmaal the same position in schools as Dano-Norwegian, and the Primary Schools Act of 1892 prescribed that all children learn to read both language forms. It was left to local option which form should be used in written work. By the turn of the century some 200 rural schools had opted for Landsmaal. This led to a demand for reform in spelling. In 1890 a committee made proposals for spelling norms to be used in schools, and in 1901 a word list compiled by Matias Skard was officially approved for school use.

These reforms fueled linguistic passions, and the defenders of both Rigsmaal, as Dano-Norwegian came to be called, and Landsmaal organized themselves into hostile camps. In 1899 the *Rigsmaalsforeninger* (Societies for the Protection of Rigsmaal) was founded, followed by the *Noregs Maalag in 1906*.

The dissolution of the union with Sweden in 1905 strengthened the defenders of Landsmaal. Spelling changes were approved in 1907 and made mandatory in government offices and schools. These reforms were based on the spoken language, but nevertheless they created much confusion in syntax and vocabulary and led to plaintive cries from Norwegians that they no longer knew how to spell their own language. The idea also was put forward by writer Moltke Moe that the two language forms should be merged into a common language called Fellesnorsk (Common Norwegian).

In the years immediately following the 1907 reforms, the language question remained a controversial one, and it even led to the resignation of Prime Minister Wallert Konow in 1912. In 1916 a new language commission was set up, and its recommendations carried the process of Norwegianizing Dano-Norwegian a stage farther. Among other things, the feminine gender was introduced, and alternative forms were permitted for certain verb endings. The proposals immediately drew fire from supporters of Dano-Norwegian, including Knut Hamsun, whose scathing pamphlet *Sproget i Fare* (Language in Danger) opposed regimentation of language. The *Rigsmaalsvernet* (Defenders of the Rigsmaal) retaliated by launching a dictionary, which was completed in 1957. Since 1913

Landsmaal has been a co-official language of the Storting. In 1917 geographical names were Norwegianized. In 1918 the Danish *amt* for county was replaced by the Norwegian *fylke*, and many places were rechristened; Thus Brasberg became Telemark, Christiania became Oslo, Trondhjem became Nidaros and later Trondheim. The names of the two languages were themselves changed, to Bokmaal (Rigsmaal) and Nynorsk (Landsmaal).

The language question gained fresh impetus after the Labor Party gained power in 1933. Halvdan Koht, the party's chief theoretician and spokesman in this debate, advocated what he called Folkemalet (Folk Language), which would coalesce the two languages on the basis of Norwegian folk speech. In 1933 the Storting set up a new language committee for this purpose and also for reducing the number of alternative word forms in both languages. The committee's report, issued in 1936, tried to achieve unity by legitimizing many formerly dialectal grammatical and lexical forms and introducing radical changes in Nynorsk grammar. The report proposed many alternative forms but was permissive regarding their usage. The report was criticized by both language camps, and its permissiveness displeased teachers. In response, the committee issued a supplementary report changing some of their recommendations, and it was approved by the Storting in 1938. The new orthography had the disadvantage of being a construction that did not correspond to the actual speech of any social group. For many words, the committee gave an obligatory form, an optional form and a side form, all equally valid, but excluded many current ones. The new orthography was adopted by the city of Oslo which, because of its importance as a textbook market, influenced the rest of the country. However, the new manuals of style and usage began to dispense conflicting advice creating a language that was more natural but less precise. Opposition to the reform came unexpectedly from poet and essayist Arnulf Overland, one of the more radical members of the Labor Party.

The Nazi occupation of Norway brought a lull to the language struggle, but it resumed vigorously as soon as the war ended. In 1949 the Education Ministry set up a committee to make recommendations for norms in both languages. The proposal engendered an intense struggle, rising to fever pitch. Protests by parents spread throughout Norway, while the Authors' Society and the Norwegian Academy for Language and Literature, led by Arnulf Overland, conducted a legal and media battle in favor of Rigsmaal. In 1958 the Language Commission delivered its report. Its task had been to propose a reduction in the number of optional spellings and thus make for greater stability in orthography and remove the need for parallel editions of texts. But the commission's recommendations were less than radical. In Bokmaal, some of the optional spelling forms were reduced to the status of side forms, and complicated rules governing the use of the feminine gender were introduced. In Nynorsk vowel changes were introduced for a large number of words to bring them in line with Bokmaal, consonants doubled in some words and the number of permitted optional forms increased rather than decreased. In 1958 the Storting approved the proposals, and they were promulgated in 1959 with a few minor changes. *Ny Lareboknormal 1959* (New Textbook Norm 1959) was published in that year, giving word lists including all the permitted forms, both moderate and radical.

In 1964 the Education Ministry set up a new committee to examine the language question. Known as the Vogt Committee, after its chairman, Hans Vogt, or the Sprakfredkomiteen (the Language Peace Committee), its recommendations, issued in 1966, called for a reorganization of the Language Commission, abandonment of the commission's mandate to promote a fusion of the two languages on the basis of the folk language and a return to traditional spelling in some areas.

The language struggle has had some positive results. The spelling of Norwegian has become more phonetic than it was at the turn of the century. Boksmal has become a more literary instrument and Nynorsk more uniform. However, statistics show that *Nynorsk* has been losing ground since the 1940s, with less than 10% of primary schools using it. Only about 5% of the books published in the country are in Nynorsk. Eventually some modified form of Boksmal may become the sole language form of Norway.

RELIGION

Christianity was introduced in about A.D. 900 by German missionaries from the Hamburg-Bremen bishopric and was established as the national religion by King Hakon the Good (945–60). Repeated conflicts between church and state during the middle ages led to easy acceptance of the Reformation and the establishment of a state church based on the Lutheran Confession. The evangelical fervor that characterized other European countries during this period did not appear in Norway until the middle of the 19th century. The renewal of the church began with a layman and farmer, Hans Nielsen Hauge, at the beginning of the 19th century. A second awakening took place through the preaching of Giles Johnson. Out of this movement grew the Luther Foundation of 1868 with a strong mission emphasis, which in 1891 became the Luther Inner Mission Society. A similar society developed in western Norway through the work of returning emigrants. Another revival, in 1880–90, led to the founding of the Luther Mission Society in 1891. The 20th century has not witnessed any similar revivals, but the church continues to be a dominant force in national life. Membership and orthodox belief continue to be high (almost 66%), although church attendance is low (3%). Other statistics also indicate the strength of religious traditions: 50% are regular listeners of religious broadcasts, 90% of the children are baptized, 80% are confirmed, 85% are married in church, 95% are buried from church, 84% of parents teach their children evening prayers, 50% pray regularly and 95% support religious education programs in school.

When the church became Lutheran in 1537 it retained a diocesan and parish structure that was basically pre-Reformation in character. At present there are 10 bishoprics sibdivided into 91 deaneries, 594 parishes and 1,078 congregational districts. There are about 1,300 chapels and churches served by some 1,000 clergy including, since 1961, a few women priests. From the 1950s there has been a brisk building of churches, particularly in the new population centers.

The earliest free church was the Baptist, founded by a Danish missionary in 1850. Methodism came to Norway in 1853 through the efforts of a Norwegian seaman converted and ordained in the United States. Other free churches grew out of the renewal within the state church, such as the Evangelical Lutheran Free Church and the Mission Covenant Church. Pentecostalism began in 1906 and has grown rapidly since then. The first Roman Catholic parish was organized in 1842 but even after about 150 years the number of Catholics was only about 11,000 of whom 65% were native-born. Nevertheless, Norway was transferred in 1977 from the jurisdiction of Propaganda to that of the Congregation for Bishops.

The Constitution of 1814 specifies the Evangelical Lutheran religion as the official religion of the state. This provision still is preserved, although various other constitutional terms have been eliminated, including the ban against "monkish priests, Jesuits and Jews." Article 4 states that the king must profess the state religion and Article 12 that at least half the cabinet must do the same.

The principal law governing church structure (Norske Kirkes Ordning) dates from 1953 and prescribes the elements of a self-governing structure: pastors, elected parish councils, bishops and diocesan councils. On the national level, the law recognizes a regular bishops' meeting and a quadrennial diocesan council meeting. The Central Council of Diocesan Councils was established by law in 1969. The appointment of ministers and bishops and control over finance are vested in the government through the Ministry of Church Affairs and Education. The financial needs of the church are met partly by the state, with the salaries of the clergy as the main item; partly by the 440 municipalities, which build churches, appoint and pay minor officials and provide clergy housing; and partly by voluntary contributions from church members. The principle of state aid to denominations outside the church system was recognized in the 1969 law and, since 1970, they have been subsidized out of the state budget by a small sum per capita.

The 1969 law also provided that (1) no one is permitted to belong to more than one religious body at the same time, (2) freedom of religion is assured for all religions, (3) religious bodies must register with the county where their principal office is located, (4) anyone over age 15 may freely join or leave a religious body, (5) no one under age 20 may take perpetually binding religious vows, (6) children born in wedlock belong to the religion of their parents and (7) children born out of wedlock follow the faith of their mother.

HISTORICAL BACKGROUND

Norway, known as Norge (Northern Way) in the early centuries of the Christian era, entered European history dramatically in the 8th and 9th centuries when the warlike Vikings embarked on their plundering raids on the undefended shores of Germany, Holland, Scotland, England and France and carried rich booty home. Olaf Haraldsson (d. 1030) was the first notable king, and he is credited with the establishment of the Norwegian monarchy and Christianity as the national religion. The archbishopric of Trondheim was established in 1152. Throughout the 11th and 12th centuries Norway was rent by civil wars. In the 13th century a common legal code was adopted and the right of succession to the crown was fixed. In the same period, Iceland and Greenland came under Norwegian rule.

Norway lost its independence at the death of Haakon V in 1319 when Magnus VII became the ruler of both Norway and Sweden. The Black Death ravaged Norway in the middle of the 14th century. After the death of Olaf V Norway entered the Union of Kalmar with Denmark and Sweden in 1397 and was ruled from the 15th to the 18th centuries by Danish governors. The economy suffered as the German merchants of the Hanseatic League dominated Norwegian trade. Wars broke up the Union of Kalmar but union between Denmark and Norway was maintained. The Lutheran Reformation was introduced in 1536. Norway was involved in the Nordic wars on the Danish side, in the course of which it lost to Sweden Harjedalen and Jamtland in 1645 and Bohuslan in 1658. Denmark's alliance with France during the Napoleonic wars resulted in the dissolution of its union with Norway. By the Peace of Kiel in 1814 Norway was ceded to Sweden, but Denmark retained the Faeroe Islands, Iceland and Greenland. A new constitution law was signed in 1814 and Christian Frederick was elected king but a short war resulted in his abdication and in union with Sweden in the same year. The union proved unpopular throughout the 19th century and was dissolved in 1905. Danish prince Carl was elected king of Norway and assumed the name Haakon VII. Norway remained neutral in World War I but was invaded by the Nazis in 1940 after 125 years of undisturbed peace. The national resistance was led by King Haakon, who escaped to

England, where he established a government-in-exile. Norway was liberated on May 8, 1945, and the king returned a month later. After the war, Norway abandoned its neutrality and joined NATO.

CONSTITUTION & GOVERNMENT

The Norwegian Constitution (Grunnloven) is one of the oldest of modern constitutions. It was signed at Eidsvoll, north of Oslo, on May 17, 1814. It comprises five chapters: (1) Form of Government and Religion, (2) The Executive Power, the King and the Royal Family, (3) Citizenship and the Legislative Power, (4) The Judicial Power and (5) General Provisions. It does not include a Bill of Rights or other specific guarantees of human rights other than those implied in its provisions.

The Grunnloven was a hastily written document; it was drafted in just six weeks. Further, it predated the introduction of parliamentary democracy by 70 years. As a result, it has been amended often, either through formal acts of the Storting or changes in constitutional practice. Thus the Constitution today is a curious mixture of written law and common law.

When the Constitution speaks of the king as the locus of executive power, it denotes in constitutional practice the "king in council" or the "Council of State," and the royal power is limited to signing cabinet papers and decisions along with the concerned minister. However, unlike in Sweden, the king, who is the head of state, has not been shorn of all formal powers, but generally he is outside the *regjeringen*, or the central government as a political unit. The head of government is the prime minister.

The Constitution specifies that "matters of importance shall be decided in the Council of State." It also enumerates these "matters of importance," including among them the church, the military, appointment of officials and the issuance and repeal of ordinances. They day-to-day political decisions made by the cabinet are prepared by the ministries and voted on at informal meetings known as *regjeringskonferanser*. They are then implemented through the central administration or other public agencies. The executive also has considerable legislative initiative. According to the Constitution, it has the right of suspensive veto against bills passed by the Storting, but this is rarely if ever done.

The cabinet generally consists of 17 ministers (half of whom are required to be members of the state church) headed by the prime minister. The tradition is to consider the prime minister as primus inter pares, a fact that distinguishes him from his U.K. counterpart. However, the entire cabinet is appointed by and resigns with him. Ministers are responsible individually and the cabinet collectively to the Storting. Cabinets may be forced to resign through a parliamentary motion of no confidence.

In addition, the central government works through the local institutions, which carry out part of the central government's functions. For example, the municipal school board is in charge of municipal schools, the price authorities are represented by the Price Boards, the Labor Inspectorate by the Labor Inspection Boards and the Agricultural Administration by the Municipal Agricultural Boards.

ORGANIZATION OF NORWEGIAN GOVERNMENT

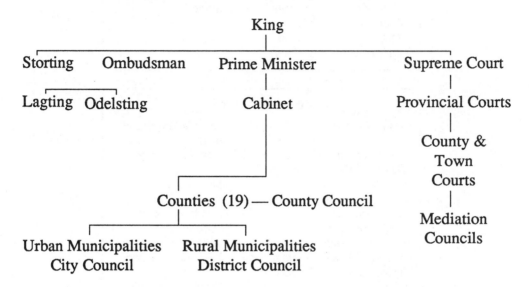

RULERS OF NORWAY

Kings
November 1905–September 1957: Haakon VII
September 1957–Olav V

Prime Ministers
May 1945–November 1951: Einar Gerhardsen
(Norwegian Labor Party)
November 1951–January 1955: Oscar Torp
(Norwegian Labor Party)
January 1955–August 1963: Einar Gerhardsen
(Norwegian Labor Party)
August–September 1963: John Lyng
(Conservative Party)
September 1963–October 1965: Einar Gerhardsen
(Norwegian Labor Party)
October 1965–March 1971: Per Borten (Center Party)
March 1971–October 1972: Trygve Bratteli
(Norwegian Labor Party)

RULERS OF NORWAY *(continued)*

October 1972–October 1973: Lars Korvald
(Christian People's Party)
October 1973–January 1976: Trygve Bratteli
(Norwegian Labor Party)
January 1976–February 1981: Odvar Nordli
(Norwegian Labor Party)
February–October 1981: Gro Harlem Brundtland
(Norwegian Labor Party)
October 1981–May 1986: Kaare Willoch
(Conservative Party)
May 1986– : Gro Harlem Brundtland
(Norwegian Labor Party)

CABINET LIST

Prime Minister:	Gro Harlem Brundtland
Minister of Agriculture:	Gunhild Oyangen
Minister of Church and Education:	Mary Kvidal
Minister of Consumer Affairs and Administration:	Einfrid Halvorsen
Minister of Culture:	Hallvard Bakke
Minister of Defense:	Johan Jørgen Holst
Minister of Developmental Aid:	Kristi Kolle Grøndahl
Minister of Environmental Affairs:	Sissel Roenbeck
Minister of Finance and Customs:	Gunnar Berge
Minister of Fisheries:	Bjarne Moerk Eidem
Minister of Foreign Affairs:	Thorvald Stoltenberg
Minister of Health and Social Affairs:	Tove Strand Gerhardsen
Minister of Industry:	Finn Kristensen
Minister of Justice and Police:	Helen Bøstrud
Minister of Labor and Municipal Affairs:	Kjell Borgen
Minister of Oil and Energy:	Arne Oien
Minister of Trade and Commerce:	Jan Balstad
Minister of Transport and Communications:	William Engseth
Governor, Bank of Norway:	Hermond Skanland

Norway was the third Scandinavian country to establish an ombudsman, after Sweden and Denmark, in 1962. The Storting's ombudsman for public administration (also called the civil ombudsman) is elected by the Storting for a period of four years after every general election. He must possess the same qualifications as a Supreme Court judge. Rules governing his work are laid down in a special act supplemented by a Storting directive.

FREEDOM & HUMAN RIGHTS

A deeply rooted democratic tradition, strong egalitarianism, a free press and a highly developed social welfare system make Norway a model country in terms of human rights. Human rights issues are marginal and concerned mainly with the rights of immigrants.

Persons may be detained for up to four hours without being charged but must be brought before a judge for arraignment within 24 hours. If there are no strong grounds for detention, the suspect is released pending trial. Although a provision for bail exists in Norwegian law, it is rarely if ever used. A person in pretrial detention generally appears before a judge every four weeks for a new determination of the necessity of continued detention. There is no legal time limit on the time a prisoner may be held before a trial. Preventive detention exists but is used rarely. In criminal cases all Norwegian subjects and aliens are entitled to free legal counsel, and in civil cases the indigent are afforded this right. Conscientious objectors who refuse alternative civil service are imprisoned for up to 16 months by an administrative order and without a trial. Wiretapping is prohibited by law but can be used in state security and narcotics cases when officially approved by the court within carefully drawn and monitored legal guidelines. The only restraints on free speech are those against slander, libel and sexist or racist remarks. The State Film Control Board has the right to censor films deemed overly violent, pornographic or blasphemous.

Women are politically more prominent in Norway than in any Scandinavian or other country. In the late 1980s they held nearly 35% of the Storting seats and 44% of the cabinet positions, including the office of prime minister. The office of ombudsman provides a direct route for individual complaints against government agencies. Other monitoring agencies include the Equal Rights Council (for women), the Immigrant Council, the Oslo Peace Research Institute and the Norwegian Human Rights Institute.

The cultural rights of the Lapps (also called Sami) are adequately protected. New minorities, such as Africans, Pakistanis, Turks and Vietnamese fare less well.

CIVIL SERVICE

Government ministries are relatively small, employing only about 4,000 of the 175,000 employees in public administration. Each ministry has one state secretary (the larger ones have two), who is appointed and resigns simultaneously with the minister. The senior civil servant in a ministry is the secretary-general.

While ministries are generally concerned with policy formulation and budgeting, actual administration is vested with the departments, each headed by a director-general. Departments are divided into divisions, of which there are approximately 350.

The majority of the departments (or directorates, as they are popularly called) are in Oslo. Most of them employ thousands of personnel. Some, like the National Insurance Administration, the Patent Office, the State Pension Fund and the Directorate of Labor, are relatively autonomous, while others, such as the Directorate of Public Works and Real Estate, come directly under the authority of a ministry. The organizational pyramid of the directorates is similar to that of the ministries, except in the case of the Defense Command. The heads of the directorates are known by various titles: director, director-general or managing director.

State and county administrative functions were bifurcated in 1975, and most central government departments have their own regional and local organization. This organization normally follows county divisions, but in some cases, such as the Norwegian State Railways and the Postal Service, may have a larger regional division. The central government has direct appointive powers for the 52 police districts and 10 dioceses and also appoints the 18 county governors.

LOCAL GOVERNMENT

For purposes of local administration Norway is divided into counties and municipalities. There are 454 municipalities in the country; the older distinction between urban and rural municipalities was abolished in 1964. Through statutory mergers the number of municipalities has been reduced from a peak of 680 in 1950. Even so, the smaller municipalities are in the majority, and 55% of them have under 5,000 inhabitants. There are 18 counties; their former Danish appellation of *amt* has been changed to the Norwegian *fylke*. Oslo is not incorporated in any county but has a separate, independent status.

Local government dates from 1837, when the Municipalities Act created two kinds of *Kommunes: bykommuner* and *landkommuner* (urban and rural municipalities, respectively). These were what was called *primaerkommuner* (municipalities of the first order).

In addition to the county municipalities, secondary local authorities have been established on a voluntary basis with limited spheres of responsibility. Thus intermunicipal enterprises have taken over responsibilities requiring larger investments, such as electricity, water supply and refuse disposal.

Until 1954 some of the municipalities had been subdivided into so-called parish municipalities, with more restricted tasks. The arrangement fell into disuse but is being revived in the municipalities of Oslo, Trondheim, Stavanger, Drammen, Ålesund, Skien, Harstad and Ski.

Political and financial authority at the local level is vested in popularly elected bodies: the County Councils and County Executive Committees in the case of counties, and the Municipal Councils and the Municipal Executive Boards in the case of municipalities. Municipal Councils are elected by direct suffrage every four years—that is, the second year after the last parliamentary elections. From among themselves the councillors elect the municipal executive board *(formannskap)*, comprising one-fourth of the total membership of the council and reflecting the proportion of the different political parties in the larger group. Meetings of the council and the board are chaired by the *ordforer* (mayor), elected for a two-year term by the council from among board members. Municipalities with a population of 10,000 or more have a *radmann* (chief municipal administrator), while in smaller municipalities this function is entrusted to a *kontorsjef* (municipal executive secretary), or in the smallest ones to the board itself. The larger municipalities have functionally differentiated subcommittees, each headed by a *kommunalrad* (alderman), who is on the payroll. Municipal administrators, auditors and treasurers enjoy special protection against dismissal to ensure their independence.

The county administration is governed by the County Municipalities Act of 1961. The Folkesting (County Council) is a popularly elected body varying from 25 to 85 members and serving a four-year term. From among themselves the councillors elect the Fylkesutvalg (County Executive Committee) comprising approximately one-fourth of the total membership of the council. This committee chooses the *fylkesordforer* (county mayor). Since 1976 the county administration has been headed by the *fylkesradmann* (chief county administrator).

By statute, both municipal and county councils are required to establish specialized agencies, such as Building Development Councils, Education Boards, Social Welfare Boards, Juvenile Welfare Boards, the Hospitals Board and the Roadworks Board.

The major items in the municipal budget are public health (20%), education (25%), building and roads (18%), social welfare (7%) and miscellaneous (30%). Municipal revenue is derived from taxes and government grants. Municipal taxes comprise the income tax, the capital tax and the property tax, of which the income tax accounts for over 90%. The counties levy only the income tax. Government grants make up 20% of total net receipts in municipalities and 30% in counties. All grants are net. The Tax Equalization Fund is administered by the Ministry of Local Government and Labor.

Counties	Capitals	Area		Population
		sq. km.	sq. mi.	(1983 est.)
Akershus	—	4,917	1,898	376,129
Aust-Agder	Arendal	9,212	3,557	92,751
Buskerud	Drammen	14,933	5,766	217,402
Finnmark	Vardø	48,649	18,783	77,394
Hedmark	Hamar	27,388	10,575	187,784
Hordaland	Bergen	15,634	6,036	394,545
Møre og Romsdalg	Molde	15,104	5,832	237,315
Nordland	Bodø	38,327	14,798	245,017
Nord-Trøndelag	Steinkjer	22,463	8,673	126,713
Oppland	Lillehammer	25,260	9,753	182,108
Oslo	Oslo	454	175	448,747
Østfold	Moss	4,183	1,615	234,751
Rogaland	Stavanger	9,141	3,529	312,576
Sogn og Fjordane	Leikanger	18,634	7,195	106,175
Sør-Trøndelag	Trondheim	18,831	7,271	246,200
Telemark	Skien	15,315	5,913	161,944
Troms	Tromsø	25,954	10,021	147,709
Vest-Agder	Kristiansand	7,280	2,811	138,745
Vestfold	Tønsberg	2,216	856	188,702
TOTAL		323,895	125,057	4,122,707

Source: Official government figures.

All decisions of the Municipal Council are subject to the scrutiny of the county governor. Certain municipal decisions also are subject to prior approval—for example, floating of loans and property transfers. County and municipal administrations also are subject to various complaints and appeals procedures, including investigations by the parliamentary ombudsman and concerned ministries.

FOREIGN POLICY

A founding member of the United Nations, Norway also is one of the original members of NATO, although its membership is qualified by two reservations: It does not permit NATO military bases on its soil in peacetime, and it does not permit the stockpiling of nuclear weapons on its soil in peacetime. Norway has been one of the leaders in Western cooperation through the Council of Europe, the OECD and the EFTA. However, in a 1972 referendum it rejected membership in the EEC. Regional cooperation through the Nordic Council is another major element in foreign policy.

Whereas relations with Nordic countries and Western allies have been remarkably smooth, those with its northeastern neighbor the Soviet Union have been periodically marred. Since 1944 Norway has been under pressure from the Soviet Union to cede Bear Island and to revise the multilateral Spitsbergen Treaty of 1920, which gave sovereignty of the islands to Norway. The Soviet Union suggested that the Spitsbergen islands be defended as a joint Soviet-Norwegian responsibility. In 1947 the Storting turned down the proposal, but this was followed by further Soviet claims regarding delimitation in the Barents Sea and Soviet fishing rights in the area. Soviet espionage activities in Oslo and frequent sightings of Soviet submarines in Norwegian waters have further soured relations between the two countries.

PARLIAMENT

The national legislature is the unicameral Storting consisting of 157 members elected by universal suffrage and proportional representation every four years. There are no by-elections, since a system of alternates or deputies ensures immediate replacement in case the seat falls vacant. The Storting also is not subject to dissolution. Once constituted, it elects one-fourth of its members to serve as an upper chamber (Lagting) while the remainder serves as a lower chamber (Odelsting). Each bill is dealt with first in the Odelsting and then in the Lagting. If both chambers agree, the act is considered passed. Should there be disagreement after two readings of the bill, the matter is settled by the Storting as a whole, with a two-thirds majority required.

As in Sweden, cabinet members cannot sit in the Storting, even though they are elected, but must relinquish their seats to their alternates. Preparatory legislative work takes place in the standing committees, while considerable time is devoted in the Storting itself to debates and interpellations. Members sit not according to party blocs but in alphabetical order of the counties they represent. Geographical loyalties are as strong as political loyalties. The northern counties elect 38 representatives, the southern and western counties 50 and the eastern counties 69. Of the latter, 15 come from Oslo. On a per capita basis, the remoter areas are somewhat better represented than the others.

The bulk of the parliamentary work is done through committees. Each member of the Storting is a member of at least one of the standing committees. Each committee broadly corresponds to one of the government departments, as follows: Finance, Fisheries, Consumer Affairs and Government Administration, Defense, Commerce and Shipping, Industry, Justice, Church and Education, Cultural and Scientific Affairs, Local Government and Labor, Agriculture, Environment, Petroleum and Energy, Communications, Health and Social Affairs and Foreign Affairs.

The committees maintain the relative proportion of party strength in the larger body. In practice, the parties nominate their candidates to the various committees on the basis of their qualifications. Committee membership must balance geographical and special interests. The most important committees are Finance and Foreign Affairs.

Despite their pivotal role in legislation, standing committees have no right to kill legislation or hold public hearings. The meetings of the party parliamentary groups are perhaps as important in determining the direction of deliberations. These meetings decide whether members should vote as a group or be free to vote as they please.

According to the Constitution, a bill may be presented by either the government or an individual member of the Storting, but in practice private member bills are rare and have slight chances of passing. Before the government prepares a bill, it is customary to appoint a commission. A draft bill is prepared on the commission's recommendations and circulated for comment by interested parties.

When the Constitution was adopted in 1814, only higher civil servants, members of the upper middle class and farmers were entitled to vote. In 1898 the franchise was extended to all males irrespective of income. In 1907 the Constitution was amended to give women the right to vote, and in 1913 they were given full voting rights. Currently the age of suffrage is 18.

The country is divided into 19 electoral districts, each district corresponding to a county or, in the case of Oslo, to the city. To minimize the risk of underrepresentation in rural areas, the "farmer paragraph" in the Constitution states that the number of urban representatives should be related to the rural representatives in the ratio of one to two. This principle works in favor of rural areas.

The Constitution prescribes indirect election of delegates, but this was abandoned in 1919 in favor of proportional representation, which is in force today. Until 1953 the so-called d'Hondt method was used to achieve proportionality, but since it favored the larger parties at the expense of the smaller, the Lague method was adopted, and finally a compromise, including both d'Hondt and Lague elements. Because even this method does not achieve full proportionality, proposals have been made to create a certain number of so-called national seats, to be awarded to parties that are underrepresented in the Storting.

The Elections Act contains detailed regulations on the compilation of the Electoral Register, election procedures, party lists and joint lists, and electoral pacts among parties.

STORTING ELECTION RESULTS, 1973–85								
	1973		1977		1981		1985	
Political Group	Vote %	Seats	Vote %	Seats	Vote %	Seats	Vote %	Seats
Norwegian Labor	35.3	62	42.4	76	37.3	65*	40.8	71
Conservative	17.4	29	24.7	41	31.6	54*	30.4	50
Christian People's	12.2	20	12.1	22	9.3	15	8.3	16
Center	11.0	21	8.6	12	6.7	11	6.6	12
Progress	5.0	4	1.9	—	4.5	4	3.7	2
Liberal	3.5	2	3.2	2	3.9	2	3.1	0
Liberal People's	3.4	1	1.7	—	0.6	—	0.5	—
Socialist Left	11.2	16	4.1	2	4.9	4	5.5	6
Red Electoral Alliance	—	—	0.6	—	0.7	—	0.6	—
Communist	—	—	0.4	—	0.3	—	0.2	—
Others	0.9	—	0.9	—	0.1	—	0.4	—
TOTAL	99.9	155	100.0	155	99.9	155	100.0	157
Turnout	80.2		82.9		81.0		80.2	

* After disputes about the local results, reelections were held in two constituencies, resulting in a loss of one seat by the Conservatives to Labor. In the 1981 Storting, these parties, therefore, held 53 and 66 seats, respectively. The voting figures in the table do not incorporate these changes.

POLITICAL PARTIES

Six political parties are represented in the Storting, of which two, the Progress and the Socialist Left, are fringe parties. Of the four major parties, the Conservative, Center and Christian People's parties together make up what is known as the *borgerlig* (bourgeois bloc). In ideological terms, the parties occupy standard niches in the spectrum, Norwegian Labor to the left, Conservatives and Christian People's to the right, and Center in the middle. Despite strong consensus among the bourgeois parties, each party retains its own ideological profile. Discipline is high, and floor crossing is very rare. Because the socialist and nonsocialist blocs are evenly matched, the balance of power often rests with the small fringe parties. In fact, after the 1985 elections, the socialist bloc had 77 seats and the bourgeois bloc 78 seats in the Storting, leaving the fate of government to the two seats of the Progress Party.

The Center Party (Sentepartiet, SP) was founded in 1920 as the Agrarian League. In the following year it changed its name to the Farmers' Party and in

1959 to the Center Party. It has shared power with other nonsocialist parties in coalition governments in 1963, 1965–71, 1972–73 and 1983–86.

Formerly the voice of farmers, the Center Party has broadened its range of policies and programs and also has adopted environmental and decentralist planks. In foreign policy it is strongly pro-NATO and pro-West but is firmly opposed to Norway's membership in the EEC. The party's support is drawn primarily from farmers, particularly large landowners. Regionally, its stronghold is Trondelag.

The Christian People's Party (Kristelig Folkeparti, KrF), the strongest Christian democratic party in Scandinavia, was founded in 1933 and emerged as a national party in 1945. It joined nonsocialist coalitions in 1963, 1965–71, 1972–73 (when it provided the prime minister, Lars Korvald) and 1983–86.

The party upholds Christian values in public life and is strongly opposed to abortion. In foreign affairs it is pro-NATO but divided on the question of the EEC. Since 1977 the KrF, like the Center Party, has found its electoral support eroding in favor of the Conservatives.

The Conservative Party (Hoyre, "The Right") was founded as a monarchist party in 1884 and has carried the conservative banner through the years. Since 1973 it has enjoyed remarkable growth, taking 31.6% of the popular vote in 1981 and 30.4% in 1985.

A doughty champion of free enterprise and a free market, Hoyre has moderated its stance over the years and come to accept the central aspects of the welfare state as irreversible. In recent years it has called for deregulation of the economy and reduction of taxes. In foreign policy it is both pro-NATO and pro-EEC. It is largely an urban party of above-average income-earners. Membership was estimated at 170,000 in 1982.

The Norwegian Labor Party (Del Norske Arbeiderparti, DNA) was founded in 1887 and became a political force with the introduction of universal male suffrage in 1898. It experienced considerable growth in the period just before World War I. After that war the party was taken over by radical leadership, which took it into the Communist International, thus precipitating a number of splits. After reuniting in the 1920s, the DNA established itself as the largest political party, a lead it maintained until recently. In 1935 the DNA began a term in office that lasted for 30 years, interrupted only by the Nazi occupation and a two-month nonsocialist coalition in 1963. From 1945 until 1961 it enjoyed an absolute majority in the Storting. The DNA's organization is characterized by close association with trade union locals, which provide its core membership.

The DNA is committed to a welfare state in a mixed economy, supported by a high degree of state planning. In foreign policy it is pro-NATO but opposed to foreign bases on Norwegian soil in peacetime as well as installation of nuclear weapons there in peacetime. Its historic strength is drawn from the industrial proletariat. Membership is estimated at 160,000, of whom more than half come from trade unions. Conflicts between the party's radical and moderate wings periodically surface, dimming its prospects of renewed electoral success.

The Progress Party (Fremskrittspartiet) was founded in 1973 by a political maverick, Anders Lange. As Anders Lange's Party for Substantial Reduction in Taxes, Duties and Governmental Interference, it took a surprising 5% of the vote and four seats in the year's election. After Lange's death a year later, the party was torn by internal strife, which cost it its Storting representation in 1977. Riding a conservative wave of resentment, it again captured four seats, in 1981. Although its representation was halved in 1985, its two seats held the crucial balance of power in the Storting.

The Socialist Left Party (Sosialistik Ventrepatri, SV) was founded in 1961 by a group of anti-NATO activists who had been expelled from the Norwegian Labor Party. Capitalizing on the success of the anti-EEC forces in 1972, the party allied itself with other far left groups to form the Socialist Electoral League. In the 1973 elections it took 11.2% of the vote and 16 seats. Two years later the League was converted into the Socialist Left Party. Since then, its fortunes have waned and internal disagreements have diminished its appeal. In 1977, 1981 and 1985 it gained two, four, and six seats, respectively.

The Communist Party of Norway (Norges Kommunistiske Parti, NKP) was founded in 1923 by left-wing Norwegian Labor Party members. The NKP was politically significant only for a brief period following World War II. From 1973 to 1975 it was part of the Socialist Electoral League.

The Liberal Party (Venstre) was founded in the early 1880s. The Venstre was the dominant party of government until World War I despite two serious splits in the right. In the interwar period it was overtaken by Norwegian Labor as the party of social reform and lost its centrist support to the Agrarian/Farmers' (Center) and Christian People's parties. With no single economic or social constituency, it coasted along on the strength of its historic traditions and vaguely liberal ideas until it split to two in 1971 over the EEC issue. In 1985 it lost its representation in the Storting for the first time in its long history. There are no illegal political parties or known terrorist groups.

ECONOMY

Norway is a free-market country with a dominant private sector. The year 1986 marked a turning point in Norway's oil era, which began with the first discoveries about 20 years ago. Following a period of rapid output and employment growth, general government budget surpluses and a strong foreign balance,

Norway is undergoing a period of severe domestic restraint accompanied by a major shift of resources and policies.

The fall in oil prices revealed the extent to which the economy had become dependent on oil revenues. Since 1973 increasing production levels had boosted oil revenues, providing the financial basis for an expansionary economy. During this period the Norwegian economy was characterized by several favorable developments.

- GDP growth rates were stronger and more stable than in other OECD countries.
- Employment growth was strong, and unemployment, despite increased participation rates, was kept down to comparatively low levels.
- The current balance of payments registered large surpluses since the 1970s so that foreign debt was significantly reduced to 8% of the GDP by the end of 1985.
- The general government budget, in contrast to virtually all other OECD countries, remained in comfortable surplus.

The issue of how to use the windfall wealth from oil was thoroughly debated in Norway in the 1970s. The initial plan was to conserve and spend it cautiously so as to minimize the social and economic costs of structural adjustments. However, while oil production and exports developed much in line with initial expectations, oil wealth was sharply increased by the rise in the price of oil and the dollar exchange rate. In these circumstances it proved difficult to resist competing and excessive sectoral claims on resources for various regional and social purposes. Sectoral policy became increasingly ambitious as concrete goals for expenditures in many sectors were established. This in turn made fiscal policy more rigid and difficult to use for economic stabilization. As a result, an overly expansionary fiscal policy was pursued during most of this period, supporting domestic demand growth as well as nonviable production structures.

The rapid absorption of oil money into the domestic economy led to inflation and a depreciation in the nominal exchange rate. Labor market conditions became tight as a result of strong wage pressures. To cushion the consequences, the government resorted to subsidization of traditional industries and repeated devaluations of the krone. The government pursued two contradictory policies. On the one hand, it permitted strong pressures for structural change to develop, while on the other it took measures to counteract them. Notwithstanding, the rise in domestic prices and costs was almost the same as the OECD average when measured in the national currency. However, when measured in a common currency, prices and costs were sharply higher. Sweden was the only country among Norway's main trading partners that had higher hourly wage costs in manufacturing. At the same time, productivity performance was much weaker. From 1975 to 1985 manufacturing output remained broadly un-changed, while it grew by more than 25% in the OECD area and employment fell by 13.5%. Norway's competitive position, therefore, deteriorated as a result by 27% from 1973 to 1977 alone. Industries exposed to competition also lost market shares both at home and abroad. This, in turn increased the economy's dependence on the oil sector. The growing importance of the offshore market was reflected in an industrial survey, which showed that:

- In the 65 largest manufacturing firms, 13% of the gross revenues during the period were related to the oil sector.
- About one-third of the turnover in large, metal, machinery and equipment companies was related to deliveries to the oil sector.
- In shipbuilding the number of hours allocated to the oil sector increased from 7% in 1978 to 40% in 1984.

Thus the growth of the oil sector allowed Norway to maintain high spending and employment levels over a period when most of the OECD area suffered from weak demand and rising unemployment. The oil dependence also was reflected in the growing share of oil revenues in the public sector and in the rapid buildup of foreign debt in the 1970s.

Large current deficits and growing inflation made it necessary for the government to revise its economic policy substantially in 1977. The growth in domestic demand was curbed, and the krone was devalued in 1978. In addition, a price and income freeze was in effect in 1978–79. This resulted in a short-lived improvement in 1978 and 1979, but the situation began to deteriorate again in 1980. When the price and income freeze was lifted, pent-up pressures led to a record rise in prices and wages in 1980–81. In 1981 inflation was 13.5% while output, profitability and productivity all remained depressed.

A new growth phase began in 1983 and 1984. The GDP rose by 3.2% in 1983, by 4.3% in 1984 and by 4.5% in 1986. Manufacturing investment also began to expand in 1984, and output grew by some 2%. Productivity grew by 4.5%, inflation was cut to 5.7%, public expenditures as a share of GDP were cut to 47.5% from 48.1% and net foreign debt was reduced to 16.8% of the GDP from 22.5%.

The oil price decline hit an overheated economy. The financial consequences have been dramatic. Real national income fell by 10% and total export earnings by more than 15% in 1986. The cumulative decline in the oil sector's foreign exchange earnings between 1985 and 1989 would be in the best case about Kr100 billion (20% of the GDP) and in the worst case about Kr140 billion. Government oil tax revenues would plunge even more sharply. If oil prices remain depressed, real GDP growth would be 1.25% per year between 1987 and 1995. In the same period production in the traditional exposed sector would decline by almost 0.5% annually, employment in 1995 would be only 2% higher than in 1987, the current external deficit would reach 8% to 9% of the GDP and the net foreign debt would rise between 25% and 65% of the GDP.

PRINCIPAL ECONOMIC INDICATORS

Gross National Product: $64.440 billion (1986)
GNP per capita: $15,480 (1986)
GNP average annual growth rate: 3.7% (1973–86)
GNP per capita average annual growth rate: 3.4% (1973–86)
Average annual rate of inflation: 7.0% (1980–86)
Consumer Price Index 1980=100
    All items: 187.4 (February 1988)
    Food: 201.9 (February 1988)
Wholesale Price Index 1980=100: 158 (February 1988)
Average annual growth rate (1980–86) (%)
    Public consumption: 3.7
    Private consumption: 3.4
    Gross domestic investment: 2.9

BALANCE OF PAYMENTS, 1987 ($ million)

Current account balance: -4,137
Merchandise exports: 21,157
Merchandise imports: –22,026
Trade balance: -869
Other goods, services & income +: 11,569
Other goods, services & income –: –13,861
Other goods, services & income net: —
Private unrequited transfers: –199
Official unrequited transfers: –778
Direct investment: –828
Portfolio investment: 444
Other long-term capital: 1,021
Other short-term capital: 5,495
Net errors & omissions: –204
Counterpart items: –1,275
Exceptional financing: —
Liabilities constituting foreign authorities' reserves: —
Total change in reserves: -515

PUBLIC FINANCE

The Norwegian fiscal year is the calendar year.

GROSS DOMESTIC PRODUCT, 1985

GDP nominal (national currency): 501.8 billion
GDP real (national currency): 336.4 billion (in 1980 prices)
GDP per capita ($): 11,976
Average annual growth rate of GDP, 1980–85: 3.4%

GDP by type of expenditure (%)
    Consumption
      Private: 47
      Government: 19
    Gross domestic investment: 26
    Gross domestic saving: 26
    Foreign trade
      Exports: 47
      Imports: -38

Cost components of GDP (%)
    Net indirect taxes: 11
    Consumption of fixed capital: 14
    Compensation of employees: 48
    Net operating surplus: 27

Sectoral origin of GDP (%)
    Primary
      Agriculture: 4
      Mining: 20
    Secondary
      Manufacturing: 14
      Construction: 5
      Public utilities: 4
    Tertiary
      Transportation & communications: 9
      Trade: 13
      Finance: 8
      Other services: 8
      Government: 14

Average annual sectoral growth rate, 1980–86 (%)
    Agriculture: 3.0
    Industry: 3.8
    Manufacturing: 0.3
    Services: 3.4

    The public sector consists of the central government, the municipalities and the counties. Two-thirds of the revenues from direct taxes are transferred to municipalities. The bulk of central government revenues is derived from indirect taxes, particularly the value added tax on sales and the investment tax. There also are a number of special taxes, such as those on liquor, tobacco, motor vehicles, gasoline and electricity. Over 70% of government expenditures

OFFICIAL DEVELOPMENT ASSISTANCE								
In $ Million								
1965	1970	1975	1980	1982	1983	1984	1985	1986
11	37	184	486	559	584	540	574	798
As Percentage of GNP								
1965	1970	1975	1980	1982	1983	1984	1985	1986
0.16	0.32	0.27	0.27	0.27	0.24	0.24	0.24	0.23

goes to the municipal and private sectors. These include Social Security, subsidies, interest and dividends, transfers to agriculture and fisheries, etc.

Controlling government expenditures is a major goal of budgetary policy. It is rendered more difficult for both political and institutional reasons. In the national budget of 1987 about 75% of central government outlays (of which two-fifths are transfers) were classified as virtually automatic due to legislation, contracts or perceived political constraints and moral obligations. Projections in the long-term program of 1986–89 point to a rise in government expenditures to about 70% of the GDP, excluding oil, by the turn of the century in the absence of effective measures to curb public spending. Transfers continue to be the strongest growing item in public outlays. Real pension outlays will increase by more than 3% annually as a result of demographic trends and the maturing of the supplementary pension system. In recent years individual benefits also have risen. Business sector support has over the past 15 years increased annually by about 8% in volume, compared to general public expenditures growth of 5%. There has been a particularly strong increase in subsidies to farmers following the parliamentary decision in 1975 to level farmers' income with that of industrial workers. Since 1982, however, overall support for the business sector has been reduced slightly in nominal terms. Interest payments also are likely to rise along with growing deficits.

Containing government deficits also has involved increases in taxation. The tax burden in Norway is among the highest in the OECD area, with marginal tax rates of up to 67%. High marginal taxes tend to increase pressures for selective deductions. This has led to a complicated tax system wherein high-income groups tend to benefit most from deductions and wherein income redistribution aims are only partially achieved. In 1987 the government announced a program for tax reform through a "gross taxation" system to supplement the ordinary income tax. The program also calls for:

- greater degree of lump sum budgeting within the central government
- introduction of a grant quota program for the municipalities
- deindexation of fiscal budget expenditures
- greater use of fees and prices for public sector services

Until 1975 government budgets recorded large supluses as a result of oil revenues, on an average equal to 2% of the GDP. However, if oil taxes are excluded, the public sector showed a deficit every year until 1987, when for the first time it showed a surplus. A strong growth in domestic demand and a substantial increase in central government assets as a result of high oil revenues from 1983 to 1985 influenced this development. The surplus also resulted from the tightening of fiscal policy in 1986 and 1987. Budget expenditures before loans increased by 10% from 1986 to 1987 as a result of higher expenditures for state petroleum activities and higher interest payments. Adjusted for these factors, the growth in spending was 7%, less than the rise in consumer prices. Local governments also contributed to this growth in expenditures.

CENTRAL GOVERNMENT EXPENDITURES, 1986
% of total expenditures

Defense: 8.3
Education: 8.7
Health: 10.5
Housing, Social Security, welfare: 35.0
Economic services: 19.5
Other: 17.9
Total expenditures as % of GNP: 40.6
Overall surplus or deficit as % of GNP: -0.1

CENTRAL GOVERNMENT REVENUES, 1986
% of total current revenues

Taxes on income, profit & capital gain: 20.2
Social Security contributions: 21.8
Domestic taxes on goods & services: 39.7
Taxes on international trade & transactions: 0.5
Other taxes: 1.0
Current nontax revenue: 16.7
Total current revenue as % of GNP: 48.4
Government consumption as % of GNP: 20.0
Annual growth rate of government consumption: 3.7 (1980–86)

CURRENCY & BANKING

The national monetary unit is the Norwegian krone (plural: kroner), divided into 100 ore. Coins are issued in denominations of 5, 10, 25 and 50 ore and 1 and 5 kroner, and notes are issued in denominations of 10, 50, 100, 500 and 1,000 kroner.

The Norwegian banking system is of comparatively recent date. The central bank, the Norges Bank (Bank of Norway), was founded only in 1816, the first savings bank in 1822 and the first commercial bank in 1848.

Norges Bank is organized as a limited company in which the government owns all the shares. The bank has a board of directors consisting of five members. The president and the vice president are appointed by the king in council, while the remaining three are chosen by the Storting. In addition to the usual functions of a central bank, it also serves as the adviser to the minister of finance on matters related to fiscal policy.

There are 10 government banks, which control a sizable share of the credit market. Of these, the largest is the Norwegian State Housing Bank. The Post Office Bank finances its loans through deposits, while others either receive government loans or issue government-guaranteed bonds.

There are 227 savings banks, with an authorized capital of NOK120 billion. Most of these are local banks, but in recent years a number of mergers have resulted in larger regional banks. The largest, Sparebanken ABC, is the fourth-largest private bank in the country.

There are 28 commercial banks, with an authorized capital of NOK190 billion. The three largest are Den Norske Creditbank, Christiania Bank og Kreditkasse and Bergen Bank.

EXCHANGE RATE Kroner per U.S. Dollar						
1982	1983	1984	1985	1986	1987	1988
7.054	7.722	9.084	7.582	7.400	6.232	6.356

In *The Banker*'s annual list of the 500 largest banks in the world in 1987, Den Norske Creditbank ranked 169, Christiania Bank 200 and Bergen Bank 245. In 1985 foreign banks were allowed to establish branches in Norway. There are 11 life insurance companies and 10 casualty insurance companies, with a total capital of NOK65 billion and NOK26 billion, respectively. A large number of finance companies are owned by the banks or the insurance companies.

The Oslo Stock Exchange, founded in 1818, is the largest stock market institution. More than 120 stocks are traded every day, and daily transactions average NOK60 million. A second stock exchange, for smaller companies, was opened in 1984.

From 1977 to 1981 there was a substantial tightening of credit policy as part of a reorientation in fiscal policy. As a result, interest rates rose in both nominal and real terms. In 1981 the government carried out a gradual liberalization of credit policy. The bond investment obligation was reduced, and since 1985 has been abolished for commercial and savings banks and insurance companies. The scope of direct regulation was scaled down and made more market-oriented. At the same time, private credit institutions gradually took over a higher share of the domestic credit supply to the private sector and municipalities. The state banks now provide about 20% of the domestic supply of credit, excluding loans to Statoil.

Monetary policy was tightened again in 1986. Primary reserve requirements were increased and marginal reserve requirements were imposed on banks. The credit supply still exceeded the target level by as much as NOK14 billion, or 37%. In contrast, the money supply expanded somewhat less, by 7%, down from 17% in 1985. However, unregistered credit flows suggest that the actual expansion rate of liquidity is much higher.

FINANCIAL INDICATORS, 1986

International reserves minus gold: $12.524 billion
  SDRs: 389.2
  Reserve position in IMF: 589.4
  Foreign exchange: $11.546 billion
Gold (million fine troy oz): 1.184
Ratio of external debt to total reserves: —

Central bank
Assets (%)
  Foreign assets: 43.9
  Claims on government: 22.5
  Claims on bank: 33.5
  Claims on private sector: —
Liabilities (%)
  Reserve money: 14.7
  Government deposits: 68.3
  Foreign liabilities: —
  Capital accounts: —

Money supply
Stock in billion national currency: 101.8
M^1 per capita: 24.390
U.S. liabilities to: $4.504 billion
U.S. claims on: $759 million

Private banks
Assets (%)
  Loans to government: 13.7
  Loans to private sector: 65.1
  Reserves: 0.7
  Foreign assets: 10.8
  Other: 9.7

FINANCIAL INDICATORS, 1986 *(continued)*

Liabilities Deposits: 486.6 billion krone
  of which (%)
  Demand deposits: 13.9
  Savings deposits: 41.7
  Government deposits: 0.9
  Foreign liabilities: 21.1

GROWTH PROFILE (Annual Growth Rates, %)

Population, 1985–2000: 0.2
Crude birth rate, 1985–90: 11.8
Crude death rate, 1985–90: 10.9
Urban population, 1980–86: 0.9
Labor force, 1985–2000: 0.7
GNP, 1973–86: 3.7
GNP per capita, 1973–86: 3.4
GDP, 1980–86: 3.5
Inflation, 1980–86: 7.0
Agriculture, 1980–86: 3.0
Industry, 1980–86: 3.8
Manufacturing, 1980–86: 0.3
Services, 1980–86: 3.4
Money holdings, 1980–86: 12.9
Manufacturing earnings per employee, 1980–85: 1.0
Energy production, 1980–86: 5.3
Energy consumption, 1980–86: 2.8
Exports, 1980–86: 5.1
Imports, 1980–86: 5.8
General government consumption, 1980–86: 3.7
Private consumption, 1980–86: 3.4
Gross domestic investment, 1980–86: 2.9

AGRICULTURE

Only a small part of the land area is suitable for agriculture. Of the total land area of 31 million ha. (77 million ac.), only 1.095 million ha. (2.705 million ac.) (3%) are classified as farmland, and of this area, 7.5% is not being farmed. Thus the per capita agricultural area is only 0.27 ha. (0.67 ac.), among the lowest in the world. As Norway extends over 13 degrees of latitude, conditions for farming vary considerably among the various parts of the country. Topographical and soil conditions also vary. The terrain in most of the northern and western districts is precipitous and rugged, thus restricting cultivation to the flat districts of Rogaland, Trondelag and East Norway.

The number of holdings has steadily decreased through the post war period, although the drop has been less marked since the middle of the 1970s. Many small holdings, particularly those between 0.5 and 2 ha. (1.2 and 4.9 ac.), have been abandoned. At the same time, the average size of the holdings has risen as the abandoned farms have been purchased by the larger ones. About 8,800 holdings are over 20 ha. (49.4 ac.), and the average size of all farms is 9 ha. (22.2 ac.). The total number of farms is 115,400, of which 20,000 are between 0.5 ha. and 2 ha. Leased land constitutes 20% of the agricultural area. More than 30% of farmers lease part or all of their holdings. The area under lease is distributed among 39,000 farmers, of whom one-fourth do not own any land.

More than 40% of the agricultural area is used for growing grass and 35% for growing grain. Of the latter, only 5% to 6% is used for growing food grains. The remaining 25% of the agricultural land is used for horticulture, root crops and other field crops.

Part-time farming is widespread. About 65% of the farmers follow another occupation beside farming: either fishing in the coastal districts or forestry in the inland ones. In areas with the poorest natural conditions, the average age of farmers has been rising in recent years, since few young men are willing to undergo the rigors of farming life.

Agricultural production meets only 40% of the nation's food requirements measured in calories, and about 50% is met by imports. Some of the staple elements of the Norwegian diet, such as sugar and citrus fruits, are not produced at all, and climatic conditions also limit the cultivation of certain types of grain, such as rye. The most common grains are barley and oats, with wheat a distant third. Norway is self-sufficient in potatoes, vegetables and fruits such as apples and strawberries. The best agricultural land is in the areas around Oslofjord, in the large valleys in the central part of southern Norway, on the plateau of Jaeren south of Stavanger, and in central Norway. Due to the climate, the growing season is generally short. But plants in the North are less susceptible to diseases than those in the South.

Animal husbandry generates about 70% of the farm income. Livestock production has gone through a period of extensive structural changes in recent years. The number of holdings with livestock of different types has decreased, while the size of the herds has increased. Greater productivity has compensated for the decline in numbers. Milk production increased by 25% and meat production by 45% between 1970 and 1985. Norway is self-sufficient in dairy and meat products and also exports some cheese.

One of the key goals of agricultural policy is to ensure parity of income between agricultural and industrial workers. This policy is governed by the Basic

Agreement for Agriculture of 1950, which states that agricultural prices should be determined by annual negotiations between the government on the one hand and the Norwegian Farmers' Union and the Norwegian Smallholders' Union on the other. In 1976 the Norwegian Association of Reindeer Lapps was given comparable negotiation rights with the government. Farmers receive their income in two different ways: as prices for the goods they sell; and as production supplements, which vary according to the size and geographic location of the holding. On the assumption that agricultural production should be as efficient as possible, efficiency norms are determined for 23 typical models of varying size in different regions. Prices received by farmers for wool and grain are guaranteed prices. Others are target prices, which producers receive only if there is a reasonable ratio between supply and demand for a given commodity. This ratio is regulated by geographical balancing of supply, seasonal adjustment by storing, and sales promotion by the agricultural organizations. Production supplements are financed by the fiscal budget. The district supplements, among them those for milk and meat, help to even out incomes in farming among the different regions. The price subsidies have production restrictions and thus favor the smaller producers. In addition to production supplements, the state also pays consumer subsidies for food items.

There is a general ban on import of agricultural products other than those in short supply. The prices of imported agricultural products also are subject to strict regulation.

Investment support for agriculture is provided by the State Bank for Agriculture, which provides loans to farmers at a rate of interest below the market rate for purchase of equipment, construction and improvement of farm property and buildings. The Agricultural Development Fund finances a major share of the grants for development, such as silo and barn drying installations, channels for watering systems, leveling of cultivated land, farm buildings, purchase of land, utilization of outlying land, planting in older orchards, and installations for hatching roe and breeding fish.

Over the years there has been a substantial body of agricultural legislation. The most important of these laws is the Land Act of 1955, which affirms the right of the state to expropriate mismanaged farms. To discourage splitting up holdings, the act prohibits partition of farms without the approval of the County Agricultural and Forestry Board. The act also prohibits use of arable land for any purpose other than agriculture. The Concession Act of 1974 provides the legal basis for the control and regulation of the sale of agricultural real estate. Farm property may be purchased by a person not related to the owner, but only to operate the farm. The farmer's relatives are required to reside on the farm within one year of transfer of the property and to operate it for at least five years. The Allodial Rights Act of 1974 entitles the eldest child to take over the farm intact. It also provides for the rights of relatives to repurchase farm holdings that have been sold outside the family. A property of at least 1 ha. (2.47 ac.) becomes an allodium when it has been the property of an owner's family for 20 years. The Marketing Act of 1936 promotes rational marketing through the state Marketing Council. The Land Reallocation Act provides the basis for consolidating properties through exchange of land or allocation of supplementary land or for dissolving joint ownership of agricultural land.

Under the Ministry of Agriculture, each municipality has its Agricultural and Forestry Committee and each county its County Agricultural and Forestry Board, each divided into an agricultural service, a forestry service and a land reallocation service. Several subordinate agencies of the Ministry of Agriculture are charged with inspection, testing and control. The ministry also administers the Norwegian Grain Corporation, which is one of the country's largest commercial enterprises.

Agricultural education is provided by the Agricultural University of Norway and the State Veterinary College. In addition, there are about 60 vocational schools for agriculture at the upper secondary level. Agricultural research is coordinated by the Agricultural Research Council, established in 1949, which funds 25% of all agricultural research. Another 42% is conducted by the State Veterinary College and the Agricultural University. There are 15 agricultural research stations, which direct the activities of 90 agricultural experimental groups.

Cooperatives are strong in the agricultural sector. The largest group is the Division of Agricultural Cooperation (LF) of the Norwegian Farmers' Union, which represents 16 nationwide cooperative farming organizations. There also are cooperatives for dairy farmers, meat producers, horticulturists and forest owners.

Although fishing employs less than 1% of the labor force, it is of critical importance to the three northern counties, which together account for more than half the number of fishermen. About 80% of the 30,000 fishermen in 1983 were registered as having fishing as their main occupation. Along with the increased exploitation of species such as capelin, mackerel and blue whiting by purse seine vessels, fishing as a part-time activity has declined. For centuries the Norwegian waters contained abundant fish resources, and fishing was one of the historic occupations of Norwegians. In 1977 Norway established a 322-km. (200-mi.) economic zone around its mainland coast and in 1980 established a similar economic zone around Jan Mayen Island.

Norway is the second-largest fishing nation in Europe after the Soviet Union. Four species—cod, capelin, saithe and prawns—make up 75% of the Norwegian fish catch. About 70% of the total catch comes from the mainland zone or the area around Spitzbergen and Jan Mayen. The fishing fleet consists of more than 26,000 boats, 8,900 of which are decked. Open boats are used in nearby waters along the coast and in the fjords by part-time fishermen. In recent years the fishing fleet has been upgraded through the addition of electronic locating equipment, freezer trawlers and factory ships for freezing and fileting fish.

The fisheries sector is strongly unionized, with well-developed cooperatives. The Norwegian Fishermen's Association in Trondheim is responsible for negotiating agreements with the government under law. Wholesale sale and processing of fish are handled by the fishermen's own sales organizations. Fishery policy is formulated by the Ministry of Fisheries, while the Directorate of Fisheries in Bergen is responsible for quality control, pricing, etc. Norway has five fishermen's training schools. Research is coordinated by the Norwegian Fishery Research Council through its special Institute for Research in Fishery Technology in Tromsø.

Approximately 66,000 sq. km. (25,476 sq. mi.), or 22% of Norway's total land area, is under forest. Of this woodland, the state owns 10%, the municipalities 10% and the rest is in private hands.

A characteristic of Norwegian forestry is its close link with agriculture. Nearly 94% of forest properties are owned by farmers. A large proportion is owned by smallholders. The productive forest area is distributed among 120,000 properties representing an average area of 55 ha. (136 ac.) per holding. Nearly 52% of productive forest consists of spruce, 31% of pine and the remainder of deciduous species.

The annual production of timber for production and sale is 8 million cu. m. (283 million cu. ft.), of which spruce accounts for 75% and pine for 20%. Domestic production meets 85% of lumber requirements. Exports of forest products account for 7% to 8% of total Norwegian exports.

The total cubic mass of growing forest below the timber line is, according to the National Forest Survey, approximately 428 million cu. m. (17 billion cu. ft.) and the annual increment 13.2 million cu. m. (466 million cu. ft.). The quality of the spruce fiber is very high. The growth rate of the forests in the northern latitudes is relatively slow, and it takes about 65 to 70 years to produce timber of the best quality.

Norway has a low proportion of national forest, with only 10% of the woodlands under the administration of the State Forestry Service, mostly in the North. Another state corporation runs five sawmills. Fifteen national parks, mostly above the timberline, with 961,000 ha. (2.37 million ac.) and 50 forestry reservations, complete the state's stake in forestry. Traditionally, local citizens have ancient and permanent rights over state forests, such as for timber, fuel-wood, grazing, hunting and fishing.

The central cooperative in the forestry sector is the Norwegian Forest Owners' Federation, founded in 1913. The federation's 19 district associations and 463 local associations have a total membership of 55,000, who together own 3.6 million ha. (8.9 million ac.), comprising 55% of the productive forest land and generating 70% of the annual felling. A second association, the Forest Owners' Association, represents 200 of the larger property owners who receive all of their income from forestry.

Some 10,000 persons are employed in forestry, of whom 4,000 are owners. Another 32,000 persons are engaged in downstream operations such as saw-mills, and total employment corresponds to 10% of the industrial labor force.

Research is conducted by the Norwegian Forest Research Institute, which is run by the Council for Forest Research. University-level education is given at the Agricultural University of Norway.

AGRICULTURAL INDICATORS, 1986

Agriculture's share of GDP: 4%
Average annual growth rate: 3% (1980–86)
Value added in agriculture: $2.580 billion (1986)
Cereal imports (000 tons): 479
Index of Agricultural Production (1979–81=100): 113.1 (1985)
Index of Food Production (1979–81=100): 113.1 (1985)
Index Food Production per Capita: (1979–81=100): 108 (1984–86)
Number of tractors: 145,800
Number of harvester-threshers: 17,500
Total fertilizer consumption: 251,800 tons
Fertilizer consumption per ha. (per ac.) (100 g.): 2,776 (1,124)
Number of farms: 102,000
Average size of holding, ha.: 9.4 (23.2)
Size class (%)
  Below 1 ha. (below 2.47 ac.): 11.9
  1–5 ha. (2.47–12.35 ac.): 26.4
  5–10 ha. (12.35–24.7 ac.): 27.5
  10–20 ha. (24.7–49.4 ac.): 24.6
  20–50 ha. (49.4–123.5 ac.): 9.1
  50–200 ha. (123.5–494 ac.): ⎤
  Over 200 ha. (over 494 ac.): ⎦   0.7

Tenure (%)
  Owner-operated: 97.4
  Rented: —
  Other: 2.6

AGRICULTURAL INDICATORS, 1986 *(continued)*

% of farms using irrigation: 9
Total area under cultivation: 954,000 ha. (2,357,000 ac.)

Farms as % of total land area: 2.9

Land use (%)
  Permanent crops: ⎫
  Temporary crops: ⎬   44.9
  Fallow:
  Meadows and pastures: 55.1
  Woodland: —
  Other: —

Yields, kg./ha. (lb./ac.)

  Grains: 3,193 (2,850)
  Roots & tubers: 24,450 (21,823)
  Milk kg. (lb.)/animal: 5,327 (11,744)

Livestock (000)
  Cattle: 976
  Horses: 14
  Sheep: 2,415
  Pigs: 693

Forestry
Production of Roundwood: 10,620 million cu. m. (375 million cu. ft.)
  of which industrial roundwood (%): 92.5

Value of exports ($000): 807,552
Fishing
Total catch (000 tons): 2,106.8
  of which marine (%): 100
Value of exports ($000): 922,460

MANUFACTURING

Norway is not a major manufacturing country by European standards. The sector employs 20% of the labor force and generates 15% of the GDP. The manufacturing base is very narrow, and Norway has not established itself strongly in the newer hi-tech sectors.

The most striking characteristic of manufacturing is its dispersion. The large plants in the power-intensive industries are in the fjord and coastal districts, close to the power sources and also the ports. Another feature is the generally small size of the plants themselves. Of the 14,000 plants, only a few hundred employ more than 200 workers, and their share of the industrial payroll is about 40%.

Of the various branches of manufacturing, the largest are the power-intensive industries producing chemicals, iron and steel, ferroalloys and aluminum. The sector comprises 30 companies, three-fourths of whose output is exported. They consume about one-third of the electric power production. Norway is the second-largest exporter of primary aluminum after Canada. All the bauxite is imported, but with cheap electric energy, the aluminum industry is able to compete successfully in international markets. The leading producer is the government-owned Ardal og Sunndal Verk, which has three plants in the fjord country on the southwestern coast. Norsk Hydro and Elkem also have large aluminum plants. In addition, Norway is a leading producer of ferroalloys, meeting 40% of West European demand. The raw material base is quartz, which is quarried from Norwegian mines. Norsk Hydro is a large producer of magnesium, which is used in aluminum alloys, as well as ammonia, which is used in the production of fertilizers and urea. Norsk Hydro plants are in the southwestern part of Oslofjord, which is one of the most concentrated industrial areas in Norway. The leading producer of pig iron and steel is the state-owned Norsk Jernverk. Following the decline of the shipbuilding industry, Norsk Jernverk has moved into the production of beams for the building industry. About three-fourths of its output is exported.

The number of government-owned enterprises is only a small share of the total industrial sector, but these play a significant role in the economy. They are mostly public utilities, and special monopolies, such as railroads. The core of the state sector consists of companies taken over as reparations from German interests at the end of World War II. The extent of state participation in these enterprises ranges from 50% to 100%. Of the total gross investment in industry, government-owned firms account for about 12.5%. Some large industrial firms partially or wholly state-owned are Statoil (petroleum); Norsk Hydro (aluminum, fertilizers, petrochemicals, power); Sydvaranger (iron mining); Norsk Jernverk (steel); Norsk Olje (petroleum products distribution); and Ardal og Sunndal Verk (aluminum). The Norwegian government also is a major shareholder in Scandinavian Airlines System. In addition, the government promotes industrial investment through the Regional Development Fund.

Foreign investment in Norway is primarily from four countries: the United States, the United Kingdom, Switzerland and Sweden. About 100 U.S. firms have direct investments in Norway, most of them in sales subsidiaries. Total U.S. investment is over $2 billion, of which 73% is in petroleum; 21% in manufacturing; and 6% in other sectors, chiefly commerce. As a general rule, licenses or concessions must be obtained for productive and manufacturing activity by foreign firms. These concessions contain a number of legislative impediments governing the conditions under which foreigners may acquire real estate or develop natural resources. Foreign investment in banking and insurance is not favored, and takeover of Norwegian companies is normally not permitted. Applications for investment in new enterprises are carefully screened. Once investment permission is granted, the right of physical establishment is controlled by the authorities in accordance with national social and demographic policies. The official policy toward foreign indirect (portfolio) investment has been highly restrictive in the past but has been liberalized to some extent recently.

MANUFACTURING INDICATORS, 1986

Average annual growth rate, 1980–86: 0.3%
Share of GDP: 14%
Labor force in manufacturing: 25.6%
Value added in manufacturing ($ million): $7,939
    Food & agriculture: 20%
    Textiles: 3%
    Machinery: 26%
    Chemicals: 7%
Earnings per employee in manufacturing:
    Growth rate: 2.5% (1980–85)
    Index (1980=100): 105 (1985)
Total earnings as % of value added: 57
Gross output per employee (1980=100): 118
Index of Manufacturing Production (1980=100): 102 (1984)

The engineering industry has become one of the growth leaders in manufacturing, accounting for more than one-third of the value of sectoral output and for an equivalent share of employment. The engineering specialties are turbines, generators and transformers, all of which were originally developed to meet domestic demands. Shipbuilding was, until recently, the largest branch of the engineering sector. Despite the current stagnation in world shipping, Norway has managed to maintain its share in the construction of specialized vessels as well as platforms and equipment for offshore drilling.

Wood-based industries have lost their former preeminence but still account for a substantial share of the exports. Further, the import component in these exports is very small, thus helping the current account position. About 80% of the production is exported, mostly to EEC countries. At the same time, Norway has to face stiff competition from Canada, Sweden and Finland in international markets. Plants in the wood-processing industry are close to the forests and the rivers. Historically, rivers have been the principal means of lumber transportation, a factor that has determined the scattered location of paper and pulp mills.

The leading concern, Borregaard, has its largest plant in the town of Sarpsborg at the mouth of the Glomma River on the southeastern side of Oslofjord.

Fish processing consists of a large number of small-and medium-size companies spread along the coast, particularly in northern Norway, and thus is one of the most dispersed of all the manufacturing sectors. Many are operated by the fishermen themselves as cooperative enterprises. The industry has undergone considerable changes, moving from dried and salted fish in the early days to canned fish, and still later, after World War II, to frozen fish. About 60% to 70% of the catch is reduced to oil, 15% is frozen and 9% is salted and dried.

Most of the other manufacturing sectors, particularly domestic consumer goods, have been stagnating for many years.

MINING

Norwegian mining production dates back to the 17th century, when two mining towns were founded: the silver town of Kongsberg, southwest of Oslo; and the copper town of Røros, on the mountain plateau southeast of Trondheim close to the Swedish border. The extraction of iron ore began at the turn of the century.

RESOURCE PRODUCTION			
	1984	1985	1986
Hard coal (000 metric tons)	451	507	580
Crude petroleum (000 metric tons)	34,682	38,342	42,451
Iron ore (000 metric tons)	2,500	2,321	N.A.
Iron pyrites (unroasted) (000 metric tons)	428	395	380
Copper concentrates (metric tons)	25,042	19,252	21,887
Lead concentrates (metric tons)	3,967	3,597	N.A.
Zinc concentrates (metric tons)	28,513	27,352	N.A.
Natural gas (million cu. m.)	27,375	26,699	27,025

Current mining is relatively modest in scope, and mining accounts for only 2% of the gross manufacturing output by value and employs only 2% of the industrial labor force. Ore deposits are of low grade, requiring extensive use of mechanical equipment and open-cast mining. Most of the mines are in northern and central Norway. In the northernmost county, Finnmark, mining is the most important industry. Outside the town of Kirkenes three large iron ore deposits are mined by the state-owned A/S Sydvaranger, principally for export. Iron ore from the Nordland mines is used by Norsk Jernverk. Known iron ore deposits are estimated to last another 100 years at current rates of extraction. There also are substantial reserves of titanium or ilmenite, used in the production of paint. Europe's largest ilmenite deposit is in the town of Egersund, which produces 10% of the world output. Coal is mined in Svalbard, which supplies one-third of the country's total coal consumption. Other minerals mined in Norway include sulphur, copper, zinc, lead and nickel, but these are of marginal importance.

ENERGY

Norway has abundant supplies of domestic energy resources. The share of hydroelectric power in this energy pie is much larger than in other industrialized countries. It covers 42% of total energy consumption, while oil covers 46% and coal, coke and fuelwood another 12%. Manufacturing obtains 45% of its energy from water power. Norway thus consumes far more electricity per capita than any other country in the world, twice as much as the United States and three times as much as West Germany.

About 60% of the country's hydroelectric potential has been developed, most of it since 1945. In 1939 total production of hydroelectricity was 10.9 TWh; by 1983 it had increased nearly tenfold, to 106.2 TWh. It is estimated that this output could easily be doubled. Norway exports electricity to Sweden and Denmark.

Norway is one of the major European oil and natural gas producers, and its resources on the continental shelf are expected to be commercial well into the 21st century. Explorations on the continental shelf began in 1966, and the first discoveries were made in the late 1960s. Production started in 1971 and increased strongly from 1975 onward following the opening of pipelines to the United Kingdom. In 1985 about 800,000 bbl. were being produced per day, and production rose to 70 million tons by the end of the 1980s. Gas production started in 1977. By 1980 it attained a level corresponding to that of oil production but remained virtually stable thereafter. Overall, oil and gas production rose from 7.8 million tons of oil equivalent in 1975 to 63.9 million tons of oil equivalent a decade later. Norway emerged as a net exporter of petroleum in 1975 and in 1985 produced more than nine times its own domestic consumption. Norway's share in world energy production is, however, small (1.2% for oil and 1.8% for gas in 1984), but its corresponding share of oil exports was larger, at 3%, and considerably higher for natural gas, at 11% in 1984, making Norway the largest net exporter of gas and oil in the OECD area.

ENERGY INDICATORS, 1986

Total energy production, quadrillion BTU: 4.0
  Crude oil: 1.78
  Natural gas liquid: 0.13
  Natural gas dry: 1.07
  Coal: 0.01
  Hydroelectric power: 1.0
  Nuclear power: 0.0

Average annual energy production growth rate, 1980–86: 5.3%
Public utilities' share of GDP: 4%
Energy consumption per capita, kg. (lb.) oil equivalent: 8,803 (19,407)
Energy imports as % of merchandise imports: 7
Average annual growth rate of energy consumption, 1980–86: 2.8%

Electricity
  Installed capacity: 23,236,000 kw.
  Production: 103,190,000,000 kw.-hr.
    % fossil fuel: 0.3
    % hydro: 99.7
    % nuclear: —
  Consumption per capita: 24,777 kw.-hr.

Natural gas
  Proved reserves: 2.612 trillion cu. m.
  (92.243 trillion cu. ft.)
  Production: 25.479 billion cu. m. (900 billion cu. ft.)
  Consumption: 1.229 billion cu. m. (43.402 billion cu. ft.)

Petroleum
  Proved reserves: 11.133 billion bbl.
  Years to exhaust proved reserves: 36
  Production: 306 million bbl.
  Consumption: 75 million bbl.
  Refining capacity: 240,000 bbl. per day

Coal
  Reserves: 30 million metric tons
  Production: 569,000 metric tons
  Consumption: 1,191,000 metric tons

The number actually employed in the oil sector is small. In 1985 only some 9,300 persons were engaged in oil production and drilling. Including support personnel in transportation, catering and construction, it employs 64,000 persons, or about 3% of the labor force. Taking into account deliveries and other services, the figure may be closer to 6%.

The major gas fields are Frigg, Ekofisk (the oldest) and Stratfjord. Both Frigg and Ekofisk attained peak production levels in the early 1980s, but a rapid decline set in after 1985. A new field commenced production in Ula in 1984, and several others were scheduled to commence production. The Troll gas field, containing and estimated 447 billion cu. m. (1.58 trillion cu. ft.) of gas, was declared commercial in 1983, and in 1984 further gas reserves, estimated at between 300 billion and 350 billion cu. m. (1.06 and 1.24 trillion cu. ft.), were discovered in a field in the Tromsø patch. A further gas field was discovered at Sleipner in 1984. Other considerable reserves are known to exist where the continental shelf extends beyond the Arctic Circle.

The increasing oil dependence of the Norwegian economy is clearly reflected in four key statistics: The share of the petroleum sector in the GDP rose from 2½% in 1975 to nearly 20% in 1985; oil investments have risen steeply since the mid-1960s, accounting for about 15% of total gross investment in 1975 and 20% in 1985; the share of oil and gas exports in total goods exports rose from 9% in 1975 to 49% in 1985; and finally, the contribution of oil tax revenues to total government income rose from 2% in 1975 to 19% in 1985.

LABOR

In 1988 the labor force consisted of 2.128 million persons, over half the population. The labor force has grown and changed substantially since 1958, when it was only 1.056 million strong, about half of what it is today. Along with aggregate growth, the work force has changed in composition and character. There is much more specialization today, with attendant enhancement of training and education. There are far more service workers and public sector workers, both in absolute terms and relative to the proportion of blue-collar workers.

To illustrate, in 1950 the labor force was evenly matched among the primary, industrial and service sectors of the economy. By 1983 two-thirds of all wage earners worked in the service sector. In 1980 the service sector contributed twice as much as the industrial sector and 12 times as much as the primary sector. Since World War II, the number of official categories of professions has gone from 30 to over 100. There are, for example, some 13 categories of nurses. This has important implications in terms of the impact education has on employability of certain groups of workers and on the changing attitude toward the trade union movement.

The increasing role of women in the work force is another important trend. Women now comprise 43% of the total work force. Of the total growth in employment between 1976 and 1984, 80% is attributed to women entering the work force. Most women work part time. In 1984, for example, half of all married women worked less than 30 hours per week. At the same time, they continue to work for lower salaries than men. This is attributable in part to the tendency for women to major in comparatively less marketable subjects and to gravitate toward traditional sector of employment for women, such as nursing and teaching. Most women are employed in the public sector and in urban areas. Even in jobs where women are in the majority, men usually supervise.

In recent years new job openings have roughly matched the numbers seeking work for the first time—on an average, about 30,000 annually. In this respect Norway has fared better than most West European countries. But there are structural rigidities peculiar to Norway that have depressed prospects of greater expansion. The first is that with a population of only about 4 million unevenly distributed over a vast area, the country is unable to take advantage of the economies of scale or to adopt innovative industrial approaches. For example, 95% of companies have fewer than 100 employees, and 80% have fewer than 20 employees. There is a wide regional dispersion of production, and many towns are dependent on single industries. In addition, many factors militate against mobility of labor, such as the harsh weather, rugged terrain, high transportation costs and strong regional loyalties. Other rigidities are caused by government social and economic policies. Managers faced with rules and costs associated with the employment of full-time workers tend to substitute overtime work in place of new full-time positions, and more work is contracted out rather than being done in-house. Higher labor costs have led to noncompetitive pricing, declining productivity and loss of export markets. Further, the government's regional development policy contributes to the already serious lack of labor mobility. By subsidizing inefficient and unprofitable companies through public funds, the government has tied major segments of the work force to economically unsustainable enterprises. The costs of doing business also are pushed up through state-mandated social payments, such as the low-wage fund, to which employers contribute to ensure that each employee earns at least 85% of the average industry wage.

Throughout the postwar years, Norway has enjoyed one of the lowest rates of unemployment in the world. This pattern was broken in 1981, when the rate began to creep up, making it a political issue for the first time. From a low of 1.3% in 1980, it rose to 1.7% in 1981, 2.4% in 1982, 3.8% in 1983 and 3.9% in 1984 before falling to 2.0% in 1988. However, Norway, like Sweden, does not include persons receiving special government "labor market measures" as unemployed. If they were counted, the unemployment rate would be much higher. The impact of unemployment varies from region to region and from one age group and gender to the other. In the Oslo area unemployment is historically low, in the 1% bracket, while in the northernmost county of Finnmark it was close to 8.7% in 1985. A comparatively high unemployment level has long been a fact of life in northern Norway, reflecting its harsh climatic conditions and the seasonal nature of its industries. About 29% of the total unemployed group is officially classified as "long-term unemployed" (unemployed for 26 weeks or longer). Elderly workers represent the largest proportion of this group. The extension of the unemployment compensation period from 40 consecutive weeks to 80 consecutive weeks has also provided an incentive for reregistration of some workers who had previously dropped off the rolls. The proportion of female unemployed has actually dropped, from 41.8% in 1980 to 37.7% in 1985, as a result of more job openings in the public sector, which traditionally absorbs more women.

The government sponsors a number of programs to combat unemployment over the short term under the general rubric "labor market measures." These include public works projects initiated expressly to create jobs, and salary subsidies to the private sector to encourage employment of workers (mostly over 50) who were laid off or were too old to find new employment readily. Vocational training and special education and subsidies to industry for apprenticeship programs cover 69% of those receiving labor market measures.

Members of the work force considered organizable number 1,710,000; of these, some two-thirds are members of a trade union. Today there are more workers in trade unions in Norway than ever before, although as a percentage of the work force the rate has not changed from the 66% reported in 1958.

There are over 70 national unions in Norway, with hundreds of union locals. Most unions are represented by one of four umbrella labor organizations: the Norwegian Federation of Trade Unions (LO), the Confederation of Vocational Unions (YS), the Norwegian Professional Association (AF) and the Oil Operators' Federation (OFS).

The LO is the largest of the federations, with 33 national unions and a total membership in 1984 of 760,074. Founded in 1899, it also is the oldest, and its members comprise two-thirds of organized labor. In addition, the LO is politically active, with political interest transcending the traditional union agenda, and it has promoted solidarity with social democratic values and the Norwegian Labor Party. The LO-Norwegian Labor Party relationship has never been defined or institutionalized except for the formal liaison Cooperation Committee, which meets weekly.

Most Norwegians regard the LO as the most powerful private institution in the country, and its membership is the highest in its history. However, its share of the unionized work force has dropped from 84.5% in 1958 to 64.1%. This decline is due partly to the faster growth of the other federations and independent unions. Originally LO membership consisted primarily of blue-collar workers. Today only one-third of LO members are blue-collar workers, and this proportion is expected to decrease to one-sixth by 2000. As the economy became increasingly service-oriented, it failed to attract white-collar workers to the same extent as the AF and the YS. Fading class distinctions and the rise of a more egalitarian society also have worked against the LO, blunting its appeal to educated youth. Increasing specialization and proliferation of professions have led to "vocational" solidarity rather than the "working-class solidarity" that the LO stands for. The LO's unwieldy size and its close identification with the Norwegian Labor Party also are liabilities in its efforts to broaden its appeal. Despite these trends, the LO's preeminence in the labor field has never been seriously challenged.

The YS, the second-largest federation, has 115,000 members in 14 national unions. It includes about 10% of all organized workers. To some extent the YS competes directly with the LO, and there are frequent jurisdictional disputes between the two. The most fundamental difference is that the YS is not linked to any political party and is pragmatic rather than ideological.

The AF has a total membership of 105,500 in 33 national unions representing those in professions, such as doctors, professors, lawyers and engineers. About 30% are civil servants.

The OFS consists of only 5,000 members in four unions. Despite its small size, it is responsible for a disproportionately large share of what little labor unrest has occurred in Norway in recent years. The new and special nature of the work in offshore oil fields has contributed to the independence and militancy of OFS unions.

There are 25 unions operating independently of the four umbrella federations. The two largest, the teachers' union and the nurses' union, with 50,700 and 33,000 members, respectively, have established formal liaison mechanisms with the LO for consultation and coordination.

The principal organization representing employers and management is the Norwegian Employers' Federation (NAF). It is responsible for negotiating all collective agreements with trade unions at the national level, and it is consulted by the Storting and the government at every stage of decision-making in labor relations. It maintains strict control over its affiliates, which must have NAF approval before signing labor agreements or staging lockouts.

Industrial relations are governed by the Labor Disputes Act of 1915, and the Basic Agreement of 1935 signed between the NAF and the LO. Provisions of the agreement standardize working conditions for all enterprises. Collective agreements are negotiated nationally or industrywide and run for two years. Local negotiations are rare.

The Basic Agreement defines the fundamental relations between labor and management, including the role of shop stewards, the right to organize, procedures for collective bargaining, grievance procedures, checkoff of union dues, election of works councils, advance notice of intended strikes or lockouts, sympathy strikes and lockouts, shift work, employment of nonunion workers, indexation of wages, and the establishment of the Information and Development Fund for training in productivity.

Cost-of-living wage adjustments are now common. Some contracts allow the reopening of negotiations on wages if the Consumer Price Index rises a specified number of points. In some years wages are frozen, as in 1978–79, in an effort to curb inflation.

Strikes and lockouts are infrequent. They are forbidden by the Basic Agreement during the life of a contract, and punitive sanctions are imposed on offending unions or managements. Mediation machinery is available but seldom used. The voluntary referral of a dispute to the National Wage Committee is more frequent. A cooling-off period is required before any industrial action is taken. If a strike threatens vital interests, the Storting may refer a dispute to the National Wage Committee for compulsory arbitration. Public employees have the same right to organize, bargain collectively or strike as private employees. However, a greements between unions and public officials must be approved either by the Storting or a municipal or county council.

Often, bargaining between labor and management is superseded by tripartite bargaining, with the government as the third party. The Contact Committee, composed of representatives of labor, management, agriculture, fisheries and government serves as the most influential forum for annual review of economic policies, trends and developments.

Tripartite cooperation is common in other areas, such as for the Information and Development Fund. There also is the Joint Committee for Research and Development in Industrial Democracy, affiliated with the Norwegian Institute for Social Research. This committee sponsors practical experiments to soften assembly line job monotony.

Under the Labor Disputes Act, disputes over rights must be taken to labor courts, and conflicts over interests or issues affecting economic benefits to mediation by the National Wage Committee. The labor courts are composed of seven members: a chairman, two public members and two members each representing labor and management. All are appointed by the government. The Mediation Agency has a chief mediator and eight district mediators, all appointed by the government for a three-year term.

The Employment of Domestic Servants Act prescribes a minimum age of 15 and a written contract for employing a domestic. Working hours must not exceed nine hours a day.

The Equal Rights Act of 1979 forbids discriminatory treatment of female workers in hiring, promotions and dismissals. Exceptions are made for affirmative action programs designed to strengthen the position of women in sectors where they were previously underrepresented.

The Joint Stock Companies Act mandates employee representation on management boards. In companies with more than 50 employees, one-third of the board members may be elected by employees. In companies with more than 200 employees, the act requires the establishment of an assembly, one-third elected by workers, which elects the board of directors having final say on investments, technological changes and other matters affecting the labor force.

LABOR INDICATORS, 1988

Total economically active population: 2.128 million
As % of working-age population: 64
% female: 43.6
Activity rate (%)
  Total: 49.9
  Male: 69.1
  Female: 40.9

Employment status (%)
  Employers & self-employed: 9.0
  Employees: 86.3
  Unpaid family workers: 2.0
  Other: 2.7

Organized labor: 66.1

Sectoral employment (%)
  Agriculture, forestry, fishing: 7.1
  Mining: 1.0
  Manufacturing, construction: 24.1
  Electricity, gas, water: 1.0
  Trade: 17.1
  Transportation, communications: 8.4
  Finance, real estate: 6.7
  Services: 34.6

Average annual growth rate of labor force, 1980–2000: 0.7%

Unemployment (%): 2.0
Labor under 20 years: 5.4

Hours of work
  Manufacturing: 30.6 hours per week

The Work Protection and Working Environment Act of 1977 is a far-reaching piece of social reform and social legislation. Its objectives are to assure workers full protection against harmful working conditions and to enhance the quality of working life. Technological changes must be assessed on the basis of their impact on worker health, safety and stress. The act sets up Work Environment Committees composed equally of labor and management to monitor compliance with its provisions. One member of the committee is designated as a safety delegate. The act also provides for a 40-hour week, limits on shift work, a ban on nonessential night work, a maximum 36-hour workweek for employees under 16, one months' advance notice of dismissal for all employees and six month's advance notice for employees over 60.

The Act on Protection Against Bankruptcy assures workers of their wages for up to six months if their employer goes bankrupt. Payments are made by the government.

The Annual Holiday Act requires a four-week annual vacation for all employees and five weeks for those over 60.

The government tries to maintain full employment through measures designed to promote productivity and training. Its wide range of stimulants include in-plant training as an alternative to layoffs, with half of its costs subsidized by the estate; training programs for youth under 20; subsidies to labor-intensive industries; subsidies to institutional sheltered employment; and relocation allowances to promote worker mobility.

There is only a small number of foreign workers in Norway.

FOREIGN COMMERCE

Norway is a charter member of the EFTA whose members have had duty-free access to each other's nonagricultural markets for over a decade. Norway also has an agreement for duty-free access covering manufactured products. The United Kingdom, West Germany and Sweden are the main trading partners.

A few commodities such as grain, alcohol and pharmaceuticals are imported exclusively by state monopolies. Private industrial associations are involved directly in the conduct of trade and the formulation of trade policies. In 1988 Norway completed its grant of duty-free concessions agreed to in the 1979 Tokyo Round of the GATT. Exports are paced by petroleum, but traditional exports such as forest products, ships and aluminum still contribute a major share of the exports. In recent years Norway has enjoyed a trade surplus, primarily as a result of substantial oil exports.

TRANSPORTATION & COMMUNICATIONS

The Norwegian State Railway dates to 1854, when the first rail connection was opened from Oslo to Eidsvoll. In 1909 the Bergen Railway was opened. The system was completed in 1962. Of its total length of 4,240 km. (2,635 mi.), 2,443 km. (1,518 mi.) are electrified. There are plans to extend the line to Tromsø. The main lines radiate from Oslo to Stavanger, Bergen, Trondheim,

FOREIGN TRADE INDICATORS, 1986

Exports: $18.2 billion
Imports: $20.3 billion
Balance of trade: -$2.1 billion
Annual growth rate, 1980–86 exports: 5.1%
Annual growth rate, 1980–86 imports: 5.8%
Ratio of international reserves to imports (in months): 4.8
Value of manufactured exports: $6.825 billion
Terms of trade (1980=100): 87 (1986)
Import Price Index (1980=100) 84.1
Export Price Index (1980=100): 67.2
Import of goods as % of GDP: 29.0
Export of goods as % of GDP: 26.0

Direction of trade (%)

	Imports	Exports
EEC	49.3	64.9
U.S.A.	6.8	5.4
East European economies	1.8	0.9
Japan	7.4	1.2

Composition of trade (%)

	Imports	Exports
Food / Agricultural raw materials	8.5	9.8
Fuels	5.9	42.9
Ores & minerals	3.1	1.5
Manufactured goods	82.5	45.8
of which chemicals	6.7	6.9
of which machinery	40.5	17.5

Bodø, Åndalsnes, Røros, Kongsvinger and Moss, where there are connections to Sweden.

Of the 79,540 km. (49,434 mi.) of roads, 64% is paved. Although the main roads are in good condition, stretches of older road are narrower and less well maintained and are full of curves, bridges and tunnels. Ferries are common. The mostly private ferry companies run 245 ferries servicing 164 routes. Bus transportation is extensive, both in the cities and in areas not served by rail lines. The longest bus route runs from the Nordland Rail terminal in Fauske to Kirkenes near the Soviet border, for a distance of 1,300 km. (808 mi.).

TRANSPORTATION INDICATORS, 1986

Roads
  Length, km. (mi.): 85,872 (53,358)
  Paved (%): 64

Motor vehicles
  Automobiles: 1,513,954

TRANSPORTATION INDICATORS, 1986 *(continued)*

Trucks: 240,673
Persons per vehicle: 2.4
Road freight, ton-km. (ton-mi.): 6,022 million
(4,125 million)

Railroads
Track, km. (mi.): 4,258 (2,646)
Passenger-km. (passenger-mi.): 2,241 million
(1,392 million)
Freight, ton-km. (ton-mi.): 2,932 million (2,008 million)

Merchant marine
Vessels: 2,107 (over 100 gross tons)
Total dead weight tonnage: 14,202,700
Oil tankers: 8,665,000 GRT

Ports
9 major
17 secondary
58 minor
Cargo loaded: 58,428,000 tons
Cargo unloaded: 17,604,000 tons

Air
Km. (mi.) flown: 59 million (36.6 million)
Passengers: 611,400
Passenger-km. (passenger-mi.): 3.960 billion
(2.460 billion)
Freight km. (freight-mi.): 137.3 million (94.0 million)
Mail, ton-km. (ton-mi.): 18.5 million (11.5 million)
Airports with scheduled flights: 41
Civil aircraft: 62

Pipelines
Refined:
Natural gas: } 53 km. (32.9 mi.)

Inland waterways
Length, km. (mi.): 1,577 (980 mi.)
Cargo, ton-km. (ton-mi.): 10.698 billion (7.328 billion)

COMMUNICATION INDICATORS, 1986

Telephones
Total: 2,579,000
Persons per: 1.6

Phone traffic
Local:
Long distance: 6,131,368,000
International: 176,257,000

Post office
Number of post offices: 2,753

COMMUNICATION INDICATORS, 1986 (continued)

Domestic mail:
Foreign mail received: } 1,602,438,000
Foreign mail sent:

Telegraph
  Total traffic: 430,000
  National: 322,000
  International: 108,000

Telex
  Subscriber lines: 10,817
  Traffic (000 minutes): 10,217

Telecommunications
  4 coaxial submarine cables
  INTELSAT, EUTELSAT, MARISAT

TOURISM & TRAVEL INDICATORS, 1986

Total tourist receipts: $828 million
Expenditures by nationals abroad: $1.925 billion
Number of hotel beds: 11,734
Average length of stay: 3.8 nights
Tourist nights: 3,460,000
Number of tourists: 1.347 million
  of whom from (%)
  U.S.A.: 19.8
  West Germany: 15.1
  U. K.: 12.4
  Other Nordic countries: 50.0

Norway's maritime traditions go back to the Viking longships, and it has maintained its prominence as a shipping nation through the centuries. The merchant fleet comprises 2,300 vessels, two-thirds of which are in coastal traffic. However, 95% of the total tonnage of 19.2 million gross tons is in international traffic, thus making an important contribution to Norway's balance of payments. The largest units are oil tankers, which account for over 60% of the total tonnage. The 160 oil tankers in the Norwegian fleet have an average size of 160,000 tons Dw, and the largest can transport over 400,000 tons of oil. In addition, the fleet has over 100 tankers for transportation of gas and chemicals, and 40 combined carriers. Half of the merchant fleet consists of specialized vessels, including ships built for transporting supplies to the offshore oil platforms. Shipping companies also operate many oil drilling platforms. Another specialty is the cruise trade, particularly in the Caribbean. The world's largest passenger ship, the *Norway* (formerly the *France*), was put into operation as a cruise ship in 1980. With an average ship age of seven years, Norway has one of the youngest merchant fleets in the world. More than one-third of the ships are less than 10 years old, and nearly 70% are less than 20 years old.

The vast majority of the shipping companies are small or medium-size, and all are privately owned. In general there has been less government involvement in this sector than in others. The fleet has declined considerably in the past decade both in absolute and in relative terms. In 1969 it accounted for one-tenth of the world's total tonnage, compared to 5% in 1985. The decline is due partly to the general crisis in international shipping and partly to the growth in flags of convenience. The merchant fleet employs about 35,000 people, of whom 18% are foreign nationals. The largest ports are Oslo and Bergen.

Norway is a part owner of Scandinavian Airlines System (SAS). In addition to SAS, two other airline services provide extensive domestic service: Braathens South American and Far East Air Transport (SAFE), and Wideroe's Flyveselskap. There are 41 airports, of which the largest are Fornebu and Gardermoen near Oslo, Fiesland near Bergen, and Sola near Stavanger.

The Postal Service was established in 1647, and the first postage stamp was issued in 1855. There are 2,753 post offices, the northernmost of which is in Ny-Ålesund in Svalbard.

The telecommunications system includes four coaxial submarine stations and 10 domestic satellite stations.

In recent years the number of foreign tourists has equaled or exceeded the total population. It is estimated that 50% come from the Nordic countries for whom no passports are required. Tourism makes an important contribution to the economy of the outlying regions along the coast and mountains.

DEFENSE

The king is the commander in chief of the defense forces, but executive control is vested in the minister of defense, while the Defense Committee of the Storting exercises legislative control. The command structure is integrated in a triservice organization headed by the chief of defense, whose deputy is the chief of the defense staff. The heads of the four services—army, navy, air force and home guard—have the title of inspector general. Operational command is held by the North Norway (COMNOR) and the commander, South Norway (COMSONOR). COMNOR also is commander of the Allied Task Force, North Norway. In situations of conflict, he is subordinate to CINCNORTH, the NATO commander of the Northern Flank, always a British general, whose headquarters are at Kolsaas, outside Oslo.

Like several other European states (Sweden, Switzerland, Austria, Yugoslavia and West Germany), Norway has adopted a doctrine of Total Defense, which aims to integrate in times of war an integrated force combining economic, psychological, law enforcement, medical, home defense and other related elements. In practice, the principal concern of the defense forces is the security of the Finnmark region bordering the Soviet Union and close to the Kola Peninsula, where massive Soviet forces are permanently stationed.

Norway is a founding member of NATO, and its Brigade North, the largest of its army's standing units, is earmarked for NATO assignment in wartime. Other army units will remain under direct national control. Certain units are earmarked for U.N. peacekeeping duties. Norway has placed certain unilateral restrictions on the stationing of alien troops on its soil in peacetime, and the country does not receive military aid. Also, it does not permit the stockpiling of nuclear weapons, or the establishment of launching sites for rockets. However, NATO forces regularly exercise in Norway.

DEFENSE PERSONNEL, EQUIPMENT & BUDGET

Defense budget, 1986: $1.737 billion

% of GNP: 2.9%

Defense expenditures per capita: $420

Defense expenditures per soldier: $44,538

Defense expenditures per sq. km. of national territory: $5,361 ($13,889 per sq. mi.)

Total military manpower: 39,000

Total mobilization strength: 495,000

Reserves: 201,000

Army: 20,000; 2 subordinate, 5 regional, 16 subordinate territorial commands; 1 brigade of 3 infantry battalions; 1 tank company, 1 field artillery battalion, 1 AA battery unit in North Norway; 1 all-arms group of 1 infantry battalion, 1 tank company, field artillery in South Norway; 2 border garrison battlions; 1 infantry battalion (Royal Guard)

Navy: 7,600; submarines, frigates, fast attack craft; 1 helicopter squadron; coastal defense; naval bases at Horten, Haakonsvern (Bergen), Ramsund and Olavsvern (Tromsø)

Air Force: 9,400; 5 fighter squadrons; 1 maritime reconnaissance squadron; 2 transport squadrons; 1 helicopter squadron

Arms imports: $180 million

Arms exports: $0

For deployment purposes, Norway is organized into two commands: Northern, with headquarters at Bodø; and Southern, with headquarters at Oslo. The Northern Command includes the Brigade North, with its separate headquarters at Bardufoss, near Tromsø. The mobilization brigades and the local defense forces are organized under four regional headquarters. The home guard is organized into 18 districts, divided into 90 subdistricts and 500 local areas.

The army is divided into 10 corps: infantry, cavalry, artillery, engineering, signals, transportation, army aviation, logistics, repair and medical. Unlike Sweden and Denmark, Norway does not maintain its historic regiments of infantry and cavalry, except for the royal footguards.

All male citizens are liable for military service from age 20 until 45. Conscription is universal for 12 months. About 85% of the soldiers are conscripts who are transferred to the mobilization brigades on completion of their terms of duty. Training lasts three to eight months at schools and training centers in southern Norway. Special courses are offered in winter warfare. Regular officers are trained at the Military Academy in Oslo, where the Staff College is located.

Officers and enlisted personnel wear khaki uniforms with a patch in the branch colors. Combat dress is an olive green smock and trousers in summer and white ski overalls in winter. A peaked cap, a ski cap, a beret or a NATO helmet are worn as appropriate.

Although Norway does not have strong military traditions, Norwegian soldiers are generally hardy and particularly skilled in winter warfare. Conscription is less unpopular and conscientious objectors significantly fewer than in neighboring countries, such as Sweden. Defense policy is guided by the present threat posed by Soviet buildup on the northern border and dependence on NATO help to repel any Soviet aggression in the future. NATO defense plans are based on transfer of reinforcements from North America in case of an attack on Western Europe. Called the Rapid Reinforcement Plan, it is Norway's principal security shield.

Norway has no significant defense production.

EDUCATION

Three factors have influenced Norwegian education in the past 300 years: geography, history and the church. One of the most sparsely populated countries of Europe, Norway contains relatively few large towns, while the rural communities are scattered over a large area. Schools thus tend to be small, with more than 50% of elementary schools having only one class for any particular age group. The influence of history is reflected in deep-rooted egalitarian traditions. The country was too isolated and too poor to cause a powerful upper class to emerge. The church's influence is constitutionally enshrined. The Act Concerning the Basic School states that "the purpose of the school is to help give pupils Christian and moral upbringing."

During the 19th century, most schools were adjuncts to parishes, and training was mostly ecclesiastical in nature. After Norway dissolved its union with Denmark, a surge of nationalism led to the founding of the University of Oslo in 1811. The first primary school act was passed in 1840, although primary schooling did not become compulsory until 1887.

The legal foundations of education are found not so much in the Constitution as in series of acts passed by the Storting, especially between 1840 and 1980:

1840: Act Concerning Compulsory Schooling
1889: Act Extending Compulsory Education to Seven Years
1954: Act Setting Up the National Council for Innovation in Education
1959: Act Extending the School-Leaving Age to 16
1969: Act Concerning the Basic School
1973: Act Concerning Teacher Education
1974: Act Concerning the Upper Secondary School
1975: Act Concerning Preschools
1980: Apprentices Act

Compulsory education ensures free schooling for all Norwegian children for nine years. More than 90% of the pupils continue their schooling after this period. Some 99% of children at the basic level and 96% at the upper secondary level attend public schools. Textbooks and other instructional materials are provided free by the state. The state provides not only free transportation to the nearest school but also free living quarters for students who live too far for commuting. Generally, schools are coeducational; further, efforts to remove sex stereotyping in the curriculum have led to the integration of boys and girls in the same classes for subjects such as domestic science, needlework and carpentry.

The school year runs from August through June for 35 to 38 weeks and is divided into two semesters, autumn and spring, separated by summer and Christmas vacations. In addition, there are short holidays in autumn, in midwinter and at Easter.

The country has two official languages: Landsmaal or Nynorsk and Rigsmaal or Bokmaal. (See the section on language.) At the basic level, local education authorities decide by ballot the language of instruction. Pupils in upper secondary school normally have to study both. The law decrees that all textbooks be published in both languages at the same price and the same time. English is compulsory for all pupils from the fourth grade.

In the general education branch of upper secondary schools, females outnumber males, but the reverse is true in vocational schools. In the higher education sphere, the share of females has been growing in recent years but has not yet attained parity. The education of Lapps or Sami is supervised by the National Council for Education of Lapps.

Examinations and grading practices have evolved through numerous reforms. In the basic school, parents must be informed at least twice a year about their children's progress at school. In the junior school, no marks are given. At the intermediate stage, pupils are given marks in compulsory subjects at least twice a year. In the seventh through the ninth years, pupils also are given marks for order and conduct. The scale of marks runs from excellent through very good, good and fair to poor. In three subjects—Norwegian, English and mathematics—these marks are relative and follow a Gauss curve, while in other compulsory subjects a percentage breakdown is used according to which 50% of the pupils receive very good, 45% good and 5% poor.

At the primary level there are no private schools. At the secondary level a few private schools are run, particularly by non-Lutheran denominations. They are similar to folk schools, and their students do not take national examinations. At the higher level, private institutions are run by commercial and philanthropic organizations but not by denominations.

Preschool education is voluntary and provided by one of three types of schools: *barnehager* (kindergartens), *barneparker* (supervised outdoor playgrounds) and *forskole klasser* (in-school programs for six-year-olds). Preschool education is governed by a 1975 law that made local authorities responsible for it, although overall direction lies with the Ministry of Consumer Affairs and Government Administration.

Primary and compulsory education lasts for nine years, from ages seven to 16. *Grunneskole* (basic) schooling comprises two cycles: *barnetrinnet* (junior) for classes one through six and *ungdomstrinnet* (youth) for classes seven through nine, with an optional 10th year in some cases. Teaching hours normally are from 8:30 A.M. to 2:00 P.M. five days a week and are divided into 45-minute periods. Weekly class hours vary from 15 periods a week for seven-year-olds to 30 periods in the sixth grade. In the junior stage pupils are taught by the same teacher in most subjects, and in many cases the same teacher follows the pupils through the grades. In the youth stage each classroom group has a teacher with general overall responsibility and special teachers for each subject. There is an upper limit of 30 pupils per class throughout the basic school. The curriculum is regulated by the Act Concerning the Basic School of 1974, which lays down a model plan emphasizing individualized learning and a common core approach. All pupils follow the same timetable throughout the first seven years, with limited subject options in grades eight (five periods) and nine (10 periods). In addition, pupils learn certain obligatory and nonobligatory topics. The former include traffic training, alcohol and drugs, tobacco, environment, family life, consumer education, nutrition, first aid, dental health and sex education; the latter include gardening and drama. At the end of the basic school, pupils take written examinations in some subjects and oral examinations in others. Grades and assessments are combined to establish a final grade.

The basic school system organized in school districts within the individual municipalities. There are 2,000 such districts, of which 270 are ungraded, and some 1,000 have no separate classes for all age grades. According to the act, basic schools shall not be established for fewer than 10 pupils except by special dispensation. The average size of the class is 20.8 students.

Each municipality has a local education board, which appoints all teachers and prepares school budgets. In each county, the director of schools represents the national government and is advised by a special body called the Basic School Council. Municipalities are reimbursed for their educational expenditures through grants that vary from 25% to 85% of the outlay, depending on their financial capabilities.

Upper secondary school (*videregaende opplaering*) is defined as postbasic school between compulsory and higher education, principally from the 10th to the 12th school year, or in the 16 to 19 age range. A comprehensive reorganization of upper secondary education took place following the passage of the Act Concerning the Upper Secondary School of 1974, which consolidated the former gymnasiums and vocational schools into one school with two tracks, general and vocational. The curriculum is divided into eight study courses, of which the *allmenfag* (general studies option) is based on the former gymnasium curriculum. The remaining seven are craft and vocational subjects. Within each subject there are branch and core groups. The average number of teaching periods per week normally ranges from 28 to 32. Most study courses consist of a one- or two-year *grunnkurs* (basic course) and a one- or two-year *videregaendekurs* (further education course). In the first year pupils consolidate their knowledge of general subjects, while in the second and third years 50% of the class schedules are filled with compulsory subjects and pupils are required to specialize along one of the four branches or lines: languages, social studies, natural sciences and music. The vocational subject groups also include a few general subjects.

Grades in the upper secondary school range from 0 to 6 and are given for overall achievement as well as for performance in written examinations. Examinations are held under the aegis of the National Council for Upper Secondary Education. In the general area, pupils take at least three written examinations, of which one is a Norwegian composition. A certain percentage of pupils whose names are drawn by lot take additional oral examinations. Examinations also are held for pupils not enrolled in schools. Since 1983 a new school-leaving-examination certificate has replaced the old matriculation certificate.

The National Council for Upper Secondary Education is vested with the control and direction of this level of schooling, including curriculum development and examinations. In the fields of teaching and examinations, each school is directly responsible to the council, while the County School Board deals with matters such as planning and budgets. The governing body of each school is the school committee. Operating expenses are met by the county municipalities, who receive reimbursement from the state equal to 30% to 75% of the school budgets. Grants also are extended to private upper secondary schools.

Outside the mainstream are the folk high schools, which were established in the 19th century by a Danish educator, N. Grundtvig. The folk schools are uniquely Scandinavian and offer general education for young adults between 17 and 21. They have no set examinations, and many are boarding schools where social activities are accorded status equal to academic studies. There are 85 folk schools.

Higher education is provided by universities and regional colleges. Until 1983, entrance to these institutions was through the *examen artium* (matriculation certificate), but since then regulations have been relaxed.

The university year is divided into two terms, a spring term between January 15 and June 15, and an autumn term between August 20 and December 20. The lowest degree in humanities and science is the *cand. mag*, which normally may be completed in four to five years, studying five subjects. There is no strict time limit for the completion of studies, but all students, except those at Norges Tekniske Hogskole, must first complete a preliminary course leading to the *examen philosophicum* within six months. In the liberal, social and natural sciences, subjects are taken at the *grunnfag* (subsidiary), *mellomfag* (minor) or *hovedfag* (major) levels. Study or research at the *hovedfag* level usually leads to a master's degree.

There are four universities in Norway: Oslo, Bergen, Trondheim and Tromsø. All are state institutions, although they enjoy considerable autonomy. The University of Oslo founded in 1811, is the country's oldest and, until 1946, its sole university. It has seven faculties. The other three universities were founded after World War II and before 1970: Bergen in 1946, and Tromsø and Trondheim in 1969. The last-named was formed through the merger of the State College of Teachers, the Museum of the Royal Norwegian Academy of Sciences and Letters, and the Norwegian Institute of Technology. In addition to universities, there are eight specialized colleges, including the Agricultural University of Norway, the State Veterinary College, the Norwegian School of Economics and Business Administration, the Oslo School of Architecture, the State

Academy of Art, the Norwegian College of Physical Education and Sports, the State Academy of Music and the Norwegian College of Fisheries.

Each county has a regional college, which provides vocational education at the university level for two or three years. It is administered by a regional college board, with a majority of its members appointed by the Ministry of Church and Education on recommendation of the county officials. Although vocational in nature, the courses are interdisciplinary and are open to part-time and adult students. There are few private postsecondary institutions.

The structure of university administration differs. Normally the Senate is the highest administrative body for the entire university, and the Faculty Board for each faculty. At the University of Tromsø, the northernmost university in the world, students have a high degree of representation but there are no faculty administrative bodies.

Higher education is virtually free. Students pay only a small fee, which goes toward welfare activities carried out by their own organizations. The State Educational Loans Fund was set up in 1947 to eliminate inequalities of opportunity due to geographical, social and economic factors. Scholarships are granted on the basis of a means test. Students over 20 living away from home are given monthly stipends. The state finances practically all higher education, both private and public.

The Storting exercises legislative control over education, but operational responsibility is vested with the Ministry of Church and Education. The ministry is advised by a number of bodies, such as the Council for Basic Schools, the National Council for Upper Secondary Education, the National Council for Education of Lapps, the National Council for Teacher Education, the National Council for Adult Education and the National Council for Innovation in Education. The principal trend in educational administration is toward decentralization in favor of local authorities, such as county school boards, school committees and municipal school boards. The ministry is represented in each county by the school director.

Local authorities collectively raise about 45% of the cost of schooling. The exact ratio of local to central government contributions varies according to the economic resources of the community.

Adult education is governed by the Adult Education Act of 1976 and is offered through a variety of sources, both public and private. These include public schools and college as well as voluntary organizations such as the Workers' Education Association, affiliated with the Norwegian Labor Party; the Evening School, affiliated with the Conservative Party; the Association of People's Academies; the Norwegian Housewives' Association; the Folk University, a national body comprising over 300 students; free teaching groups; correspondence schools; and the Norwegian Institute of Distance Education.

The law recognizes three categories of teachers: *forskoleloerer*, a teacher in preschool; *allmenloerer*, a teacher in junior basic school; and *fagloerer*, a teachers in upper secondary school. Teachers for basic school are trained at colleges of education in three-year integrated programs, while teachers for upper secondary school are required to take a six-month course qualifying in the subject of specialization after a three-year program in a college of education. The law recognizes two additional categories for determining remuneration: *adjunkt* (adjunct), for one who has completed an additional year at college or a first university degree; and *lektor* (lecturer); one who has, in addition to a degree from a college of education, either a second degree of three years of study at the postgraduate level. All teachers are civil servants and are paid according to civil service scales. Higher scales apply in northern Norway to compensate for the physical hardships in desolate regions. Teachers normally reach their maximum salary scale after 14 to 18 years of service. At the junior level a full-time teacher has 29 weekly teaching periods of 45 minutes each, and at the youth stage 22 to 26, depending on the subjects taught.

EDUCATION INDICATORS, 1986

Literacy
  Total (%): 100
  Males (%): 100
  Females (%): 100

First level
  Schools: 3,525
  Students: 534,000
  Teachers: 31,459
  Student–teacher ratio: 17:1
  Net enrollment rate: 98%
  Females (%): 49

Second level
  Schools: 920
  Students: 204,199
  Teachers: 10,087
  Student–teacher ratio: 12:1
  Net enrollment rate: 84%
  Females (%): 50

Third level
  Institutions: 228
  Students: 93,535
  Teachers: 6,961
  Student–teacher ratio: 13:1
  Gross enrollment rate: 29.3%
  Graduates per 100,000 ages 20–24: 2,217

EDUCATION INDICATORS, 1986 *(continued)*
% of population over 25 with postsecondary education:
11.9
Females (%): 49

Foreign study
   Foreign students in national universities: N.A.
   Students abroad: 4,233
      of whom in
         U.S.A.: 1,539
         West Germany: 803
         U. K.: 738

Public expenditures
   Total: $4.020 billion
   % of GNP: 7
   % of national budget: 12.9
   % current: 86.6

LEGAL SYSTEM

The Norwegian legal system is purely national in origin although closely related to other Nordic legal systems with regard to the development of jurisprudence. The influence of Anglo-American law is limited to court procedure in criminal cases. Such court procedure, formerly based on customary law, now has been codified in the revised Civil Disputes Act and Criminal Procedures Act. Judicial procedures differ to some extent in civil and criminal cases, but the Act Relating to the Courts of Justice applies to both.

With regard to civil cases, there are three ordinary courts: district courts or city courts (*herreds* or *byrett*), the High Court Appeals Division (Lagmannsret) and the Supreme Court (Hoyesterett). In certain cases a conciliation board (forliksrad) may deliver judgment. A special panel of the Supreme Court, the Appeals Selection Committee (Kjoeremalutvalg), also may act as a court of justice proper with regard to some decisions.

No action may be brought before a court unless an attempt has been made to settle the dispute through a conciliation board. Each board consists of three members elected for four years. As a rule there is one conciliation board in each municipality. At present there are 450 conciliation boards. Conciliators are paid a small fee for handling each case but receive no other remuneration. Practicing lawyers are ineligible to act as conciliators.

The main purpose of a conciliation board is to mediate disputes to effect conciliation. Only if the board fails in this respect may a judgment be rendered. Certain types of cases are excluded from the purview of the conciliation boards. These include matrimonial and descent cases; cases involving public authorities; and cases concerning patents, trademarks and industrial property. On receiving a request or summons for mediation, the conciliation board summons the parties to a meeting, which they must, as a rule, attend in person. No party may be represented or be accompanied by a lawyer.

If the board succeeds in bringing about a settlement, a formal agreement is entered, which has the same effect as a final judgment. If the parties fail to agree, the dispute usually will be referred to the courts for trial. When both parties appear and request the board to settle their dispute, the board may pronounce judgment, and it also may render judgment at the request of one of the parties in debt and real-estate cases where the value does not exceed NOK30,000 and NOK10,000, respectively. Judgments delivered by the board may be appealed to the district court or the city court.

Nearly 90% of all settled disputes are resolved by the conciliation boards, 60% of them by default and only 3.8% by conciliation.

The designations "district court" and "city court" refer to the same kind and level of jurisdiction, the former covering a rural district and the latter a town. There are 85 district courts. In nine of the larger urban areas (Oslo, Frederikstad, Drammen, Skien, Porsgrunn, Kristiansand, Stavanger, Bergen and Trondheim) the city courts are organized as collegiate tribunals comprising several judges headed by a president *(justitarius)*. The district court of Asker and Baerum also is organized in this manner. The other district and city courts are organized with one professional judge only, referred to as *byfogd* in towns and *sorenskriver* in rural areas. Of the 85 district courts, 47 are in towns and the remaining 38 in districts. The courts may also employ the services of one or more deputy judges *(dommerfullmektiger)* or temporary associate judges *(hjelpedommere)*.

For the main hearing the court is generally set with one professional judge only, but either of the parties may request that there be in addition two lay judges. The lay judges *(domesmenn)* are drawn by lot from a panel of lay judges and are elected by the municipal councils within the jurisdiction of the court for four years. Lay judges with expert knowledge in certain fields may be appointed by the court. The lay judges participate in trying the facts of the case and the application of the law. Since each member of the court has one vote, the professional judge is generally outvoted by the lay judges.

The High Court Appeals Division is the next-highest court level. There are five such intermediate appellate courts, in Oslo, Skien, Bergen, Trondheim and Tromsø, each headed by a presiding judge *(lagmann)* and including several High Court judges. A judgment rendered by a district court or a city court may be brought before the High Court Appeals Division only if the value involves amounts of NOK2,000 or more. Cases concerning matters without economic value may always be appealed to the High Court. Frequently the judges of the High Court are on circuit. Each case is heard by three professional judges, but either party may request that four or two lay judges be called in to participate in the adjudication process.

At the apex of the judiciary is the Supreme Court. Judgments delivered by the High Court Appeals Division may be appealed to the Supreme Court provided the economic value involved is NOK 12,000 or more. Otherwise the appellant must first obtain the consent of the Appeals Selection Committee of the Supreme Court. This committee is composed of three justices, who serve on a rotation basis for certain periods. In certain cases appeals lie directly to the Supreme Court from the district courts or the city courts.

The Supreme Court consists of a president or chief justice and 17 permanent justices. It is divided into two parallel sections, each of five justices. Generally, evidence before the Supreme Court is presented indirectly, since all direct evidence has been presented to lower courts. Expert witnesses may, however, give evidence directly, and the Supreme Court may examine concrete items of additional evidence. Accordingly, the main hearing is of a somewhat different character than that before the subordinate courts, but otherwise it follows the same mode of procedure. Judgments delivered by the Supreme Court are published in the *Norsk Rettidende* (Norwegian Law Gazette).

Special courts in the judiciary include the Official Assessment Court, the Land Appropriation Court and the Labor Disputes Court. There are no special commercial courts in Norway.

The main provisions of the Norwegian criminal law are codified in the General Civil Penal Code of 1902, which has been amended several times. The Permanent Commission on Criminal Law has been established to submit proposals for possible amendments and improvements. The code divides punishable acts into two categories: felonies and misdemeanors.

Criminal procedure stipulates that criminal proceedings can be launched only by the Public Prosecution Authority, headed by the director-general of public prosecutions, who is directly under the king and thus independent of the Ministry of Justice. Under him there are 17 state advocates, who also are appointed by the king. Officials in the higher echelons of the police also belong to the Public Prosecution Authority. These include the district commissioner of police, the deputy and assistant district commissioners and the superintendents. Criminal proceedings can be initiated only by the senior officers *(embetsmenn)* of the Public Prosecution Authority. All ordinary courts of justice have jurisdiction in criminal cases, even though their interdependent competence is different from that in civil cases. Prosecution may, however, be waived if the public interest does not require it or when the accused agrees to certain state-imposed conditions.

In criminal cases there are normally only two court levels: (1) the district court, the city court or the High Court and (2) the Supreme Court. When a city court or district court takes and records evidence for the use of the trial court, it is set without lay judges. In such a capacity, the court is termed the Court of Examining and Summary Jurisdiction. The Public Prosecution Authority may demand a pretrial judicial criminal investigation against an accused. Such an investigation is mandatory before an indictment. In principle, the consent of the Court of Examining and Summary Jurisdiction is necessary before arrest, detention, search and seizure. A person who is arrested must be brought before the Court of Examining and Summary Jurisdiction within 24 hours, and its judge will decide whether he is to be remanded to custody. In some cases a case may be tried and adjudicated by the Court of Examining and Summary Jurisdiction.

Criminal cases are tried by the High Court, with three professional judges and a jury of 10 members selected from a panel of 16, of whom three are eventually excused by the prosecution and three by the defense. The jury determines guilt, and in doing so is bound by the judge's interpretation of points of law but not by his opinion in other areas. Judgment is rendered on the basis of the jury's verdict, but the judges may nevertheless set aside that verdict in certain cases, or they may place the matter under a more lenient penal provision. Judgments are rendered immediately after the termination of the sitting of the court or, at the latest, within 24 hours.

Appeals lie to the Supreme Court, which is barred from trying any evidence related to the question of guilt and must confine itself to the points of law contested in the appeal. However, regardless of the points contested, it may consider whether the provisions of the substantive criminal law have been wrongfully applied to the detriment of the accused and whether the punishment imposed is too severe.

There are no special courts to try criminal cases against juvenile offenders. Juveniles may be tried and punished after age 14. Criminal actions against offenders under 18 are determined by municipal juvenile welfare boards composed of five members elected by the municipal councils for four years.

If an accused is guilty of several attempted or actual felonies of a serious nature, the court shall hold him in preventive detention after he has served his full term. The so-called security sentence may be invoked against a person whose criminal responsibility is reduced for reasons of insanity. In recent years security sentences have been imposed only in rare instances.

The death sentence has been abolished as a result of a law amendment in 1979, and the most severe punishment is imprisonment for life. Beside imprisonment *(fengsel)*, the ordinary forms of punishment are detention *(hefte)* and fine *(boter)*. Minor cases are decided by the writs of fine option issued by the Public Prosecution Authority. In some cases a convicted person may forfeit a public office, or forfeit the right to pursue a specified trade of profession, usually in conjunction with other penalties. In addition, he may be barred from living in or visiting a specific place, and the sentence also may provide for confiscation of money or personal property. The execution of the punishment may be postponed and the sentence itself suspended at the discretion of the judge in the case of occasional offenders and young first offenders. When sentences are suspended, probation periods are fixed at between two and five years. During probation, the convicted person is subject to the supervision of a designated person, an official panel or an after-care institution. Other terms and conditions also may be imposed, such as payment of indemnification and reparations.

The penal system consists of three central prisons—two for men and one for women—for those serving long terms of imprisonment; 24 regional prisons for terms of imprisonment between six and 18 months; and eight auxiliary prisons for imprisonment terms of up to 20 days.

As a rule, prisoners may be released on parole after completing two-thirds of the sentence, provided at least four months have been served. The power of pardon is vested in the king in council.

The constitutional status of the judiciary vis-à-vis the executive is one of growing importance. Courts may entertain actions by Norwegian subjects against the crown and determine whether administrative agencies have acted in compliance with the laws and statutes. However, the courts cannot try the purely discretionary part of administrative decisions except when the exercise of authority has been arbitrary, resulting in an abuse of power. Although not specifically authorized by the Constitution, the courts have the power to set aside a statute of the Storting if it is at variance with the Constitution. The courts also may set aside provisional decrees of the king in council for the same reason. The Supreme Court generally hews to its precedents in this respect and rarely departs from its own earlier interpretations. A special court, the Court of Impeachment, adjudges cases against government ministers. This court is composed of five Supreme Court judges and 10 members of the Lagting, while the proceedings are initiated by the Odelsting. Since 1814, impeachment proceedings have been initiated eight times, the last in 1926–27 against Prime Minister Abraham Berge.

Judges are chosen by public competition and appointed by the king in council on the recommendations of the Ministry of Justice. Judges retire at 70 (or 67, if they so choose) but may be dismissed only on the basis of a court judgment.

LAW ENFORCEMENT

The national police force was formed in 1936, when the municipal police forces were amalgamated with the state police, which until that time was responsible only for the rural districts and for certain specialized police functions.

The higher echelons of the police force belong to the Public Prosecution Authority. The country is divided into 53 police districts, each headed by a district commissioner of police *(politimestrene)* assisted by deputy and assistant police commissioners and superintendents, all of whom are trained lawyers. The district commissioner and the deputy commissioner are appointed by the king, and lower officials by the Ministry of Justice. Thus, by virtue of its special organization, the police force is subject to a dual subordination: on the one hand to the Public Prosecution Authority with regard to criminal investigation, and on the other to the Ministry of Justice in law enforcement. Police stations are manned by inspectors.

In the rural districts the police duties are carried out by sheriffs *(lensmennene)*, of whom there are 390. The sheriffs also discharge some functions relating to the Public Prosecution Authority. In Svalbard the governor also is district commissioner of police.

The largest police district is Greater Oslo, under a superintendent, under whom there are the Criminal Police, the Harbor Police, the Traffic Police and the Foreigners Bureau. The Central Criminal Police Bureau represents Interpol in Norway. The Mobile Police, organized into six divisions, are deployed during emergencies or riots anywhere in the country. Since Norway is generally free from civil disturbances, the Mobile Police are usually assigned for traffic duties during the peak tourist season in summer. The police also are in charge of civil defense duties. The Police Emergency Headquarters in Oslo coordinates all peacetime emergency services.

Training is provided by the Police School.

Information is not available on incidence and types of crime in Norway.

HEALTH

Norwegians are generally healthy people, with the longest life expectancy for both males and females in the world. Cardiovascular diseases account for 50% of all deaths and cancer for 21%. Road accidents account for 1.3% of all deaths but 25% of accidental deaths.

In terms of morbidity, psychiatric and nervous disorders dominate, especially abuse of alcohol and drugs. Rheumatic disorders and disorders of the musculoskeletal system are major disabling conditions. Based on the data on absence from work due to illness, the average Norwegian is ill for 30 days a year. Clearly, females have a higher morbidity rate than men. Most infectious diseases are under control, but incidences of the so-called lifestyle diseases have been growing rapidly.

HEALTH INDICATORS, 1985

Health personnel
  Physicians: 10,110
    Population per physician: 411
  Dentists: 4,397
  Nurses: 44,354
  Pharmacists: 3,041

Hospitals
  Number: 1,192
  Number of beds: 24,776
    Per 10,000: 165
  Admissions/discharges per 10,000: 1,663
  Bed occupancy rate: 84%
  Average length of stay: 9 days

Public health expenditures
  As % of national budget: 10.8
  Per capita: $539.50

Vital statistics
  Crude death rate per 1,000: 10.5
  Decline in death rate, 1965–84: 7.4
  Life expectancy at birth (years)
    Males: 72.8
    Females: 79.5
  Infant mortality rate per 1,000 live births: 8
  Child mortality rate ages 1–4 years per 1,000: Insignificant
  Maternal mortality rate per 100,000 live births: 2.0

Causes of death per 100,000
  Infectious & parasitic diseases: 7.5
  Cancer: 231.9
  Endocrine & metabolic disorders: 13.0
  Diseases of the nervous system: 16.1
  Diseases of the circulatory system: 518.5
  Diseases of the respiratory system: 105.2
  Diseases of the digestive system: 30.4
  Accidents, poisoning & violence: 65.0

The health care system represents a compromise between central control and local initiative. Health institutions are mostly owned and run by the counties.

Each commune has its local board of health headed by a local public health officer. In rural districts and small towns the officer combines the roles of general practitioner and health administrator.

Under the Hospital Act of 1970, provincial councils have full responsibility for the planning, operation and construction of hospitals, but their medical activities are supervised by the director-general of health. The running costs are met partly by the national health insurance system.

Official health policy favors primary care, responsibility for which is more diffuse. The central government employs one or more public health officers in each municipality.

Although the health service is designed to ensure equality of access to health care, the system suffers from two persistent problems. One is the regional disparity in the availability of medical personnel and resources. Oslo has one doctor for every 226 inhabitants, while Sogn og Fjordane County has one for every 904. Secondly, patients over 67 account for nearly 50% of all bed days and 37% of the health budget. On the basis of current demographic trends, this percentage is likely to increase still further by 2000, when those over 67 will constitute 26.19% of the population.

FOOD & NUTRITION

The average Norwegian consumes 3,326 calories and 104.5 g. (3.7 oz.) of protein per day. This food supply is 115% of FAO daily requirements. Food expenditures account for 15% of total household expenditures.

PER CAPITA CONSUMPTION OF FOODS
Kg. (Lb.), 1986

Potatoes: 61.0 (134.5)
Wheat: —
Rice: 2.0 (4.4)
Fresh vegetables: 28.2 (62.2)
Fruits (total): 43.4 (95.7)
  Citrus: 8.0 (17.6)
  Noncitrus: 35.4 (78.0)
Eggs: 11 (24.2)
Honey: 0.7 (1.5)
Fish: 14.9 (32.8)
Milk: 214.0 (471.8)
Butter: 4.8 (10.6)
Cream: 5.9 (13.0)
Cheese: 12.1 (26.6)
Yogurt: 2.2 (4.8)

```
PER CAPITA CONSUMPTION OF FOODS (continued)
Meat (total): 44.1 (97.2)
   Beef & veal: 17.2 (37.9)
   Pig meat: 19.2 (42.3)
   Poultry: 2.0 (4.4)
   Mutton, lamb & goat: 5.7 (12.5)
Sugar: 42.2 (93.0)
Chocolate: 7.6 (16.7)
Ice cream: 8.9 l. (18.8 pt.)
Margarine: 16.0 (35.3)
Biscuits: 5.8 (12.7)
Breakfast cereals: 2.1 (4.6)
Pasta: 8.8 (19.4)
Canned foods: 2.8 (6.2)
Beer: 44.6 l. (94.2 pt.)
Wine: 4.0 l. (8.4 pt.)
Alcoholic liquors: 1.3 l. (2.7 pt.)
Soft drinks: 60 l. (126.8 pt.)
Mineral waters: 9.5 l. (20.0 pt.)
Fruit juices: 8.8 l. (18.6 pt.)
Tea: 0.2 (0.4)
Coffee: 10.1 (22.3)
Cocoa: 1.3 (2.8)
```

MEDIA & CULTURE

Norway's press history goes back to the 16th century, when printed newssheets appeared sporadically in various towns. The first formal paper, *Norske Intelligenz Seddeler,* was founded in Bergen in 1763. The press played a significant role in the movement that led to independence from Denmark in 1814 and thereafter grew rapidly. Its golden age was the period from the turn of this century to 1940, during which time over 80 newspapers were founded. The press survived the Nazi occupation relatively intact.

```
              MEDIA INDICATORS, 1986
Newspapers
   Number of dailies: 64
   Circulation (000): 1,682
      Per 1,000: 454

   Number of nondailies: 81
   Circulation (000): 407
   Per capita: 99

   Number of periodicals: 4,010
   Circulation: —
```

MEDIA INDICATORS, 1986 *(continued)*

Newsprint consumption
  Total: 126,400 tons
  Per capita: 30,687 kg. (60.6 lb.)

Book publishing
  Number of titles: 4,152

Broadcasting
  Annual expenditures: 845.5 million krone
  Number of employees: 2,470

Radio
  Number of transmitters: 764
  Number of radio receivers: 1,505,000
    Persons per: 2.8
  Annual total program hours: 11,539 (public)

Television
  Television transmitters: 1,389
  Number of TV receivers: 1,339,400
    Person per: 3.1
  Annual total program hours: 2,414 (public)

Cinema
  Number of fixed cinemas: 461
  Seating capacity: 127,000
    Seats per 1,000: 32.2
  Annual attendance (million): 12.8
    Per capita: 3.1
  Gross box office receipts: 271.5 million krone

Films
  Production of long films: 8
  Import of long films: 284
    % from U.S.A.: 51.4
    % from France: 10.9
    % from Italy: 7.0
    % from U.K.: 9.5

CULTURAL & ENVIRONMENTAL INDICATORS, 1986

Public libraries
  Number: 1,391
  Volumes: 16,502,000
  Registered borrowers: 1,198,000
  Loans per 1,000: 4,360

Museums: 434
  Annual attendance: 4,768,000
  Attendance per 1,000: 1,150

Performing arts facilities: 13
  Number of performances: 5,098
  Annual attendance: 1,073,000

CULTURAL & ENVIRONMENTAL INDICATORS, 1986
(continued)

Attendance per 1,000: 260

Ecological sites
  Number of facilities: 55
  Zoos & botanical gardens: 7

The press reflects its political roots. A few papers are owned by political parties, such as *Arbeiderbladet*, the Norwegian Labor Party's official newspaper. Even independent dailies have strong party leanings. Norwegian Labor Party papers are more numerous, although with smaller circulations. The Conservative Party press includes in its ranks the prestigious *Aftenposten*.

Even though the majority of the dailies employ bold headlines and numerous photographs, the news and commentary generally are serious and of high quality. One feature is the *kronikk*, a signed and dated op-ed essay on an intellectual or political subject of current interest. Makeup is neat and orderly. In the case of the *Aftenposten*, the nation's leading daily, advertising takes up 65% of the space in the morning edition and 46% in the evening edition. It averages 44 pages for its morning edition and 16 pages for its evening edition, but other dailies are considerably thinner. No newspapers are published on Sundays; consequently, Saturday editions are much bigger. Since 1977, air transportation has made possible same-day delivery of dailies to even the remotest villages.

Many cities have competing newspapers, a sign of press vitality and health. Oslo leads with eight, followed by Bergen with five and Kristiansand, Molde and Stavanger with three. Seventeen cities have two competing newspapers: Ølesund, Arendal, Bodø, Drammen, Flora, Gjøvik, Larvik, Moss, Namsos, Sandefjord, Skien, Stjordal, Tønsberg, Tromsø, Trondheim, Vaden and Voss. Except for the national dailies, most newspapers have low circulations, with an average of 13,000. The mass-circulation papers are produced in Oslo, including the *Aftenposten*, the *Verdens Gang* and the *Dagbladet*, all of which also may be considered as the country's most influential papers. The *Aftenposten* is generally included among the world's elite newspapers.

In the 1960s, as the press began to falter under financial pressures caused by declining readership and declining advertising revenues, state subsidies were introduced. In 1972 the Press Fund was set up to grant cheap loans to newspapers threatened with extinction. Direct aid from the state since then has been by subsidies, loans, help with distribution, government advertising, and training and research grants. The government, in fact, is one of the biggest national advertisers. Indirect aid includes preferential postal rates, exemptions from sales taxes, VAT concessions, special phone rates, help to news agencies, and subsidies for joint distribution and production. The subsidies are based on the amount of

LARGEST NEWSPAPERS IN NORWAY	
Newspaper	Circulation
Verdens Gang	269,140
Aftenposten	232,938
Dagbladet	169,317
Bergens Tidende	94,201
Adresseavisen	83,717
Stavenger Aftenblad	63,676
Arbeiderbladet	56,000

newsprint used for the editorial portion of each newspaper and are distributed equally to all papers with circulations of less than 10,000, and to papers with circulations of up to 80,000, provided they are not the leading paper in the district in advertising revenues.

Most newspapers are privately owned, and there are no major publishing chains. The exception is the Schibsted Group, which publishes the *Aftenposten* and *VG*, the former a conservative medium and the latter a liberal one. The Norwegian Labor, Conservative and other parties have their own stakes in the press and run party organs, but party ties have been loosening in recent years. One advantage enjoyed by the Norwegian press is the relatively cheap and abundant supply of newsprint, of which the country is one of the major producers.

The Norwegian Constitution specifically guarantees freedom of the press in Article 100:

> There shall be liberty of the press. No person may be punished for any writing, whatever the contents may be, which he has caused to be printed or published unless willfully or manifestly he has either himself shown or incited others to disobedience to the laws, contempt of religion or morality, or the constitutional powers, or resistance to their orders, or has advanced false and defamatory accusations against any other person. Everyone shall be free to speak his mind frankly on the administration of the state or on any other subject whatsoever.

Journalists may legally conceal their sources, but when brought to trial, they may be subject to imprisonment if they refuse to disclose their sources in criminal cases.

Norway has two national news agencies: Norsk Telegrambrya (Norwegian News Agency, NTB), founded in 1867; and the Norsk Press Service (NPS).

Both radio and television are state monopolies financed through state subsidies and income from license fees. Sound broadcasting began in 1925 and television in 1960, and both are operated by Norsk Riksringkasting (NRK), headed by a director-general. NRK Radio operates two long-wave, four medium-wave and four short-wave stations, 46 VHF transmitters and 705 low-power relay stations. The noncommercial television service is broadcast through 52 main transmitters and 1,434 low-power relay stations.

SOCIAL WELFARE

Social welfare services cover all activities under the Social Care Act, the Child Welfare Act and the Temperance Act and include social counseling and rehabilitation; protection of children and adolescents; care of the aged; noninstitutional services to the handicapped; therapy for and care of alcoholics; and assistance to certain minority groups, such as refugees and Gypsies. The administration of these services is vested with the municipalities under the overall direction of two departments of social services within the Ministry of Health and Social Affairs. The First Department of Social Services deals with child welfare and drug- and alcohol-related issues. The second, or General, Department of Social Services deals with social aid, the aged, handicapped and refugees. At the regional level, the county administrations include social service departments that handle work related to the Ministry of Justice (such as family law), the Ministry of Health and the Ministry of Consumer Affairs and Government Administration as well. At the municipal level, the Health and Social Welfare Board is in charge of all social services under the director of the Social Welfare Office. In the larger cities, the administration of social work, under the direction of the municipal executive for social welfare, is very extensive, often including specialized subdivisions for children and other youth. These agencies offer assistance to needy residents whose requirements cannot be met through statutory social insurance and other benefits, including welfare arrangements. These efforts are partly client-oriented, such as financial aid, institutional care for the aged and the handicapped, advice and guidance, and home help; and partly of a general nature.

Social Security is based on the National Insurance Act, which went into effect in 1967, replacing the old-age pensions (1936), disability benefits (1961), widows and mothers pensions (1965), survivors' benefits for children (1957) and rehabilitation assistance (1961). In 1971 health insurance (1911), unemployment insurance (1939) and occupational injury insurance (1895–1960) also were incorporated into the National Insurance Program. The insurance program is administered by the National Insurance Department through the National Insurance Administration (RTV). The regional branch of the RTV is the County Committee for National Insurance, headed by the county medical officer, and the local insurance office in the municipalities. Disputes relating to insurance are handled by the Social Insurance Appeals Court.

Others dealing with welfare programs are the Family Affairs and Equal Status Department and the commissioner for children. Equal status between the genders is enforced by the ombudsman for equal status and promoted by the Equal Status Council. The commissioner for children promotes and defends children's interests on a broad front.

The principal benefits disbursed under the National Insurance Program are: (1) old-age pensions, (2) sickness benefits, (3) unemployment benefits, (4) rehabilitation aid, (5) disability benefits, (6) occupational injury benefits, (7) funeral grants, (8) survivor benefits and (9) benefits to one-parent families. Irrespective of citizenship, the program covers all persons domiciled in Norway. The pension age is 67, extendable to 70. The old-age pension consists of a basic pension, a supplementary pension, special supplements, compensation supplements, and supplements for spouse and children. There are related insurance programs for seamen, fishermen, forestry workers and reindeer-herding Lapps.

There is no private welfare system in Norway.

CHRONOLOGY (from 1945)

1945 — Vidkun Quisling, head of the Nazi administration of Norway, is executed; Einar Gerhardsen of the Norwegian Labor Party is elected prime minister.

1951 — Oscar Torp of the Norwegian Labor Party succeeds Gerhardsen as prime minister.

1955 — Gerhardsen returns to office as for a second term as prime minister.

1957 — King Haakon VII dies and his son Olav V ascends the throne.

1963 — The Norwegian Labor Party yields power for a month to a Conservative Party-led coalition headed by John Lyng. . . . Gerhardsen heads his third government.

1965 — Per Borten of the Center Party displaces Gerhardsen as prime minister.

1971 — Norwegian Labor returns to office under Trygve Bratteli.

1972 — Lars Korvald of the Christian People's Party forms a coalition government. . . . Norwegians reject EC membership in a national referendum.

1973 — Trygve Bratteli leads his second government.

1976 — Odvar Nordli replaces Bratteli as Norwegian Labor leader and prime minister.

1981 — Norway's first woman prime minister, Gro Harlem Brundtland, takes office as prime minister following her election as Norwegian Labor Party Leader. . . . The Brundtland government falls, and Kaare Willoch of the Conservative Party forms a coalition government of nonsocialist parties.

1986 — Willoch resigns following a no-confidence motion in the Storting and Brundtland heads a minority government.

BIBLIOGRAPHY

BOOKS

Aftenposten. Facts About Norway. Oslo, 1987.

Burgess, Philip M. *Elite Images and Foreign Policy Outcomes: A Study of Norway.* Athens, Ohio, 1968.

Derry, T. K. *A History of Modern Norway, 1814–1972.* New York, 1973.

Eckstein, Harry. *Division and Cohesion in Democracy: A Study of Norway.* Princeton, 1960.

Gustavson, Bjorn, and Gerry Hunius. *Improving the Quality of Life: The Case of Norway.* Oslo, 1981.

Hodne, Fritz. *The Norwegian Economy, 1920–1980.* New York, 1983.

Kvovik, Robert B. *Interest Groups in Norwegian Politics.* Oslo, 1976.

Lafferty, William. *Participation and Democracy in Norway: The Distant Democracy Revisited.* Oslo, 1982.

Larsen, Karen. *History of Norway.* Princeton, N.J., 1948.

Lindgren, Raymond E. *Union, Disunion, Reunion: Norway, Sweden and Scandinavian Integration.* Princeton, N.J., 1959.

Nawrath, Alfred. *Norway.* Chicago, 1965.

Olsen, Johan P. *Organized Democracy: Political Institutions in a Welfare State: The Case of Norway.* Oslo, 1983.

Popperwell, Ronald G. *Norway.* New York, 1972.

Ramsey, Natalie Rogoff. *Norwegian Society.* New York, 1974.

Udgaard, Nils. *Great Power Politics and Norwegian Foreign Policy.* Oslo, 1973.

OFFICIAL PUBLICATIONS

Ministry of Finance

De Offentlige Sektorers Finanser (Public Sector Finances), Central Bureau of Statistics

Financielle Sektorbalanser (Financial Sector Balance Sheets), Central Bureau of Statistics (biannual, Norwegian and English)

Statement of General Accounts published in Report No. 3 to the Storting

Other Units of Central Government

Annual Report and Statement of Accounts of National Insurance Administration (National Insurance Program, family allowances and pension insurance for fishermen and forestry workers and the military)

Annual Report and Statement of Accounts of National Insurance Fund

Annual Report and Statement of Accounts of Price Regulation Funds

Annual Report and Statement of Accounts of Public Service Pension Fund

Annual Report and Statement of Accounts of Seamen's Pension Insurance

Annual reports and statements of accounts of other extrabudgetary units

Local Government

Statements of accounts of counties and municipalities
Note: All sources are annual and in Norwegian only except as indicated.

SWEDEN

SWEDEN

BASIC FACT SHEET

OFFICIAL NAME: Kingdom of Sweden (Konungariket Sverige)

ABBREVIATION: SW

CAPITAL: Stockholm

HEAD OF STATE: King Carl XVI Gustaf (from 1973)

HEAD OF GOVERNMENT: Prime Minister Ingvar Carlsson (from 1986)

NATURE OF GOVERNMENT: Parliamentary democracy; constitutional monarchy

POPULATION: 8,393,071 (1988)

AREA: 449,964 sq. km. (173,686 sq. mi.)

ETHNIC COMPOSITION: Nordic

LANGUAGE: Swedish

RELIGION: Evangelical Lutheran

UNIT OF CURRENCY: Krona

NATIONAL FLAG: A yellow cross with extended right horizontal on a blue field.

NATIONAL EMBLEM: A main shield quartered by a gold cross whose arms taper toward the center. Panels display alternately three jeweled gold crowns on blue and a gold-crowned lion on diagonal blue and white stripes, the emblem of the Folkung dynasty. A small heart shield imposed at the center of the cross combines the symbols of the Vasa dynasty and the ruling Bernadottes. The charges include a gold urn displayed against a silver band on a red field, a gold eagle on a blue field with silver stars, and a silver twin-turreted castle on a blue background. Gold-crowned lions flank the main shield, which is topped by a royal crown and circled by the cherub-decorated collar of the Order of the Seraphim, its medal suspended below.

The emblem is displayed against an ermine-lined red pavilion crested with a larger gold diadem.

NATIONAL ANTHEM: Du Gamla, du Fria, du Fjallhoga Nord (O Glorious Old Mountain, Crowned Land of the North)

NATIONAL HOLIDAYS: New Year's Day; Midsummer Day; all major Christian festivals

NATIONAL CALENDAR: Gregorian

PHYSICAL QUALITY OF LIFE INDEX: 99 (on an ascending scale with 100 as the maximum)

DATE OF INDEPENDENCE: 10th century

DATE OF CONSTITUTION: January 1, 1975

WEIGHTS & MEASURES: Metric

GEOGRAPHICAL FEATURES

The largest of the Scandinavian countries, Sweden is one of the countries located farthest from the equator. It extends from north to south at roughly the same latitude as Alaska, with about 15% of its total area situated north of the Arctic Circle. Extreme length north to south is 1,574 km. (98 mi.), and the greatest breadth east to west is 499 km. (310 mi.). It has a total area of 449,964 sq. km. (173,686 sq. mi.), of which land area occupies 411,407 sq. km. (158,803 sq. mi.), and water area 38,558 sq. km. (14,883 sq. mi.), including some 96,000 lakes. Sweden is bounded on the north and northeast by Finland; on the east by the Gulf of Bothnia; on the southeast by the Baltic Sea; on the southwest by the Øresund, the Kattegat and the Skagerrak and on the west by Norway. Of its total boundary length of 4,595 km. (2,855 mi.), that with Finland is 586 km. (364 mi.) long; that with Norway, 1,619 km. (1,006 mi.) long; and the coastline is 2,390 km. (1,485 mi.) long. The two largest Swedish islands are Gotland, with a coastline of 400 km. (249 mi.), and Öland with a coastline of 72 km. (45 mi.). At present there are no border or other territorial disputes.

The capital is Stockholm, on the outlet of Lake Mälaren into Saltsjo, an inlet of the Baltic Sea. The second largest city is Göteborg, on the southwestern coast near the mouth of the Göta River, which empties into the Kattegat. It is also at the terminus of the Trollhättan–Göta Canal. The third-largest city is Malmö, on the Øresund, about 16 miles southeast of Copenhagen, with which it is connected by ferry. Malmö was ceded to Sweden by Denmark in 1658. The fourth-largest city is Uppsala, about 40 miles northwest of Stockholm. It is the seat of the Lutheran archbishopric and a famous university founded in 1474. There are seven other cities with populations of over 100,000.

Sweden is rhomboidal in shape, and the most impressive of its geographical features is its length—indeed, the Swedes speak of *vart avlanga land* (our long, drawn-out land). It shares this and many other features with its Siamese twin, Norway, but is a land of lower altitudes and less dissected relief than Norway.

Four topographical divisions can be discerned in the country, although they are of unequal size. The largest is Norrland, which commonly refers to the broad Baltic slopes from the lower reaches of the Dal River northward. This region comprises three-fifths of the country, with its rolling landscape of hills and mountains, forests and large river valleys. In this region are deposits of iron and other ores, which gave rise to Sweden's oldest industrial zone of Bergslagen. Through Värmland and Dalarna, Norrland's landscape merges with those of the faulted lands of Central Sweden, which constitutes the second region. The wooded highland region of Smaland in the South is the third region. The fourth region is in southernmost part of the country and is known as Scania or Skåne, a continuation of the fertile plains of Denmark and northern Germany.

Norrland slopes from the Kjølen Mountains along the Norwegian frontier to the Gulf of Bothnia. Its many rivers, notably the Göta, the Dal, the Angerman, the Ume and the Lule, flowing generally toward the southeast—have incised

Population of the biggest municipalities.	
Stockholm	659,030
with suburbs	1,435,474
Göteborg	425,495
with suburbs	704,052
Malmö	229,936
with suburbs	457,919
Uppsala	154,859
Norrköping	118,567
Örebro	118,043
Västerås	117,706
Linköping	116,838
Jönköping	107,362
Helsingborg	105,468
Borås	99,963
Sundsvall	93,181
Eskilstuna	88,528
Gävle	87,784
Umeå	85,108
Lund	82,015
Södertälje	79,764
Halmstad	77,151
Karlstad	74,439
Skellefteå	74,282
Huddinge	70,209

the plateau surface. Norrland falls readily into three subdivisions. The western highlands follow the Norwegian frontier and are lifted to peaks of over 1,829 m. (6,000 ft.), of which the highest is Kebnekaise at 2,123 m. (6,966 ft.). Prolonged erosion, however, has reduced much of the surface to a plateau. The depressions of this upland are filled by lakes, most of which lie somewhat more than 305 m. (1,000 ft.) above the level of the Baltic. The largest of these lakes are Torneträsk (317 sq. km., 122 sq. mi.); Luleträsk with Langas (220 sq. km., 85 sq. mi.); and the interconnected trio of Hornavan, Uddjaure and Storavan (660 sq. km., 255 sq. mi.). There are a number of small icefields above 66°N latitude. Southernmost of the lakes is Kalsjo, to the east of which opens out the lowlands centered in Storsjön, which is the second topographical subdivision of Norrland. The rivers in this region are marked by falls and rapids. This subregion continues to the Finnish border and is interspersed with spreads of peatland and some of the most extensive forest stands in the country. The piedmont zone yields to the third subdivision, the Bothnian coastal plain, which merges almost imperceptibly into the sea. Both the littoral and estuaries are crowded with islands. The Bothnian coast may be divided into three sections—lower, middle and upper—of which the middle extends from Örnsköldsvik to Skellefteå.

Central Sweden is a shatter zone of lakes and plains. The four principal lakes are Vänern, Vättern, Hjälmaren, and Mälaren, of which Vänern is the second largest in Europe, with an outlet to the west by way of the Göta River. It claims Sweden's largest catchment area. The Trollhättan Falls, on the Göta River, are indicative of the change in level between the lake and the Skagerrak lowlands. Lake Mälaren lies only about 0.6 m. (2 ft.) above the average level of the Baltic Sea. Throughout the Great Lakes region are extensive plains such as Uppland (centered on Uppsala), Västmanland, Narke, and East and West Gotland. Archaeological evidence suggests that this lakes and plains region was the core of early Swedish settlements.

To the south of Lake Vättern are the faulted landscapes of Skåne, which, although resembling the Danish landscape, have areas of much more pronounced relief, Skåne differs from much of Sweden not merely in its structure and geological history but also in the fact that its coast is free of islands.

Like other northern countries, Sweden is richly islanded. The archipelago of Stockholm shows the most intense concentration of islands, the outermost of which are separated from their Finnish counterparts by the Åland Sea. In contrast, the western coast archipelago of Bohuslan is a skerry zone where the ice, waves and winds have left the skerries bald in appearance. The Göta River cuts through this rocky back country to the plainlands of Central Sweden. Of Swedish islands, Gotland occupies a special and central place. Although it has a plateau appearance and is skirted with limestone cliffs, it has some of the finest beaches in the Baltic. Its principal town is Visby.

Since the last Ice Age, the land in northern and central Sweden has been rising, in some places up to 0.9 m. (3 ft.) per century.

Much of the Swedish landscape is dominated by coniferous forests blended in southern Sweden with such deciduous trees as birch and aspen. Hardwoods such as linden, ash, maple and elm are found throughout southern Sweden up to the border of Norrland. Because of their lime-rich bedrock and favorable climate, Gotland, Öland and part of the Scandinavian mountain range have interesting flora that include numerous varieties of orchids. Although the wolf has been entirely eradicated, bears and lynx still inhabit the northern forests. Throughout the country there are large numbers of moose, roe deer, foxes and hares. Winter bird life is dominated by a few species, but summer brings large number of migratory birds from the south. Fish species range from cod and mackerel of the deep, salty Atlantic to the salmon and pike found in the less saline Gulf of Bothnia and in lakes and rivers. In 1910 Sweden was the first country to establish national parks, mainly in Norrland.

CLIMATE & WEATHER

Climatically, Sweden is on the border between the Arctic zone and the Atlantic zone with its warm Gulf Stream. Because of the influence of the latter, Sweden enjoys a more favorable climate than its location would seem to suggest. Stockholm averages -3°C (26°F) in February and 18°C (63°F) in July. However, because of its latitudinal extent, there is a wide climatic divergence between Norrland and southern Sweden. Most of Norrland has a winter of seven months and a summer of less than three, while Skåne, in the South, has a winter of about two months and a summer of more than four. The short northern summers are partially compensated for by comparatively high summer temperatures, the greater length of day and the infrequency of summer clouds. On the other hand, the considerable cloud cover in the winter reduces heat loss by radiation.

The weather is very changeable. A few hours of rain are often followed by bright sunshine and wind followed the next day by more rain. As a result, temperature differences between night and day in both summer and winter are not great, especially in western Sweden. Another type of weather, however, creates a more contrasting climate when high pressure leads to hot spells in summer and cold ones in winter. Data are not available on prevailing wind patterns.

Annual rainfall is heaviest (58 cm., 23 in.) in the Southwest and along the border with Norway, while the average for Lapland is only 30 cm. (12 in.). The maximum rainfall occurs in the late summer and the minimum in early spring. There is considerable snowfall in the North, where snow remains on the ground for half the year, causing most ports on the Gulf of Bothnia to remain snowbound throughout the winter.

CLIMATIC VARIATIONS					
City	Average Temperature, February	Average Temperature, December	Sunrise December	June	Sunset December	June
Kiruna	-12.9°C (9°F)	+12.8°C (55°F)	never	n.a.	never	n.a.
Stockholm	-3.1°C (26°F)	+17.8°C (64°F)	8:47 A.M.	2:34 P.M.	2:45 P.M.	9:05 P.M.
Malmö	-0.7°C (31°F)	+17.2°C (63°F)	8:37 A.M.	3:28 P.M.	3:36 P.M.	8:52 P.M.

POPULATION

The population of Sweden in 1988 was estimated at 8,393,071, based on the last census, held in 1984, when the population was 8,342,621. Sweden ranks 71st in the world in size of population and 49th in land area. The population is expected to increase to 8,421,000 by 1990 and then decline to 8,328,600 by 2000.

The first complete census in Sweden was taken in 1749, and since there exists an uninterrupted series of demographic data. In addition to censuses, Sweden has since the 18th century drawn on a unique church-record system for the continuous recording of individual demographic changes at the parochial level. Each newborn child and immigrant is assigned a national registration number indicating date of birth and sex. This number is entered along with other relevant data in a personal file maintained by the registration office of the parish in which the individual is registered. This file continues to record life events such as marriage, childbirth, divorce, change of address and death. If the person moves to another parish, the file is transferred to that parish's registration office. The country's 24 county administrative boards keep regional computer registers, which are continually updated with information from parish registration offices. The county administrative boards, in turn, report to Statistics Sweden, which keeps a national register of population.

At its first census the population of Sweden was 1.8 million. It grew to 3.5 million in 1850 and 7 million in 1950, thus nearly doubling every 100 years. The average annual growth rate for the past 200 years has been 7%, but this figure masks some heavy fluctuations. Generally, a period of high fertility and high mortality gives way to a period of low mortality and low fertility, a process called "demographic transition." On this basis, Swedish demographic developments can be roughly divided into four phases: 1750–1810; 1810–70; 1870–1930; and 1930 to the present day.

The first of these periods was one of high mortality and high birth rate, but within this period the average birth and death rates of 33 and 37 per 1,000, respectively, fluctuated sharply. For example, in 1772–73 and 1808–9, the death rate was almost 60 and 40 per 1,000, respectively. Disregarding regional differences, the number of children per marriage averaged eight, of whom perhaps four or five would reach adulthood. Migration to and from Sweden was very small. Population growth during this period averaged just over 6%.

The death rate began to decline between 1810 and 1870 due partly to better food supply and partly to advances in medical science. It was primarily infant mortality and female mortality that declined; the death rate for adult men did not start to decline until about 1850. Both mortality and fertility followed a steadier course than previously, with only moderate fluctuations. Fertility increased somewhat during the close of this period, which meant that more children per family and a larger proportion of children survived into adulthood. The population growth rate rose during this period, to upward of 10% per annum.

The years between 1870 and 1930 marked a new phase of demographic transition, distinguished by a decline in the birth rate, which became more and more pronounced toward the close of the period. Only 85,000 children were born in Sweden in 1930, and the birth rate dropped from 30 to 14 per 1,000. Mortality also continued to diminish, and because it declined more rapidly than the birth rate, there was a heavy natural increase in population. Population growth, however, stopped short of an average of just over 6% due to large-scale emigration, another characteristic of this period.

The first mass exodus of emigrants took place between 1853 and 1873, when about 103,000 Swedes (just under 3% of the population) settled in North America Following a decline caused by depression in North America and boom years in Sweden, emigration once again escalated, in 1879. During the next 14 years, up to and including 1893, an average of 34,000 Swedes emigrated to North America annually. Altogether nearly 1.4 million people emigrated between 1865 and 1930, only a quarter of them returning to their native land. North America was the destination of more than 80%; the balance went to other Nordic countries.

During the Great Depression years of the early 1930s, the natural population growth rate fell to 2.8%, one of the lowest on record until that time. The marriage rate began to rise, however, and the number of births then rose steeply during the 1940s, attaining at mid decade a level that has never been exceeded since. A similar "hump" occurred during the 1960s, when the baby boomers of the 1940s themselves began to establish families. Since then, the birth rate has fallen continuously, while the death rate has remained low. A new factor was the rise in the number of nonnative immigrants from the 1930s on. Following a decline in the early years of the 1970s, net migration to Sweden has accounted for between 70% and 80% of population growth.

Changes in the birth and death rates have led to a shift in the national age structure involving on the one hand a decline in the proportion of children and a corresponding proportional increase in the elderly population. Children under 15 years today comprise one-fifth of the population, as against one-third a hundred years ago. On the other hand, persons over 64 years have doubled their share of the population during the past 40 years.

Due to a higher mortality among men, Sweden, like most other countries, has a surplus female population, but since male births exceed female births, young men outnumber young women. The national ratio is 1,000 men to 1,025 women, while the ratio of births is 1,000 boys to 952 girls. Men are more numerous up to age 51. Women today have an average life expectancy of 79.9 years; men, 73.8 years. The corresponding figures over 100 years ago were 43.5 and 39.4 years.

The nuclear family still is the most important social unit, although the family has shrunk in size, with an average of less than two children per family, slightly below the replacement rate. Cohabitation has become increasingly the norm, very often leading to marriage. The divorce rate has risen, and twice as many marriages end in divorce as in 1960. Nevertheless, 72% of children under 18 live with both parents; 15% live with a single parent, usually the mother; and 13% of all children live in "mixed families," where the custodial parent is living with a new spouse. The average Swedish woman gives birth to 1.6 children. Only 10% of the female population remain childless.

The spatial distribution of population during the past 100 years has favored the cities. Almost 83% of the population live in urban communities, of which the three largest—Stockholm, Göteborg and Malmö—account for 30% of the national population, with the 1,780 suburban communities accounting for another 10%. Whereas Norrland increased its population by 116% between 1850 and 1900 following the opening up of its timber and mineral resources, the trend has been reversed in the 20th century, and its share of the population declined from 17.8% in 1930 to 14.3% in 1984.

The average density of population in the country is 20 inhabitants per sq. km. (52 inhabitants per sq. mi.), varying from 231 in Stockholm to 3 in Norrbotten, the northernmost county. More than 70% of the country's area has a population density of six inhabitants or less per sq. km. (16 inhabitants or less per sq. mi.).

Equality between men and women is a guiding principle of government policy and has made more impressive strides in Sweden than in other developed countries. The principle is incorporated into the Swedish Constitution and is actively promoted by a number of state organizations. The Equality Affairs Division of the Ministry of Labor has overall responsibility in this field. The Council on Equality Issues, an advisory body to the minister of labor, represents 24 public and private bodies, including women's organizations. The Interministerial Committee is a coordinating body bringing together equal-opportunities programs of various ministries. The Commission for Research on Equality Between Men and Women was set up in 1983 to initiate and oversee research in this field. The Office of the Equal Opportunities Ombudsman was set up when the Act of Equality Between Men and Women at Work came into force in 1980. The Equal Opportunities Commission is a special body that enforces compliance with the Equal Opportunities Act.

DEMOGRAPHIC INDICATORS, 1986

Population: 8,393,071 (1988)
Year of last census: 1984
 Male/Female ratio: 49.36: 50.64
Population trends (million)
 1930: 6.142   1960: 7.498   1990: 8.421

DEMOGRAPHIC INDICATORS, 1986 *(continued)*

1940: 6.371   1970: 8.081   2000: 8.329
1950: 7.041   1980: 8.310   2020: 8.0
Population doubling time in years at current rate: 636
Hypothetical size of stationary population (million): 7
Assumed year of reaching net reproduction rate of 1:
  2030
Age profile (%)
0–14: 18.1   30–44: 22.1   60–74: 15.7
15–29: 20.7   45–59: 16.0   Over 75: 7.4
Median age (years): 39
Density per sq. km.: 20.4; (52.9 per sq. mi.)
 per sq. km. (sq. mi.) of arable land: 18.5 (48)
Annual growth rate (%)
1950–55: 0.70   1975–80: 0.20   1995–2000: –0.21
1960–65: 0.67   1980–85: 0.01   2000–2005: –0.20
1965–70: 0.78   1985–90: –0.14   2010–2015: –0.25
1970–75: 0.37   1990–95: –0.17   2020–2025: –0.31
Vital statistics
 Crude birth rate, 1/1000: 12.2
 Crude death rate, 1/1000: 4.2
 Change in birth rate, 1965–84: –28.9%
 Change in death rate, 1965–84: 7.9%
 Dependency, total: 51.7
 Infant mortality rate, 1/1000: 7
 Child (0–4 years) mortality rate, 1/1000: Insignificant
 Maternal mortality rate, 1/100,000: 2.1
 Natural Increase, 1/1000: 1.0
 Total fertility rate: 1.6
 General fertility rate: 42
 Gross reproduction rate: 0.72
 Marriage rate, 1/1000: 4.6
 Divorce rate, 1/1000: 2.3
 Life expectancy, males (years): 73.3
 Life expectancy, females (years): 79.4
 Average household size: 2.4
 % Illegitimate births: 43.6
Youth
 Youth population 15–24 (000): 1,162
 Youth population in 2000 (000): 945
Women
 Of childbearing age 15–45 (000): 1,686
 Children per: 3.1
 % women using contraception: N.A.
 % women married 15–49: N.A.
Urban
 Urban population (000): 7,127
 % urban 1965: 77   1985: 86
 Annual urban growth rate (%)
 1965–80: 1.0   1980–85: 1.2
 % urban population in largest city: 15

> **DEMOGRAPHIC INDICATORS, 1986** *(continued)*
> % urban population in cities over 500,000: 35
> Number of cities over 500,000: 3
> Annual rural growth rate: –1.9% (1985–90)

A major safeguard against sex discrimination is found in the Instrument of Government, which forms part of the Constitution. An important feature of Swedish family law is to place men and women on an equal footing in marriage, to divide the responsibilities for home and children equally between both spouses and to protect the financially weaker party in the event of divorce or death.

The main statute governing the practical application of the equality of women and men in Sweden is the Equal Opportunities Act, which promotes equal rights for both sexes with respect to employment and working conditions. The act consists of two parts: The first prohibits discrimination on grounds of sex; the second obliges the employer to promote equality actively at work. Disputes under this act are tried by the Labor Court. Equality between the sexes also is promoted through school curricula. Boys and girls receive identical education. Home economics, technology, typing, handicrafts, woodworking and metalworking are compulsory for all children. A special effort is made to broaden the choice of studies and occupations made by girls through summer courses in technology for girls. Despite these efforts, student career choices still are marked by traditional stereotypes. Few women go on to postgraduate studies, where they constitute only 23% of Ph.D. graduates. Only about 5% of university and college professors are women.

Although female participation in the labor force has reached parity, female unemployment rates are slightly higher. Even so women are employed on different terms and in more restricted sectors, which pay less. Women also have different hours of work, as they still do most of the work at home and assume most of the responsibility for children. In 1985 a total of 44% of the gainfully employed women worked part-time, as against 6% of the men. Although the principle of equal pay for equal work has long been accepted legally, there are pay differentials between men and women. Women earn on average less than men because women are generally employed in sectors of the economy that are less well-paying. They also have a smaller share of overtime pay. Although career choices have expanded for women, their choices remain extensions of their traditional roles. The female labor market is much narrower than the male one. Women predominate—i.e. constitute more than 60%—in 56 occupations, whereas men do the same in 121. Men and women are equally balanced in only 14. Not only do men and women work in different sectors, but they also do different jobs in the same sector. To counter these problems, the government launched a campaign in 1982 called "More Women for Industry," designed to make it easier for women to enter nontraditional careers.

The third area of equality concerns the home and family, where statutes have challenged male dominance. The Marriage Code of 1987 modified the Code of Succession and Inheritance to make financial arrangements following the death of a spouse or divorce more equitable. Divorce laws in Sweden are among the most liberal. If both parties agree and if they have no children under age 16, they are automatically entitled to a divorce. Otherwise, the law requires a six-month deliberation period. Joint custody of children is automatic unless requested otherwise. The children may, however, live with only one of the parents, who is entitled to receive maintenance allowance from the other. If such payment is delayed or withheld, maintenance advances are paid under the Social Security system. Family planning is encouraged by the state, which provides free family planning services, contraceptive devices, health care for mothers and children, and obstetric care. Restrictions on abortion were abolished in 1975, and they may be performed up to the 18th week of pregnancy upon request, although an abortion between the 12th and the 18th weeks is subject to a special inquiry. In 1985 a total of 31,000 legal abortions were performed in the country, a figure that has remained more or less constant since 1980. Since 1974 both the father and the mother have been entitled to special benefits enabling them to take care of their children without loss of income. Leave of absence with parental benefit is provided for a total of 12 months in connection with childbirth. This benefit may be spread over a four-year period. Either of the parents is entitled to receive compensation at the same rate as sickness benefit—i.e., 90% of their gross income for nine months and a fixed daily rate for the remaining three. In addition, all fathers are entitled to 10 days' leave of absence with parental benefit when a child is born. Either parent also can take time off up to a maximum of 60 days per year for the care of a sick child. Women are encouraged to return to work as soon as possible after childbirth, as a result of which only 10% of women between 20 and 64 are full-time housewives.

Public child care in Sweden is the responsibility of the municipalities and has expanded rapidly since the 1970s, when women began entering the labor market on a large scale. In 1987 a total of 47% of all preschool children up to age six were cared for in public child care facilities. By 1991 all preschool children aged 18 months to six years will be entitled to be cared for at public facilities.

The fourth area of gender equality is in public affairs, where the representation of women in decision-making and advisory bodies has increased substantially over the past 10 years. Of the 349 members in the Swedish Riksdag (Parliament) in 1985, some 31% were women, with Liberals having the most, at

39%, and Communists the lowest, at 16%. Women also have a 37% representation in the county councils and 30% in the municipal councils.

Sweden had no history of immigration in modern times until the end of World War II. During the 1950s and 1960s, Sweden experienced a steep rise in immigration such as to transform the population structure and ethnic composition. Today there are close to one million immigrants in Sweden, including children with immigrant parents. In the process, Sweden has changed from a monolingual and ethnically homogeneous society to a multilingual society with a number of ethnic minorities.

A shortage of manpower as a result of the expansion of Swedish industry was the initial impetus to the effort to recruit foreign workers. These efforts began in 1947 following agreements with Hungary, Italy and Austria. In 1954 a common Nordic labor market was created, giving citizens in the Nordic countries a free right to settle and work in the entire area. Net immigration totaled 134,000 in the 1940s and 106,000 in the 1950s. The continued expansion of Swedish industry fueled two major waves of immigration in the 1960s. The first consisted mostly of workers from Yugoslavia, Greece and Turkey. Until 1967 immigration was virtually unregulated. Growing political and trade union concern about the social and economic consequences of the large-scale importation of labor led to restrictions on non-Nordic immigrants. From 1968 the revised Aliens Act required non-Nordic immigrants to hold a work permit before entering Sweden, although non-Nordics had the right to family reunion. Continuing strong demand for labor led to a second wave of immigration in the late 1960s and early 1970s, this time mainly from Finland, with which Sweden concluded the "channeling agreement." In 1971 the last recruitment of non-Nordics on a collective basis was undertaken in Yugoslavia. Total net immigration in the 1960s was 235,000.

In the 1970s immigration to Sweden changed character once again. That from non-Nordic countries was on the basis of family reunion, and refugees became relatively more prominent among immigrants. These refugees came from all parts of the world, particularly the Middle East (such as Assyrians); from Chile, fleeing Pinochet's regime; and from Indochina. Return emigration, particularly to Finland, increased. These trends have continued into the 1980s. In 1986 roughly half the immigrants were refugees, a quarter were immigrants from Nordic countries, and another quarter were non-Nordics admitted on the basis of family reunion.

In 1986 there were about 389,000 foreign nationals, not including 400,000 immigrants who had become naturalized Swedish citizens. About 50% are Nordics, 28% other Europeans; 13% Asians, 4% Latin Americans, 2% Africans and 2% North Americans. There are 205,000 foreign nationals employed in Sweden, accounting for about 5% of the work force. A higher percentage of immigrants than Swedes are employed, mainly due to their younger age structure. About 35% of immigrants work in manufacturing, 12.5% in health care, 21% in the private sector and 8% in office jobs. Difference in income between Swedes and foreign nationals is small. However, foreign nationals are over-represented in industries with a poor working environment and irregular working hours. Often they live in more crowded conditions, as they have more dependents.

In many respects immigration policy has lagged behind the changing realities of immigration. As in other European countries, planners had underestimated the scope and misjudged the direction of immigration flows. Similarly, the number of asylum-seekers has been far greater than that forecast a few years ago.

Sweden did not have an immigration policy until the 1960s. The first laws in this field were the Aliens Act and the Aliens Ordinance, which were last revised in 1984. They recognize three types of immigration permits: a work permit, a residence permit and a permanent residence permit. There also is a section in the Aliens Act that allows the grant of a residence permit on humanitarian grounds. This clause has been developed into a full-blown refugee policy. A refugee quota, at present 1,250 persons, is determined annually by the Riksdag. The "quota" refugees constitute only a small portion of the total number of refugees admitted to Sweden every year. The bulk of refugees are granted permanent residence on the basis of individual applications for asylum on arrival in Sweden.

Since the 1960s a large number of reforms have been carried out to improve immigrants' conditions in Sweden. A large-scale program of Swedish-language instruction was started in 1965; a working commission on the social adjustment of immigrants was set up in 1966; a government-subsidized paper for immigrants was started in 1967; a bill providing for special tuition in Swedish and other subjects for immigrant schoolchildren was adopted by the Riksdag in 1968; and a new government agency, the Swedish Immigration Board, was set up in 1969 to deal with immigration and naturalization.

In 1975 the Riksdag passed a bill outlining a new immigration policy based on three objectives: equality between immigrants and Swedes, freedom of cultural choice for immigrants and cooperation and solidarity between the natives and the immigrants.

To implement this new policy, the Riksdag adopted a number of reforms. Grants were extended to 30 national immigrant organizations with over 1,200 local associations. Subsidies are given to publications in various minority languages. The Swedish Broadcasting Corporation broadcasts radio and TV programs in the major immigrant languages. Many of the reforms are aimed at immigrant children. Under the Home Language Program, instruction is now being given in over 60 languages. Every newly arrived immigrant is offered 400 to 500 lessons in basic Swedish at government expense, and employers are required to give their immigrant employees 240 hours' leave of absence at full pay to attend lessons in the Swedish language. Sweden also is among the few countries in the world to grant all aliens (resident for at least three years) the right to vote and to run for office in local and regional elections. In 1986 the Riksdag passed a bill creating an ombudsman against ethnic discrimination. There also is an advisory council on immigration policy, on which various immigrant groups are represented.

Admission of Refugees in Sweden, 1979–86		
Year	Adults	Children
1979	2,768	N.A.
1980	4,062	N.A.
1981	3,357	N.A.
1982	6,188	N.A.
1983	3,784	N.A.
1984	5,423	approx. 1,600
1985	6,553	approx. 2,000
1986	13,419	approx. 4,000

Source: *Statistics Sweden*, 1987.

ETHNIC COMPOSITION

Until the end of World Warr II Sweden was a very homogeneous country. Almost the entire population was Swedish, with the exception of two small minorities: the 30,000 or so Finnish-speaking people of the Northeast, along the Finnish border; and the 15,000 or so Sami or Lapps. Since then, Sweden has acquired close to 1 million aliens belonging to some 50 to 60 ethnic and linguistic groups. (See the Population section for these new ethnic immigrants.)

The Sami or Lapps have inhabited Sweden since pre-Christian times. The area of Lapp settlement extends over the entire Scandinavian Arctic region and stretches over the mountain districts on both sides of the Norwegian-Swedish border down to the northernmost part of the province of Dalarna. The Lapps were originally hunters and fishermen. Capturing wild reindeer was a dominant feature of their hunting culture, which came to include taming and breeding reindeer. The total number of Lapps is estimated at 40,000 to 50,000, of whom 15,000 to 17,000 live in Sweden. Of the Swedish Lapps, only 600 to 700 households are directly engaged in reindeer breeding. Two different systems of

Population with an Immigrant Background, 1986			
Country of Origin	Foreign-Born*	Born in Sweden+	Total
Nordic countries	313,023	131,669	444,692
Denmark	40,960	17,357	58,317
Finland	226,000	96,805	322,805
Norway	42,947	16,565	59,512
Other European countries	201,893	78,776	280,669
Federal Republic of Germany	37,202	14,645	51,847
Great Britain	9,680	5,090	14,770
Greece	13,138	6,219	19,357
Hungary	13,684	4,200	17,884
Poland	30,054	9,736	39,790
Yugoslavia	38,840	18,195	57,035
Africa	15,131	5,164	20,295
North America	15,969	5,090	21,059
U.S.A.	11,892	3,988	15,880
South America	28,505	4,108	32,613
Chile	15,276	1,444	16,720
Asia	87,445	21,687	109,132
Iran	13,915	1,566	15,481
Turkey	20,141	9,230	29,371
Soviet Union	6,645	1,011	7,656
Unknown	73	2,259	2,332
Total	669,876+	250,138§	920,014
Foreign citizens	305,821	85,019	390,840

* Including foreign citizens and naturalized immigrants.

+ Including Swedish citizens 0–17 years old with at least one foreign-born parent and foreign citizens born in Sweden.

+ Including about 10,000 Swedish children born abroad.

§ To this should be added more than 120,000 persons age 18 years or over.

Source: *Statistics Sweden*, 1987.

reindeer breeding have evolved in Sweden. One is a stationary system in which the reindeer are allowed limited freedom of movement within a forest region. The other system, known as mountain reindeer breeding, is more nomadic and geographically extensive. It is characterized by transhumance, or long migrations between summer grazing lands in the mountains and winter pastures in the forest regions or along the coast.

Reindeer-breeding Lapps are members of a Sami village or community that is both an administrative and economic unit and a geographical grazing area. It also is a kind of cooperative society maintaining common facilities and distributing the costs among its members. The migration of the reindeer generally follows the main river valleys and lake systems. The grazing lands have come to be divided into three main regions: summer pastures in the high fells; spring and autumn grazing lands in the low fells and adjoining birch forest belt; and winter pastures in the coniferous forests.

In the low fell region, where the mountain reindeer mate and calve, the Lapps have their most permanent encampments, or *visten*. Other *visten* have been built in the coniferous forest regions of the winter pastures.

Formerly, reindeer were raised mainly for milk and as beasts of burden. Since the 1920s the emphasis has been on meat production. As breeding techniques have changed, the reindeer are kept in larger herds without continuous surveillance. As reindeer herding in itself does not provide enough to support a family, most Lapps combine it with other pursuits such as fishing, handicrafts, hunting and tourism. The Reindeer Husbandry Law of 1971 governs the Lapp economy and safeguards their interests against those of developers and exploiters.

LANGUAGE

The national language is Swedish, a North German branch of the Germanic languages, and the Nordic language with the largest number of speakers. It also is the second official language of Finland, where it is spoken by about 300,000 Swedes.

In historical perspective, the development of the Swedish language can be divided into two main periods: Old Swedish (800 to 1526), and New Swedish (1526 to the present). The watershed between the two is the publication in 1526 of the Swedish-language version of the New Testament, which contributed to the regularization of spelling and word forms. The publication of the journal *Then Swenska Argus* and of the Swedish lawbook *Svea Rikes Lag* in the 1730s also constitute milestones in the development of the language, as they heralded the emergence of a simpler written language more akin to the spoken word.

The spoken or standard language today as encountered in the mass media is largely the Stockholm dialect. Thus the regional variants are being gradually displaced or becoming less fashionable. There is no language policy.

The language of the Lapps belongs to the Finno-Ugric group and can be divided into three main dialects: Central or North Sami (the largest); East Sami; and South Sami. South Sami is spoken in areas of central Norway and north-central Sweden. Farther north in Sweden and Norway and in the extreme North of Finland, North Sami is the most common dialect. East Sami is spoken in eastern Finland from Lake Inari and eastward to the Kola Peninsula in the Soviet Union.

Sami does not have an extensive written literature, but oral "literature" plays a prominent role in the Lapp culture. The oral tradition takes the form of yoiking, a sort of singing. There are a few Lapp literary works that have attained the status of classics, including Johan Turi's *Tale of the Lapps*, first published in 1910; Andreas Labba's *Anta* (1969); Erik Nilsson Mankok's *My Lasso* (1962); and Margareta Sarri's *When Simon Fjallberg and Others Came to a Realization* (1971), *Under the Raspberry Tree* (1980) and *Thou Mountainous North* (1983).

RELIGION

Christianity was introduced into Sweden in the 10th century by English missionaries, and the first bishop was installed in 1164, in Uppsala. By the time of the Reformation, parishes had been established throughout the country. King Gustavus Vasa was one of the principal leaders of the Swedish Reformation, resulting in the adoption of the Lutheran Confession in 1527, a year after the publication of the New Testament in Swedish. The major consequence of the Reformation was to transform the church into an instrument of the state. Thus it became a civic duty not only to be on the church rolls, but also to take regular part in the divine services. For example, the Public Worship Regulation Act of 1686 prescribed that all Swedes must take communion at least four times a year. A system of keeping population records necessary to enforce this and similar laws was developed during the 17th century and has survived to this day.

With the advent of religious and political liberalism in the 19th century, the church became less closely identified with the state. Beginning in 1860, it became possible to resign from the church. No conflict between church and state developed in Sweden as it did in other countries in Europe and Latin America. Anticlericalism was never a political issue. Further, Sweden never had a Catholic-Protestant conflict nor any religious wars.

Although Sweden is for all practical purposes a nonreligious country, about 95% of the population still belong to Christian church rolls. However, a recent Gallup poll showed that if church membership rolls were to be set at zero—i.e., if all members were to be recruited anew—some two-thirds of the population still would apply on their own accord. Church services are attended by about 1% of the population. At the same time the church remains a highly visible and pervasive social institution, too powerful to be ignored. The high festivals of the ecclesiastical calendar are popularly observed. The vast majority of the children still are baptized, and most marriages and burials are conducted in churches.

The Church of Sweden is divided into 13 dioceses, each headed by a bishop assisted by a diocesan chapter and, for financial administration, by a diocesan board. The archbishop, who has no formal authority over the other bishops, has his see at Uppsala. The central organs of the church for special tasks of evangelism and social work are appointed by the General Assembly. The parishes, which are the smallest administrative units, number 2,570. A local parish is governed by the pastor and an elected vestry. In turn, the vestry chooses a parish council, which handles the routine administration. There are about 5,000 pastors, of whom some 3,000 are serving in parishes. In 1960 women were first ordained.

About 4% of the population over 17 belong to the free churches, which grew out of the Low Church, the Evangelical Lutheran wing of the Christian Revival Movement in Sweden. A peculiarity of the Swedish religious scene is that a significant proportion of members of the Church of Sweden belong simultaneously to the free churches. The Jesus Movement and the charismatic movements have strengthened the free churches, of which the largest is the Pentecostal movement, with about 100,000 members, followed by the Mission Covenant Church, the Baptist Church and the Salvation Army.

The extensive postwar immigration has helped to increase the number of both Catholic and Orthodox adherents, although reliable figures are not available on their widely scattered parishes. Finally, there are about 15,000 Jews with eight congregations (of which three have their own rabbis) and a slightly larger number of Muslims, mostly Turks.

Relations between church and state are governed by the Ecclesiastical Law of 1686, the Constitution of 1809 and the Law of Religious Freedom of 1951. A child born as a Swedish citizen automatically becomes a member of the Church of Sweden if both of his or her parents are members. Religious and ecclesiastical affairs are under the jurisdiction of the Office of Ecclesiastical Affairs of the Ministry of Education. Ecclesiastical law is jointly framed by the government, the Riksdag and the General Assembly of the Church, with a veto vested in the last. The government is empowered to make decisions concerning the prayer books, the Psalter and translations of the Bible, with the consent of the General Assembly. The higher clergymen, including the 13 bishop, are appointed by the government, in each case from three names submitted by the Synod. Under a new law enacted in 1961, the local parishes are responsible for payment of salaries of the parish clergy and other expenses. Each parish is economically independent and has the right to levy a church tax, which is collected as part of the local income tax. Thos who have formally left the Church of Sweden still are required to pay some 30% of the church tax, this amount representing the costs of the church's civil duties, such as keeping the population records and maintaining the burial grounds. A series of efforts to separate church and state since 1958 has not borne fruit.

HISTORICAL BACKGROUND

Central and southern Sweden were ruled by a people known as Svear in the early centuries of the Christian era. They were descendants of people known to Tacitus as Suiones, a "people mighty in ships and arms." Norway and Sweden were joined in 1319 under the infant King Magnus VII, but Waldemar IV, king of Denmark, overran Skåne, the southern part of Sweden, and by the Union of Kalmar (1397), all of Scandinavia was united under the Danish throne. For over a century Sweden resisted the union and in 1523 shook off Danish rule and elected Gustavus Vasa (Gustaf I) to the Swedish throne. Gustavus laid the foundations of modern Sweden by establishing a hereditary monarchy, making Lutheranism the state religion and creating a national army and navy. His successors expanded the kingdom by incorporating Estonia and other areas of eastern Europe. The reign of Gustavus Adolphus (1611–32) is considered the golden age of the Swedish kingdom. Under him Sweden rose to the rank of one of the great powers of Europe. He was the creator not only of the first modern European army but also of the most efficient administration of his day. He defeated Denmark in 1613, Russia in 1617 and Poland in 1629 and became the savior of Protestantism through his intervention in the Thirty Years' War. He extended the borders to the east by conquering the rest of Livonia and acquiring Ingermanland and Karelia. For the following half century the Baltic Sea became a Swedish lake. Gustavus was killed at Lutzen in 1632, and he was succeeded on the throne by his daughter Christina. By the Peace of Westphalia of 1648 Sweden gained Pomerania and Bremen. By the Peace of Bromsebro with Denmark in 1645 Sweden received the hitherto Danish territories in southern Sweden. The Swedes also achieved freedom from the Sound toll (on the Øresund) exacted by the Danes against Swedish shipping.

The rise of young Charles XII marked the end of Swedish ascendancy. Further military enterprises proved too much for the country's limited military manpower, and a series of wars with a coalition of powers consisting of Russia, Denmark, Poland and Saxony left Sweden exhausted. Finally, the Peace of Nystad in 1721 reduced the country to the position of a second-rate power. Russia regained Livonia, Estonia, Ingermanland and the Keksgolm and Viipuri districts of Finland. Finland was lost partly in 1743 and wholly in 1809.

Throughout the 18th century, the kingdom was torn by internal dissension between the pro-French faction (the Hats) and the pro-Russian faction (the Caps). From 1751 to 1814 the throne was occupied by the House of Oldenburg-Holstein-Gottorp. In 1810 one of Napoleon's marshals, a Frenchman from Pau named Jean-Baptiste Jules Bernadotte (1764–1844), was invested with the crown. In 1814 he brought his adopted country over to the side of the Allies against Napoleon in the last full-scale war fought by Sweden. From 1814 to 1905 Sweden and Norway were united under one crown.

In the 19th century Sweden laid the foundations of its modern liberal democracy dominated by the Social Democratic Party. Sweden kept aloof from the European scramble for colonial possessions and remained neutral in both world wars.

CONSTITUTION & GOVERNMENT

Sweden is a constitutional monarchy in which the powers of the king are largely ceremonial. The power to govern rests with the prime minister and cabinet, who are dependent on the support of a unicameral legislature. The Constitution is based on the theory of separation of powers, but the practice evolved in the present century is a fusion of powers. The cabinet, while exercising great influence over the Riksdag, is by no means as powerful as its counterpart in the United Kingdom. The Riksdag still has considerable independance, largely through the workings of its committee system. The judiciary is independent, but there is no tradition of judicial review. The administration is semi-autonomous and is not subject to detailed and direct control by the ministry.

Respect for law and a concern for developing clear statements of the basic laws are ingrained in the Swedish political ethic. The modern Swedish Constitution is thus long, detailed and specific. It consists of several documents that have been heavily amended, by both formal and informal means. The documents are devoted much more to the organization of governmental operations than to relations among the different branches of functions of government. Their character, despite some foreign influences, is largely indigenous. With a few exceptions they contain no explicit bill of rights, but a concern for due process and the rights of Swedish citizens is clearly implicit in many of the provisions.

Not only is the Constitution detailed (the English-language version covers over 100 pages), but it also deals with a number of matters that in other countries would be found either among the ordinary laws, or even among the rules of internal organizations and procedures. The extreme specificity of the provisions is characteristic of the Swedes, who regard such details as fundamental. This concern for detail, for the organization and regulation of practices rather than grand theoretical statements, is accompanied by a kind of rationality that does not pay much attention to theory or ideological purity. Thus government for the Swedes is the art of compromise. They also consider their political institutions as malleable and are prepared to shed or change them without much fuss.

The Swedish Constitution consists of four separate documents:

1. The Instrument of Government (Regeringsformen) passed in 1974 and based on those adopted in 1634, 1720, 1772 and 1809. It has been formally amended over 300 times, and very few of its provisions have been left untouched. It is not only the oldest of the four documents but also the most important.

2. The Riksdag Act (Riksdagordningen) of 1974, which occupies a place halfway between the Constitution and ordinary statute law. The act of 1974 updated the Act of 1866, a very detailed document filled with regulations.

3. The Act of Succession (Successionordningen) of 1810, one of the shortest of the four documents and comprising only a preamble and nine brief articles. The right of succession is vested in the Bernadotte dynasty through the eldest-born male or female, according to the 1979 amendment to the act.

4. The Freedom of the Press Act (Tryckfrihctsforordningen). The first act on press freedom was enacted in 1766 and was followed by the Acts of 1809, 1810 and 1812 and the present Act of 1949.

The Constitution can be amended easily and either formally or informally. It can be amended by two joint decisions of the king and the Riksdag, with a general election intervening. Amendments therefore have been free and frequent, although the Instrument of Government has never been completely revised. Even when the Constitution is revised, amendments generally change details rather than principles and reflect the gradual evolution of political practice and needs.

The monarch (Carl XVI Gustaf) since September 1973 exercises no political power. Under the Constitution he is the ceremonial head of state. He does not take any part in the deliberations of the cabinet and does not sign any documents. His earlier role in selecting a new prime minister has been taken over by the Speaker of the Riksdag. The Swedes use their word for king—*konungen*—in two ways: either as meaning the king as a person, or more frequently, referring to kingly authority. The agency that exercises the latter is the king in council *(konungen i statsradet)*. The word "government" *(regeringen)* is commonly used to mean the cabinet exclusive of the king. The term "crown" *(kronen)* refers to the legal personality of the state.

Real power rests with the prime minister and the cabinet. The official name for the cabinet is the Council of State (Statsradet); the members of the Council of State are known as state councillors *(statsrad)*. The cabinet at present includes 21 ministers (16 men and five women) as follows: the prime minister *(statsminister)*; 12 heads of ministry *(departementschef)*; and eight ministers without portfolio, also called consultative councillors *konsultativa statsrad)*.

The office of prime minister is less than 100 years old. The office has benefited from a series of distinguished incumbents, particularly Per Albin Hansson,

Tage Erlander and Olaf Palme. The prime minister generally works not only through the Riksdag, the cabinet and the media but also through informal meetings with interest groups at his official estate, Harpsund, with the result that the term "Harpsund democracy" has come to be applied to prime ministerial initiatives in the resolution of major national problems.

Although independent experts sometimes are called on to serve in the cabinet, as a rule ministers are members of the Riksdag, and they retain their seats there while serving in the cabinet. But a substitute takes over the parliamentary duties of any MP who has been appointed to the cabinet. All cabinet ministers give up their rights to vote in the Riksdag, although they are entitled to address it.

According to the new Constitution of 1974, all formal governmental decisions rest with the cabinet and not the king. When the cabinet resigns, the speaker of the Riksdag is required to confer with the leaders of the parliamentary parties and with the deputy speakers before proposing a new prime minister for parliamentary vote. If it is approved, the speaker thereupon appoints the prime minister who, in turn, appoints all other cabinet ministers. The prime minister may be dismissed by the speaker or the Riksdag and ministers may be dismissed by the prime minister of the Riksdag.

The cabinet is responsible collectively for all government decisions. However, in practice a great number of routine matters are decided by individual ministers and only formally confirmed by the government. Plenary cabinet meetings are held under the chairmanship of the prime minister one to three times a week. At these meetings, held behind closed doors but attended by top officials, formal decisions are made but no minutes are taken. As a rule cabinet members lunch together in their private restaurant in the Government office. A third and even less formal kind of decision-making is when two or three key ministers concerned discuss the matter with or without the presence of subordinate officials and reach agreement without involving the full cabinet. There is a high degree of coordination among all the branches of government in the formulation of policies. Before becoming final, government decisions receive the comments of all officials concerned.

The 13 ministries are collectively known as the Government Office (Regeringskansliet). The ministries (departements) are small units, each as a rule consisting of no more than 100 persons. They are primarily concerned with preparing government bills to the Riksdag on budget appropriations and laws; issuing laws and regulations and general rules for the administrative agencies; international relations; appointments of officials; and certain appeals from individuals. By and large, ministries are not concerned with the details of administration.

The highest-ranking officials in a ministry are the under secretary of state, the permanent under secretary and the under secretary for legal affairs.

As a rule, the preparation of legislative and other measures is not done exclusively in the ministries. In matters of major importance, the government on its own initiative or at the request of the Riksdag calls upon a group of experts to serve on a commission of inquiry *(utredning)*. The commissioners (normally five to 10 people) are given a high degree of freedom to pursue their inquiries through hearings, research and travel. The number of commissions at work varies somewhat but is estimated at over 300. The work of the commission usually takes several years to complete, and its findings are presented in a report *(betankande)*. Most reports are published in a numbered series as Swedish Government Official Reports (Statens Offentliga Utredningar). Every commission report is sent by the ministry concerned to the various administrative agencies and nongovernmental organizations for their official comments *(remiss)*. The material thus assembled is reported as background to government bills to the Riksdag.

It is necessary to distinguish between "government authorities" *(statliga myndigheterna)*, a term that is sometimes used to refer to the entire central government administration, and "agency" or "board" *(ambetsverk* or *centralt ambertsverk)*, which normally denotes a central administrative authority responsible directly to the government in any field. There are over 200 such authorities broadly defined but the term is generally restricted to 70 or 80 central agencies. In addition, there are 24 country administrations, which have a status similar to that of the agencies. The head of an agency has the title of director general, and under him the organization is divided into departments or divisions.

Historically, the agencies antedate the departments and have had from the beginning a semi-autonomous position within the government. They are responsible not just to individual ministers but also to the entire cabinet. Unlike departments, they are concerned only with the execution of policy, and for this reason they maintain larger staffs. There is no single word common to the titles of all these agencies, and they operate under many names—*verk, forvaltning, styrelse, namnd, anstalt, kontor,* etc. Among the more prominent agencies are the Social Welfare Board, the Labor Market Board, the Housing Board, the Post Office, the National Police Board, the State Railways and the Central Bureau of Statistics, to name but a few. Some agencies are headed by a board and others by the director general only. Generally the mission and work of the agencies are described in detail in the General Instruction to Agencies (Allman Verksstadga). Some agencies have extensive regional and local organization, whereas others operate on a national level only or function via the county administration. Until recently, all but two of the agencies have had their offices in

Stockholm. However, beginning the 1970s, as part of a policy of creating better regional balance, many of them were dispersed to 16 other towns, mostly in northern and central Sweden. The seven enterprises, known as central government commercial agencies, form a distinct group. They are the National Industries Corporation, the Post Office Administration, the National Telecommunications Administration, the State Railways, the National Civil Aviation Administration, the National Power Administration and the Forest Service. The government-owned business companies *(statliga bolagen)* are, however, entirely independent of the administration.

The office of ombudsman is Sweden's enduring contribution to the lexicon of public administration. The ombudsman system is one of the checks against official high-handedness and unresponsiveness to public interests. The parliamentary ombudsmen, or the parliamentary commissioners for the judiciary and the administration, to use their full title *(justitieombuds mannen,* JO), are four in number, all appointed by the Riksdag. There are other ombudsmen, in special areas, and who are appointed by the government (and therefore come under the scrutiny of the JO) but who have similar duties of surveillance. There also is a press ombudsman who, however, is a private official sponsored by media organizations.

The JO's office dates back to 1809. Each of the four parliamentary ombudsmen is elected for four years. One of them is the administrative chief, responsible for the administration of the office. All four have the constitutional task of "supervising the application of laws and ordinances in public activities." However, JO's cannot supervise cabinet ministers, members of the Riksdag or municipal councils. Each JO has a separate sphere of supervision. In practice, the JO's office receives and investigates complaints from individuals who believe they have been wronged by civil servants or the administration. About 3,500 such complaints are handled each year, about one-third of which are unfounded. The JO has the discretion to decide which cases should be investigated, and also to investigate laws and regulations on a long-term basis. JO's serve as special prosecutors in cases of breaches of duty by civil servants or violations of civil rights and also are empowered to take disciplinary measures in such cases. In their annual report to the Riksdag, JO's often propose amendments to existing legislation that they find unsatisfactory or prejudicial to the public interest. They also make frequent inspections of agencies and departments under their jurisdiction.

The other four ombudsmen are the competition ombudsman (NO), the consumer ombudsman (KO), the equal opportunities ombudsman (JamO) and the ombudsman against ethnic discrimination (DO).

The NO's office was set up in 1954, and its activities are based on the Competition Act of 1982, which was designed to promote a desirable level of competition in the economy. Two types of restrictive business practices are prohibited under the sanction of criminal penalties: resale price maintenance and collusive tendering. Otherwise Swedish antitrust legislation is not based on criminal sanctions except when business practices restrict productivity, impede the trade of others or manipulate prices. The NO is assisted by the Price and Cartel Office, which keeps the *Market and Merger Register*. The NO may prosecute offenders through the Market Court, a special tribunal consisting of jurists, producers and consumers. It may issue a prohibition or injunction under penalty of an administrative fine. The act also prohibits mergers that may lead to market dominance by one company to the detriment of others.

The office of the KO was set up in 1971 to protect consumers under the Marketing Act and the Unfair Contract Terms Act. It covers promotion of goods and services, including advertising, and requires reverse burden of proof from advertisers to substantiate their claims. The KO may obtain injunctions from the Market Court against harmful or deceptively promoted products.

ORGANIZATION OF SWEDISH GOVERNMENT

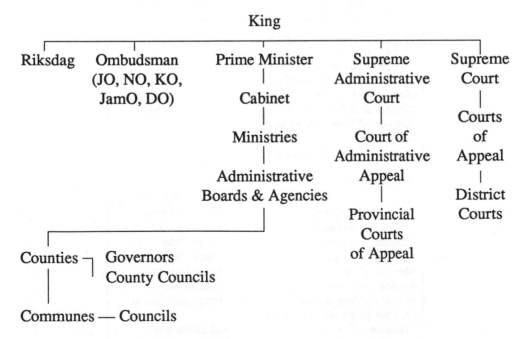

The office of the JamO came into existence in 1980 under the Act of Equality Between Men and Women at Work, to monitor discrimination on the grounds of sex and actively to promote gender equality in the workplace. It can enforce its writ through the Equal Opportunities Commission and the Labor Court.

The office of the DO was set up in 1986 to protect immigrants against discrimination in the workplace and other areas of social life.

Other checks on the government include the Parliamentary Standing Committee on the Constitution (Konstitutionsutskotet, KU), which inspects government programs annually to ensure that they comply with the laws of the land. Another check on administrative abuses is the right of appeal. Anyone affected by the decision of an authority can appeal through the Provincial Courts of Appeal to the Court of Administrative Appeal and the State Administrative Court.

The Swedish political system has been subject to constant and probing examination for the past several decades. The result is a parliamentary system that really works.

CABINET LIST

Prime Minister	Ingvar Carlsson
Deputy Prime Minister	Kjell-Olof Feldt
Minister of Agriculture	Mats Hellström
Minister of Civil Service Affairs	Bo Holmberg
Minister of Communications	Sven Hulterström
Minister of Culture	Bengt Göransson
Minister of Defense	Rolne Carlsson
Minister of Development Aid	Lena Hjelm-Wallen
Minister of Economy and Budget	Kjell-Olof Feldt
Minister of Education	Lennart Bodström
Minister of Environment and Energy	Birgitta Dahl
Minister of Foreign Affairs	Sten Sture Andersson
Minister of Health and Social Affairs	Gertrud Sigurdsen
Minister of Housing	Hans Gustafsson
Minister of Immigration	George Andersson
Minister of Industry	Thage Peterson
Minister of Justice	Thage Peterson
Minister of Labor	Ingela Thalen
Minister of Foreign Trade	Anita Gradin
Minister of Wages and Salaries	Bengt Johansson
Minister of Youth, Sports and Tourism	Ulf Lonnqvist
Deputy Social Minister	Bengt Lindqvist
Chairman, Bank of Sweden	Bengt Dennis

RULERS OF SWEDEN (from 1946)	
Kings	
October 1950 –September 1973	Gustaf VI Adolf
September 1973	Carl XVI Gustaf
Prime Ministers	
October 1946 –October 1969	Tage Erlander (Social Democratic Party)
October 1969 –October 1976	Olof Palme (Social Democratic Party)
October 1976 –October 1978	Thorbjorn Falldin (Conservative Party)
October 1978 –October 1979	Ola Ullsten (Liberal Party)
October 1979 –October 1982	Thorbjorn Falldin (Conservative Party)
October 1982 –March 1986	Olof Palme (Social Democratic Party)
March 1986	Ingvar Carlsson (Social Democratic Party)

FREEDOM & HUMAN RIGHTS

Respect for human rights is a basic value in Sweden's social and political system. However, some human rights organizations, such as the Swedish section of Amnesty International, have complained of violations, particularly with respect to refugees seeking asylum who are denied entry at the border. There also have been complaints about the treatment of Kurds in connection with the ongoing hunt for the killers of former prime minister Olaf Palme. There are some charges that policemen use excessive force in making arrests. Persons considered dangerous may be held for up to six hours without charges and criminal suspects for up to 12 hours without charges. The time between arrest and arraignment before a magistrate is set at five days but is occasionally longer if there are intervening holidays and weekends. Bail does not exist, but suspects not considered dangerous or likely to destroy evidence may be released to await trial. Foreigners are not released before trial for fear that they might flee the country. Public defenders are available where the maximum sentence is a prison sentence of six months or more. Courts are permitted to accept hearsay testimony from witnesses. Wiretaps are permitted in cases involving narcotics and

national security. The number of authorized wiretaps has increased significantly in recent years.

Swedes enjoy all civil liberties, including freedom of speech and press, peaceful assembly and association, religion and movement, Ombudsmen serve as official government monitors of individual rights in Sweden. Of particular concern
are the rights of the Lapps. In 1985 the U.N. Human Rights Commission com-
mented that Sweden lacks forceful legislation against racism. In 1986 Sweden
appointed a special ombudsman to monitor racism and discrimination. As in
other Nordic countries women enjoy full equality with men in public life and
their rights in the workplace are protected by the Equality Ombudsman.

CIVIL SERVICE

The term "civil servant" *(statstjansteman)* is used in a somewhat broader sense
in Sweden to include clergymen, judiciary, teachers and professors. All appointments are made by the government almost exclusively on merit. Theoretically,
only the very top jobs are viewed as political, but during the years following
World War II, recruitment to some of the lower position as well has been influenced by political party affiliations. Nevertheless, Sweden does not have a
tradition of political patronage, and even top officials are removed only after interparty agreement.

Sweden can point to a long history of civil service independence, first developed in the 17th century. It is one area of government to which the nobility
made a lasting contribution and in which that influence still persists. The independence of the civil service is partly due to the freedom of the civil servant to
engage in political activity and to hold political office, and to the division between policy-making and administration. The average civil servant regards
himself as having the same freedom from political interference as judicial officers in other countries. Like judges, they may not be removed from their posts
by the king without due process, nor may they be transferred to other posts except on their own application. The civil servant cannot be removed except for
gross negligence, and even then only after a proper trial in a civil court. At the
same time, all civil servants as well as lay members of the agency boards are personally responsible for the legality of their actions or lack of actions, and this liability may be enforced through criminal proceedings before a court of law, unless the accused person had expressed his dissent to a course of action in the
official minutes. Legal responsibility for illegal actions of ministries (as distinguished from agencies) rests with ministers, not civil servants. The civil servant
enjoys high social prestige in Sweden.

The civil service is organized into a well-echeloned hierarchy. The foremost
civil servants are those who hold the highest offices, as directors-general of

agencies or provincial governors. Immediately subordinate to them is a second tier of equally important positions, filled through application and competition. A third group consists of positions filled by the central agencies. The full range of positions and their hierarchy are reflected in the General Salary Agreement for Civil Servants, which divides them into three salary levels: A, B and C. Level A covers the less-well-paid positions and is divided into 30 salary classes—A1, A2 A3, etc. In turn, these classes are divided into three cost-of-living zones. Level B is composed of those in intermediate supervisory positions, such as bureau chiefs and the like. It is further divided into 10 classes, but no adjustment is made to differences in cost of living. Level C is composed of the highest-paid employees. In addition, there are some groups to whom special levels, called levels U, apply (e.g., teachers and professors).

The most important single factor in recruitment is the candidate's educational background. A law degree is the traditional passport to the civil service, and this is still largely true for higher positions. However, in recent year degrees in political science, science and social sciences have become equally important avenues to the civil service.

Sweden has neither civil service examinations nor a civil service commission. Most candidates apply directly to the departments of their choice, which exercise considerable autonomy over their recruitment and selection processes. Most positions are advertised in the *Post och Inrikes Tidningar* (Official Gazette) and other newspapers. Competition is quite keen.

A large number of civil servants come from the middle and upper middle classes, leading to frequent Social Democratic complaint about the bourgeois nature of the civil service. The retirement age is 50, according to an unwritten rule.

Data on the size of the Swedish civil service are not available.

LOCAL GOVERNMENT

Rural municipal districts were first established on the basis of medieval parish boundaries by the Local Government Ordinances of 1862. The ordinances also established a regional unit of self-government, the county council, whose jurisdiction extends over the principal regional administrative unit, the *lan* (county). Thus there now are two kinds of local governmental units: the municipalities *(kommun)* and the county councils *(landsting)*. Both units are governed by the Local Government Act of 1977, which is under revision. In addition, the Church of Sweden has local units called *forsamling* (parishes).

Local government in Sweden is more important than it is on the rest of the Continent. Municipalities and counties together account for 70% of total consumption and investments within the public sector. In 1985 the national government and local governments accounted for 9.5 and 22.5%, respectively, of the GDP.

The *kommun* is a legal personality in much the same way as a corporation. The two main types of communes are primary and secondary. There are four kinds of primary communes: (1) cities *(stad)*, (2) rural communes *(landskommun)*, (3) market boroughs and (4) municipalities. The last two are chiefly of historical interest.

For purposes of national administration Sweden is divided into 24 counties, each headed by a governor *(landshovding)*, an official appointed for life by the king in council and who serves as the chief representative of the government in the county. The governor supervises the county administration *(lansstyrelsen)*, which is responsible for all national programs for which no other administrative agency has been given jurisdiction. The county council *(landsting)*, on the other hand, is primarily a local governmental body, not an arm of the national administration. The boundaries of the council districts coincide with those of the *lan*, with the exception of the Kalmar *lan*, which is divided into two county council districts. The regularly elected city councils of Stockholm, Göteborg and Malmö also serve as county councils within their respective jurisdictions.

Until 1952 Sweden was divided into 2,500 municipal districts based on the parish boundaries in 1862. A boundary reform in 1952 cut the number to 1,037. During 1962–74 a further reorganization was carried out, reducing the number to 284. There were two reasons for this reduction: The movement of population from rural to urban areas had reduced the ability of the rural municipalities to provide essential services, and the creation of nine-year compulsory schools made larger municipalities necessary.

The 1977 Local Government Act provides the basis for grass-roots democracy at the local level. There are an estimated 33,000 elected representatives serving on municipal and county councils. The regular and deputy members of these bodies are elected by the people in general elections every three years on the same day as the parliamentary elections. Both citizens and resident aliens over 18 can vote in these elections. Council sessions are conducted by a chairman *(ordforande)* chosen by the council for one year. The administrative arm of the council is its board or executive committee, called a *kommunalnamnd* in rural districts and a *dratselkammare* in the cities. They must have at least five members but normally have between 11 and 17 members.

Some 15 to 20 other boards and committees carry out specialized tasks. It is customary to distinguish between those operating in regulated and those in unregulated areas of communal competence. In practice, this ensures central government influence over regulated boards, some of which, such as the election and tax boards, include either chairmen appointed by the county governor or civil servants as members. There is also a distinction between "strong" boards (such as child welfare, school and construction) and "weak" boards (such as civil defense).

Stockholm is governed by the special Communal Law passed in 1957. Its principal administrative bodies are the 100-member City Council; the 12-member Board of Aldermen (Stadskollegiet); and the City Director (Borgarrad), which acts as a kind of administrative cabinet. There are nine such directors elected by the council for four years, generally from among its own members. Serving under the directors are approximately 50 other boards.

In recent years an increasing number of municipalities and county councils have given full-time jobs to one or more of their elected representatives. They are called municipal commissioners (kommunalrad) or county council commissioners (landstingsrad).

The tasks of the local sector fall into two distinct categories: those granted under the Local Government Act and those based on special legislation. Those requiring a larger population base, such as medical care, are handled by the county councils. There is another distinction between the "regulated" and the "unregulated" aspects of commune activities. The latter is in the sphere of local self-government proper and is marked by considerable flexibility and variation, both in theory and in practice. These unregulated powers are derived from a section of the Commune Law that states that the commune has the right to conduct its own affairs provided its actions are compatible with general public interest, do not conflict with any statute, do not encroach on the jurisdiction of another agency and remain within the case law constraints imposed by the Supreme Administrative Court. The regulated areas involve less self-government and more decentralized administration of centrally determined policies, and the provision of services as required or authorized by national statutes or government directives. These tasks include schools (both the nine-year comprehensive school and the upper secondary schools), social services (such as child care and care of the elderly, public health and medical care, including hospitals and preventive health care and nursing, building, social planning, public transportation and fire protection.

Of the total 1985 municipal and county expenditures of SEK259 billion, municipalities accounted for 67% and county councils for 33%. About 22% of these expenditures went for education; 22% for social welfare; 14% for industrial activities; 9% for finance and investment; 6% for land and housing; 6% for environment, health and social protection; 5% for communications; 5% for recreational amenities; 4% for employment and enterprise; 1% for cultural amenities; and the balance for joint municipal administration. The largest item of income for both municipal governments and county councils is the local tax.

POLITICAL SUBDIVISIONS				
		Area		Population
Counties	Capitals	sq. km.	sq. mi.	(1984 est.)
Älvsborg	Vänersborg	11,395	4,400	425,500
Blekinge	Karlskrona	2,941	1,136	151,900
Gävleborg	Gävle	18,191	7,024	291,500
Göteborg och Bohus	Göteborg	5,141	1,985	709,700
Gotland	Visby	3,140	1,212	55,900
Halland	Halmstad	5,454	2,106	236,300
Jämtland	Östersund	49,916	19,273	134,900
Jönköping	Jönköping	9,944	3,839	301,000
Kalmar	Kalmar	11,166	4,311	240,100
Kopparberg	Falun	28,264	10,913	285,600
Kristianstad	Kristianstad	6,089	2,351	280,400
Kronoberg	Växjö	8,452	3,263	174,300
Malmöhus	Malmö	4,939	1,907	745,400
Norrbotten	Luleå	98,919	38,193	264,500
Örebro	Örebro	8,515	3,288	272,100
Östergötland	Linköping	10,569	4,081	392,300
Skaraborg	Mariestad	7,938	3,065	270,400
Södermanland	Nyköping	6,061	2,340	251,000
Stockholm	Stockholm	6,488	2,505	1,551,200
Uppsala	Uppsala	6,989	2,698	248,100
Värmland	Karlstad	17,582	6,788	281,200
Västerbotten	Umeå	55,401	21,390	245,300
Västernorrland	Härnösand	21,711	8,383	264,800
Västmanland	Västerås	6,302	2,433	257,000
TOTAL		411,506	158,884	8,330,600

Source: Official government figures.

The municipal tax rate varied from 18% to 11.3%, while the county council tax varied from 12% to 14.5%. Tax payable to the church amounted on an average to 1.1%. Local tax levels have risen substantially over the years, averaging 22.24% in 1955; 17.25% in 1965, 25.23% in 1975; and 30.34% in 1986. Local tax accounted for 41% of municipal income in 1985, while the corresponding figure for county councils was 62%. There is no special property tax, but it is built into the income tax.

The next-largest income item is state subsidies, both special-purpose and operational grants-in-aid. The operational grants-in-aid consist of a tax equalization grant paid to municipalities and county councils with a small tax base. In 1986 a total of 252 municipalities and 21 county councils received such grants, which accounted for 26% of their income. Another 20% of income comes from fees and 3% from charges paid by patients.

Municipalities and county councils together have over 1 million employees, of whom nearly 635,000 are in municipal service, including 140,000 teachers. Nearly 77% of employees are women; in the county council sector, the percentage is 84%. The major municipalities and county councils have between 50,000 and 80,000 employees, making them among the largest employers.

There are currently 21 local government federations, of which the largest are the Swedish Association of Local Authorities and the Federation of County Councils. These two also function as bargaining agents in wage negotiations with trade unions representing local government employees.

Despite considerable autonomy enjoyed by local bodies, the management of their activities in critical areas is governed by detailed rules embodied in special legislation. Decisions regarding physical and social planning need to be confirmed by the county administration. The national government also controls the quality and efficiency of local statutory activities. For example, schools are supervised by the national boards of education, and social welfare by the Social Welfare Board. State subsidy regulations also incorporate conditions and restrictions with which local governments have to comply.

As in many other large countries, demography and development are characterized by considerable regional imbalance. The uneven distribution of population between North and South has become even more lopsided as rapidly diminishing employment in agriculture and forestry in Norrland led to a further migration to the South, at the rate of 10,000 each year since 1960. After a period of relative stability in the 1970s, the demographics worsened again in the 1980s as the worldwide recession adversely affected traditionally strong economic sectors such as lumber, mining, steel and shipbuilding. Structural changes have confined industrial growth to a handful of localities with strong information networks and pools of highly skilled labor.

To correct this situation, the Riksdag in 1985 passed the Regional Policy Act, aimed at restoring interregional balance in development. The act delimited three development areas—A, B and C—of which the first two, containing 13.5% of the population and 62% of the land area, are to receive special incentives. A and B include regions with severe long-term problem such as Norrland; those with problems related to structural change, such as Bergslagen; the mining and steel district of central Sweden; and the shipbuilding communities of Uddevalla on the western coast and Malmö in the South. The administration of regional development support is delegated to the county administrative boards and the National Industrial Board. The latter is the central authority for providing regional financial assistance to enterprise. The array of policy measures varies from region to region, depending on the problems and opportunities. Inputs are of limited duration, usually lasting for two to three years.

The county administrative boards are the principal regional authorities responsible for implementation of regional policy in the counties through planning, coordination, administration, and forecasting of employment and population trends. The county administrative boards also are required to draw up regional technology diffusion programs. Location grants, investment grants, location loans and conditional support account for the major costs in the regional development support plans. A fixed-sum employment grant is paid annually for up to seven years if additional labor is taken on by firms in the development areas. The Regional Policy Act also calls for development of sparsely populated rural communities to make them economically viable and to enable them to maintain a minimum level of services. The high freight costs to the northern part of Sweden are compensated for by transportation subsidies for certain classes of goods. These subsidies vary from 10% to 50% of the freight costs. Payroll taxes are reduced in Norrbotten, the northernmost county of Sweden, where the level of unemployment is chronically high. The Riksdag also has approved funds for increased R&D activities in Norrland in conjunction with the University of Umeå and other institutions.

The Norrland Fund is a publicly owned foundation to promote industrial development in the four northernmost counties. Regional development funds have been established in every county, financed by the government and the county councils. Privately owned investment companies qualify to receive favorable government loans if their activities are carried out mainly in the development areas. The Expert Group on Regional Studies, affiliated with the Ministry of Industry, initiates and coordinates research to improve regional policy and programs. The Center for Regional Science Research of the University of Umeå also is engaged in regional policy research.

FOREIGN POLICY

The most remarkable feature of Swedish foreign policy is that it has escaped from both wars and entangling alliances since 1814. Since the end of the Napoleonic wars, Sweden has adopted a realistic international role as a minor power in keeping with its resources and has devoted its energies to peaceful internal development. In pursuit of this policy Sweden has been favored by both history and geography. Located on the outer fringes of Europe, outside the cockpit of conflicts, it had had no compelling reasons to defend itself against the superpowers. With until recent years a homogeneous population, it has no irredentist groups, no colonies, no outstanding territorial claims on others and no claims on its territory by other powers. As a result its foreign interests are and have been for the past 175 years limited to the peaceful resolution of international disputes, foreign aid to developing nations, general support of disarmament (particularly since the end of World War II of nuclear disarmament) and espousal of issues involving human rights and social justice.

The keystone of Swedish foreign policy is neutrality, defined officially as "alliance-free in peace and noninvolved in war." The Swedish concept of neutrality is quite unlike that of most other nonaligned power in the world. Sweden's neutrality is not laid down in the Constitution or otherwise proclaimed as a state doctrine. It is neither confirmed in nor guaranteed by any international agreement. It is a policy that the Swedish governments have chosen to pursue and one that Sweden could, if it should so wish, amend at any time. (In Switzerland, on the other hand, neutrality is part of a historical tradition that has gained international recognition through the Vienna Conference and the Versailles Peace Treaty. Austrian neutrality is affirmed in the Austrian State Treaty of 1955, to which the superpowers are parties). Sweden's neutrality also is different from the nonalignment of developing nations, although it does involve avoidance of spheres of influence. It is not ideologically uncommitted, nor is it passive and isolationist. It has an active policy of promoting peace by steering clear of diplomatic minefields and entangling alliances. In the context of history, the policy has saved the country from being dragged into two world wars and has transformed Sweden into a zone of safety and peace. Critical to this policy is the ability of Swedish governments to eschew alliances with their concomitant political obligations, which could reduce the confidence of the superpowers in the national will to remain neutral in the event of actual war. For this reason Sweden chose not to become a member of the EEC, despite the considerable advantages that such a membership would have brought. At the same time, because Sweden does not equate neutrality with isolationism, it was able to join the United Nations while Switzerland did not. The policy of neutrality also has not prevented Sweden from opposing the Soviet occupation of Afghanistan, U.S. involvement in the Vietnam War, or the minority regimes of South Africa or formerly Rhodesia.

Swedish foreign policy is characterized by a remarkable consensus. There is almost universal agreement among Swedish politicians and the public on its basic principles, even though there might be differences on its application in specific situations. The disposition toward a common, nonpartisan front in foreign policy is facilitated by the institutional arrangements involved in its making. The Riksdag has little power over foreign affairs, and the executive takes the dominant role. In any given year not more than a dozen questions are asked in the Riksdag on foreign policy issues. As a rule, political parties are reluctant to debate questions of foreign affairs openly. Although the Foreign Ministry is responsible for the day-to-day conduct of foreign relations, policies are discussed and formulated by the Permanent Advisory Council on Foreign Affairs

(Utrikesnamnd), chaired by the king. The council, founded in 1921 to replace the "Secret Committee," is to "confer with the king concerning the relations of the realm with foreign powers." Usually it meets about a dozen times annually. It is elected each year by the Riksdag, and it functions even between sessions. Its membership is identical with that of the Riksdag Committee of Foreign Affairs, a body created in 1937. The latter has 16 members chosen from both houses and from all the democratic parties, including the opposition, and it usually includes the various party leaders. Its minutes are secret.

The key planks of Swedish foreign policy are (1) a strong defense backed up by self-sufficiency in military equipment and strategic supplies; (2) support for multilateral disarmament, a comprehensive nuclear test ban treaty, a nuclear weapons freeze and the strengthening of the nuclear nonproliferation treaty; (3) support for national liberation movements and the struggle against racial discrimination; (4) support for a new international economic order that will ensure the progress of Third World countries; (5) respect for human rights; (6) support for the legitimate rights of the Palestinians; and (7) promotion of Nordic cooperation and unity.

Sweden was one of the prime promoters and founding members of the Nordic Council, which is not a supranational organization but one designed for regional cooperation. It includes, besides Sweden, Norway, Finland, Denmark and Iceland. The Nordic Council does not deal with matters of military or foreign policy. Unlike the EEC, it represents only what has been described as "cobweb integration," or "small-step functional integration." The concrete results of this arrangement are many. Passports have been eliminated within Scandinavia. There is a common labor market except in certain professions. All Scandinavians have a common "social citizenship" in the five countries, which entitles them to social welfare benefits without restriction. There are many successful joint ventures, as the Scandinavian Airlines System. Yet, avenues of further cooperation do not appear promising. There are subtle differences among the five countries that rhetoric often hides. The economies are not entirely compatible, and fears of Swedish domination have not disappeared. The security needs of the countries also are different.

Sweden has a long-standing and genuine interest in developing nations, a legacy of the strong moral undercurrent in Swedish political life. Development aid (see the Economy section) equals 1% of the GNP and is growing. Because Sweden was never a colonial power, it commands the trust of the Third World to a greater degree than the major European powers. The scope of Swedish aid is broadest in Africa and more narrowly distributed in Asia. The aid program is notable for the thoroughness with which it is planned. The principal administrative agency is the Swedish International Development Authority (SIDA), created in 1965. Commitments are generally made for three-year periods after extensive consultations with the representatives of the recipient countries. Sweden also took the lead in canceling debts owned by the poorest nations. Swedish assistance to the Third World comes from private resources as well as the government. The Swedish Cooperative Center administers a voluntary technical assistance progam. Sweden also has created a Peace Corps based on the U.S. model, and the first contingents were sent into the field in 1965.

In international forums Sweden has consistently spoken out against violations of human rights in various parts of the world, particularly South Africa and Chile. Sweden also leads international efforts against torture, the death penalty, summary trials, arbitrary executions and the denial of citizens' rights to leave or return to their home countries.

Sweden was not a charter member of the United Nations, but once admitted in 1946, it became one of its staunchest supporters, taking part in more peacekeeping operations than any other country. More than 40,000 Swedish troops have served with U.N. forces around the world. Since 1963 it has designated part of its military forces to be available on short notice to the United Nations.

Stockholm's traditionaly good relations with Moscow have not prevented it from speaking out against Soviet invasions of Hungary and Afghanistan. Further strains were introduced by numerous incidents involving Soviet submarines in Swedish waters (one of which ran aground on the Swedish coast) and intrusions of Soviet planes into Swedish airspace.

One diplomatic landmark in the 1980s was the restoration of full diplomatic ties with the Vatican after a 450-year break. Also, in 1983, an agreement was concluded with Denmark resolving an old offshore border dispute.

PARLIAMENT

Since 1971 Sweden has had a unicameral legislature, the Riksdag. A constitutional amendment adopted in 1968–69 abolished the bicameral system, which had existed since 1866. From 1971 to 1976 the Riksdag had 350 members. In 1976 the strength was reduced to 349 to avoid a situation where the socialist and nonsocialist blocs would have exactly the same number of seats, as happened in 1973. In relation to its population, parliamentary strength is quite large compared to other democracies.

It is characteristic of Swedish constitutional law that many rules concerning parliamentary organization and procedure are included in the fundamental laws, such as the Riksdag Act and the Instrument of Government, while some standing orders are found in the Riksdag Regulations (Rikstadsstadga). The formal rules are supplemented by a rich body of traditional and customary practice.

Sweden is divided into 28 parliamentary constituencies, which coincide with the counties except in two cases. Stockholm and Göteborg form their own constituencies. Malmö, Lund, Landskrona and Hälsingborg together form what is known as the four-city constituency. Further, Älvsborg County is divided into two constituencies. Of the total 349 seats in the Riksdag 310 are permanent constituency seats and 39 are equalizing seats for the country as a whole. The purpose of the equalizing seats is to ensure that all parties receive the number of seats strictly proportional to the number of votes cast in their favor country-wide. However, there is an important exception to strict proportionality, and that is the so-called blocking rule. A party must obtain at least 4% of the total number of votes cast in a constituency to take part in the distribution of Riksdag seats. This rule is designed to reduce the number of minor nuisance parties.

The Riksdag meets annually, as prescribed in the Constitution, on January 10 (or the closest working day). There are two sessions every year: the spring session, from January until the end of May; and the autumn session, from about October until the end of December.

A distinction usually is made between the external and the internal administration of the Riksdag. The internal administration consists of the Presidium, the chamber staff, the standing committees' staff and the Administrative Office of Parliament. The external administration consists of the parliamentary agencies—the Bank of Sweden, the National Debt Office, the parliamentary ombudsman's office, etc. The Presidium consists of the speaker, three deputy speakers, a representative of each party caucus in the Riksdag, the chairmen of the standing committees and the deputy chairman of the administrative board in the Riksdag.

The seating arrangement in the Riksdag is quite unlike that of most parliaments. Members are seated not according to party affiliation but by constituencies, arranged in order of the state calendar, with Stockholm first and Norrland-Lapland last. Within each constituency seats are distributed according to seniority.

Probably the single most important characteristic of the Riksdag is its system of standing committees, where a large part of the parliamentary work is transacted and whose decisions are generally accepted by the whole Riksdag. Currently there are 16 standing committees specializing in different topics as follows:

- Committee on the Constitution
- Committee on Finance
- Committee on Taxation
- Committee on Justice
- Committee on Laws

- Committee on Foreign Affairs
- Committee on Defense
- Committee on Social Insurance
- Committee on Social Affairs
- Committee on Cultural Affairs
- Committee on Education
- Committee on Transportation and Communications
- Committee on Agriculture
- Committee on Industry
- Committee on the Labor Market
- Committee on Physical Planning and Local Government

In addition there are numerous advisory bodies; some of the more important are: the Election Committee of Parliament, the Advisory Council on Foreign Affairs, the Appeals Board, the War Delegation and the Parliamentary Ombudsman's Delegation.

Each of the standing committees has 15 members and as many deputy members, elected on a proportional basis among the parties.

Practically all items to be considered must be referred to the standing committees for discussion, and a committee is required to report the results of its deliberations to the plenary chamber. Unlike in the U.S. Congress, a member's bill cannot be killed in a committee. Committee members who disagree with the majority may write dissenting opinions, which are attached to the report. A member who does not dissent but who wishes to emphasize an additional viewpoint may do so in the form of a special opinion. In exceptional cases a committee may initiate matters on its own. If the subject of a government or member's bill falls within the jurisdiction of more than one standing committee, they may examine it jointly or successively.

A committee often needs to obtain outside views on a proposed piece of legislation. This is done by requesting written outside opinions or by holding hearings. Ministers may be invited by a committee to take part in a hearing. The initiative to hold a hearing may also come from an outside organization. All committee meetings take place behind closed doors, and they are not recorded in the minutes.

Parliamentary party elections are held on the first day of each annual Riksdag session. The entire delegation of a party is known as the parliamentary group (riksdagsgrupp). Usually it meets once a week, but votes are seldom taken, and the group decisions are not binding on members. The group also elects the party's executive committee, which, too, meets once a week; an officer resembling a whip, who handles voting; and members to the various committees and delegations. Although the party leader in the Riksdag has no official standing, as in the United Kindgom, he is the grand spokesman as well as the symbol of party unity. A great deal of what happens in the Riksdag is a result of discussions among party leaders, especially through regular conferences held each Wednesday when the Riksdag is in session. Generally party discipline is less rigid than in the United Kingdom but much more strict than in the United States. Except in the case of the Communists, there is no requirement that the individual member follow the decision of his party, except on major issues. Discipline tends to be more strictly enforced when the parties are more evenly matched in numerical strength. The degree of discipline on the floor of the Riksdag is less important because of the nature of the Swedish parliamentary system. In most cases the differences among parties have already been resolved, either in committee or by agreement among leaders before a bill reaches the final vote.

Government bills deal with a variety of matters. These bills also may vary in length, from a couple of pages to several hundred pages. An exception is the Budget Bill, a document of some 3,000 pages. Altogether the government usually presents more than 200 bills to the Riksdag every year. A draft bill normally consists of four sections: the proposal, the main content, the recital and the submission. Bills dealing with new laws or a change in existing legislation also include the proposed text of the new law and detailed reasons for its adoption. Before presenting it to the Riksdag, the government may submit it to the Advisory Committee on Draft Legislation. This committee, which consists of judges from the Supreme Court and the Supreme Administrative Court, scrutinizes the legislative aspects of the proposal. Their comments are attached to the bill. After the delivery of each government bill a period of 15 days is allotted to the members for moving amendments. During the first 15 days after the government has first presented the Budget Bill, individual members are entitled to introduce bills on any subject.

The Riksdag meets in plenary session twice a week (on Wednesdays and Fridays), and committees meet the day before (on Tuesdays and Thursdays). There are two types of plenary meetings: The briefer type, called "tabling plenary meeting," takes place on Tuesday and Friday afternoons, when much formal work is done. The working plenary session when the real business of debate and decision-making takes place, is on Wednesdays. When the press of business is great, they may be held on other days as well or continue late into the evening.

There is complete freedom of debate, with none of the restrictive rules for closing or cutting off debate. Despite this right, detailed procedural debates or long-winded speeches are very rare. Filibusters and other obstructive tactics are unknown. Party leaders do not control the floor or determine who will be allowed to speak. Actually, the members who speak first and speak most are the party leaders, cabinet members and committee chairmen. Members have the right of a brief reply or rejoinder. Generally debates are dull, and not infrequently the Riksdag is far from full when some M.P.'s are on the rostrum. This is so because all documents dealing with matters under discussion have been circulated in advance. Most members listen to the debates in their offices via loudspeakers and get on with their other work. Meetings in the chamber also are transmitted by closed-circuit TV to clubrooms and other common premises. When debate ends and it is time to vote, a voting bell sounds throughout the Riksdag building. In minutes the assembly hall is filled to capacity as members arrive from their offices or from meetings.

Documents and not speeches thus dominate the Riksdag's work. The written work is so painstakingly compiled and so volumimous that it leaves no room for stirring speeches. Many times decisions have already been made in the committees or by interparty agreements, making debates superfluous. Further, because a Riksdag member is not personally accountable to his constituents, he does not strive to "speak for the record." The most important debate of the year takes place in the spring, when the Budget Bill is presented. This is an opportunity to review the government's general performance and for the opposition to sharpen their knives.

A member of the Riksdag may elicit information from the government through two kinds of inquiries: interpellations and ordinary questions. Neither can be voted on or sent to committee, but both can initiate debate. Ministers need not answer either kind of question, but in practice they seldom refuse. Answers to interpellations are distributed in writing and summarized orally by the minister to whom they are addressed. Not surprisingly, the opposition makes optimum use of these two types of questions. In 1964 the Riksdag introduced a question period when answers to ordinary questions could be presented on the U.K. parliamentary model.

Most Riksdag matters are decided without voting, by acclamation. If there is no unanimity, a division may be requested by any member. Voting in a division takes place in three stages: first a voice vote, then a standing vote and then a machine vote. Machine voting takes place by members depressing one of three buttons for "yes," "no" or "abstain." The results of the machine voting are photographed and made available to the public. Members may be paired to maintain the relative strengths of the parties, regardless of sickness of other causes of absence. Pairing is not officially recognized but is based on voluntary agreement among the political parties. The executive branch cannot veto a law passed by the Riksdag. All Riksdag debates are published in two editions, one provisional and the other final.

The Riksdag may, with an absolute majority, enter votes of censure, leading either to the resignation of individual members or of the whole government. However, a vote of censure is of no effect if the government calls for a new election within a week. Votes of confidence are not taken in the Riksdag as separate items and cannot be moved by a member in any form other than a motion for a vote against the prime minister or one of the other ministers. The government may, however, make a bill or proposal a "question of confidence," but this must be done before the vote is taken.

In 1984 the monthly remuneration of a Riksdag member was SKr11,662. In addition, the members receive daily allowance when the Riksdag is in session, expense allowances, traveling allowances, etc. In addition to an old-age pension and a national supplementary pension, members are entitled to receive the Riksdag member pension from age 65 and a proportionate pension until they reach 65.

Elections to the Riksdag are secret, free and direct. The electorate does not vote for an individual candidate but instead votes for a party list of candidates. Electors may add or remove names from the list, but this right has little or no practical political significance. More importantly, a party can run more than one list under the party label, and votes for this list are totaled when calculating the party vote. Multiple lists are more commonly run by nonsocialist parties. After the vote the multiple lists are merged to form one rank-ordered list. There are no by-elections. In the case of a vacancy, the seat passes to the candidate next in line on the list.

To distribute seats in the Riksdag, Sweden uses the odd-number or St. Lague method. For distribution of the 39 equalization seats, the whole country is regarded as a constituency. A calculation is made of how many seats the various parties would have won if Sweden really were a single constituency. The difference between the ordinary constituency seats and the "national constituency seats" is then adjusted with equalizing seats.

Elections are held on the third day in September every third year and take place at national, regional and local levels simultaneously. Consequently, ballot papers of different colors and markings are employed: plain white for municipal, blue with a black corner line for county municipal and yellow with two black corner lines for parliamentary elections. Voting is optional, but participation levels generally are over 90%.

Suffrage is limited to adults over 18. Aliens resident for at least three years may vote and run as candidates in local and regional elections but not in parliamentary ones.

There are no legal restrictions on campaign expenses and no laws that compel disclosure of sources of donation. However, parties tend to limit their expenditures by mutual agreement. Campaigns are brief, limited to about three of four weeks, usually beginning in August after the vacations. However, during this short period, activity is intense. Rather than personal campaigning, most candidates tend to rely on posters, meetings, rallies and media events. Since 1965 parties have received some state subsidies in proportion to their mandate, provided they have received at least 2% of the national vote.

Referenda are permitted by the Constitution in two different forms. The Riksdag may enact a law according to which a consultative referendum is to be held. As yet, only four such referenda have taken place, the latest being in 1980 on the nuclear power issue. A 1979 amendment to the Constitution permits decisive referenda on amendments to it. One-third of Riksdag members can authorize such a referendum, which then will be held simultaneously with the general elections. As yet, no such referendum has taken place.

PARTY COMPOSITION IN THE RIKSDAG		
Parties in the Riksdag	1988	
	% of Votes	Seats
Moderate Party	18.3	66
Center Party	11.3	42
Liberal Party	12.2	44
Total, nonsocialist parties	41.8	152
Social Democratic Party	43.2	156
Left Party Communists	5.8	21
Total, socialist parties	49.0	177
Ecology Party	5.5	20

POLITICAL PARTIES

Sweden has virtually a two-party political system, with the nonsocialist or bourgeois parties parties forming one group and the socialists and the Communists the other. The two sectors are more or less evenly matched, but the socialists have generally had the edge since 1932, enabling them to form most of the governments and remain in power for an unbroken period of 44 years, from 1932 to 1976. But although the political lines are sharply drawn, the five major parties have tended to downplay ideology and favor pragmatic cooperation in foreign affairs as well as on most other issues. The rhetoric of the hustings always yields to the Swedish homing instinct for the middle way. This explains why Sweden, a capitalist monarchy, has had a socialist/Communist government for most of this century.

The Constitution restricts the distribution of seats to parties registered with the National Tax Office. The basic organizational structures and functions of the three main levels of party organization are similar for all five major parties. The differences are in the working groups at the national level and the procedures for the nomination of candidates. By long-standing convention, the national leadership does not interfere in the nomination process for parliamentary candidates, which takes place at the constituency level. This also is true of the Communists, whose structure is more centralized than that of others. Party cohesion is strong and mavericks are rare in all the major parties. Those who break ranks may suffer expulsion. The local party caucuses not only choose candidates but also submit motions for submission to party regional and national congresses. Regional party officials also play a crucial role in determining the final ticket. The most important national party organ is the annual congress, which elects the national leader (who is more often than not the parliamentary group leader) and other party functionaries. In general issues are more important than personalities in election campaigns, although with more managed media coverage, this is changing. Television time is allocated equally to all parties represented in the Riksdag. However, the time-honored poster and slogan campaigns still survive.

The Social Democratic Party (Socialdemokratiska Arbetarepartiet, SAP), the "natural" ruling party of Sweden, is over 100 years old. Founded in 1889 with Hjalmar Branting as leader, the SAP soon abandoned its earlier orthodox Marxism and collaborated with the Liberals in a program that emphasized modernization of the economy, parliamentary democracy and coexistence with both monarchy and capitalism. It entered government for the first time in 1917 and until 1932 took turns with nonsocialist parties in forming unstable minority governments. In 1932 it was voted into office on an expansionist economic New Deal-type program to meet the Great Depression. In 1933 an agreement with the Agrarians began an almost uninterrupted tenure in power until 1976, although coalitions were necessary from 1936 to 1939, 1939 to 1945 and 1951 to 1957. The SAP gained an absolute majority in 1940 and 1968 and made its poorest showing in 1976, with a 42.7% total; however, even then it was the strongest single party by a wide margin. It returned to power in 1982, and its popularity has been enhanced after the tragic assassination of the Prime Minister Olof Palme.

The SAP's Marxist fervor has steadily diminished and its socialism has been considerably diluted with traditional liberal concepts. John Kenneth Galbraith and Gunnar Myrdal are the inspirations of the party ideologues rather than Marx, whose name is never mentioned in campaign speeches or manifestos. The SAP now stresses the welfare state, the middle way and economic democracy. Its major achievement has been to make the trade unions the top partners in the Swedish economy, especially after the passage of the Codetermination Act in

1976. The party has lost some support over the nuclear issue, which the nonsocialists have cleverly exploited.

The SAP has approximately 1.1 million members, of whom 70% are affiliated with the trade unions. It has more loyal and diehard supporters than any other party. As a result, SAP strength is equally spread throughout the country and all classes. Nevertheless, it still is by and large a workers' party, and it draws well over two-thirds of its support from blue-collar unionists. Although this support has declined since the immediate postwar period, the SAP has made compensatory gains among white-collar workers and among the youth (partly as a result of Olof Palme's apparent anti-Americanism). Northern Sweden is the party's stronghold. The Swedish Confederation of Trade Unions (Landsorganisationen, LO) is formally independent but is in fact the parent and ally of the SAP, supplying most of the socialist content of legislation and delivering the votes at election times. The Cooperative Movement also has a significant overlapping membership with the SAP, although its relationship is not as close or natural as that of the LO.

The SAP controls a number of newspapers, including the best-selling daily *Aftonbladet*. Christian Social Democrats have their own organization within the party, the Broderskapsrorelsen (the Brotherhood Movement).

The Center Party (Centerpartiet) is the modern successor to the Agrarian Party. It was a junior partner in SAP-led coalitions from 1933 to 1939 and from 1951 to 1957. After the second of these coalitions, the party's vote fell to just 9%, down from the 11% to 14% it polled before the war. Further, a rapid drift out of agriculture threatened the party's electoral base. To broaden its appeal, the name was changed to the Center Party in 1958. This strategy proved successful, culminating in a 25.1% vote in 1973, although the support has since then ebbed, to 12.4% in 1985. The party has provided one of the two nonsocialist prime ministers in modern times in the person of Thorbjorn Falldin, party leader from 1971 to 1985.

The party's support base is the National Farmers' Association, which has many close links with it. The party program adopted in 1970 is notable for its opposition to nuclear power but otherwise differs little from SAP positions. The membership is estimated at 140,000, drawn from industrial workers, white-collar workers and small businessmen. It retains the loyalty of a majority of the country's farmers who now provide it with a quarter of its total support. The party is strongest in the rural areas of central Sweden. As Sweden's "green" and antinuclear party, it attracts many younger voters as well as women.

The Liberal Party (Folkpartiet) was, after its founding in 1895 the main rival to the ruling party. After a national party organization was created in 1902, it concentrated on the classical liberal issues: extension of the franchise and parliamentary reform. But the final gain of these reforms left the party without issues, and it swiftly lost its electoral support, dropping from a majority at the turn of the century to slightly over 20% in 1920 and 10% in the 1930s. The decline was hastened by a 1928 schism between a rural free-church temperance wing and an urban radical wet wing. The schism was not healed until 1934. Its fortunes revived after World War II, and it bacame the strongest nonsocialist bloc, with a quarter of the national vote. It slipped again to record an all-time low of 5.9% in 1982 but rallied slightly, to 14.2% in 1985. They were in power continuously from 1976 to 1982 (first as part of a nonsocialist government, and later on their own) after having been out of power since 1932.

Under the leadership of Bertil Ohlin, the party leader from 1944 to 1967, the Liberals moved away from their traditional laissez-faire economic policies and toward a cautious social liberalism expressed in controlled private enterprise. The Liberals oppose both socialists and conservatives in principle but in practice are prepared to accommodate with both, mostly with the latter. The Liberals are strong proponents of civil rights and liberties, equal opportunities for men and women, and development aid to the Third World.

Membership is estimated at 54,000, spread across class and regional lines, with no particular strength in any. The party has lost strength in the old free church bastions, especially Västerbotten County in northern Sweden and Jönköping County in south-central Sweden, partly as a result of secularization and partly because of rural depopulation. While repelling the left radicals, the party still attracts the cultural radicals and the limousine liberals. The Liberal press is extensive and includes *Dagens Nyheter*.

The Moderate Party (Moderate Samlinspartiet, MS) is the new name for the 19th Century Conservative Party, the dominant political party until the 1917 extension of universal suffrage. Since that time they began losing ground until they reached their lowest watermark, with 12.3% of the vote in 1948. The party fortunes mended slightly in the 1950s when it became once again the largest nonsocialist party, with 20.4% of the vote in 1958. Two decades of poor showing followed until the party recovered once again, to 23.6% in 1982 and 21.3% in 1985.

The Moderates are the farthest removed from the Social Democrats on both domestic and foreign issues. The Moderates are in favor of a free market economy, reduced public sector expenditures, and nuclear power programs in the domestic sphere, and a stronger defense and greater Swedish involvement in the EC in the foreign sphere. When it changed its name in 1969, the party signalized the occasion by coming out for the first time in favor of an expansion of social welfare programs while still opposing profit-sharing programs. However, its views on fiscal restraint, EC membership and nuclear power are not shared by its nonsocialist allies in the Riksdag.

The Moderate Party has a membership of over 100,000. Unlike in other countries, they draw their right-wing support mainly from urban areas, where they command a quarter of the vote of the white-collar workers, half the vote of the higher civil servants and professional people, and almost the entire vote of the large and small entrepreneurs. In addition, the party also enjoys the allegiance of the well-to-do farmers of southern Sweden. Its support is weakest among the blue-collar workers and in the northern half of the country, which is traditionally more radical. Although the MS does not accept contributions from private industry (since 1976), the Federation of Swedish Employers and the Federation of Swedish Industry are solidly behind it. The party newspaper is *Medborgaren*; that of the youth wing is *Moderat Debatt.*

The Left Party Communists (Vansterpartiet Kommunisterna, VPK) are descendants of the left wing of the Socialists, from whom they broke away in 1917. The VPK is the smallest of the five political parties and owes its political influence solely to socialist coattails. From 1921 to 1967 it was known as the Swedish Communist Party. It experienced periodic schisms in 1921, 1924, 1929, 1967 and 1977, and after a peak of 10.3% in the 1944 elections dipped to between 4% and 5.6% by 1985. Often it has to fight hard to survive the 4% barrier. Staple electoral appeals include freezes on prices and rents; lower taxes; and a nuclear ban, on which it agrees more with the Center Party than with the Socialists. Subscribing to a strict Marxist program on the one hand and accepting parliamentary trappings on the other, the party frequently falls between two stools.

The VPK has approximately 18,000 members, with the bulk of its support coming from the docklands and heavy industrial communities and the "red" county Norbotten. One of every two VPK voters is under 30. The party also has a strong appeal for the educated counterculture groups. The party's main newspaper is *Ny Dag.*

Minor political parties barred from the Riksdag by the 4% rule include the Christian Democratic Party, which generally garners 1% to 2% of the national vote in every election on a platform opposing the permissive society; the Ecology Party, founded in 1982, that seeks less economic growth and a six-hour day; the Pensioners' Party; the Swedish Communist Party, a Maoist splinter group; and the Worker Party Communists, a pro-Moscow faction.

There are no illegal political parties or known terrorist groups in Sweden.

ECONOMY

In the mid-19th century, Sweden was one of the poorest countries in Europe, with a mainly agrarian economy. Its transformation into an advanced industrial economy was accelerated by abundant natural resources, such as iron ore, timber and water. The proportion of the total labor force employed in industry rose from 15% in 1870 to 34% in 1913. Sweden escaped both world wars. In the interwar period, Sweden's annual growth rate per capita of 1.6% was exceeded only by that of the United States. At the end of World War II, the demand for Swedish exports rose sharply, and Sweden began to emerge as an advanced industrial nation. The postwar economy has been characterized by an explosive growth in the public sector. Public sector expenditures, both per capita and as a percentage of the GDP, are higher in Sweden than in any other Western economy. The size of the public sector can be measured in various ways: It employs 31% of the work force; public sector consumption accounts for 30% of the GDP; public sector investment corresponds to 5% of the GDP. Total 1986 public sector spending, including consumption, investment and transfers, accounted for 63.8% of the GDP. Although this figure is less than the 67% reported for 1982, it is much higher than the 33% recorded in 1960, the 45% in 1970 and the 50% in 1975.

Although industrial production grew by 6.5% annually in the 1960s—helped by membership in the EFTA, of which Sweden is a founding member—sluggish economic growth and a yawning current account deficit brought it in the 1970s close to being a sick man of Europe. Critics were quick to point out that the economy was staggering under the burden of a bloated public sector. Yet, within a decade, the economy had rebounded with an impressive scorecard: an unemployment rate of only 2.7%, an inflation rate of 3.3% (both below OECD averages) and a GDP growth rate of 1½ to 2% in 1986. The balance of payments recorded in 1986 a surplus of 1% of the GNP, and the general government budget has been reduced to 1½% of the GDP. Significantly, this reduction in the government budget deficit has been achieved without much increase in the overall tax burden, which, however, at more than 51% of the GDP, remains one of the highest in the OECD area. The general improvement in economic performance since 1982 has been helped by external factors and the economic adjustment strategy introduced in the same year and continued into 1986. It was sustained mainly by a stable level of private consumption, the terms-of-trade effect of falling oil and raw materials prices, and a relaxation of monetary policy. In addition, supply-side measures, such as removal of subsidies to industry and financial sector reform, seem to have led to improved resource allocation.

Sweden's ability to adjust to external shocks stems partially from the economic philosophy that has guided it since the 1930s. Although one of the most socialist countries on the Continent, Sweden has used capitalism itself as an engine to maximize output and used the public sector to redistribute the wealth thus created through taxes and transfers. The foundations of Sweden's modern economic system were laid in the early 1950s by two trade union economists, Gosta Rehn and Rudolf Meidner, whose prescription for full employment and low inflation was to allow market forces to operate freely and to intervene via fiscal, monetary and wage-setting mechanisms. The Swedish model consisted of five main ingredients:

- A fairly tight fiscal policy.
- Nonintervention in the production of goods, permitting ownership of industry to remain primarily in private hands.
- A wage policy designed to reduce wage differentials. This was not just to achieve greater equality, but also to improve the mobility of labor. A narrowing of wage differentials speeded up the transfer of resources to force ailing companies into bankruptcy while helping productive companies to expand.
- A policy of actively tackling unemployment with measures such as recruitment subsidies and job-creation programs.
- Measures to improve the mobility of labor by retraining and grants to help workers move.

This model served the economy well until the second half of the 1970s, when Sweden, as a heavy user of imported fuel, was hit harder than most by the two oil shocks. At the same time, two of Sweden's biggest industries, steel and shipbuilding, were hurt by declining competitiveness and productivity. In an attempt to save jobs, the nonsocialist governments of 1976–82 boosted public spending, increasing the central government deficit from 2% of the GDP in 1976 to 13% by 1982. Much of the money was used to prop up collapsing shipyards and steelworks. Government subsidies to industry rose from Skr1 billion in 1975 to Skr17 billion in 1982. In an effort to keep both inflation and unemployment in check, the Social Democrats, who regained power in 1982, reversed these policies. The main elements of their program were a 16% devaluation of the krona, a cut in the central government budget deficit to 4% by 1986–87 and a virtual abolition of subsidies to failing industries. Government policy now emphasizes support for R&D, incentives for hi-tech investment and regional development in order to create a favorable climate for industry to renew itself.

Sweden can best be described as a mixed economy. Although the Social Democrats have been in power for more than 50 of the past 56 years, nationalization was never their primary objective. Within the business sector more than 90% of the companies are privately run in an open market economy. The remaining 10% are owned either by cooperative societies or by the state. The state takes over companies primarily for employment policy reasons. Particularly during the 1970s, the state initiated structural rationalization of entire crisis-hit industries, such as steel, textiles and shipbuilding. State-owned companies are run on conventional business principles and are expected to yield annual profits. A number of them are owned through the state holding company, Procordia AB. The state also influences the business sector through its regional development policy, under which companies that set up operations within certain specific regions may receive loans, loan guarantees or location grants. Although the public sector has on the whole grown rapidly in recent decades, the state accounts for only a small percentage of industrial employment. Corporate taxes are not as burdensome as generally thought because companies enjoy generous deductions for investment and reserves, and options for depreciation.

GDP. The annual growth rae of Sweden's GDP was 5% during the first half of the 1960s, a rate that has not been equaled since. It slowed down to 2% in the 1970s and to 1% in the 1980s. This pattern is not entirely dissimilar to that experienced by other OECD member countries. In GDP per capita, only the United States exceeds and only Switzerland and Norway equal Sweden. Further, income disparity is much narrower in Sweden as a result of a steeply progressive income tax system and a redistribution of wealth through Social Security.

Income. After a continuous rise in disposable income during the postwar period, real disposable household income decreased between 1981 and 1983, but it rose between 1984 and 1986 by an average of 1.8% annually. Wage earners' real incomes, however, have not risen as fast as those of other groups, such as pensioners. In 1950 disposable household income constituted 70% of the GDP. By 1987 this share had fallen to about 50%. Direct taxes and Social Security contributions have risen more rapidly than the flow of income transfers from the public sector back to households. Income taxes and Social Security contributions as a proportion of the GDP rose from 17% in 1950 to 40% in 1985. More than half of household wealth consists of real property; financial assets such as bank balances, bonds and stocks make up another two-fifths, and cars, boats and consumer durables one-tenth. Wealth is distributed less evenly than income.

Consumption. In 1985 gross household income totaled about SEK619 billion. After deduction of direct taxes and Social Security contributions of SEK182 billion, total disposable income for private consumption and saving was SEK437 billion. Private consumption in the same year was SEK439 billion, of which food and housing made up 35% each, consumer durables 9%, clothing 7% and other services 14%.

Savings. The savings rate of Swedish households is low by international standards. In the 1970s it varied between 3% and 5%, and it has been negative in recent years. The low savings rate may be attributed mainly to the lack of incentives to save for one's retirement and the low yield on investments. Most financial saving by households is in the form of bank deposits. In recent years a growing proportion has gone into tax-exempt and insurance savings programs and share-investment funds.

Investment. After an upward trend in the 1950s and most of the 1960s, total investment has fallen dramatically in relation to the GDP, from 23% in 1960 to 19% in 1986. Since 1970 this rate has, on average, been lower than in most OECD countries. Although industrial investment by state-owned companies rose sharply after 1980, that by private companies has continued to fall. Very low profitability and low expectations concerning future growth contributed to the stagnation of investment activity. Declining productivity, higher wages and high interest rates also tend to depress industrial investment.

Development assistance. Concern for reducing income disparities is not merely a goal of domestic fiscal policy but of international economic policy as well. Sweden has been contributing to international development programs for over 30 years, transferring SEK57 billion to the Third World. In 1968 the Riksdag decided to appropriate 1% of the GNP to development cooperation, a goal that was achieved in 1975–76. Sweden considers this effort as its moral responsibility as a rich nation to share its wealth with the underprivileged.

The Ministry of Foreign Affairs is responsible for multilateral assistance programs through international organizations and the Swedish International Development Authority (SIDA) for bilateral assistance. About 40% of the assistance is directly allocated to 17 selected countries, 30% to other bilateral programs and 30% to multilateral programs. Sweden's contributions to the multilateral programs are generally pledged for three years to facilitate long-term planning by recipient countries. Bilateral assistance is based on the principle of country programming, with negotiated two-year agreements. Two-thirds of the main recipient countries are in Africa, on the southern and eastern parts on the Continent. The major sectors of assistance are in rural areas and include health and family planning, soil conservation, transportation, education, forestry, women and water. Assistance is almost exclusively grants. Earlier loans have been entirely written off. Credits borrowed on the capital market and mixed with a grant element from the aid budget also are offered, and the credit is tied to the procurement of goods and services of Swedish origin. Concessionary credits also are extended, with an official guarantee administered by the

Swedish Export Credit Guarantee Board. From the 1985–86 balance of payments, support is given to qualifying countries. Humanitarian assistance was initiated in Latin America, and substantial sums are channeled to victims of oppression in Chile, El Salvador and Guatemala. The Swedish Agency for Research Cooperation with Developing Countries was founded in 1975. In 1978–79 a technical cooperation program was set up under the Swedish Commission for Technical Cooperation (BITS). BITS provides feasibility studies, consultancy services, training programs, institutional cooperation and personnel exchange.

PRINCIPAL ECONOMIC INDICATORS

Gross National Product: $109.950 billion (1986)
GNP per capita: $13,170 (1986)
GNP average annual growth rate: 1.3% (1973–86)
GNP per capita average annual
   growth rate: 1.1% (1973–86)
Average annual rate of inflation: 8.2% (1980–86)
Consumer Price Index (1980=100):
   All items: 172.9 (February 1988)
   Food: 198.7 (February 1988)
Wholesale Price Index
   (1980=100): 161 (December 1987)
Average annual growth rate (1980–86) (%)
   Public consumption: 1.5
   Private consumption: 1.1
   Gross domestic investment: 1.2

PUBLIC FINANCE

The fiscal year runs from July 1 to June 30. Work on the budget begins in the different agencies during the spring and summer of the preceding year. The local administrative bodies submit their requests *(petita)* to the central boards over them. By July the central boards begin the preparation of their own requests, which must be submitted to the ministries by September 1. After the Ministry of Finance has adjusted the estimates with the help of the paymaster general, the draft budget and the annual economic survey are presented as the Finance Bill to the Riksdag at its formal opening on January 10. After a general debate the bill is then referred to two committees: the Committee on Supply for expenditures, and the Committee on Ways and Means for revenues. In late April or early May, the government submits a supplementary finance bill, which incorporates additional bills, revised estimates of revenues and a revised economic survey. By the end of May the Riksdag decides on the final version of

```
┌─────────────────────────────────────────────────┐
│         BALANCE OF PAYMENTS, 1987 ($ million)    │
│                                                  │
│  Current account balance: –873                   │
│  Merchandise exports: 44,003                     │
│  Merchandise imports: –39,537                    │
│  Trade balance: 4,466                            │
│  Other goods, services & income +: 12,224        │
│  Other goods, services & income – : –16,170      │
│  Other goods, services & income net: —           │
│  Private unrequited transfers: –379              │
│  Official unrequited transfers: –1,014           │
│  Direct investment: –2,843                       │
│  Portfolio investment: –2,346                    │
│  Other long-term capital: 4,490                  │
│  Other short-term capital: 1,242                 │
│  Net errors & omissions: –480                    │
│  Counterpart items: 741                          │
│  Exceptional financing: 1,693                    │
│  Liabilities constituting foreign                │
│     authorities reserves: —                      │
│  Total change in reserves: –1,624                │
└─────────────────────────────────────────────────┘
```

the budget. Additional Budget I may be approved during the autumn session and Additional Budget II during the following spring session.

The budget consists of two parts: the current budget and the capital budget. The budget is by tradition very detailed, indicating how and under what conditions each sum will be used. Formerly such details were used to check royal power, but they continue to control the subordinate administrative agencies, which are nominally independent of the government. Such control is normally exercised by specifying the type of grant to which an agency is eligible. There are three types of grants:

- Proposed grant *(forslaganslag)*, which must be spent during the year, but more money than has been granted can be spent with authorization from the king. This type of grant accounts for 75% of the budget.
- Reserved grant *(Reservationsanslag)*, the total of which may not be exceeded but that may remain unused one year and reserved for expenditure the following year.
- Unmarked grant *(obetecknade)*, a grant that may neither be exceeded during the year nor reserved for the next year.

After the budget has been passed the king issues authorizations to the various branches of the administration to spend the money as granted by the Riksdag.

The two major characteristics of fiscal policy are its traditional use to effect income redistribution and the high rate of government consumption. Greater reliance on the annual budget as an instrument of fiscal policy has led to mount-

```
┌─────────────────────────────────────────────────┐
│            GROSS DOMESTIC PRODUCT, 1985           │
│                                                   │
│  GDP nominal (national currency): 662.5 billion   │
│  GDP real (national currency): 574.2 billion (in 1980 prices) │
│  GNP per capita ($): 11,860                        │
│  Average annual growth rate of GDP, 1980–85: 1.3% │
│                                                   │
│  GDP by type of expenditure (%)                   │
│     Consumption                                   │
│        Private: 50                                │
│        Government: 28                             │
│     Gross domestic investment: 18                 │
│     Gross domestic saving: 21                     │
│                                                   │
│     Foreign trade                                 │
│        Exports: 36                                │
│        Imports: –32                               │
│                                                   │
│  Cost components of GDP (%)                        │
│     Net indirect taxes: 11                         │
│     Consumption of fixed capital: 12              │
│     Compensation of employees: 58                 │
│     Net operating surplus: 19                      │
│                                                   │
│  Sectoral origin of GDP (%)                        │
│     Primary                                       │
│        Agriculture: 3                             │
│        Mining: —                                  │
│                                                   │
│     Secondary                                     │
│        Manufacturing: 22                          │
│        Construction: 7                            │
│        Public utilities: 3                        │
│     Tertiary                                      │
│        Transportation and communications: 6      │
│        Trade: 11                                  │
│        Finance: 12                                │
│        Other services: 15                         │
│        Government: 22                             │
│                                                   │
│  Average annual sectoral growth rates (1980–86) (%) │
│                                                   │
│     Agriculture: 2.5                              │
│     Industry: 2.5                                 │
│     Manufacturing: 2.3                            │
│     Services: 0.5                                 │
└─────────────────────────────────────────────────┘
```

ing deficits, especially in the first half of the 1980s. This also applies to municipalities, whose activities are not regulated in detail by law. Although the central government budget deficit diminished slightly, from Skr43.3 billion in 1984 to Skr32.5 billion in 1986, the municipal sector showed a deficit of Skr5.2 billion for the latter year. The Social Security sector showed a deficit of Skr24 billion as a result of accumulation of funds for the supplementary pen-

OFFICIAL DEVELOPMENT ASSISTANCE

In $ Million

1965	1970	1975	1980	1982	1983	1984	1985	1986	1987
38	117	566	962	987	754	741	840	1,090	1,337

As Percentage of GNP

1965	1970	1975	1980	1982	1983	1984	1985	1986	1987
0.19	0.38	0.82	0.78	1.02	0.84	0.80	0.86	0.85	0.84

sion program. The overall deficit in the public sector was Skr14 billion, corresponding to 1.4% of the GDP. A significant portion of the deficit is accounted for by interest payments on the national debt, estimated at 20% of total public spending in 1986, as against 9% in 1980.

Indirect taxes are the chief sources of revenue for the central government. In 1986 indirect taxes totaled Skr150 billion, corresponding to 50% of total revenues. Another 23% comes from direct taxes and 15% from Social Security contributions. The local governments obtain 55% of their revenues from taxes on income and property and 25% from state transfers. These state transfers are of four kinds: (1) equalization grants to municipalities with a low tax base, (2) compensation for loss of taxes, (3) grants-in-aid for specific municipal activities and (4) investment grants. In the social services sector, contributions from employers and employees make up the bulk of the income, estimated at 60% in 1986. Interest income for the National Pension Insurance Fund amounted to SrK31 billion in the same year.

The high marginal tax rates for middle-income earners have necessitated repeated adjustments of income-tax brackets, including indexation against inflation. An adjustment of tax scales was phased in between 1983 and 1985, cutting the marginal tax rate to some 50% for 90% of all income-earners while at the same time restricting interest payment deductions, especially on home mortgages. There is an extensive black economy estimated at between 10% and 20% of the Swedish GDP. The asymmetries in the tax system also invite tax avoidance and evasion.

In January 1987 the government presented proposals for a sweeping tax reform, including:

- simplification of the tax schedule to three marginal rates, with a top rate of 60%
- widening the income tax base by eliminating some deductions
- introduction of incentives to save, and taxing income from capital and capital gains more equitably
- extension of the VAT base—currently 19% of the price, including tax—which now covers only 70% of consumer spending

These changes are not expected to change the overall tax burden.

CENTRAL GOVERNMENT EXPENDITURES, 1986
(% of total expenditures)

Defense: 6.6
Education: 8.9
Health: 1.1
Housing, Social Security, welfare: 51.8
Economic services: 6.8
Other: 24.8
Total expenditures as % of GNP: 44.1
Overall surplus or deficit as % of GNP: –2.6

CENTRAL GOVERNMENT REVENUES, 1986
(% of total current revenues)

Taxes on income, profit and capital gain: 16.0
Social Security contributions: 29.8
Domestic taxes on goods and services: 29.6
Taxes on international trade and transactions: 0.5
Other taxes: 8.3
Current nontax revenue: 15.8
Total current revenue as % of GNP: 41.1
Government consumption as % of GNP: 27
Annual growth rate of government consumption
(1980–86):
1.5

CURRENCY & BANKING

The Swedish monetary unit is the krona (plural: kronor), divided into 100 ore. Coins are issued in denominations of 5, 10, 25 and 50 ore and 1 and 5 kronor, and notes in denominations of 5, 10, 50, 100, 1,000 and 10,000 kronor.

Credit market institutions fall into two main categories: banking institutions, which receive deposits from public and make principally short-term loans; and capital market-institutions, whose long-term lending is financed by either public or private insurance savings or by borrowed funds, such as bond issues. Apart from the Bank of Sweden, the central bank, there are three types of banks: commercial, savings and cooperative banks, accounting for 62%, 31% and 8%, respectively, of total bank deposits. As a result of amendments to banking legislation in 1969, the various types of banks are permitted to operate in identical areas, with the result that structural differences among them are becoming less pronounced. Customers may use not only the 3,500 bank branches but also, for certain services, the 2,160 post offices.

The major capital-market institutions are the National Pension Insurance Fund, the Swedish Investment Bank, insurance companies, mortgage institutions for housing and shipping, and some specialized credit institutions for export credits and long-term credits. These institutions act as financial intermediaries—i.e. they procure capital by borrowing in the long-term market.

The year 1986 was a landmark in the history of Swedish banking, as a result of Sweden opening its borders to foreign banks. Some limited foreign participation in the banking sector was permitted even before 1986. In 1973 an amendment to the Bank Act allowed foreign banks to open branches in Sweden, but only in 1986 were they authorized to establish subsidiaries in the country.

EXCHANGE RATE OF KRONA per U.S. Dollar						
1982	1983	1984	1985	1986	1987	1988
7.294	8.001	8.989	7.615	6.819	5.848	5.983

The Swedish credit market is regulated by statute. All banks are chartered for renewable 10-year terms and subject to the inspection of the Central Bank Inspection Board, which audits the bank's accounts, examines loan commitments and compiles statistical information. Since 1971 all commercial banks have had government-appointed directors on their central boards as well as on regional and local boards. Employees also are entitled to appoint certain directors to these boards. In 1985 government approval was made mandatory for the appointment of bank chairmen.

The Bank of Sweden, founded in 1668, is the oldest central bank in the world. The bank is charged with monitoring the credit sector as well as formulating and implementing monetary policy. Until the end of the 1970s the bank followed conventional monetary policies, emphasizing low-interest rates. However, as financial imbalances appeared by the early 1980s, the bank began to follow a more active policy, characterized by greater adaptation to the market and deregulation. The bank has increasingly resorted to open market operations and specific measures to control interest-rate trends.

Like the Bank of Sweden, the National Debt Office is subordinate to the Riksdag. The National Debt Office finances the public deficit. In recent years it has become the largest borrower in the credit market, and since 1977 it also has been a large borrower in the international capital market.

There are 20 commercial banks in Sweden, with a total of 1,300 branches. Of these, the top four account for 80% of the assets: PKbanken, Skandinaviska Enskilda Banken, and Svenska Handelsbanken cover all Sweden, while Götabanken serves southern and central Sweden. Well over half the commercial bank deposits originate from private individuals. Commercial banks are not permitted to grant loans for periods exceeding one year, but loans may be renewed and thus, in practice, be viewed as long-term. Since 1980 commercial banks have been permitted to raise long-term funds by issuing bonds. They also may assist in long-term business financing by acting as underwriters in the sale of stocks and bonds. The Bank Act does not, however, allow banks to buy common stocks for their own portfolios. The deposit business of the commercial banks includes current accounts (which, unlike in Anglo-Saxon countries, are interest-bearing), savings accounts and time deposit accounts with varying terms and interest rates. Since 1980 commercial banks have been allowed to issue certificates of deposit (CD). Commercial bank checks play a dominant role in payment transactions, and they may be cashed in a bank different from the one on which it is drawn. Since 1987 a further amendment to the Bank Act has made it possible for Swedish banks to open branches abroad.

The traditional function of the savings banks is to promote personal savings. The act governing them stipulates that the bank's capital must be contributed by its founders but may be repaid if and when sufficient reserves have been accumulated. Thus they have no share capital. As a result of mergers the number of savings banks has fallen sharply, from 450 at the beginning of the 1950s to 130 by 1986, and it is expected to fall to 70. The savings banks jointly own a commercial bank, Sparbankernas Bank, which acts as a central bank for them. Savings bank deposits are largely in the form of time deposits. Their lending has been directed mainly toward local long-term capital requirements, primarily for housing, agriculture, small-scale industry and municipalities. However, following the bank legislation of 1969, their activities have grown more and more similar to those of the commercial banks, and their range of services has widened.

Cooperative banks operate as economic associations, and their equity capital consists of the members' invested capital and retained profits. Called Rural Credit Societies until 1974, they originally performed banking services for farmers. There are 389 local cooperative banks with 695 branch offices, grouped into 12 regional banks. At the top is the central administrative body, the Federation of Swedish Cooperative Banks and a commercial bank, the Foreningsbankernas Bank. The number of cooperative bank members is over 600,000. Total bank deposits in 1986 amounted to Skr32 billion and advances to Skr23 billion.

Finance companies have been established in Sweden since the mid-1960s, grew rapidly in the 1970s and now number 244, with a total outstanding credit of Skr84 billion in 1986.

Since saving for insurance is fairly widespread, insurance companies play an important role in the capital market. There are about 500 domestic insurance companies and 50 foreign insurance companies. Most of the companies are very small, and only about 60 operate nationwide. Here, too, the degree of concentration is high, and a few companies dominate the market. The insurance companies administer capital totaling Skr260 billion invested in prime bonds, bank deposits or promissory notes secured by first mortgages on property. One-tenth of the fund may be invested in other assets, though not in shares. They may acquire shares in an individual company up to only 10% of total voting power.

The National Pension Insurance Fund, set up in 1970 to receive supplementary pension contributions from employers for their employees, administers a fund valued at Skr270 billion. The fund thus has a dominating influence on the capital market, holding about one-quarter of the total amount of bonds. The fund is governed by four separate boards, one of which was established in 1974 to acquire shares in Swedish companies.

There are other specialized credit institutions, such as mortgage companies, which finance their lending by issuing bonds or by borrowing in other ways. Among the 24 such specialized institutions, 12 are in the housing sector, nine in the business sector and three in the local authorities sector. In 1962 AB Svensk Exportkredit was set up by the commercial banks and the state jointly to finance Swedish exports at competitive market rates. State guarantees in connection with export credits are given by the Swedish Export Credit Guarantee Board.

The state-owned Swedish Investment Bank was established in 1967 to finance relatively large and risky industrial projects. To a certain extent the bank is permitted to acquire equity in other companies. Loans to the housing sector have been granted since 1985 by the StatensBostadsfinansierings AB. In addition, the government grants credit from a number of loan funds that obtain capital through the national budget. These include the National Board of Educational Assistance and the Industrial Loans Fund.

Starting virtually from scratch in 1980, a thriving money market has emerged in Sweden. Initially finance companies began issuing promissory notes at rates above the traditional bank-deposit rates for large deposits on special terms. Later, in 1980, banks were permitted to issue certificates of deposit and the commercial banks and some other banks quoted buying and selling rates for this new instrument. The real takeoff for the money market was the introduction of a new short-term, market-rate government instrument—the Treasury Discount Note—in 1982. It attracted from the start a wide range of investors, with banks, stockbrokers and new specialized institutions acting as market-markers. The government has since relied heavily on this instrument for its domestic financing, and it is frequently used by the central bank for its open-market operations. The booming trade in government securities has stimulated the creation of new instruments for other borrowers as well. Nonfinancial companies and municipalities have begun to issue commercial papers. Another new money-market instrument is the interest option—i.e., buying and selling ("call" and "put") options with government bonds as underlying securities. Forward trading and interest swaps also have developed rapidly.

As the Swedish credit market has become increasingly integrated with the international market, regulations on banks' and customers' forward trading in currencies have been liberalized. For example, banks are able to finance foreign assets in Swedish kronor without a currency risk by borrowing corresponding sums on demand.

The bond market originated in Sweden in the 1830s with bond loans issued first by mortgage funds and then by the state. Today these two sectors account for 90% of bond borrowing, and companies account for only 6.11%. On the lenders' side, the market is dominated by the National Pension Insurance Fund as well as banks and insurance companies. Rapid developments in the bond market have given greater scope for borrowers other than the state and the housing sector. These include adjustment of interest on bond loans after a certain number of years, abolition of liquidity ratios and easing of restrictions on issues, and lifting of ceilings on lending. Another step toward deregulation was taken in 1986 when the general investment obligation for the National Pension Insurance Fund and the insurance companies was abolished. This meant that all new bonds were issued at market rate. The deregulation has intensified competition in the market and stimulated creation of a secondhand bond market.

The stock market is dominated by the Stockholm Stock Exchange, the country's only stock exchange. It has 31 members, of whom 13 are banks and 18 are stockbrokerage firms. Altogether there are about 40 registered stockbrokers, of which 13 are banks and 14 are limited companies. At present 158 companies are listed on the exchange, of which 116 are on the AI list and 42 on the AII list. AI companies have a share capital of at least SEK10 million and at least 1,000 shareholders with round lots. In addition, there is an unofficial listing and an over-the-counter market. in addition to A and B shares, warrants, convertibles and other instruments are traded. Brokerage commission is determined by the market. The cost of trading also is affected by a turnover tax of 1%, introduced in 1984.

Between 1979 and 1986 daily turnover rose from SEK2 billion to SEK142 billion. Share prices also have risen rapidly—by 60% in 1980, 35% in 1982, 65% in 1983 and 50% in 1986. The Swedish market for options has, in a short time, become one of the largest in the world, with up to 40,000 contracts bought and sold daily. In 1986 index options—call and put options based on an index of the 30 shares with the highest turnover—also were introduced. Investment in the exchange is increasingly dominated by large institutions, such as the Fourth National Pension Insurance Fund, wage earner funds, insurance companies and mutual funds. Foreign investment in Swedish shares also is significant.

Monetary policy. In support of a growth-oriented full-employment policy, Swedish financial markets were among the most regulated in Europe. A cornerstone of the system was credit rationing by channeling funds to priority sectors, such as government expenditures and housing. To protect the low Swedish interest rate level, strict exchange controls were maintained. Allocation of credit was guided by liquidity quotas, investment quotas and lending ceilings, all determined by the central bank. The system worked well during the 1950s and 1960s; monetary policy worked countercyclically, and the exchange rate of the krona remained unchanged.

However, with the disturbances triggered by the first oil shock bringing higher and more variable inflation and widely fluctuating interest and exchange rates, the system began to show strains. A gray financial market developed where finance companies charged interest higher than official rates. Commercial banks began to circumvent interest rate regulation by setting up finance houses themselves. In 1978 the banks were given full freedom to set interest rates on deposit accounts, but in practice these remained linked to the central bank discount rate. Since 1970, however, banks have been free to offer a "preferential interest rate" to principal depositors. These so-called deposits on special terms or prime rate deposits expanded relatively quickly, so that by 1984 about 20% of total deposits were earning a market-oriented interest rate. By this time a considerable amount of the credit flows in the economy took place outside the system. Another feature of this development was that financing the increasing deficits of the public sector was straining the rigid credit market to its limits. Every time the government deficit increased, the obligation to buy housing and government bonds by banks and insurance institutions also was raised.

FINANCIAL INDICATORS, 1987

International reserves minus gold: $6.551 billion
  SDRs: 320
    Reserve position in IMF: 310
    Foreign exchange: $5.921 billion
Gold (million fine troy oz.): 6.069
Ratio of external debt to total reserves: N.A.

Central bank
Assets (%):
  Foreign assets: 32.7
  Claims on government: 64.3
  Claims on bank: 2.9
  Claims on private sector: —

```
┌─────────────────────────────────────────────┐
│        FINANCIAL INDICATORS, 1987 (continued) │
│  Liabilities (%):                             │
│     Reserve money: 47.6                       │
│     Government deposits: —                    │
│     Foreign liabilities: 1.3                  │
│     Capital accounts: —                       │
│  Money supply                                 │
│  Stock in billion national currency: 85       │
│  M¹ per capita: 10,155                        │
│  U.S. liabilities to: $2.907 billion          │
│  U.S. claims on: $2.152 billion               │
│  Private banks                                │
│  Assets (%):                                  │
│     Loans to government: 8.0                   │
│     Loans to private sector: 79.2              │
│     Reserves: 1.3                              │
│     Foreign assets: 11.4                       │
│  Liabilities: deposits, SKr594.8 billion      │
│     of which (%)                              │
│     Demand deposits:                          │
│     Savings deposits:         75.6            │
│     Government deposits:                      │
│     Foreign liabilities: 24.4                 │
└─────────────────────────────────────────────┘
```

FINANCIAL INDICATORS, 1987 (continued)

Liabilities (%):
   Reserve money: 47.6
   Government deposits: —
   Foreign liabilities: 1.3
   Capital accounts: —

Money supply
Stock in billion national currency: 85
M^1 per capita: 10,155
U.S. liabilities to: $2.907 billion
U.S. claims on: $2.152 billion

Private banks
Assets (%):
   Loans to government: 8.0
   Loans to private sector: 79.2
   Reserves: 1.3
   Foreign assets: 11.4
Liabilities: deposits, SKr594.8 billion
   of which (%)
   Demand deposits: ⎫
   Savings deposits: ⎬   75.6
   Government deposits:
   Foreign liabilities: 24.4

The process of deregulation began in 1978 with abolition of interest rate regulation on household deposits, followed in 1980 by abolition of controls on the issuing rates for private bonds. Quantitative controls on new issues finally were abandoned in 1983, causing a sixfold increase in the net issue of bonds by enterprises in just one year. In 1983 the liquidity quotas on housing and government bonds also were abolished. In 1986 the quantitative investment limits for priority bonds were completely withdrawn along with the banks' lending ceilings. The establishment of a money market was greatly facilitated by the introduction of two new instruments: the bank certificate of deposit in 1980, and the Treasury discount note in 1982. The latter quickly dominated the market. Their large quantities and regular issues created a good basis for secondary trading, and their short maturity and low risk made them even more attractive. This was followed by introduction of the coupon bonds, with maturities of up to seven years. The sophistication of the financial system was further enhanced by the establishment of interest rate auctions for government discount note bills and government papers. With the entry of foreign banks and the lifting of controls on finance houses in 1985, the domestic financial markets are now completely deregulated.

The Bank of Sweden adheres to an exchange rate fixed to a basket of currencies of major trading partners. Exchange controls also have been successively relaxed, but these have taken place at a considerably slower pace than credit market controls and they still remain among the most stringent in the OECD area.

AGRICULTURE

Arable area is limited to about 3 million ha. (7.41 million ac.), or about 7% of the land area. The climatological conditions for farming vary greatly between the North and the South of Sweden. Farmers in the southern coastal regions cultivate a wide range of crops, such as wheat and sugar beets. Bread grains and grass for fodder are cultivated in the plains of central Sweden. A large proportion of the northern farms are devoted to fodder.

GROWTH PROFILE (Annual Growth Rates, %)

Population, 1986–2000: 0.0
Crude birth rate, 1985–90: 10.2
Crude death rate, 1985–90: 12.3
Urban population, 1980–85: 1.2
Labor force, 1985–2000: 0.3
GNP, 1973–86: 1.3
GNP per capita, 1973–86: 1.1
GDP, 1980–86: 2.0
Inflation, 1980–86: 8.2
Agriculture, 1980–86: 2.5
Industry, 1980–86: 2.5
Manufacturing, 1980–86: 2.3
Services, 1980–86: 0.5
Money holdings, 1980–85: N.A.
Manufacturing earnings per employee, 1980–85: –0.3
Energy production, 1980–86: 7.7
Energy consumption, 1980–86: 2.4
Exports, 1980–86: 5.7
Imports, 1980–85: 4.0
General government consumption, 1980–86: 1.5
Private consumption, 1980–86: 1.1
Gross domestic investment, 1980–86: 1.2

The proportion of the labor force employed in agriculture fell from about 20% in 1950 to 4% in 1986. About half of the farmers run the farms on a part-time basis.

The value of agricultural production in 1985 was estimated at Skr25 billion, about three-quarters coming from animal products and the rest from vegetable products. In the 1980s the agricultural share of the GDP has remained relatively stable, at 2%. At the same time, productivity has risen on the farms, and the agricultural value added has risen by over 2% annually since 1970, even as the number of hours worked has fallen by about 4% annually in the same period.

Swedish farms have grown fewer in number but larger. Between 1980 and 1984 the number of farms with 2–20 ha. (4.94–49.4 ac.) of arable land decreased by about 6,000. There are over 112,000 holdings with more than 2 ha. of arable land. About 60% of them have less than 20 ha. of cropland, while over 3% have over 100 ha. (247 ac.). But about 80% of the cropland belongs to farms of over 20 ha. Farming is preeminently a family enterprise. Nevertheless, more than 40% of the total farming acreage is leased. Farmers have a high average age, as most young rural people are leaving the farms to find work in towns.

About three-fourths of the harvest consists of fodder. Animal production accounts for about 80% of a farmer's income. Cattle are the most important type of livestock. There are 1.5 million head of cattle, including 650,000 dairy cows. Most herds are small. The average yield per cow in 1983 was about 8,000 kg. (17,637 lb.) of milk. The pig herd totals 2.6 million. Producers of large herds of over 500 pigs accounts for about 44% of the total number of pigs, although they represent only 5% of the total number of producers. Egg production is being taken over by large, specialized units. Sheep farming is an alternative to beef stock. The two principal types of sheep are white sheep for meat and gray pelt sheep for early fleece as well as meat.

Under the general direction of the Ministry of Agriculture, agricultural policy is managed by two central authorities, the National Board of Agriculture and the National Agricultural Market Board. Through the County Agricultural Boards, the former oversees both farming and livestock. The latter is the central administrative authority for price controls and marketing in the agricultural sector. Legislation on agriculture and food is extensive, including policy guidelines laid down in 1947, 1967 and 1985. One important objective is to ensure farmers a standard of living equivalent to that of comparable groups, and consumers high-quality food at reasonable prices. Government support mostly takes the form of protection for domestic production and financial aid for rationalization. For the former, levies are applied on imported agricultural products. Government credit guarantees are extended to promote rationalization of structural features of the sector. In recent years there have been large surpluses of animal products, especially pork and milk, owing to declining consumption and a continued rise in production. The surplus is exported at a discount, subsidized by the state. Agricultural products are priced through central agreements between the government and the Federation of Swedish Farmers (LRF). To limit consumer food price increases, the government began to subsidize basic food products in 1973. For fiscal 1985–86 these subsidies amounted to Skr3 billion. The milk subsidies were abolished in 1987.

Basic training in agriculture, forestry and horticulture is an integral part of secondary education, comprising two-year lines of study followed by specialized courses. Higher studies are pursued at the Swedish University of Agricultural Sciences at Uppsala. The certificate program lasts five years and the masters six years.

Producer cooperatives for agricultural credit and supplies and for marketing agricultural produce are an integral part of Swedish farming. Altogether some 75% of agricultural output passes through these cooperatives. Agricultural cooperation, the antecedents of which date back to the 19th century, is based on single-purpose societies that cover 15 different branches, the most important of these being dairy production, meat production, forestry, supplies and credits. The local associations are grouped into primary district-level societies, which are grouped into national federations. The Federation of Swedish Farmers is the lead organization of the cooperative movement, which today covers 800 societies and 1,400 establishments throughout the country, with an annual turnover of Skr40 billion.

Although Sweden is not primarily a fishing nation, ample herring stocks in the North Sea led to a brief surge of activity in the 1950s and early 1960s. After a record catch of 400,000 tons in 1964, landed fish yields have decreased considerably, to an annual average of 200,000 tons. The two most important fish species are herring and Baltic herring, which together account for almost half the catch. Cod is next, with about 52,000 tons annually, although it it more profitable than the other two species combined in value. The geographical locus of the fishing industry is shifting to the Baltic Sea, but the western coast still accounts for about 50% of the yield. Employment in fishing has declined to about 3,800 compared with 7,500 in the mid-1960s. Approximately 10% of the catch is auctioned, and over half is exported. However, the volume of imports greatly exceeds that of exports.

Forests cover 23.4 million ha. (57.8 million ac.) and account for 57% of the total Swedish land area and just under 1% of the world's forests. Two-thirds are in the northern temperate coniferous belt, while the southern part belongs to the temperate mixed forests. There are few tree species. The growing stock of forest land has risen throughout this century, and Sweden has never had as many forests as it has now. Annual growth is about 85 million cu. m. (3 billion cu. ft.) and fellings are about 65 million cu. m. (2.3 billion cu. ft.). In the extreme South the rotation period lasts about 70 years; in the extreme North, about 140 years.

Of the woodlands, 25% are owned by forest companies, 26% by the state and 40% by private individuals. Most of the public forests are owned by the state, mostly in the North, while the rest are owned by municipalities and the church.

Most of the company forests are in central Sweden. Eleven large companies own about 90% of the company forests, of which Svenska Cellulosa AB is the largest, with 1.7 million ha. (4.2 million ac.). Private ownership is predominant in southern Sweden, where there are 240,000 holdings, half of which are run in combination with farming.

The Forestry Act provides the framework of fundamental public regulations for forest management. It regulates the establishment of stands, cutting, nature conservation and measures for combating insect damage. As in Norway and Finland, Sweden has a "common access prerogative," which means that everyone may walk freely in the woods, meadows and fields and pick wild berries, flowers and mushrooms. The chief responsibility for the administration of forest policy, including grants, advisory services and education, is vested in the Swedish Forestry Administration of the Ministry of Agriculture. This office comprises the National Board of Forestry and 22 county forestry boards. The National Forest Enterprise, under the Ministry of Industry, is a trading agency that administers the state's woodland and farm holdings. It collaborates with ASSI, the State Forest Industries, which runs an extensive forest industry business. Forestry know-how is marketed by a state forest service firm, Swedforest. Other associations in this sector are the National Federation of Swedish Forest Owners, the Forestry Society and the Swedish Forestry Association. Programs of forestry education are provided by 26 secondary schools, the National School for Forest Technicians and the Faculty of Forestry of the National University of Agricultural Sciences. Forestry research is conducted at this university as well as at the Institute for Forest Improvement, the Forest Operations Institute and the Swedish Forest Products Research Laboratory.

AGRICULTURAL INDICATORS, 1986

Agriculture's share of GDP: 3% (1986)
Average annual growth rate: 2.5% (1980–86)
Value added in agriculture: $3.840 billion (1986)
Cereal imports (000 tons): 140 (1986)
Index of agricultural production (1983–85) (1979–81=100): 107
Index of food production (1983–85) (1979–81=100): 107
Index of food production per capita: (1984–86) (1979–81=100): 109
Number of tractors: 190,000 (1985)
Number of harvester-threshers: 48,900
Total fertilizer consumption: 456,400 tons
Fertilizer consumption per ha. (per ac.) (100 gr.) 1,406 (569)
Number of farms: 106,000
Average size of holding ha. (ac.): 27.4 (67.7)
Size class (%)

AGRICULTURAL INDICATORS, 1986 *(continued)*
Below 1 ha. (below 2.47 ac.): insignificant
1–5 ha. (2.47–12.35 ac.): 16.3
5–10 ha. (12.35–24.7 ac.): 20.1
10–20 ha. (24.7–49.4 ac.): 22.2
20–50 ha. (49.4–123.5 ac.): 27.6
50–200 ha. (123.5–494 ac.):
Over 200 ha. (over 494 ac.): 13.8

Tenure (%)
  Owner-operated: 47.8
  Rented: 16.1
  Other: 36.1

Activity (%)
  Mainly crops: 46.0
  Mainly livestock:
  Mixed: 54.0
% of farms using irrigation: 1.8

Farms as % of total land area: 19

Total area under cultivation: 8,558,000 ha.
(21,146,000 ac.)

Land use (%): total cropland, 31.8
  Permanent crops: 0.2
  Temporary crops: 96.4
  Fallow: 3.4
  Meadows and pastures: 6.3
  Woodland: 50.6
  Other: 11.2

Yields kg/ha. (lb./ac.)
  Grains: 3,821 (3,410)
  Roots and tubers: 36,286 (32,387)
  Pulses: 2,548 (2,274)
  Milk kg.(lb.)/animal: 5,749 (12,674)

Livestock (000)
  Cattle: 1,779
  Horses: 57
  Sheep: 434
  Pigs: 2,410

Forestry
Production of roundwood: 53,339 million cu m.
  of which industrial roundwood %: 91.7
Value of exports ($ 000): 4,930,038
Fishing
Total catch (000 tons): 247.6
  of which marine %: 95.6
Value of exports ($ 000): 80,714

Productivity in forestry rose steeply in the 1960s but fell dramatically in the 1970s. In recent years annual production growth has been approximately 1%. Employment also has declined, to 1%. Unfavorable prices, low profitability and high marginal rates have depressed the sector.

The forestry sector, including forest industries, had a production value in 1985 of SEK87 billion, of which SEK26.5 billion were value added by manufacture, representing 4.5% of the GDP at producer prices. Forest industry products account for 18% of gross exports and over 50% of net imports.

MANUFACTURING

In the 1980s Sweden is undergoing a second industrial revolution. There is a gradual shift from the traditional sunset industries, such as shipbuilding, steel and textiles, to more advanced products with sophisticated technology, such as transportation equipment, electronics, electrical equipment and chemicals. The sector also is emerging from a decade of restructuring, in which its share of the GDP fell from 34% to 31.8% and industrial employment fell from 28% to 20%. Industrial profitability is again comparable to the prosperous years before 1975.

The transformation of Swedish industry into a knowledge-intensive one is accompanied by the changing composition of Swedish exports. Here the dominance of engineering is even more marked. Engineering products accounted for 42% of total exports in 1985 compared with 25% in 1950. On the other hand, exports have declined in raw-material–based industries such as paper, wood and pulp, whose share fell from 30% in 1950 to less than 17% in 1985. Another characteristic of the new industrial structure is the dominance of larger firms as well as greater concentration of production. Small units have closed down, and the more efficient ones have grown bigger. Between 1950 and 1985 the number of production establishments in the manufacturing sector fell from 16,000 to 9,000, while at the same time the proportion of employees working in establishments with over 1,000 employees rose from 20% to 22% of total employment. International competition ensured the survival of the fittest, which invariably were the largest.

The largest industrial city is Stockholm; several other manufacturing centers lie within 201 km. (125 mi.) of the capital, such as Västerås, Uppsala, Norrköping, Örebro, Köping, Gävle and Eskilstuna. Göteborg is the site of large shipyards and produces a wide range of industrial machinery and petrochemicals. Another major industrial zone is centered around Malmö and nearby cities such as Hälsingborg, Borås, Jönköping, Karlstad, Lund, and Halmstad.

Statistics on ownership and control of manufacturing do not support Sweden's reputation as a socialist economy. Private enterprise dominates the sector, accounting for 90% of industrial employment. The share of the private sector is 99% in shipping and textiles, 98% in engineering, 95% of forest industries, 94% of steel and metalworking, 93% of banking and 83% of retail trade. Not only is the economy overwhelmingly private but it is also dominated by a few large firms, as proved by the government Commission on Concentration. Antimonopoly legislation came rather late to Sweden and still is not very stringent. Like most West European countries, Sweden is generally tolerant of cartels, monopolies and oligopolies.

The 100 largest firms are responsible for about half of the country's production, and the 20 largest account for about one-third. The 10 largest Swedish firms are as follows (all of them are multinationals):

MAJOR SWEDISH COMPANIES
Operations in Sweden and Abroad

Company	1984 sales, billion Skr	Number of Employees
Volvo (machinery, espec. cars)	87.0	68,600
Axel Johnson Group (conglomerate)	41.6	30,100
Asea (machinery)	36.1	58,400
Electrolux (machinery)	35.0	89,500
Ericsson (electronics)	29.7	74,300
Kooperativa Förbundet/ Cooperative Union and Wholesale Society (conglomerate)	26.9	29,100
Saab-Scania (cars, aircraft)	26.0	43,100
ICA (wholesale)	22.5	6,400
JS Saba (wholesale/retail)	18.4	18,100
SKF (machinery)	17.8	43,900

Source:: Veckans Affärer.

Decision-making power within the private sector is even more concentrated and is exercised by some 15 family groups and two investment companies: Industrivarden, tied to Svenska Handelsbanken; and Custos-Safvean, controlled by Skandinaiska Banken. The connection with banks is not accidental, as they form the nucleus of industrial empires in Sweden. These 17 groups have a controlling interest in about 200 enterprises that generate 25% of total manufacturing output. The three largest private fortunes belong to the Bronstrom family (shipping and shipbuilding); the Bonnier family (publishing); and the Wallenberg family, the most powerful of them all, which controls a business empire of some 70 enterprises, including SKF, Asea, Alfa-Laval, Saab-Scania and Electrolux.

The public manufacturing sector is not particularly large and is estimated at about 8%, for the most part confined to specific areas of the economy, including iron ore, forests, water power, atomic energy, and transportation and communications. With one or two exceptions all state enterprises were in operation long before the Social Democrats came to power in 1936 and are not manifestations of socialist doctrine. They are organized either in the form of state trading agencies or as state companies in which the shares are partly or wholly owned by the state. The state trading agencies are referred to as *affarsdrivande verk* (government agencies that conduct business), such as the State Railways. The state companies, on the other hand, are organized as joint stock corporations (*aktiedolag*, AB). There are 11 such companies, engaged in a variety of activities, from liquor and gambling to mining and manufacturing. Together they employ about 81,000 people, or roughly a tenth of the industrial work force, and had 1984 gross sales of Skr49 billion. Most of the enterprises are grouped under Procordia AB (Formerly Statsforetag AB), a group of 30 individual companies. Other state-owned ventures include LKAB (mining), ASSI and NCB (pulp and paper), SSAB (steel), Svenska Varv (shipbuilding), Pripps (brewing) and PKbanken.

OECD countries account for more than 95% of total foreign investment in Sweden. Traditionally the United States was one of the largest investors, accounting for 20% of the total in 1981–85. However, the Nordic countries as a bloc accounted for an even larger proportion, about 40%, during this period. The Nordic share rose to 55% in 1986, with Norway accounting for 26% and Finland for 23% of a total of Skr6.6 billion in 1986. The U.S. share in that year dropped to 10%. In 1985 there were about 2,400-foreign owned companies in Sweden, about half of them in manufacturing. They accounted for 7% of employment in the business sector. Foreign ownership is concentrated in four sectors: wholesaling, engineering, chemicals and food processing.

Foreign investment is a long-standing tradition, first started by Swedish multinationals such as SKF, Sandvik, Electrolux, Ericsson, Swedish Match and Alfa-Laval. In 1986 Swedish companies abroad employed 370,000 persons, more than 30% of total employment in Swedish manufacturing. Foreign manufacturing activity is limited to multinationals; about 17 companies account for 85% of Swedish employment abroad. Somewhat over half the total personnel strength of the large Swedish multinationals are employed abroad, and their production in foreign markets exceeds their exports from Sweden. In the past 20 years Swedish multinationals have grown faster than Swedish industry in general and the multinationals' subsidiaries abroad have performed much better. Manufacturing activity abroad is concentrated in the mechanical and electrical engineering industries, chemicals and transportation equipment. About half of both production and employment abroad are in the EEC, but there are sizable investments in Latin America and an expanding industrial presence in the United States. Since 1981 the number of permits issued for direct investments abroad has risen very steeply, from Skr9 billion in 1982 to Skr35 billion in 1986. Nearly 95% of these investments are within OECD countries. The United States alone accounted for 50% in 1986. During the same period Swedish investment abroad has exceeded foreign investment in Sweden by Skr50 billion. Much of this growth is attributable to the removal of the Central Bank restriction on financing foreign ventures in kronor.

Much of Sweden's industrial dynamism is attributable to substantial investment in research and development. It spends 6% of its industrial output on R&D, placing it second only to the United States with 7.2% and ahead of Japan with 4.3% and France, Great Britain, West Germany and the Netherlands, with 4.5%. In many sectors Swedish R&D has expanded more rapidly than has investment in plant and equipment.

Engineering is the largest sector within manufacturing representing 42% of the industrial value added. Several of the largest industrial companies are in this field, along with over 4,000 other smaller firms. Another characteristic is the large number of subcontractors. Engineering is heavily export-oriented. Close to 70% of its production is exported, accounting for 45% of total Swedish exports. The second-fastest-growing sector is the chemicals industry. In recent years total annual investments in this sector have averaged Skr2 billion, equivalent to 10% of the capital expenditures in the whole manufacturing industry. In 1984 annual sales totaled Skr78 billion, of which 35% was value added. About 45% of the production is exported. The sector employed over 70,000 people in 1984. Pharmaceuticals are the fastest-growing branch within this industry, taking advantage of the high standard of Swedish medical research. Pharmaceuticals are the most research-intensive sector in Swedish manufacturing, with costs equivalent to 35% of value added, compared with the industry average of 9%.

MINING

The Swedish mineral wealth is mainly metal ores. The mining industry accounts for 1% of the market value of total industrial production and employs less than 1% of the total industrial labor force. Sweden accounts for 2% of total world iron ore output, 1.4% of copper, 3.0% of lead and 4% of zinc. Sweden ranks sixth among iron ore exporters of the world.

```
┌─────────────────────────────────────────────┐
│           MANUFACTURING INDICATORS           │
│ Average annual growth rate 1980–86: 2.3%     │
│ Share of GDP: 24.1%                          │
│ Labor force in manufacturing: 28.6%          │
│ Value added in manufacturing: $20.878 billion (1985) │
│    Food & agriculture: 10%                   │
│    Textiles: 2%                              │
│    Machinery: 35%                            │
│    Chemicals: 8%                             │
│ Earnings per employee in manufacturing growth rate: │
│ –0.3% (1980–85)                              │
│    Index (1980=100): 98 (1985)              │
│ Total Earnings as % of value added: 37       │
│ Gross output per employee (1980=100): 124 (1985) │
│ Index of Manufacturing Production (1980=100): 107 │
│ (1984)                                       │
└─────────────────────────────────────────────┘
```

Iron ore production, including pellets, concentrates and ore, amounts to 20 million tons a year. Annual production of sulphide ores is 18 million tons. Large reserves of bituminous shales containing oil and low-grade uranium as well as aluminum, vanadium, molybdenum, nickel, potassium, magnesium, phosphates and sulphur are known and may be of economic importance in the future. Both iron and copper form the basis of the modern Swedish engineering industry. In terms of value, iron ore earns about 1% of Sweden's income from exports. Ores with high phosphoric content make up one-fourth of the total iron ore production in the Lapland mines.

About 80% of the domestic production on nonferrous ores comes from the Boliden Company's fields in central and northern Sweden. Its smelting plant at Ronnskar recovers precious metals, lead, copper, rare metals, arsenic, etc. Zinc metal is not produced in Sweden, and zinc ore concentrate is exported. The production of cooper ore is not sufficient to meet domestic needs, and considerable quantities of the metal are imported in a finished or semiprocessed state. Production volumes of the nonferrous ores have increased continuously and now amount to about the same tonnage as iron ore. Production of zinc and lead is two to three times domestic needs, that of copper 80%, that of gold 100% and that of silver 60%.

The most important iron ore deposits are found in the Kiruna-Malmberget district, with proved reserves of approximately 3 billion tons. The biggest copper mine is also in this district. In the Skellefteå district, extending from Boliden in the East to the highlands in the West, and in the highland belt along the Norwegian border are the sulphide ore deposits. The largest of these is at Laisvall, where the biggest single lead ore mine in Europe is found. Proved reserves of sulphide ores are estimated at 200 million tons, most of them in northern Sweden. Both iron and sulphide ores are also found in the Bergslagen mining district in central Sweden, but only two of its mines, Grangesberg and Dannemora, are still in operation. Nearly all mines are underground, with depths averaging between 300 and 500 m. (984 and 1,641 ft.). Kiruna claims the world's largest underground mine, with an annual capacity of 20 million tons of iron ore.

Except for the Bergslagen mines, which are exploited by private interests, the mining industry is dominated by the state-owned SSAB, which has taken over LKAB, concessionaires of the Kiruna and Malmberget mines. The mining industry is continuously engaged in improving efficiency and economy. Pelletizing capacity has been expanded to over 9 million tons annually.

There is no foreign participation in Swedish mining.

PRODUCTION, IMPORTS, EXPORTS, AND CONSUMPTION OF THE LEADING NONFERROUS METALS, 1985 (in 1,000 tons)				
	Production	Imports	Exports	Consumption
Cooper				
Concentrates (metal content)	92	23	26	
Metal	101	58	51	110
Lead				
Concentrates (metal content by analysis)	76	5	25	
Metal	84	5	65	26
Zinc				
Concentrates (metal content by analysis)	207	—	211	
Metal	—	35	1	34

ENERGY

Sweden's energy situation is characterized by a high level of consumption; negligible supplies of indigenous oil, natural gas and coal; and considerable dependence on imported energy. Energy policy is based on a reduction of imported oil and phasing out of nuclear power for environmental reasons.

OUTPUT OF SWEDISH MINERAL PRODUCTS, 1974–85 (in 1,000 tons)			
	1974	1980	1985
Iron ore products (ore, concentrates, pellets)	36,955	27,184	20,454
Pyrites concentrates	425	396	407
Copper concentrates	168	181	378
Lead concentrates	104	102	113
Zinc concentrates	202	306	388
Fluorspar	4	—	—
Coal	30	—	—
Fireclay and chamotte	225	—	—
Cement	3,323	2,438	2,100
Talc	7	16	14
Apatite	21	88	193
Scheelite	0.8	0.6	0.7

Of the total 1984 energy consumption of 354 terawatt-hours or 30 million tons of oil equivalent, the industrial sector accounts for about 40%; the transportation sector for 20%; and the housing, commercial and service sectors for the remaining 40%. Total primary energy demand amounted to 413 terawatt-hours or 36 million tons of oil equivalent, or four metric tons of oil per capita.

After rising by about 5% in the 1960s, energy demand declined during the 1970s. Oil consumption fell by 2.8% a year between 1973 and 1981, and over the same period the proportion of oil in the total energy supply dropped from 70% to 60%. Energy has been used more and more efficiently since 1973, and its growth rate has been less than one-third of the economic growth rate.

Three factors explain Sweden's relatively high level of energy consumption: heating requirements in a severely cold climate, an energy-intensive industrial sector and the need for long-distance transportation. Heating accounts for 40% of the final energy consumption. Forest products and iron and steel absorb a significant share of the total energy used in industry.

Sweden's reserves of conventional fuels are negligible. There is almost no oil, natural gas or coal. There are sizable reserves of uranium, but the ore is mainly low-grade and is not being mined at present. Reserves of peat are very large. Peat bogs make up 12% of the land area, covering 5.4 million ha. (13.3 million ac.). The estimated fuel content of the reserves is 3,000 million tons of oil equivalent. On the other hand, most of the peat layers are thin, and only a fraction of the peat area can be used for fuel production. Indigenous solid fuels, chiefly peat and forest residues, accounted for 13% of total energy demand in 1984.

Hydroelectric power is the most important source of energy. Average production capacity is 66 terawatt-hours. It is estimated that another 30 Twh of hydroelectric power per annum could be economically harnessed, especially from four unexploited rivers in northern Sweden. In 1984 hydroelectric power accounted for 56% of total electricity production. In the same year, nuclear reactors accounted for 40% of Sweden's electricity production. Total capacity of the 12 reactors, the last two of which went on stream in 1985, is 9,400 MW. The uranium used by these plants is imported, but the fuel rods are made domestically. A central plant for the interim storage of the used nuclear fuel was completed at Oskarshamn in 1985. Electricity is produced by state, municipal or private companies, of which the State Power Board accounts for 50%. The electric power grid has several cross connections with Denmark, Finland and Norway. Limited natural gas supplies are being piped from Denmark. Up to 3 million metric tons of coal are used, most of them going to district heating plants. All the coal is imported, primarily from the Soviet Union, Poland and the United States.

Oil consumption in 1984 was 17 million tons, compared with almost 30 million tons at the beginning of the 1970s. In 1984 total imports of crude oil and oil products were 15 million tons at a cost of SEK27 billion, representing 13% of Swedish imports. In the 1970s imported crude came mainly from OPEC countries. In 1984 only 10% came from OPEC countries and practically none from the Middle East. Instead, the bulk of the imports come from the North Sea, almost 50% from the United Kingdom and 25% from Norway. Refined oil products are imported, mainly from Western Europe and the Soviet Union.

Annual capacity in Swedish refineries is 20 million metric tons. The largest refinery, Scanraff, is jointly owned by the cooperative oil company OK, Texaco and the government-owned Svenska Petroleum AB. BP and Shell also have refineries in Sweden.

The principal goals of Swedish energy policy are outlined in the Energy Bill approved by the Riksdag in 1985. The bill's primary thrust is in the areas of oil substitution, oil reduction, energy conservation, district heating and research into new technology. An important instrument in the search for other sources of energy to replace oil has been the Oil Substitution Fund, which invests in oil-substitution technologies such as heat pumps, solar heating, small hydroelectric plants and boilers that burn domestic fuels. Also of central importance to this policy are energy conservation measures, as a result of which Swedes today consume only two-thirds as much energy per capita as Americans do. Special attention is given to energy-saving programs in housing. District heating, in which water heated in a central place flows through a network of piping to supply many buildings with space heating and hot water, already plays an important part in heating supply. It is highly economical in sufficiently dense settlements and can use alternate energy sources such as waste heat, solar heat, heat pumps and refuse.

As a result of the 1980 referendum on nuclear power, it was decided to complete the present 12-reactor program and use the reactors during their lifetime but then to phase out nuclear power, closing down the last one not later than the year 2010. Radiation protection and environmental regulations are very stringent in Sweden. By making deliberate efforts to achieve more efficient use of electricity, energy planners intend to reduce the need for additional electric power production to replace nuclear energy when it is phased out.

ENERGY INDICATORS, 1986

Total energy production quadrillion BTU:: 1.29
    Crude oil: 0.0
    Natural gas, liquid: 0.0
    Natural gas, dry: 0.0
    Coal: 0.1
    Hydroelectric power: 0.62
    Nuclear power: 0.68
Average annual energy growth rate: 7.7% (1980–86)
Public utilities' shares of GDP: 2.6% (1984)
Energy consumption per capita (kg. (lb.) of oil equivalent):
4,703 (10,368)
Energy imports as % of merchandise imports: 9 (1986)
Average annual growth rate of energy consumption: 2.4%
(1980–86)

Electricity, 1985
    Installed capacity: 3,318,000 kw.
    Production: 136.543 billion kw.-hr.
       % fossil fuel: 4.9
       % hydro: 52.1
       % nuclear: 43.0
    Consumption per capita: 16,165 kw.-hr.

Petroleum
    Consumption: 135 million bbl.
    Refining capacity: 437,000 bbl. per day

Coal
    Reserves: 1 million metric tons
    Production: 12,000 metric tons
    Consumption: 4,143,000 metric tons

LABOR

Over half of Sweden's total population of 8.4 million in 1986 were economically active. The secular employment trend away from farming into industry and later into services has been even more pronounced in the postwar period. In 1985 a total of 35% of the labor force was employed in the production of goods, including construction, compared to 58% in 1960. In the same period, employment in the service sector, including trade and transportation, rose from 41% to 65%. Employment in the public sector also has risen substantially, from 21% in 1965 to 37% in 1986. With very slow population growth and prolonged life expectancy, the economically active 16-to-64 age group constitutes a declining proportion of the total population. However, a large influx of immigrants after World War II added to the labor force. From 1951 to 1984 the average net inflow was 13,000 persons annually, and foreign citizens now make up 5% of all employees. The inflow was particularly marked in the 1960s and in the second half of the 1970s. In the 1980s the flow has turned, and the market experienced a net outflow of some 2,000 workers a year.

The proportion of women in the labor force also increased, to 47% of 2.1 million in 1986. This change was primarily due to the increased participation in the work force of women with preschool children and the training programs offered by the National Labor Market Board to help women break into male-dominated occupations. In 1986 a total of 86% of women with young children were in the labor force. A law against discrimination at work on grounds of sex went into effect in 1980.

For most of the postwar period, the labor market has been characterized by high and stable employment. Politically, employment has been a top priority of the Social Democrat administrations. However, about 24% of the force works only part-time, less than 36 hours per week.

The four Nordic countries—Denmark, Finland, Norway and Sweden—constitute a common labor market. A Nordic citizen wishing to work and settle in another Nordic country needs no work or residence permit. He also receives unemployment insurance benefits and public assistance, including retraining.

According to the Swedish Central Bureau of Statistics, the economy created 44,000 new jobs in 1985 so that the rate of unemployment declined to 2.8%, down from 3.1% during 1984. The average unemployment rate for those aged 20 to 24 was 5.3%; for those aged 16 to 19 it was 4.6%. The number of discouraged workers averaged 36,800, or 2.2% of the population outside the labor force. According to the bureau, 72.3% of the Swedish population between ages 16 and 74 were working or looking for work during 1985. The rate for men was 76.5%; for women, 68.1%. The 2.9% unemployment rate for women remained just slightly above the general rate. Their proportion is highest in the public sector, where they constitute 76% of the payroll. The unemployment rate for aliens is 5.2%, nearly double the national average. They are granted the same wages and unemployment benefits as Swedish citizens, and the great majority of aliens are trade union members.

The Swedish Labor Market Board reported that an average of 178,000 persons, or 4% of the labor force, worked under tax-financed labor market programs and therefore were not included in the unemployment rate. The programs covered those who received wage subsidies as well as those in training courses, youth job corps and relief work. The government provides wage subsidies to private industry and local governments to help defray the costs associated with hiring hard-to-employ and handicapped persons. If those in these programs are counted as unemployed, the unemployment rate would jump to close to 7%. According to a labor market policy research study, an estimated Skr32 billion in 1984–85, or about 4.4% of the GNP, was devoted to these programs.

The Swedish labor market is characterized by strong, centralized organizations that have developed in the past 85 years. The largest of the employer organizations is the Swedish Employers Confederation (SAF), which has some 43,000 member companies organized in 35 employer associations who together represent employers of 1.25 million people, or 35% of all employees. Most SAF members are small firms—over 80% have fewer than 25 employees. However, 138 companies, with over 1,000 employees each, dominate the organization. Other important private sector employer organizations outside the SAF are the Association of Swedish Banking Institutions and the Swedish Newspaper Employers Association. In the public sector the state is represented by the National Agency for Government Employers, county councils by the Federation of Swedish County Councils, municipalities by the Swedish Association of Local Authorities and state-owned enterprises by Employers Association for Companies in Joint Ownership.

Proportionally, Sweden has the highest union membership of any country. An estimated 95% of manual workers and 75% of white-collar employees belong to unions, including the police, the military and the clergy. Although national and local unions share in the organizational leadership, power is vested in the national federations. Pension and strike funds, etc., are centralized, and money can be disbursed from them only with the consent of the national executive board.

The largest of the trade unions is the Confederation of Swedish Trade Unions (LO), with 2.3 million members, including about 85% of all blue-collar workers. It is a highly centralized federation of 24 trade unions, of which the largest are the Municipal Workers' Union, with 633,000 workers, and the Metalworkers' Union, with 460,000 workers. The national agreements signed by the SAF and the LO are administered locally by union officials, or ombudsmen, who also take part in negotiating supplementary local agreements. The LO has long stressed the principle of wage solidarity and has succeeded in reducing wage spread. If a strike threatens and more than 3% of the members of an affiliated union are involved, the strike must be sanctioned by the LO. The affiliated unions have comparable powers over their constituents. Although members of local unions are consulted in the formulation of union demands prior to the beginning of negotiations, there is no tradition of seeking membership ratification of the final agreement. Votes to strike are only advisory.

The second-largest union is the Central Organization of Salaried Employees (TCO), with 24 affiliates and over 1 million members. The TCO is decentralized federation, with most responsibilities lodged in its affiliated unions. The TCO does not engage in collective bargaining but functions primarily as a coordinating and information agency. It works with the LO on labor policies but opposes the latter's egalitarian wage demands. About 85% of white-collar workers in Sweden belong to the TCO.

The third-largest federation is the Swedish Confederation of Professional Associations (SACO), which in 1975 merged with the National Federation of Government Officers. About 60% of the SACO membership is in the public sector. The SACO is organized according to occupation and includes self-employed professionals such as doctors, lawyers, accountants and dentists, who make up about 3% of the membership. The SACO is more centralized than the TCO and more aggressive than the LO in demanding income tax reductions.

The Federation of Salaried Employees in Industry and Services (PTK) was founded in 1973. At the end of 1986 it had 564,000 members.

Whereas the TCO and the SACO are nonpolitical, the LO is closely related to the Social Democratic Party and also is involved in consumer cooperatives and housing societies. About 75% of the membership of the Social Democratic Party comes through LO affiliates. A joint party-union committee coordinates policies. All federations maintain extensive facilities for education, information, recreation, culture and travel. The LO owns *Aftonbladet*, a national daily, and several provincial newspapers are owned by local unions.

The framework for relations between labor and management is enshrined in the Basic Agreement signed in 1938 between the SAF and the LO. It provides for legislative intervention against conflicts that threaten industrial peace and bans certain industrial actions against third parties. Furthermore, it establishes a uniform negotiation procedure with far-reaching obligations to work for peaceful settlement of disputes, lays down general rules governing layoffs and dismissals and sets up a labor market council. The Basic Agreement has been fairly well observed over the years by both parties. The pledge to observe industrial peace has been incorporated into binding agreements between the SAF and the LO. In subsequent years the SAF and the LO have negotiated additional agreements on safety, job security, vocational training, works councils, protection of women at work and technological change.

The pivotal fact of collective bargaining is that it is centralized. Moreover, central agreements are adhered to by affiliates. Neverthless, the bargaining of affiliates sometimes goes beyond the terms of the Basic Agreement, leading to the "wage drift"—benefits over and above those authorized by law or central agreements. The binding force of collective agreements was abolished as early as 1915 and their enforceability clarified in 1928. In the same year the Riksdag passed the Labor Courts Act, setting up a special judiciary to adjudicate disputes arising from the interpretation of contracts. Swedish law distinguishes between justifiable and nonjustifiable conflicts. The former relate to the interpretation of collective agreements and are handled by labor courts, while the latter deal with disagreements over the terms of a new contract and come under the jurisdiction of the Labor Market Council.

In 1970 labor and management endorsed the recommendation of the EFO Report (named after the initials of its three authors, Edgren, Faxin and Odhner). It constituted a thorough analysis of the connection between wages and the national economy. Its basic conclusion was that wage policy should be consistent with central national economic aims: full employment, economic growth, reasonable price stability, income distribution and a positive trade balance. Since the Swedish economy was almost evenly divided between two sectors—one exposed to foreign competition and the other protected from it—the report concluded that the latter should become the wage leader in collective bargaining.

In 1971 the LO reported a "glaring difference between conditions at work and those outside the plant." Something needed to be done to bring industrial democracy down to the plant level. For this purpose, labor and amanagement joined in programs to redesign tools, machines, plants and general organization of work to allow workers more variety on their jobs, more discretion on how to do the job and more opportunities for advancement and individual growth. These programs include job rotation; job enrichment; teamwork; autonomous work groups; flexitime; and elimination of the assembly line, time clocks and status symbols. They also include equalization of working conditions between blue- and white-collar workers, shared setting and implementation of production goals, less supervision, and decentralized decision-making.

The traditional policy pursued by the government with respect to industrial relations has been one of nonintervention. The government has normally confined its activity to setting up legal framework for the peaceful settlement of disputes, leaving substantive issues to the parties. The pattern changed in the 1970s with legislation in several sectors and some cases of intervention. The major landmarks in the history of labor legislation are:

- The Act on Employee Participation in Decision-Making (MBL) of 1977, obliging employers to take the initiative in beginning negotiations with trade unions at the company before decisions are made on major issues such as closure, reorganization and expansion, as well as changes important to individual employees, such as transfers. The local trade union also needs to be informed on how plant operations are progressing financially and in terms of production. Management is further obliged to inform the union about its personnel policy guidelines. The act encourages the signing of collective agreements on codetermination covering management procedures, supervision of work, and pay and working conditions. These agreements are binding until terminated in writing. Workers have a residual right that entitles them to strike if the codetermination agreement is ignored or does not achieve the desired results. Labor also enjoys priority of interpretation in case of disputes, which can be set aside only by a Labor Court decision.

  Since 1972 unions of most companies with 25 employees or more are legally entitled to minority representation on the board of directors. Local union officials also have won the right to perform union functions during company time.

- The Working Environment Act of 1978 replaced the earlier workers' protection legislation and covers not only the physical but also the psychosocial environment. Its key provisions state that "working conditions must be adapted to human physical and mental aptitudes [and must be arranged in such a way] that the employee himself can influence the work situation." The act provides for safety delegates and safety committees in every plant with the right to suspend work if it entails immediate and serious danger to life when no remedy is obtained through representation to the employers. The act also obliges management to provide safety training to employees.

- The Security of Employment Act of 1974 guarantees employees a high degree of job security, with particular protection against arbitrary dismissal or demotion. The law severely limits an employer's right to lay off workers temporarily and gives priority to those who have worked longest. Another law enacted in the mid-1970s entitles the National Labor Market Board and its regional agencies to compel a company to hire or keep an employee. The act also requires one to six months' notice with pay before dismissal and provides for court reinstatement of unfairly dismissed employees.

- A 1983 law establishing wage-earner funds. These funds enable unions to acquire shares in companies with workers' pension funds.
- The Collective Contracts Act forbids industrial action during the lifetime of an agreement and empowers courts to settle disputes and assess damages.
- The Vacation Act grants an annual five-week or 25 days of vacation for all employees after one year of service, four weeks of which may be taken during June, July or August. Employees may "bank" up to five vacation days per year to be used for extended vacations once in five years.
- The Working Hours Act limits the workweek to 40 hours unless provided otherwise in a collective agreement. Shift employees work fewer hours. The act sanctions 200 hours of overtime annually.
- The Promotion of Employment Act requires management to notify county labor boards of any planned cutbacks involving five or more workers. The act mandates the establishments of adjustment groups in all enterprises to facilitate employment of older people.
- The Shop Stewards Act forbids discrimination against shop stewards who are not elected independently but appointed by the union.

The labor market policy reflects its socialist orientation. Its goal is to use the collective strength of organized labor to advance the wage claims of disadvantaged groups and thus press for the structural transformation of the economy. Capital and manpower would be moved over from unprofitable to profitable business sectors. In the 1970s its emphasis was on training, work rehabilitation and regional development. Other emphases have been added in the 1980s: sexual desegregation, working environment, geographical mobility and work for older people. Full employment has remained the one constant in labor policy that has enjoyed the unanimous support of all political parties.

The instruments of labor market policy can be divided into four main categories:

1. Employment and Counseling Services, including dissemination of job-related information and placement. Vocational and educational guidance are also provided through nine-year compulsory schools and integrated secondary schools. To promote geographical and vocational mobility, the government provides relocation assistance.

2. Programs to influence the labor supply, including training.

3. Programs to influence the demand for labor, including relief work, regional development grants and recruitment subsidies to companies that hire jobless people referred to them by the Employment Service.

4. Programs for disdvantaged groups, including older persons, women, adolescents and handicapped persons.

After all means of finding work for a job-seeker are exhausted, he is entitled to unemployment benefits. Roughly three-quarters of the labor force are covered by unemployment insurance, which is payable to employees affiliated with government-approved unemployment insurance societies. It is the heart of the economic security system. Cash payments at a lower rate are payable to those who do not belong to an insurance society, primarily new entrants to the labor market. Voluntary unemployment insurance is administered by societies closely tied to trade unions. There are currently 44 such societies, with about 3.3 million members. Government subsidies finance 95% of their expenditures, with the remainder coming from membership fees. Entitlement to benefits is conditional on a person's willingness to accept suitable work or referral to an appropriate training program. The Employment Service thus performs and important monitoring function in the system. Benefits are payable up to a maximum of 300 working days for persons under 55 and 450 days for those over 55. The benefit may not exceed 92% of previous income from work up to a daily maximum amount fixed by the Riksdag. All benefits are taxable.

Mediation in labor disputes is the function of the National Conciliator's Office. The mediator does not have the power of sanctions. The National Labor Court consists of nine members, of whom no more than seven meet at the same time. Its jurisdiction covers all labor legislation. Disputes on collective agreements form only a small fraction of Labor Court cases.

The Labor Market Administration is an agency of the Ministry of Labor with overall responsibility for labor market policy programs. It comprises:
- the Labor Market Board (AMS)
- the 24 county labor boards
- the district labor boards and the District Employment Service
- local employment services

The image of Sweden as a land of labor peace was revised in the 1970s. However, industrial unrest is less prevalent in Sweden than in other countries. There have been only three major strikes in labor history in Sweden: those of 1909, 1945 and 1980. Wildcat strikes were relatively unknown until 1969, when the country was struck by a series of such strikes. According to the SAF, the number of man-days lost through legal and illegal strikes in 1985 was 351,413, up from 31,204 in 1984. There were six legal strikes, which accounted for 4% of the number of strikes and 94% of total man-days lost.

Wage increases in the private sector have exceeded wage increases in competitor countries. In 1985 the Palme government persuaded both labor and management to hold total wage increases to 5%, the so-called Rosenbad Agreement. However, the Bank of Sweden estimated that average increases in wage costs in the manufacturing sector were double the Rosenbad limit and that

```
┌─────────────────────────────────────────────────────┐
│               LABOR INDICATORS, 1986                │
│ Total economically active population: 4.39 million  │
│ As % of working-age population: 65                  │
│ % female: 47.5                                      │
│ Activity rate (%)                                   │
│    Total: 52.37                                     │
│    Male: 56.97                                      │
│    Female: 47.97                                    │
│                                                     │
│ Employment status (%)                               │
│    Employers & self-employed: 6.8                   │
│    Employees: 90.1                                  │
│    Unpaid family workers: 0.3                       │
│    Other: 2.8                                       │
│                                                     │
│ Organized labor: 90%                                │
│                                                     │
│ Sectoral employment (%)                             │
│    Agriculture, forestry, fishing: 4.8              │
│    Mining: 0.3                                      │
│    Manufacturing, construction: 28.6                │
│    Electricity, gas, water: 0.9                     │
│    Trade: 13.7                                      │
│    Transportation, communications: 7.0              │
│    Finance, real estate: 7.5                        │
│    Services: 37.2                                   │
│                                                     │
│ Average annual growth rate of labor force, 1980–2000:│
│ 0.3 %                                               │
│                                                     │
│ Unemployment %: 2.7                                 │
│ Labor under 20 years: 5.1%                          │
│ Earnings in manufacturing: 48.27 SKr per hr.        │
│                                                     │
│ Hours of work                                       │
│    Manufacturing: 37.6                              │
│    Nonagricultural work: —                          │
└─────────────────────────────────────────────────────┘
```

overall wage increase stood at about 7%. In addition, nonwage labor costs have increased rapidly since 1972. In 1985 these costs amounted to 42% of cash wages before taxes for blue-collar workers and 46% for other employees. Based on hourly wages, the increase was 67% for blue-collar workers.

FOREIGN COMMERCE

The Swedish economy is highly dependent of foreign trade. About 50% of its manufactured goods are exported, and some companies export as much as 80% or 90% of their production. Although the Swedish content of the country's exports is decreasing, it still is relatively high. Total exports correspond to about 30% of the GDP. In the early 1970s Sweden started to lose its market shares.

The loss continued into the latter part of the 1970s, owing to rising costs and an inflation rate exceeding that of major competitors. The trend was, however, reversed after the devaluations of 1981 (by 10%) and 1982 (16%). With 1.7% of the world's exports and 1.5% of the world's imports Sweden ranked in 1986 as the world's 13th highest exporter and 15th highest importer.

The growth of Swedish exports was originally based mainly on the country's resources of timber, ores and waterpower. The share of raw materials-based industries has since fallen; in 1986 timber and pulp accounted for only 7% of exports, as against 15% in the mid-1970s. In the mid-1960s Sweden still was the world's leading exporter of iron ore. Countries such as Australia and Brazil have since overtaken Sweden, and iron ore now accounts for only 1% of exports. Instead there has been a significant rise in Sweden's world market share of processed goods. Products of the engineering industry—metal goods, machinery, electrical products, transportation equipment and instruments—now account for approximately half of exports. Swedish engineering companies have succeeded in maintaining their position in the face of stiffening competition in export markets by concentrating on specialized products. Exports of chemical products, including pharmaceuticals, have risen markedly in recent years, to over 8% of exports in 1986. Among semimanufactures, paper and paperboard account for 10% and iron and steel for 6%.

Swedish imports per capita are among the highest in the world. Swedish imports are far more differentiated than its exports. In 1986 the share of imports of engineering products came to 43% of total imports, while fuel accounted for 11%. The latter was, however, a low figure owing to plummeting oil prices.

Sweden traditionally has maintained one of the lowest tariff levels in the world. It uses a single-column tariff with Brussels nomenclature. Import duties apply to all countries receiving most-favored-nation (MFN) treatment. Most raw materials, basic chemicals, pharmaceuticals, wood pulp, newsprint, pig iron and some finished goods, including ships an aircraft, are admitted duty-free. However, certain agricultural products are subject to import fees. Sweden signed a trade agreement with the EC in 1972.

Sweden's most important trading partners are members of EFTA (of which Sweden is a founding member) and other industrial countries. Western Europe accounts for 70% of both imports and exports. Besides the Nordic countries, trade relations are closest with the United Kingdom and West Germany. The share of the developing countries has declined in the past few years, although some Far Eastern countries are strong markets for exports.

After a period in the late 1970s when the external balance deteriorated sharply, trade figures improved as a result of the 1981 and 1982 devaluations. In 1986 the trade balance showed a surplus of Skr 33.5 billion and the current account a surplus of Skr7 billion, partly owing to favorable external circumstances, such as falling oil prices and a depreciating dollar.

A substantial portion of Swedish foreign trade consists of trade in services. In 1985 service exports (excluding investment income) amounted to Skr60 billion, corresponding to 23% of total commodity exports. In 1975 this quota was below 17%.

The structure of service exports has changed in recent years. In 1975 income from shipping constituted 60% of total service exports. Owing to the weak performance of shipping in general and the Swedish shipping industry in particular, the share of shipping in Swedish service exports fell to 24% in 1985. Other service exports, such as consultancy, construction work and insurance, have offset this loss. The value of service imports (excluding interest payments and dividends) amounted to Skr54 billion in 1985. Imports of shipping and other transportation services still are lower than the corresponding exports, thereby generating an overall transport surplus of Skr12 billion in 1985. Swedish spending on foreign travel exceeded foreign tourist income in Sweden by Skr9 billion in 1986.

Another important item in the Swedish capital balance is investment abroad, which, since its liberalization in the mid-1980s, has far exceeded foreign investment in Sweden.

By tradition, Sweden has a liberal trade policy. Import duties always have been low, and there are no nontariff barriers to imports. There are no tarrifs and import quotas on industrial products from EFTA members. In 1972 Sweden and the EEC signed a trade agreement under which free trade was established for manufactured but not agricultural goods. Sweden also is a member of the OECD and takes part in meetings of the Group of Ten.

About 90% of Swedish imports from developing countries are duty-free. The Imports Promotion Office for Products from Developing Countries was established in 1974 with the specific purpose of assisting developing countries in gaining a place in the Swedish market. The Swedish Trade Council is the central organization for promoting the country's exports. The council runs some 30 trade offices worldwide.

TRANSPORTATION & COMMUNICATIONS

Sweden has the largest rail network per capita in Europe, with 1.4 km. (0.87 mi.) of track per 1,000 inhabitants. The total length is 11,160 km. (6,936 mi.) of 1.435-m. (4.7-ft.) standard gauge (of which 6,960 km.— 4,326 mi.— are electrified and 1,152 km.— 716 mi. — double track; 182 km.—113 mi. — meter gauge; 117 km.—73 mi. — rail ferry service) run by the State Railways (SJ) and 511 km. (318 mi.) standard gauge (of which

---

FOREIGN TRADE INDICATORS, 1986

Exports: $37.3 billion
Imports: $32.7 billion
Balance of trade: $4.6 billion
Annual growth rate, exports 1980–86: 5.7%
Annual growth rate, imports 1980–86: 4.0%
Ratio of international reserves to imports (in months): 2.6:1
Value of manufactured exports: $31.196 billion
Terms of trade (1980=100): 110 (1986)
Import Price Index (1980=100): 80.7 (1986)
Export Price Index (1980=100): 87.3 (1986)
Imports of goods as % of GDP: 28.5
Exports of goods as % of GDP: 32.5

Direction of trade (%)

	Imports	Exports
EEC	57.2	50.0
U.S.A.	7.8	11.4
East European economies	3.7	2.2
Japan	5.5	1.4

Composition of trade (%)

	Imports	Exports
Food / Agricultural raw materials	10.0	9.8
Fuels	10.8	2.9
Ores and minerals	1.8	1.7
Manufactured goods	77.5	85.7
of which chemicals	9.7	6.7
of which machinery	36.1	43.8

---

332 km.—206 mi.— are electrified) and 371 km. (231 mi.) meter gauge electrified under private ownership. The SJ passenger routes are divided into commercial routes comprising 40% of the total length of track, and subsidized routes for which the company receives compensation from the state for maintaining service. A maximum speed of 109–129 kph (68–80 mph) is permitted on just over one-third of the routes. Rail traffic has been stagnating since the early 1980s. The trend is toward greater differentiation with regard to fares and services. Older rolling stock is used for low-fare journeys on weekends. A number of unprofitable rail lines were closed down in 1985.

An estimated 90% of the passenger traffic and nearly all goods transportation are by road. The road network totals approximately 414,600 km. (257,676 mi.), of which 98,000 km. (60,907 mi.) are public highways, 31,600 km. (19,640 mi.) local roads, and 285,000 km. (177,129 mi.) private roads. The maximum speed limit is 109 kph (68 mph) on highways and 71 kph (44 mph) on country roads. In per capita car ownership Sweden ranks below not only the United States but also France, West Germany and Switzerland. Access to a car is greater in rural areas than in other parts of Sweden. Car density is less in the larger cities and is particularly low in the Stockholm area, where there is a well-developed public transportation system. The average length of life of a Swedish car is high, at 15 years.

The total number of buses is 13,500, and the services are distributed fairly equally among state-owned, municipally owned and private bus companies. Local scheduled traffic operates in some 50 urban districts. Interregional and long-distance services operate partly as a network of express bus services. There are county corporations for public transportation in each of the 24 counties. Special services are provided for handicapped people and for old-age pensioners. Over 100,000 motorcycles are on the roads, double the number in 1980. On the other hand, the number of mopeds has been gradually declining. The number of trucks is steadily rising and now is estimated at 210,000, with 30,000 trailers. Of the 21,000 road haulage firms, roughly half are one-vehicle businesses.

Traffic accidents have declined since the 1960s both in absolute and in relative terms. When the change was made from left- to right-hand traffic in 1967, work on road safety was intensified. Safety belts were made compulsory for front-seat drivers and passengers. In 1982 the number of deaths per 100,000 cars was 24, among the lowest in the world.

Most of the 50 important ports are municipally owned. The government is responsible for maintaining navigable channels and icebreaking in winter. In 1984 there were 475 vessels in the Swedish merchant fleet. Slightly less than half the tonnage consisted of tankers. A quarter of the fleet is engaged in coastal shipping. The merchant fleet is very young, with an average age of nine years for vessels and six years for tankers. Sweden's share of world merchant shipping fell from 2% in 1975 to 0.8% in 1983, making Sweden the 23rd shipping nation in the world. Most shipping companies are hard-pressed by sharply rising operating costs, surplus tonnage, maritime protectionism and slack world trade. They also pay the highest unsubsidized wages in the world. Göteborg is the largest harbor, followed by Stockholm and Helsingborg.

The national air carrier, Scandinavian Airlines System (SAS), is owned jointly by Swedish, Danish and Norwegian companies, with the respective governments in turn owning 50% of each parent company's share. Nominated by *Air Transport World* as the Airline of the Year in 1986, SAS is a showcase of Nordic cooperation. It serves 90 destinations in 35 countries. Domestic routes are served mainly by Linjeflyg, which is owned jointly by SAS and AB Aerotransport, parent company of SAS. Forty Swedish cities are connected by air routes. Plane travel has become popular since the reduction of air fares in the mid-1970s. Linjeflyg had 5.3 million passengers in 1985. The principal international airport, near Stockholm, is at Arlanda, which was opened for traffic in 1983.

With 894 telephones per 1,000 inhabitants, Sweden has the highest telephone density in the world.

TRANSPORTATION INDICATORS, 1986

Roads
Length km. (mi.): 97,400 (60,485)
Paved (%): 69

Motor vehicles
Automobiles: 3,151,195
Trucks: 231,442
Persons per vehicle: 2.5
Road freight ton-km. (ton-mi.): 22,986 (15,744)

Railroads
Track, km. (mi.): 12,520 (7,775)
Passenger-km. (passenger-mi.) 6,588 million
(4,094 million)
Freight, ton-km. (ton-mi.) (million): 19,289 (11,988)

Merchant marine
  Vessels: 660 (over 100 GWT)
  Total dead weight tonnage: 3,037,400
  Oil tankers: 1,243,000 GRT

Ports
  5 major
  12 secondary
  30 minor
  Cargo loaded: 41,772,000 tons
  Cargo unloaded: 55,776,000 tons

Air
  Km. (mi.) flown: 78.4 million (1984)
  Passengers: 733,500 (1984)
  Passenger-km. (passenger-mi.): 5,378 million
  (3,342 million)
  Freight, ton-km. (ton-mi.): 190.9 million (130.8 million)
  Mail ton-km. (ton-mi.): 22.7 million (14.1 million)
  Airports with scheduled flights: 36
  Civil aircraft: 65

Pipelines
Refined: —
Natural gas: 84 km. (52.1 mi.)
Total: 84 km.

Inland waterways
  Length, km. (mi.): 1,164 (724)
  Cargo, ton-km. (ton-mi.): 9,000 million (6,200 million)

```
┌─────────────────────────────────────────────────────────┐
│              COMMUNICATION INDICATORS, 1986               │
│                                                           │
│  Telephones                                               │
│  Total: 7.4 million                                       │
│  Persons per receiver: 1.1                                │
│     Phone traffic      ⎫                                  │
│        Local:          ⎬ 22,536,865                       │
│        Long distance:  ⎭                                  │
│        International: 6,345,114                            │
│                                                           │
│  Post office                                              │
│     Number of post offices: 2,034                         │
│     Domestic mail:        ⎫                               │
│     Foreign mail received: ⎬   3,333,607                  │
│     Foreign mail sent:    ⎭                               │
│                                                           │
│  Telegraph                                                │
│  Total traffic: 252,000                                   │
│  National: 110,000                                        │
│  International: 142,000                                    │
│                                                           │
│  Telex                                                    │
│  Subscriber lines: 18,174                                 │
│  Traffic (000 minutes): 48,548                            │
│                                                           │
│  Telecommunications                                       │
│     5 submarine coaxial cables                            │
│     2 communication satellite ground stations            │
│              TOURISM & TRAVEL INDICATORS, 1985            │
│                                                           │
│  Total tourist receipts: $1.332 billion                   │
│  Expenditures by nationals abroad: $2.270 billion         │
│  Number of hotel beds: 19,591                             │
│  Average length of stay: 2.2 nights                       │
│  Number of tourists: 3.5 million                          │
│     of whom from (%):                                     │
│     U.S.A.: 10.1                                          │
│     Norway: 20.5                                          │
│     West Germany: 13.8                                    │
│     Finland: 10.9                                         │
└─────────────────────────────────────────────────────────┘
```

DEFENSE

Swedish defense is organized within the Total Defense System, comprising military, economic, civil and psychological defense. Ultimate authority is jointly exercised by the king and the Riksdag, but actual constitutional control is vested in the Riksdag's Permanent Defense Committee. The prime minister serves as chairman of the national Defense Council as the Supreme Command. Its policy decisions are executed by the Total Defense Staff Committee on the civil side and by the Supreme Command on the military side. Sweden is divided into six military command areas, each headed by a commanding general on the military side and a commissioner on the civil side. Subordinate to the commanding generals are the military district commanders in each of the counties. Each defense district contains a number of regiments and corps, totaling 49 in all.

District Command	HQ	Counties
Upper Norrland	Boden	Västerbotten, Norrbotten
Lower Norrland	Östersund	Västernorrland, Jämtland, Gävleborg (north)
Bargslagen	Karlstad	Örebro, Värmland, Kopparberg
Eastern	Strängnäs	Östergötland, Södermanland, Stockholm, Uppsala, Västmanland, Gävleborg (south), Gotland
Western	Skövde	Halland, Göteborg, Alvsborg, Skaraborg
Southern	Kristianstad	Malmöhus, Kristianstad, Blekinge, Kronoberg, Jönköping, Kalmar

The mobilizable strength is estimated at 30 brigades. In addition, there are 100 mobile (bicycle) battalions of older reservists and 500 static defense companies. The voluntary home guard is a separate force. The coast jager belonging to the naval coastal artillery is a marine commando force.

The Swedish army has not seen battle since 1814, although they served on U.N. emergency peacekeeping forces in a number of countries.

There are seven arms and services: infantry, armor, artillery, air defense, engineers, signals and maintenance corps, the directorates of which are subordinate to the army chief of staff. More important are the *regimenten* and *kar* (corps), many of which trace their origins to the 17th century. There are three types of brigades: armored, infantry and Norrland. The personnel of the army is divided into four types: regular, conscript, civil-military and civilian. The regular rank structure is an unusual one, consisting of regimental officers who correspond to the regular officers of other armies, company officers who correspond to warrant officers, and platoon officers who correspond to senior NCO's.

Recruitment is by universal conscription of all male citizens at age 18. Conscientious objection is allowed, but objectors must perform alternative civilian service for 540 days within the Total Defense System.

Liability for military service extends to age 47, reservists being technically "on leave" until then. Refresher training takes place after an interval of two years from conscription service and then at intervals of four years, for a total of 18 days. Corporals serve an additional seven days and senior ranks an additional 14 days.

The principal training institutions are the Military Academy at Karlsberg, the Royal Swedish Staff College at Stockholm and the National Defense College.

Sweden has one of the oldest and largest arms industries in the world. It supplied cannons to most of the armies of Europe during the 17th century. The most important armament producers are Volvo (jet engines and tracked vehicles), Saab-Scania (aircraft and missiles), Bofors (artillery, armored vehicles, missiles, explosives), Forenade Fabriksverken (small arms, antitank weapons, ammunition and missiles), Hagglands (armored vehicles), Norma (small arms and ammunition) and L. M. Ericsson (radar, laser, infrared and air defense control systems).

The naval forces consist of the navy and the coast artillery. Emphasis is on light, fast ships and submarines. There are 50 large and small surface attack ships and minesweepers and 12 submarines. Strategic areas are defended by the coast artillery. The navy also has helicopter units designed for antisubmarine warfare.

The air force consists of 22 squadrons operating from a large number of bases all over Sweden. All components of the air defense are coordinated by an electronically automated command and warning system. Types of aircraft include the Draken, an all-weather fighter; and the Viggen, a combined fighter, attack and reconnaissance aircraft. Armament includes Sidewinder and Falcon air-to-air missiles. All services have underground installations blasted out of rock to protect against nuclear radiation.

Economic defense is a vital part of the Total Defense System, is designed to protect the country from wartime blockade and is coordinated by the National Board of Economic Defense. Stockpiling is an important ingredient of the economic defense policy. Psychological defense, also part of the Total Defense System, is designed to maintain and strengthen the national will to fight in wartime and is coordinated by the National Board of Psychological Defense.

Sweden receives no military aid, and there are no foreign military bases in the country.

DEFENSE PERSONNEL, EQUIPMENT AND BUDGET

National military budget, 1986: $3.215 billion

% of GNP: 3.1

Military expenditures per capita: $386

Military expenditures per soldier: $48,712

Military expenditures per sq. km. of national territory: $7,144 ($18,508 per sq. mi.)

Total military manpower: 66,000, mobilizable to about 800,000 in 72 hours

Reserves: 735,500

Army: 47,000; 6 military commands; 26 defense districts (*laens*); 50 regiments; 4 armored brigades; 1 mechanized brigade; 19 infantry brigades; 60 battalions; 1 army aviation battalion; 11 artillery aviation platoons

Navy: 9,650; submarines, destroyers; fast attack craft; patrol craft; minelayers; amphibious craft; icebreakers coastal artillery; helicopters; naval bases at Musko, Härnösand, Karlskrona and Göteborg

Air Force: 9,000; 524 combat aircraft; 1 attack group; 4 air defense groups; 12 wings; 6 fighter squadrons; 12 air defense squadrons; 6 reconnaissance squadrons; 1 search-and-rescue squadron

Arms exports: $210 million

Arms imports: $60 million

EDUCATION

The first grammar schools were established in Sweden soon after the Reformation in 1571. Consisting at first of eight grades, they were expanded to 12 in 1611, in which year the task of education was delegated to the church by statute. By 1700 about 10% of the population was being schooled, mostly children of privileged groups, such as the nobility and the burghers. The major academic institution, the gymnasium, was firmly in place by the middle of the 17th century, and it remained unaltered until the middle of the 19th century. The first Swedish university was opened in Uppsala in 1477, closed in 1510 and reopened in 1595. A second university, at Lund, was opened in 1668. Swedish scholars also traveled to the Protestant universities in Germany.

The literacy rate reached 50% by about 1800. Even so, much of the country did not yet have schools. In 1842 the first law to provide a national system of elementary education was passed, requiring all children to attend schools. At the same time, the first state seminary for teachers was founded. Every parish was required to maintain at least one school having at least one seminary-trained teacher. These schools, however, were different from the gymnasia. Only in 1849 were they linked by requiring three years of elementary schooling for entry into the gymnasium. In 1894 a three-year foundation school was adopted giving Sweden the distinction of being the only European country to have some form of common schooling prior to the turn of the century. The common school was extended to four years in 1928, to six years in 1950 and to nine years in 1962, completing the process of structural reform. The upper secondary school also has been integrated, since 1965, by breaking down the lines of distinction among the traditional gymnasium, the *realskola* (continuation school) and the *yrkesskola* (vocational school).

The constitutional and legal foundations of Swedish education are found in three acts:

1. The Education Act of 1927, mandating transfer to the academic secondary school after four, preferably six, years. Private schools would no longer receive state aid after the first six years of schooling. No foreign languages would be taught in the first six years. The length of compulsory school was extended by one year in six-year foundation schools.

2. The Education Act of 1950, extending compulsory education to nine years in a comprehesive school system combining the first six years of the *folkskola* and the three years of the lower secondary school or vocational school. The program of the integrated nine-year school would not be differentiated for the first eight years.

3. The Education Act of 1962, making nine-year comprehensive education universal and placing it under municipal oversight.

During the past decade enrollment in the comprehensive school has been 98%.

Approximately 70% of pupil enter some form of upper secondary school upon completion of compulsory education, and 95% do so before age 20. The one group poorly represented at the secondary level comprises immigrant children, only 50% of whom go beyond comprehensive school. The female share in enrollment is close to parity until the postgraduate level, where it drops to 25.9%.

The academic year lasts for 39 weeks, Monday through Friday. The school year begins in the third week of August, and the autumn term lasts for about 18 weeks before Christmas vacation begins about the third week of December. The spring term lasts until June 10, with a week off at Easter. School is in session for 190 days a year.

At the comprehensive school, marks have been eliminated. Report cards are issued only in grades eight and nine, with marks based on a five-point scale. Advancement to the next grade is almost automatic, although some pupils are detained in a class for a second year. Voluntary tests are administered in some grades in Swedish, mathematics and foreign languages. There are special education programs for ethnic minorities, such as the Lapps and guest workers.

Private schools are few and enroll less than 2% of primary and secondary pupils. There are three types of private schools: (1) religious schools, both Catholic and Lutheran; (2) alternative schools, such as the "Waldorf" schools; and (3) international schools. Public subvention of private schools is on a school-to-school basis.

Preprimary. There are two types of preprimary schools. The day home is a full-time program for children of parents who work. The more common play school is a part-time institution that caters to four- to seven-year-old children three hours a day. All children are entitled to preschool education for at least one year before starting school at age seven.

Primary. Compulsory school is divided into three levels—junior, intermediate and senior—each three years in duration. All pupils take the same subjects in the first two levels. English is compulsory from grades 3 or 4. Optionals, including a second foreign language, are offered in the last level. The choice of subjects must not be determined by sexual bias. There are junior and intermediate schools in every housing area, most of them with one or two classes per grade, with a total of 150 to 300 pupils. In rural areas a single class is made up of pupils from two or three different grades. State grants for compulsory schools are distributed at the junior level on the basis of the number of teacher periods per unit of 25 pupils and at the intermediate and senior levels per unit of 30 pupils. Pupils are kept together in the same classes all the way through compulsory school. At the municipal level, compulsory schools are divided into school management districts, each under a headmaster. Pupils with special learning problems or handicaps are taken care of by a remedial teacher in a "clinic," or day school. They are also offered adjusted courses of study enabling them to devote extra time to certain subjects or work away from school one or two days a week. The curriculum provides for free activities at both intermediate and senior levels, designed to develop pupils' initiative and creativity. Some municipalities have introduced an integrated school day, with free activities alternating with teaching throughout the school day.

Upper secondary. This school offers two-, three- and four-year lines of study. The lines themselves are grouped into sectors, each with lines of varying duration and specialized courses. The three- and four-year lines comprise theoretical studies of general subjects and vocational subjects. An upper secondary school region consists of several municipalities, each under a headmaster. The number of students per class does not generally exceed 30 in theoretical courses and 16 in practical lines.

Students who apply for admission to the upper secondary school greatly outnumber the 16-year-old population because of the increasing number of mature applicants who had entered the work world after compulsory school. Roughly 35% of the students take the three- and four-year lines, more than 50% take the vocational lines and 15% take the two-year theoretical lines. Students are tracked or streamed according to various lines. Each line has its own goal, and the curriculum is structured to reach that specific goal. Some common subjects remain, such as Swedish, civics and physical education, and all lines have common electives, including English, mathematics and drawing. Students are graded according to the Gaussian curve and do not have to take a final examination, although nationwide standardized tests are administered in certain subjects.

Sweden has one of the lowest teacher–pupil ratios in the world at the secondary level, one teacher for every 10 pupils. Women constitute 45% of secondary school teaching staff.

Higher. The Swedish term for higher education, *högskola*, denotes not only traditional university studies but also professional courses. Higher education has become a mass operation, especially after the passage of the Higher Education Act of 1977, which reorganized programs and courses in five occupational sectors: technology, administration and economics, medicine and health care, teaching, and culture and information. On this basis there are six types of institutions in the higher education system: universities with facilities for research, university-level institutions with no research facilities, professional colleges, colleges of art, teacher training colleges, and schools for paramedical and nautical training.

To be admitted to higher education programs, students must first fulfill general admission requirements common to all programs and then meet the special admission requirements of the particular course or program. Nonsecondary school graduates may be admitted if they are at least 25, have worked for four years and possess a working knowledge of English.

A major portion of undergraduate education is organized into about 100 general study programs established by the Riksdag and varying in length from one to five and a half years. Each program consists of various courses. For each program a curriculum has been established by the National Board of Universities and Colleges and is applicable to all locations where the program is taught. Universities also establish local study programs on their own initiative. These provide unique specialties and harness local resources. There also are provisions for individualized study programs and single-subject courses. Short-cycle technical vocational studies provide instruction in technical areas where no training is available in a formal setting.

An academic year consists of two terms for a total of 40 points; one point is equivalent to one week of full-time study. Generally, marks are given on a three level scale: fail, pass and pass with distinction. At the end of the program, the basic degree, *filosofie kandidat,* is conferred.

Postgraduate training is given at the universities, the Royal Institute of Technology, the Karolinska Institute, the Stockholm Institute of Education, the Stockholm Institute of Economics, the Chalmers Institute of Technology, and the Lulea University College and Institute of Technology. A postgraduate program consists of a series of courses ending in a dissertation, which has to be publicly defended, and generally is completed within four years. Recently, the former degree of licentiate, a research degree with a shorter qualifying period of two to two and a half years, has been reintroduced.

The teaching staff consists of three levels: full professors, senior lecturers *(hogskolelektorer)* and lecturers *(hogskoleadjunkter).*

The National Board of Universities and Colleges is the central government agency that supervises the higher education system. It is headed by a board of governors presided over by the chancellor of Swedish Universities and Colleges. The Swedish University of Agricultural Sciences functions in a somewhat different fashion. Its board of governors is an executive body and a government agency under the Ministry of Agriculture. The country is divided into six higher education regions, each with one university and several university colleges. With the exception of the Stockholm School of Economics, all institutions are state-run. Their employees are national civil servants, and their students pay no tuition fees.

All 33 institutions of higher education are administered by governing boards, each headed by a rector, who is appointed for a six-year term. Larger institutions combining teaching and research also have administrative directors. The smallest working unit is the department, governed by a board and headed by a *prefekt.* For undergraduate education there are program committees. Postgraduate education and research are organized into faculties administered by faculty assemblies and faculty boards.

All postsecondary students receive state subsidies, grants and loans irrespective of parental income. Only about 20% is a grant, and the balance is an interest free loan.

Educational administration is three-tiered. The Riksdag determines policy, the Ministry of Education implements the policy and the National Board of Education administers programs and funds. Each of the 24 counties has a *lans skolenamnd* (county board of education) constituted along the same lines as the national board. A *skolstyrelse* (local school board) is responsible for the school system in its area. The board's seven members are elected by the local council.

The operational costs of primary and secondary education are shared between the state and the municipalities on approximately a fifty–fifty basis. The central government pays all teacher salaries, material expenses related to vocational education and general upper secondary education and a portion of all school building costs. Local governments meet all other costs. Higher education in financed entirely by the central government through budget grants.

Sweden has a long history of adult education programs, which gained impetus from the folk high school movement introduced from Denmark in 1868. In 1987 there were 110 folk high schools offering free short courses lasting one to eight weeks, longer courses of 30 to 34 weeks and extended courses of two to three years.

A second impetus came from the labor movement, resulting in a peculiar Nordic institution, the study circle. First organized in 1907, they offer today over 300,000 courses. In addition, over 100,000 people are enrolled in special education centers within the framework of *gymnasieskolan*. Others are studying in *vuxenskolan*, or adult schools that qualify for university admission. Special programs of distance education by television and radio are conducted in two institutes. All permanent employees enjoy the right to take a leave of absence for study during working hours and to receive a government grant for the loss of income.

Preschool teachers are trained at special nonuniversity-level institutes in a two-year program. Teachers in the first level of comprehensive school complete a two-and-a-half-year program at a teacher training college; teachers in the intermediate levels, a three-year program at a teacher training college. Teachers at the upper level must become specialized teachers in two or three subjects, attend a university to obtain a first degree and attend a one-year pedagogical course.

General upper secondary school teachers must obtain a first degree from a university and complete a one-year course at a teachers college. Teachers in vocational school must have a diploma as master of handicraft and two to seven years of practical experience.

In-service programs are of two kinds. The first are short, part-time courses to enrich initial training, meet local school or central authority or personnel needs and improve the curriculum. The second allows teachers to upgrade themselves to teach at a higher level. These courses require extended full-time study during leaves of absence. Such leaves of absence are very common. Approximately 12% of teachers are on leave from work at any given time.

The teaching profession is generally held in high regard, and teachers enjoy a slight salary advantage over other white-collar workers. As a group they wield considerable political influence as well through the Swedish Teachers Union.

EDUCATION INDICATORS, 1986

Literacy
  Total (%): 100
  Males (%): 100
  Females (%): 100

First level
  Schools: 4,770
  Students: 959,627
  Teachers: 100,748
  Student–teacher ratio: 10:1
  Net enrollment rate: 96%
  Females (%): 49

Second level
  Schools: 520
  Students: 267,477
  Teachers: 28,636
  Student–teacher ratio: 9:1
  Net enrollment rate: 81%
  Females (%): 51

Vocational
  Schools: N.A.
  Students: 198,621
  Teachers: N.A.
  Student–teacher ratio: N.A.
  Vocational enrollment rate: 33%

Third level
  Institutions: 12 universities
  Students: 221,200
  Teachers: 17,608
  Student–teacher ratio: 13:1
  Gross enrollment rate: 38.2%
  Students per 100,000 ages 20–24: 2,651
  % of population over 25 with postsecondary education: 15.4
  Females (%): 47

Foreign study
  Foreign students in national universities: N.A.
  Students abroad: 2,524
    of whom in
    U.S.A.: 1,160
    France: N.A.
    West Germany: 448
    U.K.: 44

```
┌─────────────────────────────────────────────────┐
│         EDUCATION INDICATORS, 1986 (continued)    │
│  Public expenditures (1986)                       │
│     Total: $8,308 billion                         │
│     % of GNP: 8.1                                 │
│     % of national budget: 8.9                     │
│     % current: 88.1                               │
└─────────────────────────────────────────────────┘
```

LEGAL SYSTEM

Civil and criminal law are based on the National Law Code (Sveriges Rikes Lag), which was adopted in 1734 and still is in force, although it has been frequently amended and little of its original contents remain. Tha majority of the *balkar* (books) into which the code is divided have gradually been replaced in this century. Thus there have come into being completly new books on marriage, wills and successions, real estate, criminal offenses, judicial procedure and enforcement of judgments. Moreover, a mass of special legislation has grown outside the code in such fields as company law, copyrights, protection of industrial property, and labor relations. In the case of public law, too, important legislation has been passed in recent times, not least in such new fields as environmental protection and nature conservation.

Swedish law is based strongly on received traditions of Germanic law but has been open to other foreign influences. Roman law has had less influence on legal developments than is the case with most European countries. An important difference in relation to the majority of continental legal systems is that Sweden has abstained from large-scale codifications along the lines of the Code Civil in France or the Burgerliches Gesetzbuch in Germany. In comparison with Anglo-American law Swedish law is based to considerably greater extent on written law, while case law plays a smaller though still important role. Thus the Swedish legal system, by virtue of its systematic contents and structure, may be said to occupy a halfway house between the continental European and the Anglo-American systems.

A brisk pace of legislation has been maintained in Sweden for the past few decades. Several important sectors have been overhauled in their entirety. Another important characteristic of Swedish lawmaking is that since the end of the 19th century, much has been prepared in collaboration with other Nordic countries. The result is a significant degree of legal uniformity in Scandinavia, especially in the field of civil law.

Swedish public life is governed to an unusually high degree by the ideals of a law-governed society. While this holds true of the courts, as a matter of course it is noteworthy that the administrative authorities also have embraced judiciary forms for their own work. Thus in its broad organic aspects Swedish law exhibits a rather peculiar mixture of traditionalism and radicalism.

The old *Rules for Judges* provides that "in whatsoever matters there be no written law, the reasonable custom is to be applied as a law in judgments." However, in modern times customary law has almost entirely lost is importance in Swedish court practice. The text of the law in force is mandatory for the courts. As secondary sources, legal precedents, legislative materials or opinion of legal scholars may be used. Previous decisions of the Supreme Court are not binding for the Supreme Court itself or for the lower courts. Swedish theory and practice assert the theory of the freedom of each court to follow its own dictates. The courts never create the law but only apply it.

While the courts occupy a special position, the difference between adjudicative and administrative authorities is less in Sweden than in most European countries. The dividing line between the two is laid down to some extent in the Instrument of Government, but more detailed regulations are found in Riksdag legislation. As a general principle, courts enforce civil and criminal law. In addition, district courts perform many duties of an administrative nature related to transfers of property, land development, guardianships and probate. One reason for such a blending of functions is that both judges and civil servants are the products of legal training.

Sweden has a three-tier hierarchy of courts: the district courts *(tingsrater)*, the intermediate courts of appeal *(hovratter)*, and the Supreme Court *(hogsta domstolen)*. There are 100 district courts, which vary in size, the smallest having only a single judge. In principle there are no limitations on the jurisdiction of district courts, and their judges receive the same salary as court of appeal judges.

The chief judge of a district court carries the medieval title of *lagman*. Working with him are one or more assistant judges *(radman)* and a number of judicial trainees or court clerks. A peculiar feature of district courts is the panel of lay assessors, or *namndeman*, who take part in the main hearings. Assessors are elected for six-year terms by local representative councils, and many of them are reelected for consecutive terms. They serve mainly in cases concerning serious criminal offenses. However, they are distinct from a jury. They are concerned not only with the verdict but also deliberate with the judge on points of law. In cases where the assessors do not take part, the district court consists generally of three judges or of one judge. Sometimes technical experts may sit alongside judges. About 10% of the total number of cases in the district courts pass to the courts of appeal.

There are six courts of appeal, of which the oldest and largest, established in 1614, is the Svea Court of Appeal in Stockholm. They hear appeals against judgments of district courts. The bench consists either of four of three judges, or of two judges and two lay assessors. The preparatory work is to a large extent carried out by junior judges.

Appeals against decisions of the courts of appeal are heard by the Supreme Court, subject to special permission. Such permission is, in principle, granted only in cases with a potential for legal precedent being established. A special section of the court consisting of three justices determines whether to accept a case for review. If permission is granted, the case is then heard by a full bench of five justices.

Court judgments are based on main hearings in which all evidence is brought forward. In civil actions the main hearing is preceded by a preparatory stage in the form of oral proceedings, and in criminal cases by preliminary investigations conducted by a public prosecutor. In higher courts cases may be decided by written proceedings alone. In general, judicial procedures are time-consuming and slow.

The scope of public legal aid has been considerably expanded in recent years. The individual, however, has to contribute toward the costs by paying an amount that is determined in each particular case according to his or her financial circumstances. In criminal cases indigents accused are entitled to a public defense counsel, but if convicted they may be ordered by the court to repay the costs. In minor civil nonfamily cases the procedure is less formal, less expensive and generally is limited to one hearing.

The prosecution system is organized into local districts, each headed by a chief prosecutor. In each county there is a county prosecutor, who is responsible to the chief public prosecutor in Stockholm. Public prosecutors are responsible for preliminary investigations in criminal cases and for waiving prosecution in the case of minors.

Legal counsel is not required in court proceedings, but in practice the majority of cases are handled by attorneys. The number of attorneys per capita is low in Sweden compared to other countries. Publicly funded law offices are set up in each county. All practicing lawyers must be members of the Swedish Bar Association.

Sentencing and enforcement of verdicts are individualized and adapted to the convicted person's chances of rehabilitation. Conditional suspended sentences are used wherever possible. Prisons frequently grant furloughs, and there are few closed prison blocks. Capital punishment, last used in 1910, is now forbidden in the Constitution, both in peacetime and wartime.

The court system for administrative cases consists of the administrative courts of appeal and the Supreme Administrative Court. There are four administrative courts of appeal, in Stockholm, Götenborg, Sundsvall and Jönköping. The Supreme Administrative Court has 22 justices.

Special courts include courts-martial, land courts, water rights courts, the Labor Court, the Supreme Rent Court and the Insurance Court.

LAW ENFORCEMENT

On January 1, 1965, the county police systems of Sweden were integrated into a national police, with the responsibility vested in the National Police Board, headed by a police commissioner. Under the board, the country is divided into 23 police regions, each headed by a police commissioner. These regions are divided into 119 police districts, each headed by a police chief. Within each district is a citizen's advisory group called the Police Committee. Crowd control and emergencies are handled by the intervention police. Training is provided at several training establishments: the National Institute of Technical Police, the Police High Schools of Stockholm and Lund and the Police College of Solna.

The Swedes are generally a law-abiding people. The crime rate is low, and the number of reported murders annually is only about 100.

HEALTH

Health care is provided mainly by local authorities. Responsibility in this field rests with the 24 county councils and three large municipalities of Göteborg, Malmö and the island of Gotland. These units also operate the public dental service and mental health services. Private health care exists on a limited scale. Only about 5% of the physicians work full time in private practice. The corresponding figure for dentists, however, is 50%.

The county councils were established in the 1860s mainly to operate hospitals, and since that time their range of health services has expanded, particularly after the passage of the Health and Medical Services Act of 1983. Health care programs account for 75% to 80% of the total council budgets. Although the councils operate their health care systems independently, the state monitors these services to ensure that they meet the prescribed standards and are cost-efficient. This supervision is exercised by the Ministry of Health and Social Affairs through the National Board of Health and Welfare. The Swedish Planning and Rationalization Institute of the Health and Social Services, owned jointly by the central government and the county councils, undertakes research and development work in health care administration, including construction and equipment.

National health insurance, established in 1955, covers all Swedish citizens and aliens. Medical benefits are payable for physicians' care; dental treatment;

hospital care; paramedical treatment such as physiotherapy, convalescent care and handicap aids; and travel expenses. Compensation may also be paid for drugs and advisory services. The patient pays a nominal amount to the county council on each visit to a doctor at a public outpatient clinic and on each prescription filled by a pharmacy. Doctors themselves receive their entire salaries from the county councils. The county councils receive compensation from the state in proportion to the number of inhabitants in their area. At least 40% of a person's dental costs also are covered by the program.

In 1971 all pharmacies were organized into one single company, Apoteksbolaget, two-thirds owned by the state and one-third by the pharmacists' association.

Until recently health care had been very hospital-oriented; now it is more home-based. The number of beds is relatively high, equivalent to about 16 per 1,000 inhabitants (five general, five long-term, three and a half psychiatric and two and a half mentally retarded). There also are 7 places per 1,000 in municipal homes for the elderly.

In contrast, the number of outpatient visits to the physician is comparatively low–about 2.5 visits per year per patient, excluding public health care visits, which are about half the former rate, because of the improved level of health. Of the visits to doctors, 53% take place at the hospital, 30% to a district physician and 17% to a private physician. Outpatient care is organized into primary care districts, each with one or more health care centers and one or more nursing homes. The outpatient system also includes district nurses and district midwives. School health services and industrial health services also are under district jurisdiction. County medical care is responsible for central county hospitals, each with 15 to 20 specialties, and district county hospitals, each with four specialties. Above the county level, Sweden is divided into six medical care regions, providing services that require highly trained specialists and also special equipment. Within each region there is at least one hospital that qualifies for this role: Umeå, Uppsala-Örebro, Stockholm, Linköping, Göteborg and Lund-Malmö.

In 1984 about 440,000 persons were employed in the health sector, equal to 9% of the labor force (up from 115,000 persons and 3% of the labor force in 1960). There is a serious shortage of doctors, a situation unlikely to improve before 2000. In 1984 health care costs climbed to SEK 70 billion, or 10% of the GDP (from 3% of the GDP in 1960). Taxes cover 64% of the costs at the municipal level, state subsidies add another 14%, patients' fees 4%, compensation from the national health insurance system 8% and other state grants 10%. Medical research is coordinated by the Medical Research Council.

HEALTH INDICATORS, 1985

Health personnel
  Physicians: 20,200
  Population per physician: 413
  Dentists: 9,338
  Nurses: 72,386
  Pharmacists: 4,107
  Midwives: N.A.

Hospitals
  Number: 1,000
  Number of beds: 15,859
  Beds per 10,000: 139
  Admissions/discharges per 10,000: 1,968
  Bed occupancy rate: 86.1%
  Average length of stay: 22 days

Type of hospitals
  Government: N.A.
  Private nonprofit: N.A.
  Private profit: N.A.

Public health expenditures
  As % of national budget: 1.1
  Per capita: $63.30

Vital statistics
  Crude death rate per 1,000: 11.2
  Decline in death rate, 1965–84: 7.9%
  Life expectancy at birth (years)
    Males: 73.3
    Females: 79.4
  Infant mortality rate per 1,000 live births: 6.8
  Child mortality rate ages 1–4 years per 1,000:
  insignificant
  Maternal mortality rate per 100,000 live births: 2.1

Causes of death per 100,000
  Infectious & parasitic diseases: 7.9
  Cancer: 235.6
  Endocrine & metabolic disorders: 18.4
  Diseases of the nervous system: 10.2
  Diseases of the circulatory system: 614.6
  Diseases of the respiratory system: 92.5
  Diseases of the digestive system: 29.5
  Accidents, poisoning & violence: 59.2

FOOD & NUTRITION

The average Swede consumes 396 calories and 95.7 g. (3.4 oz.) of protein per day. The food supply is 117% of FAO daily requirements. Food accounts for 13% of total household expenditures.

```
┌─────────────────────────────────────────────┐
│        PER CAPITA CONSUMPTION OF FOODS        │
│               Kg. (Lb.,) 1986                 │
│                                               │
│  Potatoes: 66.4 (146.4)                       │
│  Wheat: 56.7 (125.0)                          │
│  Rice: 2.0 (4.41)                             │
│  Fresh vegetables: 34.8 (76.7)                │
│  Fruits (total): 52.8 (116.4)                 │
│     Citrus: 13.7 (30.2)                       │
│     Noncitrus: 39.1 (87.1)                    │
│  Eggs: 13 (28.6)                              │
│  Honey: 5.1 (11.2)                            │
│  Fish: 6.0 (13.2)                             │
│  Milk: 160.2 (353.2)                          │
│  Butter: 7.4 (16.3)                           │
│  Cream: 7.4 (16.3)                            │
│  Cheese: 14.6 (32.2)                          │
│  Yogurt: 9.2 (20.3)                           │
│  Meat (total): 52.7 (116.2)                   │
│     Beef & veal: 15.8 (34.8)                  │
│     Pig meat: 30.9 (68.1)                     │
│     Poultry: 5.0 (11.2)                       │
│     Mutton, lamb & goat: 1.0 (2.2)            │
│  Sugar: 46.2 (101.8)                          │
│  Chocolate: 4.2 (9.2)                         │
│  Ice cream: 13.3 l. (28.1 pt.)                │
│  Margarine: 17.0 (37.4)                       │
│  Biscuits: 11.0 (24.2)                        │
│  Breakfast cereals: 6.7 (14.8)                │
│  Pasta: 4.1 (9.0)                             │
│  Canned foods: 10.3 (22.7)                    │
│  Beer: 44.9 l. (94.9 pt.)                     │
│  Wine: 11.8 l. (24.9 pt.)                     │
│  Alcoholic liquors: 5.3 l. (11.2 pt.)         │
│  Soft drinks:      ⎫                          │
│  Mineral waters:   ⎬   43.5 l. (91.5 pt.)     │
│  Fruit juices:     ⎭                          │
│  Tea: 0.4 (0.8)                               │
│  Coffee: 9.0 (19.8)                           │
│  Cocoa: 1.9 (4.2)                             │
└─────────────────────────────────────────────┘
```

MEDIA & CULTURE

Statistics show that Swedes are among the most avid newspaper readers in the world. In 1986 there were 169 high-periodicity (four to seven issues per week) newspapers with a combined circulation of 4.472 million, or 574 copies per 1,000 inhabitants, and 75 low-periodicity (one to three issues per week) newspapers, which added another 10% to the circulation and per capita consumption. In contrast to the steady rise in total and per capita circulation, the number of newspapers has declined, from 216 in 1945. Most of the closures have affected competing newspapers, as a result of which a number of towns have become one-newspaper towns. Increasing concentration has claimed many casualties in recent years, including the Social Democratic *Stockholms Tidningen*, discontinued in 1966, and the Liberal *Göteborgs Handels-och Sjofarts Tidning,* which ceased publication in 1973.

Implications of this development are aggravated by the political orientation of the press. The political lineup of the press is not representative of the political preferences of the electorate. While the Social Democrats and the Communists have been sharing approximately half the popular vote for decades, their share of the daily press is only one-sixth in terms of circulation. The Conservative, Center and Liberal parties enjoy the allegiance of 73% of the press, independent nonsocialists 11% and Social Democrats and Communists 16%. As the Social Democrat press is younger and more vulnerable to economic pressures, the future press structure is expected to be more skewed than at present in terms of ideology.

The number of newspapers reached a peak in about 1920, when 240 newspapers were published, most of them in small editions of less than 1,000. The 1950s was a period of shakeout for the press during which more than 30% fell by the wayside. Since 1969 newspaper mortality has been checked as a result of a state program of direct subsidies. Circulation growth, however, tends to favor the larger dailies, 13 of which account for 50% of the total circulation. The *World's Great Dailies* named *Svenska Dagbladet* as the most influential daily in Sweden. However, it ranks only fifth in circulation, with 225,167 copies, behind *Göteborgs-Posten* (185, 135); *Aftonbladet* (434, 402); *Dagens Nyheter* (400,323); and *Expressen,* the best-selling national tabloid, which sells 552,167 copies.

The three largest cities—Stockholm, Göteborg and Malmö–produce papers appearing seven days a week. Six-day publication is more prevalent in other parts of the country. Most provincial papers appear in the morning, while the three big cities also put out large afternoon tabloids. The afternoon tabloids *Expressen* and *Aftonbladet* have near-national readership.

The average Swede regularly reads more than three periodicals, placing Sweden foremost in international periodical statistics. The periodical press comprises some 2,500 titles, of which some 175 are in newspaper format and appear at least once a week. The traditional weeklies are losing ground, with women's and men's magazines sustaining the heaviest losses. Serious literary and political magazines are rare as also are magazines for young people. Specialized magazines and consumer magazines have done well.

In comparison with other countries, Swedish newspapers have small circulations, because of the country's small population base. Only five dailies have editions of over 100,000 copies. The largest provincial papers have circulations of between 50,000 and 100,000 copies. Nevertheless, Sweden has the highest per capita newspaper readership in the world, virtually one of every two Swedes. Because consumption is close to the saturation point, the only means of increasing revenues is by raising the subscription price and advertising rates, both of which tend to make newspapers noncompetitive with other media forms.

Press ownership is quite diverse and falls into three categories: private, foundations and organizational. Despite the democratic traditions, a few press baronial families dominate the media. The best known of these families is the Bonnier group, which controls the two of the top best-sellers; *Dagens Nyheter* and *Expressen*, which together account for a quarter of the total circulation. The Hjorne family owns the *Göteborgs-Posten* and *Göteborgs-Tidningen*, which claim 8.2% of the total circulation. The Ander family owns a chain of eight provincial newspapers. As in most Western countries, three types of papers may be distinguished in relationship to the markets they serve: monopoly, competitive and complementary. There are some 70 papers in the first, 20 in the second and 25 in the third. All monopoly papers are high-coverage papers that also generate greater advertising revenues and higher profits. The Parliamentary Commission on the Press has designated newspapers with less than 50% household coverage as low-coverage and thus entitled to state subsidies.

The concept is widely held in Sweden that the press is a public utility that should not be allowed to suspend service to the people. As a result, Sweden has a unique system of industrial relations in the press whereby all disputes between publishers and journalists and production staff are subject to arbitration if the parties involved are unable to reach an agreement through direct negotiations. It prohibits strikes and lockouts and other similar actions. Under these agreements, Sweden has enjoyed uninterrupted labor peace in its newspaper industry since the 1950s. It has also helped to characterize stoppage of newspaper publication, either by lockout or by strike, as a violation of the concept of freedom of the press and thus, in effect, a violation of the Constitution.

Sweden seems to have been the first country in the world to establish freedom of the press. In 1766 Parliament adopted the Freedom of the Press Act as part of the Constitution. More recently, similar legislation has been passed for radio and television, but without yet becoming constitutional law. The present Freedom of the Press Act dates from 1949, with several subsequent amendments. As part of the Constitution, it is protected by special safeguards against abrogation or abridgment.

Not only is censorship forbidden, but also press freedom is safeguarded by an elaborate combination of measures found in few other democracies. Foremost among these devices is the designation of a "responsible publisher" for every publication. He alone is responsible for every violation of the act, and every item published should receive his approval. In the case of foreign publications, the distributor is held responsible, as the prior links in the chain are not subject to Swedish law. The net effect of this provision is to exempt sources of information from criminal liability. In fact, the law explicitly prohibits the investigation or disclosure of newsmen's sources. It follows that the identity of the informant is immaterial and thus inadmissible as a point of law. This protection is extended even to state and municipal employees, who are thus free to give information to newspapers and other media without fear of repercussion. The rationale for such protection is that government needs to be scrutinized effectively by the media. There are, of course, some exceptions to the general rule of impunity and anonymity of sources, especially where gathering or divulging information constitutes or involves high treason or espionage or related crimes.

Another remarkable feature of the Freedom of the Press Act is the principle of free access to public documents, introduced as early as 1766. This gives all citizens, even aliens, the right to obtain documents from a state agency regardless of whether the documents concern him personally. The right of access is monitored by the parliamentary ombudsman and may be enforced through the Supreme Administrative Court. Exceptions to the rule of access are spelled out in the Secrecy Act.

Offenses punishable under the Freedom of the Press Act include high treason, instigation to war, incitement to riot, conspiracy and sedition as well as threats to or contempt of minority groups on grounds of race, color, creed or ethnic origin. Pornography is no longer punishable under Swedish law. Most of the legal actions against newspapers concern libel. Public prosecutions under the act may be initiated only by the chancellor of justice and not by public prosecutors, and even then only with the consent of the cabinet. Press cases are tried by nine lay assessors, of whom six must agree for a conviction. Furthermore, the act specifies that the judge and the assessors must be guided by a special bias in favor of the media, judging the intent rather than the wording of documents.

Press freedoms also are guarded by a number of organizations, such as the Swedish Press Council, set up in 1916 as the first of its kind in the world. In

1969 the office of press ombudsman was established to supervise adherence to ethical standards in the newspaper industry.

Although while the Freedom of the Press Act guarantees surveillance of the authorities by the press, it has been more difficult to ensure competition and diversity in the press. Thus, since the 1970s Sweden has had to partly abandon its libertarian concept of an absolutely free press in order to launch a program of press subsidies. State intervention is designed to preserve variety in the press by countering market forces that favor concentration of ownership and to shore ailing papers against imminent closure. The guiding principles of press policy are to encourage the survival of competing newspapers in the same locality, discourage monopolies and chains, foster editorial independence from powerful financial pressure groups and promote efficient utilization of resources and collaborative arrangements in production and distribution.

State support for the press has been both direct and indirect. Indirect support consists of subventions to the party press, exemption from the VAT on subscription and single copy sales, lower scales of tax on advertising, privileged status with respect to publication of state and local government advertising, and special postal rates. Direct aid is disbursed in four forms: (1) state loans to help finance modernization and rationalization; (2) production loans limited to low-coverage newspapers published at least once a week (the amount of the aid is directly related to the volume of newsprint devoted to editorial comment); (3) development aid for the establishment of complementary newspapers in localities without one; and (4) aid for the promotion of collaborative arrangements. The subsidies, which are administered by the eight-member Press Subsidies Board, are financed by a 10% tax on all advertising, except newspaper advertising, where the tax is 3%.

State subsidies have produced a radical change in the economic climate in which the press operates. They have given the low-coverage newspapers breathing space and a competitive edge in an industry where the mortality rate is very high. They also have become a vital source of income to the press, and it is doubtful if they ever will be abandoned. Roughly one of three newspapers has received some form of support under the program. The most successful outcome of the program has been the joint distribution program, introduced in 1970, which has almost entirely replaced private distribution. The prevailing tendencies toward concentration also have been slowed, if not halted. Since the introduction of the program only one newspaper has ceased publication and only two have reduced their periodicity. Press revenues also have shown a marked improvement.

The only national news agency is Tidningarnas Telegrambyra (TT), a cooperative news agency founded in 1921. It works in conjunction with Reuters, AFP and dpa.

Broadcasting is the exclusive domain of the Swedish Broadcasting Corporation (SBC, Sveriges Radio AB), founded in 1925 as a joint stock company. Television began regular operations is 1956, with a second channel introduced in 1969. SBC comprises four wholly owned and independent subsidiaries: one for nationwide radio, one for national and regional television, one for local radio and one for educational radio and television. The parent company is owned by three groups of shareholders: popular movements, including evangelical groups; consumer cooperatives and labor unions; and newspaper and business organizations. Shares are distributed among the three groups in the ratio of 60:20:20. The state owns no shares, but the cabinet appoints the chairman and half the board of directors. The annual budget is appropriated by the Riksdag. Television license fees (which finance the corporation's work except for the overseas service) also are fixed by the Riksdag. Commercial advertising is not allowed on either radio or television or even on cable.

Physical broadcasting distribution facilities are owned and managed by the National Telecommunications Administration. General broadcasting policy is laid down in the Radio Act and an enabling agreement between the companies and the government. The government exercises no control over programs prior to broadcast. However, the Radio Council is empowered to raise objections after broadcasts have been aired.

There are 24 radio stations covering all of Sweden. A system of independent radio stations, run by more than 1,300 local private organizations, broadcasts in around 100 locations. The international service is called Radio Sweden.

MEDIA INDICATORS, 1986

Newspapers
  Number of dailies: 169
  Circulation (000): 4,782
    Per 1,000: 574

  Number of nondailies: 75
  Circulation (000): 467
  Per 1,000: 56

  Number of periodicals: 3,690
  Circulation: N.A.

  Newsprint consumption
  Total: 266.700 tons
    Per capita: 32.3 kg. (71.2 lb.)

Book publishing
  Number of titles: 10,373

```
┌─────────────────────────────────────────────────────┐
│           MEDIA INDICATORS, 1986 (continued)          │
│ Broadcasting                                          │
│    Annual expenditures: Skr976 million (television only)│
│    Number of employees: 3,463                         │
│ Radio                                                 │
│    Number of transmitters: 340                        │
│    Number of radio receivers: 3,330,000               │
│       Person per receiver: 2.5                        │
│    Total annual program hours: 19,112                 │
│ Television                                            │
│    Television transmitters: 803                       │
│    Number of TV receivers: 3,265,000                  │
│       Person per: 2.6                                 │
│    Total annual program hours: 4,691                  │
│ Cinema                                                │
│    Number of fixed cinemas: 1,165                     │
│    Seating capacity: 315,000                          │
│       Seats per 1,000: N.A.                           │
│    Annual attendance (million): 18                    │
│       Per 1,000: 2,200                                │
│    Gross box office receipts: Skr466.9 million        │
│ Films                                                 │
│    Production of long films: 24                       │
│    Import of long films: 318                          │
│       % from U.S.A.: 52.5                             │
│       % from France: 14.2                             │
│       % from Italy: 6.0                               │
│       % from U.K.: 7.2                                │
└─────────────────────────────────────────────────────┘
```

The electronic media came too late to be included in the Freedom of the Press Act. Instead, they are covered by the special Radio Act and the Broadcasting Liability Act, which went into effect in 1967 and which were amended in 1978. Both are modeled after the Freedom of the Press Act. A constitutional law on freedom of speech applicable to mass media other than the press was introduced in 1989.

SOCIAL WELFARE

Social welfare legislation has a long history in Sweden. The Poor Relief Act went into effect in 1763. It was followed by the Workers' Protection and Labor Welfare Act fo 1889. The Old-Age Pension Act was passed in 1913 and the Social Welfare Act in 1955. The first child welfare legislation was passed in 1902, amended in 1960 by the Child and Youth Welfare Act, which included rules for the protection of children who are ill-treated as well as juvenile delinquents. Sweden is one of the few countries with special legislation on compulsory treat-

```
┌─────────────────────────────────────────────────────┐
│  CULTURAL & ENVIRONMENTAL INDICATORS 1986             │
│  Public libraries                                     │
│     Number: 404                                       │
│     Volumes: 42,886,000                               │
│     Registered borrowers: N.A.                        │
│     Loans per 1,000: 9,262                            │
│                                                       │
│  Museums: 181                                         │
│     Annual attendance: 15,800,000                     │
│     Attendance per 1,000: 1,900                       │
│                                                       │
│  Performing arts facilities: 27                       │
│     Number of performances: 12,009                    │
│     Annual attendance: 2,335,000                      │
│     Attendance per 1,000: 280                         │
│                                                       │
│  Ecological sites                                     │
│     Number of facilities: 67                          │
│     Zoos & botanical gardens: 18                      │
└─────────────────────────────────────────────────────┘
```

ment of drug abuser and alcoholics. The first law in this field was passed in 1913, and the most recent, the Compulsory Care of Alcohol and Drug Abusers Act, in 1982. In 1982 social services were integrated in a single comprehensive piece of legislation, the Social Services Act, which places the responsibility for social services on social welfare committees in each municipality.

Social insurance forms the key element of social welfare policy and is defined to include medical, dental and parental insurance and partial, basic and supplementary pensions (all of which come under the National Insurance Act), as well as compulsory work injuries insurance and voluntary unemployment insurance.

Every citizen is covered by the compulsory health insurance program. It reimburses all costs of in-patient hospital treatment for periods of up to two years. For outpatients all costs exceeding 50 kronor per occasion—or 75 kronor in the case of house calls—are reimbursed. The cost of medicines exceeding 55 kronor per prescription also are covered, as are travel expenses to hospitals and doctors. The sickness benefit insurance entitles people to compensation for loss of income owing to illness, injury or handicap. Since 1974 the system has paid 40% of dental costs for adults, while dental care is free up to age 19.

Old-age care is based on a two-tiered pension insurance system. At the base is the national basic pension, an inflation-indexed sum paid to everyone aged 65 and up with the option to begin slightly reduced payments a few years earlier or higher payments later. On top of the basic pension is ATP, which guarantees a retired person an indexed amount related to his or her average working income during the person's 15 best-paid years. In ordinary income brackets, the basic and ATP pensions together are expected to total about two-thirds of the person's working income. Retirement pensioners with limited incomes may also qualify four housing benefits and subsidized domestic help. If a person loses half of his or her work capacity before retirement age, he or she receives a disability pension. Family pensions consist of the widow's pension and the children's pension.

In 1974 a system of general unemployment insurance was introduced, replacing earlier voluntary systems. All wage earners and salaried employees between ages 18 and 65 are entitled to compensation during periods of unemployment. Newcomers to the market and those who do not belong to an unemployment insurance fund receive cash labor-market assistance.

The main provision of the family and child welfare program is the general tax-free benefit for each child below age 16. In 1987 this was Skr5,820 per child each year, with Skr 2,910 extra for the third child and Skr 5,820 extra for the fourth and each additional child.

HEALTH INSURANCE

Allowances for Medical Expenses
- Out-patient services
- Hospital treatment
- Paramedical treatment
- Travel expenses
- Pharmaceutical preparations
- Counseling on birth control
- Dental care

Sickness Benefit
- During illness

Maternity Benefit

Parental Benefit
- In connection with the birth of a child
- and through the first four years
- For temporary care of children

PENSIONS

Basic Pension
- Old-age pension
- Disability pension
- Widow's and children's pensions
- Disability allowance
- Child care allowance
- SPECIAL BENEFITS
- Pension supplement
- Wife's supplement
- Children's supplement
- Disability allowance
- Municipal housing allowance

PENSIONS *(continued)*

Supplementary Pension (ATP)
  Old-age pension
  Disability pension
  Widow's and children's pension

Partial Pension

WORK INJURIES INSURANCE

1. Work Injuries Insurance
  Allowance for medical expenses
  Sickness benefit
  Life annuity
  Death benefit

OTHER BENEFITS

Other Benefits
  Child allowance
  Child allowance supplement
  Training allowance
  Adult study assistance
  Military and civil defense training allowance
  Maintenance advance
  Daily unemployment benefit
  Cash labor market assistance
  Compensation pay when laid off

Parental benefit is paid in connection with childbirth. This benefit compensates a total of nine months' leave, two months of which may be taken before the birth. Postnatal leave may be shared between the parents. Parents also are entitled to benefits for up to 60 days per child per year if they are obliged to stay home from work to look after a sick child below age 12.

Old-age care programs include the home helper service; the municipal transportation service; foot care; distribution of food to pensioners' homes; and activities in district day centers, such as study circles.

Housewives are entitled to a vacation grant to enable them to vacation in a holiday home if they can pass a means test.

There is no private welfare system in Sweden.

CHRONOLOGY (FROM 1946)

1946—Social Democrat Prime Minister Per Hanssen dies and is succeeded in office by Tage Erlander.

1949—The Riksdag passes the new Freedom of the Press Act.

1950—King Gustav V dies after a reign of nearly half a century; Gustav VI Adolf ascends the throne.

1969—Prime Minister Tage Erlander is succeeded in office by Olof Palme.

1973—King Gustav VI Adolf dies and his grandson Carl XVI Gustav ascends the throne.

1974—The Riksdag passes the new Instrument of Government and the Riksdag Act.

1976—The Social Democrat-Communist bloc fares badly in elections; nonsocialist coalition parties form a government under Conservative leader Thorbjorn Falldin.

1978—Falldin yields office to Liberal leader Ola Ullsten.

1979—Falldin is back in office, leading his second government.

1982—Social Democrats gain an electoral majority again and form a government under Olof Palme.

1986—Olof Palme is assassinated by unknown assassins; Ingvar Carlsson is elected Social Democrat leader and prime minister.

BIBLIOGRAPHY

BOOKS

Abrahamsen, Samuel. *Sweden's Foreign Policy.* Washington, D.C., 1957.

Andersson, Ingvar. *History of Sweden.* New York, 1968.

————*Introduction to Sweden.* Stockholm, 1956.

Andren, Nils. *Modern Swedish Government.* Stockholm, 1968.

Anton, Thomas J. *Administered Politics: Elite Political Culture in Sweden.* Amsterdam, 1980.

Becker, Harold K., and Einar O. Hjellema. *Justice in Modern Sweden.* Springfield, Ill., 1976.

Board, Joseph B. *The Government and Politics of Sweden.* Boston, 1970.

Braatoy, Bjarne. *The New Sweden.* Edinburgh, 1939.

Brinley, Thomas. *Monetary Policy and Crisis: A Study in Swedish Experience.* New York, 1983.

Carlgren, M. *Swedish Foreign Policy During the Second World War.* New York, 1977.

Childs, Marquis W. *Sweden: The Middle Way on Trial.* New Haven, 1980.

Einhorn, Eric, and John Logue. *Welfare States in Hard Times: Problems, Policies and Politics in Denmark and Sweden.* Kent, Ohio, 1982.

Fleischer, Wilfrid. *Sweden, the Welfare State.* Westport, Conn., 1977.

Fry, John A. *Industrial Democracy and Labor Market Policies in Sweden.* Elmsford, N.Y., 1979.

Gustavson, Carl G. *The Small Giant: Sweden Enters the Industrial Era.* Athens, Ohio, 1985.

Haastad, Wilhelm. *Parliament in Sweden.* London, 1957.

Heckscher, Eli F. *Economic History of Sweden*. Cambridge, Mass., 1954.

Huntford, Roland. *The New Totalitarians*. Briarcliff Manor, N.Y., 1980.

Korpf, Walter. *Working Class in Welfare Capitalism: Work, Unions and Politics in Sweden*. London, 1981.

Kublik, Steven. *Sweden's Development from Poverty to Affluence, 1750–1970*. Minneapolis, 1973.

Lindbeck, Assar. *Swedish Economic Policy*. Berkeley, Calif., 1973.

Mead, William Richard. *An Economic Geography of the Scandinavian States and Finland*. London, 1959.

Moberg, Vilhelm. *A History of the Swedish Peoples*. New York, 1973.

Ruden, Bengt, and Villy Bergstrom. *Sweden: Choices for Economic and Social Policy in the 1980s*. London, 1982.

Ruston, Dankwart. *Politics of Compromise: Study of Parties and Cabinet Governments in Sweden*. Westport, Conn., 1955.

Schwartz, Eli. *Trouble in Eden: A Comparison of the British and Swedish Economies*. New York, 1980.

Scobbie, Irene. *Sweden*. New York, 1972.

Strode, Hudson. *Sweden: Model for a World*. New York, 1949.

Svanstrom, Ragnar, and Carl F. Palmstieri. *A Short History of Sweden*. Westport, Conn., 1975.

Verney, Douglas Vernon. *Public Enterprise in Sweden*. Liverpool, 1959.

Wilson, Dorothy. *Welfare State in Sweden*. London, 1980.

OFFICIAL PUBLICATIONS

Budgetredovisning (Annual Accounts of Agencies)

Fördelning av Statsbudgetens Utgifter efter Andamal och Art (Distribution of Central Government Budget Expenditure by Function and Economic Type)

Halvårsrapport (Semiannual Report), Fjärde APfonden (Fourth Pension Insurance Fund)

Månadsrapport (Monthly Report), Allmänna Pensionsfonden (National Pension Insurance Fund)

Monthly Digest of Swedish Statistics, National Central Bureau of Statistics (Swedish and English)

National Accounts, National Central Bureau of Statistics

National Debt Office Annual Report (Swedish and English)

National Insurance Annual Report, National Social Insurance Board (Swedish and English)

Realekonomisk Fördelning av Statsbudgetens Inkomster och Utgifter (Central Government Budget Revenue and Expenditure by Economic Type)

SOS Kommunernas Finanser (local government statistical reports), National Central Bureau of Statistics (Swedish with English summary)

Statistiskt Meddelande, Serie N, Nationalräkenskaper och Offentliga Finanser
  Utfallet av Statens Budget (Statistical Review, Series N, National Accounts
  and Public Finances. Final Accounts of the Central Government Budget)
  (Swedish and English)
Statsbudgetens Utfall (Final Accounts of the Central Government Budget)
Utfall av Statsbudgeten (Monthly Report), National Debt Office
Note: All sources are annual and in Swedish only except as indicated.

STATISTICAL SOURCES

The statistical data used in the book are derived from a number of sources,
most of them published by international organizations.

(Annuals unless otherwise noted)

Banks, Arthur. *Cross National Time Series* (Binghamton, N.Y.)
Central Intelligence Agency: *World Factbook* (Washington D.C.)
Energy Information Administration. *International Energy Annual* (Washington, D.C.)
Euromonitor Publications. *European Marketing Data and Statistics* (London)
———— *International Marketing Data and Statistics* (London)
Food and Agriculture Organization. *Production Yearbook* (Rome)
———— *Trade Yearbook (Rome)*
———— *Yearbook of Fishery Statistics* (Rome)
———— *Yearbook of Forest Products* (Rome)
Institute for Strategic Studies. *The Military Balance* (London)
International Civil Aviation Organization. *Digest of Statistics-Airline Traffic* (Montreal)
International Labor Office. *Yearbook of Labor Statistics* (Geneva)
International Monetary Fund. *Balance of Payments Yearbook* (Washington D.C.)
———— *Direction of Trade Statistics* (Washington D.C.)
———— *International Financial Statistics* (Washington D.C.)
International Road Federation. *World Road Statistics* (Washington D.C.)
International Telecommunication Union. *Telecommunications Statistics* (Geneva)
INTERPOL. *International Crime Statistics* (Paris, Biennial)
OECD. *OECD Economic Outlook* (Paris) Periodical
———— *Financial Market Trends and OECD Financial Statistics* (Paris, periodical)
———— *Indicators of Industrial Activity* (Paris, periodical)
———— *Main Economic Indicators* (Paris, periodical)
———— *Main Science and Technology Indicators* (Paris, periodical)

———— *OECD Observer* (Paris, periodical)

———— *OECD Economic Sruveys* (Paris, occasional)

———— *OECD Economic Outlook* (Paris, periodical)

———— *OECD Economic Studies* (Paris, periodical)

———— *Quarterly Labor Force Statistics* (Paris, periodical)

———— *Quarterly National Accounts* (Paris, periodical)

———— *Quarterly Oil Statistics and Energy Balances* (Paris, periodical)

———— *Monthly Statistics of Foreign Trade* (Paris, periodical)

———— *Reviews of National Policies for Education* (Paris, series)

———— *National Policies and Agricultural Trade* (Paris, series)

———— *Competition Policy in OECD Countries* (Paris, series)

———— *Consumer Policy in OECD Countries* (Paris, series)

———— *Revenue Statistics of OECD Countries* (Paris, series)

———— *Trends in Banking Structure and Regulation in OECD Countries* (Paris, series)

———— *Information, Computer, and Communications Policy* (Paris, series)

———— *Reviews of National Science Policy* (Paris, series)

———— *Innovation Policy* (Paris, series)

———— *Industrial Structure Statistics* (Paris)

———— *Labour Force Statistics* (Paris)

———— *OECD Employment Outlook* (Paris)

———— *Energy Balances of OECD Countries* (Paris)

———— *Energy Statistics* (Paris)

———— *National Accounts of OECD Countries* (Paris)

———— *Sivard, Ruth Leger. World Military & Social Expenditures* (Leesburg, VA)

United Nations. *Demographic Yearbook* (New York)

———— *Monthly Bulletin of Statistics* (New York)

———— *Population and Vital Statistics Report* (New York, monthly)

———— *Statistical Yearbook* (New York)

———— *Yearbook of Industrial Statistics* (New York)

———— *Yearbook of International Trade Statistics* (New York)

———— *Yearbook of National Accounts Statistics* (New York)

———— *Yearbook of World Energy Statistics* (New York)

UNCTAD *Handbook of International Trade and Development Statistics* (Geneva)

UNESCO *Statistical Yearbook* (Paris)

U.S. Bureau of Mines. *Minerals Yearbook* (Washington D.C.)

U.S. Arms Control and Disarmament Agency. *Worldwide Military Expenditures and Related Data* (Washington D.C.)

U.S. G.P.O. *Social Security Systems of the World* (Washington D.C., occasional)

World Bank. *World Bank Atlas* (Washington D.C.)

────── *World Development Report* (Washington D.C.)

WHO *World Health Statistics Annual* (Geneva)

World Tourism Organization. *World Travel Statistics* (Madrid)

INDEX